LET'S DO IT

LET'S DO IT

THE BIRTH OF POP MUSIC:
A HISTORY

BOB STANLEY

PEGASUS BOOKS
NEW YORK LONDON

LET'S DO IT

Pegasus Books, Ltd.
148 West 37th Street, 13th Floor
New York, NY 10018

Copyright © 2022 by Bob Stanley

First Pegasus Books cloth edition September 2022

ISBN: 978-1-63936-250-9

10 9 8 7 6 5 4 3 2 1

Printed in the United States of America
Distributed by Simon & Schuster
www.pegasusbooks.com

For Tessa and Len

This book gives an account of the entertainment industry at a time, between the American Civil War and the beginning of the civil rights movement, when racism was not only endemic but overt. Offensive language has been retained in order to offer a true picture of the discrimination of the era; to erase it could suggest that these prejudices never existed.

CONTENTS

Introduction ix

Prologue xv

1 1900: Pop in the Beginning 1

2 Elite Syncopations: Scott Joplin and Ragtime 12

3 Songs for Sale: Tin Pan Alley 27

4 Doing What Comes Naturally: Irving Berlin 43

5 A Culture of Consolation: Music Hall and Musical Theatre 52

6 On the Other Side of a Big Black Cloud: World War I 62

7 A Conversation of Instruments: The Birth of Jazz 71

8 The Greatest Love of All: Louis Armstrong 86

9 The Blab of the Pave: Jerome Kern and Broadway 96

10 Let Me Entertain You: Al Jolson 111

11 I'm Gonna Do It If I Like It: The Jazz Age 121

12 In a Silent Way: Race Records 139

13 Invisible Airwaves Crackle with Life: Radio 148

14 Trying Hard to Recreate What Had Yet to Be Created: Hillbilly 165

15 Black and Tan Fantasy: Duke Ellington and the Cotton Club 174

16 Learn to Croon: Rudy Vallee and the Dawn of the Electric Era 185

17 All Hollywood and All Heaven: Talking Pictures 195

18 Ten Cents a Dance: The Great Depression 206

19 Nothing but Blue Skies: Bing Crosby 218

20 Industrial Light and Magic: The Movie Musical 229

21 Pardon My Pups: The Boswell Sisters 240

22 Make Those People Sway: British Dance Bands 246

23 Fascinating Rhythm: Fred Astaire and the Dance-Hall Boom 258

24 Eighty-Eight Key Smiles: Fats Waller and Friends 264

25	Tight Like That: The Age of Swing	271
26	Serenade in Blue: The Great American Songbook	288
27	The Winds Grow Colder: Judy Garland and Billie Holiday	298
28	Be Like the Kettle and Sing: Britain at War	309
29	Why Don't You Do Right: America at War	323
30	Hot Licks with Vanilla: Glenn Miller	337
31	Someone to Watch Over Me: Vocal Refrains	345
32	We Had to Break Up the Band: Post-War Jazz	356
33	Call Me Irresponsible: Frank Sinatra	368
34	Saturday Night Fish Fry: Rhythm and Blues	378
35	California Suite: The Long-Player	394
36	It's Mitch Miller's World and We Just Live in It: The 45	412
37	Breaks a New Heart Every Day: Peggy Lee	425
38	Almost Like Praying: Post-War Broadway	434
39	Squeeze Me: Vocal Jazz	447
40	Experiments with Mice: British Big Bands	460
41	Revival: Trad Jazz and Folk	466
42	In a Restless World: Nat King Cole	480
43	Ports of Pleasure: Exotica	489
44	Sharks in Jets Clothing: Rock 'n' Roll	495
45	The Summit: Frank, Dino and Sammy	506
46	TV Is the Thing: The Rise of Television	518
47	I Could Go on Singing: The Next Generation	526
48	The Strength of Strings: Film Soundtracks	537
49	What Kind of Fool Am I: Lionel Bart and Anthony Newley	547
50	Whipped Cream and Other Delights: Adventures in Beatleland	555
51	The Last Waltz: Tom Jones and the New Balladeers	566
52	Some Kind of Rapprochement: The 1970s	576
	Epilogue	585
	Acknowledgements	593
	Sources	595
	Bibliography	599
	Index	605

INTRODUCTION

As a kid I had a train set. My favourite thing about it wasn't the tracks or the engines, but the buildings, made by a company called Superquick, that went around the edge. One of these was a cinema, and the film showing, that week and every week, was called *The Music Man*. The name was so generic I assumed it was made up. Then, when I was about eight or nine years old, I was given my first album, a hand-me-down copy of *With the Beatles*, and I discovered – thanks to Tony Barrow's sleevenote – that Paul's lilting 'Till There Was You' was from a film called *The Music Man*. Barrow explained that it had also been recorded by Peggy Lee, whom I thought of as a grown-up singer – nothing to do with the Beatles or the glam rock acts dominating the radio. What was *The Music Man*? I guessed (rightly) it was a musical. Who starred in it? Who wrote 'Till There Was You'? How did the Beatles end up covering it? I assumed someone would tell me more about it when I grew up, but no one did. The moment had passed. *The Music Man* was a forgotten moment from my parents' youth, and if it wasn't for my Superquick cinema – freezing time in 1962 – I may never have come across it.

When I was writing *Yeah Yeah Yeah: The Story of Modern Pop*, I was constantly aware that pop music didn't begin with the Beatles in 1963, or Elvis in 1956, or even with the first seven-inch singles in 1949. There was a prehistory that went right back to the first recorded music, at the turn of the twentieth century, and that a tangled web of new musical forms – mostly American – had led to shows and films like *The Music Man*. What's more, the chronology confused me. I had clots of knowledge about the Great American Songbook writers, and New Orleans, and blues, and early Hollywood musicals. I had read exemplary books on individual genres, but they rarely mentioned the myriad other contemporaneous pop forms. So much tended to be slung into an all-purpose folder labelled 'old-time music'. I realised that no book described what popular music had sounded or felt like – or even explained what was truly popular, and when – before rock 'n' roll.

To that end, *Let's Do It* is a guide through the pop music of the first half of the twentieth century, unravelling all the genres, styles and names that can seem tangled to the casual fan of George Gershwin, Billie Holiday or Rodgers and Hammerstein, and finding the silver threads and golden needles that bind them all together.

* * *

What makes pop music exactly? For me, its essence is the record itself – the grooves, the label, the feeling of permanence. The act of listening to something more than once, of playing a record again and again, separates 'pop' from the merely 'popular'. The advent of records affected the way music was written, played and performed: if a 78 rpm disc could only handle three minutes of music, then a song couldn't be more than three minutes long. 1900 is the sweet spot, when a brand-new musical form – ragtime – linked arms with the nascent pop music industry and launched the twentieth century. And that is where this story begins.

In 1900 recording technology was still so primitive that acts had to play as loudly as possible in the studio, gathered around a giant horn. The story weaves through the fall of British pop influence during World War I, the rise of the American Jazz Age in the 1920s, the sound of swing, and the triumphs of Broadway and Hollywood musicals in the '30s and '40s. Post-war, pop's forward motion faltered. We will discover an era that created some extraordinary music but lacked direction; when the Songbook writers were in decline and jazz splintered; when Frank Sinatra made his hippest and best albums, but with songs that were mostly decades old. Rock 'n' roll moves into this vacuum in the '50s, and the Beatles presage an unlikely swing of the compass from New York back to London in the '60s. The story concludes with the beginnings of a rapprochement between the old pop world and the new age of rock and soul in the '70s. As it turned out, and with the benefit of twenty-first-century hindsight, they really weren't so cosmically different.

Pop music developed, in almost every genre, every style, thanks to a constant push and pull. For every cheeky Lionel Bart, gamely making light of the Blitz, there was a prim Ivor Novello hankering for the cucumber sandwiches of his turn-of-the-century childhood. There was the maximal rhythm of Count Basie and the minimal softness of Claude Thornhill; the furrowed Jerome Kern and the flighty P. G. Wodehouse; the bellow of Sophie Tucker and the squeak of Helen Kane; the Andes siren sound of Yma Sumac and the lounge-bound purr of Julie London; the rough Louis and the smooth Hutch. Music could be hot or it could be cool, and that didn't apply only to jazz. This was an age when mass media and pop culture were struggling to establish themselves. Multiple strands were all fighting their own corner: radio and jukeboxes did not work hand in glove; musical theatre looked down on Hollywood; Chicago mistrusted New York; Britain feared Americanisation. Binaries and dichotomies emerge throughout the story – trends and splits, the ebb and flow of the progressive and the conservative, the interplay of different classes, different cultures.

Let's Do It is about records that were made to sell, music that was intended to be heard by the largest possible audience, whether performed in travelling vaudeville shows, on West End and Broadway stages, on celluloid printed in Hollywood and Shepperton, or on 78, 33 and 45 rpm records. It is an Anglo-American story, with early nods to sounds and styles from Vienna, although outside influences are constantly absorbed and co-opted from around the globe – Hawaii, Cuba, Brazil – essentially as land-grabs.

We'll discover how calamities shaped the future. The baritone Jacob Schmidt was caught in a mustard gas attack in World War I, which permanently affected his voice; he re-emerged in the 1920s as Whispering Jack Smith, with his hit song 'Me and My Shadow'. His voice was so soft it was inaudible on stage, but it was perfect for the intimate new world of radio – the crooner was created. During World War II, the Germans used their newly invented tape recordings to give the impression that Hitler was in eight places at the same time. The technology was brought home by victorious American soldiers and adapted so that Bing Crosby could play golf while his radio show was supposedly being broadcast live. We'll see how World War II broke up the swing bands, putting the post-war focus on solo singers like Frank Sinatra and Peggy Lee, and how Tin Pan Alley's infantilism in the 1950s left the door open for the music of the underclasses – rhythm and blues, country and western – to win back the youth crowd with the schism of rock 'n' roll.

*   *   *

I love pop music that delights in trespassing formal boundaries, but I like it even more when the trespass is accidental. I'm fascinated by how the Great American Songbook, the music of the nation's second-generation immigrants, was a construct that its creators only pieced together once its commercial hold began to slip in the 1950s. I love it when a 'fake' form does something that the 'real' or 'proper' original has failed to, whether it's Irving Berlin interpolating ragtime at the wrong speed in a New York bar, or Little Walter playing blues with a distorted, amplified mouth organ, or Gene Autry singing cowboy ballads with a Swiss yodel thrown in. Or George Gershwin's 'Rhapsody in Blue', which in 1923 aimed for the 'serious' but also showed how pop could head towards new emotions, cleverness and fun; it suggested the sense of something quite different arriving, a possible future that was free of borders and discrimination.

An unavoidable fact throughout *Let's Do It*'s narrative, though, is that from the 1870s to the mid-1960s – almost the entire timespan of this book – segregation was legally in place in many American states, and for most of this time Jim Crow racism wasn't ebbing away but intensifying. As well as jazz and blues, minstrelsy always lurks in the background of America's pop energy. So, along with the creative triumphs of Louis Armstrong and Nat King Cole, there will be some horror stories.

Another thing to be borne in mind is that women having any kind of career – let alone one in the music industry – was far less common in the first half of the twentieth century than it would become in the second. The upshot of this is that hardly any women had pop careers that spanned decades, so it feels good to have the chance to acknowledge under-appreciated female talents, like the pioneering crooner Vaughn

De Leath and the bandleader Ina Ray Hutton, as well as more familiar stars such as Sophie Tucker, Peggy Lee and Barbra Streisand, who did overcome the odds to enjoy long-lived success. Delving into the stories behind the familiar and unfamiliar names, we see how both the music and the lyrics tell the story of race, class and emancipation – not just telling it, but becoming the story, with pop music acting as a driver for social change.

What is left out of *Let's Do It*? The early days of recording technology are more to do with science and patents than music, and there are already a bunch of fine books on the subject. Classical music – or 'serious' music, as it was often called – impinges on the story, but it has its own separate narrative. Modern jazz begins to follow its own non-showbiz path in the 1950s, which, as it wasn't always being produced with sales in mind, mostly made it non-pop. I won't cover rock either, the 'modern pop' age, save for rock 'n' roll's initial, explosive effects on the pre-existing pop world; those years are dealt with in *Let's Do It*'s sister volume, *Yeah Yeah Yeah*.

* * *

Historian David Lowenthal wrote that 'a past nostalgically enjoyed does not need to be taken seriously'. The way in which genres like ragtime and barbershop, not to mention music hall and the British excursion into 'trad' jazz, have been largely written up as whimsical old-time music – not least by their practitioners – is something I wanted to overturn. History can be rewritten to suit modern tastes, and the (understandably) squeamish may want to sidestep the popularity of people like Al Jolson or Stan Kenton. Other emphatic historical switches are less easy to comprehend. Though both were great innovators, in 2020 Sun Ra is undoubtedly better known to the under-forties than his band-leading contemporary, the at-the-time infinitely more popular Count Basie. The work of the great jazz pianists Hazel Scott and Mary Lou Williams now seems to be explored only by sociologists and feminist academics. Bing Crosby, one of the great technical innovators, is written off as the punchline to a David Bowie joke on *Saturday Night Live*. I've aimed to give these people's lives and their music room to breathe, to give them back their place in the story, and to bring the whole, evolving world of early pop to life.

I wanted to give personality and shape to names that are, like Irving Berlin, now just part of the furniture, and to give space to many others who are virtually forgotten but really shouldn't be, the songwriters, singers and arrangers whose collected works hover on the brink of extinction. Harry Warren, Annette Hanshaw, Reginald Foresythe, Kay Swift, Pete Rugolo, Wynonie Harris, Ethel Ennis . . . these are the secret heroes of this story.

Above all, I wanted *Let's Do It* to be entertaining. Almost everyone in this book would have considered themselves an entertainer. I'd be letting them down if I wrote an encyclopaedia.

PROLOGUE

One of the things that strikes you when you look at the world at the turn of the twentieth century, on 1 January 1900, is how surprisingly modern it was. There was refrigeration, central heating, telephones; cars and aeroplanes were just around the corner. It was a different world, but still a very recognisable one. By 1900 industrial processes had begun to reshape all lives and all culture. Popular music was not immune, and it was about to be transformed.

There was mass production in all things; this was a driving force in increased piano sales in both Britain and America between 1870 and 1910. Tens of thousands of pianos in the pubs and drawing rooms of Britain were provided by massive factories in Kentish Town, north

London.* Historian Ann Douglas has said that piano literacy was almost as high as print literacy among wealthier American women. It was a sign of affluence and culture; in New York, the Gershwin family acquired a piano in 1910, which was hoisted through the window onto the second floor of their home, originally for their son Ira. As a result, in Britain and America the sheet-music industry obligingly filled a vacuum. The piano in the parlour became more viable once mass production brought down the cost of sheet music: in the 1890s it was still common for a copy of a popular song to set you back four shillings, but by 1900 you had the 'sixpenny songsheet'.

There were record companies too, which – once someone had the bright idea to affix a piece of paper to the blank circle in the centre of a disc – also became known as record labels. Thomas Edison had discovered recorded sound in 1878, but it wasn't until 1894 that he finally agreed that the 'talking machine' or 'phonograph' that played and recorded on wax cylinders was a medium of entertainment rather than a stenographer's aid or dictating machine. Throughout the 1890s he was engaged in legal, patent and copyright disputes with the German-born inventor Emil Berliner, who had come up with the flat 'gramophone' disc. The key to making it a commercial prospect was duplication. Berliner discovered that if he made a 'negative' metal disc from the original recording and used this negative stamper to press records, then he could go into business. In 1901 the biggest American label, Columbia Records, which until then had been using Edison's wax cylinders, adopted Berliner's more convenient 78 revolutions per minute ten-inch discs, and the format of the age – right up to the rock 'n' roll era – was set.†

---

* A large piano showroom still existed on the corner of Highgate Road and Kentish Town Road as recently as the 1990s. It is now a cab office.
† Originally, in 1888, Berliner had made zinc discs coated with a fatty film; the surface was switched to black wax, then hard rubber, and finally to shellac discs – basically, the hardened secretions of beetles – in 1897. 78s were still prevalent in Britain until 1960. Cliff Richard's first half-dozen singles were issued as 78s, as well as on the increasingly popular 45 rpm seven-inch format. 78s survived into the mid-1960s in India, with Beatles songs like 'Day Tripper' and 'Michelle' appearing on what looked like a disc from a bygone age.

The advent of recorded sound and talking machines also gave us the earliest days of the music press. Early gramophone magazines, when sales of 78s were low and slow, read much the same as they would in the 1960s. *Phonoscope* (US, 1896), *Sound Wave* and *Talking Machine News* (UK, both 1906) all featured lists of new releases and reviews of this week's 78s, and they give a strong idea of what 'popular music' meant at the dawn of the recording industry: band favourites, military and otherwise; classical orchestral music; arias, operas, operettas and other musical shows; banjo duets; music-hall and minstrel songs; gospel; and, then as ever, popular ballads. Whistling solos were big at the turn of the century, as were vaudeville comedy routines. Recordings were apparently used in American schools to provide rhythms for marches, parades and assemblies.

1894 saw the first edition of an American trade magazine called *The Billboard*, a 'monthly resume of all that is new, bright and interesting on the boards'. It wasn't initially set up with the intention of covering the nascent music industry, which it didn't venture into until 1904, but was instead 'devoted to the interests of advertisers, poster printers, bill posters, advertising agents, and secretaries of fairs'. It included a page of 'Bill Room Gossip' – by 1897 renamed 'Stage Gossip' – which paved the way for what would later inform and dominate the British and American music press.

Popular music wasn't invented with the gramophone and the 78. The first truly American songwriter, and one not scared to write about current affairs, was probably John Hill Hewitt, who wrote the most popular song of the 1820s, 'The Minstrel's Return'd from the War', about a soldier torn between his girl and his country (150 years later, its theme would be revived on 'Billy Don't Be a Hero', a transatlantic number one). Hewitt was quick to spot a trend, making him the first recognisable writer of American popular song. Opera was having a moment in the 1830s? He wrote 'Gardé Vous', for an operetta called *The Prisoner of Rochelle*. Swiss yodelling families were taking America by storm in the 1840s? Hewitt swiftly produced 'The Alpine Horn' in 1844.

Most of Hewitt's songs are barely remembered today, but Stephen Foster's are: 'O Susanna', 'Camptown Races', 'Swanee River', 'Beautiful

Dreamer'. It's hard to believe they were actually written, with a pen and ink, by a human being, and not just plucked from a tree. 'Beautiful Dreamer', especially, is ageless; if you were told it had been written in the 1930s by Rodgers and Hart, or in the 1960s by Sedaka and Greenfield, you wouldn't flinch. Foster wrote it in 1862, a couple of years before he died. That was also the year in which the first stretch of the Thames embankment was built; a law was passed in Britain that meant violent robbery was to be punishable by flogging; and dear Otto von Bismarck gave his 'blood and iron' speech about unifying Germany. Lord Palmerston was prime minister, meaning any public house called the Lord Palmerston had yet to be built. It was a very long time ago. (It was also the year George 'Geordie' Ridley first sang 'Blaydon Races' at Balmbra's Music Hall in Newcastle-upon-Tyne, but more of that later.)

Foster was the first writer of songs that were recognisably pop, tunes that would later be performed by Nat King Cole, the Byrds, Bing Crosby, the Beach Boys, Jerry Lee Lewis, Charles Ives, Mavis Staples, John Prine, Bob Dylan, Foghorn Leghorn and the Beatles, without anyone noticing that they were more than a hundred years old. Foster even looks modern in photos. He tried to make a living as a professional songwriter when no such profession existed. John Hill Hewitt had taught young ladies how to play piano and written songs in his spare time, but Foster was determined to be an innovator. Unfortunately, his sheet music would be published by several different companies, and – still some decades away from secure publishing copyrights – there was little Foster could do to stop it. He couldn't phone a rogue publisher in New York and ask what the hell was going on, because there was no such thing as a phone. Instead, he moved from Pennsylvania to New York, sold his songs for a pittance and fell into poverty. One day, he slipped badly and hit the sink in his Bowery lodgings, gouging his head. He was taken to Bellevue Hospital, but they couldn't save him because there were no blood transfusions yet, nor antibiotics. A man out of time, Foster died broke, aged thirty-seven, in January 1864.

* * *

New Yorkers Alexander and Thomas Harms set up one of the very first American music publishing companies in 1875. T. B. Harms & Co. stood out as it proudly sold contemporary popular music, rather than religious or classical, and sold it well. The success of songs like Paul Dresser's 'The Letter That Never Came' (1886) led other publishers to open offices near the Harms brothers, in and around Lower Manhattan's Union Square. Max Dreyfus, who worked as an arranger for the brothers, bought them out in 1904 but kept the name, going on to turn T. B. Harms & Co. Inc. into a Broadway institution as the publisher for Jerome Kern, George Gershwin, Vincent Youmans, Richard Rodgers and Cole Porter. At one point in the 1930s the company would publish around 90 per cent of Broadway's scores and show tunes.

In 1893 a Milwaukee songwriter called Charles K. Harris wrote a maudlin ballad about a couple's misunderstanding called 'After the Ball' and thought it had potential. Rather than sell it to the likes of T. B. Harms for an 85 cent payment, he published the song himself and then set about badgering established singers into performing it. First, it was shoehorned into an existing but failing show called *A Trip to Chinatown*, single-handedly transforming the musical into a hit. As a result, 'After the Ball' became the first sheet-music million-seller.

Harris had started out with a little talent and a lot of neck. At the age of eighteen he had set up his own music publishing company at 207 Grand Avenue in Milwaukee. Outside hung a sign that proclaimed: 'Charles K. Harris, banjoist and songwriter. Songs written to order.' When John Philip Sousa's military band played 'After the Ball' every day during a six-week engagement at the 1893 World's Columbian Exposition in Chicago, the song's popularity snowballed, and Harris decided to move his office to New York. The continued success of 'After the Ball' was powerful enough to inspire other songwriters to do the same. Among his cheeky innovations, Harris was probably the first publisher to include a photograph of the singer on his sheet music. This both appealed to consumers and massaged the egos of the performers, endearing Harris to them even more.

* * *

The Wild West feel of the nascent American music industry, where foreign songs were routinely pirated and royalties were the stuff of myth, had come to an end with the International Copyright Act of 1891, otherwise known as the 'Chace Act'. One of the first songs to benefit was 'The Man That Broke the Bank at Monte Carlo', written by one Fred Gilbert, who sold it for £50 to the singer who made it famous in Britain, Charles Coborn. William 'Old Hoss' Hoey met Coborn on a trip to London and brought it back to the States, where his hoarse rasp of a voice made it an American hit. Coborn's £50 was well spent: he made thousands from the song.

These new hummable, disposable songs were commercial and intended to squash the old established musics. The classical canon, folk songs and ballads were now competing with, and being crowded out by, the din of professional songwriters in the district of lower Manhattan that became known as Tin Pan Alley. This was popular music, mass-produced to order. It was 'pop'.

1

1900: POP IN THE BEGINNING

MISS EVIE GREENE AS SHE CAPTIVATES LYRIC AUDIENCES IN "FLORODORA."
FROM A PHOTOGRAPH BY THE LONDON STEREOSCOPIC COMPANY, REGENT STREET, W.

Henry T. Finck, a forty-five-year-old critic for the *New York Evening Post*, was a Wagner man. He didn't like popular music, parlour songs or even whistling in the street, and in February 1900 he made an acute, if heavy-hearted, observation about the coming century. 'One afternoon, while I was watering flowers in the back yard, a boy in the street whistled a tune I had not heard before.' While Finck screwed his eyes up and scowled at its 'offensive vulgarity', he also felt 'certain I should hear it a thousand times during the summer. And my prophetic soul divined the truth. In the course of a week or two every boy in town was whistling that tune, every other man humming it, and every tenth woman playing it on the piano.' It was, Finck hissed, 'like an epidemic'. The song he heard was a 'hit', and for a couple of months it would be inescapable, locally and nationally. With communication getting ever faster and songwriting becoming more industrialised, this was how music would work in the new century, whether Henry T. Finck liked it or not. Hits of the day, here today and – on the whole – gone tomorrow. Just as algorithms would scare people in the twenty-first century, music lovers in 1900 worried about how organisations and capital were mass-producing music which fed on fads and left little to chance.

The first use of the word 'pop' appeared in an advert in the British theatrical trade paper *The Stage* in 1901. It ran: 'WANTED Managers to apply at once to the London Music Lending Library, the largest and best lib. in the world. All the latest Pop. Music. ALGERNON CLARKE proprietor, 18 Lonsdale Road, Barnes SW13.' It was a handy shortening; the full stop was there to make it snappier, and cheaper to print, than 'popular'. That it appeared in a London publication was not an accident: in 1900 American pop culture barely existed. So how did the twentieth century quickly become the American century? The answer will involve youth and renewal and modernity, plus a degree of class warfare. None of this would have seemed at all clear in 1900, with popular music in the US still largely in thrall to the most flowery of old-world values, producing home-grown operetta hits like Victor Herbert's 'Gypsy Love Song' (aka 'Slumber On, My Little Gypsy Sweetheart'). In some corners of the US something new and wild was stirring, as we'll soon discover, but as yet it wasn't widely known on the streets of New York or Chicago or San Francisco.

What music was genuinely popular in 1900? There were hymns and there was folk music that went back generations; there was music hall and panto in Britain; there was vaudeville and minstrelsy in America; there was parlour music, operetta and musical theatre; and there were also marching bands. There was no fundamental split between classical and popular music. The great composers and the great singers – Tauber, Caruso – could dip into the popular idiom any time they felt like swimming in a public pool. Both were annotated the same way in sheet music; both could be interpreted by any performer, it just depended on how capable you were.

What kind of popular music soundtracked the late Victorian age? Britain being Britain, in 1900 the popular music you heard, and where you heard it, depended entirely on class distinctions: for the upper classes, the aristocracy of light music was Johann Strauss; Gilbert and Sullivan were for the upper middle class, something to aspire to; the Gaiety Theatre shows of impresario George Edwardes, frothy musical comedies, were strictly middle-class; below that, there was a grading down through brass bands and Sousa marches and, eventually, music hall – the folk music of the urban working class.

People who didn't give two hoots about class distinctions were to be found in the halls, mimicking their betters with songs like 'Burlington Bertie' and 'Champagne Charlie'. Some intellectuals preferred the grit of music hall to the powdered safety of musical theatre and light opera. Ford Maddox Ford edited *The English Review* from a box at the Shepherd's Bush Empire. G. K. Chesterton wrote that 'The most serious things we have left are the comic songs.' But in the wider social scheme, where did music hall sit? The Irish dilettante George Moore said: 'The music hall is a protest against the wearisome stories concerning wills and misers. It is a protest against the immense drawing room sets, the rich hangings, the velvet sofas. It is a protest against the villa, the circulating library and the club.' In other words, it was a protest against what was becoming known as 'musical comedy'.

Everyone played instruments and sang. At the local pub, everyone joined in, so it didn't matter if you couldn't sing. Old ladies played the harp at recitals, where cultural weight might be added by ponderous parlour songs like 'Come into the Garden, Maud', which was loosely adapted from a Tennyson poem. On the streets of London there were barrel organs that sounded like hundred-year-old spirits. On the streets of Bradford there were brass and silver bands; in 1895 alone, there had been 222 brass band competitions in England. It wasn't just the north. Among the hundreds of kids in London's East End who grew up hearing both German and Salvation Army bands was Freddie Ricketts, from the particularly poverty-ridden district of Ratcliff, who was inspired to join an army band. In 1914, having ditched his none-more-cockney name for the more classless Kenneth Alford, he wrote 'Colonel Bogey'. It became a sheet-music million-seller and was adapted during World War II as 'Hitler Has Only Got One Ball', before becoming the theme to the 1957 movie *Bridge on the River Kwai* and a Top 20 American hit for Mitch Miller a year later.* 'Colonel Bogey' is an early example of popular music's longevity and time-travelling potential: you can follow it from the street-world of pub pianos, past the omnipresent marching bands, right through modern military nostalgia and into 1985's Brat Pack movie *The Breakfast Club*, in which the kids in detention whistle it. More recently, it has become a jingle for a digestif in Germany. Much of 1900's popular music is forgotten, but the marching band had legs.

Music hall was at its zenith in 1900. It was the great working-class art – its singers, writers, even its impresarios were working-class. Songs dealt with the stuff of everyday life, the secret source of most great pop music. There were songs for the homeless (Morny Cash's 'I Live in Trafalgar Square' – 'with four lions to guard me'), the poor (Ella Shields's 'Burlington Bertie from Bow') or families overrun by children (a late entry, Lily Morris's 1927 hit 'Don't Have Any More, Mrs Moore'). The Victorian idea of charity was inclined to split couples and put them into different workhouses; this horror became the subject matter of Albert Chevalier's 'My Old Dutch'.† Grim reality was

---

* Alford was stationed at Fort George in the Highlands in the weeks leading up to the outbreak of World War I. One morning he was playing golf, when his opponent whistled two notes instead of calling 'Fore!'. The inventive Alford finished the whistled melody on the spot and named the tune 'Colonel Bogey', after the Edwardian golfer's fictional foe, the spirit of the course. The colonel may be forgotten, but 'bogey' is still a golfing term.
† Music hall's origins lie in the Theatres Act of 1843. Prior to that, only the royal theatres at Drury Lane and Covent Garden were allowed to show plays; everybody else had to make do with charity benefits or musicals – in other words, variety shows. After the Act, the theatres could at last put on Shakespeare (this had previously been an offence punishable by closure). With relish, the taverns took on the variety turns that the theatres abandoned, opening a music room or song-saloon in a space adjacent to the pub. 'Every publican', wrote Willson Disher, 'would now try to lay violent hands on the building next door, whether

put to words and music. Almost nothing was out of bounds.

The queen of the halls was Hoxton's Marie Lloyd, thirty years old at the turn of the new century, who was sadly never recorded but made sauciness into an art form. With slightly crooked teeth, round cheeks and large, sad eyes, she wasn't an obvious star, but her high-kicking songs and daring deliveries were dazzling. The writer Compton Mackenzie recalled going to see her in the 1890s. She was kitted out 'in a cream dress with a cloud of amber underclothes. She sang and danced to Ta Ra Ra Boom De Ay. It was highly respectable, there was hardly any leg distinguishable at all above the knee. I was rather shaken by the freedom with which she was kicking her legs about, particularly as my grim old nurse was present. I turned to [my friend] and said "She's showing her drawers" which really was a frightful thing . . . Even until the first world war, I couldn't have told that story in public.'

Gus Elen, born in Pimlico in 1862, had made a living packing eggs for the Co-Op before he took to the stage. He made a science of complaining – 'It's a Great Big Shame' (1895), 'If It Wasn't for the Houses in Between' (1899) – the great essayist Max Beerbohm writing that Elen 'too much resembles real life to be wholly pleasurable'. Sam Mayo, nicknamed 'The Immobile One', had an almost cosmic glumness, and his recordings had some of the best titles in music hall: 'Rabbit and Pickled Pork', 'I Feel Very Bad I Do' and 'Things Are Worse in Russia'. Mayo created a record by playing nine halls in one night in 1905, and died in 1938 while playing billiards – a very music-hall way to go. Performing in blackface, Eugene Stratton scored one of the biggest hits of the new century with 'Lily of Laguna' ('I know she likes me, I know she likes me, because she says so'), which showed that music hall could be just as sentimental as operetta in its own way. You want full, teary-eyed music hall? Marie Lloyd's 'The Boy I Love Is Up in the Gallery' was a great big love-in for the entire scene. Cheeriness against all odds, that was the appeal.

---

workshop or stable-yard, school or church. No opera house was too grand for the purpose, no shanty too mean.' The Grapes in Southwark Bridge Road was the first tavern to coin the term 'music hall' when its 'Grand Harmonic Hall' was re-christened the Surrey Music Hall in 1850.

Music hall's popularity had grown in the last decades of the nineteenth century, as acts began to tour the country. From the 1880s chains of halls run by the likes of Oswald Stoll and the Moss–Thornton group began to push smaller, purely proletarian venues out of business.* Stars were still made in London, and agents and writers had to move there to make their name, but by 1900 Marie Lloyd's songs would be as well known in Heckmondwike or Hetton-le-Hole as they were in Hoxton. The first publication devoted entirely to music hall, *The Magnet*, had been published in Leeds in the 1860s; growth was steady enough that halls were built for the first time in the relatively large towns of Dewsbury and Keighley in 1901, while *The Magnet* could advertise fifteen halls in Barnsley alone as late as 1913. The popularity of family-friendly pantomime, revived commercially in the 1880s by Augustus 'Druriolanus' Harris, had also brought in a more middle-class crowd, which served only to swell the numbers.

The promoter George Edwardes, owner of the West End's Gaiety Theatre, had struck gold when he switched from burlesque and comic opera in the 1890s and introduced the Edwardian musical comedy – a mad perfumed world of romantic melodies, light songs, small plots and large hats. These shows were also notable for the hour-glass figures of leading ladies such as Ruby Miller, who remembered Edwardes's 'kindly blue eyes'. It was all extraordinarily polite – beautiful girls, suitably buttoned-up and demure – and the songs had powder-puff titles like 'What Did the Butler See' and 'Moonstruck'. These confections were inspired by Gilbert and Sullivan, but were made entirely of icing.

The big musical comedy hit of 1900 was *Florodora*, with words and music by Leslie Stuart. Its songs included 'I Want to Be a Military Man' (be careful what you wish for, Victorian England), 'The Flowers Are Blooming So Gay' (which could have been a line from *Oklahoma!*) and 'Tell Me, Pretty Maiden'. The latter wasn't much of a song, but the show stole a trick from vaudeville and the halls: when the song was performed, a bevy of beauties were brought onto the stage, twirling their parasols

---

* By 1914 just sixteen syndicates owned 140 halls, roughly two-thirds of the total nationwide.

and fluttering their eyelashes. For the target audience, this was something quite new. Like Gilbert and Sullivan's shows, *Florodora* transferred to Broadway to become an even bigger hit, its legend stretching all the way to 1930, when it was celebrated in an early Hollywood musical, *The Florodora Girl*. 'Tell Me, Pretty Maiden' might sound as if it was written by a small soft toy, but – hey! – look at those bloomers! *Florodora* sound-alike tunes proliferated for the rest of the decade. Even at this stage, popular music was a battleground for musical adventurers and bread-head reactionaries, but in the world of musical comedy, it wouldn't always be easy to tell the good guys from the baddies, as we'll see.

By 1900 the satire of Gilbert and Sullivan's comic operas had been largely replaced by the sugary world of the musical comedy. Sullivan died just as the century was born, but W. S. Gilbert continued to be a source of inspiration to younger lyric writers like P. G. Wodehouse, who remembered: 'I was taking lunch at his home in Harrow Weald. He was a great raconteur, and was telling a very long story, one of those stories where you make it as dull as possible up to the punchline, when everyone collapses and roars with laughter. There was a pause before the punchline. It didn't seem funny, but I thought it must be funny because it was Gilbert. I laughed, and he gave me the dirtiest look. I never saw anyone look so furious.'

Gilbert had taken operetta and made the lyric-writing key, creating a new popular art form. 'I know nothing about music,' he once claimed. 'I can't tell the difference between "Rule Britannia" and "Pop Goes the Weasel".' Nevertheless, he must have blanched at Edwardes's barely middlebrow offerings. Ivan Caryll and Lionel Monckton were Edwardes's chief composers for the Gaiety shows, which all translated across the Atlantic. Caryll would buy plays from France, write music for them, take them to director Florenz Ziegfeld on Broadway and tell him that they wouldn't come cheap because the authors needed paying. Caryll, naturally, had already bought sole rights for himself and was robbing Ziegfeld blind.

Londoners didn't always get away with it. When the actor Seymour Hicks 'borrowed' some of his best lines for Edwardes's show *The Shop Girl* from America after he'd played there in 1895, the papers were ready for him on his next trip, nicknaming him 'Stealmore Tricks'. 'Comedians beware!' warned *Variety*. 'Stealmore Tricks is in town. Padlock your gags! Lock up your jokes!' But at the beginning of the new century the middle-class Englishman could ride roughshod over the American immigrant, safe in the knowledge that this was the natural order of things.

* * *

In the US, 1899's big hit had been Paul Dresser's panoramic 'On the Banks of the Wabash', its 'new mown hay, sycamore, candlelight gleaming' sounding endlessly romantic to the growing number of city dwellers. One of the first heart-tuggers of its kind, 'On the Banks of the Wabash' glorified America in a brazenly sentimental way. By the turn of the century there were dozens of similar self-mythologising American songs, even though the West was still fairly wild. Mark Twain – no stranger to mixing sentimentality and American dust himself – said that in 1900 Virginia City had 'half a dozen jails, and some talk of building a church'.

'On the Banks of the Wabash' was also a pointer to the ruthless nature of the American music industry. In the British music halls, audiences would be encouraged to sing along with the choruses; once a song was a hit, no coaxing was necessary. This idea was borrowed by the nascent American music industry. Song pluggers would turn up with pianos – at racetracks, in parks, at political rallies, in factories, even at army training camps – and pass out chorus slips printed with lyrics to encourage sing-alongs. This also allowed shy listeners to hear the new songs and take home a piece of paper which mentioned the title and publisher of the song. From the start, pop music would be about interaction between the industry and the public.

Take the jukebox, a staple of American pop culture, which has its roots in the nickel-in-the-slot phonograph invented by Louis Glass, the general manager of the San Francisco-based Pacific Phonograph Company. This was an Edison wax cylinder phonograph that you stuck a coin in before putting something that looked like a stethoscope in your ears, and the very first machine was installed at the city's Palais Royal

Saloon at 303 Sutter Street in November 1889. Very soon, they could be found at fairgrounds and amusement arcades, and on the Oakland to San Francisco ferry. Four different people could listen to your selection without disturbing anyone else; it was as much a primitive Walkman as a jukebox. The nickel-in-the-slot had no amplification, and the cylinders had to be changed every day as they wore out so fast. The sound quality must have been painfully poor. No matter: at Chicago's first annual Convention of Local Phonograph Companies of the United States in 1890, the inventor and patent-holder Louis Glass claimed that his invention had already brought in more than $4,000. By 1900 there were plenty more nickels in his nickelodeon.

* * *

Vaudeville – a form of variety theatre with a dozen or so separate acts sharing a bill – was the American equivalent of music hall.* And in 1900 the biggest craze in vaudeville was the 'coon song', which had first come to prominence in the mid-1880s and was still prevalent. The illusion of the South as a serene, happy Eden for all – typified by Stephen Foster songs like 'Old Folks at Home' and 'Camptown Races' – had been ruined by the civil war of 1861 to 1865. With the mass movement of the South's black population to the northern cities, nineteenth-century minstrelsy's good-time racial stereotypes of watermelons, corn and banjos were replaced with something worse. The black caricature instead portrayed them as dumb, indolent, dishonest and 'new in town', an unwanted foreign presence. Hits of the 1890s and early 1900s included 'New Coon in Town', 'No Coons Allowed', 'I Wonder What the Coon's Game Is' and the 1901 singalong 'Every Race Has a Flag

* The impresario Tony Pastor had opened his first 'Opera House' on the Bowery in 1865, before moving up to a more respectable stretch of Broadway. His variety shows had middle-class sensibilities – no liquor, no obscenities – and he began calling them 'vaudeville' rather than 'variety' in 1876. Prior to Pastor's taming of variety, medicine shows and 'Wild West' travelling acts had provided a similar blend of music, comedy, jugglers and novelty performers to a less urbanised America.

But the Coon'.* The lyrics mocked African Americans' aspirations to a place in society, and became more violent near the turn of the century, with songs like Charles Trevathan's 'The Bully'. This was a major hit in 1896 for Scots Canadian 'coon shouter' May Irwin,† who sang it in a show called *The Widow Jones*: 'I'm a-lookin' for that bully and I'll make him bow . . . Took along my trusty blade to carve that fella's bones, just a-lookin' for that bully, hear his groans.' The violence in the lyrics was usually meted out on the black characters, but the implication that these violent interlopers walked the streets of the North was clear.

What separates the emergent world of pop music in 1900 from its twenty-first-century descendant? Most significantly, it was not associated with youth culture, because youth culture as we know it simply didn't exist.‡ There was no such thing as a teenager; in Britain, fifteen- and fifty-year-olds alike were spending their wages on a Saturday night watching the same turns at the same music halls. Most teenagers would have been in full-time employment since the age of twelve: boys labouring or down the pits; girls in domestic service, both in mills and factories.

Henry T. Finck's prophetic outburst on whistling in the street was probably unwitting; he was snobbishly reacting against an old-world version of popular music that was now being streamlined and intensified by the industrialisation of culture. Still, it hinted at an awareness of new distinctive elements that would soon remake American music. The contrasts between Britain and America were about to be amplified

---

* By 1920 there was a red, black and green pan-African flag, hoisted by the Universal Negro Improvement Association and African Communities League. One of the main reasons for its existence was to shut down the still-popular 'Every Race Has a Flag But the Coon'.

† Women were discouraged from comedic vaudeville performances. A peculiar way around this was the development of 'coon shouters': white women – usually plus-size – who roared out songs that were either parodies of black masculinity or sexually suggestive. They rarely performed in blackface, which highlighted their exclusion from minstrelsy. Coon shouters who went on to become beloved entertainers included May Irwin, Mae West and Sophie Tucker.

‡ America was willing it into existence, though. Youth as a driving value had been part of the American landscape since *New York Tribune* editor Horace Greeley had written, 'Go west, young man!' in 1865, leading to the long-held belief that California was for the young.

by the recording industry, and by Europe's slowness in coming to terms with the end of empire. Patriotism had begun to affect music hall in 1900. Songs were written to reflect the emotions of war; in the short term the messy Boer War that ran from 1899 to 1902 – 'England's Bit of Bunting', 'A Mother's Gift to Her Country', 'The Boers Have Got My Daddy'. People began to forsake the hearts and flowers of the Victorian era in a dry run for the complete takeover of the British music industry fifteen years hence. With these sabre-rattling songs, Britain was marching gloriously into its own past.

Without a pointless war to hold it back, and with the popularity of coon songs on the wane,* American popular music, starry-eyed and laughing, could look to the future. Will Marion Cook's all-black musical *Clorindy: The Origin of the Cakewalk* had opened on Broadway in 1898. 'Negroes are at last on Broadway, and here to stay!' claimed the exuberant composer. 'My chorus sang like Russians, dancing meanwhile like Negroes, and cakewalking like angels, black angels!' Cook had studied under Dvořák, and later brought the jazz clarinettist Sidney Bechet over to England; for this kindness alone he deserves a statue. Meanwhile, minstrel show music had mutated and now concentrated on the luxurious steamboats that paddled up and down the Mississippi, ending in New Orleans – the Paris of the New World. It was here and upstream in Sedalia, Missouri, that the first truly American popular music was germinating.

* It may have dropped in popularity, possibly due to the growing violence in its lyrics, but the coon song didn't go away. The banjo player sometimes called 'the grandfather of country music', Uncle Dave Macon, recorded 'New Coon in Town' as late as 1929.

2
ELITE SYNCOPATIONS:
SCOTT JOPLIN AND RAGTIME

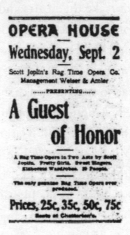

Ragtime was America's pulse. It just took a while for Americans to find it.

In 1900 European music, whether Mozart or Marie Lloyd, was the real thing as far as New York was concerned; American music was as nothing, trivial, an embarrassment. To get over this hump, and for twentieth-century pop to begin, white America had to acknowledge that African American music existed. Enter ragtime. In contrast to the family of musics that were merely popular, ragtime was identifiably 'pop'. Emerging in the last years of the nineteenth century, it was urban, it was democratic, it was innovative and it had a strong African American influence. It had a beat, it had syncopation. All of these things were unusual.

Ragtime set the template for every successive twentieth-century pop boom. For a start, it immediately made you want to dance. This really wasn't true of Victorian parlour songs or Sousa marches or music hall or even Viennese waltzes. Toe-tappers didn't really exist before ragtime. Secondly, the heyday of classic ragtime had the lifespan of a butterfly; it would be messed about with and commercialised, to the horror of its originators, but to the benefit of pop's advancement. Thirdly, it didn't have rules (even though some people *did* write ragtime rule books), because no one wanted ragtime to be homework; it was fun, it was anti-snob, it was the soundtrack to good times. Fourthly, it was a threat – to morals, to public decency, and most of all to other musicians. Most significantly, it was a black music that would be transformed by the music industry, rewritten – with both zip and slightness – into a more digestible, more widely appreciated form.

It was also a target for the press, and music-hall songs ridiculed it. It was supposedly a flash in the pan – so why wouldn't it just go away? Ragtime, once it became a piano-based music, also attracted women to compose popular songs, since the piano in the home was primarily there for wives and children. In addition, it crossed music's racial borders, which in the nineteenth century had been rigid and ugly. Ragtime was, at heart, instrumental, and so it was open to blacks, whites, profession-als and amateurs alike. Lastly, it had pop's first tragic figure, its own lost boy, the beautiful mind which could take no more. For James Carr or Donny Hathaway, Nick Drake or Kurt Cobain, read Scott Joplin. He felt the full prejudicial headwind for black composers. The pervasive legacy of minstrelsy and the coon song would provide the dark floor for Americans in the American century, and Joplin, ragtime's greatest figure, would become its saddest victim. As well as many of the good things to come in pop, the ragtime era also highlighted how black America would struggle to impose itself, would see its culture nipped and tucked by the music industry, and would watch any potential profits inevitably go elsewhere.

Where did ragtime come from? Geographically, the Mississippi basin in the 1890s. Like New York's Tin Pan Alley a couple of decades on, and Liverpool's Merseybeat in the 1960s, it was a result of immigration and trade creating a fluid society with a need for innovation to make ends meet.

Why did it catch fire? What set it apart from the popular music that had gone before? Rhythm – the explicit beat, America's heartbeat – was everything in this new music. You could play behind it, melodies and harmonies could twist around it, and the key word was 'syncopation' – in other words, putting an irregular beat over a regular beat. In ragtime the melody itself was fully syncopated; tune and rhythm were inseparable. It used oompah basslines taken from marching music and set melodies against them in 'ragged time', breaking free of conventional Western bar structures. In the European tradition, percussion had always been an afterthought.

Syncopation was created by the pianist's left hand creating a regular 'boom-*chick* boom-*chick*' rhythmic melody to get you on your feet. So completely did its relentless, euphoric sound mesmerise a turn-of-the-century audience used to maudlin ballads and cartoonish depictions of black entertainers that 'ragtime' was in the dictionary by 1902 – a 'ragtime girl' being either a 'sweetheart' or a 'harlot'. All ways up, ragtime signified fun.*

The written and recorded form would be the making of ragtime, its mass-produced driver. If it lost a little in translation from the bordello to the page, or from the bar-room to the studio and ultimately onto a shellac 78, then that was part of what made it new, industrialised and American. These ephemeral distortions were an essential part of what made it pop.

* * *

In the beginning you could hear it only in bars and bordellos. It was true tenderloin music. The first man to try and capture it from the smoky air, to write ragtime music down on paper, was Ben Harney, who had been born on a riverboat somewhere between Louisville, Kentucky, and Nashville, Tennessee, in 1872. Harney was white. He didn't invent ragtime and didn't claim to be the 'father of ragtime' (though he didn't mind too much when he was publicised as such), but he thought of himself as an adoptive parent. In 1896 the sheet music for Harney's 'You've Been a Good Old Wagon but You Done Broke Down' stated that he was the 'Original Introducer to the Stage of the Now Popular

* The first published syncopated melody was the anonymous 'Bonja Song', which had appeared in Britain as far back as 1818, pre-dating even minstrel shows. Though arranged for piano, 'bonja' meant banjo.

"Rag Time" in Ethiopian Song'. Harney moved to New York in 1896 and became a regular at Tony Pastor's 14th Street Theatre, where the *New York Clipper* wrote that he 'jumped into immediate favour through the medium of his genuinely clever plantation negro imitations and excellent piano playing'. Before the year was out, the 'rag time pianist' had also played the Weber and Fields Music Hall and the Metropolitan Opera House, spreading the popularity of ragtime music like jam. He published his *Rag Time Instructor* in 1897. A white man who could shout the blues, who wrote and produced an all-black variety show called *Ragtime Reception*, Harney was a groundbreaker and was appreciated as such. Until the rise of Al Jolson in the 1910s, he was also the highest-paid popular musician in America.

The 'rules' of ragtime would become part of its marketing. A Swede called Axel Christensen set up a school in Chicago that offered 'ragtime taught in ten lessons'. He may as well have added, 'and then you can get the money, and then you get the girls'. The ragtime pianist was the thing to be, and Christensen would end up as the 'dean of ragtime', with more than fifty schools across the States. 'In 1902 and 1903 there was no accepted method or system of playing ragtime. No two pianists ever played syncopated numbers alike,' he claimed, quite proud that he had brought some order and clarity to proceedings. Ragtime's high-pop crossover would be where the music took off. Its specific technique would turn out to be nowhere near as powerful as the unhitched idea of ragtime.

* * *

An absolute precursor of ragtime was bandleader John Philip Sousa. Many rags would basically be marches composed for the piano, with added syncopation.

There may have been no acclaimed indigenous American music in 1900, but recognisable styles were emerging, and the most popular music that could be called 'American' was that of the marching band. The most primitive early data for record sales in the 1890s have Sousa at number one for pretty much the entire decade. Among the most instantly recognisable tunes are 'Stars and Stripes Forever', 'The Washington Post' and 'The Liberty Bell', which had an afterlife as the theme from *Monty Python's Flying Circus*. In 1868, aged thirteen, Sousa had tried to run away to join a circus band; instead, his father enlisted him as an apprentice in the United States Marine Band. The boy did well and ended up running the Marine Band from 1880 to 1892, but only recorded with them for the last two years. That didn't stop them cutting 229 titles for Columbia in those two years. Whether Sousa made it to the studio or not, they bore his name, an early trademark of distinction in the fledgling record industry. In spite of the fame and prestige that records brought him, he didn't like them, coining the phrase 'canned music' to describe them. Possibly with his military hat on, in 1906 he wrote: 'Canned music is as incongruous by a campfire as canned salmon by a trout stream.' To give Sousa his due, his thin, acoustic recordings must have sounded as awe-inspiring as tinned pilchards compared to the pumping presence of a real live band. Either way, there are more than a thousand recordings listed in the Sousa Band discography.

As well as providing circus tent 'screamers',* military music was also seen as suitable for dancing, and Sousa provided both 'two-steps' ('Washington Post', from 1889, and 'Triton March', from 1896) and 'cakewalks' (borrowed from African American culture). Not satisfied with being the king of popular music, he decided to take his work into the realm of the classical. This would become a regular move for popular musicians who had reached the top of the tree, from Scott Joplin to George Gershwin to Paul McCartney, but Sousa was the first. He worked on suites, beginning with *The Last Days of Pompeii* in 1893, and following it with *At the King's Court* (1904) and *Dwellers of the Western World* (1910). Just to remind us that these were less enlightened times and that even the lowest socially acceptable popular culture was still entirely white, the *Dwellers* suite was divided into three movements: 'The Red Man' is itchy, like skittering mice or cartoon-baddie music;

* Marching music written for the circus, designed to build up excitement during a show.

'The White Man' is stately, regal, impossible to dance to, more there to accompany the swishing of gowns; 'The Black Man' is at least recognisably southern, a cakewalk, and easily the catchiest piece. But by 1910 Sousa would have struggled to hide his source material.

As fashions changed, the military bands adapted. The Victor Recording Company's house Military Band would be put to use on a bunch of dance records from 1911, as the turkey trot, tango and foxtrot were introduced to America in the immediate pre-war years. The record labels dictated their purpose, stating 'for dancing', 'trot or one step' and even – in a proto-disco move, pre-dating beats per minute – '60 bars per minute'. The Victor Military Band cut the first recorded version of W. C. Handy's 'St Louis Blues', as well as Eubie Blake's 'Bugle Call Rag' and patriotic numbers like the Caruso-written 'Liberty Forever'. They fell from favour only when the viola-and-piano-led society orchestras, like those of Victor's Joseph C. Smith and James Reese Europe, became more fashionable at dances in around 1916, ushering in the 1920s sounds of Paul Whiteman and Isham Jones. By the time electric recording arrived in the mid-'20s – a means of truly communicating a marching band's power – military bands were seen as antiques, a relic of a pre-war, more militarily innocent age. The Victor Military Band's last record was released in 1919, but they'd had a pretty good run.

* * *

Before ragtime appeared as sheet music, there for posterity and archival hounds like me, it went undocumented; there was no Cecil Sharp or John Lomax lurking in saloons and bordellos to record whatever the pianist was playing.* Every saloon bar in America had a piano, which provided a ready source of employment for anyone who could play it. Usually, they would try and blend into the wallpaper, playing familiar tunes and never refusing a punter's request. Somehow, freelance

---

* The first published rag is thought to be 'La Pas Ma La' by Ernest Hogan, a white minstrel comedian, in 1895.

itinerants invented the style, playing whatever bawdy noise suited their surroundings, but it was Scott Joplin who decided it was something more than a soundtrack for boozing, scrapping, ogling and groping.

Joplin was pop music's original Entertainer. His 'Maple Leaf Rag' was published by the local sheet-music publisher, John Stark, in Sedalia, Missouri, in 1899,* and it was the first piece of sheet music to sell a million copies. It was stately, but it had an unmistakable wink; it was sweet, but genuinely uplifting – it made you want to hold your head high. Also, it was incredibly catchy, what music-lovers a hundred years on would call an earworm. Alongside the murk, morbidity and melted butter of turn-of-the-century American balladry, it came across like a freshwater fountain. Stark took the 'Maple Leaf Rag' two hundred miles east, to St Louis, where he sold half a million copies of it and started a craze which went national, then international. It was the biggest ragtime hit of all. More than Ben Harney, more than anyone else, Joplin was the genre's creator and its leading light, and his 'The Entertainer', published in 1901, would sell two million copies as the theme from 1973's *The Sting*. There's longevity for you.†

Yet ragtime's agency would be constantly doubted. There are no contemporary accounts praising a bright new musical genre, just queries over how 'real' it was. In this way, too, it broke fresh ground: more than a century on, pop is still confronted with questions of authenticity, seriousness, whether it's too mechanised, whether it lacks heart. Fun, especially populist fun, isn't enough for some people. While he conceded the music was 'brimming over with life', novelist Arnold Bennett described ragtime as 'the music of the hustler, of the feverishly active speculator, of

---

* It would be convenient for me and the story that's about to unfold if Scott Joplin had been the first person to use the word 'rag' in a song title, but a white Chicago bandleader called William Henry Krell had beaten him to it with 'Mississippi Rag' in 1897. Tom Turpin's 'Harlem Rag' – the first by a black musician – came in December of the same year. Like trying to discover the 'first rock 'n' roll record', you can always go deeper: ragtime expert Ann Charters reckoned Charles Gimble's 'Old Black Joe', from as far back as 1877, had the syncopation of ragtime. Eubie Blake could hear it in Franz Liszt; he could hear it in the church – 'all God's children got rhythm'. It's an inexact science.
† It would also be used to sell Felix cat food in 2007.

the skyscraper and the grain elevator'. All of this and more was thrown at ragtime, and Scott Joplin bore the brunt of it.

Joplin was responsible for making ragtime the first true American music, and his tunes gave it lasting significance. He had been born in Texas in 1868, the son of a former slave, and played the piano from an early age. By the time he was in his teens he was playing across the Midwest in boarding houses, casinos and bars. The first pop music would be born, like so many later genres, in the underworld.

Many American cities had a 'tenderloin' district where men and women, blacks and whites could mix freely. Joplin found himself in Sedalia. It was a railroad town, and so had a pretty lively nightlife. It also had a college for black students, where Joplin would learn advanced counterpoint by day while earning money playing a cheeky piano at the Maple Leaf Bar by night. One night, a music-store owner called John Stark walked into the bar and heard Joplin playing a tune. Stark introduced himself and asked Joplin if the melody was his own. They struck a deal, and Stark published it; the tune was called 'Maple Leaf Rag'. With a bit of money now in his pocket, the serious-minded Joplin set himself up as a teacher in St Louis.

The American public would discover ragtime through a dance craze: the cakewalk. This had been started by black workers on plantations as they imitated and lampooned the formal European dances of the white plantation owners. It was a caricature, but as a spectacle it took on a life of its own. The cakewalk became part of the minstrel show and was in major vogue in the mid-1890s, with raggy compositions like Sadie Green's 'Cakewalk' (1896). Joplin had the idea of writing specifically for the cakewalk and other neo-folk dances, like the two-step and the slow drag. He created *The Ragtime Dance*, a modern folk ballet, in 1902. Stark initially refused to publish it, fearing it was too ambitious and wouldn't sell. Wasn't ragtime meant to be simple good-time music? Wasn't that why it was popular? After his daughter Nell convinced him to publish the nine sheets of music, Stark's fears were borne out when *The Ragtime Dance* flopped. This didn't stop Joplin from aiming high, his aspirations to serious music revealed by the subtitles of later tunes like 'Bethena: A Concert Rag' (1905) and 'Fig Leaf Rag: A High Class Rag' (1908).

Minstrelsy would have been a constant presence in Joplin's life, whereas for us today it is simply an unfortunate pop-cultural flavour which we can choose to ignore. It was the key to the entire framework of American vaudeville culture for many decades, through the nineteenth century and into the twentieth, a language everyone spoke and shared. It was culturally strong as well as culturally nasty; the minstrel archetypes – stock characters like Zip Coon, the Interlocutor, Tambo and Bones – and topics like razor fights offered a powerful and seductive comedic structure. This culture was a limiting framework within which you could nonetheless flourish as a black performer or writer, despite the self-evident moral morass. Some of the biggest 'coon song' hits were by black writers, including the most famous (and to modern ears most repellent), Ernest Hogan's 1899 hit 'All Coons Look Alike to Me'. This is what Joplin was fighting against when he was trying to get ragtime taken seriously, not only as pop music, but as a cultural representation of black America. His high ideals would cause him huge heartache in the future.

Joplin aside, who else was out there writing this music? In Kansas City there was Charles L. Johnson, who wrote the insanely uplifting 'Dill Pickles'. It was published by the Carl Hoffman Music Company in Kansas City, Missouri, the same outfit that had published Scott Joplin's 'Original Rags'. It was a sheet-music million-seller, the second after 'Maple Leaf Rag', and it single-handedly pushed ragtime's popularity up another level in 1906, just as it was starting to wane.

Then there was James Scott, a song plugger at a music shop in Carthage, Missouri, who wrote rags in his spare time. In 1905 he travelled to St Louis to find his hero, Scott Joplin, and play him one of his tunes. Joplin was impressed. John Stark published the 'Frog Legs Rag' in 1906, and it became the best-selling tune in the Stark catalogue, after 'Maple Leaf Rag'. 'Everybody called [James Scott] "Little Professor",' remembered Scott's cousin Patsy. 'He always walked rapidly looking at the ground, would pass you on the street and never see you, always deep in thought.'

In Baltimore, there was child prodigy Eubie Blake, whose parents had bought him a pump organ when he was just five. By the time he was a teenager he was playing in bordellos, as well as in church, and by 1912, aged twenty-five, he was on the vaudeville circuit playing his own ragtime tunes, such as 'Charleston Rag'. He also played with James Reese Europe's feted Society Orchestra, who accompanied the white dancing sensations Vernon and Irene Castle. Blake's stab at immortality would be achieved with another black vaudeville act, Noble Sissle, and their 1921 all-black Broadway revue *Shuffle Along*, which included the deathless, post-ragtime 'I'm Just Wild About Harry'.

Another Joplin fan, Joseph Lamb, was of Irish descent and lived in New Jersey. He shared Joplin's love of long, classical phrases. Lamb took piano lessons from a priest at school in Ontario, but quit after a few weeks because 'the good father had nothing to offer Joe'. He took it for granted that ragtime was a respectable pursuit, something his hero Joplin could never do.*

Joplin's muse may have been leading him to think of a rag opera, but with the demand for more rags came commercial necessity. Other songwriters were less high-minded, and New York's new publishing companies were happy to take advantage. You were only a marginally capable piano player, hoping to keep the wife and kids entertained? Write a rag, man! One writer who simplified the Joplin style and considerably sped up the ragtime tempo – a classic pop move – was George Botsford. His 'Black and White Rag' would be revived decades later as the manic, joyous theme to the BBC's snooker show *Pot Black*.

After John Stark, the most significant – and commercially savvy – publisher of ragtime was Charles Neil Daniels, who managed America's biggest music publisher, Jerome H. Remick. A pianist, he had been noted at college for his exquisite pen-and-ink manuscripts. In 1901, while managing the sheet-music department of the Barr Dry Goods Company in St Louis, he wrote a song called 'Hiawatha'. Daniels was offered the unheard-of sum of $10,000 for it by Detroit-based Jerome H. Remick;

---

* When ragtime was revived in the 1950s, enthusiasts were delighted to discover that Lamb was still alive; what's more, he was more than happy to sit down and talk about Joplin and the heyday of rags, and even cut an album – *Joseph Lamb: A Study in Classic Ragtime* – for Folkways in 1960. He died in Brooklyn later that same year, aged seventy-two.

with this came the offer to manage Remick's company. He accepted, and words were added to 'Hiawatha', creating a tableau of a simple, primitivist West. 'Hiawatha' sold millions of copies, kick-starting a craze for Tin Pan Alley-penned 'Indian' songs: 'Feather Queen', 'Valley Flower', 'Golden Deer', 'Red Wing' (based on a Robert Schumann melody), 'Silver Heels' (about 'the sweetest and the neatest little girl') and others, all glorious, whitewashed fabrications. Lyrics tended to revolve around 'heap much kissing', and the craze lasted right up until the outbreak of World War I. But Daniels wasn't interested in writing more faux-Native songs, because he was a ragtime fan, pure and simple; he even encouraged his staff to write rags and scoured small towns for locally published work. Remick eventually published five hundred rags, roughly a sixth of all published ragtime songs, and Daniels nurtured ragtime with a fan's enthusiasm and a businessman's nous. (He was also smart enough to realise motion pictures were going to make more money than sheet music and wrote a song for *Mickey*, a Mack Sennett film starring Mabel Normand in 1919. It would become the first-ever film theme.)

* * *

Ragtime began its spread across Europe in 1900, when John Philip Sousa introduced it as part of his repertoire on his first overseas tour. Vess Ossman, the banjo player, came over playing rags later the same year. Things moved slowly, and though the ragtime-associated dances like the turkey trot, the bunny hug and the grizzly bear crossed the Atlantic, it wasn't until 1912 that the Original American Ragtime Octet reached Britain. Without witnessing American musicians playing the music, Europeans had found it hard to grasp its syncopation, but seeing the real deal made all the difference. Also in 1912, a British revue called *Hullo Ragtime* became the first of many, with more than seventy rag-based revues running in Britain by 1913. Music hall was not allergic to the new music's charms, and Marie Lloyd's 'Piccadilly Trot' was gently ragtime-influenced, even if it did claim the territory for its own: 'No doubt you've heard about the turkey trot, some say it's rot, some say it's not. Well, I've got another one that beats the lot, and

it doesn't come from Yankeeland.' Nevertheless, it was seen by many as
a fad and didn't entirely revolutionise British dance culture, which was
still largely based on waltzes. Right up until World War I broke out,
dance programmes were still printed with threads and came with tiny
pencils. Take a look at one and it might reveal the occasional two-step,
but outside of the music halls everything dance-related was still put
together with military precision. The dancefloor revolution in Europe
would have to wait a while.

What did ragtime recordings sound like in the early scuffling days of
the music industry? Those from the first decade of the twentieth century tended to feature either a banjo (accompanied by military band or
piano), piccolo, accordion or xylophone – all high, percussive instruments that would cut through the grit and hiss of early 78s. The first
ragtime record with solo piano – 'Everybody Two Step' by Mike Bernard
– was released as late as 1912. Bernard was the orchestra leader at Tony
Pastor's Music Hall in New York; back in 1900, he had won a ragtime
piano-playing competition sponsored by the *Police Gazette* and been
rewarded with a diamond-studded medal that proclaimed him 'Ragtime
King of the World'.

Once ragtime became an international craze, it was inevitable that
things like subtlety and nuance would get lost in the rush and that writers would start adding lyrics for extra catchiness. Tin Pan Alley simplified
ragtime, which may have wrinkled the noses of purists, but ensured its
survival as the prime pop trend right up to 1917: hits included 'Trouble
Rag', 'Jungle Town Rag', 'Chocolate Creams Rag', 'Ragtime Insanity',
'Mop Rag' and 'Ragtime Cowboy Joe'. The latter was a miracle in that it
squeezed together two trends: one for modernist ragtime, and another
for melancholic, nostalgic cowboy songs. Mostly, lyrics gabbed on about
just how super ragtime was. Even Scott Joplin was paired up with a Tin
Pan Alley hack lyricist called Joe Snyder in 1910 for the self-absorbed
'Pine Apple Rag': 'That tune is certainly divine . . . Hear me sigh, hear
me cry for that "Pine Apple Rag" . . . Isn't that a wonderful tune?'
Enough, already!

The outbreak of World War I would prove to be the beginning of the
end for ragtime, as patriotic songs took over, while a new music called

'jass' – or 'jazz' – would be all the rage once peace had come. But the war did inspire a raggy unity anthem, Anna Chandler's 'The Dance of All Nations Ragtime Ball'. A mezzo-soprano, Chandler had been born on 4 July 1884 in New Cumberland, Pennsylvania, an early American settlement which was famous for little more than its annual apple festival. But Chandler sounded like a heap of new urban fun, a woman out of time, born a little too early for the Jazz Age. Though she tries to hide it, her vaudeville diction is quite apparent as she does her bit for world peace. There are 'brown-skin gals', Irish jigs and an obscure French move or two, while 'a pair of would-be Castles spinned round like a top. They wouldn't stop until she dropped.' Chandler dropped ragtime after the war, like almost everyone else, and sang exclusively in Italian and Hebrew on the Orpheum vaudeville circuit right through to the 1940s.

The music became a victim of its bad press. Though syncopation had set ragtime apart, made it modern and cakewalk-friendly, a common misunderstanding was that there was nothing more to it than a boom-*chick* bassline, and therefore you could 'rag' any old song you liked. In Britain, the pianist with the travelling Original American Ragtime Octet, Melville Gideon, recorded 'Ragtime Improvisation on Rubinstein's Melody in F' for HMV in 1912. Ragging the classics became a parlour game. Irving Berlin had early success with this gimmick on 'That Mesmerising Mendelssohn Tune' in 1909, a syncopated take on Felix Mendelssohn's 'Spring Song'. The biggest hit of all was Berlin's 'Alexander's Ragtime Band' in 1911, which disgusted Scott Joplin, who had recently arrived in New York, and made him more determined than ever to have ragtime taken seriously as an American classical music. The industry's sniffy attitude to the style, though, was epitomised by Louis A. Hirsch's 1912 recording 'Bacchanal Rag': 'Take some music, start to fake some music in a lag time, then you have some ragtime. Steal from the masters any classic you see, rag it a little bit with his melody . . .' Unable to compete with cut-throat New York competition, John Stark closed his office and moved back to St Louis.

Ragtime didn't completely die out after World War I, not in its classic form. As Tin Pan Alley moved on to jazz and beyond, the way was clear for the ragtime classicists to resume their positions. And in Jelly

Roll Morton, they found a brand-new champion, one who was happy to embellish his part in the story of jazz and pass anecdotes on for ethnographers like Alan Lomax, who ensured the legends were preserved, writ large. In the twenty-first century, original ragtime sounds more modern than what came immediately after because we're used to hearing it on piano rolls rather than scratchy, acoustic-era 78s. Enthusiasts and clubs abound. Since the 1970s, ragtime – Scott Joplin's work in particular – has been issued on classical record labels; these vinyl albums would be the music's cultural redemption. But all this came far too late for Joplin.*

He had written *A Guest of Honour* in 1903, an opera for the St Louis World's Fair, and was distraught when the fair was cancelled (any manuscripts have long since disappeared). The lure of official acceptance, of a move away from mere pop and a welcome into the classical fold, obsessed Joplin.

Treemonisha, a didactic opera about what Joplin called 'the coming of age of the black race', was finished in 1911 and ran to some 230 pages. John Stark turned it down. It contained Victorian parlour songs and extended dialogues on the betterment of black folk, and there was

---

* If ragtime had an heir, it was stride piano, a style analogous to the rise of jazz that would be perfected in the 1920s by James P. Johnson, Willie 'The Lion' Smith and Fats Waller. Like ragtime, it was built on the left hand's rhythmic action, but had a 'boom-*chang*' – alternating a bass note and a chord – rather than the single, softer bass notes of ragtime. Not a huge difference, but enough to make stride pure party music, designed for Harlem. What's more, unlike purist ragtime pianists, stride players were happy to play the day's popular songs in the stride style. Johnson's 1921 'Carolina Shout' became a classic 'test piece' for young jazz pianists (Duke Ellington learned it note-for-note from a piano roll), while his 1923 song 'Charleston' (from the Broadway show *Running Wild*) still works as a two-minute precis of the Roaring Twenties. With Waller, stride seeped into swing; on recordings like 'Truckin'', 'Paswonky' and 'Yacht Club Swing', you can feel the disparate American sounds of the early twentieth century coalesce. But, like Joplin, stride's big names still aspired to the classical tradition. Willie 'The Lion''s own compositions often referenced Impressionist painters; Johnson spent the 1930s writing mostly forgotten orchestral pieces; Fats Waller was never happier than when he was playing Bach on an organ, and never really got over his parents' disapproval of his music. Tellingly, no one used the term 'stride piano' in the 1920s; they just called it 'ragtime'.

barely a rag in sight. You couldn't blame Stark – what was a third-rate Verdi compared to a first-rate Joplin? It played once in a hall in Harlem, with Joplin playing all of the orchestral parts on piano, with no costumes, no funding, no other musicians. As a black pioneer, he experienced shut-outs and disrespect whatever he did: the classical world shut him out and, after a while, so did the popular market. There was no space in between for Scott Joplin.

Joplin and other black American musicians weren't deludedly following a snobbish call to cultural quality. They were hoping to make the best of their lives at a self-set distance from the most appalling policing, cultural and literal, using whichever moves and tricks and masks and digressions allowed them to fashion music they could be proud of. They were forced to tread a difficult line between the 'serious' and the 'popular', between the 'fake' and the 'proper'; what blocked them from their desires and ambitions in any given state or city was the inherited dynamics of a segregated country in which – until recently – they themselves could literally have been bought and sold.

Treemonisha wouldn't be entirely ignored: it went on to win the Pulitzer Prize, but not until 1976. Joplin would be committed to the Manhattan State Hospital for the Insane by his wife in 1916, suffering from the delusion that a black man could stage a grand opera. Then came death, and oblivion. He was buried in an unmarked grave, only to be honoured with a stone by ASCAP in the 1970s, after his name and his music had been miraculously revived. It turned out Joplin hadn't been insane at all.

After the success of *The Sting* and Joshua Rifkin's million-selling recordings of Joplin's rags in the 1970s, Eubie Blake said, 'Ragtime wasn't considered anything. Some people, if they don't understand something they cry it down, they don't give it a chance. I've spent all of my lifetime saying that ragtime was art, see?'

3
SONGS FOR SALE: TIN PAN ALLEY

Ragtime's rise to national, then international, prominence took a full decade. The first decade of the American century would see the creation and rapid rise of the music industry, which, once in place, both made ragtime a phenomenon and broke the spirits of its innovators. Recorded music needed to be marketed and sold, and songs needed to be written in order to be recorded. Lower Manhattan didn't lack for a 'can do' spirit.

In the 1900s dozens of would-be writers saw Charles K. Harris rolling around in 'After the Ball' dollars and, hoping lightning would strike Lower Manhattan again, bought themselves a little office space on West

28th Street, between Broadway and Sixth Avenue. It became a warren of songwriters' offices that was soon nicknamed 'Tin Pan Alley' on account of the noise issuing from multiple bashed pianos, not to mention the wastepaper bins – filling up with abandoned songs – that were being kicked in frustration.*

Art and commerce were interchangeable on Tin Pan Alley. 'Meet Me in St Louis' was written as an advert for the Louisiana Purchase Exposition, otherwise known as the St Louis World's Fair, in 1904; it would become a hit all over again in 1944 as the theme to one of Judy Garland's best-loved films. The very soul of cockney London, Florrie Forde's 'Down at the Old Bull and Bush' (1903) was actually American in origin: 'Here's the little German band, just let me hold your hand' was a lyrical clue. It had been written by Harry Von Tilzer, whose real name was Harry Gumm; his mother's maiden name was Tilzer, and he'd added 'Von' for a bit of Tin Pan Alley class. The song was an ad for Budweiser, brewed by Anheuser-Busch – you can imagine the original jingle. Von Tilzer also gave us the boisterous cheeriness of 'Wait 'Til the Sun Shines, Nellie', first recorded in 1905 by minstrel singer Byron G. Harlan, and fifty years later by Buddy Holly.

The era's biggest American hits, emanating from the Alley – as yet untouched by Missouri's ragtime – were largely lachrymose stuff. The sentimental 'In the Shade of the Old Apple Tree', written by one Egbert Van Alstyne, was recorded straight by the Peerless Quartet and Henry Burr in 1904, but was so sappy that it was almost immediately parodied, nearly as sappily, by Billy Murray ('I climbed up the old apple tree, 'cos a pie was the real thing to me'). More blubby yet was 1906's

---

* The first music publisher to move to the block was the successful M. Witmark and Sons – Isidore, Julius and Jay – who moved uptown from 14th Street to 49–51 West 28th Street in 1893. Others soon moved into close proximity: Paul Dresser and Harry Von Tilzer from Indiana; and Charles K. Harris from Milwaukee, who had written the schmaltzy but wildly successful 'After the Ball' in 1893. By 1900 West 28th Street had the largest concentration of popular-music publishers in the US. A chance hit and a couple of hundred dollars could secure you an office. Tin Pan Alley quickly became so effective at the publication and distribution of sheet music that publishers in other American cities were marginalised.

'My Gal Sal', a last flourish from Paul Dresser, the writer of 'On the Banks of the Wabash', who cried every time he sang one of his own songs. The portly Dresser, in his cups, was legendarily generous – to his author brother Theodore Dreiser, to the homeless of New York – and gave all of his songwriting royalties away. He died in 1907, aged forty-eight, and so never lived to see himself played on screen by Victor Mature – in the 1942 biopic *My Gal Sal* – nor to delight in the fact that his on-screen persona would cavort with Rita Hayworth (the film remains one of Hollywood's most complete rewrites of history – half of the songs in the film were written by Leo Robin rather than Dresser).

The biggest home-grown name, the most celebrated American composer of the decade, wasn't really American at all. Victor Herbert had been born in Dublin in 1859 and moved to the States in the early 1890s; by 1898 he had his first operetta on Broadway, *The Fortune Teller*, featuring 'Gypsy Jan', 'Romany Life' and 'Slumber On, My Little Gypsy Sweetheart' – telltale titles that gave away his Viennese inspiration. New York remained largely immune to the charms of American music. What it needed was some pride, some self-mythologising, and the person to do that was a smug-looking man in a straw boater called George M. Cohan.

Cohan became the first undisputed king of Broadway with a batch of songs he wrote in his mid-twenties, between 1904 and 1906, and a two-pronged attack that stood his work apart from Herbert's light operas and home-grown ballads like the Haydn Quartet's 1905 recording 'In the Shade of the Old Apple Tree'. First, he was heavily patriotic – he was all about the New World. Secondly, he mythologised Broadway as a place of glamour ('Give My Regards to Broadway'). No hokum about apple trees; it was all city slicker sentiments and love for the new century. Cohan had been born on 4 July 1878, which entitled him to a certain amount of loud-mouth chauvinism; in 1904 he wrote the most patriotic pop song of the lot, 'Yankee Doodle Dandy'. He reacted to critical reviews of his work with a sharp 'So long as they mention my name'. Along what lines did he write his plays? one critic asked. 'Mainly on the New York, New Haven and Hartford line.' He's recognisably modern and even has a statue in Times Square, so why isn't Cohan's name better remembered? Well, he damaged his legacy by singing his own songs, which wasn't a great idea, given his inability to stay in tune. Still, it makes for an entertaining listen today: 1911's 'Life's a Very Funny Proposition' suggests the odd rising and falling cadence of Bob Dylan, only sung in a half-Scottish, half-French accent.

* * *

As American songwriters like George M. Cohan began to create American theatre music free of any debt to Vienna or Gilbert and Sullivan, and Will Marion Cook introduced ragtime rhythms to Broadway with his 1903 show *In Dahomey*, so the gramophone was reinvented for the burgeoning American age in the shape of the Victrola. Thomas Edison himself had thought that any use of the gramophone beyond dictation was in the realms of novelty, and he had a point: it recorded the human voice much better than it did the violin; for any other use it was a squeaky mechanical toy. *Talking Machine World* was under no illusions and wrote that 'the high-brow element professed to find nothing of merit in the talking machine'. The piano, on the other hand, continued to be a source of spiritual succour beyond the Victorian age. It took the business savvy of Eldridge Johnson of the Victor Talking Machine Company to make the gramophone an equally acceptable and desirable piece of household furniture in the Edwardian age.

Johnson invented several things which any record collector or twenty-first-century vinyl obsessive would be familiar with today: a straight tone arm, a recess in the middle of the disc on which you could place a paper label, and a box under the turntable in which all of the mechanical parts were neatly contained. This was his new record player, and in 1906 it went on the market as the Victrola. It came in a four-foot-tall mahogany cabinet; Edison's machines looked like industrial lathes by comparison. Soon, President Taft had a Victrola in the White House, and Johnson milked this news for all it was worth, using photos of Taft in his sales literature.

Taking the gramophone away from penny arcades and fairgrounds and making them respectable by placing them in a mahogany cabinet was one thing, but Johnson also appealed to the snobbery of classical fans by starting the Victor Red Seal label. In 1904 he poached the operatic tenor Enrico Caruso from the British-owned Gramophone Company and sold the resultant recordings at $5 each, while a Harry Lauder or George M. Cohan 78 would sell for just $2. Caruso's recordings included works by Verdi, Bizet and Puccini, but also 'O Sole Mio' (later adapted by Elvis Presley as 'It's Now or Never', and in the 1970s as the 'Just One Cornetto' ad jingle) and sentimental numbers like P. J. O'Reilly's 'For You Alone'. The power of suggestion is a wonderful thing: because Caruso had recorded 'For You Alone', it would later be recorded by other popular operatic singers, like Mario Lanza and Richard Tauber, though the song had more to do with Irish whimsy than Puccini. What Johnson had realised was that by putting a high-class sheen on his records, he could appeal to people with money, allow people with less cash to feel classy, and essentially hype his own product. A Red Seal record in your living room expressed social power – you felt better about yourself. The class split between 'serious' and popular music was now laid bare in monetary terms.*

Eldridge Johnson's foresight also created the record collector. His Victrola cabinet included a shelf for storing your records; you were immediately tempted to fill it and create your own musical library. What's more, the Victor Red Seal label itself was hugely appealing: deep red with gold-coloured script, which would continue to be used until the mid-1950s. Victor was unashamedly classist. It used blue and purple labels for Vaudeville and music-hall acts, and black ones for comedy and marching band records, which sold for just 75 cents. Unsurprisingly, Victor sold three times as many blue, purple and black label records

---

* While the classical world shouldn't impinge too heavily on our story, it would be wrong to ignore early recordings by opera singers, because they were often given popular songs to record. Alma Gluck, the celebrated Romanian soprano, cut several Stephen Foster songs, as well as James Bland's 'Carry Me Back to Old Virginny'. John McCormack likewise recorded plenty of Irish songs that didn't even qualify as folk, like 1910's 'Dear Little Shamrock' – things you were never likely to hear in opera houses. This was down to technology. The human voice was much easier to record than an orchestra, and the strongest voices sounded best of all. The first symphonic recording wasn't attempted until 1915.

– American popular music, rather than compressed European culture –
than it did the high-end Red Seal records.

* * *

Let's look at a Victor record catalogue for July 1910 to get an idea of
what was available. It features fifteen pages of 'band records' (virtually
all by Pryor's Band and Sousa's Band); five of 'orchestra records' (essentially light music, from a Harry Lauder medley to Verdi, Puccini and
something called the 'Don't Be Cross Waltz'); two of 'Victor records
for dancing' (mostly waltzes but also covering other dancefloor needs,
from 'Cakewalk in the Sky' and 'Black Man Two Step' to a handful
of barn dances and quadrilles); ten pages of solos (including twelve
banjo solos by Vess Ossman and church bell-ringers in Hastings); four
of 'sacred numbers' ('Abide with Me', 'Ave Maria', a few sung by the
Haydn Quartet); and forty pages of Red Seal records (printed on different coloured paper and in the centre of the catalogue, so that record
dealers could easily detach them and separate them from the riff-raff).
There are also fifteen pages of 'popular songs', with dozens by Ada Jones,
Billy Murray and Henry Burr, a few Vesta Victoria music-hall sides like
'Waiting at the Church', and Collins and Harlan's 'Nigger Loves His
Possum' ('a real old-fashioned darky shout', says the catalogue, with a
nostalgic tear for the fading minstrel scene).

Victor had cut their first proper recording sessions with Enrico
Caruso in March 1902, and these records became an object of desire,
a cultural artefact in your front room. 'Vesti la giubba', from *Pagliacci*
and sung by Caruso, became the first classical million-seller in 1907.
But it was not the first record to sell a million copies: rather less well
remembered is Arthur Collins's 'The Preacher and the Bear' from 1905
(later revived by Baloo the bear himself, Phil Harris); and it's probable,
though not officially documented, that Len Spencer's 'Arkansas Traveler'
achieved the feat in 1902.

Len Spencer was possibly the world's first million-selling recording
artist. What do we know of him? Born in Washington DC in 1867,
his mother was a suffragette and political activist, while his father, Platt

Rogers Spencer, was an education pioneer, creating Spencerian script, the de facto standard writing style for business correspondence until typewriters became standardised in the early twentieth century. Just as Spencer Sr's career was running out of steam, his son became the first nationally known American recording star. *The Arkansas Traveler* was a popular comedy sketch on the vaudeville circuit, involving a city slicker trying to get information from a local farmer; the punchline comes when the city slicker turns out to be a better fiddle player than the farmer. It's easy to see why historians might like to claim the great Caruso had the first million-seller rather than this trifle, but it was Len Spencer, accompanied by Charles D'Almaine on the violin, who most likely got there first.

Spencer was an adaptable fellow: his other recordings saw him mug his way through 'The Transformation Scene from "Dr Jekyll and Mr Hyde"' (1905) and impersonate a menagerie on 'A Barnyard Serenade' (1906). Oddly, it's his recordings from the 1890s, which tended to be actual songs rather than sketches, rather than the ones from the early twentieth century that sound like harbingers: the inescapable vaudeville hit 'Ta Ra Ra Boom De Ay' (1892); 'A Hot Time in the Old Town' (1897), on which he was accompanied by ragtime banjo player Vess Ossman; his 1896 recording of Ben Harney's 'You've Been a Good Ole Wagon but You've Done Broke Down', which he introduced, rather dismissively, as 'a little ragtime foolishness', yet it was quite probably the first time the term was captured on record.

What was a recording session like in the early days of the industry? Everyone sang and played facing a large horn made of tin; the horn was connected to a hose, and the hose was connected to a needle which cut the sonic impulses into grooves on a disc. Noises that were too loud or sharp could cause the needle to jump out of the groove. If this happened, the wax would be melted with gas jets and smoothed out again, and the performers would start again. Initially, singers had to make do with little more than piano accompaniment, but by the 1900s whole bands would be crammed into tiny, stifling rooms. Wires holding musical scores hung from the ceiling. Londoner John Stroh invented the Stroh violin in 1899, which was designed exclusively for the recording studio and had two specially attached horns: one to face the recording horn, the other so the musician could hear what he was playing. It made quite a distinctive sound, but, boy, it looked crazy. Any mistake meant the recording session had to start again, as there was no possibility of editing. Tenor Walter Van Brunt remembered, 'On the interludes between verses we'd duck down to let the sound of the orchestra past us. If you had a headache, it wasn't so good.' Until the advent of electric microphone recording in the mid-1920s, this was the norm.

Who was buying these records? It was mostly women. Gramophones in the Edwardian age were thought of as furniture, interior design, which in polite society was entirely a woman's domain. Music – to be played to the husband when he returned from a hard day's work – was most definitely a wife's job. She was expected to be an educator of her husband, her children, her community. Before the age of recorded music, she would be expected to play the piano and give recitals over afternoon tea. Given that they also had a home to run and kids to look after, it wasn't surprising that many women jumped at the chance of playing records rather than spending months and years learning to play the piano. Social refinement could be bought, on Victor Red Seal.

Good music was the order of the day, something Victor would drum into women by sending reps armed with the latest talking machine out to parent–teacher meetings, sorority gatherings, coffee mornings and afternoon teas at private homes. The only time men were involved in this business would be in writing a cheque that evening.

* * *

The dominant American sound on record in the 1900s was created by a cappella male quartets in close harmony. Some years after its popularity faded, the sound would become known as 'barbershop'. Quartet singing cut through particularly well in the primitive age of recording. The names of the three dominant acts on record – the American Quartet, the Peerless Quartet and the Haydn Quartet – left no doubt as to how they might sound, and their line-up – first tenor, second tenor, baritone and bass – was similarly unwavering. The record that defined the sound was the Haydn Quartet's 'Sweet Adeline' (1904), with its curious, affecting mix of jollity and an instantly nostalgic ache. Notes slipped and criss-crossed in a silvery way, and sometimes the whole group would slide up a note as one, which was particularly heart-tugging. Songs with giveaway titles like 'Absence Makes the Heart Grow Fonder' (Harry Macdonough, 1901), 'In the Shade of the Old Apple Tree' (Haydn Quartet, 1905) and 'Let Me Call You Sweetheart' (Peerless Quartet, 1911) were deeply sentimental but deftly arranged and performed. Among the more up-tempo hits, Billy Murray and the American Quartet's 'Casey Jones' from 1910 – written about the 1900 Cannonball Express train crash – survived to become a kids' TV theme in the 1950s, while the Peerless Quartet's 'On Moonlight Bay' (1912) would later be swung by Glenn Miller in 1937 and even lampooned by the Beatles, with the help of Morecambe and Wise, in 1963.

Before the recording era, quartets had harmonised on street corners and, when the sun went down, under lamp posts. While the best-known names were all white, there were also black quartets, though these were barely recorded (an exception was Polk Miller's Old South Quartet, who first recorded for Edison Standard in 1909, though Miller – a white banjo player – probably had a lot to do with that). The earliest reference to 'barbershop' on record was 1910's 'Play That Barbershop Chord', recorded by the American Quartet. It may have been related to a common sign outside American barbershops that read, 'Four seats, no waiting', but no one seems to have any hard evidence that white American barbers or their customers harmonised together. On the other hand, quartet singing in black barbershops was documented during the late nineteenth century: as racial prejudice barred black men from theatres and concert halls across the South, the barbershop was one of the few places they could get together and sing. By the time barbershop singing was revived in the 1930s, as a nostalgic memory of an innocent age that countered the Depression, the scene – and its rewritten history – had become entirely white.

Given this, you might expect the story of close-harmony quartet singing to be another case of African American expression, alienated from its origin, consumed and appropriated by dominant white America. For once, though, here was a real example of musical miscegenation. There had been forerunners in New Orleans's black gospel quartets (Louis Armstrong would remember harmonising on street corners), but the hybrid sound of the Peerless Quartet and their kin also drew on German and Austrian sources. The Tyrolese Minstrels had toured the US several times between 1834 and 1843 (during which they premiered 'Silent Night', among other songs), and they were soon followed by other singing groups from Germany and Austria who inspired choral societies to be formed across the US, as well as college 'glee clubs', which specialised in three- and four-part harmonies. Yale's first glee club was founded by a German immigrant called Gustav Stoeckel in 1863.

Barbershop went on to play a peculiar part in American misremembering: the idea that it was all about amateur community performance, untainted by commerce (members of the Peerless and Haydn Quartets, like Arthur Collins, Henry Burr and Harry Macdonough, were well-known singers in their own right), was a nonsense; and the perceived innocence of small-town American life before World War I which it came to represent was just as mythical. Norman Rockwell's 1936 illustration *Barbershop Quartet*, which appeared on the cover of the *Saturday Evening Post* – there had been a hugely popular barbershop contest in New York in 1935 – helped to construct a national myth around cultural erasure. Rockwell's image is almost camp; the music by then was regarded as little more than amusingly corny. This is a real shame, as barbershop was a rare crack in the wall of racial separation and segregation in the early-twentieth-century US, a cross-cultural sound, a hybrid that characterised the young country.

The quartets would remain popular until the Jazz Age, gamely keeping up with the news through the 1910s. The Peerless Quartet alone would come up with 'That Raggedy Rag' ('Oh, that beautiful rag!') in 1912, 'Since Mother Goes to the Movie Shows' ('Everything is on the blink, dirty dishes in the sink!') in 1916, and a bunch of songs during World War I, including 'We Don't Want the Bacon (We Want a Piece of the Rhine)'.

* * *

What was happening with the rise of barbershop and other nascent American musics was one of the most significant developments in pop: the natural American voice was gradually becoming more dominant. The light American accent would become the basis of a classic tradition, the lingua franca of pop music, conversational in tone, with a touch of gentility. Even now, a love song sung in an upper-middle-class English drawl (Ed Sheeran's natural speaking voice) or a working-class London accent (like Adele's) would sound awkward, basically unacceptable in pop terms, and so both singers lean on the same Americanisms. Back in nineteenth-century America, it hadn't been just the home-grown songs that were seen as tawdry; the American voice itself had confidence issues, and the Old World – in particular the Italian operatic school, with its trills, ornamentation and exhibitionism – had squashed nativism in the local pop music scene. In Britain, untrained singing was still regarded as music for labourers, the soundtrack of the saloon bar; likewise, respectable Americans thought of American pop culture as low and barbarous. The rapid industrial changes of the twentieth century's first decade made a huge difference. Single urban life, with no family to shame you with subtle class differences, meant a great thawing.

Aside from the barbershop quartets, one of the key names responsible for this cultural thaw was Florenz Ziegfeld, a twinkle-eyed character of German and Belgian parentage who had been born in Chicago in 1867. The Follies were Ziegfeld's adaptation of the French Folies-Bergère, with songs, colour, comedy and – the thing he cared about most – the notion of 'glorifying the American girl'.* The costumes were superlative; the girls needed 'to have personality, to have grace', claimed Ziegfeld. 'The eyes should be large and expressive . . . proportions of the figure should be perfect.' And, as P. G. Wodehouse noted drily, an outstanding selection of dancing girls could push any show 'over the

* They also have a precursor that Ziegfeld may have been aware of in H. G. Pélissier's *Follies*, a satirical annual show that started in 1903 and was run by the Finchley-born Pélissier with some extravagance; King Edward would request a Royal Command Performance by Pélissier's troupe at Sandringham in 1904. The *Follies* ran until 1913, when Pélissier died of cirrhosis, aged thirty-nine.

thin line that divides the flopperoo from the socko'. The first Ziegfeld Follies show was staged in 1907 at the Jardin de Paris and provided a first bridge between vaudeville and musical theatre. The Follies would become a Broadway institution, introducing an extraordinary number of American songs and stars to the world, Eddie Cantor, Fanny Brice and Sophie Tucker among them. Before Hollywood, getting a part in the Follies was the most fail-safe way for an actress or singer to make her name. Ziegfeld's basic but clever idea was to use the name Follies and simply add the year; this way he always made it feel like an event, something to look forward to in the calendar, which neatly hid the fact that he was basically putting on the same revue every year.

Ziegfeld had an embarrassing habit of forgetting to pay his writers their fees. P. G. Wodehouse wrote: 'You feel that $100 bills mean no more to him than matches to a cigar store. And half the time he hasn't enough to buy a knitted waistcoat for a smallish gnat.' Unsurprisingly, Flo was not a popular man. In 1908 he was thrown into the swimming pool designed for a chorus-girls routine. More seriously, in 1912 a love rival tried to kick him to death outside the stage door of his own theatre.

A 1910 article in the *New York Times* remarked that 'the consumption of songs in America is as constant as the consumption of shoes, and the demand is similarly met by factory output'. Tin Pan Alley was a machine, where rhyming 'moon' and 'June' wasn't yet a cliché; indeed, it seemed to guarantee popularity. The 1908 Ziegfeld Follies gave us 'Shine on Harvest Moon'* – a hit recording as a duet for Ada Jones and Billy Murray, and also for 'Ragtime' Bob Roberts – and a year later Gus Edwards wrote the equally popular 'By the Light of the Silvery Moon'. Edwards, who sang at the Café del Opera on 42nd and Broadway, was quite the showman; he would emerge from a dark corner with a flashlight on his face and sing a

---

* The married vaudeville couple Nora Bayes and Jack Norworth took the writing credit, though the song was likely to have been written by Bayes's piano accompanist Dave Stamper. As he couldn't read or write music at the time, Stamper had been unable to copyright the song – though he'd tell anyone who'd listen that it was his – so Bayes and Norworth forced him to wear Japanese stage make-up, hoping that would put off inquisitive journalists. After he left their employ, he wrote dozens of songs for the Ziegfeld Follies, which rather backed up his claim.

song about a sentimental crook called 'Jimmy Valentine', who sounded rather like a forefather to the Sweet's 'Block Buster': 'Now, if you see a figure crouching in the ghostly pale moonshine, and the bullseye gleam through your startled dream, then it's Jimmy Valentine.'

The most significant song in the development of American pop, written by a scrawny twenty-two-year-old called Irving Berlin, was 'Alexander's Ragtime Band'. We may have been more than a decade on from 'Maple Leaf Rag', but a Tin Pan Alley song that finally acknowledged ragtime's existence took the form to a new level, out of the rare and into the everyday. It was such a colossal hit that everyone wanted a slice of the pie. On vaudeville stages every single act wanted to perform it; theatre managers had to tell four out of five acts that they couldn't. It had initially broken in Chicago – which had loved ragtime from the off – in 1911, sung by coon shouter Emma Carus. By the end of the year a million copies had been sold in America; by the end of 1912 twice as many had been sold in Britain and across Europe. Tin Pan Alley's adoption of ragtime led to it displacing the sentimental ballad (for now, at least), the dialect song and the coon song (which both more or less disappeared), and rendered music-hall and vaudeville ditties part of an older musical world.

'Alexander's Ragtime Band' worked so well because it was an invitation to the masses ('Come on along . . . let me take you by the hand') that was so sure of itself. 'Come on and hear,' it said. Don't be afraid. Embrace the new age. 'People say "Alexander's Ragtime Band" started ragtime,' Irving Berlin said. 'It did not. Ragtime was written years before I even thought of the phrase. But it did crystallise it.' 'Alexander' alone was enough for Berlin to be labelled the 'king of ragtime' by the press in 1912, when he paraded down Broadway; a photo of the event shows Berlin grinning underneath his top hat, on top of the world, the toppermost, unimaginably successful. He had his own copy of the photo, and on it he'd written, 'This is the life.'

Among the biggest, post-'Alexander', Tin Pan Alley ragtime hits was 'Oh You Beautiful Doll', sung by Billy Murray and the American Quartet and written by Nat Ayer of Boston, who had also written songs for Ziegfeld and *Hullo Ragtime*, a show that would conquer London in

1912. High on the show's success, Ayer stuck around for shows at the Hippodrome, where he was drolly reviewed by *The Times*: 'Mr Harry Williams and Mr Nat D. Ayer are an American pair of a type now becoming familiar to London. One sings, one plays the piano and sings; both wear pronounced evening dress, and both perform ragtime. For complicated syncopation perhaps one of the songs sung by the gentleman at the piano is (in ragtime's native idiom) "the limit".' That London in 1912 was still seen as the beginning and the end for songwriters – with few suspecting its popular culture was about to be put on ice for four years – was demonstrated by Ayer's keenness to write for the London stage. His other song for the ages was 'If You Were the Only Girl in the World', a duet first sung by Kennington's George Robey and Kentish Town's Violet Loraine in the 1916 show *The Bing Boys Are Here*. It was a lush romantic piece, instantly nostalgic, but Ayer's cruder, more effervescent number about a 'great big beautiful doll' was the one that would echo down the decades, with Nancy Sinatra going on to cut it as late as 1967.

No singer was more indicative of America's new-found effervescence than the insatiable Sophie Tucker, who emerged in 1912, aged twenty-six, as 'The Last of the Red Hot Mamas', though no one had previously been aware that red-hot mamas were endangered. Tucker was a Russian–Jewish émigrée whose family had opened a restaurant in Hartford, Connecticut, where young Sophie sang for tips. After eloping in 1902, aged sixteen, she left her son Bert with her parents and moved to New York in 1906 to seek fame and fortune. Told by promoters that she was too fat and ugly to be a star, she was only given work in blackface, and spent a year and a half touring as a minstrel singer. She hated it and began to sabotage her act: first, she would take off a glove at the end of her performance, revealing a white hand; emboldened, she would then rip her wig off to show her blonde hair. The crowd went wild. This got Sophie Tucker noticed.*

---

* Her vaudeville years gave her the opportunity to meet black performers, and her style was indebted to them. She was tight with the dancer Bojangles, aka Bill Robinson. At a party she threw in New York, Bojangles was told by the doorman that he had to come in through the kitchen rather than the main door. A furious Tucker insisted that everyone would have to enter via the kitchen.

Her big break came with the 1909 Ziegfeld Follies, where she sang as the sets changed behind her. After two jealous leading actresses got her sacked, the vaudeville agent William Morris picked Tucker up and helped her to become a star. The louder she was, the better she was. There was no room for subtlety in Tucker's world, and men were crushed and broken in her clutches: 'You've Got to See Mama Every Night or You Can't See Mama at All'. She ruled her men, flaunted her brooches, bangles and feathers, and shamelessly used sex to keep them in line. Given that there were barely any songs written from a woman's perspective in the 1900s, let alone feminist ones, this was a major breakthrough. Her fan club was called the Amalgamated Red Hot Mamas of the USA. During the Prohibition years, when you had to keep the Mob sweet to get any club work, Sophie would play cards with Al Capone until six in the morning. The cross-dressing J. Edgar Hoover once asked for one of her dresses. 'You'll never get into it,' she replied.

Singing off the beat, Tucker's style pre-empted jazz singing, and by 1929, the year of *The Jazz Singer*, she was the highest-paid female singer in America. Age did not diminish her; it simply gave her extra repertoire, such as 'Life Begins at Forty' ('That's when love and living start to become a gentle art . . . a good man when he's forty knows just how to take his time'). Her signature songs were the gentle 'Some of These Days' (1911) and 'Second Hand Rose' (1920), but on her raunchier numbers she could get away with murder: 'I Don't Want to Get Thin' claimed that 'The sweetest tasting peach is one that's round and ripe,' while on 'My Extraordinary Man' she boasted, 'I've had 'em short, I've had 'em medium, I've had 'em tall'; when the band step up, she laughs, 'I'll take care of you boys later.' In this way she made the songs her own, almost impossible for anyone else to perform without seeming second-rate. A smart cookie, she dubbed the Tucker-adoring Judy Garland 'the next red hot mama' after they appeared together in *Broadway Melody of 1938*. Tucker's fame was still strong enough in 1945 that her recording of 'My Yiddishe Momme' was blasted out on a gramophone by GIs when they reached the Brandenburg Gate.

* * *

One-man melting pot Irving Berlin created a whole undiscovered borough for Americans to move into. This place was fun, it was modern
(kick out that dark Victorian furniture!), and it opened up vistas beyond
for other young writers who had been struggling to find their way.
Among them was twenty-seven-year-old Jerome Kern, who soon discovered a place between Berlin's high-kicking gait and the mooning, waltz-
friendly romance of what had come before. George Gershwin would
have been just fourteen in 1912, soaking it all up as his dad introduced
him to the local New York nobility at the Turkish baths and various restaurants he ran. The Gershwins may have arrived in America as paupers,
but they carried themselves like gentry, and this would come across in
young George's songs. One of his first hits was another American classic,
'Swanee', which Al Jolson snatched from his hand in 1920. Berlin, Kern
and Gershwin became friendly competitors who would egg each other
on to more dazzling melodies and wittier lyrics, much as Lennon and
McCartney, Dylan, Jagger and Richards, and Holland/Dozier/Holland
would forty years later. In 1935, when Gershwin took his foot off the
pedal to write *Porgy and Bess*, Cole Porter, Hoagy Carmichael and
Richard Rodgers would step up, trying to snatch his hit-maker crown.

But more on these names later. The point is that these writers and this
music owed everything to 'Alexander's Ragtime Band'. It's the mother of
American song. Tin Pan Alley songwriters would go where the money
was, and in 1912 stilted rhythms and syrupy lyrics were dropped like
hot potatoes. At one stroke, 'Alexander' consigned all other kinds of
popular music to the past. It also indicated where the action would be
once the mud had dried in Western Europe.

4
DOING WHAT COMES NATURALLY:
IRVING BERLIN

I sit at my window and the words fly past me like birds – with
God's help I catch some.
    Jean Rhys

Meter, melody, and everything else that relates to the construction of a song are secondary. All that is necessary is to have
something to say and to say it as quickly as possible.
    Irving Berlin

Irving Berlin is the first in line. Top of the bill and front of the queue.
His name will crop up in almost every chapter of this book because he

wrote hit songs for more than half a century. And that still allowed for a long, and somewhat tragic, retirement – but we'll get to that.

In the beginning, Israel Beilin had nothing. The Siberian village where he was born in 1888 was razed to the ground by Cossacks, and his family fled to New York's Lower East Side when he was five years old. Israel Baline, as he had been rechristened at Ellis Island, became a waiter; then, once he started writing novelty songs in his spare time, he became a singing waiter. When he got an office, the first thing he did was to put a picture of Stephen Foster on the wall – the forefather of all pop music, the songwriter who had died in poverty in the mid-nineteenth century because the business of show business wouldn't be invented for another half-century. Nothing else on the walls. This was modernity: immigration and integration, suffragettes and skyscrapers just outside the door, a telephone on his desk, an automobile to take him home. It was 1908.

By 1911 Berlin* had already had more than two hundred songs published, which had earned him a very tidy £100,000 in royalties. 1911 was also the year he came up with 'Alexander's Ragtime Band'. He was waiting for a train to Palm Beach, Florida, and had twenty minutes or so to kill before he left his office; the song was finished before he picked up his tan leather suitcase and locked the door. Berlin was twenty-three years old, and even if he had written nothing else, he could have lived quite comfortably for the rest of his life. 'Do I believe in inspiration?' he wrote years later. 'In having things hit you from nowhere? Big things you've never dreamed of? Occasionally – yes. I have never given Irving Berlin any credit for "Alexander".' It exploded, the hit of the year, everywhere. It's possibly the first song that springs to mind if anyone brings up ragtime, though, in truth, it's closer to a Sousa march. It's ersatz ragtime, with no time for rule books, but it absolutely accords with the spirit that those rule books were meant to deliver.

Berlin went from writing lyrics on napkins and slopping soup onto people's laps to being tagged a revolutionary almost overnight. He hadn't found his own sound before, but he did with 'Alexander'. Some

---

* His final name change had come in around 1908, when someone misspelled 'Baline' as 'Berlin' on some sheet music.

said it wasn't ragtime at all, that it lacked the classic syncopation, and they were quite right. What Berlin did was to dip in and out of ragtime norms, throw in some vaudeville, have fun with his songwriting and create a definite New York sound. These were ragtime songs, rather than ragtime itself; this difference would go on to provide fertile ground for academics and sociologists ever after, but no one outside of purists in St Louis and Sedalia gave two hoots at the time.

What Berlin had created was a hybrid pop song. It had a great hook and a memorable title, and it was easy to sing. It also melded a slight melancholy, which Berlin reckoned he had learned from 'Slavonic and Semitic folk tunes', with the vogueish ragtime style, which is what gave it a subtle urban edge (he later wrote an essay called 'Song and Sorrow Are Playmates'). It became so ubiquitous a hit that it lent itself to multiple soundalikes and follow-ups, not least from Berlin himself: 1914's 'He's a Rag Picker' was based on the charge that he had stolen the tune for 'Alexander's Ragtime Band' from Scott Joplin. 'Naturalness', he found, came to him as long as he followed his own basic lyrical rule: 'Easy to sing, easy to say, easy to remember and applicable to everyday events.' More than seven decades later, Bill Drummond would write *The Manual* on how to make a number-one record, but the first edition was Berlin's. And as Drummond would with 'Doctorin' the Tardis', a UK number one in 1988, Berlin added already familiar musical quotes to 'Alexander's Ragtime Band', with a bugle call and a smidgen of Stephen Foster's 'Swanee River'. He wrote songs in the way a good cook can work with whatever is hanging around in the fridge. No one had done this before.

Why was 'Alexander' *so* big a deal? It was the first major hit to emphasise the chorus, which was twice as long as it was on most songs, and Berlin dispensed with the second verse entirely. He was more interested in the sound and feel of the lyric than the narrative. The first verse was simply there to build up anticipation for the singalong chorus – 'Come on, you know it!' Music historian Alec Wilder reckons it to be the first popular song in which the verse and chorus are in different keys – C and F respectively. Berlin, writing in 1913, had little doubt about why it worked: 'The whole art of a good ragtime song lies in giving it a rhythm that is snappy, and in making it so simple that the artiste can sing it, a baby can sing it, anybody and everybody can sing it. Its appeal is to the masses, not the classes.'

Sat in his office, though, he constantly worried it would all suddenly end. He had no formal training; he had never learned how to read and write music. He would look at the picture of Stephen Foster on the wall and think about the number of deathless standards he'd written. Maybe the most important song Berlin ever wrote was 'Everybody's Doin' It' in 1912. It was as big as 'Alexander's Ragtime Band', and it pushed forward, utilising America's new-found dance-craze bawdiness. Tea dances in cafés and restaurants now lasted all afternoon, and tea wasn't the only beverage on offer. Couples grasped each other as they did the turkey trot and the bunny hug. F. Scott Fitzgerald would recall how the dance craze of 1912 'brought the nice girl into the café, thus beginning a profound revolution in American life'. This seemed to open the songwriting floodgates for the freshly confident Berlin, but there was another reason why his output became even more prolific.

In 1913 he married, but his wife Dorothy died of a fever as soon as they returned from their honeymoon in Cuba. They had been together for barely five months. Berlin decided to throw himself deeper into his work, which resulted in his first ballad, the troubled and highly personal 'When I Lost You'. He also branched out into publishing; other songwriters would send material to Irving Berlin Inc., and if he liked it, they would become part of the family. He toured Britain, billed as the 'King of Ragtime', which enabled him to call himself an international star on his return. And at this point he launched his first Broadway musical, *Watch Your Step*. It seemed he had ridden out the tragedy and darkness in his life, that he had it all planned out.

What Berlin was repressing was his grief. It's rumoured that he stayed celibate for a full decade after Dorothy's death. The year of the Charleston, 1923, was soundtracked by 'What'll I Do'; the following year by 'All Alone'. Maudlin ballads were hardly what Mr Ragtime was known for, but both were huge hits.* It was widely known that Berlin,

---

* 'What'll I Do' became the theme to the British TV series *Birds of a Feather* as late as 1989. 'All Alone' became the title track of a 1964 Frank Sinatra album, which also included 'What'll I Do'.

a Russian Jew from the Lower East Side, was now dating Ellin Mackay, an author with Algonquin Round Table friends and the daughter of the man who ran the *Postal Telegraph*. Ellin's dad did not approve, and Berlin poured his distress into these ballads. His mood had hardly improved by 1925, when his heartache led to a pair of waltzes, 'Remember' (a hit for Ruth Etting) and 'Always'. An underwhelmed Algonquin circle play-wright, George S. Kaufman, laughed that the latter's opening line of 'I'll be loving you, always' should have been 'I'll be loving you, Thursday'. When Irving and Ellin finally married in 1926, he wrote 'At Peace with the World'. This run of hit songs is one of the first, if not the very first, to qualify as autobiographical pop, something that wouldn't become commonplace until the 1960s.

Irving and Ellin's first date, on 24 February 1924, had been at a Paul Whiteman concert at the Aeolian Hall which aimed to raise jazz to the level of classical music. His medley of Berlin songs, unfortunately, was dreary and entirely eclipsed by a new George Gershwin piece called 'Rhapsody in Blue'. We'll hear more about the Aeolian Hall and 'Rhapsody' later, but it was clear to Berlin that he would have to up his game; it was equally obvious to him that he had found a muse, one who would take his songwriting to a whole new level.

Ellin was fifteen years his junior, and an heiress. As her father had refused to let them marry, they had had to elope. It was a Jazz Age fairy tale, and the press loved it – a wealthy, literary Catholic girl and a Jewish immigrant who had started out as a singing waiter. In 1925 Ellin became one of the very first writers for *The New Yorker*, a weekly maga-zine for the smart, young and sexy, writing a piece called 'Why We Go to Cabarets: A Post-Debutante Explains'. Class and social distinctions tumbled down; it was all super-modern.

* * *

The unlikeliest thing about Berlin's huge success is that he never believed he was a genuine talent. He thought he'd just got lucky, and that if he ever learned about musical theory or chord sequences, or how to write down quavers and crotchets, his run of luck would end – he'd be revealed as a fraud, as if his whole life was an unending version of *Sparky's Magic Piano*.

Whenever it looked like he might be flagging, another hit would push him back to the summit. In 1926 he'd managed to insert a song into a Rodgers and Hart stage musical called *Betsy*, when the show's star, Belle Baker, complained to him that none of the songs struck her as show-stoppers. He went round to her apartment with half an idea – a song called 'Blue Skies' that he was writing for his baby daughter Mary Ellin – and had the whole thing finished before Belle had made a pot of coffee. Berlin excitedly called the show's producer, Florenz Ziegfeld, who told him it was Rodgers and Hart's show, and there were contracts and moral issues to take into account, no matter how much Ms Baker loved the song. Baker then told Ziegfeld she wouldn't go on unless she sang it. Ziegfeld rolled his eyes and relented, just as long as Rodgers and Hart had no idea who the extra song was written by.

On the opening night *Betsy* seemed to drag. Belle Baker did her best but could feel she was losing the crowd, until, just as the show was about to stall completely, she sang 'Blue Skies'. The crowd went bananas, calling Baker for encore after encore. Rodgers and Hart sat in the audience, confused; then a spotlight picked out Berlin, sat in the front row, lustily singing the chorus, and the decibels grew further still. Lorenz Hart headed to the bar.

*　*　*

Time frames melt into each other when you talk about Irving Berlin. More than a quarter century after 'Alexander's Ragtime Band', he wrote the best-selling record of all time, with sales figures that – in the digital era – are unlikely ever to be surpassed. In December 1937 work began on the film of *Alexander's Ragtime Band*. Berlin was in Hollywood, away from his family for Christmas, and unsurprisingly feeling homesick. Rather than wallow, he decided to write a song about his circumstances. Originally, 'White Christmas' had a verse about palm trees and swimming pools: Berlin imagined it being sung by elegant west coast types, sipping cocktails and reminiscing about the Christmases of their childhood.

Berlin would often get out a sheet of paper, write a new song title at the top, then work on it for days, weeks, sometimes years. He called these 'square songs'. Other times he'd stay up, work through the night and have a ready-made classic by breakfast. 'White Christmas' was one of these 'round songs'. When Bing Crosby was handed the sheet music, he gave it a look, took his pipe from his mouth and smiled, 'You don't have to worry about this one, Irving.'

The melody of 'White Christmas' is simultaneously cosy and melancholy, and almost entirely downward. Just the odd line climbs incrementally up and then down ('just like the ones I used to know'), as if trying to conjure the shape of a Christmas tree out of thin air. With Crosby's warm blanket of a vocal, and a performance designed for film rather than built for the stage, it's an incredibly intimate song. Yet it's all about Christmases past, with the singer wishing everyone else future white Christmases. Lurking throughout is the melancholy of times long gone, of Berlin's heritage, and the knowledge that Christmas can be the loneliest time of the year.

It's typical of Berlin's work rate and astute commerciality that while he fretted over 'White Christmas', knowing its power and hoping Crosby and its parent movie *Holiday Inn* would do it justice, he was at the same time writing 'square songs' that were all for the war effort and unlikely to endure any longer than an open packet of crisps. There was the fierce 'When That Man Is Dead and Gone', which likened Hitler to Satan (and was sung in Britain by precocious child star Petula Clark), while 'Arms for the Love of America' was written especially for the US Army's Ordnance and Ammunition Department; another song, patriotic and brave enough to take on the most unromantic of subjects, was called 'I Paid My Income Tax Today'.

Throughout his life Berlin worried that the music would suddenly elude him, that he'd just wake up one morning and there would be nothing. It caused him sleepless nights. He went to the doctor about his insomnia and said that he had even resorted to counting sheep. The unsympathetic doctor told him he should try counting his blessings instead, and another hit was born. 1954 saw two movies based entirely on nothing more than a three-minute Irving Berlin song: *There's No*

Business Like Show Business and *White Christmas*. The latter was an easy-going retread of *Holiday Inn*, but the soundtrack included Berlin's last great song, 'Count Your Blessings (Instead of Sheep)'. In the film it was sung as a duet between Rosemary Clooney and Bing Crosby, but contracts prevented Clooney from appearing on the single. Instead, Bing sings it alone, with great sleepiness, backed by an ominous low-key arrangement by J. J. Lilley. String lines jump octaves with no warning and counter Bing's beautifully somnambulant delivery with an edge that threatens to drag the song down throughout. The effect is unnerving and truly beautiful. If any one song reflected the state of Berlin's mind, it was 'Count Your Blessings'.

His other hit of 1954, 'There's No Business Like Show Business', reprised 'Alexander's Ragtime Band' and 'Puttin' on the Ritz', as well as reviving 'Heat Wave', first made famous by Ethel Waters in 1933 and now performed, in glorious Cinemascope, by Marilyn Monroe. Even as his legend was being amplified for the umpteenth time, Berlin was riddled with self-doubt. He took a rest week during filming, and when asked if he was feeling better, laughed, 'I've just eaten the biggest lunch . . . never felt better.' Later, though, he admitted to depression. During the filming of *White Christmas*, Bing Crosby had gone to his house to hear the new songs. Berlin was a bag of nerves, and Crosby, sensing his discomfort, asked, 'Do you like them, Irving? Well then, they're good enough for me.'

In 1955 Berlin wrote very little, save for the ironic 'Anybody Can Write'; in 1956 there was nothing at all. He took up painting, and wasn't much cop, which at least inspired a song called '(You Can't Lose the Blues with) Colours'. He wrote songs for his children, then for his grandchildren, but not for the world outside. 'I got to a point I didn't want to leave my room when daylight came,' he remembered. He would live this way for decades.

An unseemly number of the twentieth century's great songwriters would be hit by misfortune, illness and depression, but Berlin – the first and the greatest – seemed to be haunted by his own jukebox. One of his earliest songs was 'I'll See You in C-U-B-A'; his first wife would die after contracting typhoid fever there. He wrote 'My Little Feller' for Al Jolson's second talkie, but also for his son Irving Junior, born in December 1928, who died three weeks later on Christmas Day. After this tragedy, every Christmas Eve the Berlins would tell their daughters that they needed to pop out for some last-minute Christmas preparations, when they would lay flowers on the grave of baby Irving. Song and sorrow were playmates.

For Berlin, then, 'White Christmas' had an entirely different meaning to the one it had for the rest of the world, for whom it became their favourite secular carol. Once his daughters left home, he never celebrated Christmas again. But by then much of the calendar, social or seasonal, had a Berlin song to match – 'Easter Parade', 'Tell Her in the Springtime', 'Anna Liza's Wedding Day', 'Call Me Up Some Rainy Afternoon', 'Five O'Clock Tea', 'Top Hat, White Tie and Tails', 'Our Day of Independence', 'Happy Holiday', 'Snow', 'Let's Start the New Year Right' – and in times of peril his adopted homeland would sing his 'God Bless America'. His songs became folk songs, in the air, everywhere; they had flown past his window, and he had been smart enough to catch them.

When asked to consider Berlin's position in the hierarchy of American songwriters, Jerome Kern said that 'Irving Berlin has no place in American music. He *is* American music.'

5

A CULTURE OF CONSOLATION: MUSIC HALL AND MUSICAL THEATRE

In 1909 Europe seemed to be sleepwalking towards disaster. A music-hall hit of that year claimed 'There'll Be No War as Long as There's a King Like Old King Edward' (because 'he 'ates that kind of thing!'), but unfortunately for all concerned, King Edward died in 1911.

In the US, popular music continued to grow and develop in a peaceful world. The country's immediate pre-war music scene was quite different to Britain's and wasn't about to be frozen solid for four years. America was ushering in new names, new voices and new styles that would seem even more important in Europe after the war. Its songs were now being mass-produced.

Britain's Edwardian age had been separated from its Victorian era by technology. In 1901 Marconi had sent a radio signal across the Atlantic; in 1904 came the first purpose-built cinema; and in 1906 the extended Bakerloo and Piccadilly lines were able to transport the working classes from Lambeth and Elephant and Castle to the more moneyed environs of Oxford Street and Regent's Park in minutes. This new mobility – along with the football boom, the decline in religious observance, Electric Theatres showing 'moving pictures', and even the first roller-skating craze – were all meaningful strides away from tight British class strictures. The ermine-clad music-hall singer Vesta Victoria stuck it to lower-middle-class snobbery in 1907 on her recording of 'Poor John', where she found herself slowly being taken apart by a prospective mother-in-law, until the final verse: 'She gave a sigh and cried, "I wonder what on earth he wants to marry for?" That was quite enough, up my temper flew. Says I, "Perhaps it's so that he can get away from you."'

Poor John's mother would almost certainly have gone to see the Gaiety musical play *The Merry Widow*, brought to London by George Edwardes in 1907, in which the Austro-Hungarian bandleader Franz Lehár depicted a colourful Paris and an impoverished Balkan state in the 1860s. It was a huge hit. Edward VII came to one of the first performances, which made it a must-see. But it says a lot about recorded music's lack of popularity in Britain in 1907 – partly because of the limitations of the two-minute cylinder or shellac format – that no English-language version was made at the time, and there wouldn't be one until 1942. Sheet music and pianos were still a better outlet for home reproduction of musical theatre.

The Merry Widow's star, Lily Elsie, was earning £10 a week from the show, but music-hall chorus girls were more likely to be on 35 shillings, even though the halls were more popular than ever. Grand London venues like the Empire Leicester Square, the Hippodrome and the Palace Theatre at Cambridge Circus – within yards of each other – were all late-Victorian, purpose-built music halls; they were also the work of architect Frank Matcham, who was keen on grand refinements, like the Indian-style interior and pagoda domes he added to the Empire Palace, Nottingham. Not to be outdone by Matcham, the Moss–Thornton group had cupids painted on the ceiling of their Liverpool Empire. These halls were now called 'variety theatres', the 't'-word distinguishing them from the older halls, which had been as much dining rooms and beer halls as places for entertainment.

Music hall had always been thought of as coarse and vulgar (which of course it often was), and had been battling against the moralists from the get-go. Yet, perversely, some of music hall's strongest supporters were the ones trying to curtail its grubby charms. The Coliseum on St Martin's Lane was built in 1903 by Oswald Stoll, a Liverpudlian impresario who was ashamed of music hall's honest vulgarity and planned to improve it, clean it up, bring in some of the folks going to see *The Merry Widow* by making music hall a wholesome family entertainment – everything it hadn't been. Signs appeared backstage: 'Please do not use any strong language' and 'Gentlemen of the chorus are not allowed to take their whips to the dressing rooms'. In other words, said Stoll, mind your manners.

In 1906 came a new bill that recognised a worker's right to withhold their labour. The music-hall strike began almost immediately, in January 1907. The strikers' demands seemed quite reasonable: 'No artist can be transferred from one theatre without artist's consent'; 'Times shall not be varied without artist's consent'; and 'No bias to be shown against any artist who has taken part in this movement'. Oswald Stoll led opposition to the strike, while Marie Lloyd stood by the striking performers. Stoll dismissed her 'utterances' as being down to her 'innate partiality for dramatic effect'. Twenty-two halls were picketed, and the strike lasted until June, when it was ended by arbitration in favour of the artists.

Stoll needn't have fretted so. What his fellow sensitive Edwardians had begun, new distractions for the working classes – the growth of spectator sport, the cinema, World War I and the advent of radio – all helped to finish.* By 1933 the Garrick was staging an evening of

---

* The same new pastimes meant that choral societies and brass bands – staples of the Victorian age – went into decline. In 1910 *The British Bandsman*'s Yorkshire correspondent asked, 'Can anyone account for the apathy of the younger generation against becoming bandsmen?' One answer was to be found in the centre of Bradford a year later, when Bradford City paraded the FA Cup for the first and only time, and 'the multitude surged and swayed in Town Hall Square, Forster Square and Peel Square . . . a solid mass of people some of whom swarmed up lampposts in order to catch a glimpse of the Cup. The cheering swept through the streets in waves, and the teeming populace seemed almost frantic with joy.'

'Old Time Music Hall'; within thirty years of the Coliseum being built, music hall was essentially a thing of the past.

When the halls became a political battleground, the combative atmosphere put off many aspiring new acts, preventing fresh blood from joining the ranks. Ten-year-old Bud Flanagan was a budding conjuror but quit his music-hall gig as Fargo the Boy Wizard to go to sea as a ship's electrician in 1910.*

The strike didn't kill music hall; it just weakened its previously un-assailable position. In 1909 Harry Champion brought the house down at the Metropolitan Theatre on Edgware Road with 'Boiled Beef and Carrots': 'Don't live like vegetarians on food they give to parrots. Blow out your kite from morn 'til night on boiled beef and carrots!' (Champion also sang 'A Little Bit of Cucumber' to appease vegetarians.) 1912 saw the first Royal Command Performance at the Palace Theatre, London. Irving Berlin's 'Everybody's Doin' It' was taken off the bill at the last minute, which must have pleased the rag-phobic George Robey. 'The Palace girls danced charmingly,' he recalled. 'They actually dared to wear knee length skirts. I was surprised . . . some of my normally boisterous colleagues suffered at the hands of the censor who went through it with a fine comb.' Robey sang alongside Harry Lauder and most of the music-hall greats, with the notable exception of Marie Lloyd. It was a respectable but very dull affair without her. Music hall hadn't necessarily become more serious – Harry Champion's 'Any Old Iron' ('You look dapper from your napper to your feet!') had been a hit in 1911 – but bawdiness was almost entirely eliminated. With the royal assent, music hall was now officially respectable, and its new status would be ridiculed in Wilkie Bard's 'I Want to Sing in Opera': 'I simply love Wagner, Mozart, Puccini, their music is really tip-top. So I mean to change my name Bloggs to Bloggini and see if I can't get a shop . . . Signor Caruso told me to do so.'

---

* Ironically, Bud Flanagan, with partner Chesney Allen, would later became one of the last hold-outs of music hall. A gentle singing comedy duo, they didn't work together until the mid-1920s, but had become beloved stars of the Palladium by the end of the '30s. Their sound was somehow very comforting, with Flanagan singing and Allen vaguely harmonising in a semi-spoken voice. Flanagan's own 'Underneath the Arches' became their signature tune.

The slow demise of music hall would also see the end of a potent weapon in the social struggle. 'Boiled Beef and Carrots' may have sounded boisterous enough, but songs about food – and the scarcity of it – were a reflection of working-class life that would never really be replaced. In 1901 J. A. Hobson had written: 'Among large sections of the labouring classes, the music hall is a more potent educator than the church, or the school, or the press. The glorification of brute force and an ignorant contempt for foreigners are ever-present factors, which at great political crises make the music hall a serviceable engine for generating military passion. The art of the music hall is the only popular art of the day. Its songs pass quickly from the Empire and the Alhambra across the country, through a thousand provincial halls, clubs and saloons, until the remotest village is familiar with its songs and the sentiments.'

Given their often very localised material, the stars of the halls were surprisingly popular in America. The songs could just as easily set off the tears of America's homesick immigrants, whatever their country of origin. 1905 saw thirty-five-year-old ex-miner Harry Lauder become a star with 'I Love a Lassie', a song he had written for a pantomime at the Theatre Royal, Glasgow; by 1908 he was doing a private performance for Edward VII at Sandringham. Lauder had been working as a music-hall performer in Scotland and the north of England, mostly as a comedian, but became an international star when he decided to tone down his accent, drop the jokes that were dialect-dependent and appear on stage fully kitted out in kilt, sporran and tam-o'-shanter. This must have been a weird throwback for someone who had worked for a decade down the mines of Hamilton, Lanarkshire, starting when he was fourteen years old, but it was a look that seemed to fit his own stirring, romanticised, Scottish-esque songs: not only 'I Love a Lassie', but also 'Roamin' in the Gloamin'' and, most memorable of all, 'Keep Right on to the End of the Road' (written in 1916, a few days after his son had been killed in action).

Songwriter Irving Caesar's family had arrived in New York from Romania in the 1890s. 'Harry Lauder wasn't loud, but he was a volcano,' Caesar recalled. 'My father had only been in this country ten or fifteen years. If he could go to a Harry Lauder presentation and come away and buy the records, and make the records part of their cultural experience, that proves something, doesn't it?'

Caesar was one of a rising tide of American songwriters whose work would eventually eclipse Austro-Hungarian operettas and British music hall, but for now the US wept to 'I Love a Lassie' and swooned to the decidedly non-American, Viennese sounds of Franz Lehár, Emmerich Kálmán (*The Countess Maritza*) and Oscar Straus (*The Chocolate Soldier*). These were the descendants of Offenbach, but this was operetta largely without the raised eyebrow, romantic rather than witty. Gypsies seemed to be their major lyrical preoccupation. Lehár's *The Merry Widow* wowed New York as it had London. A phenomenon at the time, its charms are largely untranslatable – like the Goons or *Frampton Comes Alive!* – to modern ears.

The Merry Widow had opened at George Edwardes's Gaiety Theatre in 1907 and ran for more than two years. The Gaiety shows often made stars of their actresses, all of whom had hour-glass figures and milk-white skin, and *The Merry Widow* made Lily Elsie a huge star. Edwardes had originally signed up Mitzi Gunther, the original Merry Widow, who had made the operetta a hit in Germany and Austria, before he had met her; when she arrived in London, he got a shock and declared, 'She has the voice of an angel, but no waist.' The reality of weighty Teutonic operetta wasn't for Edwardes, so he commissioned librettist Basil Hood to lighten the load and make *The Merry Widow* gayer and younger. The script now included the Ruritanian ambassador in Paris, Baron Popoff, and his troublesome pet, Hetty the hen. Lehár, a serious man, was unimpressed. Actor Joe Coyne, playing Prince Danilo, was such a lousy singer that he recited every song. When Lehár turned up to rehearsals, Edwardes convinced him that Coyne was 'saving his voice'. None of this mattered. Lily Elsie became one of the most famous women in the country, and soon her face featured on chocolate boxes and biscuit tins. Middle-class women wore her wide-brimmed hat, and the 'Merry Widow Waltz' – reversed, in the Viennese style – was a sensation, selling over two million sheet-music copies.

The actresses in Edwardes's shows were maybe the closest thing Britain had to pop stars. Appearing in *Havana*, Hope Hillier remembered meeting her co-star Gladys Cooper for the first time: 'She came into the dressing room looking so beautiful that I had to gasp for breath.' Stage-door johnnies had to be kept at bay, and Edwardes always felt slighted when his actresses married. Ruby Miller, with her spectacular red hair, became a favourite of the 'mashers' – Miller recalled them as 'resplend-ent young men in their tails, their opera hat and cloak lined with satin, carrying tall ebony canes with gold knobs and gardenias in their button-holes'. Max Beerbohm was a regular at both the Gaiety and Edwardes's second theatre, Daly's, and wrote about the allure and 'surpassing joy' of the actresses: 'The look of total surprise that overspreads the faces of these ladies whenever they saunter onto the stage and behold us for the first time, making us feel that we have taken rather a liberty in being there: the faintly cordial look that appears for a fraction of an instant . . . the splendid nonchalance, all so proud, so fatigued, all seeming to won-der why they were born, and born to be so beautiful.'

In 1908 George Bernard Shaw's sister Lucy returned from Germany and contacted Edwardes to tell him that Oscar Straus had turned Shaw's *Arms and the Man* into an operetta called *The Chocolate Soldier*, and it was doing very well. The cocky Edwardes turned it down flat as Shaw had been sniffy about the Gaiety shows before, when he had been drama critic for the *Saturday Review*. His pettiness caused him to miss out on a huge hit – almost on the scale of *The Merry Widow* – and *The Chocolate Soldier* went straight to Broadway instead.

Edwardes opened a third theatre, the Adelphi, in 1911, but he was stretching himself and overestimating the lasting appeal of his style of poperetta. *The Count of Luxembourg* premiered there with great fanfare. Lily Elsie – now on £100 a week – was its star, Franz Lehár conducted, and King George V and Queen Mary were in the royal box on opening night. The *Daily Chronicle* wrote that Elsie gave 'the strange impression of being from another world, where stage romances are life-and-death affairs, and a touch of the fingertips, a glance, a whisper, are matters of almost religious ecstasy'. Unfortunately, the paper also noted that 'it is delicious while it lasts, but one comes away with few definite musical memories'. *The Count of Luxembourg* did poor business; the craze for waltzes was fading. And in worse news for Edwardes, Lily Elsie told him that she was to marry and retire from the stage. Soon after, he suffered a stroke from which he never fully recovered.

Changing musical tastes, ailing theatrical impresarios and the shadow of imminent war aside, the bioscope – or cinema, as it was soon to be known – was poised to replace the physical space of the variety theatre. Silent films threatened the musical play, so Edwardes came up with *The Girl on the Film*, a crude parody, in 1913. But a bigger threat came from the 'revue', an American import which didn't have a need for a plot, just sketches, solo turns, songs and dances linked together by a vague central theme. Albert De Courville, a reporter for London's *Evening News*, travelled to the US to study the way Americans produced their shows; he returned full of ragged-up enthusiasm and booked the Hippodrome to stage *Hullo Ragtime* in 1912. He brought a 'trap' drummer, cornet player and trombonist over to join the Hippodrome's own orchestra. Its leader, Julian Jones, initially loathed this intrusion – 'This is not music,' he told De Courville, 'it's against all the principles of music!' – but when the non-stop show was a runaway hit, he eventually conceded it was 'quite effective'. De Courville allowed for no curtain waits and brought in an American dance instructor who drilled the chorus girls in a manner that was alien to Edwardes's delicately staged routines. Everything about *Hullo Ragtime* moved faster, faster.

* * *

The difference in the pace of Edwardian Britain and America could be summed up by the story of James Bland, a black middle-class New Yorker.

Genuine black minstrel troupes – known as Georgia Minstrels rather than Nigger Minstrels, who were in blackface – had been popular in Britain since the 1870s, in the halls as well as when performing for nobility (Queen Victoria was alleged to have cracked a smile for one Billy Kersands of the Hague and Hicks troupe). Bland arrived in London in 1882, with his five-string banjo, as part of the Haverly troupe. He was quickly acclaimed for his own compositions: 'Oh Dem Golden Slippers', 'Hand Me Down My Walking Cane', 'Carry Me Back to Old Virginny' ('where the cotton and corn and taters grow') and the sweet barbershop harmonies of 'In the Evening by the Moonlight'. The pre-war South in all its mythic honeysuckle gentility was evoked by Bland's songs, and Britain hailed him as a successor to Stephen Foster, slapped his back, bought him drinks and treated him with due respect. When it was time for the Haverly Minstrels to go home, Bland decided to stay on in London.

His billing was 'James Bland – the Idol of the Halls', and he began to sing songs about London life while dressed immaculately in a suit. English hospitality began to catch up with him, though, and his fondness for pubs led him to turn up late for shows and stumble over his words, which his hosts put down to southern eccentricity. Yet when he returned to New York at the turn of the century, his homeland saw him as yesterday's man, washed up. Ragtime was taking over, and his songs seemed old-fashioned, embarrassing, an echo of a past that newly urbanised America – especially black America – was keen to forget. Bland died, broke, in 1911.

In the shadow of a war that some knew was coming, Britain felt like it was in a state of flux. In stark contrast to the metallic brashness of Sophie Tucker and 'Oh You Beautiful Doll', the pre-war gentility of Britain was summed up by one of 1912's biggest hits, Sidney Baines's 'Destiny Waltz'. A piece of light music that led to a series of Baines waltzes – 'Ecstasy', 'Mystery', 'Victory', 'Witchery' and the language-mangling 'Frivolry' – it sold a million copies and couldn't have been more date-stamped; it was allegedly one of the tunes played on the *Titanic*. The light classical sound of the English tea dance, as much as the newly tamed world of music hall, met its nemesis in ragtime. J. B. Priestley saw the revolution at close quarters: 'Of all the new exciting things that were crowding into our lives, the most urgent hit me when I went over to Leeds to a variety show at the Empire and heard Ragtime. Suddenly, I discovered the 20th century, glaring and screaming at me. The syncopated frenzy of this was something quite new – shining with sweat, the ragtimers almost hung over the footlights, defying us to resist the rhythm, drumming us into another kind of life in which anything might happen.'

Sophie Tucker was the physical embodiment of emancipation, and her American voice was the sound of Britain's near future. In 1913 she began calling herself the 'Mary Garden of Ragtime' (Garden being a contemporary Scottish opera singer); she would have the pop nous to switch her nickname after the war to 'The Queen of Jazz' and picked up a new backing band called the Five Kings of Syncopation. Britain in 1913 was whistling a new music-hall song that still retains a sadness almost too great to think about. Florrie Forde recorded 'It's a Long Way to Tipperary' as a lament from an Irish worker in London; a year later, it signified a far greater homesickness.

ON THE OTHER SIDE OF A BIG BLACK CLOUD: WORLD WAR I

TAKE ME BACK TO DEAR OLD BLIGHTY. (1).

Jack Dunn, son of a gun, over in France to-day, —
Keeps fit, doing his bit, up to his eyes in clay;
Each night, after a fight, to pass the time along,
He's got a little gramophone that plays this song.

Up until 1914, Germans had usually been referenced in popular song as jolly, sausage-loving fellows (Arthur Collins's 'The Leader of the German Band', 1906) or cuddly, ever-hugging gals (Irving Berlin's saucy 'Oh How That German Could Love', recorded in 1910 by Sam Bernard). Along with Viennese operetta, songs that spoke warmly of Germans came to an abrupt end in 1914.

The world would survive the loss. More surprisingly, Broadway and Tin Pan Alley in America and London's West End and Denmark

Street,* which had been growing more supportive of each other in the years leading up to 1914, began to diverge dramatically. With the declaration of war, music hall became fiercely militaristic, and the halls themselves quickly resembled recruitment offices. The stars of the day were enthusiastic supporters of the cause, with cash prizes offered to willing conscripts: backed by a military band, Harry Lauder offered 'ten pounds for the first recruit tonight'; George Robey promised 'a shiny florin for every recruit who signs on tonight'; while, in male drag, Vesta Tilley sang 'Your King and Country Want You', 'In Dear Old England's Name' and 'Jolly Good Luck to the Girl Who Loves a Soldier' (all 1914), guilt-tripping dozens of drunken lads into signing up one night at the Sunderland Empire. She earned the nickname 'England's finest recruiting sergeant' and later publicly regretted her role in the slaughter.

In Britain, it was the passing of an age. Initially, when war was declared, the theatres were packed, with many in khaki, yet to be sent abroad. Sad-eyed, long-haired Ruby Miller provided glamour. She was the latest star to emerge from George Edwardes's Gaiety Theatre and was the sweetheart of the West End by 1914, when a Romanov grand duke asked to drink champagne from her slipper. Neither would be quite the same carefree soul four years later. Miller's husband was killed in action in 1918, and she retired, aged twenty-nine, seeking solace – like many others suffering bereavements – in clairvoyancy and astrology.

There were still a handful of popular songs written in Britain that didn't directly reference the war. Unity Moore's 'I'm Mary from Tipperary' – an answer song to Florrie Forde's smash hit 'It's a Long Way to Tipperary' – was in a show called *Business as Usual*, though it couldn't help but remind crowds of what was happening on the continent. Lord Kitchener's face was everywhere. Down in Bath, Fred Weatherly was a retired barrister who had taken up songwriting, rather successfully, with the deeply evocative 'Danny Boy' in 1913. Two years later, he wrote the equally successful 'Roses of Picardy', which at its peak was selling

---

* Like the creation of Tin Pan Alley, music publishers in London began to coalesce on this short street off Charing Cross Road after the firms of Lawrence Wright and Campbell Connelly both moved there in 1911. It would remain the heart of the British pop industry until the 1970s.

50,000 copies of sheet music a day. Still, even with this innocuous song
to a girl with 'sea-blue eyes', there was the suggestion of death: Picardy
was the area of northern France that contained the Somme.

There were also songs about our gallant allies, though Britain being
Britain, these had paternalistic titles to make you wince: Violet Loraine's
'Three Cheers for Little Belgium', Harry Fay's 'Bravo Little Belgium'
and military song specialist Fred Godfrey's 'Good Luck, Little French
Soldier Man' were popular in 1914. African and Asian members of the
Empire who had fought in the Boer War had been rewarded in 1901
with the Nat Clifford song 'John Bull's Little Khaki Coon' ('I'm not a
common darkie, that's why I'm dressed in khaki'); British Jews in World
War I had to suffer Gus Harris's 'Sergeant Solomon Isaacstein' (1916),
which called for Jews to be integrated into the war effort, while at the
same time being casually anti-Semitic. The chorus was jolly enough
('Sergeant Solomon Isaacstein, he's the pet of the fighting line. Oy, oy,
oy! Give three hearty cheers for the only Jewish Scotsman in the Irish
Fusiliers!'), though the verse saw the protagonist set up a pawn shop in
the trenches 'with money lent at 90 per cent'.

As the months passed, the euphoria faded; what was wanted was no
longer courage but endurance. The biggest hits looked forward to the
end of the conflict. With 'Keep the Home Fires Burning', Ivor Novello
would become the leading romantic songwriter of the post-war period.
In 1913, when he was twenty, he moved to London from Cardiff with
his mother. They found a flat above the Strand Theatre, and Novello
would stay there until his death in 1951. Within months of arriving
in the capital, he had written 'Keep the Home Fires Burning', a song
as gallantly affecting as a Wilfred Owen poem. In the 1920s he would
begin a run of hit musicals that never let up. His style was operetta,
very English, often very pretty, and he remained entirely unaffected by
the outside influences of ragtime or jazz. His melodies – maybe the
best being 'Some Day My Heart Will Awake' (from *King's Rhapsody*,
1949) – swooped like swallows. Novello was also stupidly handsome
and decided to turn to acting in the 1920s, acing that too, making a
brief foray into Hollywood as the star of D. W. Griffith's *The White Rose*
and landing a lead role in Alfred Hitchcock's debut, *The Lodger* (1927).

Novello had a reputation for flings, though his fame as a matinee idol meant he was usually labelled a flirt rather than a philanderer. His songs were perfectly chaste: 'My Dearest Dear', 'I Can Give You the Starlight', 'Fly Home Little Heart' and, ultimately, 'We'll Gather Lilacs'. Listening to his catalogue now, with the exception of 'Keep the Home Fires Burning' the songs are almost impossible to place in any kind of social or historical context. When he described Noël Coward's 1929 musical *Bitter Sweet* as reminiscent of 'a vanished, kindly, silly, darling age', Novello could have been writing about his own entire oeuvre.

In the halls, the songs would remain upbeat throughout the war, but the emphasis changed over time. Hardly any gung-ho songs about signing up were released after Christmas 1914, when it was commonly thought the war was due to end. Still, the sentiment was very rarely anti-war; instead, later songs heard in the halls had glum titles like 'Slog on, Slog on for 1917' (1917), 'On the Other Side of a Big Black Cloud' (1917), 'We Must Keep on Keeping on' (1918) and 'It's No Use Worrying Over Yesterday' (1918). Inward-looking, cheerily mournful things appeared, such as 'Take Me Back to Dear Old Blighty', sung by both Dorothy Ward and the reliable Florrie Forde, which rather desperately pleaded, 'Take me over there, drop me anywhere – Birmingham, Leeds or Manchester, well, I don't care!' War was neither challenged nor celebrated, but was instead given the same weight as other everyday disasters of working-class life. The halls relied on singalongs, and a politically freighted song that went even slightly against public opinion was never going to be performed.

America looked on, unimpressed. British songs may have danced around the subject, but international politesse didn't stop Irving Berlin from writing the openly pacifist 'Stay Down Here Where You Belong' in 1914, recorded by Henry Burr: 'To serve their king they've all gone off to war, and not a one of them knows what they're fighting for.' When the US eventually entered the conflict and the national mood changed, Berlin became embarrassed by the song.* The Peerless Quartet

---

* After the war, Groucho Marx playfully enjoyed singing it, and Berlin allegedly offered him money to stop.

and Morton Harvey released the even more forthright 'I Didn't Raise My Boy to Be a Soldier' ('I brought him up to be my pride and joy. Who dares to put a musket on his shoulder to shoot some other mother's darling boy?'). The two songs were major American hits, both on record and as sheet music.

The music hall did not allow dissent or protest songs to slip through easily. The relatively low sales of records in Britain suggests that there wasn't a market for them. Ten years later, a niche peacenik market could have sustained such releases, but the halls made hits, and the priority of the theatre industry was to fill them, not sow discontent. Consensus politics kept dissent at bay.

Ambiguous statements could filter through, though. In 1917 'Oh It's a Lovely War', a rarity in that it was sung from the perspective of soldiers, was a huge success: 'Up to your waist in water, up to your eyes in slush, using the kind of language that makes the sergeant blush. Who wouldn't join the army? That's what we all enquire. Don't we pity the poor civilian, sitting beside the fire.' There were also soldiers' songs, none of which would be recorded without being sanitised first. In 1916 General Douglas Haig heard a column of soldiers, marching on their way to the Somme, singing 'Do Your Balls Hang Low'. He rode to the head of the column to point out this ill-discipline, only to find the sergeant singing the song as well: 'Do they rattle when you walk? Do they jingle when you talk? Can you sling them on your shoulder like a lousy fucking soldier?' An embarrassed Haig told the sergeant he had a fine, strong voice and that 'I like the tune, but those words are inexcusable.' It was cleaned up after the war as 'Do Your Ears Hang Low', supposedly about a dog, and would be sung this way by children's TV character Barney the Dinosaur in 1993. Likewise, 'Bless 'Em All' ('the long and the short and the tall'), one of the best remembered World War II songs, first recorded by George Formby in 1940, had been copyrighted by one Fred Godfrey back in 1917. Godfrey would have heard its original lyric – 'Fuck 'em all' – while he was in the Royal Naval Air Service, and he cheekily pinched it, changing one crucial word.

The strongest anti-war songs – 'Teddy McGrath', 'The Kerry Recruit', 'Glen of Aherlow' – came from Ireland, unsurprisingly. None of them would have been heard in the halls, and they were barely played in public. 'The Recruiting Sergeant' was regarded as treasonous by the British government: 'Come rain or hail or wind or snow, I'm not going out to Flanders – there's fighting in Dublin to be done. Let your sergeants and commanders go, let Englishmen fight English wars.' Anyone heard singing it in public faced six months' imprisonment.

Clues as to what might happen to both musical taste and rigid class structures after the war could be found in the works of doomed poet Wilfred Owen. 'Smile, Smile, Smile' ironically took its title from the chorus of 'Pack Up Your Troubles', while 'Anthem for Doomed Youth' could work as a twenty-first-century neo-Gothic song title. Owen was twenty-five when he was killed in action, a week before Armistice Day. Along with automatic respect for your elders, the bloodbath of the war also killed off several of Europe's monarchies and empires, including the Russian, the Austro-Hungarian and the Ottoman. The notion of fighting for king and country was no longer sacrosanct, no longer something you might sign up to die for without giving it a second thought. It made sense that the US, a country with no history of a monarchy and no need for hand-wringing, reparations or revolution at the end of the war, would be best placed to steer international culture.

* * *

British popular music had effectively pressed the 'pause' button for four years. The West End may as well have still been in the late nineteenth century. Viennese operettas were now *verboten*. Instead, the ravaged theatres featured upper-class British problems in *Betty* (in which the anti-hero laughingly proposes to a servant girl); Ruritanian fantasy with *The Maid of the Mountains*; and a mind-boggling 2,238 performances for Frederic Norton's *Chu Chin Chow* (based on *Ali Baba and the Forty Thieves*), a record not surpassed until 1958's *My Fair Lady*. Watching from the sidelines, there was to be no break in continuity in American pop during the war. As if to affirm that, unlike the West End, it wouldn't be preserved in Edwardian aspic, the 1914 Broadway season provided Jerome Kern's game-changing, intimate 'They Didn't Believe

Me', the very first song that would later be regarded as a Great American Songbook standard.

Intimacy would take a while to become a force on Tin Pan Alley, where, on 1916's 'Naughty! Naughty! Naughty!', the fetching Marguerite Farrell was rolling her 'r's and singing, 'I'm going to take you right across my knee, I want you though you're unruly.' Homesick ballads for émigrés still sold. You would have thought Ireland to be a mythical utopia, such were the number of glassy-eyed best-sellers written about it: Chauncey Olcott's 'When Irish Eyes Are Smiling' (1913) and 'Too Ra Loo Ra Loo Rai' (1914), the latter eventually forming the foundations for another US number one, Dexys Midnight Runners' 'Come On Eileen' in 1982; George MacFarlane's 1915 recording 'A Little Bit of Heaven (Sure They Call It Ireland)'; and – a sentimental double whammy – 1916's 'Ireland Must Be Heaven for My Mother Came from There' by Charles Harrison. Ireland was seen as a symbol of peace, which, bearing in mind the 1916 Easter Rising and Roger Casement's execution for treason, seems quite eccentric. The biggest hit was a revival of 1912's 'It's a Long Way to Tipperary', a success in the States for both the American Quartet and John McCormack at the end of 1914.

In 1917, when America did eventually join the conflict, Tin Pan Alley began looking around for war songs, happy to play its part. The US War Industries Board decreed that 'music is essential to win the war' and provided as much paper as was necessary for the booming sheet-music sales. Yankee Doodle himself, George M. Cohan, re-emerged after years in the shadows and blew the bugle loudest with 'Over There', a number-one best-seller for the shamelessly populist Enrico Caruso.* It wasn't a hit in Europe, and must have seemed naive to the war-weary British.

American pro-war songs generally felt more robust than the British ones. Irving Berlin's surname may have been decidedly out of step with American loyalties, but he wasn't about to change it to Windsor, or

---

* Almost a century later, it would become ubiquitous in Britain as the jingle for the GoCompare ad, in which a portly opera singer dressed as Caruso is seen in multiple insurance-related situations, one of which sees him crawling from the wreckage of a car crash, still trying to sing the blasted song.

even back to Baline. He would recall: 'I wasn't very much of a soldier, so I suggested writing a show for them, which was quite a success.' He also came up with a song, late in the war, that poked fun at the army: 'Oh How I Hate to Get Up in the Morning'. The same year, tenor Sam Ash sang the interventionist 'We're Going to Celebrate the End of the War in Ragtime (Be Sure That Woodrow Wilson Leads the Band)'. And having read reports of the slaughter on the Western Front, Berlin did a complete turnaround and came up with 'Let's All Be Americans Now': 'Lincoln, Grant and Washington – they were peaceful men, each one. Still they took the sword and gun when real trouble came.' It was recorded on the Edison label by Adolph J. Hahl, who, unlike Berlin, decided his name was becoming problematic and soon changed it to Albert Hall.

*　*　*

World War I acted as a giant wooden spoon, stirring music around countries and across continents. It brought together potential musicians, would-be songwriters and stay-at-home singers who may have chosen a career in the army before all this insanity but were now moved in an entirely different direction. It's hard to know how much influence the wind-up gramophones in the trenches might have had, but the commingling of the American, British and French working classes could push popular culture in only one direction, and that was away from starchiness. Patriotic parlour songs wouldn't cut it any more. Mistrust of the military, bitterness towards the older generations, and the new liberated noises coming out of America would turn a generation's heads.

By November 1918 London and New York must have seemed like they were on different planets. So much had changed in four years. Bronx-born Moss Hart, the future Broadway producer (*My Fair Lady*) and playwright (*The Man Who Came to Dinner*, *You Can't Take It with You*), travelled to Broadway for the very first time in 1918, when he was fourteen years old. Years later, he could still remember his excitement as the subway doors opened at Times Square: 'I shall certainly never forget the picture that greeted me as I dashed up the stairs and stood gaping at my first sight of Broadway and 42nd Street. A swirling mob of shouting happy people filled the streets, and others hung from every window of every building. Confetti and paper streamers floated down from the buildings, and traffic stopped dead in the middle of the street. Soldiers and sailors climbed happily onto the tops of taxis, grabbing girls up to dance with them. My first thought was 'Of course, that's just the way I thought it would be.' But what I took to be an everyday occurrence was Broadway celebrating that the armistice had just been signed. The First World War was at an end. I had merely stumbled into a historic moment.'

7

A CONVERSATION OF INSTRUMENTS: THE BIRTH OF JAZZ

On 6 April 1917 America had joined Britain, France and Russia in trying to end World War I. More than two million US soldiers would eventually fight in Europe (where a fifth of them had been born). President Woodrow Wilson, talking to the entire country, including the many citizens who wanted to stay neutral, knew this was a defining moment: 'Woe to the man that seeks to stand in our way in this day of high resolution.' He was addressing Jewish Americans, Italian Americans, Irish Americans and, in particular, German Americans. Eighteen months later, the war was over, and Europe ceded the remainder of the twentieth century to the US.

What the Old World needed from the New World in 1918 was its newness. Europe was trying to find paths out of the hellhole of Ypres. It was clear that the old order wasn't fit for purpose and Europe had to start from scratch. It found other ways of seeing, hearing, being; through Dada or Vorticism, Alban Berg or André Breton, Bolshevism or fascism, Kibbo Kift or the Woodcraft Folk, the new chipped away at the old, made huge efforts, invested in much toil. How clear and fresh and effortless the US must have suddenly seemed. And jazz was America's musical skyscraper. It was ecstatically modern; it created spaces that weren't simply a rejig of the pre-established 'serious' or 'popular' categories. Jazz really was a new thing under the sun.

Here's one way in which jazz was entirely new. Notation had evolved in Europe over a thousand years. Jazz trashed this. Notation indicated what should be played, but not how. Swoops on the trombone or in a vocal needed supplementary symbols, which were a new language. With improvisation, and endless variations in phrasing and accenting, the old school was lost. The unity of the whole idiom, of the whole centuries-old Western tradition of music, was gone for ever.

What's more, jazz overthrew the binary of 'serious' and 'popular'. Via Sidney Bechet and George Gershwin, as much as Stravinsky or Varèse, the potential of the word 'serious' began to shift. It would turn out to be an evolving encounter, with the three terms – 'serious', 'pop' and 'jazz' – dancing around the roles they played.

* * *

Jazz did not grow directly out of either ragtime or blues. It would suit my story if that were the case, and going forward popular music would have no bother combining elements of all three, but jazz grew up in New Orleans – the Paris of the New World – in splendid isolation.

A tranche of land that had been sold to the US by Napoleon, New Orleans was proud of its French heritage and flush with plantation and shipping money. The younger generation looked to spend this money on earthly pleasures, with the result that New Orleans was ripe with bordellos as ornate as a shipping magnate's palace. Each of these became a site for musicians and one strain of the earliest purely American music: Dixieland.*

New Orleans city councillor Sidney Story is one of the accidental heroes of this book. In 1897 he rose, cleared his throat and addressed the issue of the city's bordellos, bands, brothels and bacchanalian behaviour. 'Members of the city council,' he huffed, 'I propose the following ordinance be adopted by the city of New Orleans. From and after the

---

* Other new musical subcultures grew in the working-class areas of rapidly growing industrial cities at roughly the same time. Buenos Aires created the tango, for example, while Havana developed the rumba.

first of October 1897, it shall be unlawful for any prostitute to occupy, inhabit, live or sleep in any house not situated within the following limits: from Custom House Street to St Louis Street; from Northern Basin Street to Robinson Street; from the riverside of Franklin to the woodside of Locust and from Upper Perdido to Lower Gravier.'

One of the first experiments in legalised prostitution, the area would be nicknamed 'Storyville', and it became a hedonistic fantasy land that gave us popular-music standards like 'Basin Street Blues' and 'When the Saints Go Marching In'. The district's performers were all black. Among the best known were the Spasm Band, also known as the Razzy Dazzy Spasm Band. If you scoff at the idea that they could have been the antecedents of hip hop, ragga, or DIY punk acts, check out their line-up: Cajun, Stalebread Charlie, Chinee Whisky, Warm Gravy and (there's always one who won't play ball) Charlie Stein.

The music of the bands, however, wasn't heard in the brothels and bordellos, where you would find only a lone pianist, playing either some form of ragtime or popular classics like 'Tales from the Vienna Woods'. There were four or five cabarets which did accommodate some of the bands, but jazz was primarily an outdoor music (for starters it was too loud for the confines of a bar or bordello) that was played on riverboats and at parades, picnics and lawn parties. When it did move indoors, it was played faster, as the bar owners thought that was more suitable for a fast-living situation.

So it was a localised event, part of New Orleans's unique musical development, until the closure of Storyville by the Department of the Navy in 1917. Black jazz musicians who had needed the district in order to thrive and make a living then started to move northwards, up the Mississippi, via rivers and canals, on riverboats, all the way to New Orleans's geographically predetermined successor as jazz capital, Chicago. And from Chicago, jazz began to spread across the country, then over the Atlantic, its popularity building even faster than ragtime. This being the early twentieth century, it took a white band to make the global breakthrough. For now, the New Orleans originators would remain in the shadows.

* * *

The most succinct description of jazz I've ever come across was by cornet player Nick LaRocca, who, as someone who played on the very first jazz record, knew a thing or two about it. The sound of the Original Dixieland Jazz Band (originally 'Jass Band' – the word was too new to have a fixed spelling in 1917) was 'a conversation of instruments', said LaRocca, in which he and gangly clarinettist Larry Shields would talk and ad-lib on the subject of a tune. Chairing the debate was trombone player Eddie Edwards, interjecting when he felt the need, while the pianist and drummer nodded, laughed and buoyed up the chat.

The word 'jazz' had been knocking around for a while before the ODJB released 'Livery Stable Blues' in 1917, either in the phrase 'jazz it up' (move a little faster) or in the same way that 'rock and roll' would later be used – as a euphemism for sex – before it too became the name of a musical genre.

If you're going to use a sexual phrase to describe your music, then it probably isn't going to be a pub singalong, a tea-drinking accompaniment or the militarily square noise still being made by many dance bands, orchestras and vaudevillians in 1917. Yet jazz wasn't the only possible future for American dance bands, as they skipped from bar to restaurant to hotel in New York: there was also jug music, a fashion for Middle Eastern exoticism (Joseph C. Smith and His Orchestra released 'Allah's Holiday', as did Prince's Orchestra, who followed it with 'Arabian Serenade') and, most intriguingly, Hawaiian music.

There had been a smattering of Hawaiian recordings since 1900, but they exploded in 1916 thanks to a bunch of records by Helen Louise and Frank Ferera: 'Aloha Land', 'Everybody Hula', 'Hawaii I'm Lonesome for You'. Ferera was a steel guitarist in the Royal Hawaiian Quartet, the house band at the 1915 Panama–Pacific Exposition in San Francisco. At the Expo, Ferera met Thomas Edison, who quickly issued his 'Ua Like No Alike'/'Medley of Hawaiian Hulas'; by the Expo's end, seven months later, he was duetting with his wife, Seattle-born Helen Louise. They became a sensation, signing to Victor and selling around 300,000 copies of 'Drowsy Waters'. The couple both played Martin guitars. Louise strummed gently, while Ferera played high, clean, lonesome lines over the top. They had little to do with traditional Hawaiian music, but in the pre-electric recording era Ferera's playing cut through beautifully on 78s. A measure of his fame was his December 1916 appearance on the cover of *Edison Phonograph Monthly*, which claimed that Ferera 'first introduced the Hawaiian style of playing the guitar into the United States. It was in 1900 that he brought the first ukulele here and commenced to charm vaudeville audiences with the weird and plaintive effects he produced.'* Exotic and naive, these are wonderful records. Their success encouraged others to cash in: erstwhile ragtime banjo king Vess Ossman cut 'My Hawaiian Sunshine'; vaudeville act Arthur Collins and Byron Harlan had a bash with 'They're Wearing 'Em Higher in Hawaii'; and even the now-fading Peerless Quartet gave us 'Along the Way to Waikiki'. An even bigger wave of cod-Hawaiian recordings would emerge in the 1950s, as the islands became incorporated into the United States. And here's a thing: while Louise and Ferera's records are now almost completely forgotten, they were likely a major generational influence. Ferera's style – its sliding notes, its melancholy – foreshadowed both bottleneck-playing on blues records and steel guitar on country tracks. Both came, indirectly, from Hawaii.

The Hawaiian craze was short-lived but suggested that the American public were ready for something quite new. The collapse of civilisation in Western Europe was psychologically encouraging them to loosen cultural ties and start afresh.

* * *

'Jazz' was a word loaded with insouciance, freedom and general naughtiness. It caught on, became the hip phrase to drop, and when 'Livery Stable Blues' became the first-ever jazz 78, it was an instant and massive hit. The Original Dixieland Jazz Band weren't the first to use 'jazz' in their name, but they were the first to use it to describe their music. Their front line of cornet, trombone and clarinet became the template.

---

* The Louise/Ferera team was abruptly broken up when in 1919 Louise mysteriously fell from a ship travelling from Los Angeles to Seattle. Ferera was also on board.

On every level, the ODJB were a recognisable modern pop group, like the Rolling Stones or Public Enemy or Take That, with glamour and gimmicks and a sense of purpose. They were just one of dozens of bands in New Orleans, where anything from saucepans to strips of sandpaper could be used as instruments. But the ODJB stood out. Drummer Tony Spargo had a teddy bear on his cymbal which jumped up whenever he hit it, which was frequently. They'd lift up their coat-tails and point their instruments to the ceiling when they hit the high notes. Each wore a top hat with a letter on it, spelling out the word 'DIXIE'. They had razzamatazz; they were incredibly exciting. In 1916 they got a gig at a café in Chicago, where other southern bands had played and moved on – it was no big deal. The ODJB caused a sensation. Al Jolson caught their act and was so excited he burst into tears. He got them a slot at Reisenweber's Restaurant on Columbus Circle in New York, which had twelve dining rooms, a thousand employees, the 400 Club cabaret room (where Sophie Tucker was a regular performer) and the Paradise dancefloor.* The swells took to the ODJB's anarchic sound just as easily as Chicago had. Reisenweber's undersold them, describing them as 'the fad of the hour' under a bigger claim for its 'exceptional beefsteak dinner – $1.50'. But it wasn't a fad; it was the beginning of club nightlife for New York.

The ODJB were also incredibly *loud*. In New Orleans, bands had played outdoors; they were street bands. Bringing them inside was quite new. They also played *fast* – compare their 'Tiger Rag' to a stately Scott Joplin rag. And they gave a good interview. 'You see, I cut the material,' explained LaRocca, 'Shields (clarinet) puts on the lace, and Edwards (trombone) sews it up.' They had a manager, Max Hart, who coaxed phrases out of them for a hungry press. 'I am the assassinator of syncopation,' said LaRocca. If someone came up with that line today, I'd want to hear their music immediately. No wonder people got excited in 1917.

The new sensation, the band that effectively gave us the first true pop hit single, actually had a strong link to ragtime, the sound they

* No other restaurant in New York had such a dancefloor. It had been built in 1916 to accommodate the Hawaiian dance craze and was hosted by actress and dancer Dora 'Doraldina' Saunders.

destroyed overnight. ODJB pianist J. Russel Robinson had been a rag-time writer and player, still a teenager when he had his first rag published ('Aggravatin' Papa', which was given lyrics and recorded by Bessie Smith and Sophie Tucker). He was especially fond of tributes to girls – 'Mary Lou', 'A Portrait of Jennie', 'Margie'. But the ODJB didn't mention this in interviews, giving the impression that their music came from nowhere and was entirely spontaneous, and people wanted to believe that. That, above all else, is what made them the first pop group.

The ODJB settled in London after arriving on April Fool's Day 1919 via New Orleans, Chicago and New York.* Initially, they were booked by promoter Albert De Courville to play in a show called *Joy Bells* at the London Hippodrome, but after one night a member of the cast issued De Courville an ultimatum. This was George Robey, a one-man rep-resentation of music hall and decades of tradition, and he wasn't about to share a stage with this anarchic, primitive racket. Either he went or they did. Robey was too big a name to lose, so De Courville arranged some short residencies for the ODJB at Rector's on Tottenham Court Road and the Embassy in Old Bond Street. It was probably for the best, as a seated theatre was no place for 'Tiger Rag'. Around Easter 1919 they played a fortnight at the London Palladium, a quote on the poster outside claiming they 'made the feet ache to dance'.†

* The influenza pandemic claimed more than half a million American lives in 1918 and 1919, one of whom was the ODJB's Henry Raga, who died two days before they sailed for England. Recording pioneer Fred Gaisberg lost his brother William, then head of the Gramophone Company's London recording studios. He contracted flu recording a Royal Garrison Artillery bombardment on the Western Front that was released on an HMV disc.
† The London Palladium poster for the ODJB also claimed that they were 'quite unlike the various renderings already heard in this country'. Almost forgotten to history are acts like Murray Pilcer's Jazz Band, who had been playing in London since 1916. Their sound was based on ragtime banjo, with the emphasis on percussion. The band, who were from New York, played commercial ragtime sets at the Trocadero, the Oxford Theatre and the Savoy Hotel between 1916 and 1922, and even cut a couple of singles before the ODJB arrived. Listen to 'K-K-K-Katy' (1916) and, prominent banjo aside, wonder how they ever got to call themselves a jazz band. It's anarchy all right, but it sounds more like Bagpuss leading an oompah band down Tring High Street than anything you'd associate with New Orleans.

The English climate didn't suit J. Russel Robinson's wife, an asthma sufferer, so he left the band in 1919 and returned to the States. Robinson was replaced by English pianist Billy Jones, who, quickly absorbing the work of the other players, effectively became the first British jazz musician.

The Southern Syncopated Orchestra, a huge agglomeration of black musicians put together by Will Marion Cook, sold out the Philharmonic Hall on Wigmore Street in 1919. They never released a record but pulled in crowds by word of mouth, thanks largely to the praise of Ernest Ansermet, a friend of Stravinsky and the conductor for Diaghilev's Ballets Russes. He had been blown away by one of the Southern Syncopated's clarinet players: Sidney Bechet, reckoned Ansermet in October 1919, was on 'the highway the whole world will swing along tomorrow'. Given the antipathetic line most of his contemporaries were taking, this was an extraordinarily brave and forward-looking observation. Bechet quit the orchestra and returned to New York. Just as well for him, as in October 1921 a ship carrying the Southern Syncopated to Dublin was in a collision in the Irish Sea, and several band members drowned.

Bechet would turn out to be one of jazz's earliest international ambassadors. As part of the *Revue nègre*, he played in Paris in 1925 with Josephine Baker; a year later, he put together a band and played in Russia. France loved him, until he accidentally shot a woman while involved in a drunken duel with a Frenchman who said Bechet had played a wrong chord. After leaving prison, he went back to New York, recorded some formative Latin jazz with stride pianist Willie 'The Lion' Smith in 1939, opened a tailor's shop in the 1940s, and then moved permanently to France in the 1950s, where he wrote maybe his best-remembered song, 'Petite Fleur'. He was a truly beautiful player, under-appreciated at home; you get the feeling his life might not have been so peripatetic had he been white.

* * *

So, what was so new about the jazz band?

Wind instruments in bands, whether in tight-spot nightspots or bigger ballrooms, were unheard of before jazz. London's most popular pre-jazz dance band was the Savoy Quartet (residents of the Savoy Ballroom), which consisted of two banjos, piano and drums*; their lead banjoist, Joe Wilbur, was also their vocalist.

The formula for the Savoy band, without fail, was instrumental verse, vocal chorus, vocal verse, a second vocal chorus and an instrumental chorus. I cannot lie: it's hard work listening to the squareness of too many Savoy Quartet recordings a century later, though it's of historical interest to compare their 1918 banjo-led 'Darktown Strutters Ball' – all Keystone Cops effects and percussive gags, not quite ragtime, not quite jazz – to the swing of the ODJB version recorded a few months earlier.

Of the other 'hot' and syncopated orchestras who snuck through the door behind the ODJB, Earl Fuller's cannily named Famous Jazz Band – hurriedly put together by Fuller and signed by Victor to fulfil the huge demand for jazz records created by 'Livery Stable Blues' – would become one of the most commercially successful, with sides like 'Slippery Hank' (1917) and 'Jazbo Jazz One Step' (1918).† The bulk of its members had started out in a circus band at Coney Island, and their clarinet player, Ted Lewis, would employ his vaudeville background, looning around on stage in the hope that the crowd wouldn't notice that he could do little more than parp weakly on his instrument. A Victor catalogue, presumably attempting to sell Fuller's 78s, explained, 'The sounds as of a dog in his dying anguish are from Ted Lewis' clarinet.' Fuller's band were ragged, but there's still fun to be had in their slapdash recordings. Aside from anything else, they recorded 'Twelfth Street Rag'

---

* The drum kit – still referred to as 'traps', short for 'contraptions', in 1917 – also had its roots in New Orleans. One of the first to use a foot pedal for the bass drum, keeping the beat while liberating the hands to be more percussive, was Dee Dee Chandler, drummer with the John Robichaux Dance Orchestra in the 1890s, who fashioned it from a Magnolia Milk Company carton, attached to a chain and spring. John MacMurray, drummer with cornetist Buddy Bolden around the same time, built his own kit, including a snare drum that was apparently 'a banjo head set on a chair'. In 1909 the Ludwig brothers patented the first factory-built bass-drum pedal, and the modern drum kit was on its way.
† The latter was described as 'a real, red-hot jazz dance of the most ultra modern variety' in an Edison catalogue – quite possibly the first time that a jazz record was promoted as 'hot'.

and W. C. Handy's 'Beale Street Blues' in 1917, helping to popularise a brace of songs that would become jazz staples.

In 1919 Lewis left Fuller and, in a sneaky move that Malcolm McLaren would use sixty years later with Adam and the Ants, took the rest of the band with him in a coup. Ted Lewis and His Band featured in *The Passing Show of 1919* and the *Greenwich Village Follies* of 1919 through to 1922. Lewis, the self-titled 'High-Hatted Tragedian of Jazz', had picked up a catchphrase – 'Is everybody happy?' – and when they weren't playing in shows his band performed in Manhattan nightclubs, such as the Bal Tabarin and the Montmartre. Lewis may have had the roots of a clown, something exaggerated by his scruffy top hat, but he had incredible taste when it came to finding new musicians: passing through his ranks in the 1920s were such significant players as Muggsy Spanier, Jimmy Dorsey, Benny Goodman, Jack Teagarden and Fats Waller. More on them later. He also knew how to milk his catchphrase: there were no fewer than three films entitled *Is Everybody Happy?* His 1930 recording of Jimmy McHugh and Dorothy Fields's 'On the Sunny Side of the Street' will come as a melancholy surprise to anyone more familiar with Jack Hylton's near-contemporary version, let alone Frank Sinatra's or Billie Holiday's jaunty takes. Bad times suited Lewis's battered hat. Talking his way through 'In a Shanty in Old Shanty Town', where 'the roof is so slanty', he would score one of the biggest hits of Depression-drenched 1932. Despite his game attempts to hold a note, Lewis had staying power: he was still on TV and playing Vegas when he died in 1971.

Meanwhile, out on the west coast, at San Francisco's St Francis Hotel, were Art Hickman and His Orchestra, a far smoother, slicker-sounding set-up that kept a pre-war string section but was fronted by three saxophone players.* Hickman's band followed the ODJB's path, arriving in

---

* This wasn't entirely new: an act called the Six Brown Brothers (an antecedent of 1960s trio the Walker Brothers in that they were led by Tom Brown, with five other players who were neither called Brown nor related to him) had played *nothing but* saxophones and scored a Broadway revue hit with 'Chin Chin' in 1914, though their sound wasn't built for the dancefloor. The saxophone would become a more significant part of a jazz band's make-up when tenor saxophonist

New York in summer 1919 to play at the Biltmore Hotel and record
with Columbia. They were soon offered a part in the Ziegfeld Follies,
still one of the hottest show-business tickets, before sailing to London
in autumn 1920, where they played as a quintet at the Criterion Roof
Garden. Nick LaRocca's ODJB had returned home in the summer of
1920 – Hickman's band was the Dave Clark Five to the ODJB's Beatles.
They did leave a significant footprint for British jazz, however, showing that the music could be more mellow than manic on recordings
like 'Alice Blue Gown' (from the show *Irene*) and 'I'm Forever Blowing
Bubbles'. Waltz time, yes, but thanks to the band's line-up and gentle
improvisation, still identifiably jazz.

Hickman hadn't accompanied his band on the trip to London as he
had a contract with Ziegfeld's Follies, instead sending out what was
effectively a franchise. In Art Hickman's New York London Five, the
'Hickman' name alone was seen as a stamp of quality. His style and
business nous had little to do with the rambunctious New Orleans/New
York jazz axis but had plenty in common with another San Francisco
orchestra, led by a balding, puffy-faced man called Paul Whiteman, who
said he was 'trying to make a lady out of Jazz'.

Portly Paul Whiteman, with his liquorice-confit moustache, thinning, Shredded Wheat hair and broad-bean-shaped head, looked like
a grocer but turned out to be jazz's greatest champion. He had a few
ideas about what jazz needed to make it big with the masses, some
of which he may have picked up from his music-teacher dad while
growing up in Colorado, others from stints in the Denver and San
Francisco symphony orchestras. After serving as bandmaster with the
fifty-seven-piece US Navy orchestra, he launched the Paul Whiteman
Orchestra in 1919. During a stint at the Ambassador Hotel in Atlantic
City, he worked with arranger Ferde Grofé and jazzed up some classics.
The Whiteman band's first record would be 'Dance of the Hours', from

---

Coleman Hawkins joined Fletcher Henderson's ascendant orchestra in 1923;
the instrument was then embraced by Chicago jazz players, helping to move the
sound away from its New Orleans roots. Pianos and guitars would also become
part of the Chicago amalgam, shifting the sound further away from that of the
classic New Orleans trumpet–clarinet–trombone–bass–drums ensemble.

Ponchielli's *La Gioconda*, backed with 'Avalon', an adaption of an aria
from Puccini's *Tosca*. If you're thinking that this all sounds a very long
way from New Orleans funeral marches and that Whiteman was the
white-bread interloper he was painted as for many decades, then you'd
be half right. Whiteman, though, was a genuine enthusiast for the new
music and had an exceptional ear for a talented player. That he was
white and relatively old – thirty-two when he scored with the million-
selling 'Whispering' in 1922 – simply meant he could open more doors
than Sidney Bechet or Kid Ory. He took this for granted and used his
leverage well.

His musicians followed carefully prepared arrangements, with
solos allowed only for Whiteman's best players. George Gershwin, Ira
Gershwin and Buddy De Sylva's 'I'll Build a Stairway to Paradise' (1922)
was outstanding, with a gorgeous muted cornet solo by Tommy Gott.
Whiteman's sound was novel not only for its arrangements, but for the
size of the band, nine players being three more than the usual. For these
reasons, people bandied the word 'symphonic' about when they talked
of Whiteman's brand of jazz. Making foxtrots from spirituals (Samuel
Coleridge-Taylor's 'Deep River' became 'Dear Old Southland') and the
classics ('Song of India' adapted Rimsky-Korsakov) led *The New Yorker*
to happily cry, 'Jazz draws the line nowhere!' Whiteman liked to incorporate guest stars on his records (something that wouldn't become commonplace until the 1990s), including the American Quartet, whistler
Margaret McKee and Hawaiian guitarist Frank Ferera. He became one
of the first 'name' bandleaders, and one of the very first to broadcast live
on the radio, from the WJZ studio in Newark, New Jersey, as early as
February 1922. No question, Whiteman was usually at the front of the
queue, and it paid dividends – his was the best-selling jazz orchestra of
the 1920s. By 1923 he was already being labelled the 'King of Jazz'.* He
never took the nickname seriously, but it was pretty useful for publicity.

---

* This is a stick that has been used to beat Whiteman with ever since. 'Jazz' was
a pretty loose term in the media and was generally used as short-hand for 'dance
music'. As late as 1930 Rudy Vallee's autobiography claimed that 'today "Jazz"
is applied to almost any form of orchestra or band music which is not strictly
classical'.

Like Scott Joplin before him, Whiteman had an urge to make his music acceptable, respectable, to have the press take it seriously, and in late 1923 he began to plan a jazz *concert*, in a real concert hall. Whiteman felt symphonic jazz's moment had arrived and, as ever, he wanted to be in there quick. He was right to feel a sense of urgency. On 23 November 1923 impresario William Morris put together *Vincent Lopez's Jazz Concert* at the Metropolitan Opera House. Lopez, a bandleader, prepared by taking lessons from the lead conductor at the Met, and created pieces like 'Eccentric' ('a genuinely imaginative handling of jazz values'); the evening's centrepiece was a collaboration with W. C. Handy called 'Evolution of the Blues', which Lopez's programme notes claimed was a 'symphonietta in jazz style' which presented 'in free-form fantasy the evolution of that specifically American negro emotional quality known as the blues'. There were songs from Irving Berlin ('All Alone'), Fletcher Henderson ('The Meanest Blues') and Rimsky-Korsakov, climaxing with a 'programmatic tone poem' called 'A Jazz Wedding'.

Lopez probably thought he had upped the ante, pushing jazz closer to the art world. Maybe he would now be hailed the 'King of Jazz'. But Whiteman had the trump card. On his side was the leader of a movement that didn't exist yet. George Gershwin was the kind of songwriter who always wanted to hear the competition, and encourage it, in order to up his own game. In other words, he was the kind of songwriter who drives music forward, who breaks formality, seeks out newness, cleverness, fun, new emotions.

The purpose of Whiteman's Aeolian Hall concert on 12 February 1924 was to try and answer the question, 'What is American music?' His plan was to show how jazz was a new classical form, and he planned to give a whistle-stop tour of the genre so far, beginning with the cacophony of 'Livery Stable Blues', moving through 'Yes, We Have No Bananas' and a suite of Victor Herbert songs, and eventually landing in the present with George Gershwin's 'Rhapsody in Blue'. Whatever Whiteman's misguided notions, they gave lift-off to the Jazz Age.

* * *

The Gershwins had arrived in Brooklyn from Russia in the 1890s with little money but a great sense of their own style. There had been no music in their home, until one day in 1910, when Papa Gershwin bought his eldest son Ira a second-hand upright piano. It was hoisted through the window of the front room on 2nd Avenue, and to slack-jawed amazement, Ira's little brother, twelve-year-old George, sat down and rattled through a few tunes off the top of his head. He had never studied a note. Later, George would recall hearing an automated piano playing Rubinstein's 'Melody in F', and how he had sat outside a penny arcade, hypnotised by it. Music saved him. 'Studying the piano made a good boy out of a bad one,' he said in 1924. 'I was a changed person after I took it up.'

By 1924 Gershwin was best known for 'Swanee', a song he'd written in ten minutes with his mate Irving Caesar while they were sitting on a bus going across Manhattan. Initially, it had been a gentle parody of Stephen Foster's 'Old Folks at Home', borrowing chunks of its lyrics, and was a show-stopping number in a mildly successful 1919 revue called *Demi-Tasse*. It took on a life of its own after Al Jolson heard Gershwin playing it at a party and decided to use it in his current show, *Sinbad*. Jolson recorded it on Columbia in 1920, and it was inescapable. Given its lack of Gershwin-like qualities, it's surprising that it would remain the biggest hit of his entire career.

The success of 'Swanee' meant Gershwin could afford to take a chance on entire musical comedies and, most intriguingly, longer-form pieces of music. There was a market out there waiting for something new: something more melodic than the adventurous but hard-to-hum works of Stravinsky or the new Viennese sounds of Schoenberg; something American that didn't scare the matriarchs like the Original Dixieland Jazz Band and those anarchic noises coming out of New Orleans. The demand was for something that sounded modern, urban, urbane. Something that sounded, essentially, like New York.

Oddly, 'Rhapsody in Blue' would also be an ending of sorts, and Gershwin's work would never really be treated seriously – by serious-minded classical listeners, that is – again. In the autumn of 1924 Aaron Copland returned to New York after studying in Paris, and

Louis Armstrong arrived in the Big Apple from the clubs of Chicago; Gershwin's extended works would end up stranded between the two. Ahead of his *New York Concerto* (aka *Concerto in F*) premiering at the Carnegie Hall in 1925, the *New York Times* wrote that 'There would not have been as much excitement if Brahms had come to town.' The reviews, though, were terrible. There was suddenly no place for music that didn't cause riots in theatres, like Stravinsky's, or crazed abandon on the dancefloor, like Louis Armstrong's. Gershwin's concerto was lukewarm; no one needed it. Gershwin was left smarting but decided to focus his energy on a different stage. A few months earlier, his Broadway show *Lady, Be Good* had opened, in which Fred and Adele Astaire had performed a song called 'Fascinating Rhythm'. Gershwin would reinvent himself for a new age and become the most celebrated songwriter of the pre-rock era.

8
THE GREATEST LOVE OF ALL:
LOUIS ARMSTRONG

In the summer of 1970 a newspaper in South Africa conducted a poll to see how many people could name the Apollo 11 astronauts, the first men on the moon. They were asked who was the very first man to set foot on the lunar surface. One person wrote the name 'Louis Armstrong'.

He may have achieved a lot of things in his life, but in 1969 Louis Armstrong wasn't walking on the moon. Instead, he was singing the hit song from the current James Bond movie, which barely sounds plausible for a man who had been born in 1901 into the poorest social stratum in America, was raised in a brothel, had pushed a coal cart as a child labourer and danced for pennies on the street – he would pick them up and put them in his mouth to stop other kids from steal-ing them, earning him the nickname 'Satchelmouth', or 'Satchmo'.

He was sent to reform school after firing a gun one New Year's Eve. The school was the Coloured Waif's Home for Boys, which happened to have a brass band, in which the young Louis began to play the cornet – similar to a trumpet but with a shorter horn and a slightly duller sound. Louis loved it so much that he was reluctant to leave the school eighteen months later. He then worked in menial jobs, playing in New Orleans clubs at night and gradually becoming a local phenomenon, until in 1922 he received a call from his hero and teacher Joe 'King' Oliver asking him to join his band in Chicago. At this point Armstrong, very modestly, gave jazz its voice. No battered top hat or bouncing teddy bears were necessary; the sound rang like a bell, a call to arms. Without him, much of what followed simply wouldn't have happened. His story unfurls until, nearly fifty years later, a South African student is quite prepared to believe that Louis Armstrong eats his breakfast on the moon.

When we think of Armstrong now, who do we see? In the twenty-first century we don't see his face on T-shirts, that's for sure, or student walls. John Coltrane is far more likely to be cited as a jazz hero. Still, Armstrong was there right at the beginning, and without him there would be no Bix or Duke or Miles or Coltrane. He had entered the jazz world in its absolute infancy; it never occurred to him that what he was doing would be regarded as art. At that point, he was just pleased to occasionally get paid for doing what he loved and trying to dodge bullets, like every other black man in America.

New Orleans jazz, before Armstrong added his two cents, had been a great syncopated street pageant, but with no real flexibility. 'Music was all around you,' recalled Armstrong, 'music kept you rolling.' There was a cornet playing the main melody, with a clarinet adding counterpoint and a rhythm section giving a beat that moved it along, a jalopy of a sound that tried to apply its brakes without skidding to a halt. Everybody in New Orleans played jazz the same way; if a cornet player was ill, there was a ready-made replacement on the next block.

Armstrong maybe wasn't the first to stretch the fabric of New Orleans jazz, but in establishing the cornet solo – eight bars, sixteen bars, maybe more – he encouraged others to jump in with invention and variation.

You could look at, say, Benny Goodman's band in the 1930s and say that everyone was playing in the style of Louis Armstrong.

The musical achievements of the Jazz Age are all the more astonishing when you consider the life that black Americans had to endure. It was still unwise for a black citizen of a southern community to be seen walking too fast or talking too loud; trying to make a living by playing music was some way down the list of concerns when lynchings were still a regular occurrence.* The situation led to more musicians moving to New Orleans, Memphis, Chicago and Kansas City, each one an oasis of hope and opportunity.

* * *

In New Orleans, in the first years of the twentieth century, men had played the cornet. The city's first cornet king was Buddy Bolden, inventive and fast-living, a local hero who, aged thirty, seemed to lose his mind while playing in a 1907 parade and was committed to an asylum from then until his death in 1931. The race to succeed Bolden was keen. Freddie Keppard, his heir apparent, would cover his right hand with a handkerchief so that his rivals couldn't work out his fingering. More fool Freddie: when jazz was first recorded in 1917, he declined to be captured on wax, thinking that other players would pinch his style.

Joe Oliver had served his time in marching bands before becoming a soloist and was the first cornetist to move a mute in and out of the bell of the horn, creating a 'wah-wah' sound.† He headed to Chicago when Storyville was closed down and jazz migrated north, and put together the Creole Jazz Band (with Louis Armstrong, second cornet; Lil Hardin,

* There were more than a hundred lynchings each year between 1910 and 1919; what's more, these were only the officially reported murders. In 1920 the number was sixty-five; by 1927 it was down to eighteen. But still, that's eighteen lynchings. Cross-burning would remain a quaint pastime in 1950s America, as Nat King Cole would discover.
† Mutes didn't really exist – Oliver was known to improvise with a condensed milk tin or even a doorknob – so he invented what became known as the 'Harmon mute', which became standard issue for all trumpet players, though someone else patented it and made all the money.

piano; Johnny Dodds, clarinet; and Warren 'Baby' Dodds, drums),
effectively the first supergroup.

Louis Armstrong had been on his way back from a funeral when
he received a telegram from Oliver asking him to come to Chicago.
The city was jumping. 'And when I joined King Oliver,' he recalled,
'the news spread everywhere. "Joe Oliver got a second cornet player.
You gotta come and see him." Paul Whiteman came, the Boston High
School boys [Bix Beiderbecke and friends], that's how I got to meet
them. Me and Joe Oliver played duets, and all the musicians thought
that was great. They tried it and everything but they didn't concentrate
like we did! They couldn't do it, couldn't do it . . . unless they wrote it
down. We never did write anything down.'

In his autobiography, Armstrong explained a trick that led to their
seemingly miraculous harmonic cornet breaks on recordings like 1923's
'Weather Bird Rag': 'King and I stumbled on something that no other
two trumpeters ever thought of. While the band was just swinging, the
King would lean over to me moving the valves on his trumpet, the notes
he was going to make when the break in the tune came . . . When the
break came I'd have my part to blend right along with his. The crowd
would go mad over it.'

* * *

Lil Hardin's childhood in Memphis had been very different to the
relentless poverty of Armstrong's. She had been taught piano at Mrs
Hicks' School of Music, then studied at Fisk University in Nashville. In
1918, when Lil was twenty, her mother moved the family to Chicago.
The timing couldn't have been better. New Orleans's finest jazz players,
post-Storyville, were all moving there, and it became the heart of the
burgeoning jazz world. Lil got a job at a music store, where she met
pianist Jelly Roll Morton and bandleader King Oliver. Before long, Lil
herself was making a decent living as a pianist. When Armstrong was
summoned to Chicago by Oliver, his idol and mentor, he met Lil, and
they soon became an item. This band, the Creole Jazz Band, recorded
'Krooked Blues' and 'Alligator Hop' for Gennett Records in 1923, and

it is where we first get to hear Armstrong play. It was pretty much the first time anyone got to hear a black jazz band on record.

With so much dusty jazz history since, it's worth looking into exactly what was so special about the Creole Jazz Band. They added breaks and solos to their spare technique, gave ebb and flow to the New Orleans formula, and used tension and release to maximise their impact. They unthreaded the tightly knit ensemble jazz of New Orleans and created a role for the soloist.

Louis was unique, an innocent. He knew his own ability but didn't have any ambitions to be a star; he was happy just to blow his cornet with his friends. King Oliver was quite aware of this and knew that if Armstrong left the band, he would go on to become the bigger attraction. Lil Hardin finally got through to Louis, convincing him to leave. First, he went to New York for a stint with Fletcher Henderson's orchestra in 1924, where he also played on sides by Ma Rainey and Bessie Smith. On the latter's 'You've Been a Good Ole Wagon', Smith taunts her former lover, and Armstrong comes close to making it a duet, growling and moaning on his cornet like the abandoned sad-sack boyfriend.

When Armstrong was tempted back to Chicago with a deal from Okeh Records, he discovered that Lil had put a band together for him in his absence, a supergroup of the city's very best players. His Hot Five and Hot Seven recorded more than seventy titles over the next three years, and the best of these are possibly the most exuberant music ever recorded by anyone. It's the sound of Louis and close friends lifting up and glorifying the traditions of Buddy Bolden and King Oliver, calling out around the world, spreading joy. Lil played square, defiantly unflashy piano; Baby Dodds was on drums, providing a steady, close-to-ragtime backdrop; Kid Ory was on trombone; and Johnny Dodds played high, dizzying clarinet. Louis was the boss, and you waited for his solo the way you waited for the Busby Berkeley set piece. If you were to reduce their catalogue to just one song, you could do worse than 'Potato Head Blues', cited at the end of Woody Allen's *Manhattan* as reason enough for living.

'Heebie Jeebies', recorded on 16 February 1926, was the first record to give the world an idea of what 'jazz singing' could entail. Armstrong would claim that he had dropped the lyric sheet and been forced to improvise. It had come naturally: he had to explain what he wanted to his fellow band members, and so opened up his satchel mouth and sang a horn solo. There are examples of scat singing that pre-date 'Heebie Jeebies' – including 'Old Fashioned Love' by Cliff 'Ukulele Ike' Edwards (Pathé, 1923), later the voice of Jiminy Cricket in *Pinocchio* – but it was Armstrong's imagination that made the song such a jump forward.* We can hear the nuance, swoops, bends and vibratos of his cornet-playing in his singing. He knew that the voice is the greatest musical instrument, and so he took this to its logical extent, the original human beatbox, tossing out rhythms and bass, brass growls, having a ball as his Hot Five mates cook up a storm behind him. The song itself barely exists.†

In 1929, at the end of the Jazz Age, Armstrong was still playing for mostly black audiences on Chicago's South Side. The Hot Five and Hot Seven records had sold well, but only in black neighbourhoods. He signed with Tommy Rockwell, a Mob-connected booking agent who planned to make him a superstar by introducing him to a white audience, then moved to New York and sang songs from Tin Pan Alley: 'Lazy River', 'I'm Confessin' (That I Love You)', 'Stardust'. Louis's version of 'Lazy River' is a hoot. He waits patiently as the band plays the melody straight. 'Uh huh . . . sure,' he nods politely, like a parent listening to a child playing 'Chopsticks', then comes in with a barely believable one-note melody, the song loosened from its structure, the melody as minimal as can be, his timing entirely free-form. 'Boy, am I riffing tonight!' he laughs, midway through the first verse. Beautiful!

He appeared in the 1929 revue *Connie's Hot Chocolates*, singing Fats Waller's 'Ain't Misbehavin'' and making it a hit, launching his career as

* Stylistically, Armstrong was probably more influenced by Alberta Hunter, the early jazz/blues vocalist who had already done several recording sessions before she recorded with the Red Onion Jazz Babies, including Armstrong, in 1924. The precise, theatrical diction he used on 'Heebie Jeebies', and throughout his career, was acquired through his experience working with the clear-voiced Hunter.
† There are pointers here to Britain's pop future: the breakdown of banjo and scat midway through could also be the first recorded 'spasm', or 'skiffle', music. The banjoist on 'Heebie Jeebies' was Johnny St Cyr, the name (maybe coincidentally) of John Leyton's character in the 1961 TV series *Harpers West One*, in which Leyton first sang his number-one hit 'Johnny Remember Me'.

a crossover entertainer. Initially, he sang and played the song from the orchestra pit, but the *New York Times*' review singled out this 'highlight of the premier' by 'an unnamed member of the orchestra'. His reputation among New York's theatre crowd grew with each performance, with both the white audience at Connie's and the black one at Harlem's Lafayette Theatre, where he was fronting an orchestra during the *Hot Chocolates* run. With his new profile, he became the most influential singer America had yet produced. His style touched everything and everyone.*

'Ain't Misbehavin'' also proved to be the end of an era. With its success, Armstrong abandoned his original jazz compositions, though he continued to improvise and play around with his phrasing on each fresh recording. He cut Hoagy Carmichael's 'Stardust' twice in 1931, and they are wildly differing versions. Here are some of the songs that Satchmo made his own between 1929 and the 1942 musicians' strike: 'When You're Smiling', 'I'm Confessin' (That I Love You)', 'Just a Gigolo', 'Them There Eyes', 'Thanks a Million', 'Swing That Music' and 'Jeepers Creepers'. Given the competition, that's not half bad. His voice was usually described as 'gravelly', but Humphrey Lyttelton likened it to 'astrakhan', which is nicely off-centre and sounds a lot more enjoyable.

The bulk of these sides would be recorded without Lil Hardin at his side. They had married in 1924, a year after he joined her in King Oliver's band. Lil saw the potential in her husband that he modestly couldn't; it's a sad irony that her convincing him to travel from Chicago and play around the country contributed to their split in 1931. At her suggestion, Louis was on the road almost every night of the year, and it wrecked their home life. According to Lil, Louis had changed his outlook on life, complaining that Lil was 'too old-fashioned'. They split,

---

* Armstrong now became the foremost practitioner of jazz adaptations of popular songs, moving towards Hollywood and beyond. His use of wordless vocals as a key instrument within a band set-up was pursued by Duke Ellington on recordings with Ivie Anderson ('It Don't Mean a Thing (If It Ain't Got That Swing)', 1931) and Kay Davis ('Transblucency', 1946), as well as by Dizzy Gillespie, with his jittery bebop vocals ('She's Gone Again', 'Swing Low, Sweet Cadillac') in the late 1940s and early '50s.

and Lil returned to Chicago.* Louis swiftly moved from being a New York cult figure to a black entertainer who was acceptable to Americans of every stripe – something no other jazz musician had been. He became a touchstone, a caricature – and a 'popular entertainer', the gravest sin in the eyes of purists.

* * *

Louis Armstrong's true significance is somehow easy to overlook. It is almost as if there were two Louis Armstrongs: the unique talent who took jazz out of New Orleans and Chicago, who made people understand it was a philosophy rather than a pop craze; and the genial Satchmo, mopping his brow as he sang 'What a Wonderful World' on ITV. By the 1960s his version of jazz seemed profoundly out of step; to young jazz fans he must have appeared closer to the nineteenth century than the late twentieth, with traces of vaudeville and crowd-pleasing minstrelsy in his apparent gratitude. The dirt-poor kid who had learned to play the cornet, changed the world and then deservedly put his feet up was seen by contemporary black musicians as old-timey, or worse.

Armstrong had to laugh this stuff off. People had short memories. In 1931 police in Memphis had arrested him for sitting next to a white woman on a bus, even though she was his manager's wife. In 1956 his home town of New Orleans had banned integrated bands, so Louis publicly stated he wouldn't play there again – and he didn't, until the 1964 Civil Rights Act changed the law. In 1957 he had played to an integrated audience in Knoxville, Tennessee, only for the place to be bombed by segregationists.

'What a Wonderful World' was offered to Armstrong in late 1967, when he was sixty-six years old, soon after the race riots in Watts, Newark and Detroit. It was written specifically for him by Bob Thiele

* Lil's career in music continued after her separation from Louis in 1931. She appeared on Broadway and recorded vocal sides for Decca, not leaving the music business until the late 1960s. In August 1971 Lil was performing at a memorial concert in Chicago for Louis, when she collapsed and died on stage, just a month after he passed.

and George Weiss, who thought there was a gulf opening between Jews and blacks in his home town of Newark and believed Louis was the perfect ambassador to help rebuild the community. The lyrics were focused on nature, not urban life, and America as a whole regarded it as Disneyfied. It failed even to reach the *Billboard* Hot Hundred. In Britain, though, it was a surprise number-one hit in 1968, and eventually became a standard, a song that could be taken straight (Rowlf sang it to a puppy on *The Muppet Show*), sarcastically (Nick Cave and Shane MacGowan's faux-drunken version) or as a hymn to chemically enhanced nirvana (on the Wu-Tang Clan interpolation 'The Forest'). But to young black America in 1967, the song maybe sounded more like accommodation, Armstrong playing a role for a whites-only crowd. The 1957 Knoxville bombing, an attempted assassination of Armstrong, counted for nothing in a more polarised era; with his endless succession of clean white handkerchiefs, Armstrong had come to be seen as Uncle Tom rather than Brother Louis. 'Cats of any colour can come together and blow,' he would calmly respond. 'Love, baby, love. That's the secret.'

His permanent smile was understandable. Slavery had been a grim reality for black Americans just two generations before Armstrong was born. How did you escape from working-class life? Either on stage or in the boxing ring – those were the only options. For a boy who had already been in reform school, Armstrong wasn't about to complain about earning a living from entertainment. It was about making people laugh or dance, about making the audience happy; it had nothing to do with self-expression. That was something Louis Armstrong pretty much invented. No one expected art on the vaudeville stage. There would have been no space for a Miles Davis in 1923.

What about the criticism that his music didn't progress? We can't all be Duke Ellington, and I'm pretty sure Louis thought he had done his bit. In his hands, music progressed so far and so fast in the 1920s and '30s that the next thirty years were, to a large extent, about filling in the gaps he had opened up. Besides, he progressed in different ways; they just happened to be ways that the critics weren't as happy about. With age he became a showman, and it was a part he enjoyed playing. You could read things into what he was doing – yes, in *High Society* he was literally sitting at the back of the bus as he commentated on the rich white folks' story – but for some younger performers this wasn't enough. They wanted fellow black performers to stand together, to be more outspoken, and they came to see his wide-eyed, brow-wiping antics as offensive. Miles Davis thought 'his personality was developed by white people wanting black people to entertain them by smiling and jumping around'. Dizzy Gillespie called Armstrong a 'plantation character'.

I'd like to think they were saying what they thought a hip young crowd might want them to say, because they were talking bollocks. It made sense that jazz-players like Davis and Gillespie and John Coltrane and Albert Ayler would want to pioneer new forms of jazz, pushing its limits, testing its boundaries, but Armstrong had been the pioneer. It was his Hot Five that had originated the idea of a small-band setting with an improvisational lead instrument. Everybody else – including Davis and Gillespie – was indebted to the originator, Louis Armstrong. Everybody else was merely following his lead.

'You'll always get critics of showmanship,' said Armstrong, in a 1971 biography. 'Critics in England say I was a clown, but a clown? That's hard. It's happiness to me to see people happy, and most of the people who criticise don't know one note from another.'

9

THE BLAB OF THE PAVE:
JEROME KERN AND BROADWAY

At the turn of the twentieth century Broadway was not a glamorous place. It was 'provincial and parochial', according to the *New York Times'* Brooks Atkinson. 'It bore no serious relation to art or life.' In 1900 there was no original American musical theatre, just Viennese imports and Victor Herbert's cod-European trifles, like the Mother Goose-inspired *Babes in Toyland*. Songs were rarely integrated into the dialogue of a show; even the omnipresent 'After the Ball' had been shoehorned into an existing successful play. It would take a New York-obsessed Englishman and an Anglophile New Yorker to create the modern Broadway show. The faux Englishman was Jerome Kern; the very real one P. G. Wodehouse.

Back in 1900 there had been four physical spaces in which American songwriters could operate, four different stages where they could pitch their work. All displayed their European roots quite clearly. First, there was the revue, borrowed from France, a mix of music, dancing and sketches centred around high-kicking girls and viewed by a high-class audience, which was dictated by high ticket prices. The revue had blossomed under the eye of Florenz Ziegfeld and given opportunities to writers like George Gershwin, Richard Rodgers and Lorenz Hart, and performers like W. C. Fields, the Marx Brothers and Eddie Cantor. It survived well into the Hollywood era and would give us some of the most diverting examples of early cinema. Secondly, there was vaudeville, essentially an Americanised version of British music hall, working-class and without the pricey costumes a revue could afford. Burlesque was essentially a cheaper version of vaudeville, with striptease, fewer songs and lewder jokes; we can be grateful to it for giving Mae West a break. Operetta – the classiest of the four options, shaped from London cheese-cake or swathed in Viennese fondant cream – had nothing to do with America at all, beyond the idea that it was ambitious, and that was very American. These shows would be imported wholesale from Europe, with the occasional new song bolted on. All four spaces survived into the 1940s, into the American age which would eventually subsume them.

But songwriting had not been a respectable job in 1900. Nobody had ever come out of a Harrigan and Hart show feeling any cleaner than when they went in; nobody had a glass of rosé waiting for them in the interval. Edward Harrigan and Tony Hart's earthy, rambunctious, late-nineteenth-century musicals – some seventeen of them – had been born from the strong Irish influence on New York, at that time probably the roughest city in the Western world. Spitting on the street was still commonplace, and at the Theatre Comique on Broadway, where you could hear comic accent songs like 'Down Went McGinty' and 'Throw Him Down, McCloskey', directing spitballs into the orchestra pit wasn't unknown (though a security guard would whack you with a bamboo pole if you tried it). Harrigan and Hart developed their skits into musicals, featuring Irish, German, Italian and black caricatures. By the time of their biggest success, *The Mulligan Guard Ball* in 1880, they had taken over the Theatre Comique. The polyglot, stereotyped humour of late-nineteenth-century New York was slapstick and chaotic, bordering on violent, and built to burn out fast. 'The Old Bowery Pit', an ode to a theatre, ran: 'You talk about blood, it was thicker than mud, you could not see action for smoke.' Harrigan and Hart split in 1885, a year after their Theatre Comique had been physically razed to the ground. The Irish influence on popular music would mellow into nostalgic waltz-time ballads by the 1890s; the tension between what Harrigan called 'melodious rowdyism' and this sweet melancholia would remain throughout twentieth-century pop.

* * *

One thing Broadway lacked in 1900 was elegance. Jerome Kern changed it fundamentally. If Irving Berlin invented Tin Pan Alley, the cheap pop thrill, then Kern was the first modern Broadway writer, the first master of the twentieth-century American musical. He was the greatest single inspiration for everyone who came after – George Gershwin, Richard Rodgers, Lorenz Hart, Yip Harburg, Arthur Schwartz, Howard Dietz, Gus Kahn, Walter Donaldson, Stephen Sondheim – and moved musical comedy away from high-end operetta and low racial stereotypes, Americanising it, his light touch and melodicism lifting the weight from heavy Viennese shows.

Kern had been born in Sutton Place, on the east side of Manhattan, in 1885 – at that time the brewery district – and was named after the racetrack where his mother had spent the day before she went into labour. This thrilling and slightly illicit beginning didn't really rub off on Kern's personality.* He looked like a sulking owl, with a round face, his round glasses perched over disappointed eyes and even rounder, pouched, sagging cheeks.

From 23rd Street to Times Square, Broadway was effectively closed to American writers in 1900. You had to be English or European;

---

* This doesn't mean he wasn't an eccentric. One day in 1923, looking out of his bedroom window, Kern noticed that his extensive lawns needed cutting. Rather than hire a gardener, he decided to buy a flock of sheep. He probably hadn't realised that they were male and female – at least not until lambing time, when Kern and his neighbours were kept awake all night. The bags under his sad owl eyes grew larger and darker; the sheep would be sold on.

producers wanted music with an English accent. Kern was still a teen-ager and not taken too seriously. He needed to know more people, make more contacts, earn a bigger reputation, and so in 1904 he headed to London, his spiritual home and the town where Broadway hits were most often created. Kern not only wrote music as if he was wise to the ways of a steak-and-kidney pudding, he looked the part too. He wore a homburg (like the king), trousers with a crease at the front (not at the side in the old-fashioned American way) and, to top it off, he always carried a cane. At a pub in Walton-on-Thames, while ordering a pork pie and a pint of mild from a barmaid called Eva Leale, he fell in love, and he and Eva soon became man and wife. In London, Kern met Broadway theatre-owner Charles Frohman and played him a song called 'How'd You Like to Spoon with Me'. Frohman took Kern for a true son of the North Downs and asked him if he would like to sail with him back to America. 'How absolutely marvellous,' replied Kern, stirring his milky tea.

It wasn't long before Frohman realised he'd been duped, but Kern was an obvious talent and an instant success on Broadway, a New Yorker with the English touch. 'How'd You Like to Spoon with Me' ended up as the hit song in the 1905 Broadway production of *The Earl and the Girl*, but could just as easily have been a hit for Marie Lloyd or Vesta Victoria on the bare boards of Wilton's Music Hall. Being an American hit, though, it had a startling stage set-up to accompany it: 'I don't know why I am so very shy, I always was demure, I never knew what silly lovers do.' Angela Lansbury would coyly flutter her long lashes to this one in the 1947 Kern biopic *Till the Clouds Roll By*,* but back in 1905 the performance had been accompanied by girls in the flimsiest of skirts and black silk stockings, singing on flower-strewn swings that swung out into the audience. It was a smash hit: the *Dramatic Mirror* called it 'the most successful number ever introduced here'.

* In *Till the Clouds Roll By*, Kern – played by Robert Walker – says he has had enough of arranging songs for 'girlie shows and beer halls'. He was going 'to England for some peace and quiet' and 'liberation from mediocrity . . . no mushy little melodies for public consumption . . . I'm going to write a symphony. Try to be somebody.'

Kern followed it with songs for *The Little Cherub* ('Under the Linden Tree', 'Meet Me at Twilight', 1906), *The Rich Mr Hoggenheimer* ('Don't You Want a Paper, Dearie', 'Bagpipe Serenade', 'Poker Love', 1906), *The Dairymaids* ('Little Eva', 'I'd Like to Meet Your Father', 1907), *The Dollar Princess* ('Not Here, Not Here', 'A Boat Sails on Wednesday', 1909) and *The King of Cadonia* ('Every Girl I Meet', 'Catamaran', 1910). All of these shows were imports, with Kern's decent but derivative songs bolted onto the book. By 1912 he had contributed more than a hundred songs to more than thirty shows, yet most of the time his name was missing from the programme. He yearned to be a composer rather than someone who was just brought in to fix other people's shows.

He was also an arranger, decades before that became a job description. An unremarkable 1913 musical called *Oh I Say* saw Kern take a step forward with musical orchestration: he added two saxophones – then regarded as a military band instrument – to the line-up, a good four years before anyone was using the term 'jazz'.

Kern's first real standard was 'They Didn't Believe Me', a song from a 1914 comedy about Mormon polygamy of British origin called *The Girl from Utah*. The show was very lucky to get it. It is the first truly modern pop song, from its transportive rhythm – suggestive of a horse and trap in 1914 New York, or a Sunday drive through the Yorkshire Dales a hundred years later – to its lyric. Starting with the word 'and' was bold enough, but when it reaches the line 'And when I tell them, and I'm certainly going to tell them,' it transcends time. The second half of the line is effectively a wink to the camera; it is something any twenty-first-century songwriter would be peacock-plumage proud of – Rodgers and Hart would make a whole career out of this kind of cleverness. Songwriter Arthur Schwartz was fourteen years old when the song first appeared and knew it was utterly different: 'Now, what has that got that all the others did not have? The first word that occurs to me is intimacy. It has a non-pretentiousness. It is not flamboyant. It is not to be sung loudly. It is not to be shouted. And it has therefore a more drawing room sound than a great big operatic theatre sound.' 'Intimacy' was a word that had never been heard in a world of operetta and coon shouts. What Schwartz was saying was that 'They Didn't Believe Me' was built for gramophones and quiet contemplation; it was a new form of pop. The melody was easy and gorgeous, the whole song warm, inviting and believable, light years away from the clockwork Victorian clunk of *Florodora*. 'They Didn't Believe Me' was so out of the ordinary that on its own it convinced the young George Gershwin to chuck in his job and move to Broadway so he could try and better it. Even now, it anticipates the style of the 1930s and '40s so precisely that it's hard to credit that the song was written at the dawn of World War I.

Kern was made by 'They Didn't Believe Me'. By the time *Love o' Mike* opened in 1917, he had finally gained full control of songs and orchestration, adding banjos, mandolins, bassoons and a set of drums, but no brass, bar the odd muted trumpet. He was going for something quieter yet more intimate. Record production was still totally incapable of picking up such subtle arrangements, but Kern was laying foundations for the future – the electronic age. In other respects, he was surprisingly untogether. On *Love o' Mike* he worked with the witty Hertfordshire-born playwright Guy Bolton; the songs, sadly, were way below par (one had the unpromising title 'Moo Cow'), but nonetheless it ran for 192 performances. Kern also cared little about his singers: 'If people really want to hear a good singer, they'll go to the opera,' he said. 'It's much more important that a singer gets the words over. The orchestra can do the rest.'

The other Englishman who helped Kern to create an American space on Broadway was a comic writer whom most of his fellow country-folk still assume never set foot outside the cloistered Home Counties. It's slightly mind-blowing – to a country ignorant of anything beyond Jeeves and Wooster – that their creator was the first great lyricist of American musical theatre. 'Before Larry Hart,' said Richard Rodgers, 'only P. G. Wodehouse had made any real assault on the intelligence of the song-listening public.' And Wodehouse loved the American song-listening public. 'From his earliest years,' he wrote in his memoir *Bring on the Girls*, 'America had been – to this pie-faced young dreamer – the land of romance.' In 1909 he was writing a daily column for *The Globe* in London, a steady job that earned him £3 a week and five weeks holiday per annum. He took the latter in one hit, sailing for a three-week vacation in the US, thinking he might try to sell his work there at the same time. Within a week he had sold one story to *Collier's* and another to *Cosmopolitan*, both on the same day, and each for $300; the going rate in London was £7 and 10 shillings per piece. Wodehouse, soon to turn thirty, felt the wind of change on his back, tendered his resignation to *The Globe* and settled down in Greenwich Village, 'with a second-hand Monarch typewriter and plenty of paper'.

Wodehouse soon became the drama critic for *Vanity Fair*, and in 1915 met up with Guy Bolton and Jerome Kern after seeing the opening night of their *Very Good Eddie*. It was Kern's second musical comedy at the intimate Princess Theatre.* 'Enjoyed it in spite of lamentable lyrics,' Wodehouse recorded in his diary. 'Bolton, evidently conscious of this weakness, offered partnership. Tried to hold back and weigh suggestion, but his eagerness so pathetic that consented. Memo: Am I too impulsive? Fight against this tendency.'

Very Good Eddie had taken its name from ventriloquist Fred Stone's catchphrase. The lyrics were similarly second-hand and under par: 'Any old night is a wonderful night, if you're there with a wonderful girl.' Wodehouse sat and frowned. Yet *Very Good Eddie* was groundbreaking in almost every other respect. Bolton's comedy was strong enough to have survived without any songs and, unusually, relied on lines and jokes from the principal characters rather than having a series of slapstick interludes from comedians to break up the romantic story. The songs were uniformly in 4/4 time rather than Viennese 3/4, and there was no starring role, the load being shared by the six actors. The 300-seater theatre was compact and bijou, the performances cohesive and witty. With *Very Good Eddie*, the Princess shows became a Broadway institution.

---

* Built in 1913, the Princess Theatre on 39th Street had been run since 1915 by Bessie Marbury, a theatrical agent who represented Oscar Wilde, George Bernard Shaw and Jerome K. Jerome, among others, and lived – relatively openly – with her lover Elsie de Wolfe for some forty years. The theatre was struggling, but Bessie was never short of sharp ideas. She decided to stage musical theatre on a much smaller scale than Broadway was used to: nothing too large, heavy or laced-up, just hungry new talent. Bessie couldn't afford Victor Herbert anyway, but she trusted her nose. The first show she put on was *Nobody Home*, with a book by Guy Bolton and songs by Jerome Kern.

The biggest of all was Wodehouse's first with Kern and Bolton, *Oh Boy*, which opened in 1917 and ran for 463 performances. It included the sumptuous 'Till the Clouds Roll By' and some striking modernism from Wodehouse. 'Nesting Time in Flatbush', for example, was about the ups and downs of contemporary living: 'Our little home may have defects like all these flats in town, it's wiser not to lean on the walls because they might fall down. It's rather badly lighted, which makes it hard to see, and the neighbours play the gramophone each night till after three.' The *New York Times* wrote a feature with the headline 'The Inexhaustible Mr Kern'. According to Wodehouse's *Bring on the Girls*, another critic turned to verse:

> This is the trio of musical fame,
> Bolton and Wodehouse and Kern:
> Better than anyone else you can name,
> Bolton and Wodehouse and Kern.
> Nobody knows what on earth they've been bitten by,
> All I can say is I mean to get lit an' buy
> Orchestra seats for the next one that's written by
> Bolton and Wodehouse and Kern.

In the years following World War I, America found its place as an affluent world leader. To the outside world, it must have seemed that everyone in this new paradise wore silk shirts and went to the theatre. Kern put the audience's new appetite for sophistication down to Prohibition: 'I wrote this music with a view of having it appreciated by people who come to the theatre without any alcoholic stimulation.' His music offered more than just 'the jazzy types of entertainment'. A great new middle class sprang up with, as Yip Harburg noted, 'the liberty of having money for the first time'. Expense accounts were a new invention, and Broadway was a major beneficiary.

* * *

What else was happening on Broadway in the 1920s? There was Jesse Lasky's Folies Bergère, which was based on another European model:

the French cabaret show. It was at once a café, a music hall, a theatre, a restaurant and a club. Like an uptown adaptation of the saloon bars where Scott Joplin and Irving Berlin had played piano and sung, the Folies Bergère had orchestras and singers entertaining patrons from the moment the doors opened at 6 p.m. It was more informal than vaudeville – men and women could mingle. This was a selling point.

As for the theatres themselves, they were almost all owned by two big-time operators: the Shubert Organization (still going today, it currently runs seventeen Broadway theatres and six off-Broadway), and A. L. Erlanger (or Abraham Lincoln Erlanger, as it said on his birth certificate). His office had a punchbag in one corner and a barber's chair in another for his daily shave. One wall was a bookcase filled with Napoleon's diaries; the smooth-faced Erlanger kept a loaded revolver in his desk and believed he was Napoleon reincarnated.

Once Kern opened the door to these venues, other young American writers were inspired to try their luck. Richard Rodgers and Lorenz Hart symbolised the link between Tin Pan Alley's new sophistication and the modern Broadway musical. Songs poured out of them but for the longest time went nowhere. Having met in 1919, when Rodgers was just seventeen, the pair spent six years enjoying piecemeal success,* mostly writing songs and librettos for amateur venues like the Park Avenue Synagogue. Rodgers had strong support from his family but also knew that at some point he was going to have to either write a major hit or rely on his back-up option, a job in the children's underwear business. Hart was fast approaching thirty when they wrote their first true classic for *The Garrick Gaieties* in 1925; simply called 'Manhattan' ('The great big city's a wondrous toy just made for a girl and boy. We'll turn Manhattan into an isle of joy'), it meant they joined the immortals.

The sophistication in the duo was, apparently, all down to Rodgers. His memoir *Musical Stages* paints a gloomy picture of a well-off middle-class family. Luckily for young Richard, his mother played the piano, which 'was where we met before dinner, and where we went after

---

* In 1919 their 'Any Old Place with You' ('I'd go to hell for ya, or Philadelphia') was included in the Broadway musical comedy *A Lonely Romeo*.

dinner. There was music every day, every day, every day.' Music aside, it sounded like a snobbish, joyless home. Hart, on the other hand, revelled in telling people that his father was a 'crook' who apparently, impatient for a cubicle, once pissed out of a window. The Hart household was party central. Rodgers, many years later, would say they were 'unstable, sweet, lovely people'.

It was all a matter of timing. Hart's lyrics were in the vernacular and suited the world that Kern had opened up. They were about the urban, automated, tipsy feel of America; they could be understood by every-body and avoided the romantic flights of fancy of the Viennese operetta writers: 'We'll go to Greenwich, where modern men itch to be free.' As Walt Whitman would have said, they had 'the blab of the pave'.

* * *

If the gay 1920s allowed room for more nuanced, urban lyrics, creating space for Larry Hart, they also saw a slight thawing in race relations in New York. There had been black shows on Broadway, but the rules were slightly different for black performers. While Jerome Kern's pre-war shows had couples cosying up to each other on romantic songs like 'They Didn't Believe Me', this was pretty much forbidden for black actors – they would be booed, or worse. If love songs were part of the show, they had to be downhearted efforts, blues songs from shouters like Ma Rainey. Singing and playing their own material was the most straightforward way for black musicians to get their work heard, and to get paid for that work. The irony remained that if you were black, it was easier to get onto the stage than it was to get a seat in a theatre.

The musical that broke the mould, unifying uptown and downtown, was 1921's *Shuffle Along* by ragtime hero Eubie Blake and Noble Sissle. One love song in particular, 'Love Will Find a Way', was a hit with both black and white audiences, while 'I'm Just Wild about Harry' was an irresistible screamer. During its 504-performance run, *Shuffle Along* would feature black stars like Paul Robeson, Josephine Baker and Adelaide Hall. There was still a limit as to how many all-black shows the flippant tastes of Broadway's white habitués could take, and waiting for the next vehicle to come along could be a thankless task. Leading your own band was one ticket – Duke Ellington would thankfully take this route – but after Sissle's and Blake's breakthroughs, other black songwriters did manage to cross the colour line. Splinters and shards from these early black pop hits have survived into our own time, occasionally as songs you might hear on Saturday-night TV, more often as magazine headlines or memes, or echoes of memes. New Orleans's Spencer Williams wrote the deathless 'Everybody Loves My Baby' in 1924; New York's Maceo Pinkard gave us the standards 'Sweet Georgia Brown' and 'Them There Eyes'. Then there was Andy Razaf, nephew to the queen of Madagascar, who had a lyrical turn to match Kern or Hart. He teamed up with Eubie Blake to write a series of ballads – 'Memories of You', 'You're Lucky to Me', 'I'd Give a Dollar for a Dime' – and also wrote a string of shows and revues that included *Ain't Misbehavin'* and *Squeeze Me* with a Harlem stride pianist and songwriter called Fats Waller (of whom more later).

Elsewhere on Broadway, the Ziegfeld Follies – now an annual jamboree – continued to boom. One of the biggest names to emerge from the Ziegfeld pack was Marilyn Miller, who usually played Cinderella-type characters, capturing saps like me when she was down at heel in overalls and a cloth cap, smudges of dirt on her sad face, before doing a dance routine and ending the show triumphant, decked out in diamonds. You can see why both Dorothy Parker and Patti Smith wrote poems about her.

Miller got her break in the *Ziegfeld Follies of 1918* at 42nd Street's New Amsterdam Theatre, singing Irving Berlin's 'Mine Was a Marriage of Convenience' and stealing the show. She got star billing in the *Follies of 1919*, and in 1920 became the biggest star on Broadway in Kern's *Sally*, about a dishwasher who joins the Follies and marries a millionaire. How popular was she? There were only half a dozen Marilyns in America at the turn of the century; by the 1930s, following Miller's stardom, it was the sixteenth-most-popular girl's name.

Almost no Broadway footage of her exists, but you can see her singing Jerome Kern's 'Who' in the film *Sunny* (1929), her light opera voice slightly behind the beat, slightly drunken maybe, and most definitely suggestive. She may not have been the best singer or dancer or actress, but she had such charisma it didn't matter. This made her, in a very modern way, a 'star'. Miller died in 1936 after suffering complications during a dental operation. Alexander Calder's sculpture of her, as Sunny, can still be seen on top of what was the I. Miller Shoe Company building at 1552 Broadway.

* * *

As the world turned in the 1920s, at seemingly twice its usual speed, popular culture shifted rapidly away from London. Broadway's boom meant the West End suffered, and by the end of the decade power had almost completely switched to New York. Anyone who made their name on the West End stage was now likely to head to the States after their first hit. An exception was Ivor Novello, writer of 'Keep the Home Fires Burning', whose songs sounded like a caricature of English fopdom.*

Novello was all about melody and romance, but there was a lack of Wodehouse's or Hart's wit, or indeed of any comedy in his work. With help from lyricist Dion Titheradge, Novello did write one uncharacteristic comic delight called 'And Her Mother Came Too' (from *A to Z*, 1921), a hit for the equally handsome Jack Buchanan, a Scottish-born silent-movie star. Broadway writer Johnny Green talked memorably about the largely forgotten Buchanan: 'Jack was one of those fellas who really couldn't sing and really couldn't dance, yet on the stage looked like the greatest – this was pre-microphones but you heard him in the back row, he moved so gorgeously . . . God-given sense of humour. Six foot three, shoulders 8 feet wide, waist ten inches, and he wore these sensational clothes. It's illegal to be as handsome as Jack Buchanan. He looked like someone had drawn him, the handsome Britisher.'†

* Novello would make a brief attempt at working in Hollywood, which didn't really know what to do with his talents (though they really outdid themselves when they tasked him with writing the dialogue for *Tarzan the Ape Man*). Less surprisingly, decades later, some Novello songs made it onto the soundtrack of Robert Altman's performatively English *Gosford Park*.

† Buchanan's best-remembered song is 'Everything Stops for Tea', from the 1935 film musical *Come Out of the Pantry*, in which he was cast opposite Fay Wray, a few years on from her starring role as King Kong's girlfriend. The song, rather

'And Mother Came Too' was closer to the work of Novello's friend, protégé and – eventually – rival, Noël Coward. Six years younger than Novello, he was just as much of a dandy, but he was no romantic. Instead, he represented a post-World War I sense of disruption, where love was to be snorted at and duty was a joke. 'I am related to no one except myself,' he said, a throwback to Beau Brummell and a role model for those future pillars of English detachment Ray Davies and Morrissey. He was loaded with what novelist Stella Gibbons called 'amusing malice' and would go on to boss the London stage in the 1930s. But more of that later.

* * *

The most groundbreaking show of the late 1920s, without question, belonged to Jerome Kern and his new writing partner. Most of the lyrics for *Showboat* were written by Oscar Hammerstein, whose career would split neatly into two. Later, he would become Richard Rodgers's lyricist, achieving unprecedented international success, but his first wave of hits would still have been enough to make him immortal. Unlike the instinctive Wodehouse, Hammerstein used lots of reference books and rhyming dictionaries, and did a lot of research. His son later said that 'like Tchaikovsky, he didn't believe in inspiration'.

Showboat was adult entertainment: not only were its tunes sophisticated, but it had a daring theme – racial discrimination, if only at the edges of the storyline. Kern was circumspect about its success. He said it meant he could 'go on being uncommercial, there's a lot of money in it'.

With Hammerstein's furrowed brow replacing Wodehouse's ruddy cheeks, *Showboat* became a kind of American opera. The centrepiece is 'Old Man River', sung as Miss Julie is thrown off the boat for miscegenation: 'I get weary, I'm sick of trying, I'm tired of living but scared of dying.' It's the opposite of Sam Cooke's 'A Change Is Gonna Come':

---

surprisingly given its regional accuracy ('They may be playing football, and the crowd is yelling "kill the referee"! But no matter what the score when the clock strikes four, everything stops for tea'), was written by the American trio of Al Hoffman, Al Goodhart and Maurice Sigler.

'Old Man River' said nothing, just silently paid witness, and life just kept rolling along. Civil rights marches would have to wait.*

Nevertheless, even approaching the subject of race made *Showboat* a revolution compared to the Viennese fancies that still filled so many halls on Broadway. Untouched by the speed of 1920s life, Sigmund Romberg carried on writing hit operettas like 1927's *The New Moon*, whose big hit was 'Lover Come Back to Me', based on a Tchaikovsky melody. 'Romberg knew what he was doing commercially,' said wise-cracking songwriter Irving Caesar. 'I'm not saying he was a plagiarist, but the audience sang the music on the way in.' A friend of Caesar's told him that he was thinking about Romberg the wrong way: 'When you go to see a Romberg operetta put on your smoking jacket, put on your slippers, fill the old pipe, lean back, and prepare to spend an evening with the old masters,' he advised. In many ways, *Showboat* was just as escapist as *The New Moon*; set safely in the past, it made audiences feel good about themselves and their country. This was the New World, not perfect, but young, with a brighter future ahead. Kern and Hammerstein would take their new roles as New World social historians quite seriously.

'The moon belongs to everyone, the best things in life are free,' Wodehouse had written. Maybe Kern – with his library of rare books, a collection he sold for $1.8 million in the late 1920s – was always a fundamentally more sober character, and *Showboat*'s heft and huge success were something the old team could never have achieved. 'He changed very much,' sighed Wodehouse. 'After *Showboat* he became "the music master", you know, a fellow who takes himself very seriously, above what he'd been doing up to that time. But before, he was very good company.'†

Still, Kern could be forgiven his airs: he was one of the half-dozen most important musical innovators of the century. Songwriter Arthur

---

* In the London production, 'Old Man River' was sung by Paul Robeson – so impressively that he was invited to Buckingham Palace to perform it. The Robesons ended up buying a house in Hampstead.

† Kern and Wodehouse had split in a row over money, which explains the latter's uncharacteristic sourness.

Schwartz would later say: 'Kern had real influence on all the people who followed him. Gershwin and Rodgers said their first songs were exactly like Kern's. If there had been no Kern maybe other composers would have developed, but not in the same way.' The same was true of Broadway.

In 1927, within a few blocks of *Showboat* you could have also seen George and Ira Gershwin's *Funny Face*, Vincent Youmans's *Hit the Deck* or Rodgers and Hart's *A Connecticut Yankee*. This was a high-water mark for musical theatre – for great American songwriting, even – but then two things came along to spoil the fun: the Wall Street Crash and talking pictures. In 1928 there were sixty-two shows along Broadway; this would decline to thirty-four in 1931. During the whole of the 1930s, the Great White Way would host only sixty-eight new musical comedies.

With a very real lack of cash and opportunity for the New York songwriter, the lure of Hollywood – just about the only place in 1930s America where there seemed to be a silver lining – would prove irresistible.

10

LET ME ENTERTAIN YOU: AL JOLSON

> If Jolson came down for breakfast he made an entrance. When
> he went into the bathroom he made an exit. When he came
> out he wanted applause. Sure, Jolson was full of show business.
>   Irving Caesar

Al Jolson, brash and egotistical, a throwback in blackface, would be the
biggest star of the 1920s. His chutzpah knew no limits. He had rhythm,
volume, the moves, the grace; in modern parlance, he was always 'on'.
His saving grace was that he could deliver the goods.

Jolson thrilled people. He was the ultimate extrovert, the greatest star
the world had ever seen – at least, according to Jolson. He was all about
spirit, feel and verve. He took out an advert in *Variety*: 'Watch me, I'm a

wow!' He chatted up Barbara Stanwyck with the line, 'I've got $30 million in the bank – wanna help me spend it?' He had enough money to give handouts to friends and colleagues, an act that was simultaneously generous and domineering.

Jolson is at once ancient history, a cultural embarrassment and the first major pop star of the twentieth century. He understood that singing and performing were only two aspects of the job. Scoring a hit was just the beginning; you had to be in a constant state of vigilance if you wanted to stay at the top. There was a Jolson brand to maintain, endless lunches and drinks parties, and new acts and shows had to be seen to keep the image fresh. He understood the rules of celebrity, and marketing opportunities were never passed up. In 1928, aged forty-two, Jolson married his third wife, the wise-looking singer, dancer and star of *42nd Street* Ruby Keeler, who was exactly half his age. On their wedding night Jolson decided to go out for a walk. Passing a fire station, he popped in and asked the firefighters if they'd like to hear a song. Four hours later, he returned to find his new bride in a silk negligee and a pretty foul mood.

* * *

Jolson was an entertainer first and foremost, learning his craft on the vaudeville stage. Like Irving Berlin, his story began in Russia, or at least Russian Lithuania, from where his father, a cantor, fled with his family in 1890, ending up in Washington DC. Aged eight, Asa Yoelson and his brother Harry would stand in front of the Hotel Raleigh and sing for senators and congressmen; the small change they collected would be spent at the theatre. After serving an apprenticeship in the Mayflower Burlesque Company with Harry, he joined Lew Dockstader's minstrels in 1909, aged twenty-three. Given a solo spot, he completely stole the show from the headliner, Dockstader himself. *Variety* wrote, 'Haven't seen such a demonstration for a single act, or any act for that matter, as given to Al Jolson.'

In 1903 he had been to see a singer called Eddie Leonard in a Washington theatre and had been mesmerised. While Leonard sang

'Ida, Sweet as Apple Cider', Jolson encouraged the audience to sing along with the chorus. Amidst the dog-voiced dentists and shrill secretaries, Jolson's voice, sounding as sweet as Ida herself, sailed across the theatre. After a hush fell, the audience – and Leonard – burst into applause. Jolson had been a comedian and a vaudeville bit-part player for at least three years at this point, but never again would he be afraid to seize a moment, grab an audience by its throat or upstage anyone. Al Jolson was born that night, and for the next fifty years blackface gave him the opportunity to mimic this memory.

The first signs of Jolson's magnetic appeal and massive ego came in 1911, when he featured in a show called *La Belle Paree*, which was opening the Shubert brothers' Winter Garden Theatre. Reviews of the opening night had been lousy. On the second night, Jolson binned the script and started talking to the audience about the reviews. Would you rather just hear me sing? he asked them. The rest of the line-up were kept waiting in the wings as Jolson sang song after song. The reviews this time were ecstatic, and Jolson was given carte blanche to ignore his fellow artists, dump all over the script and act like an egomaniac for the rest of his days. The Winter Garden became his playground, and he was soon on $2,500 a week. 'As Jolson enters the stage it is as if an electric current has been run along the wires under the seats,' wrote *Life* magazine. 'He speaks, rolls his eyes, compresses his lips, and it is all over. You are a member of the Al Jolson Association. He trembles his lip and your heart breaks with a snap.' A year after *La Belle Paree*, Jolson was starring in *The Whirl of Society* on Broadway. He had the theatre's middle row of seating ripped out to give him a runway down which he propelled himself, bobbing up and down with imaginary oars as he sang 'Row, Row, Row'. The man was a living Merrie Melodies cartoon.

His most famous line was a put-down to arguably the world's most famous singer. In 1918 Enrico Caruso was on the bill of a benefit show with Jolson. As the tenor left the stage, Jolson strode on and roared, 'You ain't heard nothin' yet!' He seemed oblivious to any offence his unbelievable cheek might cause. The line became a hook in *The Jazz Singer*, some nine years later, by which time the late Caruso wasn't in a position to be offended all over again. Jolson's characteristic kneeling pose came, almost unbelievably, from an ingrowing toenail. During a marathon set, he couldn't take the pain any more and went down on one knee, gesticulating like mad, which the audience couldn't get enough of. No fool, it became part of his routine.

Jolson's contemporaries often weren't enamoured of his antics. Arthur Tracy was also a Jewish émigré from Eastern Europe, and an altogether different kind of performer. He had been an architecture student and then a furniture salesman, until 1924, when, aged twenty-five, he moved to New York and began singing part-time in vaudeville and Yiddish the-atre. William S. Paley of CBS caught his act in 1931 and offered him a radio programme of his own. Tracy was worried he would flop, embar-rassing his family and jeopardising his vaudeville career, so he used the alias 'The Street Singer'. His shyness made him a star: the audience were desperate to know the identity of the man singing 'Marta, Rambling Rose of the Wildwood', and CBS wisely kept it under wraps for five months, so his 'Street Singer' nickname stuck. A year later, Tracy was in Hollywood performing in *The Big Broadcast* with Bing Crosby and the Boswell Sisters; by 1933 he was singing at Franklin D. Roosevelt's inauguration. 'Jolson loved to be noticed,' said the retiring Tracy: 'He was quite vociferous. Instead of sitting like most people do, like most civilians, he would stand up suddenly on a chair, and start to wave at somebody, pretending he saw somebody on the beach. Or he'd be yell-ing at somebody on the boardwalk to attract attention.'

Jolson would get into the box office and sell the tickets for his own shows. Every little stunt helped to sell more tickets.

'He had charisma,' admitted songwriter Harry Warren. 'They were just crazy about him. He stopped the show cold . . . I never liked him. He was a good entertainer, but I don't particularly like him as a person.'

It isn't hard to find stories that explain the antipathy of otherwise gentle souls like Harry Warren. Jolson would take a notepad to bur-lesque houses and vaudeville theatres, write down the best jokes, use them in his next act, and then get his lawyer to write to the original comedian, saying, 'I heard you used Mr Jolson's material in your act last week. Don't. Or else.' The world's greatest ego could brook no room for competition. 'He was a cruel man,' said 20th Century Fox's musical director Walter Scharf. 'He was cruel to people who worked for him. He had no patience. His tolerance spanned fifteen seconds, or something.' It was this temper, this flare-up, that propelled him across the stage and fired up his songs. The deference of Arthur Tracy was completely alien to Jolson, and his brazen gate-crashing of theatrical values – using noise, flash, any gimmick available – didn't always impress the critics.

'It is not talent which has landed him where he is,' ran *Billboard*'s review of Jolson's 1921 show *Bombo*. 'His small stock of ability has been capitalised with the cynical assurance of a successful clothing salesman. If he can get his finger in the buttonhole of your lapel, you buy the pants. That's all there is to it.'

Subtlety never came into it. 'Sonny Boy' was sung three times in his film *The Singing Fool* and it became so popular that, in 1928, there were forty different recordings available in Britain alone: eighteen vocal, sixteen dance-band and six piano or organ renditions. Jolson's, on Brunswick, was the best-seller, with Layton and Johnstone, John McCormack and Paul Robeson not far behind. Parlour mawkishness and songs about dying children were clearly still box-office gold at the height of the Jazz Age.

If he was not on stage, Jolson was permanently champing at the bit. He needed an audience to work his personal magic. Even allowing for his overbearing personality, Jolson is the biggest name in this book whose enormous success seems hard to fathom today, whose crude, untutored megaphone voice seems impossible to listen to as entertainment. If Jolson's neediness and manic self-promotion seem to prefigure Madonna or Robbie Williams, musically and vocally he seems little more than an object of mere historical interest, like an adding machine.

So what was so great about Al Jolson? What am I missing? How come his contemporaries, almost without exception, agreed with Jolson's description of himself as 'the greatest entertainer the world has ever known'? He had the same level of peer approval as (the slightly younger) Charlie Chaplin, unquestioning, unwavering. This singer still wearing blackface in the 1940s, decades after it should have been wiped off, this bellowing ham, more of an orator than a singer – what was so good about him?

Let's examine his voice. It was nasal, for a start, and he mangled and stretched his vowels horribly. Like blackface, it was an approximation of black culture, borrowing vocal stylings – moans, hollers, raw emotion – from the church. When Irving Berlin wrote 'Revival Day' in 1914, it was Jolson who introduced it. And, like the singing in a revivalist meeting, it was loud and uninhibited.

The Jazz Singer was the first talkie, and Jolson was its star. Some might say this is an abomination: a man in blackface calling himself a jazz singer is bad enough, but *the* jazz singer? Yet Jolson took a vocal melody and cut it up, stretched it out, spat out lines or caressed them. His voice was limited, one-paced, but he made up for this by giving it texture. In anyone's language, he was a jazz singer. Not only this, but Jolson had been working on his technique since he was thrown in with ragtime performers on the vaudeville stage at the turn of the century. He also mimicked horns, could chatter along like an old piano roll, speed up a lyric, slow it down, holler the words like an auctioneer, bend them all out of shape, and he was doing all this before any other recorded pop star. He didn't waste a syllable, freeing them from the straight rhythm of the song, toying with them but clearly loving his ability to do so. When the words couldn't do the job for him, he'd break into a whistling solo.

Where did he pick all this up? Clearly, he wasn't the first singer to slur and slide around a vocal, and Jolson would reminisce about popping into black clubs in Chicago and New York to check out the competition and pick up tips. He certainly borrowed from gospel, even shouting out 'Glory hallelujah!' on occasion. Yet his style owed at least as much to his Eastern European Jewish background. Like Afro-American songs and tunes, Jewish music – its techniques, inflections and scales – had to adapt itself to the Western European diatonic scale in America, and the junction points are where the excitement happened. Jolson exaggerated slurs and scoops, which to an opera singer like John McCormack or Enrico Caruso would have been seen as a disgrace. These days, the only time you don't hear singers incorporate these slurs and slides between notes is at the opera. It's entirely standard, and Jolson was one of the pathfinders.

He always had a fresh hit song. Again, this was quite unheard of. Most singers would stick with their signature tune and hammer it for years, happy to be associated with something everyone could hum. Not Jolie. Maybe his signature tune was 'Sonny Boy', but this had been recorded in 1928, some twelve years after his first starring role on Broadway. In between, his career highs had included 'You Made Me Love You' (1913) and 'California, Here I Come' (1924). He was the first pop singer from whose back catalogue you could genuinely configure a *20 Golden Greats*. Before the hit parade existed, he was a hit-maker; if he sang a song at the Winter Garden on a Sunday night, it would be in the repertoire of every other singer by the end of the following week. 'Swanee' was a case in point. One night, Jolson was throwing a party at a joint called Bessie Bloodgood's after a Winter Garden show. George Gershwin was there and played 'Swanee' for Jolson, who turned to his musical director Al Goodman and said, 'I'll break that in Thursday night.' Within ten days it was a hit. He never wrote anything, even though his name often appeared on sheet music. Who would refuse the request?

After his huge success with 'My Mammy', the term 'coon song' was reborn as 'mammy song'. Jolson had redefined the genre, yet it is one that is kept locked away today; the music is a tough listen. The singers who came after him – Crosby, then Sinatra, then Presley – built on Jolson's primitive foundations and would become less problematic role models for successive generations.

Still, his legacy is surprisingly mixed. Jolson's name can be used as shorthand for blatant cultural appropriation and popular music's unfiltered racism. He's largely remembered as the king of blackface. His mask allowed him to convey sentimentality, to exaggerate, to reach the balcony. It gave Jolson himself an electricity he couldn't always muster otherwise; according to his contemporary Groucho Marx, Jolson was so insecure that he would leave the tap running in his dressing room during performances so that he couldn't hear the applause for the opening acts.

So Jolson gave minstrelsy its final moment of prominence, that ugly tool of white supremacy sticking its teeth into pop well into the

twentieth century's fourth decade.* Yet for many he also evoked nostalgia: for home cooking, for family members left behind, for the green
fields and rolling hills of the Old World. In the 1920s he was the underdog, the poster boy for displaced persons. For immigrants, he was about
stability in a rootless new world that had carelessly wiped their history,
anglicising their names on arrival at Ellis Island. Italian, Irish, Slavic and
(naturally) Jewish households across America wept to his music. For
them, unlikely as it may seem now, Jolson's music and his anonymising
mask of make-up had nothing at all to do with plantations.

* * *

The Jazz Singer would make Al Jolson seem like an innovator, the first
multimedia star (on stage, on record, on screen), but it would prove to
be a short-lived victory. By the early 1930s Hollywood musicals had
found their feet. An actor and singer like Maurice Chevalier was per-
sonable, a confidant; in the 1932 Rodgers and Hart musical *Love Me
Tonight* his charm didn't need the help of any make-up or wild gestic-
ulations. Less could be more, though Jolson would never have believed
it. He was still working the crowd on screen, giving it 110 per cent and
looking rather small, shrill and silly. What worked on the stage quickly
became wearing on the screen, and after 1933's *Hallelujah, I'm a Bum*,
audiences moved on. The sensuality and technical wizardry of *42nd
Street*, released the same year, showed just how much Jolson was past his
prime. It was an important backstage musical, set in the contemporaneous Depression, which immediately gave it a modern sheen; also, it
didn't pre-exist as a stage musical, being based on a novel by Bradford
Ropes, which made it seem fresher still.† Worse for Jolson's fragile ego

* It lived on, with the BBC's *Black and White Minstrel Show* still broadcast
regularly in the 1970s, though this was more of a nostalgic look at Jolson than an
ongoing genre.
† Bradford Ropes's other claim to fame was writing screenplays for Abbott and
Costello. *42nd Street*'s music was by Al Dubin and Harry Warren – their first
musical together – and they came up trumps with 'You're Getting to Be a Habit
with Me' and 'Shuffle Off to Buffalo'.

was that it starred his wife, Ruby Keeler, who now eclipsed him. *Go into Your Dance* (1935), also based on a Ropes novel, was meant to launch Jolson and Keeler as a team to rival Astaire and Rogers. But Jolson soon realised he didn't like to be a co-star – not even when the co-star was his own wife – and the experiment wasn't repeated.

Jolson remained a star until the turn of the 1950s, but essentially he was still living in 1900. A man out of time, he should have been finished by the advent of the microphone, which he never came to terms with, always singing to reach the balcony. It's ironic that he starred in the first talking picture, a feat that guaranteed immortality, as he hated cinema and radio, both of which he saw as taking him away from a real live audience, there before his eyes. Until *The Jazz Singer* gave his career a massive boost, his radio show had pulled in disappointing figures; he was clearly singing for the hundreds in the studio audience, and the millions listening at home sensed this. Jolie was a turn-off. Several years later, bidding farewell on his last *Chevrolet Hour* in 1932, he threw the microphone to the floor and growled, 'The radio business is not for Jolie. It's a sad day when Jolie needs a mike to sing into.'

World War II re-energised Jolson and he toured the world, from Scotland to Africa, where he caught malaria, forcing him to be laid up for the rest of the war. True to form, he married his nurse in 1945. Given his attitude to change, it's unsurprising that by 1946, when *The Jolson Story* was released, Jolson was considered to be a figure from the past. Though the film starred Larry Parks, the actual singing was done by Jolson; he had even put himself forward to play his own part, even though by now he was in his sixties. Sales of his records picked up, thanks in part to girls buying music which appeared to be sung by the handsome young Parks. No matter – Jolie didn't mind! Three years later, Parks and Jolson repeated the exercise in *Jolson Sings Again*, by which point the ageing Jolson had only one lung. Both films make an attempt to explain away the blackface, and in a way they are quite touching.

His contemporary in the 1920s Eddie Cantor remembered him after the huge success of *The Jolson Story*: 'Still he was insecure. We were neighbours in Palm Springs. We walked together, talked together, ate together, and I knew him better than I had ever known him through the years. What amazed me was that this great personality had never learned how to live. He couldn't; there was something chemically wrong. The minute the curtain rang down, he died.'

The biopics turned out to be Jolson's last will and testament. In 1950 he went to Korea to entertain the troops and, Jolie being Jolie, completely overdid it. A month later, he died.

11

I'M GONNA DO IT IF I LIKE IT: THE JAZZ AGE

When lovely woman stoops to folly and
Paces about her room again, alone,
She smoothes her hair with automatic hand,
And puts a record on the gramophone.
  The Waste Land, T. S. Eliot

We may owe the permissive society to the Charleston.
  Jazz Writings, Philip Larkin

From the 1920s onwards, popular music would be inextricable from memories of youth, something a generation could share that no one else could fully understand. This was an unprecedented perceptual change and meant that the '20s became the first and only decade to be thought of entirely in musical terms – the Jazz Age.

The Jazz Age began on 20 January 1920, shortly after the Volstead Act prohibited interstate commerce in alcoholic beverages; it ended, firmly, with the stock market crash of 1929. Three months after the Volstead Act passed, F. Scott Fitzgerald's *This Side of Paradise* was published. George Gershwin wasn't Fitzgerald's musical twin, but he may have been Gatsby's. They shared a dream-state charm. Gershwin would throw parties, and when he played the piano, no one moved except slowly, slowly, towards the piano. He was always seen with beautiful women – usually married ones – though he never tied the knot. He was open, gregarious, but still unknowable, and there is a hint of sadness, a dark streak of blue, in not only his music, but also his photos. The eyes can't hide it.

It is hard to overestimate the impact of 'Rhapsody in Blue' after its debut in 1924. It can be measured in a passage from the working manuscript of *The Great Gatsby* about the fictional Vladimir Epstein's *Jazz History of the World*, a recent sensation at Carnegie Hall. At a summer party, Gatsby requests the piece to be played in full, and Nick Carraway compares its heady effect to champagne: 'Girls were swooning backward playfully into men's arms, even into groups knowing that someone would arrest their falls.'

Gershwin spent the Jazz Age as the brightest star in music, popular or serious. Though the two musics were heading in different directions, he was still regarded as their one potential unifier. The *New York Times* expected him to do something 'racially important', just when Henry Ford's *Dearborn Independent* newspaper was writing of 'the International Jew, the world's problem', and – in case Gershwin didn't already get the hint – 'Jewish jazz' and its 'abandoned sensuousness of sliding notes'. Gershwin could rise above this and took Ford on as a challenge, beginning work on the *Melting Pot* piano preludes. To American youth, though, he was still a true American hero.

In the meantime, Broadway songs fell from his fingers. Back in 1918, just out of his teens, Gershwin had become the rehearsal pianist for Ann Pennington, the top attraction in the Ziegfeld Follies.

Four foot ten, with dimpled knees, a shoe size of one and a half, and a smile that left your knees buckling from a mile away, Pennington was a Jazz Age heroine several years ahead of schedule who would make the Black Bottom a sensation when she danced in *George White's Scandals of 1926*. Looking for the perfect early muse, Gershwin couldn't have got any luckier, and within eighteen months he was writing songs for her, like the saucy 'On My Mind the Whole Night Long' in White's very first *Scandals*.

In 1924 George began to work on musical comedies with his older brother Ira, and each one included a gold-plated future standard. First up was *Lady, Be Good*, which included 'Fascinating Rhythm'; they followed this with *Oh, Kay!* in 1926 ('Someone to Watch Over Me'), *Funny Face* in 1927 (''S Wonderful') and *Strike Up the Band* in the same year, which included a brace of imperishables in 'The Man I Love' and 'I've Got a Crush on You'.

Between 1924's *Lady, Be Good* and the crash of 1929, the Jazz Age musical would develop in parallel with new technological, good-time developments. There was radio, there were record players, and shellac began outselling sheet music for the first time. In America, sales of gramophones (or 'phonographs', as they were still known) had risen from $27.1 million in 1914 to $158.7 million in 1919. In tandem, record sales boomed, climbing past 100 million in 1921. Despite these changes, the librettos for musicals remained for the most part cruddy; unless Guy Bolton and P. G. Wodehouse were involved, the storylines and scripts were generally just as featherweight as the operettas and vaudeville revues that preceded them, and they had the shelf life of strawberries. But Gershwin's songs were so forward-looking, so adventurous, that they attracted the most boundary-free singers, people who recognised that his work was reinventing the possibilities of jazz and creating a new space for vocal jazz. Ethel Waters, for one, who recorded 'I Got Rhythm' from 1930's *Girl Crazy* – such an instant classic that it would be recorded by more than seventy acts in the next dozen years.

Not everyone was thrilled by this cultural leap. The *Ladies Home Journal* wrote that 'Jazz originally was the accompaniment of the voodoo dancer, stimulating the half-crazed barbarian to the vilest of deeds.' The saxophone was suddenly seen as sinful. The gyrations of the foxtrot were an abomination. Jazz was unhealthy, immoral, it had to be wiped out. The *Atlantic Monthly* drily commented that 'jazz is vastly more calamitous than was the material havoc wrought by the World War'.

This wasn't really about music; it was about sex, as well as booze and crime and (of course) race. The National Association of Orchestra Directors – an entirely white organisation – would send snoopers around hotels and nightclubs checking up on what was being played, just in case it was the wrong kind of jazz, the kind that might lead to dirty dancing. Congress was badgered about censoring music on radio and record; eventually, the 1927 Radio Act stated that 'no person within the jurisdiction of the United States shall utter any obscene, indecent or profane language by means of radio communication'. Internal censorship meant that within a decade NBC had a banned list of 290 songs. In short, 'sweet jazz' won out over 'hot jazz'.

The 'sweet' band was an extension of the American society orchestra of the 1910s and '20s. In Britain, they played palm courts in hotel lobbies and restaurants, and the repertoire would include the folk-inspired light music of Eric Coates and Percy Grainger. In America, they were mostly based in New York, playing local dances and debutante balls across the metropolis every weekend. Initially, they played easily recognisable versions of familiar tunes; the switch to sweet jazz meant the bands still played together, with very few solos, and the tempo was still strictly mid, but elements of jazz were now sneaking in, whether it was through the band's line-up (saxophones, cornets and drum kits) or in the repertoire. In Britain, the new order were simply known as dance bands, and home-grown hot jazz was virtually unknown.

There were exceptions. Drawing crowds to London's Savoy Hotel on the Strand was Bert Ralton's Savoy Havana Band, initially a six-piece in 1922, then expanding to a ten-piece dance band once they had their feet under the table. Ralton was an American saxophonist and clarinettist (which partly explains his chops) who had originally come to London in 1920 to sell sheet music and musical instruments. Recording for Columbia, the Savoy Havana Band made some of the hottest British jazz records of the 1920s – De Sylva and Henderson's 'What Did I Tell Ya' (1926) could have got an elephant to dance the Black Bottom. Ralton died the following year in the kind of incident that could only have happened to a star performer in the Jazz Age. The band were touring in Rhodesia, spending a rare day off hunting deer. The boys were enjoying a picnic when Ralton fell against a gun and shot himself in the thigh. While waiting three hours for an ambulance, he apparently played a ukulele and sang to keep his spirits up. He later died in the Salisbury hospital where the band had given a performance for the patients and staff a couple of days before.

Americans in London were exotic creatures. Crossing over all of Britain's racial and class boundaries were the close-harmony duo of Turner Layton and Clarence 'Tandy' Johnstone, who scored a best-seller with their first 78, coupling 'Hard Hearted Hannah' ('When she's nasty, she's as sweet as sour milk') with Isham Jones and Gus Kahn's 'It Had to Be You' in 1924. They had played society dos in the States, and on arriving in Britain played private shows for Prince Edward (later King Edward VIII). They sold an incredible eight million records, before their career suddenly ended in 1935, when Tandy was named in the divorce case of bandleader Albert Sandler. According to *The Times*, the judge warned the jury that when deciding damages they should 'get out of their heads any idea of vindictiveness because of colour'. Johnstone went on to marry the former Mrs Sandler, but his career was over.

The archetypal British figure of the 1920s was the decidedly cool Noël Coward. A brilliantined polymath with a genius for self-promotion, Coward claimed to have written his best-known play, *Private Lives*, in four days flat. Like Gershwin, he remains an improbably modern figure. He nurtured friends with influence. Coward had made his stage debut in 1901, aged eleven, as Prince Mussel in a children's play called *The Goldfish* – his dad may have been a humble piano salesman, but his mother had naval blood and thought Noël deserved a higher station. Aged twenty-four, he was writing and starring in *The Vortex*, which put a mirror up to the bored, cocaine-taking upper-class circles he was now swanning around in; in 1925 *The Vortex* was just one of four Coward plays running simultaneously in the West End. He said the two most beautiful things in the world were Ivor Novello's profile 'and my mind'.

Coward wrote the words and music for eight musicals between 1928 and 1963, the most successful of which was *Bitter Sweet* (1929), which ran in the West End for 697 performances between 1929 and 1931. Full of romantic waltzes from a previous age, it was set in nineteenth-century Vienna and London, and Coward thought of it as an operetta, a counterpoint to the hyper-speed sounds all around. In the States, Jerome Kern or Cole Porter would have heard 'I'll See You Again' and been a little jealous of its seductive heart-on-sleeve romanticism, which had possibly been born out of circumstance – it had been written in the back of a cab during gridlock in New York. Coward proudly told people how quickly and easily he could dash out a classic, songs that felt preserved in amber the first time you heard them. Still, he hardly lacked for ambition: 1933's *Cavalcade* would be nothing less than a dash through British history from 1899 to 1929, as seen through the eyes of a family far more aristocratic than Coward's. He managed to imbue them with humanity and wit, which was wishfully autobiographical.

Cold Comfort Farm author Stella Gibbons wrote that Coward represented 'the myth of the twenties: gaiety; courage; pain concealed'. Coward realised, like Jolson, the need to maintain a star-like persona, and he worked hard to see every new show, every new play when it opened, which, inevitably, he would be withering about in the fewest possible words. In 1947 he was in Chicago, where Tallulah Bankhead took him to see Miles Davis perform in 'a beastly little club'. He wrote in his diary that they were 'given a table right under the trumpet, whereupon I walked out and came home. I am forty-seven and sane.' He became fast friends with Lionel Bart after *Oliver!* opened in 1960, ringing him up to congratulate him on his success and introducing himself with the line, 'Hello, this is Noël.' Bart didn't know anyone called Noël. Noël who? he asked. 'Noël Coward, you cockney cunt.' By the late 1950s he would be a habitué of Las Vegas supper clubs, like a gaunt Elvis in a silk dressing gown, trying to conjure up a revival for all things 1920s, which – sure enough – arrived in the early 1960s: 1962 would see a hit revival of *Private Lives*. Noël Coward always seemed in total charge of his own destiny.*

* * *

At the Ritz-Carlton Hotel on New Year's Eve 1923, a party was thrown by William Randolph Hearst. The ballroom had been decorated as a Japanese garden, with dozens of lanterns and hundreds of imported palms. More than two hundred of New York's wealthiest and most respected residents drank and dined, then danced to the Paul Whiteman Orchestra.

This was not a good time to be poor. In America, the economic downturn of 1920 hit demobilised soldiers hard, with 25 per cent of blue-collar jobs disappearing in the early '20s. Thanks to Prohibition, you couldn't even drink away your sorrows. People got by on a new invention – credit – and a mass market of consumers was born. 'Just charge it!' ran an ad in New York's *Daily News*. People aspired to a better life.

Some didn't want to bother with credit. A gun-toting bandit was at large in Brooklyn in early 1924. Unlike the usual craggy lowlifes, she was notable for her sealskin coat and Jazz Age style. Celia Cooney was working in a laundry for $12 a week, a pittance even then, and wanted more from life. She was a big fan of *True Detective* magazine and bought herself a pistol, which she used to rob a dozen grocery stores, while her husband Ed waited outside in the getaway car. The press loved her, one newspaper headline reading: 'POLICE ARE BAFFLED BY BOB HAIR BANDIT'. As she recalled in her serialised memoir: 'Gosh! What they said about me. Right away some wise guy had pulled that line about how I must have been a dope fiend, and leader of a band in the underworld. I had to stop and laugh at that. I said, "Here, Ed, wait

---

* Coward even managed his legacy astutely. He knew what he was doing when he appointed BBC arts presenter Sheridan Morley as his literary executor and cultural torchbearer. He needn't have worried: in their scuffling years David Bowie ('Conversation Piece') and Joy Division (*Ideal for Living*) would lift the names of his plays.

a minute while I take a shot in the arm and play you a tune on the slide
trombone. Pipe your little wifie. See who I am! I am the Bobbed Haired
Bandit! I am a dope fiend and the leader of a band!" Gee! I felt big!'

An 'underworld' band was not the kind that would play in hotels or
restaurants, or even Brooklyn chop suey houses; it would play in speakeasies, gin mills, and at dances run by the Mob. The papers did not picture
the Bobbed Haired Bandit playing slide trombone with Paul Whiteman.
Clarinettist Joe Marsala, who played in Ben Pollack's band, recalled: 'At
one time we were working at a place in Chicago and of course it was run
by what they called the Mob or the Syndicate, something like that. And
they asked us to play at a job in the afternoon – according to the union
scale, it should have paid about $18 per man, but they said all you guys
are gonna get is $10 whether you like it or not. Of course, we went. We
played the job, they fed us well, and we drank "champagne" – it was
spiked up cider or something – and we got paid. I was the last one out
the door, and as I was about to leave I heard a voice say "Hey kid, come
here." It was Al Capone. He said, "Here's a little tip for the boys," and he
gave me $1,000, which was $250 apiece, we were a quartet. I thought it
was funny they would cut you down eight dollars on your pay, then give
you a thousand-dollar tip. It was kinda cute.'

Milt Hinton, who would later become the bassist in Cab Calloway's
Cotton Club band, grew up in Chicago and had no doubts about the
symbiotic relationship between gangsters and musicians in the Jazz Age.
Chicago was known for its rent parties; if anyone had trouble finding
the readies for the rent, they would find a pianist, throw a party and
charge admission. 'We looked on Al Capone as more or less a Robin
Hood in the black community,' remembered Hinton. 'Capone had
decided to come to the South Side of Chicago and sell alcohol to the
people who gave house-rent parties.'

Working with his uncle, Hinton sold Capone's bootleg alcohol at
rent parties from cleverly disguised vehicles. 'We had three trucks. One
was El Passo Cigars, one was Ford Cleaning and Pressing . . . it was a
thriving business. The only thing you needed to do was sit there, take
the telephone calls, and deliver. And Al Capone came every Thursday or
Friday in a big car, bullet-proof. He'd come with his bodyguards with a

bag full of money. He would park that car and walk in the back of that place, and the police would be lined up, like they were waiting for a bus. He paid every one of them five dollars, and every sergeant ten. He paid 'em off, so we had no problem with the police at all. You'd never have your house raided. I was getting something like fifty dollars a week.'

Milt's future was looking bleak when one evening, taking a delivery of bootleg liquor to a rent party, someone hit their truck side on. 'I went right out the driver's side, out the window. Alcohol was all over. I tried to get up. My arm was broken, my leg was broken, my hand was broken. The finger next to my pinky on my right hand was off, hanging by skin. By the time they got me to the hospital my legs and hands were starting to swell. I was in excruciating pain. And I'm screaming. The doctor said, "I've got to take this finger off." And I was studying violin. I said, "Please don't take my finger off."' Capone heard about the accident, picked up Hinton's mother and raced to the hospital. 'Capone said to the doctor, "If he says don't take the finger off, then don't take it off." They didn't take it off.'

* * *

Flapper Phone Girls Blamed for Bad Service.
Brooklyn Eagle, 20 March 1924

Bobbed-Haired Teachers Inefficient.
New York American, 18 April 1924

Are Our Women Becoming More Barbaric?
New York American, 11 May 1924

Sometimes it was hard to know who the press were more afraid of, the Mob or emancipated women. The 1920s also saw the consolidation of newspapers into national chains, such as William Randolph Hearst's empire. Local news started to take a back seat to syndicated stories; agony aunts were born, sports gossip became an industry, and comic strip characters became national celebrities. People across America could now share Dorothy Parker's Algonquin quips. Tickling the mass mind, the papers were abetted by radio and magazines, so that some stories

– Babe Ruth's record-breaking feats, Charles Lindbergh's transatlantic flight – became inescapable. Flappers became one of the biggest of all.

Flappers were generally single working women, alone in the city, who were using upper-class bohemian women as role models. Young middle-class women, still living at home, started copying the working-class flappers, and soon they seemed to take over. They cut their hair short, wore their dresses shorter and de-emphasised their curves. They smoked and drank in public. Mostly, they were known for dancing alone, without the need for a man to lead or give them an unwanted embrace. Newspapers and pulp magazines loved them. Men gawped at them. Jazz babies! Their anthem was vaudeville singer Marion Harris's 1920 recording 'I'm Gonna Do It If I Like It'.*

The new urban single life could also lead to a sense of isolation and emptiness: among Irving Berlin's biggest hits of the decade would be 'All Alone', 'All By Myself' and 'What'll I Do'. But stay-at-home singletons would find a new friend in the gramophone, which was critical to the cultural change in post-World War I life; records took more from the American purse than any other form of recreation in the early 1920s. In Britain, the *Daily Telegraph* started running record reviews – classical, initially – in 1919. Their reviewer, Compton Mackenzie, set up monthly magazine *The Gramophone* in April 1923, which covered popular music as well, even adding a 'Collectors Corner' in 1925 for hardcore seekers of rare jazz and classical 78s. The following year, the weekly *Melody Maker* was launched, aimed primarily at jazz and dance-band musicians.

In the mid-1920s women still bought more records than men. Since the industrial-scale commodification of music began in the 1890s, the woman's traditional role as domestic educator – to her husband as well as her kids – had been propelled into the shellac age. And women not only bought records to be played in the home, they sold them too. In

* The term 'flapper' pre-dates the 1920s. As far back as April 1914 the *Daily Mirror*, writing about an anarchist conference in Newcastle, noted that 'the delegates are in reality the mildest people imaginable. There are between thirty and forty of them, including three girls in the "flapper" stage. They dress like respectable Unionists or Liberals.'

1925 *Talking Machine World* wrote: 'The sale of records is to a very great extent in the hands of the fair sex and on the proficiency of those hands rests the musical education of the nation. She has her reward in spreading the gospel of good music and, incidentally, she receives it later in her commission check.'

The dramatic rise of women working in record departments and stores was down to several factors. One was cheap labour. The women were behind the counter; they almost never owned the shop. Less prosaically, in the 1920s it was still held as a truth that women knew more about art, literature and music than most men, who wouldn't have had time for such frivolities. So women would be better positioned to find their way around Victor's, Columbia's and Edison's ever-expanding catalogues; it was their place to know Haydn from the Haydn Quartet, and a polka from a cakewalk. Department stores became incubators of a gentle, female record-buying culture. Kaufmann's Department Store in Pittsburgh had a Japanese tea room adjacent to the record 'demonstration rooms', which were three-sided affairs with sofas and rugs. The female clerk, with no need for the masculine hard sell, could radiate sincerity, enthusiasm and friendliness to the women who were there to buy records. This was a great help when, according to Jane Barth of the Eberhardt Music Company in Wichita, 'quite a big proportion of those who come in to hear our records have in mind no particular numbers they want. They just say, "What have you got that's new?"'

* * *

A new whirl of dance steps finally threw off the pre-war era. The Charleston was the biggest, and a reminder that popular music is there for dancing. 'Not since Tango has so devastating a dance agitated town,' gasped *The New Yorker* in August 1925, in the hastened style of a telegram. 'Very intricate. Even by semi-professional dancing males Charleston not done very well. Urchins do dances on streets, while one keeps eye open for police. They do it well.' The song of the same name was a huge hit for Arthur Gibbs and His Gang in 1924 and for Paul Whiteman's a year later. Most of those doing the Charleston appeared to be slim young women, at least if newsreels and newspapers are to be believed. Whiteman's 1920 million-seller 'Whispering' had mainly been bought by young women. A 1923 edition of *Talking Machine World* said, 'If it were not for the flapper, the Victor people might as well go out of business. They buy 90% of the records, mostly dance records.' If they didn't already own one, teenagers would pressure their parents into buying a gramophone, and their pocket money would then go on 78s. Out shopping with her daughter, the mother 'always allows her to make her own choice of records', according to the same magazine.

One gramophone manufacturer, Sonora, aimed its record players squarely at women. The girl who owned a Sonora 'made every evening a cheerful one', according to their ads, with friends round to listen to records and spend 'enchanted hours together . . . subdued lights . . . music . . . beauty . . . romance! As the record plays so too does their imagination, and to the tune of its mystic music they build their air castles and plans for tomorrow.' It's a wonderful thing that records and record players would be aimed so squarely at women, given their subsequent largely masculine association, and that girls could use records as a tool of seduction. Not that Sonora would have used such language.

There was certainly a new liberty for women on records, as elsewhere, in the 1920s. Marion Harris's 'The Blues Have Got Me' (1924) summed up the flapper's appreciation of popular music, which showed little respect for the recently deceased Caruso: 'Classics don't mean a thing at all, give me a hot band in a hall . . . I like my music hot, I'm off my nut about the strut.'

The archetypal flapper singer was Helen Kane, who had turned sixteen as the 1920s kicked off. A living cartoon, with massive eyes, apple cheeks and a pouty Cupid smile, she would be transformed by animators – with very little exaggeration – into Betty Boop in 1932. All her records were a collection of squeaks and squeals, stratospheric sighs, and were partly sung–spoken in her none-more-Bronx accent. All of this was perfect for naughty flag-waving tunes like 'Button Up Your Overcoat' (1929). She had been a vaudeville singer and dancer for several years before Oscar Hammerstein's *Good Boy* gave her the chance to seize the spotlight in 1928. Singing 'I Wanna Be Loved by You', she ad-libbed a little scat 'boop boop da boop' hook and was an overnight sensation. By 1930 she was starring in her own pistol-toting movie *Dangerous Nan McGrew*, pouting for the state of New York as she sang the title song: 'I've been a bad girl all my life, I pick my teeth with a carving knife.' Real life was harder on Kane: she was deserted by two husbands, and the Depression would render her uninhibited flapper shtick deeply unfashionable. In 1939 she married Dan Healy, with whom she had worked in *Good Boy*. They opened a New York restaurant called Healy's Grill and remained married for the rest of Kane's life.

Kane sang as if her tongue tingled with rumour, gossip and mild obscenities. But as everything she sang was delivered in a wide-eyed cartoon voice, the definition of ditsy, no one minded. Annette Hanshaw was her coy partner-in-crime. She was close friends with Kane, who even coached her through an impression of herself on 'You Wouldn't Fool Me, Would You'.

When Hanshaw cut her first record in 1926, aged twenty-four, she had cheerfully murmured, 'That's all!' as it ended. Pathé Records knew a hit gimmick when they heard one, and for the next eight years Hanshaw finished up pretty much all of her records with the same distinctive sign-off. She was the 1920s' ultimate girl next door, cute as a button, with both a fluttering shyness and a flapper's *joie de vivre*. Her voice was versatile enough for her to play confidante ('Get Out and Get Under the Moon') or seductress ('Moanin' Low') or gold digger ('Is There Anything Wrong in That'), and it took a special kind of ingénue to sing 'I Want a Good Man (And I Want Him Bad)', with a helpful wink and a nod from her regular backing band, the Sizzlin' Syncopators. She couldn't miss, really, and after debuting in 1929 she became one of the biggest radio stars of the early 1930s. Hanshaw would sing on air with Glen Gray's Casa Loma Orchestra and be the featured star of *Maxwell House Show Boat* from 1932 to 1934; they called her 'The Personality Girl'.*

---

* The show's theme tune was 'Here Comes the Show Boat', written by Maceo Pinkard, from Bloomfield, West Virginia, one of the most successful black songwriters of the 1920s. His other writing credits include 'Sweet Georgia Brown', first introduced by Ben Bernie's orchestra, and Whispering Jack Smith's 1926 hit 'Gimme a Little Kiss, Will You, Huh'.

All the while, the shyness was no act. Hanshaw hated what she was doing. Thinking about her radio performances, she wept, 'I'm so afraid I'll fail . . . suppose I should have to cough? And all those people listening!' She winced at 'that corny little baby voice' on record; in a 1978 interview she complained that she was 'most unhappy when they were released. I just often cried because I thought they were so poor. I'm ashamed to say I just did it for the money. I loved singing, you know, jamming with the musicians when it isn't important to do, but somehow or other I was terribly nervous when I sang. I happen to be an introvert, and I just wasn't happy.'

Alongside the flappers were the vaudeville vamps, older and more unbridled, with a curvaceous sexuality that put the flappers back in the nursery. One was Lee Morse, with the sleepy-eyed looks of Bette Davis and the sound of a more tuneful Mae West. Her brandy-aged voice was deep enough that she had to be credited on her earliest records as Miss Lee Morse. With bluesy phrasing and what sounded like the occasional hiccough, Morse initially accompanied herself on guitar, ukulele and kazoo; what's more, she wrote a lot of her own material. By the late 1920s she was recording some terrific sides ('I'm an Unemployed Sweetheart' and the self-penned 'There Must Be a Silver Lining' and 'Be Sweet to Me') with a fine band dubbed the Bluegrass Boys, even though Morse was from Oregon, and the players – including the Dorseys, banjo ace Harry Reser and guitarist Eddie Lang – had probably never been within a hundred miles of Kentucky. No matter, these were terrifically rich and sensuous recordings. Booze helped to batter Morse's career and she spent the 1930s singing in small nightclubs, which was a real shame as she had the talent to become something far greater.

Another frustrating talent was Kay Swift, whose songwriting hot streak lasted from 1929 until 1934. She was playing in a classical trio when she met George Gershwin at a party in 1925; it's fair to assume Gershwin's musical *Oh, Kay!*, which opened a year later, was titled with an eye to impressing his beautiful new friend. They composed together (though not on the same song), they critiqued each other, they became lovers. Not that it bothered Gershwin, but Kay was married to lyricist Paul James, who by day was the wealthy banker James Paul Warburg;

he wrote under an assumed name lest his clients were scared off by his affiliation with the demon jazz. Poor James had only begun writing lyrics to Swift's melodies in an ultimately vain attempt to steer his wife away from Gershwin, whom he called 'the self-centred genius'. Still, he did a more than adequate job: they collaborated on 1929's *The Little Show* (featuring 'Can't We Be Friends', which received the ultimate accolade, ending up on Frank Sinatra's *In the Wee Small Hours* in 1955 and Ella Fitzgerald's *Sweet Songs for Swingers* in 1959) and 1930's *Fine and Dandy* (big hit – 'Can This Be Love'). Swift would become the first woman to write an entire Broadway score. It would have been the biggest musical of the year, if it hadn't been for the 'self-centred genius''s *Girl Crazy*. James couldn't keep up, and his marriage to Swift ended in divorce in 1934.

Having lost her lyricist, Swift started working at Radio City Music Hall in 1934, writing new music for the Rockettes' routines every month or so. Five years later, she became light music director for the World's Fair (where the Aquacade had its own theme, 'Yours for a Song', written by another songwriter dubbed 'the girl Gershwin', Dana Suesse). Swift then eloped to Oregon, lived on a ranch and wrote a memoir called *Who Could Ask for Anything More?*, which was turned into a Hollywood musical, *Never a Dull Moment*, with Irene Dunne playing Kay. After Gershwin's death in 1937, Swift devoted herself to his work. She was trusted by Ira Gershwin, and they worked together on the first posthumous piece of George Gershwin music, 'Dawn of a New Day', which became the theme for the 1939 World's Fair. Kay and Ira also managed to complete George's unpublished score for the 1947 movie *The Shocking Miss Pilgrim*. They managed to elaborate on so much of Gershwin's work posthumously because, among her other skills, Kay was blessed with total recall. She died in 1993, aged ninety-five. It had been a life well lived.

* * *

At a Park Avenue cocktail party in 1928, members of Ben Pollack's band mingled with those of Paul Whiteman's. Jimmy McPartland, cornet player for Pollack, complained to Whiteman trumpeter Bix Beiderbecke about his band's struggle to find work, saying they were having trouble finding money for food. Bix opened up his wallet, which was bulging with dollar bills and uncashed cheques, and offered McPartland a couple of hundred-dollar bills. McPartland politely turned him down but borrowed $20 and got a good anecdote.

Beiderbecke had been born in Iowa in 1903, into a staid, German American family, lumber barons, and extremely wealthy. The jug-eared lad ended up at school in Chicago, where he used to bunk off to hear the great jazz players, in particular Louis Armstrong. Bix had apparently been picking out tunes on the piano before he was in kindergarten, and when he heard jazz from the riverboats that came up the Mississippi to Davenport, his life's curve was mapped out. It was unthinkable that this lad, born into wealth and privilege, would throw away his lineage to play jazz, but that's how legends are made. At twenty-one he was the trumpet-playing star of a group called the Wolverines, who became a campus sensation while touring in 1924 and ended up in New York. Bix was their key player, and when he left them, everyone expected him to become a major star. It turned out that the dozen or so records he made with the Wolverines would be arguably the best he ever cut.

In New York, he joined Paul Whiteman's band, adding his extraordinary, unfiltered solos to the sweetly conservative sound and lining up alongside future superstars Tommy Dorsey and Bing Crosby. Listen to his intro to 'Mississippi Mud', and you're hooked from the off. Jazz purists may wish there was more than just sixteen bars of Bix on recordings like 'There Ain't No Man That's Worth the Salt of My Tears' (1928), but he loved the discipline of the Whiteman set-up, the Ferde Grofé arrangements and George Gershwin's songs. Clarinettist Mezz Mezzrow later recalled sadly how Bix 'drifted clean out of our sphere. Losing his head over serious music made him go way tangent.' It's interesting that Mezzrow considers Gershwin 'serious music', but maybe that's as serious as Bix wanted to be. It's impossible to know. 'He didn't know how to say no,' said Louis Armstrong, 'and he didn't know how to say goodnight.' Constant partying, alcoholism and mental-health issues left him as the

Chatterton of the Jazz Age, dead by 1931, at the age of twenty-eight. 'Perhaps Bix would have been better off with either more gifts or less,' said Philip Larkin wisely.

* * *

Pop's push-and-pull, with the reactionary rubbing up against the modernist, means that in times of rapid forward motion, some will grasp tightly to the past to steady themselves. In the 1920s conservatives desired something that was neither 'sweet' nor 'hot', and so during the Jazz Age there was, paradoxically, a period of lush escapism on Broadway, a renewed thirst for European operetta. Sigmund Romberg's *The Student Prince* (1924) and *The Desert Song* (1926) were romantic tales of impossibly foreign climes and distant pasts, with no hint of the train, let alone the aeroplane. In spite of the humiliating demise of the Austro-Hungarian empire, the Viennese influence was revived on Broadway in 1924, when Czech-born composer Rudolf Friml wrote *Rose Marie*, with book and lyrics by Otto Harbach and Oscar Hammerstein II. Edith Day, who starred in the London production, recalled that '*Rose Marie* was above all romantic. It cut right across the hard-boiled, jazzed-up gaiety of the mid-twenties. It was American [in spite of the music it was set in the Rockies, rather than Vienna], probably the first American musical ever seen at Drury Lane. So its music had a touch of syncopation here and there, yet it had sentiment and glamour just as the old-time musical plays like *The Merry Widow*.' Thanks to Harbach and Hammerstein, the book and the lyrics were integrated; that was their cause, and eventually it would become the standard musical theatre format. *Rose Marie* ran for 851 performances in London and gave us the immortal 'Indian Love Call' ('When I'm calling yoooo-hoo-hoo-hoo'), which was rurally revived with huge success by Slim Whitman in 1954.

The Hungarian-born Romberg managed to write for the English market without ever mastering the language. By 1926, aged thirty-nine, he was also working with the socially conscious Oscar Hammerstein, and their *Desert Song* was inspired by the 1925 Berber uprising in Morocco against French colonial rule.* There was a London cast recording in 1927, but it refused to go away, and the full score would be cut in 1951 by the baritone superstar and operetta throwback Nelson Eddy. The mid-1920s would be the last period when musical theatre was a bigger draw than the movies. These musicals were genuine commercial hits, and it should be remembered that at the time New Orleans jazz was only gradually making inroads into pop culture. Though 'Drink! Drink! Drink!' (in the middle of Prohibition!) was the cry of *The Student Prince*, its Old World setting was a reminder that the Jazz Age wasn't for everyone.

The 1920s would be looked back on as the most modern of twentieth-century decades. Almost the minute they ended, though, they would be regarded as nothing more than an exciting and frantic interlude. The stock market crash of 1929 provided a cold, conclusive end to the party and precipitated the biggest American crisis since the Civil War. In spite of what F. Scott Fitzgerald might have said, though, few had wasted their youth; they had memories which would keep them going through the fallow years that followed and provide storylines for generations that they couldn't even imagine. Music would always be wanted, and radio waves – just there, like air – would be needed like at no time before or since.

---

* This might sound like rather rococo subject matter, but North Africa was in vogue in the mid-1920s: see also P. C. Wren's French Foreign Legion novel *Beau Geste* (1924) and Rudolf Valentino's final film *The Son of the Sheik*, a huge posthumous hit in 1926.

12

IN A SILENT WAY: RACE RECORDS

No one would have guessed back in 1912, when it first made its presence known on vaudeville stages, that the blues would become one of the defining sounds of the twentieth century. No one in the nascent music industry thought of it then as anything more than a fad, a subset of ragtime even, only with a bunch of guitar or banjo notes played together and a vocal style that hovered around a tune, occasionally hitting the note, but more commonly sounding like a moan. For the white record-buying public, the blues had briefly surfaced with the Victor Military Band's recording of W. C. Handy's 'Memphis Blues' in 1914. It had been a dance-hall craze, nothing that stood out any more than the turkey trot, and then sank for the duration of the war and seemed to have been folded into jazz come 1917.*

Like ragtime, the blues could have remained part of the music in the mist, unrecorded and undocumented. It had been plucked from the air and pressed on shellac by W. C. Handy, a thirty-eight-year-old dance-band leader who had heard some poor unknown soul whistling sadly to themselves at Memphis railroad station in 1912 and decided he'd quite like a slice of that sound. He went back home and channelled what he remembered of the melody into 'Memphis Blues', quickly following it with 'St Louis Blues'. Moments could be caught and monetised; indus-trialisation had changed everything about music, even whistling.†

The music industry, based almost entirely in New York, was happy to sell records by black Americans to black Americans, as long as the labels doing the business were white-run. Reducing the fluid, com-plex variety of southern American music into distinct genres based around racial and ethnic identities made the salesman's life easier, and by the 1920s record companies would be printing catalogues of 'race' and 'hillbilly' records. These cultural economics – binding and divid-ing races, regions and musics – were brand new. Previously, black and white artists alike had played not only blues, ragtime and string-band music, but also nationally popular sentimental ballads, minstrel songs, Tin Pan Alley tunes and Broadway hits. It may have made financial sense to New York-based record labels like Brunswick, but it was cul-tural Jim Crow.

* * *

From the vantage point of almost any time since then, it seems quite remarkable that black female singers were so popular in the 1920s.

* Aside from the song structure and the minor chords, Handy's 'Memphis Blues' and 'St Louis Blues' certainly sound closer to ragtime and more proto-jazz than the blues that would emerge in the 1920s.
† Although recorded music had been around for a decade or so, in 1912 pop music was still heard on the street more than anywhere else, through people whistling or singing the vaudeville hits to themselves.

What's more, most of these women wrote their own material, essentially inventing what would later be thought of as the 'authentic' blues form, on paper and on record. Ma Rainey was there first, the 'Mother of the Blues'; all the rest followed her – Mamie Smith, Bessie Smith, Clara Smith,* Georgia's 'Uncrowned Queen of the Blues' Ida Cox, the glamorous Victoria Spivey, Alberta Hunter (who went on to appear in London's first production of *Showboat*, in 1928, opposite Paul Robeson) and the beautifully dressed Memphis Minnie, who, according to singer Homesick James, was fond of chewing tobacco. Male blues singers couldn't get a look-in. The impact of Chicago blues shows in the early 1920s was huge. Here was music that a few years previously had been played at rent parties and in tawdry joints now taking centre stage in theatres like the 500-seat Grand in Chicago's South Side. Songwriter Thomas Dorsey's† description of a Ma Rainey show is hard to beat: 'The room is filled with a haze of smoke, she walks into the spotlight, face decorated with Stein's Reddish Make-Up Powder. She's not a young symmetrical streamlined type; her face seems to have discarded no less than fifty-some years. She stands out high in front with a glorious bust, squeezed tightly in the middle . . . When she started singing, the gold in her teeth would sparkle. She possessed her listeners; they swayed, they rocked, they moaned and groaned as they felt the blues with her . . . the bass drum rolled like thunder and the stage lights flickered like forked lightning.'

Rainey, from Columbus, Georgia, had started out in 1900, in a talent show called *A Bunch of Blackberries* at the city's Springer Opera House. Gold teeth flashing, she sang her self-penned 'Bo Weevil Blues', 'Don't Fish in My Sea', 'Louisiana Hoo Doo Blues', 'Rough and Tumble Blues', 'Titanic Man Blues' and 'Weepin' Woman Blues'. She met Bessie Smith on the road and corralled her into joining her travelling show. They got

* There were also Trixie Smith and Laura Smith. They were all unrelated, though when they were playing together the posters would often proclaim, 'The Smith Girls Are in Town'. Sometimes Bessie and Clara – who later recorded 'Far Away Blues' and 'I'm Going Back to My Used to Be' together – pretended to be sisters.
† Dorsey wrote gospel standards like 'Peace in the Valley' and 'Take My Hand, Precious Lord'.

on immediately. Ma was a lesbian, Bessie was bisexual, but the relationship was like mother and daughter.

In 1920 every aspect of the American record industry was white and northern. It was so rare for a so-called 'race record' to exist that the *Chicago Defender* newspaper urged its black readers to buy Mamie Smith's 'Crazy Blues' on the Okeh label out of racial pride – and they did, making it an unexpected million-seller.* It would take a savvy furniture manufacturer in the upper Midwest to monetise the blues and effectively create a parallel pop culture – a black, female alternative.

The catalogue of Paramount Records would end up as one of the twentieth century's most significant and fetishised. The label had been set up by the Wisconsin Chair Company of Grafton, Wisconsin, which specialised in selling furniture to black customers in Detroit and Chicago. The furniture included gramophones, and the Wisconsin Chair Company wisely realised it could sell records to play on these machines. Paramount aimed to give Wisconsin Chair's customers an introduction to the sounds of the city they had just arrived in, as well as memories of the rural South they'd left behind.

Between 1922 and 1932 Paramount would release straight blues records by Ida Cox and Alberta Hunter; country blues by Big Bill Broonzy, Blind Lemon Jefferson and Charley Patton; and more urban Chicago blues by Ma Rainey. They pressed 100,000 records a day for the African American market. One of Paramount's executives was Jay Mayo Williams, a fascinating figure and the most successful African American in the music industry prior to Motown's Berry Gordy.

Born in 1894, Williams had enrolled at Ivy League Brown University on an athletic scholarship; in 1922 he was one of only three black players in the newly founded National Football League. The pay for pro footballers was so bad that Williams sold bathtub gin to Chicago jazz

---

* The *Defender* had been set up by southerner Robert S. Abbott in 1905. Abbott revealed the horrors of lynching and enticed the black population upon whom the South relied for cheap labour to move north in an exodus that became known as the Great Migration. By the 1910s the *Defender* had achieved national reach and was the most important black publication in America. It used its influence to help to shape both the blues audience and its tastes.

clubs on the side; he also wrote a column for the *Chicago Whip* news-paper, whose editor, Joseph Bibbs, gave him his first break in the music industry. The black-run Black Swan label had been formed in 1921 and was run from Harlem by Harry H. Pace, and Bibbs was in charge of the label's distribution in Chicago; Williams started out working for the company's treasurer. Black Swan had the young Fletcher Henderson as recording director and chief accompanist, and it was aimed at the black middle classes who wanted to buy opera performed by black singers rather than raucous, earthy jazz and blues. Mind you, Pace didn't com-plain when Ethel Waters's 'Oh Daddy' sold half a million copies in 1921 – that wasn't 'too coloured', apparently. In spite of its high standards, like other nascent black record labels Black Swan struggled with dis-tribution issues and the arrival of radio, and was sold to Paramount in 1924. The experience with Black Swan taught Williams that the music industry didn't want to associate with black customers; it didn't even want to associate with black artists. What it needed, Williams realised, was a go-between, and his time with Harry Pace put him in an almost unique position.

At Paramount, Williams was an invisible man. He had no job title or contract. The label's directors gave him a salaried job, but the title of recording director went to someone called M. A. Supper, even though in reality Williams was cutting all of their race records: 'They didn't want me to be identified with the white records, or the white side of the situation at all.' Black artists on Paramount made blues records because Williams was under strict instructions that they could not record any white material. His acts bristled at the notion, but there was nothing he could do; he had nothing but the blues.*

Another man in the black recording business had a far higher pro-file. Chicago-born Jack Kapp was at Brunswick and still in his twenties when he became the first person to divide a record company's product into different genres. The Brunswick catalogue was split into three cat-egories – 'Popular', 'Old Time Tunes' and 'Race Records' – making

---

* A rare exception was Blind Lemon Jefferson's playful, semi-spoken 1927 rag 'Hot Dogs'.

it easier for retailers who knew what their customers wanted. This removed 'Race' and 'Hillbilly' records from the 'Popular' category, laying the groundwork for the concept of 'hit records', chart manipulation and the future record industry, one that's still easily recognisable today. The old industry model had been to market the widest possible variety of military, opera, folk, minstrelsy and so on, with the result that catalogues became ever lengthier and more unwieldy. Kapp found a solution in categorisation and musical segregation. Mayo Williams would remain invisible.

* * *

Paramount was also at the forefront of a more minimal blues sound that became commercially successful in the late 1920s. The popular caricature of the blues singer – one man, alone, playing guitar on a back porch – post-dates the Smith sisterhood. Blind Lemon Jefferson was a Texan with a high, unnerving voice and no little guitar-playing skill who sold more than 100,000 copies of his 'Got the Blues' in 1926. Recording in Paramount's primitive Chicago studio, Jefferson's 78s sounded decades older than, say, Louis Armstrong's contemporaneous 'Heebie Jeebies'. This wasn't by design; the owners of Paramount had no interest in their acts or their studio or their customers, so long as they bought the records. Legacy wasn't on their minds. Jefferson recorded a hundred tracks for them before his early death from a heart attack in 1929; the most he ever saw from his record sales was a Ford automobile – not much use to a blind man. His success led Paramount to search out other rural blues performers, so they brought the ragtime-influenced Blind Blake up to Wisconsin in 1926, followed by the Mississippi trio of Charley Patton, Son House and, lastly, Skip James in 1931, just as the grim reaper of the Depression was about to claim the label. Almost by chance, Paramount had assembled the greatest blues roster of the 1920s, largely because most other record companies thought the music was beneath them.*

* Jefferson's influence would later be all over the rock era. The 'Mama, that's all right, mama, that's all right for you' refrain from his 'Black Snake Moan' would

The racial division of music in the 1920s led to some odd subterfuge. White guitarist Eddie Lang played on Bessie Smith's 'I'm Wild
About That Thing' and was a regular player with his fellow guitarist Lonnie Johnson (whose name would later be the inspiration for
Anthony James 'Lonnie' Donegan). Lang's duets with Johnson were
spectacular and spectral – beginning with 1928's 'Two Tone Stomp'
and becoming more atmospheric on 'Blue Guitars', 'Blue Room Blues'
and 'Midnight Call Blues' – but he had to adopt the name Blind Willie
Dunn to mask his racial identity. He enjoyed playing in disguise so
much that he put together Blind Willie Dunn's Gin Bottle Four with
pianist J. C. Johnson, Hoagy Carmichael on vocals and drums, and
New Orleans innovator King Oliver on cornet. They recorded a warming, sweetly melancholic side for Columbia in 1929, playfully titling it
'Jet Black Blues'.

* * *

In May 1924 Bix Beiderbecke, then barely out of school, caught Bessie
Smith's act in Chicago, and it blew his mind. When she returned the
following spring, according to guitarist Eddie Condon, he 'told everyone who would listen that she was the greatest singer in the world . . .
Bix turned his pockets inside out and put all his dough on the table to
keep her singing.' Between March and May 1925 Bix and his jazz bud-
dies would go back to the club to listen to Bessie at every opportunity.

The first time she had stepped on stage – still a teenager – she had sung
in her street clothes, knowing she wouldn't need to dress up to tear a
place apart. Working constantly in tent shows through the summer and
theatres through the winter, Bessie became one of the highest-paid black
entertainers in America. She could belt it out, and it sounded entirely
natural. In spite of the antiquity of the acoustic recording equipment,
her early records still sound impressively powerful a hundred years on.

---

be rejigged by Arthur 'Big Boy' Crudup as 'That's Alright Mama', which would
become Elvis Presley's first single in 1954. 'Matchbox Blues' was lifted almost
whole for Carl Perkins's 'Matchbox', which the Beatles would cover in 1964.

With her first electrical recording – 'Cake Walking Babies from Home' in 1925 – the sheer power of her voice became even more apparent. Smith also benefited from the new technology of radio broadcasting. After a show for a white-only audience at a Memphis theatre in October 1923, she performed a late-night concert on radio station WMC for a desegregated audience. During the 1920s, she cut almost 150 sides for Columbia, backed by the best musicians in the land – Louis Armstrong, Coleman Hawkins, Fletcher Henderson, James P. Johnson. No question, you listen to these records and you can hear her influence on generations to come.

Smith had spent her childhood in a cabin, but by May 1924 she was being called 'the Empress of Blues singers' by the *Chicago Defender*. Her empire would be destroyed by the Wall Street Crash and the Depression that followed in the early 1930s. Theatres closed down; if they somehow survived, stage shows were replaced by the more economically viable talking pictures. Record sales fell through the floor. In 1932 Columbia only pressed 400 78s of Smith's 'Shipyard Blues'; a few years earlier, they had sold 780,000 copies of 'Downhearted Blues'. Who had the money or the inclination to buy blues records in the middle of a depression? Bessie could still make money on tour, but she had to share the bill with lesser blues singers. The other big names in raw blues had moved on to jazz, while Alberta Hunter toured with *Showboat*. What's more, the tastes of the crowds in the North had changed dramatically, pulled in by the allure of new, more sophisticated urban sounds. 'Nobody Wants to Know When You're Down and Out' was way too close to home, and the blues seemed to be a dying musical form when Bessie was killed in a car crash in 1937.

If she had wanted to, Smith could have moved into jazz: her timing, her swoops and her long-held notes were all entirely as one with the jazz singers who came along in the 1930s to replace her – Mildred Bailey, Ella Fitzgerald, Connee Boswell and, most notably, Billie Holiday. But Bessie was essentially a folk singer – *Showboat* just wasn't her cuppa tea – and so she simply went out of fashion. The sad upshot of this was that she barely recorded once the Depression hit, though she did cut four terrific sides with John Hammond in 1933, backed by a band that included Benny Goodman and Jack Teagarden.* They were possibly her best-ever recordings. One of the tracks was the delicious 'Do Your Duty', which was later recorded by Billie Holiday. Three days after Bessie had made these final recordings, in November 1933, Billie walked into the studio to cut her first. Beyond that coincidence are grislier parallels in their lives: booze, violence, early death. The major difference was Bessie's apparent happiness to stay within a largely black world, singing for a black audience, while Billie – produced by John Hammond, singing with Benny Goodman – saw her career destroyed by the white media's gaudy fascination with her sexuality and capacity for drink and drugs.

* * *

Tape recording and, especially, amplification, would add further chapters to the story of the blues. Technology would help to make the blues a far richer genre than the pure, uncompromised streams that were supposedly to be found away from the taint of commerce. Fifteen years after Blind Lemon Jefferson's death in 1929, the likes of Wynonie Harris and Amos Milburn would be creating electrified blues for bars, for rent parties, for dancing. Sometimes it was filthy, violent or just eerie; mostly it was fun. Another decade and a half later, the blues would achieve unlikely counter-cultural hegemony when 400,000 people travelled to the 1969 Woodstock festival to witness multiple white rock acts trying to dredge up field hollers and pacts with the devil, to summon up a lost American spirit. It wasn't a coincidence that the best, most futuristic acts on the bill were Jimi Hendrix and Sly and the Family Stone. The blues, after all, was still essentially party music.

* Hammond is a curious kind of hero, whom we will come across again several times. A scholar, fan and historian, in 1962 he would put together a well-received compilation called *King of the Delta Blues*, which beatified Mississippi singer Robert Johnson, disseminating the spooky yarn that he had met the devil at the crossroads and leading to cover versions of his songs by British bands like Cream and the Rolling Stones a few years later. An unexpected result of this was that for some decades, Johnson's profile would be higher than that of any of the Smith women.

13

INVISIBLE AIRWAVES CRACKLE
WITH LIFE: RADIO

Olden days had different ways,
Their pleasures then were fewer;
Modern days will get my praise,
Our wireless ways are newer.
'Radio Times', Henry Hall

Electricity, air travel, the gramophone and the telephone were technologies that played with concepts of time and space. Broadcast radio was possibly the most extreme step yet, enabling a mass audience – city-wide, nationally, even internationally – to hear exactly the same thing at exactly the same time. For the first time, the outside world was being brought into the home. 'The radio was like a religion,' Frank Sinatra remembered. 'They were even shaped like cathedrals.'

The structure and programming of radio broadcasting would help to define our perception of twentieth-century life. Just as the eighteenth-century Bath of Beau Nash had effectively given us the correct times for morning coffee, afternoon tea and the cocktail hour, so radio gave us the breakfast show, *Housewives' Choice*, the half-hour sitcom, drive time and the late-night, underneath-the-blanket hour. It measured out your day in bite-sized chunks. It was also the first time that popular music, and the way it was heard, became politically charged; regular ads inured us to consumer capitalism.

This cultural realignment led to some purple, but valid, prose. 'Formerly the only music in a man's head, week in week out, was the church organ on Sunday. Now he hears several hours of assorted music a week,' claimed *Radio Broadcast*.* Thanks to radio, popular music gave people a sense of time and place, a personal feeling for history. What's more, the fact people heard more of it led to the turnover of popular music becoming much more rapid, and the new sounds were coming from both black and white cultures. In the early 1920s classical music magazine *Etude* predicted that 'America is now on the threshold of one of the greatest musical awakenings the world has ever known.'

In the beginning, radio was there only for air–sea rescue and military purposes. In 1916 twenty-five-year-old Russian American David Sarnoff – on his way to becoming head of the Radio Corporation of America, but then an underling at Marconi – wrote to his employers with a plan to make it a household utility: 'The idea is to bring music into the home by wireless. The receiver can be designed in the form of a simple radio music box.' But, to Sarnoff's chagrin, it was Marconi's rivals Westinghouse who set up the first radio station at their East Pittsburgh plant in December 1920. It was called KDKA.

---

* *Radio Broadcast* ran from 1922 to 1930. Unlike engineering-based radio publications like *Radio Age* and *Popular Radio*, it talked about the state of the industry ('Is there a radio monopoly?'), while still featuring pieces like 'How to Build a Raytheon Tube'.

What did the first radio station look like? It was a room that could take three people at a squeeze, located on the ninth floor of the nine-storey Westinghouse building, and it sat directly beneath a two-hundred-foot antenna. Initially, it was there to disseminate news that in more isolated areas would otherwise take a day or two to arrive in print. Luckily, someone thought to bring a few records along and announced that a 'concert' would be played. It took a few broadcasts before KDKA realised that people might like to know which songs they were listening to, so they found an announcer to relay the titles. Stores in Pittsburgh were then flooded with requests for these records, and Westinghouse realised that they had unleashed something very powerful. Within two years of KDKA's launch there were six hundred local stations in America. Music was a cheap way of filling the American airwaves, and it was open season for song pluggers and sponsors, the latter being something that would never go away.*

Radio stations, heavy with velvet curtains to soften the acoustics, were in competition with hotels for hiring dance bands, so alliances were quickly formed. Choicer hotels leased broadcasting rights, which meant the stations got a glamorous ambience and hotels gained free publicity. 'Remote' shows were fed via a telephone line back to the station, but if the hotel was tall enough, then a transmitter was placed on the roof and the broadcast took place from the hotel itself. Brooklyn-born Vincent Lopez was the first bandleader to broadcast from a nightclub. In 1921 his band's performance came live from the Pennsylvania Hotel Grill, opposite Penn Station, and the restaurant was inundated with reservations. It was as much as the nervous Lopez could do to say,

---

* Radio stations playing records wouldn't become the norm, though; they almost exclusively used live musicians until the 1950s. Licences were dependent on stations emitting a significant proportion of live music in their first few months. Musicians and unions deplored records being played, as this cut into their work – a show that broadcast only pre-recorded music wasn't helping them to pay the rent. This began to change when Martin Block began broadcasting his *Make Believe Ballroom* programme on New York's WNEW on 3 February 1935. *Make Believe Ballroom* was the first radio show on the eastern seaboard to contain no live music; everything you heard was a record. In 1941 Walter Winchell would come up with the term 'disc jockey' to describe the way Block operated.

'Hello, everybody, Lopez speaking,' which then became his catchphrase, much as the spry 'Nola' became his signature tune. 'I like the way you introduce numbers,' Calvin Coolidge later told Lopez, when they met at the White House. 'You just give the name of the song, then play it. Most announcers talk too much.' Lopez's sidemen would include future bandleaders Glenn Miller, Artie Shaw, Charlie Spivak and Xavier Cugat; he also gave singer and actress Betty Hutton her first break. He would still be broadcasting from an oak-panelled room at the Hotel Taft as late as 1966.

For the bands there was work; for the hotels, clubs and restaurants there was kudos and publicity; for the listeners in Zaleski, Ohio, or Mechanicsburg, Illinois, there was a whiff of the high life in their own homes. The names of places like Glen Island Casino, Frank Dailey's Meadowbrook, the Baltimore Hippodrome and the Paramount Theatre, New York, had a dusting of magic, impossible dream palaces to picture as you listened. Classics and parlour songs would share the airwaves with emergent jazz.

Initially, what to broadcast had been the issue. As with the earliest commercial 78s at the turn of the century, there was an assumed need for quality high-culture output. The recital music played in hotel palm courts – the Classic FM of its day – was a natural fit, as were arias sung by female sopranos. There was also a conservative impulse to play oldies like 'After the Ball' and 'My Gal Sal' – songs that held memories for the listeners – which meant that 'oldies radio' was there from the off. More progressive elements had to battle to get airplay.*

Chicago was arguably the radio capital of America in the 1920s. A station called KYW had been broadcasting as early as 1921; the downside was that the only music it broadcast was the Chicago Civic Opera Company's afternoon and evening performances. The city had an all-opera radio station, which hardly suited its shifting demographics – the population had increased by 60,000 since the end of World War

---

* A 1924 survey of Chicago listeners by *Radio Age* magazine found that 'only 1.7% of the listeners want grand opera . . . almost one-fourth wanted classical music'. *Radio Age* initially neglected to mention that 29 per cent of those polled wanted popular music.

I due to black migration from the South. What's more, the authorities had closed down the city's red-light district under the guise of 'war-time precautions', meaning there was nowhere to hear the New Orleans musicians who had moved north; the result was a huge build-up in the demand for jazz on the radio, and an 'all-opera, all day' station wasn't going to cut the mustard. Here was a ready-made market, waiting for someone to find it.

They wouldn't have to wait too long. After President Hoover loosened government restrictions, the big four broadcasters – the American Telephone & Telegraph Company (AT&T), General Electric, the Radio Corporation of America (RCA) and Westinghouse – all set up shop in 1922. American magazine *Radio Broadcast* complained in 1924 that the programming on 'all kinds of stations' was 'monotonous'. The new commercial radio stations needed to stop worrying about broadcasting 'improving' music, so they began to move away from the sedate safety of the palm court and the opera house and started to reflect the music that was in the air. *Popular Radio* wrote that commercial broadcasters 'are interested in results rather than in philanthropy . . . they are making every effort to entertain as many listeners as possible'.*

American stations had looked to sponsorship to help pay for professional musicians and announcers, and the audience's reaction, surprisingly, had been positive. Adverts were a small price to pay for high-quality local programming. Among the first out of the gates had been the Happiness Candy Company, who purchased time on New York's WEAF in August 1923. Billy Jones and Ernie Hare were dubbed the 'Happiness Boys', with a regular slot – 'Your Friday date, seven-thirty until eight' – and their own theme tune, both innovations that would soon become

---

* In late 1923 Arthur Gibbs and His Gang were the first to record James P. Johnson and Cecil Mack's 'Charleston'. The song would go on to become synonymous with the 1920s and would be the number-one record across the US by January 1924. It was originally featured in the musical comedy *Runnin' Wild*, which had opened at New York's New Colonial Theatre in October 1923 and ran for 228 performances. If people weren't out doing the Charleston, they were watching other people doing it on Broadway or listening to Gibbs's 78 at home. It was notable that the one place you didn't hear it was on the then jazz-phobic, live-music-only radio.

the industry norm. Their half-hour show consisted of three duets and four solos, with piano accompaniment and comedy skits between the songs, and they plugged Happiness Candy and WEAF at least seven times, once after every song. By 1927 a *Radio Broadcast* survey showed that the Happiness Boys' show was among the nation's most popular programmes, along with *Maxwell Hour Coffee Time* and *The Eveready Hour*. They could do topical songs on flappers ('Don't Bring Lulu'), Prohibition ('Pardon Me While I Laugh'), the Model A Ford ('Henry's Made a Lady Out of Lizzie'), the opening of Tutankhamun's tomb ('King Tut') and even broadcast radio. On a show called *Twisting the Dials* they parodied an evening's entertainment on radio station OUCH with operatic singing (an aria from *La Bum* by Miss Loudon-Screeching), a cookery slot sponsored by the 'Bicarbonate Soda Association' and time checks – 'When you hear the beautiful chimes, it will be exactly six and seven-eighths split seconds past eight o'clock Eastern Daylight Standard Railroad Western Mountain Central Time.'

Why did Happiness Candy take the plunge and sponsor a radio show? Because radio was still seen as frivolous in 1923, its possibilities still not realised, and so only small-to-medium-sized companies – Smith Brothers cough drops, Ipana toothpaste, Clicquot Club ginger ale, Eveready batteries – would take a risk on an unknown audience, in both size and composition. Radio-set manufacturers, unsurprisingly, were an exception and advertised their own goods frequently. Recording artists were granted anonymity in order to get the sponsor's name mentioned as often as possible: a Palmolive show featured the singers Paul Oliver and Olive Palmer, quite probably not their real names. In 1925, on Thursdays at 10 p.m. on WEAF, there was a show featuring the 'Goodrich Silver-Masked Tenor'. His identity was a sworn secret, allowing the B. F. Goodrich tyre company more plugs. The Silver-Masked Tenor found such fame on radio that when he sang with the Silvertown Orchestra on the vaudeville circuit, he needed a police escort.*

* In 1930 the Silver-Masked Tenor was finally revealed to be Irish tenor Joseph M. White, who had been recording since 1915, much in the style of John McCormack.

In 1926, the same year Warner Brothers would reveal their Vitaphone sound-on-disc film technology, network radio was born. Forward-looking WEAF, the home of the Happiness Boys, was purchased by the Radio Corporation of America (RCA), which then formed a subsidiary called the National Broadcasting Corporation (NBC), created to transmit WEAF's commercial programmes to affiliated broadcasters across America. With this national network, NBC could for the first time offer advertisers access to local radio stations in every state. In its first year NBC earned $7 million. Almost immediately, the Columbia Broadcasting System (CBS) was set up by the Columbia record label, not wanting to lose ground on a rival after it heard that RCA and the Victor label were set to merge. By 1931 NBC had sixty-seven affiliated radio stations, while CBS had ninety-five. It was a commercial duopoly.

* * *

In the mid-1920s the *Ladies' Home Journal* had warned that jazz had a 'blatant disregard of even the elementary rules of civilisation', while the National Association of Orchestra Directors had its own jazz czar to police nightclubs and hotels, rooting out 'the kind of jazz that tends to create indecent dancing'. American self-censorship (the 1919 National Prohibition Act, or Volstead Act; the 1930 Motion Picture Production Code) showed a country going through uneasy times. Radio had been a listener-friendly free-for-all until the 1927 Radio Act, which spelled out that 'no person within the jurisdiction of the United States shall utter any obscene, indecent or profane language by means of radio communication'. Networks began to impose internal censorship, and by the late 1930s NBC had 290 songs on its blacklist.*

This was too late to stop the spread of hot jazz. New city life could not be contained. One of the earliest radio performances by a black musician was a 1921 broadcast of seventeen-year-old Earl 'Fatha' Hines

---

* Keen not to show any bias when World War II broke out, they even banned Noël Coward's 'The Stately Homes of England'.

on Chicago's KDKA. Hines would go on to broadcast from the Grand Terrace, the first of Chicago's black bandleaders to be networked.

Ethel Waters was the first black female voice to be heard when WVG broadcast a 1922 performance of hers at New Orleans's Lyric Theatre, backed by Fletcher Henderson's band, which could be heard over five states. Bessie Smith's 'Empty Bed Blues' may have been banned in Boston for its sexual candour ('He boiled fresh cabbage and he made it awful hot . . .when he put in the bacon, it overflowed the pot'), but her music was broadcast by WMC in Memphis and WSB in Atlanta – both stations with largely white audiences – in 1923. A year later, with thousands locked out of a sold-out theatre in Pittsburgh, the local WCAE station broadcast a whole Bessie Smith show.

Both Fletcher Henderson's band, performing at 44th Street's Club Alabam, and Duke Ellington and His Washingtonians had first appeared on New York's WHN in 1924. The popularity of these shows led to Henderson's regular broadcasts from the Roseland Ballroom, where he would be joined by Louis Armstrong from 1926 to 1928. WOR broadcast them every week, and WHN three times a week. Henderson's eleven-piece band swung (check out 1926 recordings like 'Dinah' and 'Variety Stomp'), and were seeding the ground for Swing with a capital 'S', the biggest sound of the 1930s, both commercially and literally. Henderson was a bachelor of chemistry and mathematics, and had quit his job with a chemical company in downtown Manhattan to apply his lab-technician skills to music, breaking the band into different sections (trumpets, saxophones), which could play either call-and-response or supporting riffs. It's easy to imagine Henderson working in his lab late at night, beads of sweat on his brow, test tubes replacing musicians, searching for the perfect formula as he wrestled with the new music (jazz) and the old platforms (orchestras). As we'll see, he would have a foundational role in the growth of bands, in both size and popularity, even as he was nudged into the background.

CBS, meanwhile, broadcast Duke Ellington nightly from the Cotton Club. The club may have had an entirely white, wealthy audience, but CBS was broadcasting to the whole of America – no colour bar, no entrance fee. Writing for *The Dial*, Gilbert Seldes said that 'in their music the negroes have given their response to the world with an exceptional naïveté, a directness of expression which has interested our minds as well as touched our emotions'. On a huge scale, this music fed the rebellion of white youth against the hangover of pre-World War I decorum. For the first time, there was a generational, oppositional culture. There were tens of thousands of other listeners out there just like you. You couldn't see them, but over another pealing Armstrong solo or through the conversation of 'Baby, Ain'tcha Satisfied', you knew they were there, and that was enough.

* * *

There was little to no jazz played on the radio in Britain. The country's first live public broadcast, from the Marconi radio factory in Chelmsford, had taken place in June 1920, sponsored by the *Daily Mail*'s Lord Northcliffe and featuring Australian soprano Dame Nellie Melba. While it had piqued public interest in radio's possibilities, it had displeased the authorities, who claimed similar ventures would interfere with military and civil communications; radio broadcasters had to know their place. The GPO was put in charge of radio broadcasting licences and was receiving requests on a regular basis: almost a hundred by 1922, mostly from wireless societies. Rather than giving the amateurs what they wanted, the GPO and Marconi conspired to issue a single broadcasting licence to just one company. It would be called the British Broadcasting Company (BBC),* and it was to be financed by a licence fee and by royalties from the sale of BBC wireless sets, which had to be made by officially approved manufacturers. The first executive of public service broadcasting in Britain, appointed in December 1922, was a fierce-looking Calvinist called John Reith. There would be no advertising.

* As a commercial company, the original BBC broadcast programmes that were sometimes sponsored and paid for by British newspapers. In December 1926 the Company would be dissolved and its assets transferred to the state-run, non-commercial British Broadcasting Corporation, which launched in 1927. It is unlikely that many people could tell the difference.

Aside from the news, the day's broadcasting would include a children's slot, religious programming and 'a recital of gramophone records'. To get an idea of what music the BBC deemed suitable, let's look at what you might have heard in the palm-court atrium of a prestigious hotel or on the pier in a seaside town. Violin and piano were the predominant instruments. While hymns and chamber music were acceptable, classical pieces would generally have been seen as too heavy, so specially written orchestral pieces called 'light music' evolved. Conductor Thomas Beecham called them 'lollipops', which would later become abbreviated to 'pops'. These were often written by heavyweights. Edward Elgar's 'Salut d'amour' and 'Chanson de matin' had suitably light French titles and were melodious and undemanding.

The king of light music was Eric Coates, who wrote and conducted 'attractive music, skilfully orchestrated', according to a 1934 Pathé newsreel. A graduate of the Royal Academy of Music, he always wanted to create 'pictures in sound', as he called them, and had no interest in writing anything as heavy as a concerto. In his youth, he was quite happy playing viola parts for Gilbert and Sullivan in theatre-pit bands and writing melodies to Robert Burns poems. He was especially drawn to British folk melodies that evoked the British landscape, like 'Londonderry Air'. One of his first published melodies on leaving the Academy in 1908, aged twenty-two, was called 'Devon to Me'.* By the 1920s Coates was writing fifteen-minute suites – 'Joyous Youth' (1922),

---

* 'Londonderry Air' had first been collected by Jane Ross in the early 1850s, then passed on to collector George Petrie, who published it in *The Ancient Music of Ireland* (1855), accompanied by a lovely bit of ahistorical fluff: 'The name of the tune unfortunately was not ascertained by Miss Ross, who sent it to me with the simple remark that it was "very old".' Petrie called the anonymous piece 'Londonderry Air', after Ross's home county. It is better known today as 'Danny Boy', thanks to lawyer and lyricist Frederic Weatherly's lyric, which was written in 1913. Kindred spirits, Coates and Weatherly went on to write many folk-based ballads together in the 1910s and '20s, beginning with 'Stonecracker John' in 1909. Weatherly's obituary in *The Times* in 1929 summed up the high-culture knee-jerk response to light music, while still praising it: 'Though it is easy to be contemptuous of his drawing-room lyrics, sentimental, humorous and patriotic, which are said to number about 3,000 altogether, it is certain that no practising barrister has ever before provided so much innocent pleasure.'

the child-friendly 'Phantasies' (1926) – as well as orchestrated ballads, and conducting them in light-music havens like Scarborough, Hastings and Bournemouth.

In 1931 the broadcaster, songwriter and *Radio Times* editor Eric Maschwitz was putting together a new Saturday-evening programme called *In Town Tonight*. For the introduction he had recorded the sound of traffic and flower-sellers in Piccadilly Circus, but decided at the last minute to also include some London-themed music. Coates and the London Philharmonic Orchestra had just recorded 'The Knightsbridge March' as part of his *London Suite*, and having hurriedly bought a stack of records from Chappell on Bond Street, Maschwitz chose the piece twenty minutes before the programme went on air. Coates had been at home in Baker Street, developing photos in his dark room, when *In Town Tonight* was first broadcast. His wife Phyllis called out to him, 'They're playing something of yours on the radio; I can't think what it is.' He stuck his head out of the dark room, listened for a moment, said, 'No, neither can I,' and went back to his photography. Half an hour later, Phyllis called him again. 'Dear, they're playing this thing again; it must be a signature tune or something.' He emerged again, paused and said, 'Yes . . . well, I don't suppose it will do any harm.' Within six weeks of the first broadcast, the BBC had received 30,000 letters asking about the music.

Coates was a dream for Lord Reith's programmers, who were entrusted with keeping Americanisation at the door. Soon he was commissioned to write pieces like 'Calling All Workers', which became the signature tune for *Music While You Work*. The gentle Coates was interested in writing for everyone: 'I have tried to convey a picture of the thousands of people who walk across London Bridge every day, to and from their work in the City.' 1930's 'In a Sleepy Lagoon', inspired by a stretch of coast at Selsey in Sussex, would be picked as the theme for a new BBC show called *Desert Island Discs* in 1940, and has been used ever since.

Violinist Albert Sandler, the wronged husband in 1935's Clarence 'Tandy' Johnstone affair, led the Palm Court Orchestra, who were also BBC regulars, broadcasting from the Grand Hotel, Eastbourne, from 1925 until Sandler's sudden death, aged forty-one, in 1948. 'I have no fixed programmes,' he said in 1929. 'I play what I think will suit the audience who happen to be present, and what I myself feel like playing.' He had started out playing in Lyons' Corner Houses and knew that without radio he would not have travelled much further: 'No doubt that had there been no wireless, few people would have been aware of the existence of Albert Sandler.'* Max Jaffa would be Sandler's successor in the 1940s, and his Palm Court Orchestra's repertoire would be preserved on ten-inch albums from early in the vinyl era: Stephen Foster ('Jeannie with the Light Brown Hair', 'Beautiful Dreamer') rubbed up against Strauss ('Roses from the South'), Saint-Saëns ('Samson and Delilah'), folk melodies ('D'Ye Ken John Peel') and Tin Pan Alley (Buddy De Sylva's 'When Day Is Done'). Jaffa was happy to merge these disparate sources in medleys, using Sandler's wide brief as a blueprint. The Palm Court Orchestras – found in Eastbourne and Scarborough, as well as the hotels of London and New York, and now almost invisible to pop historians – were a ghostly pre-echo of something bigger in the future. Here are the roots of the exotica and easy listening to come.

Like the Proms at the Queen's Hall, with which Henry Wood had been intending to musically educate the great unwashed since 1895, light music was loosely seen as educational, as well as mere entertainment. It wasn't bawdy like music hall or vulgar like jazz, and it had acceptable roots in the sweeter end of serious music. It was a safe pair of hands. With the birth of the BBC and national radio broadcasting, it found a natural home and an ideal outlet.†

In 1924, not long after the BBC started up, twenty-six-year-old bandleader Henry Hall convinced the Company to do remote programmes from the Gleneagles Hotel in Perthshire. Peckham-born Hall had a Salvation Army background, which chimed with Lord Reith's Calvinist background and might well have swung the deal. The

---

* The first of these performances was also the very first national BBC broadcast from a hotel ballroom. Earlier hotel broadcasts – like Dante Selmi's orchestra in Sheffield and the Clifford Essex Band in Leeds – had been regional.
† Light music's reach increased with the launch of the BBC Light Programme in 1945 and new programmes with bossy titles like *Music While You Work* and *Friday Night Is Music Night*. The BBC was always a tool of civil obedience.

business-like Hall understood not only the need to get people on their feet, but the prestige that came with radio broadcasts. No jazz snob, he also ran every band that played at the thirty-two hotels run by the London, Midland and Scottish Railway. With his head bowed, eyes looking up, eyebrow ever-so-slightly raised, Hall had a serious if gently murderous look, which may have been down to his insane workload. Initially, his band featured no singers. He was suspicious of raising passions with real human voices, and after taking over the BBC Dance Orchestra in 1932, he convinced the Corporation to keep crooners at arm's length. Hall's favourite singer was Val Rosing, the son of a Russian tenor, and Rosing's pronunciation on songs like 'Teddy Bears Picnic' was faultless and entirely jazz-free.*

With his round wire glasses and full evening dress, Hall was all about melody, initially nothing hotter than a lovely cup of tea. At 5.15 p.m. each weekday he played his signature tune, 'It's Just the Time for Dancing', and concluded his broadcast forty-five minutes later with 'Here's to the Next Time'.† Even though he could sell out the London Palladium, Hall had become so tied to the BBC that he recorded the super-catchy 'Radio Times' in 1934, a hymn to the Corporation's weekly listings magazine.‡ They would never admit it was anything as gauche as an advert, of course.

* * *

* Rosing ended up in Hollywood at the behest of Louis B. Mayer, who decided he was the English Bing Crosby, but, unsurprisingly, it didn't work out. Changing his name to Gilbert Russell, he moved from pop to opera, and by the 1960s was a Hollywood vocal coach to the likes of Natalie Wood.
† Hall's name was synonymous with unpleasantness at Frickley colliery in South Elmsall, Yorkshire. Miners at the pit referred to the unpopular late shift as 'Henry Hall's shift', or simply 'Henry's', as it began at 6 p.m., just as Hall's broadcast ended. When he died in 1989, the local Frickley Athletic football club marked the occasion in their matchday programme with a page dedicated to Hall entitled 'No More Henry's'.
‡ As a mouthpiece for the Corporation, you could find articles in the *Radio Times* like February 1933's 'Sobs and Sentimentality', with the writer George Alexander 'deploring the spinelessness of the contemporary popular song'.

Radio's smoothness and warmth, its microphones, its electricity, led the sales of records to plummet in the mid-1920s. They sounded scratchy and primitive by comparison. The obvious solution was to use radio technology to make better recordings, but the record companies – already struggling to stay afloat under the triple-pronged assaults of radio, the dance-hall boom in Britain and Prohibition in America – lacked the funding, as well as the know-how.

The answer came from the New Jersey research laboratories of Western Electric, an engineering company whose 1,200 technical staff worked to capture higher and lower frequencies in the grooves of 78 rpm shellac. Victor bought into Western Electric's impressive recording technology in 1925, as did the British arm of Columbia Records, whose head, Louis Sterling, was able to buy out the separate US parent company, knowing he had a gold mine at his disposal. 'England is now top dog,' said a 1925 edition of Britain's *Talking Machine News*. 'The tremendous developments of the Columbia Gramophone Company places that company in the position of the leading and most powerful gramophone company in the world.' And, as such, it overtook Victor.

We were entering the electric era. It was a sea change for pop, but the new technology had some initial problems. As they were used to projecting from a stage or bellowing into a horn for a gramophone recording, many singers often broke the tubes of radio transmitters. Sopranos were the worst. A softer style had first been developed in 1920 by America's 'First Lady of Radio', an apple-cheeked twenty-five-year-old called Vaughn De Leath, who sang for WJZ in Newark, New Jersey. The first singer to grasp the notion of caressing the microphone like a delicate lover, De Leath's style was tailored for radio, not the stage. The effect it gave was that she was singing in your house, just for you, and for you alone. In 1927 she recorded 'Are You Lonesome Tonight', a song that was at once a love letter, a plea and a desperate confession of devotion to an unfaithful lover: 'Is your heart filled with pain? Shall I come back again?'

De Leath had alluring dark eyes, a deep-set dimple in her chin, a permanently saucy expression on her face and constant quips on her lips; she was built for the Jazz Age and deserves a book all to herself. She had started as a soprano with a three-octave range, was quite possibly the first woman to make a radio broadcast, played the ukulele, wrote between three and four hundred songs (including 'Drowsy Head' with Irving Berlin), and – three decades before Glenn Gould – studied her own recordings to work out how she could improve them.* 'I discovered that my voice seemed to register best only in the lower range. So I concentrated on that alone . . . I find that the microphone seems to accept the crooning range much more easily than the higher notes, so I'm sticking with that.' By 1923, at the age of twenty-eight, she was running a radio station, WDT in New York.

The *Miami Daily News-Record* caught up with De Leath in 1930, as her star was starting to wane: 'Leaning close and almost affectionately towards the cold cylindrical microphone, Vaughn De Leath moves her lips and sends her crooning voice into it, hardly heard by the few onlookers in the studio. But that's all she needs to convey to the fans back home a type of singing that has made her famous. "I don't want just to entertain," she says wistfully, "I want my fans to feel, through my voice, the unity of mankind."'

By the end of the decade she had an apartment in New York, where she sang for NBC, and a home in Westport, Connecticut, with a garden 'developed from seeds sent to me by fans in every state of the union'.

* * *

By the early 1930s fast-paced, tight radio shows were being built around advertising and star names. Smaller companies had been hit hardest by the Depression, and radio advertising was now taken over by corporations like Standard Brands (makers of, among other products, Chase & Sanborn coffee, Fleischmann's Yeast and Royal Jell-O) who could still afford to buy airtime. Ad-libbing was replaced by scripts and as much product placement as the audience could take. Most significantly, the cash and flash of the bigger companies lured star names to present the

---

* One of her biggest hits was 1925's 'Ukulele Lady' on Columbia, later revived in the 1999 movie *The Cider House Rules*.

shows. It was out with the Interwoven Pair – a sock act, for crying out loud – and in with tried and trusted star names. Top of the shop was that raucous vaudeville star Eddie Cantor.

A rival to Al Jolson, with hits like 'If You Knew Susie' (1925) and 'Makin' Whoopee' (1928) on his record, Cantor had retired from the stage as a wealthy man in the late 1920s, but then lost almost everything in the Wall Street Crash of 1929. Suddenly, he needed to work again to support his wife and five daughters. Between 1929 and 1931 he made several appearances in Hollywood and on Broadway, even writing a book to try and pay his way.* But after years of honing his craft on stage he understood an audience better than almost anyone, and when he was hired by Chase & Sanborn to host a radio show, he became enormously famous all over again. The concision and verbal – rather than physical – basis of his Jewish humour made previous radio shows, still largely based on relaxed, whimsical minstrelsy and anonymous musicians, sound antique. Songs aside, there were jokes, skits and stories about Eddie's wife Ida and their five kids. It was more urban, more working-class and more exciting. At one time, 50 per cent of east coast radios tuned in between eight and nine on a Sunday evening were listening to Eddie Cantor. By 1931 he was once again flush enough to write a book called *Yoo Hoo, Prosperity! The Eddie Cantor Five Year Plan.*

* * *

What was lost with the rise of radio? Music had been regarded as one of the womanly arts throughout the nineteenth century and into the early twentieth. Radio continued what the gramophone had started – the de-feminisation of music appreciation. In 1922 85 per cent of music students in America were women, as were 75 per cent of concert-goers. The gramophone – something made of wood and metal, something that needed to be cranked by hand, like a motor car – gave music a muscularity. Men were drawn to gramophones, but generally, until the

---

* Another sideline was songwriting: in 1935 he came up with 'Merrily We Roll Along', which became the Merrie Melodies cartoon theme two years later.

mid-1920s, it was still women who chose the records that would be played on them (jazz buffs were the exception). Radio was even more technical than the gramophone and helped to legitimise music as a masculine pastime. The valves! The wiring! This in turn led to men feeling more comfortable with music as a soundtrack to their life, something that might echo their emotions and their identities, as well as their aesthetic judgements.

Unseen radio waves, filling the night air, touching tin roofs and marble floors alike – it felt like magic (still does to me), and it's easy to see how families were happier to part with a sofa during the Depression than their radio. At the same time, and for the same economic reasons, radio killed the vaudeville star. As American networks moved to a variety-show format in 1932, with a permanent orchestra and MC, they effectively subsumed vaudeville. Smarter stars of the boards, like Eddie Cantor, had already moved into radio. Music publishers, likewise, moved away from plugging songs to stage performers and began to concentrate on getting radio airplay. Rudy Vallee, the soft-voiced successor to Vaughn De Leath, made the switch with ease and by the mid-1930s was presenting his Thursday-evening *Fleischmann Hour* coast to coast. The greatest beneficiary of radio would be the crooner.

14

TRYING HARD TO RECREATE WHAT HAD YET TO BE CREATED: HILLBILLY

Country music as a genre did not exist in 1923, when Fiddlin' John Carson recorded 'The Little Old Log Cabin in the Lane'. It was not based in Nashville, it did not feature pedal steels, it was not codified in any way, and yet millions of people right across North America – in towns and rural areas, playing the fiddle and the guitar – knew country music intimately and instinctively.

None of these people were in the record industry. Ralph Peer, the thirty-one-year-old New York executive for Okeh Records who recorded 'The Little Old Log Cabin in the Lane', thought of himself as 'a businessman . . . a prophet, and a gambler'. He had recorded music for every conceivable American immigrant community: Okeh's catalogue included records in Italian, Yiddish, German, Lithuanian and Slovakian. His biggest payday as a gambler had come in 1920 with 'Crazy Blues' by Mamie Smith and Her Jazz Hounds, Okeh Record No. 4169 – the first recording aimed at a black audience. It was while on a scouting trip to Atlanta in 1923 that he was introduced to local radio station WSB's biggest celebrity, mill worker Fiddlin' John Carson, and recorded the minstrel song 'Little Old Log Cabin'. Back in New York, Peer declared it was 'pluperfect awful' and refused to release it. A local distributor in Atlanta, Polk C. Brockman, was convinced he could shift five hundred copies, and so Okeh relented. When it sold out in a few days, Brockman asked Okeh to press him a thousand more. When these sold out just as quickly, Peer and Okeh realised what they had. So did Fiddlin' John Carson, the Atlanta mill worker who publicly reinvented himself as a bumpkin from north Georgia.

The keening, nasal voice, the threadbare instrumentation, the evocations of farms and the olden days – not to mention the double entendres – all of this confused an industry which strove for sophistication, from the mixture of hotel-lobby dance bands and conservatoire-trained singers they recorded to the gold-leaf lettering on a record label. If you came from a hick town, you did your best to hide your roots. As the cash registers were ringing, though, New York's music industry knew there was something going on; they just couldn't agree on what it was. Look through mid-1920s editions of *Variety*, *Billboard* and *Talking Machine World* and you'll see a bunch of names for this unpolished genre: old-time, old time tunes, old familiar tunes, hearth and home, hill and range, hill country music . . . the industry tried the lot. In 1925 Ralph Peer settled on a shorter name which summed up the industry's patronising attitude towards this white rural music: hillbilly.

This disparaging term was the cherry on the cake. It had been almost impossible to be a country singer and also part of the popular-music industry in 1923. For a start, there was exclusion from the American Society of Composers, Authors and Publishers (ASCAP), who wouldn't accept you unless you could read and write music (they seemed to make an exception for Irving Berlin). Secondly, the American Federation of Musicians used sight-reading tests to intentionally exclude country musicians and performers; every large venue in a major city was contracted to use only union musicians, with a few exceptions in the South and South-West. *Variety* ran a front-page story on hillbilly on 29 December 1926, describing its advocates as 'poor white trash . . . with the intelligence of morons . . . the "hillbilly" is a North Carolina or Tennessee mountaineer type of illiterate whose creed and allegiance are to the bible, the Chautauqua, and the phonograph'. Luckily for John Carson, the *Atlanta Journal* hadn't been as proscriptive when it had launched the radio station WSB (or 'Welcome South, Brother') in 1922.

New York industry people sensed that the appeal of Carson and his ilk had to be that their music was steeped in tradition, something that made it feel real and relatable. Carson was in his mid-fifties when he recorded 'The Little Old Log Cabin in the Lane', and record companies decided to seek out other men of roughly Fiddlin' John's age – so they didn't *quite* understand why his rustic music was commercially engaging. Possibly, they thought his relatively advanced years equated to a grasp of history. In fact, the appeal of 'Little Old Log Cabin' lay in its romanticism, its nostalgia for a past that was half real, half imagined. This music selectively edited collective memory to serve the needs of the present day; accuracy was actually a hindrance.

If the New York-based record industry was going to laugh at country music, even as it was making money from it, then the musicians would become intentionally insular, have their own rules, build walls. Even now, 'real country' and 'hard country' are issues, and the music's continuous tightrope walk of commercial grasping and self-proclaimed authenticity is something to marvel at, quite unique in pop. That such high country legends as the Carter Family sang songs like 'Mid the Green Fields of Virginia' (a weepie written by 'After the Ball' author Charles K. Harris) and 'Little Old Log Cabin in the Lane' showed how the folk song and the popular song fed each other. They were simply called 'old-time songs'; unless you were an academic, you didn't really care about the source. Jimmie Rodgers, a foundation stone of country music, didn't pick the country yodel up from the Appalachians, nor was it a deep-rooted, soulful outpouring; he had seen a travelling Swiss act, liked the sound, and incorporated it into his music.*

---

* The yodel wasn't exclusive to nascent country: Georgian minstrel singer Emmett Miller's 'Lovesick Blues' (1928) incorporated yodels over a drunken

Rodgers, born in Meridian, Mississippi in 1897, had been a water boy, then a brakeman on the railroad between Meridian and New Orleans. In 1924, when he was twenty-seven, he contracted tuberculosis, which meant his days working on the trains would be limited. Luckily for him, in his new role at Victor, Ralph Peer was looking for more acts to sign and was holding auditions in nearby Bristol, Tennessee. Soon, Rodgers would be making jazz-, blues- and country-influenced records for Victor: not just his celebrated blue yodels (starting with No. 1, 'T for Texas') but intriguing non-country titles like 'Mean Mama Blues', 'Gambling Polka Dot Blues' and 'In the Jailhouse Now', songs from the wrong side of the tracks. By 1930 he had become the number-one country star at Victor Records and was wearing diamond rings on his fingers. Alabama newspaper the *Mobile Register* wrote a piece with the headline 'Blues Singer, Once M. & O. Brakeman, Realizes Dream'.

Rodgers 'could record anything', said Peer, and he had an address book to help him back up the claim. He knew Louis Armstrong from his days at Okeh Records and was probably responsible for 'Standin' on the Corner' ('Blue Yodel No. 9'), cut in Hollywood by Satchmo and the now thirty-two-year-old Singing Brakeman in 1930. Lil Hardin Armstrong played piano on the track,* an astonishing example of pop music escaping from genre straitjackets. Rodgers would go on to record thirteen blue yodels before his TB-related death in 1933, but sadly no more with Satchmo or Lil.

As with all other popular music, the birth of radio made a huge difference to country. The microphone embraced a soft voice and repelled shouters. Even for radio barn dances, the advent of the microphone meant that old-style banjo pickers were rapidly replaced by sweeter, more nuanced singers such as Bradley Kincaid, Scott Weisman and harmony acts like the Delmore Brothers. Intriguingly, Kentucky-born Kincaid

---

Dixieland backing. It sounded *southern*. 'Lovesick Blues' would later be recorded by Hank Williams and Frank Ifield, both of whom accented Miller's vocal jumps, cementing it as a country song.

* Some kind of brief reconciliation for the estranged couple, it turned out to be the last recording Louis and Lil would make together. Neither was credited on the label, and it was believed for decades that Earl Hines was the pianist.

made his name in Chicago, on WLS-AM's *National Barn Dance Show*, which proved the reach and appeal of country-folk songs like 'Barbara Allen' and 'In the Hills of Old Kentucky' outside the South. Kincaid's 'A Picture from Life's Other Side' (1931) was a cautionary heartbreaker, a precursor to Phil Ochs's 'There but for Fortune', while 'The Little Shirt My Mother Made' was closer to British music hall than 'The Little Old Log Cabin in the Lane'. His voice was a sweet, light tenor, quite unlike Fiddlin' John Carson; more like a proto-John Denver.

By the early 1930s two separate forms of American music were becoming strangely entwined: the 'western' and the 'country' traditions. Cowboys (a direct translation of the Spanish *vaquero* – hence 'buckaroo') were based in the West. The country tradition, by contrast, was purely from the South (which has a slightly counter-intuitive meaning in the US, inherited from the Civil War: Arizona and New Mexico are in the West much more than they are in the South, despite the geography).

The romantic image of the cowboy dates back to 1887, when Buffalo Bill Cody's touring circus introduced a new character called Buck Taylor.* As well as having the classic cowboy name, Taylor transformed the image of the spitting, cussing herdsman into a heroic, square-jawed loner, whistling to himself as he rode across a cartoon landscape under a starlit sky. The term 'cowboy' was almost unheard of before Taylor's fame; they were frontiersmen, explorers, herdsmen, but never cowboys. Taylor's popularity quickly led to the cowboy appearing on the vaudeville stage and in Tin Pan Alley numbers: Billy Murray's 'In the Land of the Buffalo' (1907) and – cross-breeding two pop crazes – 'Ragtime Cowboy Joe' by Bob Roberts in 1912. By the late 1920s, when Jimmie Rodgers was issuing his blue yodel records, a cowboy hat, knotted scarf and chaps were de rigueur for rural singers.

Like Appalachian hillbilly, western music could be linked back to English, Irish and Scottish folk ballads, and – again, like the music of

---

* Western pulp novels had first emerged in numbers soon after the Civil War. Buffalo Bill's own fame had actually started with a novel about his adventures, which was serialised in eastern newspapers and mostly made up.

the Appalachians – string bands were common. Westward-heading pioneers also favoured the pocket-sized harmonica, a German invention of
the early nineteenth century that had first been brought to America by
the manufacturer Matthias Hohner during the Civil War. Songs like 'I
Ride an Old Paint' – collected by Carl Sandberg in his 1927 *American
Songbag* – had a mystery and language of their own and a clip-clop
rhythm borrowed from the hooves of horses. The western 'tradition',
though, wasn't even as old as the country one, and neither was remotely
old in the European sense. Oklahoma, New Mexico and Arizona – all
prime cowboy country – had only recently become states in the union;
before this they were only territories, as Guam and Western Samoa are
today. This was still the frontier; it had myths more than it had traditions, and they had often been invented within the living memories
of people alive in the 1920s. The myths persisted in the Depression,
pulling desperate people westward: in 1933 the Southern Pacific railroad company alone reported that 683,000 transients had been found
travelling west in the company's boxcars.

The cowboy helped to broaden the appeal of both western and southern country music, from coast to coast. By the mid-1930s nearly every
major city had a radio station broadcasting a show with the suffix 'barn
dance' or 'jamboree'. Even New York had the *WHN Barn Dance*, starring Tex Ritter, who later headed west to become a movie star and sing
the theme for *High Noon*. Small-town radio stations were no different,
seeking out fresh local talent so they could emulate the networks. Rural
musicians found they had to adopt a new polish, poise and professionalism in front of the microphone.

The cowboy was a caricature of non-urban America, but he was
also a far more flattering stereotype than the grass-chewing hillbilly.
Mississippi-born Jimmie Rodgers knew that dressing in overalls – the
country look of the 1920s – wasn't going to cut it, unless you wanted
to be thought of as a backwoods pauper. So the Singing Brakeman took
to wearing a wide white hat, a clean scarf knotted at the neck, fringed
leather chaps and boots of Spanish leather with spurs that jingle-jangled.
Cowboy gear suggested skill – lassoing, riding at speed, shooting with
unerring accuracy, something to separate the singer from the audience

and make him heroic. Country and western may have started as equal partners, but the western look quickly became the dominant one, which also eased the music's image away from the racially divided South and into another domain.*

One major difference between country and western was the venues. In the southern Bible belt, dancing was a sin and drinking wasn't allowed. Country singer Roy Acuff once complained that he played schoolhouses, churches and tent meetings, while fiddle player Bob Wills got to play dances. Wills had been born in 1905 in Texas, south of Waco, in an area settled by Germans, Bohemians and Mexicans, and the culture was all about beer-drinking and dancing. He had a peripatetic life: in 1913 he moved to the Texas Panhandle and was winning regional fiddle contests with his dad before he was ten; he heard cotton pickers playing the blues; he learned New England and Cajun fiddling; he spent time in New Mexico, incorporating Mexican American players and writing things like 'Spanish Two-Step'; and he moved to Forth Worth just before the 1929 crash, where he absorbed the big-city jazz in the air. Wills had his own sound, and it was decidedly 'western'. We'll come across him again.

Country's breakthrough act as far as popular music was concerned – nationally, then internationally – was another Texan, Gene Autry. Single-handedly, he changed the image of country music and orientated it towards the West, towards California and Hollywood. Autry had started off recording budget 78s of Jimmie Rodgers songs on New York discount labels like Conqueror. Half the price of Rodgers's versions on RCA, this was a way to make your name when so many people were strapped for cash. After recording his own hit weepie, 'That Silver Haired Daddy of Mine', in 1931, Autry became a radio star, the Oklahoma Cowboy, on Chicago's WLS National Barn Dance. His own highly evocative recording 'Home on the Range' – which had first been published in folk collector John Lomax's Cowboy Songs and Other Frontier Ballads back in 1910 – led to Autry dressing in ornate,

---

* This was scarcely less problematic, though – the cowboy seeing off 'Indians' with his rifle and claiming their territory.

eye-catching cowboy gear: neckerchiefs, brightly studded shirts and boots of Spanish leather. Soon everyone was following Cowboy Gene's sartorial lead and Rodgers's yodelling style. It's most likely that no one in nineteenth-century America had ever yodelled to their herd like Kansas City's Tex Owens did on 1934's 'Cattle Call' – later a major hit for Eddy Arnold – but who cared? Everybody loved cowboys, especially singing cowboys. Whether from West Virginia or East Texas, singers dressed as cowboys and cowgirls. They all yodelled. No one thought of the look or the sound as inauthentic. This was the beginning of the codification of country music.

It was only a matter of time before Hollywood called. At the age of twenty-seven, Autry became a movie star, beginning with an appearance in 1934's *In Old Santa Fe*. Soon he was fighting not only cattle rustlers (*Rootin' Tootin' Rhythm*, 1937), but corrupt land developers (*The Man from Music Mountain*, 1938) and even aliens living beneath the earth's crust (*The Phantom Empire* series). He almost always played himself and got to sing his own songs, leading to the hits 'Tumbling Tumbleweeds' (1935), 'Mexicali Rose' (1936) and his signature tune, 'Back in the Saddle Again'. Literally hundreds of cash-in singing-cowboy movies would be made. Dorothy Page starred as *The Singing Cowgirl*, while black audiences were catered for by the mixed-race jazz singer Herb Jeffries in 1939's *The Bronze Buckaroo*. Demand was so high that the Sons of the Pioneers – a harmony act who would have a major hit with 'Cool Water' in 1941 – essentially formed to fulfil a need for more songs, as there were so many successful singing-cowboy movies. By 1941, when he became a sergeant in the air corps, Public Cowboy No. 1 Gene Autry's annual income was $600,000.

Even after he signed up, he managed to score a 1944 number one on *Billboard*'s new Jukebox Folk Records chart with 'At Mail Call Today', about a serviceman opening a 'Dear John' letter from his girl back home. Every kid in America went to the cinema to see Autry's movies, and – assuming they didn't have anywhere to hide a horse – they ended up wanting a guitar for Christmas. During World War II, many American servicemen from the metropolitan North would be introduced to country music by their southern comrades. This pattern would be repeated abroad, with GIs on troop ships and stationed across Europe during and after the war spreading the word internationally.*

* * *

Country also began to harden into a business model. When the US entered World War II in 1941, the Grand Ole Opry, which took place in Nashville's Ryman Auditorium, had been just another local barn dance on the radio, broadcast on WSM in Nashville since 1925. It became more prominent during the war, a much bigger deal commercially than its rivals, a touchstone. Country music wished for a spiritual home, somewhere free from non-country contamination, and the easiest thing was to simply create one. The Opry became something of mystical significance.

Hillbilly music learned not only how to manage its name (the *Billboard* chart had been renamed Hot C&W Sides by 1958), but to maintain its myths and legends. 'Rock music almost smothered out country music,' Porter Wagoner would recall in the 1970s. 'Even though I had the number one song [with "A Satisfied Mind" in 1956] about the only thing we could work was the little clubs, the skull orchards, the dives.' The music also had to fight geographic and demographic shifts: in 1940 southerners earned roughly 60 per cent of the average American income; by 1960 that figure had risen to 75 per cent and was climbing fast. When they listened to music, these folks didn't want to be reminded of their roots, yet they were still fiercely proud of them. Embracing this paradox, hillbilly music overcame the cowboy fad, the demise of western swing and the rock 'n' roll explosion to become 'country', an infinitely adaptable genre.

* In 1950 a newborn Anglo-Indian baby in Lahore was christened Gene by his mischievous, Autry-loving older brothers, who had been entrusted by their mum to take him to the registry office and have him named Anthony.

15

BLACK AND TAN FANTASY: DUKE ELLINGTON AND THE COTTON CLUB

> The three greatest composers who ever lived are Bach, Delius and Duke Ellington. Unfortunately Bach is dead, Delius is very ill, but we are happy to have with us today The Duke.
> Percy Grainger

I know people who have said, quite seriously, that they could spend the rest of their lives listening to nothing but the works of Bob Dylan, that there's so much in there to navigate and attempt to understand that you'd never get bored. Mark Perry, founder of ur-punk fanzine *Sniffin' Glue*, once told me he felt the same way about Frank Zappa, and I don't think he was joking. I can't imagine tying myself down in such a way, but if some-one put a gun to your head and made you choose one twentieth-century performer, and one alone, you could do worse than Duke Ellington.

He understood (quite rightly) that popular music should be taken seriously. He also knew that getting involved in conversations about what and what wasn't jazz was pointless; the *Christian Science Monitor*, in a 1930 Ellington feature, wrote that 'From jazz, as a subject, he shies as if he had suddenly touched something red hot.' The same year he told Florence Zunser of the *New York Evening Graphic*, 'I am not play-ing jazz. I believe that music, popular music, is the real reflector of the nation's feelings. I am trying to play the natural feelings of a people . . . Blues is the rage in popular music. And popular music is the good music of tomorrow.' He was the Duke – Sir Duke to Stevie Wonder – and he followed no rules, no critics, but knew enough about staying in touch with popular music to avoid the fate of Scott Joplin. His 1932 hit 'It Don't Mean a Thing (If It Ain't Got That Swing)' is often said to be the moment when the industry picked up on the word and turned swing into a genre. In private, Ellington would say, 'Jazz is music, swing is business,' but he was commercially savvy enough to write and record the dancefloor-friendly 'Exposition Swing' in 1937 and the cooler 'Swing Time in Honolulu', with a gorgeous Ivie Anderson vocal, a year later. On the other hand, after his years-in-the-making piece on the history of black America, the forty-eight-minute-long *Black, Brown and Beige*, was panned ('Formless and meaningless,' said Paul Bowles in the *New York Herald Tribune*), he just carried on writing suites until they got better reviews, right through the 1950s and into the '60s. No fool when it came to new technology, he also understood the importance of the album to pop before almost anyone (including Frank Sinatra), and at the turn of the 1950s would write music to fit on two sides of the new 33⅓ rpm vinyl format.

Edward Kennedy Ellington may have gone to a segregated school, but it was one that taught African history. The Washington DC that he grew up in had a black population that was schooled to believe race barriers would dissolve if the white population could see how civilised and intelligent its black neighbours were. Ellington was adored by his musical mother, who always reminded him he was 'blessed'; his father was a butler who ensured the Ellington family table was laid correctly. A kid at his school, probably during a history lesson on the Duke of Wellington, came up with the nickname, but it absolutely suited his demeanour, aloof and regal, and considerably more presidential than Woodrow Wilson.

Part of this was an unknowable disguise. Ellington's sister Ruth thought that he hid himself under 'veil upon veil upon veil'. To rise above, to stay on top, he knew that he had to keep his mystery caged. Biographer Harvey G. Cohen discovered that Ellington once wrote an uncharacteristically angry letter to a white business associate he was trying to escape from; even then, he signed it 'with great respect'.

Ellington was a synthesizer. He learned to surround himself with talent, which enabled him to constantly move forward. Billy Strayhorn was the Hal David to Ellington's Burt Bacharach, unsung but a trusted sidekick for more than twenty years. I love the story of how Strayhorn wrote the melody for 'Take the "A" Train' after he received an invitation from the Duke to meet up in New York. In a state of super-excitement he wrote possibly Ellington's most recognisable tune, one that would later crop up in the funniest bits of seemingly every Woody Allen film. I also love that the Duke took what was a basic, if ultra-catchy, swing tune and over the years made different train journeys out of it: first in 1948, as the half-speed, brassier 'Manhattan Murals' (which started 'up at Washington Heights, and right down through the island', Duke explained on a radio broadcast); and better still in 1952 for the *Masterpieces* album – bluer and smokier, it featured Betty Roche's siren bebop vocal and unexpected tempo changes to make you catch your breath.

You wouldn't have guessed what was coming from listening to Ellington's first recordings. In 1926 he was playing piano, leading a six-piece band at the Kentucky Club on Broadway through novelties like 'Animal Crackers', which was slightly embarrassing, especially compared to the great pianists with whom Ellington – new in town – was hanging out after hours in Harlem, fisty players like Willie 'The Lion' Smith and James P. Johnson.

A year later, Ellington made a giant step with a crop of recordings that placed trumpet player Bubber Miley and his plunger mute at the heart of a new, deep blue sound, rich in minor chords: 'Black and Tan Fantasy', 'The Mooche', 'Creole Love Call' and 'East St Louis Toodle-Oo'. Ellington would revisit them over the decades, using them as a canvas to colour with his own piano – sometimes basic stride, sometimes abrupt and modern, sometimes flowingly romantic – and, post-war, as building blocks for his own adventures in arrangement. The only constant was that the trumpet players were asked never to stray too far from the original parts played by Miley, who had died of alcohol poisoning in 1932, aged twenty-nine.*

Prohibition and bathtub gin killed Bubber Miley, but it had given him and Ellington an unlikely base from which to launch their careers. At the height of the Roaring Twenties, the wealthy and glamorous of New York descended in their droves on the north-east corner of 142nd Street and Lenox Avenue to hear the latest compositions, see the newest dances and revel in the cultural and creative crucible of Harlem's most famous nightclub: the Cotton Club. It was nicknamed the 'Aristocrat of Harlem', but this may not have felt like the case if you were one of the musicians or dancers. The illustrations on the menu also laid bare the fact that the Cotton Club's clientele were all white, its entertainers all black.† The interior of the club was covered with African jungle motifs and clichéd southern imagery, mixed with lurid eroticism. It didn't really look like the kind of place that would foster a talent so

---

* Miley taught his growl technique to trombonist Joe 'Tricky Sam' Nanton before he left Ellington's band. Tricky Sam in turn taught it to Bubber's replacement, Cootie Williams. 'After a while, it became me. Or I became it,' said Cootie, a player who cavorted with so much energy that he once broke his leg on stage.
† People understandably throw their arms up in horror at the idea of a white audience/black performer venue, but I was struck by how, on the day Fats Domino died in 2017, British TV kept showing a clip of him playing 'Ain't That a Shame' in the 1956 movie *Shake, Rattle and Rock!* 'As long as it's for the kids, that's OK,' says Fats, but 'the kids' are all white, the racial divide absolute. And this was in a movie from as late as 1956. Moreover, the news channels showing the clip in 2017 did their own segregation by cutting out the now-offensive all-white audience, suggesting this was a regular live show, Fats at his best in his native New Orleans.

boundary-breaking that he would become the first African American to have a postage stamp to himself.

Walking into the Cotton Club, you'd have been forgiven for thinking the Civil War had never happened, let alone the birth of record players and radio. The bandstand would have been dressed up like a colonial mansion, the walls behind featuring paintings of slave accommodation nestling among the cotton plantation. Facing away from the stage you'd have seen nothing but white faces, well fed and moneyed. In the depths of the Depression, a look at the menu would have revealed that a bottle of Budweiser cost a dollar, as did ham and eggs, and you could have ordered a Perrier, if you so desired, to wash down your shrimp foo yong (there was a whole separate Chinese menu). On the stage would have been a band that had recently gone by the name of the Kentucky Club Orchestra, and they were all black; the dancing girls were mixed-race or paler-skinned blacks. In the most cosmopolitan city in the world, its biggest nightclub was living out a fantasy of half a century before.

It had opened in September 1923, launched by gangster Owen 'Owney' Madden while he was in prison for manslaughter. Initially a means by which he could sell his bootleg beer, it operated almost continuously until Prohibition ended, and Ellington was the bandleader for most of those years. At the piano he was orchestral, and in time he would turn jazz into a modernist art form. At the Cotton Club, still restricted by the three-minute playing length of a 78, he concentrated on shorter pieces. He was there to provide incidental music for revues, comedians, dancing girls – whatever turns the venue threw his way. The revues extended the racial divide – Ellington had to soundtrack playlets about black savages and white damsels in distress – and the bandleader played up to it. They wanted jungle music? He wrote them pieces called 'Jungle Night in Harlem', 'Jungle Fever' and 'The Mooche'. The titles suggest not only the America of fifty years earlier, but also Brooklyn at the turn of the twenty-first century. You'd think it would have taken just one faintly raised eyebrow from the drummer, one snigger from the trombonist, and the ironic facade would have been revealed. But it was no joke: Ellington and his band had to ask the management before they could bring black guests. Irony is often a very necessary mask for very uneasy seriousness.*

Even this early on, and with punters to keep happy, the Duke was always looking to break esoteric new ground. Breaking the standard three-minute recording time, 1930's 'Creole Rhapsody' was a five-minute-long multi-part song that featured segments – like 'Good Vibrations', 'A Day in the Life' or 'Bohemian Rhapsody' down the line – rather than just solos, and it had to be split over two sides of a ten-inch Brunswick 78.† Then there was the atmospheric 'Creole Love Call'. Ellington heard one of the club's dancers, Adelaide Hall, singing a counter-melody to it while she was waiting in the wings one night in 1928. The band were recording the tune a few days later, so Ellington got Hall to sing on it, with highly sensuous results. She effectively sang a duet with Miley's plunger-muted horn, mimicking its moans and growls, an abstract filter on human language.‡

'I don't think he's racial,' said the Duke's right-hand man Billy Strayhorn in the 1950s. 'He is an individual.' Still, it's hard to read something like 'Black and Tan Fantasy' as non-political: 'Black and Tans' was the name for the few Harlem clubs that allowed, even encouraged, blacks and whites to mix. In 1943, at his *Black, Brown and Beige* concert at Carnegie Hall, Ellington would ask, 'Harlem, how'd you come to be permitted in a land that's free?' Nonetheless, at the Cotton Club he was

* Irony is also a tool of modernism: the classical Greek *pilotis* in Berthold Lubetkin's 1935 Highpoint apartment block in London were seen by some as a sop to traditionalists – a defeat, even – but Lubetkin used them to hide drainpipes.
† The twelve-inch 78 rpm format did exist but was reserved almost exclusively for classical music, for no reason other than snobbery.
‡ Adelaide Hall's story is remarkable, and her talent something else: she discovered blind pianist Art Tatum in 1931; moved to Westchester County in 1933 and faced down racists who broke into her house; and starred in 1934's *Cotton Club Parade* for nine months, singing Harold Arlen's 'Ill Wind' (written especially for her), as nitrogen smoke, or dry ice, covered the floor around her feet – the first time it had ever been used on stage. Hall's scat vocal, sensuous swoops and wordless eroticism on 'Creole Love Call' would become a touchstone for the vocal-jazz boom of the 1950s. She was just about the only act from the venue still with us when Francis Ford Coppola's film *The Cotton Club* screened in 1977.

immaculately turned out, so dignified, and he had unshakeable faith
in his music. Regular radio broadcasts by the Columbia Broadcasting
System introduced Ellington to the rest of the US, and so subtly, word-
lessly, before even Louis Armstrong, Duke Ellington became the first
well-known and accepted black performer for white America.

From the start, he was a sensation. In 1927 Abel Green reviewed
Ellington's first appearance at the Cotton Club for *Variety*: 'In Duke
Ellington's dance band, Harlem has reclaimed its own after Times Square
accepted them for several seasons at the Club Kentucky. Ellington's jazz-
ique is just too bad.' That's 'bad' meaning good, even in the 1920s. Was
Ellington given free rein to play his own material in this entirely white-
run establishment? Of course not. In spite of his creativity, Ellington
and his players still had to do what a regular band did and play other
people's songs. Harold Arlen and Jimmy McHugh wrote songs for the
Cotton Club; Ellington had to play them. Any resentment or envy was
well hidden by Sir Duke, but he would have had to be superhuman not
to feel either.

Arlen, the writer of such turbulent songs as 'Stormy Weather' and
'Blues in the Night', probably deserves more than a diversion here,
given his list of songwriting credits. Like Elvis Presley, he should have
been a twin, but his brother died after just one day. That must play
on your mind for ever; maybe you feel you have to make amends,
do twice as well. Both Arlen and Presley certainly overreached: Elvis
became the biggest pop star in the world; Arlen wrote the most popular
song of the twentieth century, 'Over the Rainbow'. Throughout Arlen's
life, his parents – the fine-voiced cantor Samuel Arluck and his wife,
Celia – refused to call him by his adopted American first name. To his
family and close friends, Harold was always Chaim, the Hebrew word
for 'life'.

Maybe the Cotton Club wasn't quite so much about black and
white, and more about white privilege and social underclasses, because
the Eastern European, Jewish Arlen and the Cotton Club house bands
of Duke Ellington and later Cab Calloway seemed to reach propin-
quity. Then again, it's possible Arlen's father had something to do with
him writing jazz standards like 'One for My Baby', which his fellow

Jewish writers, like the radio-ready Irving Berlin and the owlish, uptight Jerome Kern, could never have written. Samuel Arluck was Orthodox but no snob; criss-crossing the South he would have heard other sacred music of all types, and the sound of Louis Armstrong would have come as no surprise to him. His son in turn would have been exposed to the same music, and his father encouraged him to play and write and sing; he even let young Chaim bring a Victrola into the house. 'Pop had a perfect genius for finding new melodic twists,' Arlen would tell *The New Yorker*. 'I know damned well now that his glorious improvisations must have had some effect on me and my own style.' Soon he was also 'aping what jazz I heard at the time and superimposing on that my own idea, which led to orchestrating, and my beginnings'. In 1930 Arlen got himself a stopgap engagement as rehearsal pianist for a show by songwriter Vincent Youmans. 'I was hired to be an actor/singer in Great Day. During the rehearsal, Fletcher Henderson, who had the orchestra, took ill, and Vincent asked me to play for the cast. I played the piano and before each song I would play the usual vamp, a traditional vamp that we all knew. I would improvise, a little differently each time. One day the cast asked what it was and I realised I had something, and I developed it into a theme. That's how I happened to write my first professional song, Get Happy.'

The end of Prohibition in 1933 would mean the end of the Cotton Club, which, after all, had only been a glorified speakeasy. Arlen went to Broadway, then Hollywood. It took a pair of white entrepreneurs to help Duke Ellington step beyond the Cotton Club's confines. The first was music publisher Jack Robbins, a man who could safely be described as rakish. One evening in 1925 he walked into the club, and soon his eyes were on stalks, dollar signs replacing his pupils. He approached the Duke and asked if he could write the music for a show he was putting together (there was no such show). The Duke asked when he would need it by. Robbins, entirely clueless, said, 'Tomorrow,' and Ellington agreed. He'd never written the music for a show, had no idea it usually took a few months, but went home and bashed it out. To pay Ellington's $500 advance, Robbins pawned his engagement ring, then added a few extra songs to the four Ellington had written in a night and sold the show – which he titled *Chocolate Kiddies* – to Berlin's Admiralspalast theatre. An all-black revue, it was a huge success, and moved from Berlin to Hamburg, then Scandinavia, Austria, Czechoslovakia and Hungary, eventually running for six months.

Europe would freak for the Duke when he first toured there in 1933. A London critic wrote, 'Girls wept, and young chaps sank to their knees.' He was described as 'an African Stravinsky'. In 1939 he played two consecutive shows: the first was an all-night party in a tobacco warehouse in North Carolina, a true rave; the second was in Paris, where, according to *The New Yorker*, critics claimed his performance revealed 'the very secret of the cosmos' and contained 'the rhythm of the atom'. So elegant, such greatness. What did his bandmates make of him? Trombonist Tricky Sam Nanton remembered how Ellington once ate thirty-two sandwiches during an intermission at a dance in Old Orchard Beach, Maine. 'He's a genius, all right,' he said, 'but Jesus, how he eats!'

Ellington was aware that public perception was key: you needed to be in the press and constantly look fresh. The Original Dixieland Jazz Band had had manager Max Hart to ratchet up their newness, every quote, every song a revolution. Irving Mills became Ellington's manager, and he was the person responsible for dropping the word 'genius' into every other sentence. An advert for the 'Solitude' single in 1935 ran, 'Again! The stamp of Ellington's genius.' Mills hinted that Ellington's ascent to the stage of Carnegie Hall was only a matter of time*; meanwhile, Ellington, in his benign yet regal way, casually told the press that he was working on a symphonic suite about the history of American blacks. Like Scott Joplin before him, Ellington considered himself an artist. Unlike Joplin, he also had one eye on his bank balance and, with Mills's help, knew exactly how to maximise both critical acclaim and record sales. In 1937 he released 'Diminuendo and Crescendo in Blue', a step beyond 'Creole Rhapsody', so long and complex that it stretched beyond the A- and B-sides onto a second disc. The same year he released 'The New East St Louis Toodle-Oo', on the tenth anniversary of his breakthrough hit, 'The East St Louis Toodle-Oo'. Ellington certainly

---

* He would eventually get there in January 1943.

had a genius for measuring just what the public wanted. 'Art is dangerous,' he said. 'When it ceases to be dangerous, you don't want it.'

* * *

In 1959 the National Association for the Advancement of Colored People
(NAACP) would give Duke Ellington its highest award, the Spingarn
Medal, won in the previous couple of years by Martin Luther King Jr
and the Little Rock Nine. *Time* magazine was confused. Hadn't he been
a Cotton Club stalwart, playing for white-only audiences? Didn't he still
play 'for segregated audiences on his annual swings through the South'?
The answer, of course, lay elsewhere. Critics had 'not been listening to
our music', said Ellington. 'For a long time, social protest and pride
in black culture and history have been the most significant themes in
what we've done.' Further, he thought there was more than one valid
approach. On a private level, music historian John Edward Hasse discovered that Ellington had written to Harry Truman in the early 1950s,
suggesting that Margaret Truman, the president's daughter, could be the
honorary chairwoman for an NAACP benefit whose stated aim was 'to
stamp out segregation, discrimination, bigotry'.* When Hasse found
the letter in the Truman Library, he saw that Ellington's request had
been dismissed without a response, just the word 'No!' underlined twice
on the Duke's original letter. A decade later, in 1963, the government
would be less uptight: the Ellington band went on a State Department-
organised tour as ambassadors representing America in places like Syria,
Afghanistan, Iran, Iraq, Pakistan, Sri Lanka and Yugoslavia.

Ellington would be an ambassador for music and for humanity. At
a seventieth-birthday tribute to the Duke in 1970, four years before he
died, Ralph Ellison remembered seeing the Ellington band in Oklahoma
City when he was a kid, sounding like 'news from the great wide world'.
The Duke was so worldly, so elegant, 'so mockingly creative'. Who,

* Following the 1957 school desegregation battles in Little Rock, Ellington
recorded a new, moving version of 'Come Sunday', the spiritual piece from *Black,
Brown and Beige*, with Mahalia Jackson.

asked Ellison, 'treated the social limitations placed in their path with greater disdain?'

Ellington embodied American style and grace. He was *all* of American music; no one had a comparable skill for blending jazz, blues, gospel, ragtime, even folk and classical. Everybody identified with it, it was all-inclusive, but still he was beautifully guarded, a sophisticated mystery. A *New Yorker* piece from 1944 captured the Duke on tour, in the Pullman, in quiet solitude: 'At night, particularly if his train is passing through certain sections of Ohio or Indiana, he will remain at the window (shifting to the smoker if the berths are made up), for he likes the flames of the steel furnaces. "I think of music sometimes in terms of colour," he says, "and I like to see the flames, licking yellow in the dark, and then pulsing down to a kind of red glow."'

16

LEARN TO CROON: RUDY VALLEE AND THE DAWN OF THE ELECTRIC ERA

LAMBERT & BUTLER'S CIGARETTES

RUDY VALLEE

DANCE BAND LEADERS

A SERIES OF 25

23

RUDY VALLEE

Rudy Vallee is not only America's premier crooner, but is the most popular young orchestra leader in that country. He is a product of the wireless age. He left college to become saxophonist in a small band at £4 a week—now his income is anything from £25,000 to £75,000 a year. Probably no idol of the amusement world has received a greater fan mail than Rudy Vallee; his voice on the radio is an irresistible lure. He popularized *The Stein Song* with one broadcast, and within a fortnight 250,000 copies were sold. Rudy Vallee, who starred on the screen in *The Vagabond Lover*, has been married twice.

LAMBERT & BUTLER

ISSUED BY THE IMPERIAL TOBACCO CO. (OF GREAT BRITAIN & IRELAND) LTD.

A degenerate form of singing . . . They are not true love songs.
They profane the name. No true American man would practise
this base art. Of course, they aren't men.
  Cardinal O'Connell, Cathedral of the Holy Cross, Boston,
  10 January 1932

Nineteen twenty-five had seen two new, important developments in pop. First, commercial radio had created a brand-new use for the pop song: as a way to sell a product. Secondly, developments in electrification had led directly to the rise of the intimate singer; when you heard a Vaughn De Leath record, you knew she was singing to you, rather than at you. Rudy Vallee and the male crooners who followed him were disruptive and corruptive. They became the first pop pin-ups.

Crooning may sound tame to anyone raised on Jimi Hendrix, the Ramones or Daft Punk, but that was the point – tameness, or any remotely soft sound, hadn't been possible until the mid-1920s. Before the invention of the carbon microphone, singers had had to shout for their voices to register on shellac; following its arrival, all shades of singing beyond just tearful caterwauling could be accommodated. You heard subtlety, softness and sensuality on record for the very first time, and a way of singing we still recognise today.

Records made before the mid-1920s are tagged 'acoustic' by enthusiasts; after this came the 'electric' era.* In the electric age, having a naturally loud voice suddenly became unimportant, the width of your chest entirely irrelevant. The microphone removed the competitive aspect of singing; the turn of a knob was all it took. If you wanted to stand out as a singer, you needed to look beyond mere volume. In a heartbeat, a generation of performers sounded corny and old-fashioned; worse, they sounded phoney, their powers of persuasion forced. But most significantly, the rest of the world finally got to hear the natural, conversational, confident and friendly American voice.

Vaughn De Leath's delicate, refined style had reflected the growing urbanity of American life in the early 1920s, and by 1925 white-collar professionals outnumbered manual workers in the US. As the Jazz Age started to run out of puff, dancing itself to the point of exhaustion, the country looked for other sophisticated role models inside the world of entertainment.

Whispering Jack Smith fitted the bill. His style, which gave the impression that he was wearing a monocle while holding a glass of milk, was the result of a German gas attack during World War I (which was tough on Smith, given that he was originally Jacob Schmidt, whose German parents had emigrated to New York). After his father died, Smith's mum worked as a laundress, doing extra hours to pay for Jacob's piano lessons. These initially reaped a dividend after the war, when he

---

* Though earlier attempts had been made, the very first 78 recorded electrically was 1924's 'You May Be Lonesome' by 'The Whispering Pianist' Art Gillham, a songwriting crooner who was well ahead of the pack. It was released on Columbia, a month before rivals Victor managed an electric recording. Gillham was a radio pioneer who had pulled off the trick of broadcasting from airfields with a portable keyboard. His loyalty to Columbia paid off: by 1930 he had two CBS radio shows, *Breakfast with Art* and the beautifully named *Syncopated Pessimism*.

Americanised his name and found work in New York's cafés and cabarets. Without the benefit of a stentorian Jolson voice, Smith developed a clipped, clearly enunciated vocal style, which enabled customers to hear the words, even at a low volume. By day, he worked for Irving Berlin's publishing company, sat in a booth behind a piano, playing songs in-house for the music trade; in such a cramped setting, his small voice was ideal. To sell the song, Smith would play the melody with his right hand, while cupping his cheek with his left, looking nonchalant and distinctly unthreatening, the complete anti-Jolson.

Radio was made for Jack Smith. The stations had informed Tin Pan Alley writers that a range of no more than five melody notes best suited the capabilities of radio broadcasting, which was ideal for his limited voice. On top of this, whereas established vaudeville singers often wanted too much money or, worse, damaged the studio equipment with their bellowing, Smith did neither, and he became a regular on New York's WMCA in 1925, selling songs and domestic products alike. He was, it transpired, very popular with housewives.

Eddie King, manager of the Victor label, called him in to record a few sides, just as the new electrical technology was being incorporated into the company's studios. It took a month of trial-and-error recordings, but eventually 'Cecilia' became Smith's first 78. He was a dapper man, hair slicked back to reveal a widow's peak, and he became an international star with 'Baby Face' (1926), his signature tune 'Me and My Shadow' and the 'moon'/'June'-rhyming, Bryan Ferry-anticipating 'Half a Moon' (both 1927). There was also a tongue-r-r-rolling take on Paul Whiteman's million-seller 'Whispering', which revealed a sly humour, and by 1930 he was making Hollywood appearances in *The Big Party* and, as himself, in *Cheer Up and Smile*.

The star of both movies was the bright-eyed Dixie Lee, whom Smith could hardly help but notice. Dixie would go on to marry a crooner – Bing Crosby. Quite possibly this messed with Smith's equilibrium, and he began to drink heavily, once threatening to jump from the top of a skyscraper, before being talked down by his manager and his valet. Such behaviour hardly befitted the svelte figure with the widow's peak. Hollywood never called again, and Whispering Jack Smith fell from grace, leaving the door open for other crooners to take centre stage.

One of the biggest hits of 1927 was Gene Austin's 'My Blue Heaven', an upbeat reading of late-1920s domesticity. Austin had a gentle smile and looked a little like the young Brian Epstein. He had a kind voice to match. Backed by soft piano and a big teddy bear of a cello, he sang: 'A smiling face, a fireplace, a little nest that nestles where the roses bloom. Just Molly and me, and baby makes three, we're happy in my blue heaven.' He even allowed room for a little whistling and throw-away dum-de-dums and tra-la-las. Less clipped than Jack Smith, Austin sounded more like a singing postman, taking his sweet time to complete his round.

He became the first million-selling crooner, though the term still wasn't in common usage. His publicist was Colonel Tom Parker, who clearly had fond memories of the crooner era, convincing his new charge Elvis Presley to re-record De Leath's 'Are You Lonesome Tonight' in 1961. But Austin wasn't the first crooner to cause concern about gender roles in American society. That honour went to a sweet-voiced Yale graduate called Rudy Vallee, who recounted: 'I took a year out of Yale to play the Savoy Hotel in London. When I got home in June 1925, I was on the back porch with my sister, and she said, "There's a singer who's very popular on Victor records." We had a little phonograph there, and she put on one of Gene Austin's records. I hadn't heard of him, but at that time he was probably selling two or three million copies of every record he made – "Ramona", "My Blue Heaven" and all the rest.'

When Vallee opened at New York's Heigh Ho Club on 8 January 1928, with a honeyed voice borrowed from Gene Austin and a mega-phone covering half his face, he took his first step towards superstardom.*

---

* Some crooners were too idiosyncratic to sustain a career. Little Jack Little had hits with versions of Dana Suesse's 'You Oughta Be in Pictures' (1934) and Dorothy Fields and Jimmy McHugh's 'I'm in the Mood for Love' (1935), but later honed his deep breathy voice until he sounded more like Lou Reed than Bing Crosby. Career highlights include 1934's lascivious 'I'd Like to Dunk You in My Coffee' ('spread you on my bread . . . fe fi fo fum, I'm overcome with a cannibalistic feeling') and the gently menacing war-effort number 'I've Always Wanted to Waltz in Berlin' (1943).

A crooning, soothing woman like Vaughn De Leath had been fine, and the square-bothering age of the flapper was nearing its end. But Vallee provided fresh problems for a society in which notions of manhood involved sweat and toil and square jaws. He had the look of a fall guy in an early Disney cartoon, with a squishy marshmallow face, saggy and soppy, and wavy hair that poured like syrup over his milk-white head. Women swooned and sighed over him both in live performance (which men maybe could accept) and at home on the radio (which they couldn't), and by 1929 he was radio's first matinee idol. To other men, Vallee was an intruder, a serial philanderer, his beseeching voice breaking into front rooms and seducing tens of thousands of women across the country simultaneously. Clara Bow was the 'It' Girl, and everyone knew what 'it' was. Vallee, in spite of his eyebrows flying off his head and his mouth sliding around the right-hand side of his face, had 'it' by dint of his soft, conversational singing style. Vaughn De Leath and her mothering bosom were one thing. What did Rudy Vallee mean when he sang 'I'm Just a Vagabond Lover'? Rudy Vallee meant business.

What was so different about the effect of the crooners? This was technologised intimacy. Singers had been making listeners weep since the Victorian era, at the very least. Vallee fans talked about his 'sincerity', which isn't a word you'd have used for Eddie Cantor's style, but this is where radio made all the difference. The listener could be alone with Vallee's voice, and radio stations were keenly aware of this; you were being addressed as an individual, not a mass audience. The effects could be – and this again was new – sexualised; fan letters used phrases like 'burning up'. Vallee was very much a pop star, causing sexual panic, with the same erotic effect as later creamy-voiced singers such as David Cassidy and George Michael.*

Vallee's choice of material hardly seemed designed to make this so. 'The Stein Song' was an old University of Maine drinking song, with

---

* Like any craze, crooning lent itself to novelty hits. One of the cutest was Elsie Carlisle and the Ambrose band's 'My Kid's a Crooner': 'He won't say "mummy", chucks his dummy, wants a microphone . . . now my kid's a crooner. Though he's only two, he goes "boo-boo-boo-boo". I think I'll write to Crosby and ask him what to do.'

a march beat dating from 1910; 'The Whiffenpoof Song' was a barbershop piece associated with Yale, backed only by the merest tinkle of piano: 'We're four little lambs who have lost our way, we're little black sheep who have gone astray.' More on point was 1929's emotionally loaded 'Tears' ('Turn those tears of regret once more to tears of happiness').* Vallee had to have a lot of self-belief. His parboiled face hardly seemed to matter when his plaintive voice came over the air. 'I think you are endowed with "It",' wrote one fan, 'that's why I sit up night after night losing my beauty sleep to hear you.' Another fan from Brooklyn wrote, 'A long time ago, I listened to you sing "Rain" and all sorts of shivery thrills ran up and down my spinal column.'

What it all added up to was essentially a novelty. Vallee's name would crop up every so often years later ('Give me the good old Rudy Vallee days,' moped Milton Berle, after he was mauled by Elvis Presley fans in a 1956 skit), but he registered as the distant past. If his songs are forgotten, what we shouldn't forget is Vallee's contribution to pop stardom. Before Les Paul or King Tubby, and way before Marshall stacks, there was the patented Rudy Vallee sound system. In 1930 he told Paul Whiteman that he had 'borrowed an old carbon mike from NBC, hooked up a homemade amplifier with some radios, and I've got a sort of electronic megaphone. I had the legs sawn off the radios so they don't look so strange.' He had charm enough to stand on stage and sing through this 'electronic megaphone' without fear or embarrassment; the likes of Jolson were spitting feathers, screaming about gimmicks, but it worked. In this way, Vallee helped to introduce the value of artifice to popular music. The traditional objectives of the singing voice – reach, volume, power – would be permanently altered. With Vallee's Heath Robinson public address system, live music also entered the electronic age. Vallee probably knew his fame wouldn't last, but radio was always good to him, and he became the respected host of the *Fleischmann Yeast Hour*.†

* 'Tears' would go on to be the best-selling single in Britain in 1965, when it was re-recorded by comedian Ken Dodd.
† As a radio star, Vallee's influence would extend beyond his soft singing style. His *Fleischmann Yeast Hour* introduced America to future stars for the first time, American institutions like Milton Berle, Alice Faye and the Mills Brothers. In

* * *

If Rudy Vallee looked like he might dissolve if you hit him, most men would think twice before picking a fight with Russ Columbo. He took the bedside nature of the croon and made it into a sensuous lullaby on 'Goodnight Sweetheart'. He didn't have a soft cartoon face. His jaw was square, his brow was knitted in seriousness, and his lake-deep, tremulous baritone matched his saturnine looks. 'Goodnight Sweetheart' and 'Prisoner of Love' were the two stellar sides of the twenty-three-year-old's 1931 debut, and they had legs; the latter would go on to become a 1946 hit for both Billy Eckstine and Perry Como, then a 1963 hit for James Brown and one of the highlights – head bowed, down on one knee – of his live set.

From Spokane, Washington, came another youngster who could also sing quite beautifully: the serene, almost lackadaisical Bing Crosby. Vallee and his megaphone would be over by 1931, but by then Columbo and Crosby would be neck and neck.* They had an unspoken gentleman's agreement: Bing recorded 'Goodnight Sweetheart', but only after it had been a hit for Russ. The treaty was torn up when Russ recorded De Sylva, Brown and Henderson's 'When the Blue of the Night (Meets the Gold of the Day)' in November 1931, knowing that Bing had booked a studio to record the same song just five days later. Bing had been on the west coast, away from the heat and the action, and Russ was capitalising. 'The thing that decided me to go to New York,' Crosby told *Screenland*, 'was hearing a chap who had substituted for me at the [Cocoanut] Grove, on my numerous nights off, singing my stuff over the air in a brazen imitation of me.' Crosby was very much about the sunrise, the morning, long before cocktail hour; Columbo's singing, and his looks, had something of the night about

---

1937, at Vallee's insistence, Louis Armstrong hosted the show while he was on holiday; this made Armstrong the first African American to present a national network radio programme.
* Crosby never really regarded Vallee as a rival at all: 'He came out of Yale University, and he had that Ivy League sort of flair, you know. He had an appeal that was all his own.'

them. Crosby and Columbo had a neat symmetry for the media, rivals in the gossip columns.

Their radio sponsorship gave away their fanbases: Crosby had Cremo cigars; Columbo had the housewife's favourite, Maxwell House coffee. Every morning Columbo would be woken by his black valet, Gordon K. Reid, with a quote from Shakespeare and a splash of cold water. He had the stuff of legend about him.

By the early 1930s crooning was international. In Britain, Al Bowlly was a Vallee equivalent, sliding between notes, singing from just behind his teeth. His father was Greek, his mother Lebanese, and he spoke and sang in an accent that was meant to be faux-American but sounded decidedly London. He recorded 'Learn to Croon', from the 1933 Bing Crosby movie *College Humour*, and made it doubly mellifluous, backed by little more than a florid, Art Tatum-inspired pianist and what sounds like a Hawaiian guitar. 'You'll eliminate each rival soon,' he sang, and he wasn't joking. Lew Stone's band backed him on another Crosby song, the sardonically gloomy 'My Woman' (1932), which Stone embellished with a verse drawn from the melody of Chopin's 'Funeral March'.*

As a freelance singer, Bowlly was also fortunate enough to work with Ray Noble's orchestra. Noble was a rarity in that he wrote in the American style, beautiful things like 'The Very Thought of You'. What's more, he didn't regard a run in the West End as the pinnacle of artistic achievement, and would eventually move to the States. In 1929, aged thirty-one, he had been at the BBC, working under Jack Payne as arranger for the house band. 'I was very keen, and listened to every band. I was very fond of the corporation. Of course, we did still have a lot of chaps who really should have still been in the army. Awfully nice fellas, even if they really didn't know anything about broadcasting.' Noble was the archetypal British dance-band leader, with thin, narrowed eyes like Rex Harrison, a pencil-thin moustache and sunken cheeks. He left for New York in 1934, an incredibly bold move, but it paid off. He had just written 'The Very Thought of You' and packed it in his trunk.

---

* Stone's motif would later be revisited by soundtrack writer John Williams as Darth Vader's theme in *The Empire Strikes Back*.

Union restrictions meant he couldn't take any British musicians, but Noble did travel to New York with singer Bowlly. 'He was one of these simple chaps,' said Noble. 'He either thought a fella was the nicest guy in the world, in which case he'd empty his pockets for him. Or he was the dirtiest scoundrel unhung, in which case Al could rip him apart – he was an extremely strong man. It was either black or white, there were no greys. He laid a trail of female destruction across the United States that I don't think has ever been beaten.' Bowlly never became a major star in America, and his time spent in the States diminished his popularity in Britain. Some of his best-known work, though, was still ahead of him.

Crooning aggravated British conservatives as much as it did Americans. The Manchester-based *Daily Dispatch*'s radio correspondent wrote an open letter to Lord Reith, headlined 'PLEASE SIR JOHN, SUPPRESS THIS NIGHTLY WAILING': 'Since the time over three years ago when I wrote an open letter to Jack Payne asking him to stand against the emasculated, wailing songs which were spoiling the late evening dance broadcasts for so many listeners, practically every radio critic throughout the country has expressed his personal abhorrence of crooning. What has been the effect on the BBC? Absolutely none . . . The apostles of uplift during the afternoon and evening [continue to broadcast songs that] are in their essence quite against the national character, particularly to that of the hard-working people in the North of England.'

Nevertheless, the BBC were in broad agreement: in 1933 an internal memo called crooning 'a particularly odious form of singing'. Directness and sensitivity were clearly undesirable. During a general discussion about broadcasting dance music, they talked about the 'general policy of the elimination of crooning', which 'should be obliterated straight away'. It makes you wonder if it really was the Germans who dropped the bomb on Al Bowlly's Jermyn Street flat in 1941, killing the singer instantly.

A 1932 edition of *Radio Guide* featured Russ Columbo on the cover and called him 'Radio's Valentino'. They unwittingly predicted his fate: like Bowlly, Columbo would die young. In 1934 a friend was toying with an antique pistol that Columbo kept on his desk and accidentally shot him dead. In America, Bing Crosby would have the rest of the 1930s all to himself.

17

ALL HOLLYWOOD AND ALL HEAVEN: TALKING PICTURES

LOUNGE CINEMA,
MARGATE.

TALKIES.
MONDAY, FEBRUARY 17th, AND ALL THE WEEK.
AL JOLSON
— IN —

The Singing Fool

The picture occupies most of the programme, and owing to
:: its exceptional attraction there will be ::
THREE DISTINCT PERFORMANCES DAILY at 2.30, 6.30 & 8.30.

PRICES AS USUAL.

Old Age Pensioners admitted to MATINEES ONLY during
this week.

Cinemas were cathedrals of pop culture, pleasure domes that combined the Doric pillars of ancient Greece, the domes of the Taj Mahal, star-sprinkled high ceilings like a night out on the prairie and red velvet drapes straight out of Mata Hari's boudoir. Yet Hollywood hadn't been in any kind of position to reflect the Jazz Age. P. G. Wodehouse and the Gershwins' *Oh, Kay!* had been made into a movie in 1928 – a silent one. No matter the crispness of Colleen Moore's bob or the Rodchenko-goes-Californian playfulness of the poster, no silent movie was going to get within a mile of capturing the Jazz Age.

Before *The Jazz Singer*, the film and music industries had lived in entirely separate worlds. *The Jazz Singer* ushered in not only the age of 'talkies', but the cinema as a platform for song and, most significantly, the age of the Hollywood musical. Music was the best way to show off cinema's new technology. Movie moguls moved fast. The Hollywood studios descended on Tin Pan Alley and Broadway; it was a rapid and wholesale buyout. Almost all the songwriting and publishing firms moved from New York to southern California in the late 1920s and early '30s. Warner Brothers alone bought out publishing giants such as

Witmark, T. B. Harms, and De Sylva, Brown and Henderson. It was hard to believe the company had been struggling on the brink of non-existence before it made *The Jazz Singer*.

The 'talkie' aspect of *The Jazz Singer* must have seemed a little primitive, even while it dazzled audiences. Antiquarian bookseller Fred Bason saw the British premiere at the Piccadilly Theatre on 27 September 1928: 'As you see the man singing, you *hear* the man singing,' he wrote in his diary. 'If it wasn't that the noise blares forth like twenty gramophones at once or six strong voices singing at once, it would be a miracle. I suppose it is a miracle.' The excitable Bason got eleven autographs from the assembled VIPs, but it was just as well the star of the show wasn't there: 'A. Jolson is the Jazz Singer. I don't like him: Sings Awfull [*sic*].'

Al Jolson himself would have been equally sour-faced, as he didn't see much money from one of the film's stand-out songs, 'Mother of Mine I Still Have You', which he claimed to have written. As so few cinemas were equipped to screen it, *The Jazz Singer* became a film that far more people had heard about than actually seen. But it became a legend: by the time of *The Singing Fool* in 1928, a Jolson picture was guaranteed to create a hit song, and 'Sonny Boy' became a monster hit, even by Jolson's standards.

* * *

Silent films had often had scores written for them, but only the major city picture palaces could afford either a Wurlitzer organ, complete with special effects, or a full-scale orchestra to play them. Cue sheets were normally presented by distributors along with the film reels. Joseph Carl Breil's score for D. W. Griffith's *Birth of a Nation* was written for a seventy-piece orchestra, which toured the country. More often, though, in small-town or rural cinemas, the accompaniment was from a piano or violin, and the music was a patchwork of Tchaikovsky, Brahms and Grieg.*

---

* The musicians who had soundtracked movies in theatres across America were hit hard by talkies: there were 22,000 of them in 1926; by 1934 there were just

There had been experiments in sound and vision. Unsurprisingly, king inventor Thomas Edison was in there at the beginning with his Kinetophon in 1894, but he decided to concentrate on sound, leaving other experimentalists to pick up the visual side. French photographer Clément Maurice captured short, minute-long films of Little Tich, Sarah Bernhardt and Vesta Tilley with separate sound discs, introducing his Phono-Cinéma-Théâtre at the Paris Exposition of 1900, but the rudimentary sound meant that it remained no more than a low-level novelty for the next two decades. Lee De Forest, of Council Bluffs, Iowa, first developed a method of imprinting sound directly onto film, recording it in striations of greys and blacks on one edge of the strip. Much like Edison, he spent an unfortunate amount of his career fighting lawsuits. In November 1922 he set up the De Forest Phonofilm Company in New York, but none of the Hollywood studios expressed any interest in his invention. They controlled the major theatre chains, which meant De Forest was limited to showing his films in independent theatres; the Phonofilm Company filed for bankruptcy in September 1926.

Why weren't the film studios interested? As audiences seemed perfectly happy with silent film, they didn't want to rock the boat. However, as soon as there was a dip in attendances, Warner Brothers – at this point a minor Hollywood player – decided to gamble on sound as a quick-fix gimmick. Instead of using Phonofilm, though, they reverted to Maurice's sound-on-disc – which had been further developed by Bell Telephone Laboratories in the early 1920s – and renamed it Vitaphone. Each cinema required a special turntable to play the 33 rpm, thirteen-to-seventeen-inch discs the Vitaphone system needed for each eleven-minute-long reel of film. It was only in 1926 that Warners first had their own showcase cinemas, but with a unique product – the talkie – they could break into the big four chains (Fox, Famous Players, First National and Metro). On 6 August 1926 they showed *Don Juan*, starring John Barrymore. *Cinema Art* magazine reported how 'pictures were

---

4,100, and you have to wonder how even that many were finding work. Plenty of these musicians were either African Americans or women (who often played piano or organ accompaniment in smaller cinemas) or both. Their jobs went south just as the Depression arrived.

projected on the screen, and the music reproduced with such perfection, that it was difficult to believe that [the orchestra] were not actually in front of the audience'. When a messenger came for Don Juan, there was a close-up 'showing his hand knocking at the door three or four times, and [the sound] very distinctly can be heard . . . not one knock too many, mind you!' Professor Michael Pupin of Columbia University bravely went on record, saying that 'no closer approach to resurrection has ever been made by science'. Jack Warner wasn't about to undersell the impact of *Don Juan*'s debut. In Hollywood, he said, 'the reverberations triggered a panic, as though the Black Death had struck the land. No one had openly discussed the potential crisis of talking pictures, but the pros knew Armageddon was at hand. There would be suicides, mental crack-ups, emotional illnesses. There would be financial losses in the millions for those who had invested in that unstable commodity, the silent picture star.'

Warners' gamble paid off in full with the release of *The Jazz Singer* in October 1927. A schmaltzy tale of a cantor's son who chooses Broadway over his father's synagogue, it was originally set to star George Jessel, but when he asked for too much money, Warners looked to Broadway's biggest name, Al Jolson. It's hard to imagine the gloopy script (has a film ever had a more misleading name?) would have sold it alone; it was Jolson's 'You ain't heard nothing yet, folks!' antics that made it a sensation. Warners' profits increased seven-fold in a year, and the silent era was over.

* * *

The most obvious way to mimic the success of *The Jazz Singer* was to include songs in movies, so, inadvertently, Warners invented the Hollywood musical. Who was on hand to write songs in that dusty outpost in 1927? Nacio Herb Brown and Arthur Freed, that's who. Their names might not be the first that spring to mind when you think about Hollywood music today, but in the late 1920s they were the first names any film producer would have turned to. Brown was an apprentice tailor whose father happened to be the sheriff of Los Angeles, so he grew up watching Hollywood expand from a few shacks into a virtual city. At this early stage in its development, the stars weren't so starry, and so gentleman's tailor Nacio could just walk right up to them and ask if they needed a new suit. By night, he played piano in local bars, which was how he met lyric-writing hustler Arthur Freed. Given Brown's in as a tailor – which gave him access to all the hottest gossip – these two would have been highly visible to any director, and once *The Jazz Singer* had broken the ice, they were an easy pick for MGM's *Broadway Melody* of 1929. They would go on to soundtrack possibly the ultimate Hollywood musical moment, writing 'Singin' in the Rain'.

If Brown and Freed were tied up, it was easy for studios to pillage ready-made musicals from Broadway. Musical theatre had been revitalised in late 1927 by *Showboat*, which had been quickly followed by the 1928 Eddie Cantor smash *Whoopee!* (songs by Gus Kahn and Walter Donaldson, including 'Love Me or Leave Me', which became Ruth Etting's signature tune) and *Rio Rita* ('Ziegfeld's mammoth girl music spectacle', as RKO called it). Hollywood, naturally, saw a ready source of material. Silent films still in production quickly had music added; hastily written numbers which unexpectedly became standards included 'Charmaine' (from *What Price Glory?*), 'Diane' (from *Seventh Heaven*) and the title song to 1929's *Ramona*. This song, almost single-handedly, made the film $1.5 million at the box office.*

Silent stars were dropped like hotcakes by the studios and replaced with Broadway stars. Harold Lloyd's playmate Bebe Daniels never even got a chance to do a voice test for Paramount before her contract was cancelled, so she went to RKO and starred with John Boles, singing the sweet, airy 'You're Always in My Arms' in their hugely successful 1929 adaptation of *Rio Rita*.

After *The Singing Fool* and *Rio Rita*, pretty much anything with music was signed up. *On with the Show* and *Gold Diggers of Broadway* (both 1929) were static films with static sets. The camera had gained

---

* Fans of the 1960s Irish balladeers the Bachelors might spot a pattern here: all three songs gave the group Top 10 hits in 1964. 'Charmaine' had been an even bigger hit for Mantovani in 1952, but more on him later.

a voice but lost the use of its legs. Microphones now had to be stuffed
into vases filled with flowers and hidden just behind the rigid actors.
Cinematography skills learned in the silent era were now largely worthless, given that a rustling beaded dress could ruin a take. 'If you had a
letter in a scene,' recalled director Rouben Mamoulian, 'it had to be
soaked in water, like that it didn't make a thunderous crackle. But, of
course, it looked like a Dalí watch.'

Rather more inventive was the access-all-areas 'backstage' musical, a
trend that began with *Broadway Melody* (1929). 'The microphone and
its twin camera poke themselves into dressing rooms, into rich parties
and hotel bedrooms,' said *Photoplay*. It was 'alive in turn with titters and
tears' and was the first musical to win an Oscar. Two dozen dancing girls
featured in its set piece, Arthur Freed's 'The Wedding of the Painted
Doll', which celebrated 'all the little dollies from the Follies with their
painted cheeks'. An ex of Freed's, and a D. W. Griffith veteran, Bessie
Love starred as half of a sister team with Anita Page: 'When we were
doing the musical numbers, the orchestra was playing right along with
us. It was all direct recording. By the time we did *Hollywood Revue of
1929*, though, a few months after *Broadway Melody*, we recorded the
musical numbers first, and then acted to them on playback, like they do
now. So you can see how fast things were happening.'

Anything successful was cloned by every other studio. *Hollywood
Revue of 1929* was the first all-star movie, and being an MGM film, it
had the very biggest stars: Norma Shearer, Joan Crawford, Laurel and
Hardy, John Gilbert and Bessie Love (it was also the first place most
people heard Arthur Freed and Nacio Herb Brown's song 'Singin' in the
Rain', performed by Cliff Edwards and the Brox Sisters). Within months
it was a formula, aped by *Fox Movietone Follies*, Warner Brothers' *Show
of Shows*, *Paramount on Parade* and Universal's *The King of Jazz*, with
Paul Whiteman. *Photoplay* wasn't fooled by this rapid-fire output: 'The
situations have whiskers,' it said of 1929's *On with the Show*. 'The conversation consists of snappy come-backs, 1910 variety.'

It's worth remembering that *The King of Jazz* was made in this spirit
– a cheapie compendium of star names, filmed with static cameras, and
loosely linked by the biggest bandleader of the day, Paul Whiteman. It

was no history of jazz, wasn't taken as such by anyone other than miffed Bix Beiderbecke fans, and the title was probably thought up in less than a minute – something to pull in the folks who'd paid to see, or at least tried to see, *The Jazz Singer*.

When the studios weren't trying so hard to make all-star blockbusters, they made short films that accompanied the newsreels before the main feature, and these brought stars of stage and vaudeville into main-street cinemas, including Rudy Vallee, Sophie Tucker, Red Nichols and His Five Pennies, Ethel Merman and Ruth Etting. *Favourite Melodies* was the title of Etting's 1929 five-minute Paramount short, which introduced her as 'the sweetheart of Columbia Records'. She sang the weepie 'My Mother's Eyes' (later recorded by Frankie Valli as his debut single, a few years before he joined the Four Seasons) and a jazzier tune called 'That's Him Now', which allowed her to stretch the odd vowel and sigh the occasional line in a very fetching way. Wearing a dark evening dress with a rosebud trim, Etting stayed rooted to the spot, and between the two songs you can hear – in a ridiculously endearing way – the singer clear her throat and swallow before launching into 'That's Him Now' with vim. You couldn't pause a Vitaphone disc once the recording had started, so Etting's shy cough was preserved for the ages.

By 1929 Los Angeles was estimated to have 2,000 Broadway refugees, from Marilyn Miller and Al Jolson down, and it needed songwriters badly. An advance party was sent in the form of Buddy De Sylva, Lew Brown and Ray Henderson, the team who had already written standards like 'Sonny Boy', 'Button Up Your Overcoat', 'The Best Things in Life Are Free' and 'The Birth of the Blues'. They immediately struck gold with the musical comedy *Sunny Side Up*, about shop girl Janet Gaynor, who lives above a New York grocery store, and unhappy millionaire Charles Farrell. Gaynor and Farrell became the screen sweethearts of 1929, and the film was clearly a cut above warmed-over, whiskered Broadway oldies. Its songs included 'Turn on the Heat', cut in 1929 by Fats Waller, and 'I'm a Dreamer, Aren't We All', which would be recorded by Bing Crosby (with Paul Whiteman), and later by John Coltrane. De Sylva, Brown and Henderson's success with *Sunny Side Up* convinced other New York songwriters to move west. 'We had all sorts of ominous warnings,' said Richard Rodgers in 1930, 'all the routine fables about stars who ate peas with their knives.' On the train to Hollywood, he wrote home that he was anxious about 'what it's like, and how I'm going to get along with this strange business and these strange people'.*

* * *

Richard Rodgers and Lorenz Hart were contracted to Warner Brothers, who, according to a 1930 interview with Rodgers, bent over backwards for their new influx of New Yorkers: 'They gave us the cast we wanted. They've put every facility at our disposal, given us intelligent co-operation . . . My God, offices with oriental rugs, studio cars at your disposal, and people to carry your papers so you won't strain yourself.' Their first musical was *The Hot Heiress* (1931), with Ben Lyon and Ona Munson, who were a toothsome enough couple, but neither songwriter saw Lyon or Munson as singers. They had no say in the matter.

In the meantime, Rodgers and Hart were due to fly to London, where their show *Ever Green* was opening. Rodgers remembered Gertrude Lawrence sending her car to collect them, 'with a polite but firm request to appear' at the residence of one Major Butler: 'It seems that Prince George (the Duke of Kent) had asked for us to be there. There were only the Prince, Gertie, Noël [Coward], Larry [Hart], the Butlers and me, but the King of Greece was there for a while as well. We had supper and played and sang til quite late, which was a lot of fun. Larry only knocked over one glass.' He had less fun when Tallulah Bankhead turned up unannounced at his rooms with 'three bright young things. Bankhead got badly boiled on champagne, which she demanded, broke glassware, did imitations, looked awful, and finally left at 3.45 a.m.

---

* Anita Loos recalled in her memoir *Kiss Hollywood Goodbye* that the journey from the east to the west coast took five days and two trains, 'but what a de luxe five days! Compartments glittered with polished mahogany, shiny brass and red brocade; the seats flaunted antimacassars of heavy lace . . . the maître d'hôtel would come to the compartment to announce that he'd acquired some trout caught that morning in an icy mountain stream of Colorado.'

Good old London!'

The much-anticipated *Ever Green* opened at the New Adelphi Theatre in December 1930. Its star was the melancholically pretty Jessie Matthews, who twirled around inside a massive chandelier. The sets were so large and elaborate that rehearsals had taken place at Alexandra Palace, the only space in London large enough to take them all. *Tatler* called it 'a peep show, a kaleidoscope, a merry-go-round, a miracle, all Hollywood and all Heaven'. It featured 'Dancing on the Ceiling' and 'Dear Dear', both of which were singled out for praise. The *Observer* called it 'the Ascot of musical shows', and Rodgers and Hart had another hit on their hands. Matthews remembered Rodgers as 'a wonderful worker. Larry Hart couldn't care less about anything. You had to pin him down to get any lyric from him. He would wander round the theatre and you had to grab him. I did "My Heart Stood Still" but there was no verse. We had to pin him down, and suddenly he took an envelope out of his pocket.' He handed Matthews the envelope, dictated the lyric immediately off the top of his head and said, 'How's that?' So Rodgers played the verse 'and I sang from this tatty little envelope'.

Rodgers missed the premiere of *Ever Green* – he had already gone back to the States with his pregnant wife. On arriving back at their new Hollywood home, he discovered that *The Hot Heiress* had done so badly that Warner Brothers had bought Rodgers and Hart out of their contract.

* * *

The legend 'From the Broadway hit of the same name' seemed to feature on every other film poster. The market was flooded in 1929 and 1930, and the original Broadway stars brought in to reprise their roles were often ill suited to the screen. Marilyn Miller came out west to film *Sally* (1929) and *Sunny* (1930), but ended up making only three films; it was now ten years since she had appeared in *Sally* on Broadway. Any Broadway scrap could be filmed in a fortnight and slung out. Reviewing 1930's *Viennese Nights*, English trade magazine *Bioscope* wrote, 'One of the last in the fast-fading breed of film operettas, which this sort of story helped to kill.'

What Hollywood musicals really needed in order to survive was to lose their static performers; in other words, the movies needed to move again. Ernst Lubitsch, a silent veteran who initially thought the talkies would rob cinema of a certain magic, wanted something more than sound for its own sake. His first attempt was *The Love Parade* (1929), an operetta which introduced the world to soprano Jeanette MacDonald, who co-starred with French comedian Maurice Chevalier; he followed it with *Monte Carlo* (1930), which had MacDonald playing opposite quintessential Englishman Jack Buchanan. The train sequence, during which she sang the evocative 'Beyond the Blue Horizon' – words by Leo Robin ('Diamonds Are a Girl's Best Friend', 'Thanks for the Memory'), music by Richard Whiting ('Too Marvellous for Words', 'On the Good Ship Lollipop') – was worth the price of admission alone, free and exuberant, with the train's motion wedded to the rhythm of the song. Robin later recalled the strange and lonely life of a Broadway writer stranded on the west coast: 'We didn't work, there was nothing to do. You had to report every day. But as long as you reported, it didn't matter whether you stayed there. I had the producers convinced that I could work better at home, or that I couldn't come in early in the morning because I worked late at night. They didn't mind as long as you came in with a song. We managed to pass the time someway, I dunno, playing golf in the afternoon.'

The other Hollywood musical of 1929 to suggest that the fast-sinking genre had a possible future was Rouben Mamoulian's *Applause*, about a washed-up burlesque performer called Kitty Darling, played by Helen Morgan. Mamoulian dared to shoot on location in Manhattan – a first for a musical. Paramount wanted Mae West to play Darling, insisting it needed a glamorous star and that nobody would want to see a blowsy leading lady. Mamoulian held out: 'Naturally, I was not very popular on the lot. Then the reviews came out and they were sensational, saying things like, "Why doesn't Hollywood learn from this?" So it antagonised the people on the coast, who thought of me as an upstart.'

But Hollywood did learn. It was inherently conservative, and would remain so, at least until it was handed a proven winner (which, of course, Mamoulian and Lubitsch had scaled mountains of bureaucracy to achieve). So in 1932 Paramount called up Rodgers and Hart. Things were different now, they said. Rouben Mamoulian will be directing *Love Me Tonight*. This time, you really can do things your way. The post-crash, post-Jazz Age 1930s would be quite another matter. Residents of Hollywood in the '30s included Aldous Huxley, Arnold Schoenberg, P. G. Wodehouse, Berthold Brecht, F. Scott Fitzgerald and Dorothy Parker: the full flower of the arts in the shadow of a giant estate agent's sign – 'Hollywoodland'. It was the lure of the lucre. Certainly, very few people in Hollywood had a clue what to do with this amount of talent. The big names waited – by pools, under lime trees, sipping grenadine – and waited.

18

TEN CENTS A DANCE:
THE GREAT DEPRESSION

In September 1929 the Jazz Age suddenly crashed and crumpled like a Keystone Cops sedan. As the 1930s began, a quarter of America's population was out of work – more than fifteen million people. The price of wheat, corn and cotton was so low that crops were left to rot in the fields. In Britain, the 'land fit for heroes' promised by Lloyd George in 1918 never materialised – war heroes were often not even employable.

In American cities, legitimate nightclubs continued to struggle under Prohibition. In Hollywood, the Paramount-Publix studio went into receivership soon after the 1932 Bing Crosby vehicle *The Big Broadcast*. The Depression set in. A songwriter could come up with either socially conscious hits or songs to make you forget the hard times. Both schools flourished. They may have been in the minority, but when hard times songs arrived, they made their point.

For Yip Harburg, the crash meant losing his electrical appliance business and starting a new profession. 'Here I was in this silly business which I hated, detested, and then 1929 came along and I was left with a pencil. That was it.' Harburg, the most left-leaning of the Broadway writers, wrote 'Brother, Can You Spare a Dime' for a show called *Americana* in 1932 and was well aware of its significance: 'It was a time of bewilderment. The reason the song is important is because it's really a sociological statement. The question the man asked, in the lyric, it wasn't about a hand-out . . . "I built a railroad. I built a tower. I fought your wars. Why am I empty-handed? I produce, why don't I share?" It made a big event an individual statement.' The song was recorded by Bing Crosby and Rudy Vallee, and became the biggest hit of the year.

It wasn't the first major hit of its kind. In 1930 Rodgers and Hart had written another song oozing with social realism, written from the perspective of a woman hiring herself out on the dancefloor: 'Trumpets are breaking my eardrums . . . Come on, big boy, ten cents a dance.' 'Ten Cents a Dance' had been a hit for the Nebraska-raised Ruth Etting, who first made her way to New York in 1927 as an art student, dressed in flapper fineries and with a curled bob, and finding success on Broadway almost immediately. Her friend Irving Berlin introduced her to Florenz Ziegfeld, and pretty soon she was singing Berlin's 'Shaking the Blues Away' in the 1927 Follies, playing alongside Eddie Cantor. She was cute enough to be thrown in at the deep end. 'I was supposed to do a tap dance after I sang the song,' Etting later recalled. 'I worked hard on it, but I was a lousy dancer. When I was halfway through the final rehearsal, Ziegfeld said, "Ruth, when you get through singing, just walk off the stage." I got the message.' By 1928 she was concentrating on her singing, and sang Walter Donaldson's intense, minor-key 'Love Me or Leave Me' in *Whoopee!*, whose Broadway run was cut short by the crash.*

---

* Walter Donaldson was a rare writer in that he straddled Broadway, Hollywood and Tin Pan Alley (which, by the late 1920s, meant the record industry).

Etting had started out in the Chicago nightclubs, where local gangster Martin Snyder – a short, brutish man with a pronounced limp – saw her act and moved in fast. Snyder had ties to show business, introduced her to Irving Berlin and took over her management. You might be able to guess the next part. Etting and Snyder married in 1922, at which point he became violent and controlling. Etting stuck with him out of fear and pity, but her friends finally helped her to get a divorce, after which, in October 1938, the wildly jealous Snyder put a bullet in her new lover, Myrl Alderman. Happily, Myrl wasn't killed, and he married Ruth in December 1938; they stayed together until he died in 1966.

Apart from the fact she's a great singer – and that 1954's *Love Me or Leave Me* (with Doris Day as Etting and James Cagney as Snyder) is one of the great musical biopics – I tell the story of Ruth Etting as a pocket-sized reminder of the grimness of the early 1930s and an explanation for why her quietly desperate 'Ten Cents a Dance' is so effective.

As with any calamitous event, there is always someone who can benefit. In times of starvation, said the gold diggers, get what you can when you can. Hollywood being Hollywood, the philosophy of cute blondes gravitating towards wealthy old men was celebrated on screen with *Gold Diggers of 1933*. Still, even this Busby Berkeley frothery found the smouldering Joan Blondell leaning on a lamp post, singing Harry Warren and Al Dubin's 'Remember My Forgotten Man': 'You put a rifle in his hand, you sent him far away, you shouted, "Hip-hooray!" But look at him today.' The tune is Ashkenazi melancholic; it's amazing Warren and Dubin got it through conservative Hollywood.

These were nervous, disastrous days. But life went on, and mostly, instead of soundtracking the Depression, songs began to remind people how therapeutic music can be. British bandleader Ray Noble reckoned that 'people knew about the social climate and, when it came to songs, they were trying to get away from it. They didn't want to know about

---

Strangely, the 1930 film of *Whoopee!* – the first for Busby Berkeley – dropped 'Love Me or Leave Me', though it added Gus Kahn and Donaldson's delicious 'My Baby Just Cares for Me'. Sung on screen by Eddie Cantor, and a UK success for singer Sam Browne, it would be recorded definitively in 1957 by Nina Simone.

social comment. Songs were for relaxation. And listening to popular songs, you could escape. It's not a means of introducing the mind to what's going on in the world. It's a different thing entirely.'

The Great Depression rapidly put an end to the jazz scene of the Roaring Twenties, as people were no longer attending clubs or buying music, forcing many musicians out of work. Gramophones were put away or thrown out, and radios provided free entertainment. The black community was hit hardest; as a result, the bulk of the major record labels deleted race records from their catalogues.* The hollow-cheeked Hoagy Carmichael had a low-paying but stable job as a songwriter with Southern Music and was fortunate to retain it. Of the new school of Broadway writers, Carmichael was an odd man out. He emerged neither from the conservatories, like Kern, nor from the stage, like Rodgers and Hart, nor from the Tin Pan Alley world of song-plugging, like Gershwin. He appears to have drifted into songwriting almost by accident. As a Midwest college boy, he had been fortunate to strike up a friendship with Bix Beiderbecke, and this exposure to jazz would eventually lead him into the world of songwriting. Hoagy always talked of his debt to Bix.

At Indiana University, Hoagy had been influenced by a Dadaist character called William 'Bunkhaus' Moenkhaus, who built a collective of acolytes around him called Bent Eagle and set up a Midwest version of the Cabaret Voltaire at the Book Nook in Bloomington. According to a Prom-Day Scandal Sheet, under the headline 'BOOK NOOK DEMOLISHED: Disciples of Bent Eagle wreck ancient establishment', 'Hoagie [sic] Carmichael opened hostilities with a cornet solo', which led to 'the crashing of cups, saucers, spoons and other foreign matter'. Moenkhaus's love of hot jazz and spontaneity also encouraged Hoagy to pursue songwriting.

In 1931 Moenkhaus died of a ruptured stomach ulcer; not long after, Bix Beiderbecke drank himself to death. Carmichael was deeply shocked;

---

* Happily, Victoria Spivey proved to be an exception, starring in King Vidor's *Hallelujah!* in 1929, then later appearing in the surreal musical *Hellzapoppin* in 1938. By 1962 she had set up her own label, Spivey Records.

he later wrote that the early 1930s found him 'tiring of jazz and I could see that other musicians were tiring as well. The boys were losing their enthusiasm for the hot stuff . . . No more hot licks, no more thrills.'*

For other, younger writers, the Depression was a kind of blessing. Author John Cheever wrote about the giddy freedom he felt, cut loose from his predestiny with the Whiffenpoofs of Yale. Johnny Mercer was unshackled when his father's real-estate business collapsed. There were no sensible jobs left, so you may as well work on your dream of becoming a novelist or songwriter. The charming Mercer soon hooked up with Hoagy Carmichael, and proved to be just the tonic the ailing Hoagy needed. Together they wrote 'Lazy Bones' in 1933, with its southern vernacular to the fore. Mercer's first hit, it effectively invented a new Tin Pan Alley sub-genre of southern hyper-realism, of which Carmichael and Mercer would become the kings.

The Broadway show took a great leap forward when, in 1931, the Pulitzer Prize went to George and Ira Gershwin for the political satire *Of Thee I Sing*. This was the first such award for a musical, and it did a great deal to raise the status of popular music. The Gershwins' sequel was a different matter. In 1933 *Let 'Em Eat Cake* had the same producer, writers, stars and characters as *Of Thee I Sing*, but it was much darker: President Wintergreen loses his re-election campaign and returns to running his clothing store; when it goes bankrupt because of the Depression, he and former vice president Alexander Throttlebottom organise a Fascist movement to take over the government. It ran for less than a hundred performances.

Most people wanted to hear happy songs, even if they dealt with tough times ('Button Up Your Overcoat', 'A Cup of Coffee and You', 'Get Happy'). One of the more ambivalent but relatable hits came from writers Howard Dietz and Arthur Schwartz, while they were working on a revue called *The Band Wagon*. One night at Dietz's house, Schwartz said, 'I wanna write a song that has more than a romantic meaning, that

* According to Ian Fleming's *Casino Royale*, James Bond bears a strong resemblance to Hoagy Carmichael – though Fleming had a touch of Hoagy about him too. Fleming would repeat the comparison in *Moonraker*, the third James Bond novel. It was quite a claim to fame.

says something about man's existence. I don't want to be pompous about it, but let's try and think of a mood for such a song.' He had a library, and Dietz went from book to book looking for ideas for titles. He came across a book called *Dancers in the Dark*. Schwartz recalled his words: "'That's it. 'Dancing in the Dark'." I got his meaning immediately, in the sense that all of us are dancing in the dark. I went home and played this melody as if I'd known it all my life.' In the dark, confusing days of the Depression, people could empathise with 'waltzing in the wonder of why we're here'.

* * *

'Sweet' bandleader Guy Lombardo reckoned the Depression 'helped the band scene, oh sure. The Depression made it possible for people to be entertained and sit at home. You wanted to dance on Saturday night? Lift up the rug and away you go. And the bands made money, because the hotels made money, because the people went to the hotels. Every band of any importance had a commercial [radio] programme.' Sweet music was a style designed for dancing. After all, dancing was something that everybody in the Depression could afford to do. Even if you didn't think you had much talent for it, Lombardo made sure you could dance to his records. A slow, two-beat tempo played quietly – that way you could talk to the boy or girl you were dancing with. He scored the biggest hit version of Walter Donaldson's 'You're Driving Me Crazy' in 1930, which would go on to become a UK number one for megaphone-led revivalists the Temperance Seven in 1961; other Lombardo best-sellers included 'Goodnight Sweetheart' (1931), 'Paradise' (1932) and 'The Last Round Up', from the *Ziegfeld Follies of 1934*. Playing what they called 'the sweetest music this side of heaven', Lombardo's Royal Canadians outlasted everyone. They were around from 1918 to 1977, performed new year shows on radio and TV starting in 1929, and performed at the inaugurations for seven presidents. They played music straight and stuck to the way a melody was written, and people loved them for that.

Dance bands tended to be predominantly 'hot' or 'sweet', but Roger Wolfe Kahn's fell somewhere in between. He was the son of a wealthy German–Jewish banker; by 1923, when he turned sixteen, he had already learned to play eighteen instruments. At this point he precociously formed his own orchestra. With money in his pocket, Kahn smartly hired some of the best jazz musicians available, particularly for recordings – Joe Venuti, Eddie Lang, Artie Shaw, Jack Teagarden, Red Nichols and Gene Krupa – and in 1927 he even made the cover of *Time* magazine. Highlights included his own 'Crazy Rhythm' (1928) and Fats Waller's 'Sheltered by the Stars, Cradled by the Moon' (1932), on which he was helped out by silky harmony act the Kahn-a-Sirs. Oddly, Kahn never played on his band's recordings. Not having to make money from the band meant he was always doing it for fun, but by the mid-1930s Kahn got bored and decided to become a pilot instead.

For those who couldn't handle anything remotely spicy, for whom Guy Lombardo might be too edgy, Freddy Martin pioneered the 'tenor band' sound in the Marine Room of New York's Bossert Hotel. Martin took the melodic lead, fronting an all-tenor sax section with a lilting style that was soon taken up by sweet bands in provincial hotels and ballrooms across America. Starting with 'Bless Your Heart' and 'April in Paris' in 1933, they were rarely off best-seller lists until the rock era, even scoring sweet-band hits with things like 'The Warsaw Concerto' (1943), 'I've Got a Lovely Bunch of Coconuts' (complete with bizarre English accent, in 1949) and Guy Mitchell's 'My Truly, Truly Fair' (1951). No one would confuse these records with jazz.

As well as Bessie Smith's 'Poor Man's Blues' (possibly) and 'Brother, Can You Spare a Dime' (definitely), you might have heard the Boswell Sisters' 'We've Got to Put That Sun Back in the Sky' on the radio in 1932. Everyone needed that kind of pick-me-up; everybody was struggling. Vaudeville blamed radio for its demise, radio blamed costly star names, and meanwhile, in Chicago, freezing men were burning gramophone records to keep warm. Only six million records were sold in America in 1932, around 6 per cent of 1927's sales figures. Gramophone production fell from 987,000 units to 40,000. Victor, the biggest record company in the first three decades of the twentieth century, ceased to manufacture record players altogether and started producing radios – as well as radio programmes – instead. Radios provided free music in straitened times, which would help soothe a frightened world.

In Britain, though, the Depression didn't kill the record at all. For a start, American radio stations couldn't be heard in Britain, just the buttoned-up BBC. Another less obvious reason is that jukeboxes were far less prevalent: fewer than a hundred could be found in the country during the Depression. If you wanted to hear American music, you had to buy records, so you had to stay loyal to your gramophone. They remained a fixture in the parlour, and record sales barely dipped.

Who was doing well? In Britain, Jack Hylton's dance band became the very biggest thanks to a great deal of clever self-promotion, scoring a hit with 'We're in the Money', from *Gold Diggers of 1933*. Impresarios still commanded attention. The greatest was Charles 'CB' Cochran, the British equivalent of Florenz Ziegfeld. His shows were put on so beautifully that the overheads ruled out any profit, and in 1930 he put on a Cochran Revue at the London Pavilion whose cast included future star Leslie 'Hutch' Hutchinson.

Naturally, there were still class distinctions in Britain, which came across in the various ways music was consumed. The masses bought gramophone records, listened to the wireless and acted out their dreams of being Fred and Ginger, tripping the light fantastic at the local palais. But if you were well-heeled, you would go to the great London hotels for your music, where the bands of the day played what was called 'society music'. By now, American songs were so dominant that more than one hotel manager brought in an American bandleader to add some class to their joint. The Savoy had pianist Carroll Gibbons from Boston, a bespectacled man with pursed lips who allegedly couldn't stand Americans and who, after a brief fling with Hollywood in 1931, became a far bigger name in the UK. A year later, he was leading the Savoy Hotel Orpheans, who cut hundreds of sweet-dance-band sides between 1932 and Gibbons's death in 1954, all featuring him on piano. As a writer, his 'On the Air' was recorded by Rudy Vallee in 1933, but the most fun things he ever wrote were the atypical, rickety piano instrumentals 'Bubbling Over' and 'Moonbeams Dance'.*

---

* Unusually, Gibbons and his orchestra spurned the BBC for a sponsored radio show on the borderline legal Radio Luxembourg. Hartley's Jam got the plugs.

* * *

In 1931 Buddy Bolden and Bix Beiderbecke – the first jazz player and the first jazz superfan – both died. The music's current figurehead, Louis Armstrong, moved from Okeh Records to Victor, confirmation that he was crossing over into mainstream entertainment. In New York, the Fletcher Henderson orchestra recorded a song called 'Radio Rhythm', with Henderson's drummer Walter Johnson switching his basic beat from the bass and snare drums to bass drum and hi-hat, for a subtler, more danceable rhythm. It was a move quickly borrowed by an emerging band in the outpost of Kansas City; led by Bennie Moten, it featured trumpeter Oran 'Hot Lips' Page, bass player Walter Page and the insistent piano of Bill 'Count' Basie. Almost uniquely, the Moten band worked around riffs. It was hard, it stomped.

Like Chicago, Kansas City had been a place you travelled through, maybe stopping, maybe staying. Musicians found it a home-from-home, whether they were jazz players criss-crossing the country or blues players escaping from the South. And in the 1930s Kansas City went out of its way to make them feel welcome. One result was that the division between blues and jazz became non-existent. They were joined at the hip. Musicians certainly made no distinction between them.

One reason jazz and blues blossomed in Kansas City was the corrupt Tom Pendergast regime, which essentially operated as an independent state, ignoring Prohibition, encouraging clubs, effectively setting up a successor to Storyville and accidentally engineering a unique jazz scene. Pendergast had started out running a saloon in the 1890s, and by 1915 he was the leader of the city's Democratic Party, an independent influencer who worked his unelected way up to running the entire city.*

* The Pendergast era would undoubtedly be a high point for Kansas City's cultural relevance and place in American history. The University of Kansas City and the city's art museum were built during this period. Pendergast owned Ready-Mixed Concrete, which was guaranteed the contracts, meaning that construction continued through the Depression as the city's economy and population boomed in the 1920s. It's really hard to know what conclusions to draw from this story.

With a Ten-Year Plan that kicked debts into the long grass, Kansas City's citizens weathered the Great Depression better than almost all other Americans. And thanks to the non-existent local enforcement of drinking laws, the city's nightlife was second to none. Count Basie later described it as a 'wide-open city. That's where life began! You could do anything, go anywhere.'

In the mid-1920s Bill Basie had been a honky-tonk pianist with the Gonzelle White travelling show, a vaudeville act that broke up while playing in Kansas City in 1925. Broke, and with no way of getting back home to New Jersey, Basie took a job playing in a silent-movie cinema, before ending up in Bennie Moten's band. The biggest in the city, with a five-man brass section, by 1932 it had recorded telltale titles like 'Moten Swing', with Basie's piano groove front and centre. Moten died suddenly in 1934, when a surgeon accidentally severed his jugular vein while trying to perform a tonsillectomy. His band, unsurprisingly, broke up soon after, but Basie essentially put them back together under his leadership when they found a residency at the Pendergast mob-connected Reno Club in 1935. The Basie band worked on the Moten band's riff-based sound, using it as a bed for soloists, and brought in singer Jimmy Rushing and stellar tenor saxophonist Lester Young. The sound was pummelling. What's more, the Reno, fortunately for Basie, had broadcasting facilities for the local W9XBY radio station.

Record producer John Hammond happened upon W9XBY while he was in Chicago with Benny Goodman in 1935, and he freaked: 'I had a twelve-tube Motorola with a large speaker, unlike any other car radio in those days. I spent so much time on the road that I wanted a superior instrument to keep me in touch with music around the country. It was one o'clock in the morning. The local stations had gone off the air and the only music I could find was at the top of the dial, 1550 kilocycles, where I picked up W9XBY, an experimental station in Kansas City. The nightly broadcast from the Reno Club was just beginning. I couldn't believe my ears.'

The timing couldn't have been better. Hammond took the Basie band's hard-swinging Kansas blues to New York and cut some of the greatest records of the era: 'One O'Clock Jump', 'Topsy', 'Jumpin' at the Woodside', 'Jive at Five', 'Sent for You Yesterday'.*

Hammond had never wanted for money and used his position to encourage and support the music he loved. He was the great-grandson of railroad owner Cornelius Vanderbilt, and had been raised in a house which had its own ballroom, as well as sixteen servants to look after the infant Hammond. From the age of twelve he had collected records, and he dropped out of Yale to write about jazz. 'I was a New York social dissident,' said the boy who had been going to Harlem speakeasies since he was seventeen. 'I heard no colour in the music.' He was possibly the first person in the music industry to understand that music was an agent of change, the first significant 'artist-friendly' industry man, and his money gave him muscle in the Depression. By 1932, through his columns for Britain's *Melody Maker*, Hammond arranged for the struggling US Columbia label to provide recordings for its UK namesake, recording Fletcher Henderson, Benny Goodman, Benny Carter and Joe Venuti when record sales were so bad that many of them wouldn't have otherwise had the opportunity to enter a studio.†

* * *

The end of the Depression came into sight when, on 8 November 1932, Herbert Hoover was destroyed in the presidential election. The

---

* After Tom Pendergast's fall (and imprisonment) in 1938, Kansas City lost its clubs. Jazz musicians moved on to New York and the west coast, leaving just the blues players. The result was an intensification, a new urban blues, written and recorded for a black audience by black musicians featuring loud, amplified, electric guitars and high, wailing vocals. Accommodated, adapted, it became the bedrock of rock 'n' roll, the key root of modern pop. For now, it would stay localised. The exception was Louis Jordan, who became a huge star in the 1940s. When the jazzers left town, he couldn't have cared less: 'Those guys really wanted to play mostly for themselves, and I wanted to play for people.'

† Hammond also bought a Lower East Side theatre for black musicians in the 1930s and would go on to advance the careers of not just Basie but Fletcher Henderson, Teddy Wilson and Billie Holiday. And he later signed Bob Dylan, Leonard Cohen and Aretha Franklin to Columbia. If he had a high opinion of himself, it was justified.

Democrat Franklin D. Roosevelt took every state, bar a handful in the north-east. Could he turn things around? In 1933 he pledged the New Deal, raising spirits immediately by repealing Prohibition after thirteen dry years. Within weeks, 52nd Street was awash with new bars. On the radio was FDR's secret running mate, a constant voice of kindness, empathy and reassurance. Through the Depression and on to the end of the decade, Bing Crosby was never far away.

19

NOTHING BUT BLUE SKIES: BING CROSBY

You get the feeling that he's letting you in on something very important to you, something he wants to tell you about, now that you and he are alone together.

Charles Henderson, *How to Sing for Money* (1939)

The Jazz Singer had been the first movie in which the human voice was heard. The next significant voice to be seen and heard at the cinema, one that was way less stentorian, was Bing Crosby's. He popped up as part of a trio that sang with Paul Whiteman's band in *The King of Jazz*, and he would be the first singer to use technology to shape his sound. Al Jolson had piggy-backed onto new technology with *The Jazz Singer* but didn't see any advantage to it beyond short-term gain, a way to temporarily stave off his own redundancy. Crosby was very different; he understood microphone technology was the future of recorded sound. Technology helped him to become the world's first multimedia star.

Crosby also had a quality that Jolson lacked and probably wouldn't have wanted: intimacy. It helped him to become the first jazz-ballad singer. The intimacy is there from the beginning, in a brace of songs from *Showboat* – 'Ol' Man River' and 'Make Believe' – recorded with Paul Whiteman in 1928, when he was twenty-four years old. They were sung deep, with strong currents, but also in a voice that was warm and gentle and clean. Though he worked at his apparent nonchalance, Bing had total control. He was a natural. His younger brother, bandleader Bob Crosby: 'I think first of all, to be an innovator, to be a musician of any creativity, you have to have ears. You know what I mean by ears? You have to hear the sound, recognise it, and know what to do with it. And I think Bing has a great ear for music. He certainly had no vocal training. I think it came natural to him – he did his thing, and he did it different to anyone else.'

Bing had 'swing', an ear for timing and a voice to articulate it, and that's something you can't fake. His timing was strong enough that musicians followed him, which is rare for a singer. And his voice was elegant and effortless, a rich, two-octave baritone that he used like a painter, playing with shades and shadows, colouring the music. Ralph Gleason, reviewing Crosby's autobiography *Call Me Lucky* in 1953, wrote that 'Bing is the personification of the whole jazz movement – the relaxed, casual, natural and uninhibited approach to art.'

Rudy Vallee recalled being in Baltimore in 1927 to play a debutante ball in a gymnasium. Bing's trio the Rhythm Boys were lower down the bill and were playing to a disinterested crowd, accompanied by only a piano. 'Suddenly one of them walked to the centre of the floor and delivered "Montmartre Rose". There were no amplifying systems in those days and I could scarcely hear his rendition. When he had finished there was a deafening roar of applause which called for at least one

or two encores. Instead he walked off . . . You might have thought him
deaf, so unaware he seemed of the sensation he had created. But then,
this insouciance has always characterised Bing Crosby.'

It's almost obscene how big a star Crosby once was, and how little he seems to mean now. His hugeness can be proven with science.
During the war, his radio programmes attracted fifty million listeners in
America. Of the five highest-grossing Hollywood movies in 1946, three
of them – *The Bells of St Mary's*, *Blue Skies*, *Road to Utopia* – starred Bing
Crosby; he was the number-one box-office star for five years straight,
from 1944 to 1948. He recorded nearly four hundred hit singles, an
achievement no one – not Frank Sinatra, Elvis Presley, Beyoncé or
Kanye West – has come remotely close to matching, and probably no
one ever will. Beyond all this, he played a major role in the development
of tape-recording, so influencing recording and radio broadcasting for
years after his hit records ended.

* * *

In the beginning he had been Harry Crosby from Spokane, and he sang
in a harmony trio called the Rhythm Boys, who were signed up to Paul
Whiteman's organisation. Whiteman singled out Bing as the star, luring
him away from the trio and giving him instruments to play, as in 1927
no jazz band – or orchestra – had ever featured anyone who merely sang.
Bing could just about bash a dustbin lid, but that was it. And so, to look
the part, Whiteman gave him a horn without a mouthpiece and a rubber-
stringed violin. He was effectively miming half of his performance.

The Rhythm Boys weren't an immediate success. On Broadway their
routine seemed cornball, their jokes stale, and so they were ignomin-
iously shunted down the pecking order, left to perform in clubs' lobbies during intermissions. Luckily for them, another fringe Whiteman
organisation member was Harry Barris, who wrote a song for them
called 'Mississippi Mud': 'They don't need no band, they keep time by
clapping their hands. Just as happy as a cow chewing on a cud, when the
darkies beat their feet on the Mississippi mud.' It would later be revived
by Dean Martin, Dinah Shore and the Muppets, among others, though

the offending chorus line now ran, 'It's a treat to beat your feet on the Mississippi mud.'

There were traces of Mississippi mud in Bing's voice, even without the jazz melisma he was gradually adding. Bing was – literally – colour blind. During their Broadway sojourn, he and his fellow Rhythm Boy Al Rinker would venture up to Harlem and the Cotton Club. He learned a lot from those trips. Later, Bing would sing alongside Eddie Lang's picked, rhythmic jazz guitar in the Whiteman band; he worked out how to rest the chassis of his syllables on its wheels.

Crooning had made him a star, but there didn't seem to be a long-term career in it. It was a pop sensation, a great big joke to some, who thought being intimate and natural was a bit unnatural. People said it was 'girlish' for a grown man to speak tender words of love, not like those manly Sousa marches or old Caruso with his leathery lungs. People were used to the Jolsons and Cantors of this world throwing themselves all over the stage and shouting at the tops of their voices. Once the Depression hit hard under Hoover, crooning felt tied to the carefree, Dionysian 1920s. You needed to be special to outlive the craze.

In 1931 Bing left Whiteman and went solo. The same year, Mack Sennett helped Bing escape from the straitjacket of crooning by featuring him in a few short films, taking his fame to another level by giving him a face and a body. To the surprise of his detractors, it turned out Bing didn't take himself too seriously. In fact, he made fun of himself – the singing star, the playboy, the cocktail aficionado. In films, he always played 'Bing'; in 1932's *The Big Broadcast*, his full film debut, his name cropped up twenty-three times in the opening five minutes. Like Elvis, there was only ever going to be one Bing.* By 1931, with Crosby as America's brightest singing star, adored by men and women alike, as well as musicians, CBS had given him a radio show that would run weekly from coast to coast for the next quarter of a century.

As a crooner, Bing was smart enough to be flexible, and he liked to loosen his tuxedo and add a little jazz to the menu (compare his flowing

---

* Unlike Elvis, he always took co-billing on his films, wary of accepting all the credit for their success or failure.

'The Very Thought of You' to Roy Fox's stiffer take). He was also smart enough to distance himself from a fad. 'I am not a crooner,' he insisted. 'A crooner is a person who sings with half a voice and takes the top notes with a falsetto. I always sing in full voice.' He was far more adventurous than Rudy or Russ, dancing around a melody, unexpectedly breaking out into scat-singing or a whistling break, teasing the song but always eventually landing back on the melody. He had learned his phrasing from Louis Armstrong, and his scat-singing was so on the beat, a perfect rhythmic extension of his performance. Armstrong aside, he was the most influential jazz singer of the early 1930s, and the two men genuinely loved each other. Crosby said Armstrong was 'the beginning and the end of music in America', while Armstrong claimed Crosby was 'a natural genius the day he was born. Ever since Bing first opened his mouth, he was the boss of all singers and still is.' In the 1960s Tony Bennett would call Bing 'a pop singer who sang jazz. He created a psychological way of performing . . . how he learned to communicate on radio. He actually had people hypnotised for many years, no one could get past that. There was really no one else. He was like fifteen Beatles.' And, as with the Beatles, a bunch of acts got off the ground by aping him closely – Dick Haymes, Perry Como, Dean Martin, Frank Sinatra.

Once he'd loosened his tie, he also loved to drink. Prohibition was no boundary. Singing when he drank quite possibly helped that melisma, that slide, the easy charm, the mumble. Dean Martin would package it all together years later as a lifestyle choice, swaying and slurring on TV while being secretly sober, but for Bing it was real, and it was quite definitely a help. It was also most certainly a hindrance. He was originally due to appear in a couple of solo spots in *The King of Jazz*, but crashed his car in front of the Hotel Roosevelt and was slung in jail for forty days. Paul Whiteman was understandably furious and gave the solo showcases to John Boles. Bing got no more space than the other Rhythm Boys, singing 'A Bench in the Park' with the curly-mopped Brox Sisters.

Bing had never been trained to sing, and so, like most amateurs, he sang from his vocal chords rather than his diaphragm. The combination of this, his workload and the nights spent in speakeasies drinking the country dry meant he was quickly destroying his voice. It's worth remembering that at the turn of the 1930s there was still a blurred line between classical and popular music. Irish tenor John McCormack was most definitely seen as a popular singer, and operatic baritones like Lawrence Tibbett, John Charles Thomas and soon-to-be Hollywood star Nelson Eddy were recording the same songs as Bing. It's also worth noting that his early-1930s recordings can sound un-Bing to anyone used to his rich, casual baritone, partly because to keep up with his operatic pop rivals he would try and reach for high notes that just weren't in his natural register, giving him a Jolson-like blare. He was a star but still hadn't entirely worked out how he sounded best. What made his voice stand out was that bottom end, the same thing that would make Johnny Cash's impossibly cellar-deep 'I Walk the Line' stand out in the late 1950s. Bing also made it seem so easy, so conversational; if John McCormack had tried a low E flat, he'd have sounded like an impatient frog. In 1933, just as Bing turned thirty, nodes developed on his throat; doctors said he urgently needed an operation. Instead, Bing saw this as an opportunity for an extended-rest cure. When he returned to the radio, his voice had changed noticeably: it was softer, warmer, slightly raspier, but more nuanced, and any trace of Jolson blare was gone. By putting his feet up, he'd become an even better singer. There's a lesson for all of us in there.

Crosby was so comfortable in Hollywood that it may as well have been his front room. *The Big Broadcast* (1932) was a good place to start a film career, and it still stands up. There's a super-modern, slightly surreal scene with the Boswell Sisters as singing telephonists, a mass of bare arms and cables. In another scene, the Mills Brothers bomb through 'Tiger Rag', one of the most joyous noises ever recorded. It wasn't a musical as such; songs were in the film but, with the exception of 'Here Lies Love', sung by a downhearted Bing as he builds a pyre of photos of his wicked ex, they didn't relate to the storyline. It didn't matter. He was already comfortable laughing at himself. In another scene, he tries to cheer up a lonesome drunk in a bar. 'You've got a nice face,' says the stranger. Bing smiles. 'Take a good look at it . . . You don't recognise me? Bing! *Crosby!*'

On screen he casually romanced Joan Fontaine, Rhonda Fleming, Frances Farmer, Betty Hutton and Dorothy Lamour. Rudy Vallee and Russ Columbo had been too busy wooing the ladies off screen, Columbo even having to ditch his girlfriend, the gorgeous Dorothy Dell, to stay available for the masses. Looking like any other Joe, Bing sang 'I Don't Stand a Ghost of a Chance with You' to his leading lady. The boys related, the girls melted, and so he became the number-one romantic lead, while also keeping the male population onside. Singing in the shower, many thought they were just like him, and Crosby was as aware of this relatability as Sinatra would be two decades on. But until then Bing ruled. Joel Whitburn's chart books credit him with thirty-seven number ones between 1931 and 1948. Among the best were 'Out of Nowhere' (1931), 'Brother, Can You Spare a Dime' (1933), 'Pennies from Heaven' (1936), 'I've Got a Pocketful of Dreams' (1938), 'Moonlight Becomes You' (1942), 'Don't Fence Me In' (1944) and the ultimate homecoming song, 'It's Been a Long, Long Time' (1945). These records were era-defining.

He was funny too. Back in 1932 he had met another radio personality, twenty-nine-year-old Londoner Bob Hope, at New York's Capitol Theatre, and they got on just swell. It would be another eight years before they starred together in 1940's *The Road to Singapore*, but thereafter they made a whole string of *Road* movies that gleefully messed about with Hollywood norms, like a real-life Bugs and Daffy: 'He's gonna sing, folks. Now's the time to go out and get the popcorn.' In 1942 Bing danced with Fred Astaire in *Holiday Inn* and wasn't disgraced. (Astaire said Bing was his favourite dance partner. He was probably kidding, but still . . .) Two years later, he won an Oscar for *Going My Way*, the film that gave us 'Swinging on a Star': 'I couldn't be more surprised if I won the Kentucky derby,' he smiled. (It was rumoured that he used his Oscar as a doorstop.) *Holiday Inn* also contained an Irving Berlin song that, no matter how little else they recall about Crosby, people will remember him for. 'White Christmas' – a festive song with a plangent, decidedly Jewish feel – went beyond the popularity of any song before or since. Unsurprisingly, it was the number-one hit on the *Billboard* record charts in 1942. But then it repeated the feat in 1944. And again, louder, in

1945. You had to feel for anyone writing other seasonal songs while the war was still on, but none captured the feeling of home as well. It was so popular that the original recording stamper wore out from being used so many times, and the song had to be re-recorded in 1947. In 1954 they built a whole movie around it.* Eventually, it sold fifty million copies.

Technology had made him. Crooning aside, Crosby was one of the best-loved radio presenters. In 1934 he became the host of *Kraft Music Hall* on the NBC Red Network,† a live production that solidly topped the ratings for a decade, thanks to Bing's humour and easy charm, rubbing along with glamorous guests like Lucille Ball and the Andrews Sisters,‡ or talking about baseball and hitting it straight down the middle with Nat King Cole.

He would get his opportunity to give something back to the tech world in the summer of 1945, with the war finally at an end. Bing had decided that doing a live show every week was too demanding, and when NBC wanted him to broadcast the *Kraft Music Hall* live twice, once for the west coast and once for the east, that made his mind up. After eleven years at NBC, he quit. He wanted to spend time with his family, he told them. More than that, he wanted to play golf.

Meanwhile, something was brewing in a tiny electronics lab in San Francisco. One of the spoils of World War II would be the Magnetophon tape recorder. The Germans discovered in 1943 that an oxide coating on magnetic tape created sound reproduction that was incredibly close to the real thing, way ahead of anything yet created in Britain or America (Hitler used Magnetophon tapes of his speeches to enable him to be in more than one place at the same time). Jack

---

* The song is introduced in the movie with typical Bing-like grace. 'What's that you're playing?' Rosemary Clooney asks him. 'Oh, just a little tune I've been fooling around with.'
† 'You've got that something in your voice so right for selling cheese,' sang Bob Hope in 'Put It There, Pal'.
‡ Maxene Andrews of the Andrews Sisters: 'The first thing that you learned about Bing was that he was the epitome of the singing partner. The second thing you learned was that though he was a great, great gentleman he could be just a little moody. If that hat was planted firmly on his head, don't kid around; if that hat was real jaunty – why, then you could kid him. A little.'

Mullin was in the US Army Signal Corps, his unit tasked with uncovering the formulas behind German electronics. The Magnetophon he found in Frankfurt was one of the great secrets of the Axis propaganda machine. Mullin managed to liberate a pair of Magnetophons from a German radio station in Bad Nauheim (where Elvis Presley would later serve his time in the US army), plus fifty reels of tape, and had them shipped back to the States a few pieces at a time in numerous mail sacks. Back home in San Francisco, he rebuilt them and, a year later, gave a demonstration of his adopted, slightly adapted machine at MGM studios. He had hoped to interest the film industry, which snubbed him, but one of Crosby's assistants was there and relayed the news back to his boss.

Bing quickly realised that pre-recording his radio show on tape would solve all his problems. He was so impressed that he sent a tiny Californian company called Ampex a cheque for $50,000 to help their research into tape recording and ensure he would get the first machine they produced. He didn't even bother with a covering letter. Thanks to Crosby's largesse, Ampex's six-man operation would expand and begin production of the Ampex 200 reel-to-reel tape recorder. Bing switched to ABC and began to broadcast his *Philco Radio Time*. It was pre-recorded, but nobody knew.* Just for good measure, he would give one of the first Ampex 200s to Les Paul, who, with his wife Mary Ford, would go on to create the first, outrageous-sounding multitrack hit records with 'Mocking Bird Hill' and 'How High the Moon' in 1951. Crosby had just made possible the production of recordable master tapes, which revolutionised not just radio entertainment but recording-studio facilities, the quality of vinyl records and, later, TV production and (posthumously for Bing) home videos. Even his time on the golf course was well spent: Bing not only got nine holes-in-one during his lifetime, but

---

* On one live show Crosby went down a little too well, his audience laughing so long and so hard that it cut into the show's running time. Jack Mullin was about to chuck the excised tape in the bin when Crosby told him to save it for future use. Crosby's editor Bob Phillips cut the laughter into forty-two separate segments, from outbursts to sniggers to groans from the audience, as well as the reactions of the orchestra. This was the birth of the 'laugh track'.

invented the pro–celebrity golf tournament. The original fundraising pop singer, he made millions for charity.

Can someone who meant so much to so many people for so long have nothing to say to us now? Why has his star dimmed? There are a few reasons. For a start, a large chunk of his catalogue was banal, the result of singing everything he was given by Jack Kapp at Brunswick. The forays into Irish ballads, cowboy songs and jazz cool may have been key to helping Bing lose his crooner tag, making him so beloved as to become a member of everyone's extended family, but in becoming an everyman figure his feel for jazz, as well as his sex appeal, got somewhat lost. (Not many would hold a torch for Bing things like 1934's tulip-crazed 'Little Dutch Mill'.) Secondly, he wasn't adventurous enough with his arrangers, working mostly with the thoroughly competent John Scott Trotter and letting his voice do the heavy lifting. Thirdly, and most significantly, he didn't manage his legacy at all well. Given that he prophetically understood the possibilities of technology, it seems odd that he struggled to take advantage of the album era. He should have found the transition a piece of cake. Frank Sinatra would begin to eclipse him in popularity by the mid-1940s, but that's no reason why Bing couldn't have cut a string of concept albums with top arrangers in the 1950s. Besides, he began the post-war era strongly, with one of his biggest hits, 'Galway Bay', spending five solid months at the top of *Melody Maker*'s sheet-music chart in 1947, while the very first UK singles chart in November 1952 would include his 'Isle of Innisfree' at number four.*

At the start of the 1950s the usurper Sinatra's career already seemed to be fading, while Bing's position – on film, radio and gramophone – seemed unassailable. Back when albums were still collections of bound 78s, Bing had recorded hugely popular collections of songs from his films: *Blue Skies*, *The Road to Utopia*, *Going My Way*. Then there was 1947's *Drifting and Dreaming*, eight late-night tunes with a soft Hawaiian feel courtesy of Les Paul's trio, and including a deeply affecting, somnambulant take on Irving Berlin's 'When I Lost You', backed

---

* 'Galway Bay' is still remembered, largely thanks to being referenced in the Pogues and Kirsty MacColl's 'Fairytale of New York'.

by a murky mix of organ and vibraphone. It's a beautiful collection. But in the 1950s the triumphs became scattered and seemingly random. Get-togethers with pally contemporaries resulted in *Bing and Louis* (1960) and a delicious travelogue suite with Rosemary Clooney (*Fancy Meeting You Here*, 1958), but part of the problem was the number of vinyl albums that appeared simultaneously collecting his dozens of 78s from the 1930s and '40s. The sheer weight of his past held him back; new things were lost among the several volumes of *Past Masters* and collections with titles like *Golden Memories*. Then again, pictured with a pipe on the sleeve of a 1956 album called *Songs I Wish I Had Sung (The First Time Around)*, the signals were strong that Bing just wasn't bothered about staying on the treadmill. Maybe the jet age mirrored by the sharp artwork of Sinatra's *Come Fly with Me* just didn't sit well with the soft edges of a cardie-wearing man who had turned fifty three years before his final major hit, 'True Love', a 1956 duet with Grace Kelly that featured in *High Society*.

Even the later patronage of his erstwhile rival Sinatra, who signed him to his Reprise label in 1963, couldn't extract more than a few cosy, unchallenging sessions from Bing. More's the pity. In 1967 his space-race challenging 'What Do We Do with the World' was evidence on its own that he could easily keep pace with the Rat Pack, if not the Beatles. It turned out to be a one-off great single, but Bing cut little else of note between then and his death in 1977.

Crosby was in Spain, having just finished a round of golf, when his heart gave out. He had ardently guided America through the Depression, and would ease it gently through World War II. He had shown the world how to love jazz, and made us laugh out loud on damp, grey, BBC2 Saturday afternoons. He had defined what it was like to be an American in the middle of the twentieth century. Everything Bing did fitted together as part of his persona. Everything came easy to him, even dying.

20

INDUSTRIAL LIGHT AND MAGIC:
THE MOVIE MUSICAL

The whole history of making pictures is 'how much is it gonna cost?'
  Harry Warren

By 1930 Hollywood had nearly destroyed itself with static, wafer-thin musicals that were released seemingly every other day. Even minor Broadway shows were adapted: none of Rodgers and Hart's *Present Arms*, *Spring Is Here* or *Heads Up!* had been major hits, but all were rushed into production out west. And yet Hollywood not only survived the Wall Street Crash, it thrived during the Depression that followed. The musical re-emerged as a viable movie staple with *42nd Street* in 1933. Escapism was the order of the day. What's more, the movie musical made the stage seem obsolete, and Broadway would – for the entirety of the 1930s – be stripped of much of its talent and its customers.

Western Electric and RCA had begun to create directional microphones in 1932, which not only meant that cameras didn't have to remain static any more, they also improved sound recording, giving gentler voices and softer timbres a chance. Also key to the rebirth of the Hollywood musical was the arrival of someone who had never been behind a camera, had never written or sung a note, and had never even taken a dance lesson. Busby Berkeley had worked as a choreographer on Broadway before the inevitable move west led to his early work on Samuel Goldwyn's Eddie Cantor musicals. Their first together was *Whoopee!* in 1930; a year later came *Palmy Days*, which summed up the Berkeley spectacle. Cantor excitedly sang 'Yes, Yes', looking forward to a honeymoon in Niagara Falls ('We're gonna do things, we're gonna do new things, my honey loves new things, she told me so!'); he then danced with a new and more delightful chorus girl every five seconds, until they formed a chain, kicking their legs in delicious all-white outfits that looked like so much carefully positioned whipped cream. Then came Berkeley's overhead shot, with each girl appearing to be holding a giant mint imperial; the effect was, literally, kaleidoscopic. As fun and cheeky a song as 'Yes, Yes' is, the memory you took home was of the choreography. Berkeley called his dancing girls 'pattern makers rather than hoofers', and used camera zooms and swooping panoramic shots as a key part of the choreography, turning a stage set into a pool filled with a hundred mermaids or into a towered, all-female wedding cake, all moving in perfect symmetry. Nothing from the MTV era comes close.*

* * *

* This kind of choreography was new to film and amplified by the camera, but its on-stage predecessor goes back to the 1890s and the Tiller Girls' long, disciplined lines of legs.

George Gershwin had spent 1928 in Paris, which he had initially visited intending to study composition with Maurice Ravel, only to receive a rejection letter which read: 'Why become a second-rate Ravel when you're already a first-rate Gershwin?' He didn't waste his time, though, writing his 'rhapsodic ballet', *An American in Paris*. In 1929 he would be brought down from his classical cloud by Fox studios, who needed a score for their movie *Delicious*. While the premiere of *An American in Paris* had received rapturous applause at Carnegie Hall a few months earlier, Fox left all of Gershwin's work for *Delicious* on the cutting-room floor, bar a dream sequence and the playful, zigzagging opening theme, 'Manhattan Rhapsody'. With his letter from Ravel tucked inside his jacket pocket, Gershwin knew he was dealing with dolts and didn't work in Hollywood for another seven years.

Other writers couldn't pick and choose. Hollywood was just about the only place where paid employment wasn't a rarity in the early 1930s. Jerome Kern was enticed over after making a catastrophic decision. He had been an avid collector of rare books, but in 1929 he decided to sell his collection. Instead of spending the proceeds on a mansion, a yacht or dancing girls, he foolishly put it all into the stock market. By the turn of the 1930s he was flat broke. His first job, which he fully expected to be a roaring success, was dumped by MGM in favour of a film version of Rudolf Friml's ancient, creaky *Rose Marie*. Chastened, he decided to work with smaller studios, who he hoped would show him a little more respect. The Fred Astaire movie *Swing Time* (1936) would edge him closer to jazz, which up until now had brought him out in a cold sweat.

Astaire and lyricist Dorothy Fields were the best thing that happened to him – out poured 'A Fine Romance', 'The Way You Look Tonight', 'I'm Old Fashioned', 'You Were Never Lovelier'. Native New Yorker Fields had previously written lyrics for Jimmy McHugh, placing their work ('I Can't Give You Anything but Love' in 1928, 'I Must Have That Man' in 1929) with Duke Ellington at the Cotton Club, but they split as neither was especially fond of the other. She clicked with Kern, who was one of her heroes. Though nineteen years younger, she would call Kern 'Junior' as she was a full five inches taller. Both were finicky and understood each other's temperament. Fields wrote Kern a pep talk and a half for *Swing Time*: 'Pick yourself up, dust yourself down, start all over again.' Too bad that after this he went back to working with Oscar Hammerstein, on 1937's *High, Wide and Handsome*, which at least gave us 'The Folks Who Live on the Hill'.*

Hollywood had a salon atmosphere. There were wild parties. There was tennis with the Gershwins. Still, Broadway songwriters mostly hated it as they had so little say in the finished product. After Rodgers and Hart's miserable hiring (1930) and firing (1931) by Warner Brothers, they had returned warily in 1932 – Rodgers this time with his wife Dorothy and baby Mary – to work for Paramount with the far more sympathetic Rouben Mamoulian on *Love Me Tonight*. Its star was the forty-four-year-old Maurice Chevalier, who had started out in cabaret in Marseilles, then Paris; after becoming besotted with jazz in 1917, he went to London, where he had great success at the Palace Theatre. He would never be shy about playing up his French street accent (his last recording was the virtually unintelligible theme to *The Aristocats* in 1970). What Chevalier learned on stage was the personal touch. For him, the ideal setting was a café, where he could go from table to table, singing each line to a different mademoiselle. So he was perfect for Hollywood's new musical direction.† It was about 'artistic coherence', wrote Richard Rodgers in his diary, and Mamoulian was the perfect director for him. It was the first time that Rodgers and Hart's songs had been fitted to a movie. In one scene, Chevalier, playing a Parisian tailor, starts humming 'Isn't It Romantic' while giving a bridegroom a fitting. The groom walks out humming the tune; a cabbie hears it and joins in; his passenger is a composer, who writes down the notes, boards a train, and then a whole platoon of French soldiers start singing it. This was a massive step on from the fixed-camera boredom of *The Hot Heiress*.

---

* Hammerstein's politics were rarely harder to follow. The plot of *High, Wide and Handsome* pits baddie Walt Brennan, who wants to build a railway, against goodie Peter Cortlandt, who uses a herd of circus elephants to stop the railway's construction and instead builds an oil pipeline through the town. Oil and railway politics were very different in 1937, of course, but my word, this reads strangely in the twenty-first century.

† Chevalier was apparently so tight-fisted that when he was offered a cigarette, he would put it in his top pocket and save it for later.

The Al Jolson vehicle *Hallelujah, I'm a Bum* (1933) included rhythmic dialogue – another step forward – but even though it contained an instant standard in 'You Are Too Beautiful', Rodgers felt too defeated by a movie about jolly tramps in Central Park to write a score that satisfied as a whole. 'The subject of homelessness', he wrote, 'didn't strike many people as something to laugh about.' Even as musicals began to boom again, Rodgers and Hart seemed to encounter trouble with everything they worked on. There was *Hollywood Party*, starring Jean Harlow as a wannabe actress. They wrote her a song called 'Prayer' ('Oh Lord, if you're not busy up there, I ask for help with a prayer, so please don't give me the air'), but the scene was cut before Harlow even had a chance to record it. Luckily, Rodgers and Hart thought enough of the song to rewrite the lyric as 'The Bad in Every Man', for a movie called *Manhattan Melodrama*. This time Shirley Ross sang, 'Oh Lord, what is the matter with me? I'm just permitted to see the bad in every man.' It was not a hit. Larry Hart was not trying his hardest, figured MGM's head of music publishing, and one-time Duke Ellington associate, Jack Robbins. Try something more commercial, Robbins suggested, and I'll promote it coast to coast. At the third time of asking, Hart came up with 'Blue moon, you saw me standing alone, without a dream in my heart, without a love of my own.'* Still, virtually none of the films Rodgers and Hart worked on after 1932's *Love Me Tonight* did any business. One day in 1934 Rodgers picked up the *Los Angeles Examiner* and read the headline 'Whatever Happened to Rodgers and Hart?' His hands started to shake. He called Larry, and they headed back east, once again back to Broadway, slump or no slump.

* * *

* Robbins was true to his word and licensed the song in October 1934, as a theme tune for William Powell and Louella Parsons's radio show *Hollywood Hotel*. Connee Boswell recorded it for Brunswick in January 1935 and scored a hit; Elvis Presley gave an extraordinarily haunted reading of it at Sun in 1955; the Marcels added nonsense syllables and sang it three times as fast to score a transatlantic number one in 1961; and it has since been heard in films ranging from the Marx Brothers' *At the Circus* to *Grease*.

The movie musical barely existed in Britain, which seems entirely baf-fling given the songwriters, music-hall stars and actors and actresses at its disposal. This was partly down to a lack of funds, which kept British cinema years behind America and the Continent; partly due to plays that had transferred to Broadway being picked up by Hollywood; and partly because of the British attachment to the stage, to going up to town to take in a show.

Of the music-hall acts who transferred to film, Rochdale's Gracie Fields was the best and most beloved. Though never a pin-up, everyone could imagine her as their best mate. She debuted in 1931's *Sally in Our Alley* – an excuse to reprise her best-known song, 'Sally' – when she was already thirty-four years old. She hit her stride with *Sing as We Go* (1934), which was scripted by J B. Priestley and found 'our Gracie' looking for work in Blackpool after being laid off from her mill job.* As a Depression-buster, the grand finale had workers returning to the mill, led by Gracie, desperate to spend another eight hours a day amid the deafening roar of mill machinery. The Priestley/Fields team reunited a year later for *Look Up and Laugh* (also notable for being Vivien Leigh's first film appearance), in which Gracie tried to stop Birkenhead market from being demolished to make way for a department store. This wasn't the sleek deco modernism of *Top Hat*; this was about Britain clinging to the little it still had, mistrusting the future and seeing warmth and glory in its crumbling brickwork. Unlike her Lancashire music-hall comrade George Formby, she could also sing incredibly affecting ballads. By rights the waltz-time 'When I Grow Too Old to Dream' (1935) should sound like a Victorian parlour antique, but Gracie's voice is such a blend of sweetness and strength; the soprano notes towards the end give you goosebumps. It's not too surprising that years later Yoko Ono would choose it as one of her Desert Island Discs.

Wigan-born George Formby was a bigger star yet. Initially, he worked in the long shadow cast by his father, music-hall performer George

---

* The title song of *Sing as We Go* was later adapted by Monty Python as 'Sit on My Face'. It's hard to imagine that Gracie would have been shocked, as she was cut from similar cloth to Marie Lloyd: on 'Walter, Walter, Lead Me to the Altar' she invited you to guess where her tattoo might be.

Formby Sr, but in 1923 he met his wife Beryl Ingham, a champion clog dancer from Accrington.* They worked briefly as a double act, but Beryl saw his potential and encouraged him to play the ukulele, and by 1934 – just as he turned thirty – he was starring in his first movie, *Boots! Boots!*, a low-budget affair that was allegedly filmed above a fire station. After *Boots! Boots!* Formby made eighteen more films between 1934 and 1946 and would be British cinema's biggest crowd-puller for six consecutive years.

If Gracie Fields rose above her circumstances, Formby revelled in his. In spite of his fame and fortune he still smoked Woodbines, and his favourite food was beef dripping on toast. His songs – 'When I'm Cleaning Windows', 'With My Little Stick of Blackpool Rock', 'You Can't Keep a Growing Lad Down' – were like saucy postcards, and his cheery, nasal voice cut through bad times like a stiff gin. His label, Regal Zonophone, awarded him the first-ever silver disc in 1936 for selling 100,000 copies of 'When I'm Cleaning Windows' (from *Keep Your Seats, Please*); a year later 'Leaning on a Lamp Post' (written by Denmark Street songwriter Noel Gay for *Feather Your Nest*) sold twice as many, and in 1941 he signed a contract with Columbia Pictures for more than £500,000, making him officially the world's fifth-highest-paid actor, ahead even of Bing Crosby. His appeal was his cheek, and his songs were genuinely funny: 'There's Uncle Dick without a care discarding his underwear, but his watch and chain still dangle there, in my little snapshot album.' When he died, aged fifty-six, in 1961 – by which time Elvis Presley was cinema's biggest attraction – Formby was still a huge star: 150,000 people attended his funeral.

Music-hall acts aside, the one fresh British musical film star was Jessie Matthews, whose saucer-eyed blend of naïf and sexpot was made for the cinema. 'She had a heart,' said director Victor Saville. 'It photographed.' Her voice was pure operetta, not a modern touch in sight, but Jessie

---

* George Formby Sr had made Wigan Pier famous before George Orwell. He claimed it was his 'favourite bathing spot', though in reality it was just a landing stage on the Leeds and Liverpool Ship Canal. Known as the 'Wigan Nightingale' thanks to his industrial cough, he had been a big music-hall draw; Marie Lloyd said the only acts she'd pay to see were Dan Leno and George Formby. Always in poor health, he died of pulmonary tuberculosis in 1921, aged forty-five.

was a blessed star and was given box-fresh Rodgers and Hart, Irving Berlin and Cole Porter songs (Porter wrote 'Let's Do It' for Jessie and her husband, Sonnie Hale). Barred from going to America by producers the Balcon brothers, who knew she'd never come back, she banged out a string of British musicals in the 1930s, all directed by Saville. When the war began, musicals were quickly dropped: they may have cost only £50,000 to make, but that was £50,000 Britain didn't have. Finally, Jessie got to go to Hollywood, but only to feature in the 1942 fundraiser for Britain, *Forever and a Day*. 'Everything was so much trouble, so much bother,' she said of the British musical. 'I suppose it's because as a race we don't like to learn. We don't like to admit that we don't know ... Unfortunately we were very stubborn. We wouldn't learn from the Americans. It's sad, as we might have been better technically.'

* * *

When Hollywood produced its own versions of Broadway hits, the studios would frequently ditch all but the biggest songs and fill the rest of the movie with songs by in-house writers. Even when the original material came from George and Ira Gershwin (*Strike Up the Band*, which lost everything bar the title song) or Rodgers and Hart, future standards were cast out: in 1939 Busby Berkeley's *Babes in Arms* thought 'My Funny Valentine' and 'The Lady Is a Tramp' were expendable.

Here's a funny thing, though: while Hollywood poached songwriters from Broadway on a daily basis, the traffic never, ever went the other way. You could write the biggest hits in Hollywood – Oscar-winners even – and still be unknown to the wider public. Possibly there was snobbery involved: arranger Gordon Jenkins said that at Paramount 'there were twenty-seven people in the music department and only three of us could do anything: Victor Young, myself and Irving Thaler. Period. That was it, nobody else did anything, they were either there 'cos they were related or because somebody owed them a favour. Three out of twenty-seven.' This is not exactly true: Leo Robin was also at Paramount, and he wrote the delicious, Academy Award-winning 'Thanks for the Memory' ('of motor trips and burning lips, and burning toast and prunes'), sung by Bob Hope and Shirley Ross in *The Big Broadcast of 1938*, a song that pulled off the rare trick of being very funny and deeply moving at the same time. Robin, who had moved to Hollywood in 1932 after a handful of middling Broadway shows, might prove the point. You know 'Thanks for the Memory' – heck, it became Bob Hope's theme tune, his gravestone inscription – but would you have a clue who wrote it?

The ultimate case in point is Harry Warren, one of the half-dozen greatest songwriters in this entire story, and the man who – with lyricist Al Dubin – got the movie musical back on its feet in 1933, with the saucy, hit-packed *42nd Street*. If he'd stuck to his birth name, Salvatore Guaragna, his name would at least have stood out in the credits. But his dad anglicised the family's names to the point of total anonymity, and so it was Harry Warren rather than Salvatore Guaragna who headed west during the Depression, having broken through a little too late for Jazz Age Broadway. While the songs became immortal, the movies – and especially their creator – may just as well have been shut away in a Warner Brothers vault. His face – two melancholic panda eyes above a Roman nose and a down-turned banana mouth – remained unknown. When he went to collect his Oscar for best song, 'Lullaby of Broadway', in 1935, he couldn't get into the theatre because nobody recognised him.

You don't have to dig deep in Warren's catalogue for perfect nuggets: 'I Only Have Eyes for You', written for *Dames* and sung by Ben Selvin in 1934, later a doo-wop hit for the Flamingos in the 1950s and a UK number one for Art Garfunkel in the '70s; Joan Blondell's Depression torch song 'My Forgotten Man', from *Gold Diggers of 1933*; Glenn Miller's twin bolts of lightning, 'Chattanooga Choo Choo' and 'I've Got a Gal in Kalamazoo'; *42nd Street*'s 'Shuffle Off to Buffalo', a favourite of *Sesame Street*'s Oscar the Grouch*; the daft but enduring slice of baloney 'That's Amore', Warren's last big hit and Dean Martin's epitaph; and, with the longest tail of all, 'At Last', which was written for

---

* They shared a trait. Warren affected a professional grouchiness, having an affable, long-running feud with Irving Berlin, whom people always assumed wrote Warren's hits. At the end of World War II he was widely quoted (finally!) for his wisecrack 'They bombed the wrong Berlin.'

the barely recalled Glenn Miller vehicle *Sun Valley Serenade* in 1941, but more than six decades later became, in effect, the anthem of the first black US president.

Did Warren's anonymity bother him? Possibly not. He was a Capricorn, born on Christmas Day (so, cracked writer Wilfrid Sheed, he was upstaged by someone more famous from day one), and had the Capricornian fear of public appearances. If he ever had to give an acceptance speech, he would need a stiffener or two first, and he never went to Hollywood parties, though he must have known that to do so would have raised his profile. He was sociable enough, a drinking buddy of both Harold Arlen and Terry-Thomas, and would always be out socialising with his lyric writers, Al Dubin and Mack Gordon. Big crowds and the spotlight weren't for Harry Warren, but he lived to be eighty-eight and was never under-appreciated by his friends in New York. It feels good to give him a bit of space here.

Warren's most frequent collaborator was Al Dubin, whom Warren described as 'a 6' 3" fella, weighed 310 pounds, and he ate like Henry the Eighth. While he was eating a steak, he'd ask the chef to make him another one.' Dubin would drive down to Mexican border towns just for the food. One time, Warren rang him at one of his favourite haunts: the studio needed him to write a lyric. 'I've written it,' said Dubin, nestling behind a tower of burritos. 'Pick up a pen.' And he wasn't bluffing: off the cuff he dictated the beautiful lyric for 'The Shadow Waltz', the biggest hit from *Gold Diggers of 1933*, later recorded by Bing Crosby, Sonny Rollins and Sheena Easton.

Rodgers and Hart's *On Your Toes* would be the biggest hit of the 1936 Broadway season; most significantly, it brought ballet into the American musical, with George Balanchine choreographing two sequences. The 'Slaughter on Tenth Avenue' sequence was a completely integrated part of the narrative, a love-triangle play within a play, life imitating art, people playing mobsters before the play ends with real mobsters busting in. Significantly, Hollywood loved the kinetic, back-alley jazz feel of Rodgers's 'Slaughter': they didn't mess with it when they made a movie of *On Your Toes* in 1939, even bringing in Balanchine as choreographer (but they did ditch every other Rodgers and Hart song from the show).

'Slaughter on Tenth Avenue' was a pointer to the future of musical theatre, to integration and dance, if only Lorenz Hart had known it.

1940's *Pal Joey* was centred around a handsome, self-serving anti-
hero. The cast was 'nothing but villains except the ingénue', said Richard
Rodgers, 'and she was stupid'. This was a brand-new concept in musical theatre, and it allowed Hart to run riot with the lyrics. The show
featured fifteen songs, all written inside three weeks, including two of
the team's greatest in 'I Could Write a Book' and 'Bewitched, Bothered
and Bewildered' ('I'll worship the trousers that cling to him'). Opening
night was Christmas Day 1940. Rodgers remembered that 'approxi-
mately one half of the audience applauded wildly while the other half
sat there in . . . stunned silence'. The reviews were harsh. Hart read the
one in the *New York Times* – 'How can you draw sweet water from a foul
well?' – and broke down sobbing. *Pal Joey* would be revived in 1952 and
run for 542 performances, becoming recognised as Rodgers and Hart's
masterpiece. But Hart was broken by its initial lukewarm response; by
1942, dumped by an impatient Rodgers, he had drunk himself to death.

21

PARDON MY PUPS: THE BOSWELL SISTERS

The Boswell Sisters were just about the most inventive and fun act of the early 1930s. They caused a revolution in close-harmony singing, which, at the turn of the '30s, was still in a world of glee clubs and barbershops, and became the first singers to use their voices as part of the orchestra, rather than singing over it.

With a few exceptions, women don't figure heavily in jazz history books. The textbook cases we'll come to later, but the Boswells have been almost entirely overlooked. The reasons for this, beyond gender, are their ready availability (they sold lots of records and made enough money) and their Hollywood appearances. Hidden in plain sight, they seem to provide no angle, no apparent grit or gain for historians. Always, they sound like an enormous heap of fun. They would take a song like 'There'll Be Some Changes Made', speed it up to Charleston tempo, slow it down to a twelve-bar blues, then Connee would do her trumpet impression, and finally the girls sang together, aching like a mournful coven of clarinets. Keys changed at the drop of a bobby pin. If jazz is about digging into the core of a song and reinterpreting it, then the Boswell Sisters were its Marx Brothers.

Originally, they were Martha (born 1905), Connie (1907) and Helvetia (1911), and they were raised in a large white house on Camp Street, New Orleans. Money was not a problem for the Boswells. They performed chamber music together locally. This was the early 1920s, though, and the dawn of the Jazz Age meant more in New Orleans than anywhere else. As teenagers, the Boswell girls couldn't help but fall for it. They went to local shows when they could and, after studying the classics, switched allegiances. 'The saxophone got us,' shrugged Connie. Soon the Boswells' parlour was a hot meeting place: Louis Prima was a regular, as was Bix Beiderbecke's cornet-playing mentor Emmett Hardy, who had fallen in love with Martha.

Helvetia was 'Vet' to everyone; Connie, who sang from a wheelchair as a result of polio, decided to spell her name 'Connee' once they became famous, as that made it easier and quicker to sign autographs. As kids, Martha played piano, Connie cello and saxophone, with Vet handling banjo, guitar and violin. They were initially spotted by a Victor scout at a local talent contest, and they cut some sides without Vet, who was still too young. Vaudeville and a local west coast radio show on KFWB followed in 1929, without anyone getting too excited. Connee remembered 'a pretty gruelling stint at a movie house. We got into bed at our hotel when I noticed Martha seemed very quiet. Something made me ask how much we'd earned, and she shook her head and handed me the cheque – this would have been at the start of the Depression. I looked at it and it was pretty bad, so I tried to cheer her up and said, "Don't worry. $30 isn't much but it'll pay for our lodgings and get us to the next date." She just stared at me and said, "Connee, better look again." I did, and it was for $3.'

Things turned around when they played New York's Paramount Theatre in 1931. People fell in love with their lazy river stylings on the spot. Brunswick Records' Jack Kapp grabbed them, putting them in a New York studio with the cream of the city's white jazz players – Jimmy and Tommy Dorsey, Bunny Berigan, Eddie Lang and Joe Venuti – and William Paley signed the Boswells up for his nascent CBS radio network. By the end of the year they were stars and had appeared on the first public television transmission. Sadly, none of this – neither radio nor TV – has survived, but the Boswells were preserved on film by Hollywood. In 1932 they appeared alongside Bing Crosby in *The Big Broadcast*, and later appeared in *Transatlantic Merry-Go-Round* (1934).

The films don't really do them justice, but luckily the seventy-plus sides they cut between 1931 and 1935 survive and had the sisters at the controls. Most of their best sides were cut in 1932: the woozy hurt of 'Was That the Human Thing to Do', with Connee's pain backed sympathetically by Tommy Dorsey; the big city girls laughing at their finger-wagging aunt on 'Hand Me Down My Walking Cane'; the wild, Depression-defying joy of 'Put the Sun Back in the Sky', with spine-tingling, syncopated vocal swoops and tempo changes left, right and centre. Connee later told writer Michael Brooks, 'If you think these sides are way out, you should have heard the first versions. Jack Kapp howled and insisted they be remade more conventionally.'

They would record between midnight and dawn. After finishing a show at the Paramount or Roxy, the sisters would go to a speakeasy called Plunket's on West 53rd Street to get musicians, who would always be there. Connee, Vet and Martha would pump them full of black coffee, then record Connee's arrangements onto wax (Bing Crosby's tape-recording philanthropy was still a good few years away). The musicians were usually hammered, and upwards of twenty waxes would be wasted before they got a satisfactory take. 'They were pretty tightly scored,' Connee recalled, 'although I always tried to get a loose swinging sound. They were just the greatest bunch of fellows to work with. Crazy, but all wonderful musicians who understood exactly what we were trying to do. We had a ball.'

The drinking in the studio got so bad, and so many waxes were wasted, that a liquor ban was imposed. It made no difference. One night everyone was particularly well refreshed, and bassist Artie Bernstein was slumping lower and lower. The Boswells couldn't work out where the booze was coming from. Then their manager Harry Leedy saw Artie open a trapdoor in his bass, pull up a string and, like a ruddy-faced fisherman, take a bottle of whisky from the end of a hook. This drunken bonhomie could also lead to a late-night fireside warmth on Boswell recordings like Fats Waller's 'If It Ain't Love' or their take on Duke Ellington's 'Mood Indigo'.

The popularity of the Boswells inspired the nascent big-band scene to incorporate women as singers. Bandleaders knew that an attractive girl would pull in a male audience, and the female singer – known as the thrush or the canary – was soon a mainstay. The very first had been Mildred Bailey, who had joined Paul Whiteman's band in 1929, while the Boswells were still scrabbling around doing shows for dimes. Female jazz singers were a real rarity at this point, and Bailey's innovatory style – high and light, but forceful – was clearly an influence on future giants Billie Holiday and Ella Fitzgerald.

As Mildred Rinker, she had been raised on the Coeur d'Alene Reservation near De Smet, Idaho. Her mother, who died in the World War I tuberculosis epidemic when Mildred was fourteen, was Native American. Her father was Swiss American, and the family had moved to Spokane, Washington, when she was thirteen. A mean stepmother forced Mildred out of the family home, and after making a name for herself singing in Seattle speakeasies, she was on the bathtub-gin circuit, from Los Angeles to Spokane and back. On a typical night, after taking requests from contraband-happy drunks, Mildred would go back to her bedroom, peel off her bloomers, and a shower of $20 bills would rain down.

Back in Spokane, her brother Al became friends with a kid from Gonzaga Prep, Harry 'Bing' Crosby. Mildred, Al and Bing had relocated to California by the mid-1920s. Mildred then followed Al to New York, married bandleader Red Norvo in 1930, and joined his band in 1934, at which point her throaty style, her diction and phrasing, took on a sensuous swoop and swing. Listen to her version of Irving Berlin's 'I've Got My Love to Keep Me Warm' or Johnny Mercer's 'The Weekend of a Private Secretary': like the very best records of the decade, they sound like an idealised picture of 1930s urban America – sophisticated, casual, frankly uninhibited. Norvo and Bailey were dubbed Mr and Mrs Swing, scoring hits both together and apart. Mildred was first in line for songwriters; Hoagy Carmichael even sat in on piano when she recorded the definitive version of his 'Rockin' Chair' (1937). Other times she was backed by both Dorseys, the Casa Loma Orchestra, and Benny Goodman. John Hammond produced her small-group sessions, as he would for Billie Holiday a few years later. But retirement to upstate New York meant Bailey was quickly forgotten after the big-band era. She died in penury, aged forty-four, in 1951.

Bailey was at the forefront of modernity: her ethnic ambiguity, with a voice to match; a plus-size star; a woman who could lose her temper and get her own way in an age when that was a male prerogative. Quite why Bailey doesn't get her due these days, I don't know. One reason could be the miserable but banal way in which she died: from diabetes complications brought on by overeating. Billie Holiday numbed the pain with narcotics, and she's a legend. Mildred Bailey chose chocolate eclairs, and she's forgotten. History can be a mean judge.

* * *

The Boswells weren't the biggest sister group (commercially, the Andrews Sisters trumped all-comers), nor were they the first. The Brox Sisters hadn't been jazz singers – no solos, always harmony-singing – but they were perfect for the Jazz Age and anticipated the Boswells' look, if not their sound. Originally the Brock sisters from Tennessee, they had been raised in Canada and got their break in 1921, when they sang 'Everybody Step' in Irving Berlin's *Music Box Revue*. Berlin took a shine to the trio, casting them in two more *Music Box Revues* (1923 and 1924), as well as the Marx Brothers' 1926 musical *Cocoanuts*. By the end of the decade they had moved to Hollywood and got first dibs at 'Singin' in the Rain' – alongside Cliff 'Ukulele Ike' Edwards – in *The Hollywood Revue of 1929*; they also arrived in time to make an appearance in *The King of Jazz*. The Brox Sisters were very 1920s, though, all flapper 'dos and dresses, and close, sweet harmonies, with vestiges of their Tennessee accents for added ingénue value. They broke up for the same reasons girl groups would break up for decades to come – marriage, kids – and their retirement in 1932 left the door open for the Boswells, who were very much built for the 1930s.

Writing for *DownBeat* in 1944, John Lucas said that 'no single group had such a hand in shaping our popular music as the Boswell Sisters'. Their heirs would be the wartime heroines the Andrews Sisters. Maxene Andrews admitted her sisters 'imitated them, even their accents. We all loved the Boswell Sisters. The Boswells had broken down the barrier between semi-classical and New Orleans jazz for white singers. Laverne [Andrews] had a wonderful musical memory. She would listen to a Boswells record and then teach me and Patty the parts.'

The Boswells' reign was brief. In February 1936 Martha married an RAF major and became Mrs George L. Lloyd. And that was that. Vet and Martha retired from music, but Connee married Harry Leedy, who supported her solo career. There would be duets with Bing Crosby, but nothing to match the madcap innovation of the sisters' recordings. Connee eventually retired to Manhattan to paint, making the odd personal appearance prior to her death in 1976.

When Steely Dan's Donald Fagen put together his compendium of *Eminent Hipsters*, the Boswell Sisters were right at the front, Chapter One. Fagen talked about how Connee never lost her instinct for rhythm, and how he thought she had used her disability to create something startling and new, comparing her to Frida Kahlo. He also reckoned that the Boswells' 'Sentimental Gentleman from Georgia' contained the first recorded use of 'Yowzah!' – and I can think of no better word to sum them up.

22

MAKE THOSE PEOPLE SWAY: BRITISH DANCE BANDS

Roll up the carpet, push back the chairs, get some music on the radio.
    'Roll Up the Carpet', Ray Noble and Al Bowlly

Once she used to love a highbrow music man, but that's over now 'cause she's a rhythm fan.
    'Why Did She Fall for the Leader of the Band', Gracie Fields

The sense of continuity in British life had been broken by World War I. The American influence then seeped in and quickly took over.

The Home Counties politesse of the Palm Court Orchestra would be replaced by the dance band, and its repertoire very often came from across the ocean. The seeds had been sown in 1919, when the Original Dixieland Jazz Band and Southern Syncopators arrived in London with what sounded to British ears like banjo, clarinet, cornet and trombone all playing different melodies at the same time. It was confusing but thrilling, and the dance-band scene grew out of this. Hundreds of budding musicians thought they could do what the ODJB did; the cockier ones thought they could even do it better. Initially, British jazz bands were just the imitative ragbag you might expect, copying ODJB instrumentation from available 78s and making a noise that passed for jazz. After the Savoy Hotel introduced its first dance outfit in 1922, though, bands took on a new, localised look. In dinner jackets, with hair slicked back, they were generally seven or eight players, plus a bandleader and occasional vocalist. If it was still jazz, it was tamed and anglicised, respectable and army-disciplined.

This, it turned out, was exactly what Britain wanted, with the string bass and Spanish guitar smoothly replacing the sousaphone and banjo. Boiling-hot jazz didn't really suit the British reserve, so Britain created something of its own. It was modern, streamlined, and it felt like the future – a sophisticated future. Ray Noble's rhapsodic, gliding 'Midnight, the Stars and You' was several worlds away from the Bovril and damp village halls evoked by 'Over There' or 'Keep the Home Fires Burning'.

The interwar dance-band scene can be easy to dismiss, as it has almost always been seen through the lens of jazz. Essentially, the British bands played harmonies with the odd solo, so they don't really qualify as jazz. Most importantly, they had something that remains close to the British heart: a good beat. There was a reason why they called themselves 'dance bands' rather than 'jazz bands': a nation of factory workers who would later devote themselves to the metronomic rhythms of northern soul and Chicago house had heard the loose sounds of New Orleans and decided they'd like something a little different.

* * *

The West End in the 1930s was the hub of the dance-band scene: Ambrose at the Mayfair; Jack Jackson at the Dorchester; Maurice Winnick at the San Marco; Harry Roy at the Café Anglais; and the imported Americans Carroll Gibbons at the Savoy and Roy Fox at the Monseigneur on Jermyn Street. The foxtrot had started off the craze. High-end restaurants and hotels cashed in, and customers danced the night away. Al Bowlly's 'Dinner at Eight', a Ben Selvin cover taken from a 1933 Jean Harlow movie, was the height of sophistication with its hint of the illicit ('Two gardenias at my plate . . . under the table our hands will meet, we should be able to be discreet'). The biggest hotels – the Savoy, the May Fair, the Hotel Cecil – could afford the fifteen-piece bands. Tables and chairs would be placed around the dancefloor (which wasn't huge – everybody danced close together), with the band squashed up on the stage. In the Savoy Ballroom, society people and diners danced to Gibbons's Savoy Havana Band.

Star musicians switched between bands regularly, drove Aston Martins and lived in mock-Tudor houses in the stockbroker belt. The bandleaders were superstars. It was a golden age, and the only problem was that the musicians, playing the same unvarying set of show tunes and Tin Pan Alley hits ('Night and Day', 'They Can't Take That Away from Me', all American) as either quickstep or foxtrot from 9 p.m. to 2 a.m. every night, were often bored stiff. They would try to liven things up for themselves by snaffling food from the trolleys when the waiters weren't looking.

The hotels and supper clubs didn't usually get to hear the sound folks heard on the radio or the gramophone. It's unlikely Bert Ambrose would have risked playing the sinuous 'Singapore Sorrows' in front of the well-heeled diners at the Mayfair. However, if a small white card was on each table with the warning that 'Ambrose and his orchestra are broadcasting tonight and, therefore, the band is playing considerably louder than usual,' then the patrons and hotel staff would be roundly ignored. The drummer would ditch his soft wire brushes for sticks, and the millions of people who weren't eating their dinner a few feet from Danny Polo's clarinet would have a fine time dancing around their front rooms.

When the BBC launched in 1922, John Reith knew that dance music had to be included. The bands who bossed clubland, a small area of central London – Piccadilly, Leicester Square, Regent Street – had become famous across the country, accessible to everyone – in magazines, on the radio every day except Sunday. Entertainment bosses told Reith that that was what the public wanted.

The BBC was incredibly uptight about advertising and very aware of its role in the promotion of dance music. Likewise, record companies realised that if Ambrose played his latest record during his ninety-minute show on the BBC (with help from Evelyn Dall, Sam Browne, Max Bacon, Vera Lynn and the Manhattan Three), then people would go out the next day and buy it. So in 1929 the BBC took a stand to eliminate song-plugging: 'The announcer's microphone is to be removed from each dance band and only the balance microphone used.' Bandleaders couldn't plug anything; they were effectively gagged. More than ever, the broadcasts became music to dance to.

Outside of London, huge dance halls had already been built to meet the seasonal demand in working-class seaside resorts like Blackpool, Morecambe, Margate and Douglas, on the Isle of Man, so the dance boom of the 1920s was instantly catered to by venues that were now renamed 'palais de danse'. New halls would be built in every major industrial town. The first was the Hammersmith Palais, which had flagged itself up as a jazz venue by booking the ODJB in 1919. It was here and in palais de danse across the country that the British dance bands developed their own take: not only smoother, but generally a little faster than the American original.

The classic dance band was made up of twelve or fourteen players, usually dressed in identical uniforms, who were employed by a hotel or restaurant. The better-known bandleaders – Henry Hall, Jack Hylton, Harry Roy, Lew Stone – were national celebrities, brilliantined and stick-thin, usually serious-looking but with the faintest upward turn in one corner of their mouths. Every fifth or sixth song they played would be a hot number; if there were any jazz-loving players in the band, here was their chance to shine. 'Tiger Rag' was played by almost everyone. During World War II, Harry Roy toured a smaller band called the Tiger Ragamuffins, while Nat Gonella kept a cuddly tiger on the piano to indicate his preference for hot numbers.

One of the early heroes of British jazz, someone who took it to the masses, was a wealthy Filipino called Fred Elizalde, who had been a student at Cambridge when he first formed a band in 1927, giving a break to young British players like trumpeters Jack Jackson and Norman Payne, clarinettist Jack Miranda and drummer Max Bacon. Elizalde blended them with American players, like the wonderfully named trumpeter Chelsea Quealey, and got the band a job playing at the Savoy. It was among the first to be broadcast by the BBC.* Needing a singer, he brought the peripatetic but as yet unknown Al Bowlly over from South Africa in 1928. The new jazz weekly *Melody Maker* voted Elizalde 'best radio bandleader', but the BBC received complaints from listeners that his music was too hard to dance to. Elizalde couldn't care less. He returned to Manila in 1930, breaking up his hot band after being offered a job as conductor of the Manila Symphony Orchestra; he was still only twenty-three. Next, he wrote music to accompany Federico García Lorca's *Títeres de Cachiporra* and *Don Perlimplín*. Who needed Lord Reith now?†

What were the biggest dance-band hits? 'The Music Goes Round and Round' was one of BBC Dance Orchestra leader Henry Hall's biggest-selling records. By 1936 he had relented on his vocal-free rule and had begun to work with the exciting George Elrick, a friend of Al Bowlly, who had a decided swing and an unmistakable Scottish burr. Jack Jackson's signature tune was 'Make Those People Sway', a terrific self-descriptive piece that broke the band's sound down into its propulsive constituent parts, then built it back up, like a Barnsley-chopped precursor of Sly

---

* The very first had been a band led by Marius B. Winter, broadcasting from the BBC's Savoy Hill studio in 1923, while the first broadcast from a hotel was by alto saxophonist Ben Davis and his resident band at the Carlton Hotel. There were few licence-holders, and the amount of static would have been migraine-inducing.
† 1936 saw him volunteering for the Spanish Civil War, fighting in the Basque country for – rather surprisingly, given his bohemian life in the UK – Franco's fascists. People were oddly forgiving, though. He composed an opera about Gauguin, broadcast by French national radio in 1948, and three years later he was conducting the London Symphony Orchestra for the Festival of Britain. He also captained the Philippines shooting team at the Asian Games in 1954, so maybe people were scared to say no to him.

and the Family Stone's 'Dance to the Music'. Harry Roy always looked like he was on the verge of telling a filthy joke and somehow got away with 'My Girl's Pussy' in 1931. Jack Hylton's 'Life Is Just a Bowl of Cherries' was a Depression-buster: 'The sweet things in life to you were just loaned, so how can you lose what you've never owned?' Ray Noble wrote the rather more romantic 'Love Is the Sweetest Thing'; with its baroque string quartet intro and a beautiful horn vamp between choruses, it anticipated Nelson Riddle's sensual, string-led build for Frank Sinatra's 'I've Got You Under My Skin' and even the mid-section of the Beach Boys' 'God Only Knows'.

Bert Ambrose had been born in Warsaw in 1896 and fled the pogroms with his family to London's East End. From there he moved up to become a West End fixture. He was able to pull together some of the best musicians and writers, but sharp enough to know that the very best players were in America. Ambrose had played in the States – playing at Reisenweber's restaurant before forming his own fifteen-piece band at the tender age of twenty – and had absorbed the modern sounds. Back in London in 1922 he played at the Café de Paris and the Embassy Club, an exclusive supper club on Old Bond Street frequented by, among other wealthy worthies, the Prince of Wales. By 1927 Ambrose was leading the band at the ultra-prestigious Mayfair Hotel, had a record deal with Brunswick, a contract that allowed his performances to be broadcast by the BBC and an annual salary – from the Mayfair alone – of £10,000; he got a hotel suite thrown in for nothing and took up residence there.

He paid his musicians more money than other bandleaders and knew exactly what he wanted. Royalty and the aristocracy danced to him, which in a country still with a stiff class structure really meant something. Edward, Duke of Windsor and Wallis Simpson danced to Bert Ambrose, who remembered saxophonist Billy Amstell looking down Mrs Simpson's dress. Still, he never forgot where he came from: in 1930 he recorded 'Cryin' for the Carolines', an urban lament with a Jewish blues influence.

* * *

Britain was, as ever, isolationist, but nevertheless reached for the exotic, yearned for the foreign, struggled with the tension between its hatred of boiled cabbage and its fear of garlic. By the 1930s, searching for novelty, dance halls had begun to employ Hawaiian bands, gaucho tango bands and the successful Primo Scala and His Accordion Band, made up of four accordions, two pianos, violin, bass, guitar and drums. 'Primo' turned out to be a Londoner called Harry Bidgood, the musical director for George Formby's films, who also recorded as 'Rossini' and 'Don Porto'.*

Sometimes an exotic name would be enough, just a whiff of foreign climes, nothing to scare the islanders. Geraldo, leader of the Gaucho Tango Orchestra, was really Gerald Bright, who had studied piano at the Royal Academy of Music. The most mysterious, most adventurous character to emerge from the whole scene was the Mayfair-raised Reginald Foresythe. He originally came from a classical background, got into popular music as a way of making a living, was intrigued by black American culture and ended up being feted by the biggest names in jazz. Even for a Briton, he had a particularly detached view, which resulted in a very singular, often melancholic sound; at first listen you might think he was influenced by Duke Ellington's late-1940s albums or Raymond Scott's odd arrangements, but Foresythe's own blend of woodwind-heavy jazz and classical was fifteen to twenty years ahead of schedule. Black, gay and British, he must have seemed like he'd been beamed down from Mars.

Foresythe's Nigerian father had died when he was a child, and he was raised by his Scottish mother on Curzon Street in Mayfair. A prodigious pianist by his teens, he swanned off to Italy, Australia and Hawaii,† before arriving in California in 1930, where he soon found work as a

---

* They were regulars on *Music While You Work*, though to stop listeners thinking the BBC might be employing Italians, the band became 'Primo Scala's Accordion Band directed by Harry Bidgood'. They were still on the show as late as 1957.
† In Australia, he played with Harlem musical theatre tenor Walter Richardson, and the pair discovered they had similar politics. In August 1929 the *Adelaide Advertiser* wrote that Foresythe 'hoped to roll away something of the cloud of racial prejudice against the negro by proving that negroes can not only be singers and entertainers, but gentlemen . . . "Culture is something more than skin deep," he asserted.'

pianist with Paul Howard's Quality Serenaders, a band that included Lionel Hampton (on drums and vocals) and trombonist Lawrence Brown (who would soon go east to play with Duke Ellington). Foresythe also worked on myriad early talkies, including D. W. Griffith's *Abraham Lincoln*, and toured the US's southern states to get an insight into the living conditions of black Americans and to hear some jazz and blues at close quarters.

His odd, classically tinged, unshowy style quickly picked up a reputation. Most of 1931 was spent with Earl Hines's band at Chicago's Grand Terrace Café and Ballroom, arranging and orchestrating, leading rehearsals and even writing Hines's signature tune, 'Deep Forest'. In January 1933 his 'Southern Holiday' premiered when Paul Whiteman broadcast it from the Biltmore Hotel, with Foresythe at the piano. Duke Ellington was so impressed he let Foresythe stay in his apartment as a semi-permanent house guest. Foresythe repaid him by drinking heavily and regularly getting into fights in gay clubs and bars. You might have already guessed, but this story doesn't have a particularly happy ending.

Having made his wildly impressive American connections, Reggie returned to London in 1933 to show Britain what he was capable of. *Melody Maker*, in a glowing introductory piece, called him a 'wonderful musician'. Ambrose also considered Foresythe to be something very special, and chose him to be the in-house bandleader at Swallow Street's new Café de la Paix, which was looking for something more progressive and exotic than the usual dance orchestra. This was where 'The New Music of Reginald Foresythe' would be unveiled on 17 October 1933, the most forward-looking British sound of the decade. There was no brass, just reeds and a wind section, and the titles were as outré as the music: 'Lament for Congo', 'The Duke Insists', 'Volcanic (An Eruption for Orchestra)', 'Bit', 'Berceuse for an Unwanted Child' and 'The Autocrat Before Breakfast'. The press described it as 'something quite distinctive in dance music', but also as 'difficult to dance to', though the Café's clientele didn't seem to mind. 'The Serenade for a Wealthy Widow' and 'Angry Jungle' were recorded for Columbia as an opening salvo, with eight more slices of 'new music' recorded over the following year, including the eerie masterpiece 'Garden of Weed'.

Reggie Foresythe was quite aware of how good he was. In December 1933 he wrote a piece for *Tune Times* called 'This New Music of Mine', which read like a manifesto and revealed him to be a true modernist: 'Symphonic jazz is quite tasteless to me, and I was very amused a short while ago when a well-known critic and composer said he thought I was really a Gershwin at heart. The essence of all art lies in the extremist simplicity of expression. This is my aim . . . the omission of the obvious . . . the suppression of the superfluous . . . the most expression with the greatest economy of means. It may be that I am on the wrong track . . . perhaps it will even prove to be a cul-de-sac . . . I do not think so.'

By 1935 it seemed everybody loved Reggie. Truly Anglo-American, his musical futurism was not only accepted, but could be turned into actual hits by Benny Goodman or Henry Hall or Earl Hines or Ambrose; even Louis Armstrong had recorded his 'He's a Son of the South'. He could say things like, 'I believe music is a form of higher mathematics. That was how the Greeks dealt with music, and all their disciples. It was only during the eighteenth century that music began to be regarded as a romantic art.' No one feigned horror or called him out as pretentious. He was on his own, a visitor from the future, a creator of 'third stream' jazz twenty years ahead of schedule who was so talented and confident he could tell Duke Ellington where he should be taking his music.

So why isn't Foresythe's name better known? It would be easy to say it's because he was black and gay when neither was readily accepted by the Establishment, but that hardly seems to have held him back. How did his crown slip so suddenly? That's a little easier to explain. In January 1935 another high-profile admirer, John Hammond, set up a recording session for Foresythe in New York with no less than Benny Goodman and Gene Krupa, on four of his own compositions: 'The Melancholy Clown', 'Lullaby', 'The Greener the Grass' and 'Dodging a Divorcee'. The sides, released under the name 'Reginald Foresythe and his New Music', were terrific but sold poorly.

Within eighteen months, the session seemed like an odd portent. Goodman had become a star, and swing – a more basic, much louder form of the new music – was king. Foresythe's tone poems, his dislike of soloing and his carefully put-together woodwind line-up seemed fussy and fusty overnight. He had played the part of Phil Spector to Benny Goodman's Beatles. And then came the war. Foresythe joined the RAF and emerged with distinction, but by 1945 he had been diagnosed with 'war nerves', or what we would now call PTSD. A decade on from his heyday, his confidence shot, Foresythe became a full-blown alcoholic and spent the late 1940s and '50s playing clubs in Britain, where his name had been forgotten. He died in 1958, by which time the 'third stream' music he had pioneered in the early '30s was just achieving a commercial breakthrough.

* * *

Given the collectability and fetishisation of the interwar British dance bands in the 1960s and '70s – with full discographies and insanely detailed sleevenotes by the likes of Brian Rust and Sandy Forbes – why has the music not really travelled into the twenty-first century? Possibly, it's the lack of intensity. If you listen to Dixieland jazz – and it doesn't need to be anyone as accomplished as Louis Armstrong – then there's a raw thrill, the basic noise of joy. Likewise, the swing bands feel mightily alive, still sound like they could get a corpse to twitch its toes. British reserve hampers the sound of the dance bands. Democratic and populist, it rarely cuts loose. We love a good beat and a good tune, and we don't like a show-off.

Take the case of Spike Hughes, string-bass player, arranger and a reviewer for *Melody Maker* who specialised in hot jazz, under the pseudonym 'Mike'. His break came when he was offered a job playing in the pit orchestra for Charles B. Cochran's *1931 Revue*, which led to friendships with the West Indian trumpet player Leslie Thompson and black British singer Joey Shields. Both were in Spike's studio band during many 1931–2 sessions. Joey was credited for the vocals on records from the September '31 sessions (unfortunately, Decca printed his name as 'Jerry' on the labels), singing on Hughes's hot arrangements of the spirituals 'Roll, Jordan' and 'Joshua Fit the Battle of Jericho'. The BBC, predictably, banned them on the grounds that they were jazzing God's own music.

When he decided to visit New York for a holiday, Spike was met off the boat by John Hammond, a fellow *Melody Maker* writer, who invited him to stay at his Greenwich Village apartment. They visited the Cotton Club (where Hughes felt so uncomfortable at the racial split that he wrote that it was 'a waste of time'), saw Bessie Smith ('Empty Bed Blues', he wrote, was 'not for the squeamish'), visited Irving Mills's offices, just as Harold Arlen was presenting a new song called 'Stormy Weather', and attended Noël Coward's farewell party at the end of *Design for Living*'s Broadway run. At Monette's Supper Club, Billie Holiday sat at Spike's table and sang to him. He even fitted in a wild affair with an English woman called Georgina. By now he was having such a good time that he decided to stay a bit longer. The only catch was that he needed to record some sides for Decca. He wired them: could he record in New York instead of London? The result was an ad hoc band called Spike Hughes and His Negro Orchestra, including Benny Carter, Coleman Hawkins and Chu Berry, which cut fourteen sides arranged by Spike; 'Fanfare', 'Sweet Sorrow Blues' and 'Donegal Cradle Song' were his own compositions, to boot. These players could see around corners. The sound was a true amalgam of British dance band and New York jazz, and Spike Hughes was a respected colleague and artistic equal.

What did Spike do with his new-found knowledge and crazily impressive address book? He never played the double bass again. 'Anything that came later would have been an anti-climax,' he wrote in his memoir. 'I left jazz behind me at the moment when I was enjoying it the most, the moment when all love affairs should end. To have returned to Europe and to have tried to take up jazz again where I had left it in New York would have been folly and an impossibility. When at the end of May 1933 I sailed to Southampton in the *Aquitania*, I carefully threw all Georgina's letters to me into the Atlantic; figuratively I threw jazz into the ocean too.'

Spike had got closer to the flame than any other British musician. Billie Holiday had sat at his table. And he backed away, slightly embarrassed. Still, he didn't give up on music completely: throughout the 1960s and '70s he could be seen on television, presenting Southern TV's annual coverage of the Glyndebourne Festival.

So much for the musicians. The public, too, had some peculiar ideas about how dance bands should behave. 'The central tradition of British mass dancing', wrote Eric Hobsbawm, 'moved away from jazz towards a curious phenomenon called "strict tempo" dancing, which was to become a competitive sport on British television.' No improv, nothing left to chance – plenty of people in Britain wanted their popular music rigidly ordered, with a rule book and marks out of ten.

A good beat and a good tune. That, for Britain in the 1930s, was enough.

23

FASCINATING RHYTHM: FRED ASTAIRE AND THE DANCE-HALL BOOM

Astaire and Rogers were fortunate: they embodied the swing music, white telephone, streamline era before the Second World War, when frivolousness wasn't decadent and when adolescents dreamed that 'going out' was dressing up and becoming part of a beautiful world of top hats and silver lamé.
    Pauline Kael, *The New Yorker*

By 1935 dancing was becoming a lyrical preoccupation, and this was mostly down to one emaciated man with thinning hair and a jutting chin who just happened to have a very nimble tread: Fred Astaire. 'The dancing crowds look up to some rare male', wrote Lorenz Hart in awe, 'like that Astaire male.' Their popularity had been bubbling on the screen for a while, but it wasn't until 1935 that RKO realised they had box-office gold in Astaire and his partner, Ginger Rogers. Later on he would dance with better dancers (Cyd Charisse, Rita Hayworth) and more charismatic actresses (Judy Garland, Betty Hutton), but none of them was Ginger, none of them looked quite as happy to be dancing with Fred.

Tin Pan Alley began writing for a situation in which the hero was always about to break into a dance. Luckily for the writers, Astaire had a voice that was adaptable and likeable, breezy even, the perfect blackboard for George Gershwin, Irving Berlin and Cole Porter to draw character sketches on. He was the embodiment of the new sounds on the east and west coasts. Urban and urbane, he would never have touched the novelty songs, country corn or Irish tear-jerkers that Bing dotted throughout his catalogue. He was pure top hat, white tie and tails. His only question was, 'Shall We Dance'. He could also be smoothly seductive: there is passion in 'Night and Day' and 'Let's Face the Music and Dance'. George and Ira Gershwin's 'Slap That Bass', from the 1937 Fred and Ginger vehicle *Shall We Dance*, had an ahead-of-its-time call-and-response levity ('Well, slap my face!'); much more in thrall to rhythm than melody, it anticipates Louis Jordan, or even the more riotous Prince items like 'Housequake' ('Shut up already, damn!'). Astaire sings like a dancer. Most often he would calmly communicate the lyric, the story, with the minimum of fuss and the friendliest of dispositions. He was a lyric writer's dream.

Top Hat (1935) was the film that heralded a new age of dance halls and available urban sophistication. It was there from the start in the art deco font of the titles, with Astaire swapping the stuffy gentlemen's club for a sparse modernist apartment in the opening scene. The storyline was a minor comedy of misunderstandings. Astaire reckoned: 'It certainly is escapist fare, but it's timeless. It's certainly going to hold up.' Its songs – 'Cheek to Cheek', 'Isn't This a Lovely Day (To Be Caught in the Rain)', 'Top Hat, White Tie and Tails' – came from Irving Berlin.

'I've seen several of my pictures previewed and thought they were terrible,' fussed Berlin. 'You take *Top Hat* – we went to Santa Barbara for the preview, and I thought the thing was a complete flop. But after it opened, we knew what we had.' What they had was the world on a string, a modern American world that looked like a beautiful, possible tomorrow, a necessarily hopeful one given the grim economic news and even worse from continental Europe.

Pretty quickly, people would become nostalgic for this future that never arrived. In 1946 *Blue Skies* teamed Astaire with Bing Crosby, with a score, again, by Berlin. It was flagged in detail at the beginning of the film that the story took place in the mid-1930s, as if to emphasise how much Berlin had soundtracked the era. There were a few new songs, notably 'You Keep Coming Back Like a Song' (it's hard to think of a more self-referential film), but it was most memorable for a rewrite of 'Puttin' on the Ritz', which had been a best-seller for Harry Richman in 1931.

In *Blue Skies* the song belonged to Astaire (Richman's version is all but forgotten), and he had a dance routine to match. He moved in slow motion; he toyed with his cane, alternately playfully and violently; he made it look effortless and graceful, but at the same time was clearly at full stretch, challenging anyone to match his technique. One reason for this ferocity was that Astaire intended it to be his last Hollywood performance: now forty-seven, and with Gene Kelly and Judy Garland hot on his heels, he didn't want to cut corners or fade away; he wanted to leave the world remembering possibly his greatest dance routine.

* * *

The suave modernism of *Top Hat* wasn't confined entirely to Hollywood. The London revue *Spread It Abroad* (1936) featured one of the most romantic and sensuous songs of the decade. 'These Foolish Things' was a 'list song', the kind that Cole Porter had mastered with 'You're the Top' ('You're Mahatma Gandhi!') in 1934, and which the Gershwins would lampoon beautifully ('the way you sing off key') in 1937 with 'They Can't Take That Away from Me'. It had been written by relative unknowns Eric Maschwitz and Jack Strachey. Maschwitz, born in London to Lithuanian parents, also worked under the name of Holt Marvell and had been a BBC radio producer and the editor of the *Radio Times*. He was dating the Chinese American film star Anna May Wong – feline star of 1929's silent, Limehouse-set shocker *Piccadilly* – at the time he wrote 'These Foolish Things'. Quite the Jazz Age playboy, he had also had a dalliance with the writer Jean Ross, Christopher Isherwood's model for his 'divinely decadent' Sally Bowles in *Goodbye to Berlin*.

The equally dapper, dashing Leslie 'Hutch' Hutchinson made 'These Foolish Things' a smash, a Grenada-born British star who also led a divinely decadent life: before he had even moved to Britain, his lovers had included Cole Porter, Merle Oberon and Tallulah Bankhead. He made his name in London by playing after-hours private parties for society's aristocratic bright young things. With this crowd, Hutch would slip into an Oxford-educated accent; with friends, he used American slang. He may have been the epitome of mid-1930s style, but there had to be more than one Hutch to fit into a country that viewed him as not just a talented singer but an exotic creature. A terribly handsome man, women would pass their cards to him backstage, and he didn't hesitate in following up with a dalliance; he would eventually father seven children by six different mothers. But when he performed in Liverpool, a city with one of Britain's larger black communities, he had to use the rear entrance to the hotel where he was playing. He wasn't even allowed a room there.

When Hutch visited Eric Maschwitz's studio one afternoon in 1935, searching for new material before a Parlophone recording session, he found the sheet music to 'These Foolish Things' on top of Maschwitz's piano. He picked it up, played it through and asked if he could use it. Within weeks it was simply known as 'Hutch's song'; within a year it had been recorded by Carroll Gibbons, Benny Carter, Teddy Wilson (with Billie Holiday) and Benny Goodman. Before Hutch happened to pick it up, Maschwitz had spent two years just trying to get it published.

Hutch's voice was slick, tremulous but powerful, and on his versions of 'Begin the Beguine' or 'The Way You Look Tonight' you can hear an emotional richness that was largely absent from British singers of the era and closer to the French *chanson* singers. His fame even survived a media furore around his affair with Lady Mountbatten (who had first seen him in New York and had convinced him to come over to London). At least it seemed like he had survived: he would never receive any acknowledgement for the work he did entertaining the forces in World War II, was shunned by high society, and would eventually die poor and largely forgotten in 1969. Such is the snide way racism in Britain can operate, almost invisible but more than obvious to the victim. Accompanying himself on the piano, Hutch was captured in the full flower of his fame by a Pathé news team in 1933, singing Irving Berlin's 'How Deep Is the Ocean' at London's Café Malmaison. It is a remarkably intense performance. The clip survives, but sadly a 1965 TV appearance on a show called *That's for Me*, hosted by Annie Nightingale, on which Hutch performed alongside Lulu and Cleo Laine, has been wiped. How strange to think of Hutch and Annie Nightingale, symbols of such totally separate eras, sharing a TV studio.

Like Hutch, American session players came over to Britain and stayed – too many of them, according to the Musicians' Union, which argued that British musicians were losing out. In March 1935 *Melody Maker* ran with the headline 'NO AMERICAN BANDS NEED APPLY': 'Whatever plans may now be hatching to bring any American bands to this country, for any class of work whatsoever, are likely to be completely frustrated as a result of an entirely new policy adopted by the Ministry of Labour. The immediate effect will be to veto projected visits on the part of Duke Ellington's Band and Fred Waring's Pennsylvanians.' The American musicians' union did likewise. The cross-fertilisation between British and American bands came to an end and, the war aside, American bands weren't seen here again until the 1950s.

* * *

Other than *Top Hat*, maybe the most significant musical event of 1935 was the Academy of Motion Picture Arts and Sciences coming up with the Best Original Song Written for a Motion Picture category at the Oscars. The first winner was 'The Continental', a wonderful swish of a song from another Fred Astaire and Ginger Rogers vehicle, *The Gay Divorcee*. 1935's best song, awarded the following year, turned out to be Harry Warren and Al Dubin's 'Lullaby of Broadway', beating Berlin's 'Cheek to Cheek' (from *Top Hat*) and Jerome Kern, Dorothy Fields and Jimmy McHugh's 'Lovely to Look At' (from *Roberta*). It was a worthy winner, sung by Dick Powell and Ruby Keeler as the soundtrack to Busby Berkeley's beautifully bogus version of Broadway, *Gold Diggers of 1935*. Actor George Raft called it 'something to wipe out the dirty smell of Depression. All you had to do in those days was go to a movie and Berkeley could do the rest: give you a date with a great-looking dame; give you a top hat and tails; put plenty of green stuff in your pocket; and get you to hit all the right joints on the Great White Way.' Crooners emerged from waterfalls; chorus girls created the shape of a daffodil. Of course, Berkeley's Hollywood was choking the life out of Broadway. But the clubs and dance halls were full, and the next wave of new music meant theatres and cinemas, too, would soon be bursting at the seams with dancers.

24

EIGHTY-EIGHT KEY SMILES: FATS WALLER AND FRIENDS

From the radio, you heard a different kind of modern America. As much a marker of the age as Astaire, Corbusier and Schiaparelli were the great pianists. And the most famous pianist, the most fun and – with his one-size-too-small bowler hat, fat 'tache and fat cigar – the most recognisable was Fats Waller. In a fairer world, Fats would have had a filmography to match Fred Astaire's. He was incredibly charismatic, influential, and his musical taste – like his taste in everything – was all-consuming.

Thomas Waller had been born in Harlem in 1904. His mother was the organist in the local church, and that interested little Thomas greatly; she hired him a piano tutor, and he learned how to read and write music. By the age of fifteen the lad was playing the organ in a silent-movie theatre for $23 a week. When his mother died in 1920, the sixteen-year-old Waller moved into the home of his piano tutor, Russell Brooks, and took a giant step forward. It was Brooks who introduced him, musically and personally, to James P. Johnson and Willie 'The Lion' Smith, the two greatest stride-piano players in the world. Recognising a kindred spirit, they took him under their wings.

Waller's playing was so special that it became a threat to his own safety. Leaving a show in Chicago in 1926, he was grabbed and bundled into a car, then ordered inside a place called the Hawthorne Inn with a gun in his back. Sweating, terrified, he was rather surprised to be pushed through the doors and find a party in full swing. He was the unwitting 'surprise guest' at Al Capone's birthday bash. No one was going to kill him; they just wanted him to play the piano. Making the most of a tricky situation, Waller stayed at the Hawthorne Inn for three days, drank the place dry and earned thousands of dollars in cash-money tips from Capone and his cronies.

The 1920s saw Waller playing in clubs and revues. There he was, happily working on his mentor James P. Johnson's stride style, working it into New York's jazz and theatrical vanguard with dense and dextrous pieces like 'Handful of Keys' and 'African Ripples'. At the end of the decade he was commissioned to write songs for the revues *Hot Chocolates* and *Loads of Coal*, turning out 'Ain't Misbehavin'', 'Black and Blue' and 'Honeysuckle Rose' – fun-loving, copper-bottomed jazz standards.

But it was a run of recordings from 1934 to 1939 with a six-piece band, Fats Waller and His Rhythm, that made him an international figure. He recorded hundreds of sides. Some were filler, but his calming, easy style could make silk purses out of almost anything. He stepped up from ragtime, blew through 1920s jazz and breezed into the swing era. He rarely rehearsed, recorded as much as he could, made sure he was never seen out of his dandy uniform and became one of the era's beloved entertainers. 'Then I'll Be Tired of You', 'Blue Turning Grey Over You', 'Keeping Out of Mischief Now', the daffy 'You're Not the Only Oyster in the Stew', his takes on Hoagy Carmichael's 'Two Sleepy People' and Sammy Cahn's 'Until the Real Thing Comes Along': on all these titles he mixed geniality and a feather-light ease with real emotional heft. 'This Is So Nice It Must Be Illegal' was a title that summed Fats up.

His workload was prolific and his taste admirably catholic. In December 1938 a new show was broadcast by WABC called *This Is New York*, which attempted to capture the feel of the city in words and dialogue. *Radio Guide* previewed it as 'The sidewalks of New York and the people, famous and obscure, who tread them.' Fats Waller would be the show's very first guest, taking the listeners on a musical tour of Harlem. The host was critic Gilbert Sedes: 'There are exactly 243 pounds of Mr Waller tonight,' he deadpanned. 'There are also ten fingers that weigh nothing, because they are composed of pure genius.' A week later Waller was jamming with Louis Armstrong on Martin Block's WNEW show *Make Believe Ballroom*, breezing through 'I Got Rhythm', 'Jeepers Creepers', 'On the Sunny Side of the Street' and his own 'Honeysuckle Rose'; days later he was recording a sprightly 'Sweet Sue' and 'I Can't Give You Anything but Love, Baby' with crooner Gene Austin. As soon as the new year kicked in, Waller was in London, where he wrote and recorded his six-part *London Suite*, blending hot jazz ('Piccadilly'), European classical references ('Chelsea', 'Whitechapel') and hands-in-pockets mooches on 'Soho' and 'Limehouse'.* It was as if he knew he had to beat the clock. His huge appetite – for steaks, for gin, for women – was always going to catch up with him, and he died of pneumonia just before Christmas 1943. He had achieved a lot in thirty-nine years, even getting to play his own songs on the organ at Notre-Dame cathedral.

* * *

One night, Fats Waller was playing in a club, and Art Tatum walked in. Waller paused and told the audience, 'I only play the piano, but tonight God is in the house.'

---

* Waller's recording of *London Suite* wouldn't be released until 1951; in the meantime, Ted Heath's British jazz band had released a version, which turned out to be hotter in its swing than Waller's near-legendary, then-unheard recording.

No pianist played more piano than Art Tatum. He had learned by ear and was playing hymns on the piano by the time he was three. George Shearing called him 'the most pianistic of jazz pianists'. Ask other jazz players, and you'll hear similar reverence. You can see why fellow musicians were stunned by his ability: one listen to a Tatum record and you're in no doubt of his skill. Is it even at the right speed? How does he do that? The man was dextrous. His fans included not only Waller and Shearing, but Sergei Rachmaninov and Vladimir Horowitz. Almost blind, he was also a ridiculously calm presence at the piano, given the endless high-speed runs and harmonics he was coming out with. After earning a reputation at clubs in Toledo, Ohio, his arrival in New York – to perform in clubs with former Duke Ellington singer Adelaide Hall in 1932 – was much anticipated. He cut his signature 'Tea for Two' for Brunswick the following year, and it was a hit record, irresistibly sprightly, but his showiness – faster, *faster!* – could also drive a listener nuts. Post-war, in the album era, his records sounded flowery and overbearing. No question, his technique was dazzling and influential, and he inspired Teddy Wilson and almost every modern player who came after, but I'll bet Richard Clayderman was a fan too.

Earl Hines's style was just as baroque and compelling. Like Tatum, he could sweep up and down the keyboard, but there was no showiness, only absolute cheek in his playing. He would add off-beats, sudden stops, silent interludes, and no one had done this before. It made sense that he worked with Louis Armstrong when he first moved to Chicago from Pennsylvania in 1925: a good match, both always communicated humanity and real joy.

On 28 December 1928 – Hines's twenty-fifth birthday – his band opened at the Grand Terrace, which was to Chicago what the Cotton Club was to New York. Hines picked up the nickname 'Fatha' from Ted Pearson, an NBC radio announcer at the Grand Terrace: as the band played its radio theme, Reginald Foresythe's 'Deep Forest', Pearson cooed, 'Here comes Fatha Hines, leading his children through the deep forest.' The nickname stuck and led to a regular radio skit on all their broadcasts. A voice would call, 'Fatha Hines! . . . Fatha!!!' Then there would be a distant reply: '. . . *Yeeeess?*' Applause would ring out, and the

NBC announcer would confirm, 'Yes, it is, ladies and gentlemen – it's Earl "Fatha" Hines and his great band, playing for you from the Grand Terrace on the South Side of Chicago!'*

Hines and his band were on the radio sometimes seven nights a week, coast-to-coast across America. Chicago was in the perfect spot to deal with America's live-broadcasting time-zone issues, and Hines's band picked up more broadcasts than any other outfit. Among his bigger radio hits were 'Blue Drag', Fats Waller's 'I've Got a Feeling I'm Falling', 'On the Sunny Side of the Street' and – you can't really blame him – an original called 'Fifty Seven Varieties'.

Though he was given protection and work security by Capone's mob throughout the 1930s Depression, Hines wasn't able to take his career beyond the Grand Terrace. Nor was he free to say anything to the police when they occasionally buttonholed him: 'They had a habit of putting the pictures of different people that would bring information in the newspaper, and the next day you would find them out there in the lake somewhere, swimming around with some chains attached to their feet if you know what I mean.' Eventually, in 1940, Hines went into litigation with the club's owner, Capone henchman Ed Fox. The Grand Terrace then abruptly closed, and Fox disappeared. In spite of a huge offer from Benny Goodman to become his pianist, Hines instead took his band on the road for the next eight years.

Unusually, the Hines band played extensively in the South. Back in 1931 they had been the first black band to do so, and were rewarded with a bomb that exploded under the stage as they played a show in Alabama. ('None of us got hurt,' said Hines drily, 'but we didn't play so well after that either.') Travelling by train, 'they would send a porter back to our car to let us know when the dining room was cleared, and then we would all go in together. We couldn't eat when we wanted to. We had to eat when they were ready for us.' He was famously good to work for. Hit by the draft in World War II, Hines briefly had a twelve-piece,

---

* Earl Hines and Duke Ellington were once, unbeknownst to them, staying at the same hotel. Ellington was waiting for the lift. When the door opened, Hines stepped out. 'Fatha!' shouted a surprised Duke. 'Motha!' replied Hines.

all-female band, before expanding it to twenty-eight, with fourteen male and fourteen female players. This was pretty much unheard of for a name band. Earl Hines was a gentleman.

* * *

Not long before he died in 1943, Fats Waller became the first black composer to write the music for a Broadway musical with a white cast (it did employ one black couple, described in reviews as 'dusky', who danced to hot numbers during the set changes). *Early to Bed* became a legend: even though it was a hit, no score survived, and thanks to a musicians' strike during its run, there were no recordings of any of the songs. Before it opened, Waller had taken a friend to a bar, sat at the piano and played him the whole score. Waller 'was excited about every song, stopping to repeat, again and again, phrases and chords he particularly fancied . . . filling the room with études of ecstasy, sentimental songs and rocking riffs', said the friend. '*Early to Bed* was a triumph for Fats, every song was a gem.' There were thirteen of them too. It opened in the same year as *Oklahoma!* The scriptwriter for the book was George Marion, who had scripted Fred Astaire and Ginger Rogers's breakthrough movie *The Gay Divorcee*. Just how good must *Early to Bed* have been? Waller's death might have ruled out a third wave of 'Black Broadway', which had flowered briefly in the early 1900s with Will Marion Cook's *Clorindy*, and in the 1920s through Noble Sissle and Eubie Blake's musicals. *Early to Bed*, largely unheard, felt like a lost possible future.

A few songs eventually resurfaced in the 1978 Waller revue *Ain't Misbehavin'*; then painstaking research yielded an incomplete version in 2009, which made it onto the stage in New York. One Waller enthusiast, John McWhorter, wouldn't leave it there, and eventually in 2013 he found the grail. Waller's son had inherited his dad's effects and, during a low point, had given his lawyer a box of papers, letters and manuscripts in lieu of payment. McWhorter managed to trace the lawyer (now deceased) to Tenafly, New Jersey, where the man's son had inherited the box. When McWhorter opened it, the box contained not only the missing songs from *Early to Bed*, but original sketches for the score, complete with first tries, instrumental breaks and even melodies that never made the show. 'In short,' said McWhorter, reining in his enthusiasm, 'the *Early to Bed* tunes are good.' One of the lost songs was called 'The Girl Who Doesn't Ripple When She Bends'. What a title! Decades after he died, an unheard, unknown scrap of Fats Waller's oeuvre could still make an undertaker laugh.

25

TIGHT LIKE THAT: THE AGE OF SWING

At the time, swing music, big-band music, and Benny Goodman in particular were so boundlessly popular that people who made room for it in their lives have never forgotten it. I get calls from people who are in a kind of time warp.
  Benny Goodman pianist Mel Powell, 1990

America's big-band era threw up more big names, real star names that have lasted, than any previous popular-music boom: Benny Goodman, Glenn Miller, Tommy and Jimmy Dorsey, Jimmie Lunceford, Duke Ellington, Artie Shaw, Woody Herman, Charlie Barnet, Lionel Hampton, Count Basie, Gene Krupa, Les Brown, Stan Kenton and more. They were loved, fawned over, the band line-ups memorised, heroes lionised, and great arguments would break out among schoolboys over trombone players. If there had been Panini stickers available in the 1930s, then a big-bands collection would have given football a run for its money.

The swing bandleaders were a new breed of pop star, unlike any before or since. Some, like Artie Shaw and Billy Eckstine, looked the part of a pin-up, but mostly they were furrow-browed, even when they were smiling. Mono-minded, they could think of nothing – not base-ball, not women, not food – beyond sound. Their glazed eyes gave them away. They might have been smiling for the camera, but you could read it in their eyes: their mind was on the logistics of getting to Minneapolis in a snowstorm, or the positioning of the third clarinet on that corner stage in Pomona. In this respect, the bandleader was more like a football manager than a conventional pop star. Benny Goodman was closer to Arsène Wenger than Al Jolson.

* * *

The dancing boom, popularised by Fred Astaire, had led to the construc-tion of some spectacular venues. The ballrooms, via radio broadcasts, created a soundtrack without a picture, and listeners tried to imagine the sumptuous spaces from which the music was being broadcast. The Glen Island Casino, with its high ceiling criss-crossed by heavy wooden beams, was built on a small island near New Rochelle; it was said you could see the moonlight on the water of Long Island Sound through its windows. Former bandleader Frank Dailey's Meadowbrook Ballroom in Cedar Grove, New Jersey, was biggest with the white college kids in black-and-white saddle shoes, with tables around the dancefloor and a large balcony on three sides. Hollywood's Palladium had 12,500 square feet of dancefloor, was large enough to include two restaurants, and once pulled in 35,000 Harry James fans in a single week. In Manhattan, at 1658 Broadway, Roseland – with its mirrored walls and ceiling studied with hundreds of tiny lights – was refined enough that it inspired stories by John O'Hara, F. Scott Fitzgerald and Sherwood Anderson. Swing was born at Roseland in the late 1920s, thanks to Fletcher Henderson's groundbreaking orchestra; he ruled there for a full twenty years.

Henderson was the arranger and architect who laid the foundations for swing's extraordinary success in 1935 and 1936. He had shown a feel for big bands as far back as 1923. Prior to that, he had been a touring pianist for Ethel Waters, who would roar at Henderson to try and knock the classical sensibilities out of him (listening to his intro on her 1923 recording 'Ain't Goin' Marry', you can see her point). When he put his own jazz band together, there could be eight, nine, ten or more players, which was highly unusual. Along with his co-arranger Don Redman (on clarinet and saxophones), he knew how to write, and what, for a larger band. He wrote for a section rather than individual players, with call-and-response parts built in, while allowing room for improvisation. The band's syncopation gradually became smoother, and pent-up power was channelled into simple punchy riffs that band members like tenor saxophonist Coleman Hawkins could solo over. When a jazz player was secure, relaxed and comfortable with the rhythm, he could soar, stay airborne, as if on a swing above the ground. He was swinging.

It would take years for Henderson to smooth the join between the Original Dixieland Jazz Band's rickety racket and the bigger sound in his head. You can trace the growing confidence – and volume – through 'Hop Off' (1928) and 'Sugar Foot Stomp' (1931) to a dozen sides cut in September 1934 with a thirteen-piece orchestra that had a strikingly new, clean sound. He had the sound nailed: listen to 'Harlem Madness' and hear how Buster Bailey's clarinet and Henderson's own piano are talking to the orchestra, while drummer Vic Engle emphasises the off-beat. Pleased as punch, Henderson titled one of his 1934 recordings 'Hotter Than 'Ell', and no one was going to bet against it.

It may have taken a decade, but Henderson had created something quite new. 'Camp Meeting' and 'Wild Party' anticipated the sound of swing's biggest name, the Benny Goodman band, on 1935's 'King Porter Stomp'; 'Wrappin' It Up' effectively invented the sound that Glenn Miller would pick up and run with five or six years later. On the verge of the swing era, though, there still wasn't enough work to hold the Henderson orchestra together, and his entire personnel handed in their notice. Henderson's misfortune was Goodman's gain: he had decided to put a large band together at just the right time.

The big band may have evolved with the tenderloin sound of Fletcher Henderson in the 1920s and early '30s, but it wasn't until 1935 – the same year as *Top Hat* – that America fell in love with the sound, and the man who would soon be known as the King of Swing was twenty-six-year-old Benny Goodman. When Goodman took his band on the road, the results astonished everybody, and within three years he was a major celebrity, film star and millionaire.

Goodman was an intuitive talent and a beautiful clarinet player, with a total liquidity of sound.* He was also a highly professional popular musician. In 1932 he had decided to learn how to read and execute any musical score he was given – be it by Harry Warren or Mozart – as this would be the best way 'of riding out the worsening Depression'. Goodman had cut his first record, 'He's the Last Word', with Ben Pollack and His Californians in 1926, when he was just seventeen. Coming in after a saucy nasal chorus from the Williams Sisters, his solo is incredibly assured and notably rougher-edged than the more familiar Goodman of the 1930s. Compare it to his playing on Ethel Waters's recording of Irving Berlin's 'Heat Wave' (1933), shortly after he had made the hard-headed decision to study the classics: 'Heat Wave' is hot enough, but it has a purity of sound; you can hear Goodman moving away from his Chicago jazz roots into something more scholastic.

So how did Goodman gain his crown as the King of Swing? He was obsessed with precision. He figured that if his musicians were so famil-iar with their charts that they didn't need sheet music, then they could

---

* Initially, Goodman was just one of a series of gifted Chicago clarinettists, all in thrall to local heroes Johnny Dodds and the poised, smoother Jimmy Noone, who had emerged in the late 1920s. There was the pre-fame Jimmy Dorsey, the scratchy and angular Frank Teschemacher, the lugubrious playing of Buster Bailey, and the intuitive, almost chaotic Pee Wee Russell. Bailey played with King Oliver before moving to New York and joining Fletcher Henderson's orchestra at Louis Armstrong's behest; Russell turned down all approaches from big bands and played in small groups (including a Newport Jazz Festival ensemble with Thelonious Monk) all his career; Dorsey thrived in the swing era with his own band; while Teschemacher was killed in a car crash before the swing era got going. Goodman's sound was closest to Noone's, just as fluid but more sharply focused, more mathematically precise.

think more about how they played. His phrase for this was 'digging out', and it worked. Fletcher Henderson may have had better soloists in his band, but their work sounded sloppy and ragged in comparison. Goodman's band was tight, but it swung.

His professionalism and screwed-down mentality made him a perfect candidate for running a band. In 1934 he was offered a four-month residency to open the Billy Rose Music Hall at 52nd and Broadway, so he put an orchestra together. They recorded 'Moonglow' for Columbia and scored a major hit, which in turn led NBC to hire the Goodman band for their Saturday-night show *Let's Dance*. Sponsored by Nabisco as a means of promoting their new Ritz crackers, *Let's Dance* premiered in December 1934, with the Goodman outfit one of three regular bands, alongside the sweet, society jazz of Kel Murray and the Latin fare of Xavier Cugat. The auditions for the show had been piped into the offices of NBC to see if the secretaries would get up and dance, Goodman had squeaked in by a single vote.

Indulging a whim – and utterly unaware that there would be an appetite for his sound just months down the line – Goodman chose Fletcher Henderson to be the arranger for the band (his first choice, Duke Ellington, was otherwise detained). With this new platform Henderson's sound would no longer be the esoteric doodling of a chemistry student; it would be pop. The collaboration didn't start with a bang. A few months into 1935, just as *Let's Dance* was taking off, the show was cancelled when there was a strike at Nabisco. A coast-to-coast Goodman band tour had already been booked for July; with no money, the musicians had to drive themselves. It was a disaster. Most venues were expecting sweet jazz. In Grand Junction, Colorado, they played behind chicken wire to keep themselves safe from flying bottles.

The tour finished with a three-week residency at the Palomar Ballroom, Los Angeles, where – to their great surprise – they were met by huge crowds. Unsure, playing it safe, the band started the first show by performing waltzes and stock arrangements, and got no reaction. Drummer Gene Krupa called Goodman over: 'If we're gonna die,' he whispered, 'let's die playing our own thing.' So they played Henderson's arrangement of 'King Porter Stomp', the Jelly Roll Morton piano tune; in a moment of terror and faced with restive white teens, Goodman, Krupa and the band turned back to a storied post-rag/pre-jazz moment. Immediately, it was clear that was what the people wanted to hear – the stuff they'd heard on *Let's Dance*. After the show, Goodman realised that time-zone differences had meant that while his band weren't heard until midnight on the east coast, after Kel Murray and Xavier Cugat's bands, in California their stint on *Let's Dance* had been broadcast at 9 p.m., peak party time. The dancers at the Palomar went bananas, and a new era was born.

* * *

Three places are milestones in the Benny Goodman story: the Palomar, the Paramount and Carnegie Hall. Each not only provided a significant step up in Goodman's career, but their size and social significance showed how quickly jazz was being accepted into mainstream popular culture in the 1930s.

After their three-week residency at the Palomar had finished, the band took on a booking at the Paramount Theatre in New York in March 1937. They would play between screenings of Claudette Colbert's *Maid of Salem*. Before the first show, they turned up at seven in the morning for an early rehearsal and were pleasantly surprised to see a couple of hundred kids lined up outside the box office. 'We couldn't help feeling', said Goodman, 'that every one of our most loyal supporters in the five boroughs was already on hand.' The crowd whistled and cat-called poor Colbert, impatient for the intermission. The Goodman band finally appeared in front of the screen on a rising platform. 'The noise', gasped Goodman, 'sounded like Times Square on New Year's Eve.'

By 1937 they were in their pomp and cut a version of Louis Prima's 'Sing, Sing, Sing'. Gene Krupa's drum intro – something that was pretty much unheard of – was so distinctive that Elvis Presley would use it as his walk-on music at every show from 1970 until his death.

Behind the professorial public image, Goodman didn't try too hard to win friends. He rarely took the time to learn the names of his sidemen, just calling them 'Pops' until he remembered their real names. The first time a nervous Peggy Lee sang in a studio with the Goodman band, her hands were shaking so hard as she held the sheet music that the first take sounded like she was standing next to a bonfire; Goodman calling her 'Pops' probably didn't make her feel any more at ease. As a master of technique, he also wanted riddles to solve, the kind that Broadway and Tin Pan Alley weren't providing. The results were such odd concoctions as 'Mozart Matriculates' (1939), 'Clarinet à la King' and 'Caprice Paganini' (both 1941). It wasn't depth Goodman was going for here, just trickier technique.

Still, there was equality among his musicians. Trumpet player Cootie Williams joined from Duke Ellington's band in 1940, with Duke negotiating the contract of $200 a week. Cootie also played in Goodman's sextet and enjoyed featured solos with the full band. 'That Goodman band,' said Cootie, 'I loved it. It had a beat and there was something there I wanted to play with.' So did vibes player Lionel Hampton and pianist Teddy Wilson. Goodman was the first white leader of a racially integrated band. Cootie was diplomatic: 'He's just Goodman, not one way with this man and another way with someone else. The same with everyone. I think I was happier in music the first year I was with him than I ever was.' Not everyone was so happy: Raymond Scott's band marked the occasion of his perceived defection with a lament called 'When Cootie Left the Duke'.

The peak of Goodman's fame came with a show at Carnegie Hall – it had been good enough for the King of Jazz, so why not the King of Swing? – on 16 January 1938 that paid tribute to twenty years of jazz. Harry James, who was then Goodman's main trumpet player, handled Louis Armstrong's 'Shine'; Johnny Hodges and Cootie Williams were best placed to pay tribute to Duke Ellington on 'Blue Reverie'; Lester Young played Fats Waller's 'Honeysuckle Rose'. The quartet played 'Stompin' at the Savoy' and the Goodman/Wilson/Hampton tune 'Dizzy Spells', and they encored with Fletcher Henderson's 'Big John's Special', which pre-dated the Goodman band by a year. It was a complete triumph, and the recordings would be endlessly compiled, anthologised and reissued for decades to come. Gene Krupa's mad tom-toms and rimshots on 'Sing, Sing, Sing' – and the image of the drummer lost to the rhythm, eyebrows flying over his grinning face – remains one of the immovable foundation stones of pop. What a noise!

With the Carnegie Hall concert, Goodman took jazz into America's front room. On top of the music, he set up a swathe of pop habits that would endure for decades: he had the first band fan club; he made end-of-year polls for musicians a sport; and he was the first jazz musician to be played on film by a Hollywood star, Steve Allen, with Mrs Goodman transformed into the divine Donna Reed. Whether he was on radio or the big screen, whether he was leading his Orchestra, Trio or Quartet, Goodman was a hero to young America. Swing was the musical material-isation of the American Dream, and it wanted a Jimmy Stewart figure to be its physical incarnation. Benny Goodman was young, white and working class. He'd made it to the top of the pile. He got the gig.

* * *

After the breakthrough at the Palomar, it hadn't taken long for rival bandleaders to start cutting in on Goodman's action. The touring dance bands now became the new arbiters of public taste. After Cole Porter had introduced 'Begin the Beguine' to audiences in a 1935 show called *Jubilee*, it had disappeared from view, and Porter had written it off. Three years later, Artie Shaw recorded it as a B-side and it became the biggest hit of the year; what Broadway couldn't do, the big bands appar-ently could. No wonder the highways of America were clogged with orchestra coaches.

Another fine clarinettist, Shaw had a very clear idea of what the new Swing Age had to offer. It was very different to the Paul Whiteman approach: 'Swing music was regarded by most people as noisy, blatant, full of drum riffs and trumpet riffs and so on. The contribution I made musically was to show that you could use the swing idiom and apply it to music that was accepted – Jerome Kern, Porter, Gershwin, even Sigmund Romberg and Victor Herbert. So, y'know, the idea of swing-ing a tune like "Yesterdays" by Kern, or "The Man I Love", or "Lover Come Back to Me", or "Begin the Beguine" for that matter, that was a rather strange notion at that time.'

One of the other competitors in this race for fame was Bing Crosby's kid brother Bob, whose orchestra was essentially Ben Pollack's band with a new leader. Bob had originally been a singer, always in the shadow of his brother, but when he started leading a band in the mid-1930s, they had a huge hit with their goosed-up, conurbation-sized 'South Rampart Street Parade'. Crosby ran with it, and almost everything they recorded was a close cousin, but Irving Fazola's limpid clarinet rising over eastern seaboard drums and crash cymbals was always a lot of fun. Within the orchestra was a smaller Dixieland band called Bob Crosby's Bob-Cats, who showed where Crosby's heart really was; he was a good decade ahead of the British 'trad' revival of original New Orleans jazz, but that's a story we'll come to later. He stubbornly stuck to playing older New Orleans standards, in the spirit of their tradition, but thrillingly translated into a big-band context. On a melancholy 1938 original, 'My Inspiration', Fazola floated, and the orchestra, after picking up mid-song quite beautifully, was at once reverential and good-time.

All this time, there were other better but less popular musicians. They were neglected by the entertainment business because black skin was not exploitable on a national scale. Goodman, Shaw, Crosby, they all looked up to Duke Ellington. Artie Shaw named names: 'You talk about men like [bandleaders] Abe Lyman, Ben Bernie, Irving Aaronson, with whom I worked . . . These men weren't musicians. They weren't particularly interested. They purveyed music. It's like a man who sells television sets – he's not an electronics man, he's not particularly interested in the quality of the set or what makes it work. They're not creators, they're simply purveyors. There's always room for entrepreneurs. Now, let's take Duke Ellington. It's a rare talent that can maintain that organisation, but not allow that to dampen his creative qualities.'*

* * *

---

* This is unnecessarily harsh on Irving Aaronson and His Commanders. Their mid-1920s sides for Victor are tricksy but fun, with short solo bursts and inventive ensemble choruses. Shaw would dismiss them as a 'funny hat band', but their 1928 recording of Cole Porter's 'Let's Misbehave' is the Jazz Age bottled.

Not every big band considered itself a swing band. Duke Ellington's was in a world of its own, blending colour and harmony in a manner that was simply referred to as 'Ellingtonia'. Count Basie's blues-based band was probably the toughest of all, thanks to the Count's emphasis on rhythm and stomps, often four square on the beat, hi-hat fizzing like proto-disco – the band had a groove unlike any other. There was no tension, just the easy propulsion of guitarist Freddie Green, Walter Page's walking basslines and the spare, sensitive brushed drums of Joe Jones, who knew exactly when to let fly.

After breaking out of the Kansas City scene, Basie was brought to the Roseland Ballroom in 1937 by John Hammond, and then taken into the recording studio, where his band cut a bunch of classics for Decca*: there was the panther-like piano intro from Basie on 'Jumpin' at the Woodside', with Herschel Evans's high-kicking clarinet; a version of Ray Noble's 'Cherokee', with its ooh-wah brass a forerunner of the narcotic Glenn Miller sound; and 'Topsy', futuristic enough to become a number-three US hit when closely revisited by drummer Cozy Cole in 1958. Maybe they didn't sound as big as other big bands, but their riffs were punishing. Added to this, fleet-footed tenor-sax man Lester Young was modern before the term existed in jazz. At their best – with 'One O'Clock Jump' (1937), 'Time Out' (1937) or 'Doggin' Around' (1939) – they caused more dancefloor damage than any swing band.

It wasn't always simple. Basie vocalist Jimmy Rushing: 'We went to New York and we had a lot of trouble trying to please the people. Our band was mostly on the blues kick and at that time people didn't know too much about the blues. But they would nod their heads, and as long as they would nod their heads we were satisfied.' Woody Herman saw them at the Roseland and was smitten, and asked Basie, 'What is that you're playing with such a great beat?' 'Oh, that's just the blues,' replied the Count, and maybe that was the ingredient other bands lacked, the grit in the oyster.

---

* Basie thanked Hammond for his break with the urgent, Eddie Durham-arranged 'John's Idea'.

Count Basie did OK, but capital 'S' Swing wasn't such great news for most black musicians – unless they actually worked with Benny Goodman. Black pioneers like Fletcher Henderson had often been cheerfully pushed into ancillary roles, creating a frustration and a pressure that would build up and explode in the mid-1940s. Hollywood also now had less time for black bandleaders, even Duke Ellington, given that there were prominent white alternatives. *Symphony in Black* (1935) would be the Duke's last leading role. *The Big Broadcast of 1937* would give Goodman's band acres of celluloid, while in the same year Ellington was given scraps with *The Hit Parade*, sharing the screen with pin-up Eddy Duchin.

Ultimately, there was *Birth of the Blues* (1941). You could tell it had its heart in the right place from the opening titles: it was dedicated to the musical pioneers of Memphis and New Orleans who favoured 'the hot over the sweet' – those early jazz men who took American music out of the rut and put it 'in the groove'. The problem with it was, this being Hollywood in 1941, it was entirely about white players. It starred Bing Crosby as a Bix-alike. Black players still said, 'Yes'm.' In 1940 *DownBeat* ran a piece about black bandleaders earning only half the money of their white counterparts; the subheading was: 'Negro leaders could make more money running a rib joint'. Things would turn again, of course, but the swing experience must have been chastening for the likes of Ellington and Basie. If the black bands were the hot bands that swung the most, how much did it hurt that the phenomenon that became swing largely swept these outfits aside?

* * *

How much tougher it must have been for a mixed-race woman to lead a big band. It is mind-blowing that Ina Ray Hutton's name remains so obscure. To get noticed in the 1930s, with so much conventional male competition, Hutton had to dance like Mata Hari, sing like Betty Boop's big sister and make herself up like a Hollywood star. She was happy to oblige: 'I'm selling this show as a music programme,' she'd say with a wink, 'but if curves attract an audience, so much the better.'

Smart enough to work out that a top-quality, all-girl jazz band would take the Swing Age by storm, 'the Blond Bombshell of Rhythm' led her band, the Melodears, right through the 1930s, popping up on screen in *The Big Broadcast of 1936* alongside Bing Crosby and Al Bowlly. This was a remarkable feat, when you consider there were so few acknowledged female jazz musicians in the '30s. The most visible were vibes player Margie Hyams and trumpeter Billie Rogers, who both had stints in Woody Herman's band. Hyams would later recall the instantly dismissive looks when she walked into a room full of male jazz musicians: 'You weren't really looked upon as a musician, especially in clubs. There was more interest in what you were going to wear or how your hair was fixed – they just wanted you to look attractive, ultra-feminine, largely because you were doing something they didn't consider feminine. Most of the time I fought it and didn't listen to them.'

Ina Ray Hutton had been born Odessa Cowan in 1916 and grew up with her half-sister June (also a successful singer) in a black neighbourhood in Chicago's South Side. US census records listed her as being 'negro' and 'mulatto', but Hutton 'passed' as white throughout her career. She studied dance, picking up a rave review in the *Chicago Defender* when she was just seven, and made her Broadway debut at fourteen. She was eighteen when Duke Ellington's manager Irving Mills convinced her to put together the all-female Melodears and made her the leader. They were an instant hit, touring solidly for five years and appearing in several Paramount film shorts of their own, including the racily titled *Feminine Rhythm* (1935), *Accent on Girls* (1936) and *Swing, Hutton, Swing* (1937). The latter included the excellent 'Truckin'', and a surviving clip reveals them to be an extremely tight and exciting band: guitarist Helen Baker keeps time by bobbing her head, as Ina Ray does her best to tap-dance in a tight black gown that pretty much glues her knees together. You half expect the camera to pan round and reveal a crowd of cartoon wolves, leering and cheering. Safe to say, Ina Ray Hutton was not short of charisma.

The Melodears' outfits included boyish trousers, but also long, ultra-feminine, sequinned outfits; *DownBeat* reported that Hutton's stage wardrobe included four hundred gowns. Hutton would pave the way for a wave of female bands who took off in the 1940s, when many leading male musicians were serving in the US armed forces. However, in 1939 she made the contrary decision to disband the Melodears and recruit an all-male band. She was tired of her outfit being seen as a novelty act – reviews were uniformly snippy – and she told *DownBeat* she was 'through with glamour'. To emphasise the point, she even went brunette. It wasn't until the 1950s, by now fronting the *Ina Ray Hutton Show* on TV, that she got the girls back together, winning an Emmy in the process. Her last recorded performance came in the 1975 film *Brother, Can You Spare a Dime?*, and she died in California in 1984.

One possible reason Hutton has been so overlooked is that she cut very few records. Her recordings were mostly for Okeh and Elite in the early 1940s, but radio broadcasts make up the bulk of a 2011 compilation, the sole collection of her work. Also, so many details of her story seem frustratingly buried. Interviews were rare, and there is precious little available online, but the bare bones – a platinum blonde pioneer for women in music, fashion and television – cry out for a biopic.

Hutton was happy to flash her smile. If you wanted to get by purely on musical talent, it was harder still. Margie Hyams would end up in George Shearing's high-profile quartet by the late 1940s, though her name remains obscure. Looking back, she was angry: 'I just thought at the time that I was too young to handle it, but now I see that it was really rampant chauvinism.'

* * *

By the late 1930s the local dance hall had been added to cinemas and theatres as a venue for hearing new music. It wasn't long before everyone could identify their favourite band by their signature tune, like Tommy Dorsey's 'I'm Getting Sentimental Over You'. Things could happen very fast: a hastily put-together band like Bunny Berigan's could have a massive instant hit with 'I Can't Get Started' in 1937; Bob Crosby's orchestra likewise struck gold with the minimalist 'Big Noise from Winnetka'.*

---

* Crosby: 'It came about because of a bunch of kids who came in the Blackhawk restaurant from a Chicago suburb called Winnetka, and were making so much

The bigger-name bandleaders could afford to experiment a little. Artie Shaw and His Orchestra featured in *Second Chorus*, a 1940 Fred Astaire movie in which a student jokes about writing a dissertation on 'the future of the harpsichord in swing music'. It was a gag that was based in reality. Shaw's splinter group the Gramercy Five – named after his local telephone exchange – included Johnny Guarnieri on harpsichord. 1940's 'Summit Ridge Drive' was terrific, with Basie-like riffs underpinned by Guarnieri's rugged, rhythmic playing. You have to wonder why no one else picked up on this new baroque direction – at least not until Mitch Miller stuck a distorted harpsichord under Rosemary Clooney on 'Come on-a My House' a full ten years later.

On the west coast in the late 1930s an intriguing swing variant sprung up. Since 1934 Bob Wills and His Texas Playboys had been packing up to six thousand people into Cain's Ballroom in Tulsa, Oklahoma, scoring radio hits with records like 'New San Antonio Rose' (1939), a blend of horns, steel guitar, hard-thrummed acoustic guitar and a dash of Mexicana. These shows were broadcast on KVOO, which declared, 'Tuesday night at nine is Bob Wills time.' Bit by bit he added saxophones, clarinets, call-and-response vocals and jazz solos. The organisation was just like a swing band. On stage Wills was a showman, with interjections that could be introductions to his musicians ('Ah, play it, Tommy!') or just joyous hollers ('Ah *haaa*!'). He always looked like he was having an incredible time. He had an intense look in his eyes, which could have been down to his enjoyment of the music or his boozing and womanising – he chalked up five divorces in six years.

By the early 1940s Wills and his Playboys had moved, like so many Dust Bowl refugees, to California, expanding to twenty-three members

---

noise for encores that one night in desperation, after we'd played everything in the book, I said to Ray Bauduc and Bobby Haggart to play a bass and drum duet. They started to play the blues, and Haggart started that silly whistle which no one else has been able to copy because he had this cleavage in his front teeth. We wound up with one of the biggest hits ever recorded in the jazz field. Nothing but a bass and drum and a silly whistle.'

and taking the sound with them.* This sound was a country–jazz amalgam that had no name until 1942,† when Los Angeles DJ Al Jarvis
threw a competition to uncover the most popular swing bandleader.
To his surprise, Spade Cooley won, and Jarvis duly tagged Cooley the
'King of Western Swing'. No fool, Cooley then took the best players
from the LA scene, bought them white suits and gave them suitably
countrified names, like Smokey Rogers and Deuce Spriggens. Before
too long he had his own TV show, *The Hoffman Hayride*, which ran
for ten years from 1947, with guests of the calibre of Frank Sinatra,
Bob Hope, Frankie Laine and Dinah Shore.‡ By this point, the swing
element was fading in popularity, and 'western' would be folded into
'country' to become a more malleable, united and marketable sound.

* * *

Here's a paradox. Though he did more than almost anyone to put hot
jazz into the mainstream, Benny Goodman was also responsible for the
splintering of jazz and popular music in the 1940s. His band-within-
a-band – initially the Benny Goodman Trio, later the Quartet – was a
safety valve that allowed Goodman and his fellow players to escape the
rigours of ensemble-playing for the masses, to let off steam and experiment a little. They could play the same repertoire every night and sound
different each time. They had no need for a Fletcher Henderson.

The hierarchy within big-band swing, in which composers and
bandleaders got to boss the players around, to select the 'best' ones
according to their own needs, drove the players towards their intense
after-hours, musicians-first jams. Their day job was self-repression for a

---

* Wills's career would fade as quickly as swing's popularity, and he was forced to
sell the rights to 'New San Antonio Rose' in 1949. The changing radio formats
of the early 1950s locked his sound out from both pop and country-and-western
stations. He would be sidelined until the early '70s, when Merle Haggard and
others brought him back into the limelight briefly. He died in 1975.
† This is an educated guess. The exact date seems to be lost in time.
‡ One good reason why Cooley's name doesn't come up so often in swing
conversations is that in 1961 he was sent to prison for torturing and brutally
murdering his wife.

white audience – musical self-repression, as well as all the social kinds. Late nights at places like Minton's Playhouse in Harlem were when they could fully cut loose. The pop modernism of the big bands, their ushering of jazz into everyday American life, may have been a useful weapon against prejudice, but the black jazz players were less likely to embrace this new inclusivity if they were still going to be shut out. Even with swing, segregation was imposed on the black creative community, not generated from within. By the end of World War II the small, experimental group would prove not only more economically viable, but also more of a thrill for musicians hacked off by the commercial restraints of the big band. Now free to indulge its own fancies, jazz would turn its back on pop's massive audience, and the two would never fully be reconciled.

The Benny Goodman Sextet, though, had one foot placed firmly in the past. While guitarist Charlie Christian and vibes player Lionel Hampton gave them a feeling of the modern jazz to come, glancing towards 1950s west coast cool, a Sextet recording like 'Flying Home' (1939) still suggests the formalism of the big band, with its unison background hum of guitar and clarinet. In other words, it was an attempt to impose the formalism, the premeditated melodic structure of swing, onto the new small-group format. Possibly for this reason, it sounds remarkably light and nimble. It feels like a French new wave movie starring Fred Astaire and Ginger Rogers. It could have been a way forward, but time had caught up with Goodman. He had been sliding since the early 1940s: in the pop stakes, he was eclipsed by Glenn Miller; in jazz, Billy Eckstine's and Claude Thornhill's bands would make him seem antique. Hollywood made *The Benny Goodman Story* in 1956, suggesting finality, that his story already had a beginning, a middle and an end. He was only six years older than Frank Sinatra but already he was a relic, seen as an artistic void, doomed to play the nostalgia circuit for folks who preferred to think of their lives before the war.

Goodman had helped to take jazz further away from its barrelhouse reputation. He had been an important bridge for jazz – a clarinet player of conservatoire standard, a key reason for its presence on BBC Radio 3 in the twenty-first century – and his period as possibly the most influential popular musician had stretched from the end of the Jazz Age to the dawn of the modern. This had been a time of growing commercial possibilities for jazz bands, as well as increasing sophistication. The taciturn Benny Goodman had been crucial in the growth of both.

26

SERENADE IN BLUE: THE GREAT AMERICAN SONGBOOK

Look at George Gershwin. Why, his music's as good as Beethoven
or Bach. Better, maybe. Best of all, it's American!
  Mickey Rooney, *Strike Up the Band*

The 'Great American Songbook' is the unofficial term for a collection of
standards that began with Jerome Kern's 'They Didn't Believe Me' and
ended at some point in the early 1950s. It's an era that would only be
set in amber many years later. Ella Fitzgerald's *Song Book* albums of the
1950s would focus on individual writers and help to firm up the param-
eters of a golden age, but the phrase itself doesn't seem to have been used

before Carmen McRae's 1972 album *The Great American Songbook*. The age may have ended abruptly in 1950 for historians like Alec Wilder – whose *American Popular Song*, also from 1972, was the first academic study of the era – but some writers, like Johnny Mercer ('Moon River', 1961), were still capable of writing a rare new entry some years later. Another way of measuring the Songbook's boundaries is to look at its writers: Kern was born in 1885, Jimmy Van Heusen in 1913, and no one born before or after is really considered a Songbook writer by its adherents. The likes of Stephen Sondheim were already writing with a reverence for the near past in the late 1950s. But Sondheim knew the gates had already closed. You can understand why people look at these songs and their writers with such awe: they aren't just songs, they are components of the twentieth century. When push comes to shove, collectively they are America's greatest cultural achievement.

So you'd think the Songbook's contributors would all be the subjects of biopics starring Gary Cooper or Tom Hanks – or at least of airport biographies – or that there would be long essays about them by Gore Vidal; certainly they'd be household names. And these assumptions lead to another: everyone assumes that all the great hits in the American Songbook were written by George Gershwin, Irving Berlin or Cole Porter, by Rodgers and Hart, Hoagy Carmichael or, maybe, Johnny Mercer. That's about it for the A-listers; even Harold Arlen's name can get a quizzical look. But beyond the half-dozen big names of Broadway and Tin Pan Alley, plenty of other songwriters were scrapping who occasionally struck gold, but sadly for them, people still think their nugget was written by Cole Porter.

Let's look at a handful of Frank Sinatra-recorded standards. Who wrote 'In the Wee Small Hours of the Morning'? Answer: David Mann and Bob Hilliard. Then there's 'Young at Heart' (Johnny Richards and Carolyn Leigh), 'Angel Eyes' (Matt Dennis and Earl Brent) and 'You Make Me Feel So Young' (Josef Myrow and Mack Gordon).*

* Matt Dennis also wrote the music for 'Let's Get Away from It All'; Bob Hilliard went on to be Burt Bacharach's first primary lyricist, writing 'Any Day Now', 'Tower of Strength' and 'Please Stay'; and Mack Gordon co-wrote 'At Last' with Harry Warren. But still, none of these writers was Cole Porter. Coming up with a

Look at bandleader Isham Jones, forgotten to all but the hardcore, who – with lyricist Gus Kahn – wrote an incredible run of hits in the mid-1920s that dried up as quickly as it had begun: 'It Had to Be You', 'Swinging Down the Lane', 'I'll See You in My Dreams', 'The One I Love (Belongs to Somebody Else)'.* Or take a song like 'As Time Goes By'. It was written by thirty-seven-year-old Herman Hupfeld of Montclair, New Jersey, for the 1931 Broadway musical *Everybody's Welcome*. In the original show it was sung by Frances Williams; later that year it would be recorded by Rudy Vallee, giving him a modest hit. When the song was revived in 1942 in *Casablanca*, it became a huge hit, though not for Dooley Wilson, who sang it in the film (Wilson could justifiably curse the musicians' strike that prevented him from recording it). Instead, Victor reissued Vallee's 1931 recording, giving him a number-one hit eleven years on. As for Hupfeld, he lived at home with his mother, until dying from a stroke in 1951, aged fifty-seven. What else did he write? The charming post-party piece 'Let's Put Out the Lights (And Go to Sleep)', which Dean Martin recorded for his *Sleep Warm* album; 'Sing Something Simple', which became a simpering theme tune for the Cliff Adams Singers' long-running (1959 to, implausibly, 2001) Radio 2 pro-gramme of the same name, mostly remembered now as the epitome of slow-witted, un-pop BBC mediocrity that preceded the Top 20 chart show on a Sunday; and a nutty effort called 'Goopy Geer (He Plays Piano and He Plays by Ear)', which Carroll Gibbons and Jack Hylton recorded in Britain. Knowing that the agoraphobic Hupfeld rarely left his Montclair home and – war duties aside – never travelled further than New York City in his entire life makes 'Let's Put Out the Lights' and 'As Time Goes By' feel rather claustrophobic.

Berlin, Kern and the Gershwins had been the first wave, but in their wake came dozens more like Hupfeld: artful, mostly Jewish, often middle

---

couple of big hits and then disappearing from view was just as possible in 1940 as it would be in 1980 and 2020.

* Jones had extraordinarily unkind eyes and was not popular with his players. According to Benny Green, he made musicians walk on stage in line, like prisoners, and banned them from drinking, even on days off. The result was a band that had some of the heaviest boozers in the business.

class. Unlike Hupfeld, they were almost always New Yorkers, and they often liked to work in teams: Richard Rodgers with Lorenz Hart and later Oscar Hammerstein; Arthur Schwartz and Howard Dietz; Harold Arlen and Yip Harburg. Some, but not all.

Cole Porter couldn't have lived a more different life to 'Brother, Can You Spare a Dime''s openly communist lyricist Yip Harburg or the hard-living, perpetually single Lorenz Hart. He wasn't just comfortably off like the Gershwins, either; instead, he was, as he liked to say, 'rich-rich'. At the age of forty he owned sixteen – *sixteen!* – dressing gowns; this was in 1932, when most Americans didn't have $16 to hand. With the Depression and Prohibition peaking, he was an insight into other, different, glamorous ways of life (after all, he had spent much of the previous ten years abroad, absorbing sounds and feels as varied as Moroccan music, which found its way into 'Night and Day', and the dance rhythms of the Dutch East Indies that informed 'Begin the Beguine'). He was easily bored, rarely said 'no' to anything and composed lyrics while pacing on a zebra-skin rug. With deadpan, dead-on self-awareness he called 'You're the Top' 'the tinpantithesis of poetry'. He had a sturdy faith in his own intelligence. In the darkest of times, he seemed to radiate light.

'As Time Goes By' wasn't written by Porter, but he should worry. He was an extravagant man. He was wealthy, always, and given the amount of travelling, partying, horse-riding, polo and poker he got up to, it is astonishing that he had any time to write songs. Two of his best known are 'Let's Misbehave' and 'Let's Do It (Let's Fall in Love)'; hardly hiding his light under a bushel, Porter had Crowley-like openness to indulgence in whatever guise it came. While his contemporaries wrote about love – eternal, unattainable – Porter wrote about sex. He was the funniest writer of his age, but he wasn't a romantic. This made him a very modern writer. Before the Jazz Age, love had gone hand in hand with the briefest possible courtship followed by inevitable marriage, which, of course, lasted for ever. Porter didn't see it that way. For a start, he was enthusiastically homosexual. He loved the company of his wife, Linda, who was some eight years older, but their relationship was more like brother and sister than red-hot lovers. 'Always true to you,' he wrote, 'in my fashion.' He also wrote about his dalliances quite graphically, most memorably on 'All of You': 'I'd love to make a tour of you, the eyes, the arms, the mouth of you, the east, west, north and the south of you.' In New York, his liaisons had been discreet; on moving to Hollywood in 1934, surrounded by the country's most beautiful beings, his sex life became prodigious. Linda Porter played the part of a beard, not just in terms of his sexuality, but also his workload: whether he was in Venice or on the Riviera, if he needed to get some writing done, he could claim, 'Sorry, boys, gotta go, the wife'll kill me.' She was an excuse for everything and, unsurprisingly, Linda eventually got tired of this humiliating existence. By 1937 their lavender marriage was on the rocks, and Linda had moved to their Paris home when Cole fell from a horse; the horse also fell, rolling over his legs and crushing them. Linda moved back in and became his nurse as well as his wife; he would never walk again without a stick.

Now approaching fifty, Porter kept working, mostly with diminishing returns. Still, even his less successful musicals contained the occasional elegant smoke ring: 'Ev'ry Time We Say Goodbye', Ella Fitzgerald's best-remembered song, initially appeared in a 1944 bomb called *Seven Lively Arts*,* and he scored hits right up to 1956, when he wrote the very simple, very truthful 'True Love' for *High Society*. The week that movie opened, Elvis Presley scored his second US number one with 'I Want You, I Need You, I Love You' – the world seemed to be turning faster. Almost haiku-like, and gently philosophical, Bing Crosby and Grace Kelly's recording of 'True Love' would be Porter's last major triumph and almost his last word. There had been thirty or so operations before surgeons finally decided to amputate his right leg in 1958; his mother had died in 1952, and the long-suffering Linda had been taken by emphysema in 1954. Noël Coward visited him in hospital and wrote that Porter was free from pain for the first time in twenty years, but the light had gone out. He lived for another six years, watching the rise of both Elvis and the Beatles, but he never wrote another song.

---

* This was also the title of a 1923 book, of which Porter was certainly aware, by pioneer jazz critic/enthusiast Gilbert Seldes that extolled the virtues of American 'vulgar' culture.

* * *

In 1937, though, it must have felt like Cole Porter and his acolytes in New York and Hollywood had reached some kind of pop-culture peak. Of the year's biggest-selling 78s, three were big-band instrumentals: Benny Goodman's 'Sing, Sing, Sing', Count Basie's pump-a-tronic 'One O'Clock Jump' and Duke Ellington's delicate, sinuous 'Caravan'. In Britain, Noel Gay's musical *Me and My Gal* debuted 'The Lambeth Walk' and 'Leaning on a Lamp Post'; Porter gave us 'In the Still of the Night' and 'Rosalie'; and in Hollywood, Harry Warren and Al Dubin had another gold-plated year, providing the seductive chill of 'September in the Rain' for the easily forgotten *Melody for Two* (if you include shorts and Porky Pig cartoons, Warren contributed songs to seventy-eight different films that year alone).

And yet, and still, anyone suspicious of these cosmopolitan dandies, fearful of the future, could fall back on Sigmund Romberg, Rudolf Friml (both only slightly older than Porter) and the sureties of old Vienna. The duo of baritone Nelson Eddy and former chorus girl Jeanette MacDonald were at their towering commercial peak in 1937, purveying old-time melodies in lacy outfits, with voices to bring down the balcony. Part of the pop dynamic, a counter-balance to Porter's metal-frame-window modernism, was conservative revivalism, and the Bohemian/Viennese strand had had an unexpected revival in 1935, when Eddy and MacDonald were teamed up for the first time in surprise Hollywood hit *Naughty Marietta* (its hit song 'Ah! Sweet Mystery of Life' had earned Eddy his first gold disc). Eddy was already a successful opera singer who had performed Strauss at Carnegie Hall, but he was also handsome enough for Hollywood to come knocking and make him an offer he couldn't refuse. *Maytime* was the duo's 1937 hit, wherein MGM managed to attach an old Romberg operetta from 1917 to Noël Coward's storyline from *Bitter Sweet*.* Coward thought

---

* Not one to miss a trick, MGM's boss Louis B. Mayer made a film of *Bitter Sweet* itself in 1940, but changed the story enough that most would never have noticed its similarities to *Maytime*.

the film 'vulgar', with MGM bulking out his story with chunks of Wagner, Tchaikovsky and Rossini. It climaxed with Nelson's ghost coming to take the ageing Jeanette up to heaven. They sang Romberg's 'Sweetheart, Will You Remember', surrounded by an angelic choir and white rose petals, and hit the inevitable long-held high note just before the credits rolled.

You knew exactly what you were getting with Nelson Eddy and Jeanette MacDonald movies: Viennese comfort food, schnitzel and potatoes, with your tears plopping into your gravy after precisely ninety minutes. Their private lives were far more interesting and genuinely more heartbreaking than their movies. Though they had been secretly dating, they were forbidden to marry by the heartless Louis B. Mayer; instead, they made do with a mock wedding ceremony at Lake Tahoe while they were filming Rudolf Friml's *Rose Marie* in 1936. They continued to see each other on the sly – although both were married – until MacDonald died of heart failure in 1965.

From *Animal Crackers* (1930) onwards, the Marx Brothers' movies provided a necessary Hollywood palate-cleanser. Their comic foil Margaret Dumont, as the society woman who didn't seem to get the jokes, played the living embodiment of Romberg's and Friml's musicals. In 1937 the Marx Brothers' *The Big Store* featured Tony Martin's 'Tenement Symphony', with its Kellys and Vermicellis 'living cheek by jowl' – a hat-tip to the city where all of Hollywood's writers had started, and where few of them now remained. Richard Rodgers and Lorenz Hart were exceptions, back after their miserable time in Hollywood, and they had a ridiculously good 1937: 'My Funny Valentine', 'Where or When', 'Have You Met Miss Jones', 'The Lady Is a Tramp', 'I Wish I Were in Love Again', 'Johnny One Note'. It was hard to imagine that their final collaboration would be just five years away.

* * *

Though no one had been expecting another 'Rhapsody in Blue' of him in the 1930s, George Gershwin still worried that the songs he was writing for throwaway shows and movies might be seen as equally disposable.

With songs like 'I Got Rhythm' and 'Embraceable You' (both from 1930's *Girl Crazy*) he really didn't need to worry, but he still hankered to write more symphonic works.

In 1926 Gershwin had been intrigued by *Porgy*, a novel by DuBose Heyward set among poor blacks in and around Heyward's native Charleston. When in 1932 its run as a play was set to finish, Gershwin wrote to Heyward, and the pair decided to work on an opera. They made a trip to the sea islands off South Carolina to get an understanding of the local Gullah population, descended from slaves, most of whom never left the islands. Sitting around a fire, Gershwin listened to them singing spirituals. He was inspired, and by mid-1935 the opera was ready.

Gershwin had started writing his own spirituals with 'Summertime' in late 1933, while Ira provided the lyrical urban sass of 'It Ain't Necessarily So'. The correspondence between Gershwin and Heyward shows they were agreed on the necessity of an all-black cast, although Al Jolson, true to form, tried to cut in with a blackface version. The show was a hit in Boston: 'When the cries of genius subside, George Gershwin's *Porgy and Bess* will take its place indubitably as the first American opera,' read the *Boston American* review. But the three-hour performance had been heavily cut by the time it reached New York and less sympathetic critics. The *New York Times* feigned confusion, casting shade over the show before anyone had seen it: '*Porgy and Bess* opens this evening at the Alvin Theatre, throwing the entire Broadway amusement field into confusion; is it drama or opera? George Gershwin, who has written the score, calls it a "folk opera".' The paper may just as well have added, 'Well, hark at Mr La-Dee-Dah!' More worrying for Gershwin was the reaction from Virgil Thomson, a modern classical composer and critic. He found it racially objectionable, saying, 'Folklore subjects recounted by an outsider are only valid as long as the folk in question is unable to speak for itself, which is certainly not true of the American Negro in 1935.' Duke Ellington was also cross with Gershwin for treading on territory that wasn't his to claim. When Samuel Goldwyn's film version was made in the late 1950s, black actors would shy away, with Harry Belafonte saying, 'DuBose Heyward wrote a very racist story. What makes *Porgy and Bess* work is the remarkable music. But the images were highly distasteful.'*

The remarkable music alone wasn't enough to save *Porgy and Bess* in 1935, and it closed after just over three months, losing all of its investment. Gershwin took it hard. Critics shrugged; it had been a highbrow miscalculation, as they'd known all along. Singer Margaret Whiting had read the lukewarm reviews and remembered her father Richard coming home after seeing it. He was sad and angry: 'What's wrong with these people? This man is the genius of American music. He's written something that none of us could ever write.'

Two years later, in 1937, Richard Whiting would co-write the beloved 'Too Marvellous for Words' ('like glorious, glamorous, and that old standby amorous') with Johnny Mercer, a hit for Bing Crosby. That same year a reluctant George Gershwin was back in Hollywood, back writing movie songs instead of operas. This time, Hollywood didn't treat him like the golden boy. 'I had to live for this,' Gershwin complained, 'that Sam Goldwyn should say to me, "Why don't you write hits like Irving Berlin?"' It wasn't as if he'd lost the knack. That spring Fred Astaire starred in *Shall We Dance*, with a jazz-ballet score by the Gershwins and songs which included 'Let's Call the Whole Thing Off', 'They All Laughed (At Christopher Columbus)' and the magical 'They Can't Take That Away from Me'. It's hard to believe Goldwyn wasn't thrilled skinny.†

Aside from *Shall We Dance*, George Gershwin didn't write many other hits in 1937. He had been complaining of headaches for some time, and by the spring he was living at his brother Ira's house, mostly in darkness because the light was painful. He could hardly play piano – that gave him a headache too. Doctors could find nothing wrong and

---

* *Porgy and Bess* would be rescued and redeemed by Miles Davis and Gil Evans in 1959, as part of their modal recasting of jazz and light classical music.
† Astaire and Rogers knew it couldn't get any better. They split, with Ginger wanting to do more dramatic roles, it was said. Gossip columnists talked about feuds and enmity; only one, the Leeds-born *Hollywood Today* writer Sheilah Graham, was perceptive enough to note that 'the combination was terrific, Fred was never as good with anyone else. So, being a smart person – he's not an idiot – I doubt if he would allow himself to dislike Ginger.'

suggested psychiatric help. Ira's wife Leonore was frightened by George's mood swings, so he moved into Yip Harburg's vacant house nearby. He was working on the score for Samuel Goldwyn's first Technicolor film, *The Goldwyn Follies*, when he collapsed and fell into a coma. He died of a brain haemorrhage two days later on 11 July, aged thirty-eight.* The only people with him were a nurse and his valet, Paul Mueller, whose job had once been to guard the great hope of the Jazz Age from the crowds outside.

* The film was lucky to get 'Love Is Here to Stay', with its beautifully definite opening line 'It's very clear, our love is here to stay', which became a bigger hit when Gene Kelly sang it to Leslie Caron in the far better *An American in Paris* in 1951. Frank Sinatra would give it the gold seal on *Songs for Swingin' Lovers* five years later.

27
THE WINDS GROW COLDER: JUDY GARLAND AND BILLIE HOLIDAY

More than anyone else in this book, Judy Garland and Billie Holiday seem relatable to twenty-first-century pop. They have permanence. Holiday's slightly-behind-the-beat wooziness may well have been the single most important influence on female singers of the last two decades. Garland's blend of blow-the-roof-off talent and insecurity – 'I can sing! Wanna hear me? Is that OK?' – has correlated to the new century's TV talent-show winners. They are also modern totems because of the grimness of their pre-fame years, their dysfunctional upbringings, and because of how they were first abused by men, then used by the entertainment industry's machinery, before being left out in the rain, dying without the final act they deserved. Both have wisdom in their voices (an illusion, of course). Both were thoroughly tuned in to the songs they were singing. Both had the touch of the universal. Both made singing sound so easy early on; they made *living* seem so easy – the cushion of fame, the precious ability to convey real joy – and then they made it seem so tough, so impossibly tough that they couldn't take it.

Musicals didn't need a link to Vienna, a Jeanette MacDonald or a Howard Keel, to be valid. Judy Garland's delivery was unrelated to opera, or operetta, or jazz for that matter; she was pure pop, a star with pipes who could walk onto a stage or appear on a screen and everyone looking at her immediately felt better. She was no one's idea of a rebel.

The last film that she made as a child, *The Wizard of Oz*, found her singing the Harold Arlen and Yip Harburg song 'Over the Rainbow', which would become a frozen moment in popular culture; three decades later, it would also be the last song she ever sang in public. Even in 1939, aged just seventeen, she said the song made her feel 'like a grandmother in pigtails'.

She had been in pigtails – and a rustic smock, living on a melon farm – in her very first film, 1936's *Pigskin Parade*. It was one of many interchangeable 'college' musicals that Hollywood turned out in the decade following *The Jazz Singer*, a forerunner of the 1960s beach movie, and fourteen-year-old Judy got to sing a few songs of her own (none of which was as good as the film's highlight, Tony Martin's 'You're Slightly Terrific'). Her presence and her voice were so instantly infectious that songs were shoehorned into her next few movies: in *Thoroughbreds Don't Cry* (1937) she started off playing a Chopin piece, then ragged it; *Everybody Sing* (1938) was essentially a screwball comedy with a bunch of Judy songs thrown in because they made the second-rate script fizz. She didn't come from jazz, but in *Everybody Sing* she was the embodiment of the swing era's energy: 'Mr Mendelssohn's had his day,' she sang, 'Benny Goodman is here to stay.' Judy's character was expelled from school for her troubles: 'You've corrupted this school for the last time!' squawked her headmistress. Judy Garland was youth, America's future, and here, she said, was the music to prove it.

Deanna Durbin had previously been MGM's musical star. Apple-pie pretty, Durbin was not an obvious force for conservatism, but her light operatic voice sounded as stuffy as a Chesterfield compared to Garland's. They appeared together in a short called *Every Sunday*, just before Garland's star rose with *Pigskin Parade*, and Durbin left MGM for Universal. Their styles are complementary, but one is singing in Italian, a remnant of the old world, while the other soars skyward, more a Western Air Express than a nightingale.

In 1935, having just turned thirteen, Garland had sung 'Broadway Rhythm' on the *Shell Chateau Hour*, hosted by Wallace Beery, who asked her, 'What do you want to do when you grow up to be a great big girl, huh?' It's easy to forget that, as a child star, there was a more or less copper-bottomed guarantee that she would be washed up at sixteen. Judy at this time was one of a string of Hollywood child stars, with Shirley Temple at the top of the tree and Bobby Breen just behind. The difference was that she did not sing 'On the Good Ship Lollipop' – it would have seemed ridiculous. Like Brenda Lee in the 1960s (who was just thirteen when she raspily sang of her know-how on 'Sweet Nothin's'), or Michael Jackson at the turn of the '70s, Judy sang adult songs, always. Unlike the frighteningly whisky-aged Brenda, she had a voice that blended childish fear and teenage insecurity with zeal, and the assurance to make it relatable to all ages.

Her singing always felt spontaneous, as close to 'free' as anyone mentioned in this book; the word you want to use is 'innocent', though you also want to wince as you say it. Garland's style was warm, both shy and aggressive, artless even, the polar opposite of Peggy Lee (who had an equally limited range but patrolled it like a hawk), and the likely reason for this – as with every other aspect of her life – was that her approach had been frozen as a child. Listen to something as ebullient as 'The Trolley Song', and you hear both a child's enthusiasm for singing and an odd wisdom. Garland was aware that this was what people liked in her voice, and so she never really lost this naivety, hanging on to it in spite of everything. It helped to make her ballad-singing in the 1950s and '60s, by then freed from her destructive MGM contract, all the more powerful. You had all *this* and you lost it? And no one *cared*? It was often a tough listen, but it won her an adoring audience of outcasts, even as her voice failed and her vibrato became like an off-centre record. Jerry Lewis said that 'all the people whose insides have been torn out by misery identify with her'. And, of course, there were plenty of fans who still thought of her as Dorothy, even after she turned forty, and were surprised that she didn't appear in red Mary Jane slippers. Derek Jewell of the *Sunday Times* wrote of a live performance: 'She walks the rim of the volcano each second. Miraculously she keeps her balance. It is a triumph of the utmost improbability.'

What else do we hear in her voice, in happier times? Jolson's eagerness to please is in there, but it never overpowers. Some of Jolie's nasal sound too, and his bowing of words ('Rock a booyyye your baby'). Sadness was already there: take the self-referencing 'Play That Barbershop Chord', from 1949's *In the Good Old Summertime*: 'When you start that minor part, I feel your fingers slipping and gripping my heart.' Who could she have had in mind? In 1941, aged nineteen, she had been engaged to composer David Rose, who later went on to write 'The Stripper', the bawdiest piece of music ever written. But Judy began seeing songwriter Johnny Mercer; she married Rose in a bid to squash the affair, but it didn't work. Mercer wrote 'I Remember You' about her, first sung by Dorothy Lamour in *The Fleet's In* (1942), but best remembered via Frank Ifield's yodelling 1962 UK number-one hit: 'When my life is through and the angels ask me to recall the thrill of them all, then I will tell them I remember you.'

By the turn of the 1950s Garland had been dropped by MGM, having played the lead in twenty-three movies in fifteen years and suffering a nervous breakdown in 1949. There's gratitude for you. When she was nineteen and still seen by MGM as a child star, the studio and her mother had arranged for her to have an abortion, to save her career. She was married at the time. By 1950 her second marriage, to director Vincente Minnelli, was falling apart, and still Louis Mayer wanted her to play a cheerleading ingénue. So Garland returned to her vaudeville roots and reinvented herself on the stage as a singer. The turning point was a run of shows at the London Palladium in April 1951, landmark live performances which she referred to as 'an autobiography in song'.

Thanks to the gossip-greedy media, the drugs, the breakdowns and the attempted suicides would all be played out in full view of the cameras. To the public, she became the opposite of her MGM self, though the sadness had always been there. One film – after four whole years off the screen – combined the new and the old Judy Garland: 1954's *A Star*

Is Born. Its hit song was 'The Man That Got Away', with Ira Gershwin's lyrics over a blue Harold Arlen melody that rolled like a boulder being slowly pushed up a muddy hill – the complete opposite of the grace, ease and lightness of a George Gershwin song. Ira may well have been writing about life after his brother – 'The road gets rougher, it's lonelier and tougher' – and, maybe not coincidentally, he retired from songwriting almost immediately after *A Star Is Born*.

Instead of her most frequent co-star, potato-head Mickey Rooney, featuring alongside Garland on screen was James Mason, an actor with a velvet voice who could turn on a sixpence, his eyebrows switching from an amused pair of French accents to thunderous. He's such fun one minute, a violent drunk the next. And as such, he's the perfect foil for the sharp contrasts in the Judy Garland story, the black and the white, the dippy and the doomed.

Mason talked about her with his measured Hollywood-via-Huddersfield manner: 'There's the school of thought that believes that the bosses at MGM were the real villains because they encouraged her to take uppers and downers and get into these bad habits. And I think that's probably true. Anyhow, she was a unique instance of a girl who had lived a most unsavoury and unhealthy lifestyle, shall we say, and therefore was a girl who was disinclined to discipline, and she could get into terrible depressions. But she wasn't typical in any way. I thought she was wonderful. I adored her. Everybody knew about Judy, we all knew about Judy, but instead of getting one hundred percent behind her and just trying to do the best, there was an awful lot of bitching and complaining.'

After they'd shot the final scene of her final film, *I Could Go on Singing*, at Shepperton, Judy paused, looked at director Ronald Neame and his crew, and said, 'You'll miss me when I'm gone.' Then she walked away.

In 1962 Garland released her final studio album. The late 1950s had seen her on Capitol, in the company of Nat Cole, Peggy Lee, Dean Martin and Frank Sinatra: there had been 1957's graceful assemblage of torch songs, *Alone*, arranged by Gordon Jenkins; 1958's terrific, upbeat, Nelson Riddle-led *Judy in Love*; and there was a fascinating oddity in the 1959 concept album *The Letter*, written and arranged by Jenkins, with narrative interruptions from actor John Ireland. From this point sales dipped, Garland wasn't given the top-notch arrangers any more, and 1962's *The Garland Touch* had to be pieced together from random sessions. Recordings of her final London shows show that despite received wisdom – and given that she was approaching fifty – her voice stayed strong to the end. Everything else, though, had been disappearing slowly. By the time she died in 1969 Judy Garland was stick-thin, her speech was slurred and her film and recording careers had gone completely. Her relentless optimism had finally left her.

She admitted that her life had been a hard one. 'Do you know how difficult it is to be Judy Garland,' she asked in *Parade*, 'and for me to live with me? I've had to do it. What more unkind life can you think of than the one I've lived?'* The great movie musical effectively died with her. What was left? *Cabaret*, starring her daughter, Liza Minnelli.

Billie Holiday could counter that with a litany of horrors. Garland had been fed sleeping pills by her mother – 'the real Wicked Witch of the West' – from the age of ten to help her sleep while on the road. Holiday's great-grandmother had told her in detail about life as a slave; she grew up with a cousin who beat her; aged ten, she was raped by a neighbour; she left school at twelve and travelled to New York alone, where she worked as a maid and then as a prostitute, which landed her in jail. It is understandable that she is remembered, like Garland, as a victim. Both of their names have been used, and abused, as shorthand for self-destruction, but instead let's look at why Holiday's life was so special.

There is one significant stylistic difference between Judy Garland and Billie Holiday: Garland epitomised the singer who asks what a song can give her, while Holiday only considered what she could give to a song. She inhabited the song, personalised it and internalised it to a degree that no one had done before, and in this way she influenced the very biggest

---

* Her afterlife has been very different, beginning with the day of her funeral in Manhattan, on 27 June 1969. The streets were lined with fans, many of whom were gay and weren't used to being visible in numbers. There was an energy in the air. The riots and protests that began at the Stonewall Inn later that night became a rallying call for the gay rights movement. It was her final encore and her final triumph.

names who came after her – Frank Sinatra, Peggy Lee, Elvis Presley. Like Bing Crosby, Holiday wasn't just a jazz singer, she was a jazz musician; as an innovator – though not a virtuoso in the usual sense – she was still the equal of the era's best instrumentalists. What's more, unlike Bing, she got to perform with these instrumentalists on a regular basis.

It's safe to say that John Hammond had a more high-concept vision of the artists he was working with than they generally had for themselves, and Holiday fell into this category. Her debut recording – in 1933, aged eighteen – was on Benny Goodman's daffy 'Your Mother's Son-in-Law'; it's a flapper frippery, and Billie's singing is straighter and more girlish than you would expect, but straight off her voice grabs you with its grit and occasional crack. Pianist Teddy Wilson, who never liked her voice, likened her to a female Louis Armstrong, by which he meant she was unoriginal. The public thought Wilson had a tin ear, and by 1946 she was billed as 'America's No. 1 Song Stylist'.

Wilson was, nonetheless, one of the most important musicians in the Billie Holiday story. Back in 1935 Hammond had talked Brunswick into recording some sides with Wilson, after Fats Waller's small-group 78s had started clogging jukeboxes nationwide. Wilson was a far more elegant player, a musical descendant of Earl Hines who softened the Hines sound with a gentler left hand, becoming, unwittingly, the forefather of cocktail jazz. Where Hines was earthy, Wilson was genteel, propulsive but polite. Between 1935 and 1942 he recorded some three hundred understated but cool, controlled sides for Brunswick, which featured stellar singers like Ella Fitzgerald, Lena Horne and Billie Holiday. When they first recorded together, Wilson was twenty-two and Holiday twenty. Her voice was pretty, and higher than we would become used to, but already the sensuality was there. The jukeboxes were happy to have these records.

The other key figure on Holiday's best records was horn player Lester Young; they had played together in Count Basie's band. Young called everyone 'lady', male or female, and pioneered the classic post-war jazz look with his pork-pie hat. He had been a boarder at Holiday's mother's house in 1934, and he and Billie were musical soulmates. 'I think you can hear that on some of the old records, you know,' Young later reminisced. 'Some time I'd sit down and listen to them myself, and it would sound like two of the same voice.' He nicknamed her 'Lady Day', and she called him 'Prez'.

Wilson, Holiday and Young improvised in the studio, which saved A&R man Hammond and Brunswick Records a bundle in arrangers' fees. These were Tin Pan Alley songs, not Broadway, but still Wilson and Holiday spun gold, creating swing hits and jazz standards: Richard Whiting and Leo Robin's 'Miss Brown to You'; Benny Goodman, Irving Mills and Edgar Sampson's 'If Dreams Come True'; Harry M. Woods's 'What a Little Moonlight Can Do'.*

A couple of years later, Holiday was enjoying a cold drink with Artie Shaw, who told her that he'd had the idea of putting clarinet and drums front and centre, but wanted 'something sensational to give it a shove'. 'That's easy,' said Holiday. 'Hire a good Negro singer.' For Shaw's all-white band, in 1938, that took a lot of courage. Holiday had sung with unknown black pianists, then with Teddy Wilson and Count Basie, but this move would put her in the public eye, especially when Shaw wrote the sumptuous, seductive 'Any Old Time' ('and any place where you may be') for her.

That summer Shaw played at the Ritz-Carlton in Boston, and its white audiences became avid Billie Holiday fans. Other venues still wouldn't let her appear, though, and Billie had to sit on the bus as Helen Forrest sang the songs Shaw had arranged for her. Eventually, after being told by one hotel that she'd have to use the freight elevator, she quit.

---

* A Massachusetts-born sometime London resident, Woods was the epitome of the Tin Pan Alley backroom boy, the kind that is almost entirely forgotten today. He had written 'What a Little Moonlight Can Do' in 1934, when he was contracted to Gaumont British Studios, but he had been a hit-maker since 1926, when his 'When the Red, Red Robin (Comes Bob, Bob, Bobbin' Along)' was recorded by Whispering Jack Smith, Cliff Edwards and Al Jolson. His other major hits included Annette Hanshaw's 'We Just Couldn't Say Goodbye'; 'Side by Side', a 1927 hit for Cliff 'Ukulele Ike' Edwards, but a bigger one for Kay Starr in 1953; 'I'm Looking Over a Four-Leaf Clover', performed by everyone from Coleman Hawkins and João Gilberto to Porky Pig; and 'Try a Little Tenderness', also written in London (with Britons Jimmy Campbell and Reg Connelly) and first recorded by Ray Noble, but revived in 1966 by producer/arranger Isaac Hayes and singer Otis Redding.

She fell into the welcoming arms of Café Society. This was the first integrated club in New York – the name was a joke – and had been opened by shoe-shop salesman Barney Josephson in 1938 to highlight black talent and allow black people to enjoy it; he had borrowed the idea from European cabaret clubs. This was where Holiday developed her trademark look – head tilted back, gardenias in her hair – and debuted two of her signature songs, 'God Bless the Child' and 'Strange Fruit'. Columbia wouldn't record the latter. They were afraid of their southern dealers – they didn't want trouble with their distribution – and it ended up on a new independent jazz label called Commodore in 1939. The song itself had started life in 1937 as a poem, written by a school teacher and openly proud communist called Abel Meeropol. He approached Josephson and personally explained to Holiday why the harrowing song would be given maximum impact by her languid but powerful delivery. Holiday was blown away, and told her band, 'Some guy has brought me a hell of a damn song.'

Unsurprisingly, 'Strange Fruit' was not an instant number-one hit – a song about lynching wasn't anyone's idea of entertainment. 'Southern trees bear strange fruit. Blood on the leaves and blood at the root.' It made people feel sick or angry. One man hastily wrote a note at the end of a show – 'Here's some strange fruit for you' – and handed her a drawing of genitalia. Another evening, a woman followed Billie into the powder room. She was crying. 'Don't you dare ever sing that song again,' she said, 'don't you dare.' She then told Billie that when she was seven or eight years old, she had witnessed a lynching.

* * *

It wouldn't be until 1946 that Billie Holiday, aged thirty-one, was offered her first film role, in a movie about the last days of Storyville called *New Orleans*. One look at the cast – Holiday, Louis Armstrong, Woody Herman, Meade 'Lux' Lewis – and the shooting on location might lead you to think it was something special. But, no: Billie played a maid. 1946 was the year McCarthyism began making its presence felt in Hollywood, and producer Jules Levey and writer Herbert Biberman were under pressure to avoid looking too liberal, and that included suggesting black people might be responsible for the creation of jazz. They needn't have bothered: Biberman was imprisoned anyway, a year later, as one of the 'Hollywood Ten'.

Not long after, the authorities came after Billie, and she spent nine months in prison for possession. When she came out and played Carnegie Hall in 1947, the voice was still there, nothing about her drink and drug intake was affecting her performances, but a condition of her release was that she couldn't play in clubs with a liquor licence, just in the big theatres that didn't serve booze. They were cutting off her oxygen.

Britain in 1954 wasn't as proscriptive. When her microphone failed at the Manchester Free Trade Hall, she walked to the front of the stage and sang 'My Man' unaccompanied, to wild applause. In London, she shopped at Simpsons, bought a ski suit and knitted cap, then crossed the road to the Studio Club in Swallow Street, where she could drink triple brandies with Cointreau floats without the cops breathing down her neck. She said that she never went to people's houses to socialise because 'the drinks don't come fast enough, honey, and you can't leave when you want to'. When she played at the Royal Albert Hall on Valentine's Day, the reception was so warm, the appreciation of her voice so great, that she seriously considered moving. 'I want to settle in Britain, because I love the people,' she said. 'They call me an artist, not just a singer.'

You have to wonder what might have happened if Billie Holiday had moved to London. An album with Tubby Hayes? A role in Anthony Newley's *The Roar of the Greasepaint*? A duet with Dusty Springfield on her TV show? But she stayed in New York. As a young singer, Maya Angelou saw Billie in her audience one night. She pointed her out, called her a 'great person', and had the crowd on its feet applauding. But during her next song, 'Baby, Please Don't Go', Holiday stood up and started shouting at her: 'Shut that bitch up. Shut up! You remind me of my mother. *Shut up!*' After the show, Angelou walked up to her and confronted her: didn't she understand how much the audience loved her? 'No,' said Billie. 'They just wanted to see a black woman who'd been in trouble for drugs. That's the only reason they look at me.' The conditions of her death in 1959, aged forty-four, were so appallingly cruel it beggars belief. Suffering from cirrhosis, she had been under arrest in a bed at Harlem's Metropolitan Hospital for five weeks, after police found a small amount of heroin in her room; books, her radio and record player, even flowers had been confiscated. She had been fingerprinted without her consent.

Holiday's final album, *Lady in Satin*, is not unlike Marianne Faithfull's celebrated, post-heroin *Broken English*. Some would say there's a whole life in that voice; others hear a desiccated croak. It was certainly a lived-in voice, but who else would want to live there, or even stay over? I'd prefer to hear someone's life without the inevitable downturns, the misery, the cobwebs, the clutter, the years of ingrained dirt you can never scrub away. I'm kind of glad that no one got Judy Garland into a recording studio after 1962. 'Meet Me in St Louis' and 'Did I Remember', 'Over the Rainbow' and 'God Bless the Child', 'The Man That Got Away' and 'That Old Devil Called Love' – these are clear high points of twentieth-century culture.

28

BE LIKE THE KETTLE AND SING: BRITAIN AT WAR

In 1941 there were at least 50 clubs in Soho, probably more – bottle clubs where you were supposed to order drinks in advance – nobody obeyed the law. I worked in a first floor club all through the air raids, no stopping for bombs. People were fatalistic but tremendously happy. Everybody had the feeling that death was on the doorstep, so they all had a good time. As I walked back to Aldgate at 3 or 4 in the morning the whole of the City of London would be alight. We walked on through it almost every night, bomb stories were two a penny. It wasn't bravery, there was nothing you could do about it – it just went on night after night.

Tony Crombie, jazz drummer

When World War II was declared on 1 September 1939, the BBC made a decision to cut all music – whether pop, light or serious – from its schedule. It badly misjudged the national mood. Over the next six years, entertainment – especially popular music – would come very close behind food and shelter in the list of needs of a nation at war. Vera Lynn would sing directly to the troops – 'The London I Love', 'It Always Rains Before the Rainbow' and 'The White Cliffs of Dover' – and receive a thousand letters a week that were more like thank-you notes than fan mail. The BBC's stance led to a sudden boom in record sales in 1939, as people still wanted and needed to hear Joe Loss's 'Let the People Sing' ('any sort of song they choose, anything to kill the blues'), with its odd blend of church-bell brass, maudlin middle-European violin and a chorus message that seemed to be aimed directly at the BBC.

War or not, people in Britain still liked to get drunk and sing. By the end of 1939 half a million sheet-music copies of 'Beer Barrel Polka' had been sold in Britain, and it mutated into 'Roll Out the Barrel', the country's most popular singalong, with the possible exceptions of 'The Hokey Cokey' and 'Happy Birthday'. The BBC, facing a storm of criticism ('The most pitiful exhibition of complacent amateurishness to be heard on the whole of this planet during the first weeks of war,' roared *Gramophone*'s Compton Mackenzie), relented, setting up a 'slush committee' to decide what to broadcast.* Cecil Madden, a BBC programmer, recalled, 'Every week we had to go through mountains of songs and records. We existed to ban songs, which was very unfortunate, because one likes to be creative.' To sum up its new role, BBC producer Wynford Reynolds coined the phrase 'victory through harmony'. The Corporation began to broadcast from factories and military camps. Sometimes young non-combatants, like child stars, would drop in. Even regular Joes would get to sing on a show called *Private Smith Entertains*.

---

* The slush committee would be wheeled out on a regular basis. In 1942 there was a ban on 'numbers which are slushy in sentiment'; in 1943 they blacklisted crooners – 'anaemic or debilitated performances by male singers' – who might somehow emasculate our servicemen; and in the same year the Corporation decided to promote Britishness over 'pseudo-American' music, which left the swing-friendly house band of Geraldo out in the cold.

The Harry Roy Band's tribute to 'a stately gentleman we love so', 'God Bless You, Mr Chamberlain', was a big hit during the 'phoney war' in 1939: 'You look swell holding your umbrella, all the world loves this wonderful fella.' But as the years rolled on, with no real light on the horizon, Vera Lynn's 'We'll Meet Again' would become the melancholic anthem: 'don't know where, don't know when'. When bombs started falling, the BBC had to acknowledge popular music's power and the nation's shared affinities, and, to be fair, it did. The phoney war ended abruptly on 7 September 1940 – Black Saturday – when 430 people were killed in London and a further 1,600 were injured. The city was then bombed for fifty-seven consecutive nights.

* * *

Vera Lynn came from the halls and variety theatres, and she rose to fame thanks to the long run of *Apple Sauce* at the London Palladium, in which she starred with comedian Max Miller. But Vera was made for radio and would go on to become as associated with World War II as Churchill. Quite long-faced and rather toothy, she wasn't Betty Grable, but her voice was perfect for the job in hand; her songs projected the values of home and family, and her heartfelt, slightly melancholic voice conveyed a powerful imagery over the airwaves. The *Radio Times* noted that by the spring of 1941 her blend of girl-next-door glamour and reassurance had made her the number-one 'sweetheart of the forces', and by the end of the year, with *Sincerely Yours*, Lynn was on the air. Covering a lot of ground, she had to act as lover ('Yours'), lucky talisman ('We'll Meet Again'), mother (the lullaby 'Baby Mine' from *Dumbo*) and seer ('White Cliffs of Dover'). She turned longing and absence into a communal experience. Still, it wasn't enough for the BBC: Basil Nicholls, controller of programmes, said 'the programme is solidly popular with the ordinary rank and file of the Forces. On the other hand, it does not do us any good to have a reputation for flabby amusement.' And so even Lynn's position was constantly under review. At one point she was off the air for a year, only returning in 1944, with *Thirty Minutes of Music in the Vera Lynn Manner*. But then it was quite un-BBC that a working-class Londoner who refined her accent only moderately for broadcast represented the unity of the nation.

* * *

Having decided that popular music was good for morale (a decision it would still rescind at various points in the war), in late 1939 the BBC broadcast a variety concert from RAF Hendon, where Mantovani's orchestra played 'We're Going to Hang Out the Washing on the Siegfried Line', with a vocal refrain from Adelaide Hall, the Cotton Club legend. She had just arrived in London from Paris; with help from bandleader Joe Loss, she found herself in the BBC's employ within a matter of days.

Hall's contract with the BBC, and her theatre shows around the country, contrasted sharply with her Cotton Club days, when the colour divide between stage and audience had been absolute. Still, Britain had its own race issues to deal with. In 1932 the Paramount Ballroom on Tottenham Court Road opened underneath the huge art deco Paramount Court apartment block. It was black-run and welcomed an almost exclusively black crowd; a few white girls might have braved the dirty looks, but certainly you never saw white men. This was somewhere to come at the weekend to meet other people of your own skin colour, listen to West Indian musicians and relax without anyone giving you trouble. At the end of the night the banquettes were often occupied by people who couldn't find a home in their often unwelcoming host country. Britain didn't have a colour bar, but there were plenty of problems, and housing was already a serious issue for Caribbean émigrés.

Habitués of the Paramount would have struggled to find genuine swing on the radio, but for thirty minutes every week the BBC provided an alternative to the soma-like *Music While You Work*. Broadcasting a solid half-hour of swing every week, *Radio Rhythm Club* began in June 1940. Record collecting played a vital role in British jazz fandom. Almost no one heard swing in the flesh, unless it was a token number played by a British dance band; everyone's accrued knowledge came from records. This led *Radio Rhythm Club* to have a scholarly tone – catalogue numbers would have been mentioned frequently – and it was, unsurprisingly, male-dominated. Out of 211 broadcasts, only two featured women as announcers or guests. Mary Lytton and Bettie Edwards wrote together under the gender-free name B. M. Lytton-Edwards for *Swing Magazine* and were just as likely to make references to catalogue numbers as the guys. They also had a glamorous/not-glamorous back story, pretending to have grown up on a farm in Iowa, where they were subjected to 'Sweet Adeline' endlessly, before hot jazz saved their souls. Gender balance aside, *Radio Rhythm Club* was popular with the fans. It was presented by Charles Chilton, a genuine jazz enthusiast who was not only hip enough to describe something hot on Savoy as 'the last word', but also had a very non-BBC, relatable London accent.

The show even had space for jitterbug-friendly jam sessions with Harry Parry's Radio Rhythm Club Sextet, a decent outfit led by the Goodman-influenced Parry that featured black British guitarist Joe Deniz, drummer Bobby Midgley, 'vibraphone ace' Roy Marsh and future superstar pianist George Shearing. They caused a near-riot when they played in Deniz's home town of Cardiff, and one lad who enthusiastically jumped on stage had to be wrapped up in a curtain and carried off by stagehands.

A rare out-and-out British jazz bandleader, Parry had started out in Llandudno and had been playing at Mayfair's St Regis restaurant – the group was called the St Regis Quintet at this point – before the BBC called. The sextet's records on Parlophone are a delight (especially their ace signature tune, the Parry-written 'Champagne'), and their popularity led to the over-subscribed Cavendish Swing Concert, a public jam session that spun off from *Radio Rhythm Club* in January 1942. 'Swing fervour reached a new high level in this country . . . when 2,500 eager, enthusiastic, foot-stomping and wildly applauding fans packed the London Coliseum to capacity,' wrote *Melody Maker*. Back in 1941 the paper had been rather less excitable: 'The BBC *Rhythm Club* is the final and ultimate gesture, a sort of non-aggression pact between swing and officialdom, and everybody is happy.' By 1945 the scene had grown so much, thanks to Harry Parry and Charles Chilton, that small-group swing programming at the BBC – from combos led by Frank Weir,

Johnny Claes and Stéphane Grappelli, as well as Parry – had become almost commonplace.

* * *

The Squadronaires were formed as a 'service dance band', with a nucleus of players from the Ambrose band. They pilfered swing arrangements from Bob Crosby and made a British wartime hit out of his 'South Rampart Street Parade'. George Chisholm had been Bert Ambrose's trombonist and remembered how half a dozen band members 'decided to volunteer in the RAF, not through bravery, I'm sure. Six of us went up like idiots and said, "Here we are, we're a band." We went to Uxbridge, a parent station for a few weeks, sweeping floors, cleaning lavatories, and in the evenings we'd sit and have a little blow. It strayed into the office of the commanding officer, and he said, "Splendid, why don't you play in the officers' mess this Friday?" Consequently we were sent to Germany and France and Holland and what have you, and we joined the entertainments there.'

The Air Council objected most strongly to the name. They insisted the band was called His Majesty's Royal Air Force Dance Orchestra, with the bossy credit 'by permission of the Air Council', on Decca 78s, such as 1941's ominous, atmospheric, multi-part 'There's Something in the Air'. As time went by, the Air Council began to allow the use of 'the Squadronaires' in small print; the more the band played, the larger the print became.

This system – or lack of it – also created 'supergroups' the Skyrockets (officially known as the Number One Balloon Centre Dance Orchestra) and the Blue Rockets (the Royal Ordnance Army Corps Dance Orchestra) from the cream of Britain's existing bands.* Ivy Benson's outfit played alongside the Squadronaires and Skyrockets at the Jazz Jamboree of 1943, and it is worth dwelling on her band. Benson was

---

* The Squadronaires included saxophonist Cliff Townshend, father of the Who's Pete Townshend. A clarinet player in the Blue Rockets was Edwin Astley, who went on to write TV themes for *The Saint*, *The Champions*, *Department S* and *Danger Man* in the 1960s.

one of the few women to lead an all-female band, along with Blanche Coleman* and Gloria Gaye (whose band wore silver lamé dresses and were coached by Geraldo), though all three are barely remembered now. Ivy had been a regular performer on the BBC's *Children's Hour*, broadcast from Leeds, since she was nine, and worked in a factory until she could afford to buy her first alto saxophone and move to London. By the early 1940s she had become a bandleader herself, and her out-fit landed an unofficial gig as a resident dance band at the BBC in 1943. She wanted to lead a group of female musicians 'who not only looked good but sounded good', and who worked hard too. Most of her players arrived from works' brass bands in the north of England. Trumpet player Gracie Cole had won so many awards with bands in Yorkshire (the Grimethorpe Colliery Band, the Besses o' th' Barn brass band) that it took £18 a week to lure her down to London in 1945; she later joined the higher-profile Squadronaires. Holding on to musicians proved tricky: they were also magnets for GIs and frequently quit the band to get married. 'I lost seven in one year to America,' moaned Ivy. 'Only the other week a girl slipped away from the stage. I thought she was going to the lavatory but she went off with a GI. Nobody's seen her since.'

The fact that so many male musicians were away certainly furthered the cause of the Benson band, but they were still a constant target for sniping men; the Dance Band section of the Musicians' Union even sent a delegation to Broadcasting House to vent their fury. 'It was the plum job in the country. The reviews for the first broadcast were vitriolic,' remembered Benson trombonist Sheila Tracy. *Melody Maker* labelled it 'The Battle of the Saxes'. Ivy's three hundred fan letters a week from servicemen suggested it was nothing more than jealousy and misogyny.

Still, men ultimately ran the show. At the personal request of Field Marshal Montgomery, the Benson band were flown to Berlin to play at a concert celebrating the end of the war. And with that, Britain decided

---

* Andrew Motion reckons that Blanche Coleman was the inspiration for the pseudonym Brunette Coleman, under which Philip Larkin wrote risqué girls' school stories, though Larkin hate figure Ornette Coleman seems just as likely.

that all-female bands had pretty much served their purpose. The men were back now. 'Every door slammed in her [Benson's] face,' said Tracy. 'Even the BBC turned their back on her. A committee of bandleaders was set up and they all closed ranks – with the band circuit booked up there was nowhere to go.' After the war, the Ivy Benson band would be largely relegated to playing American army bases and Butlin's holiday camps.

* * *

In the autumn of 1940, as the Blitz raged on and dance bands were decimated by the call-up, the BBC's options were limited. It could call on all-female bands, but it was also within its remit to support the civilian dance-music profession during the war. With the Skyrockets and Squadronaires covering musicians in service, the BBC decided to offer Jack Payne's and Geraldo's outfits indefinite contracts as house bands. They were signed up to the Corporation's Dance Band Scheme, which meant the band members would be exempted from the draft; each band would have a stable line-up and, therefore, some guarantee of quality players. To add a bit of variety, these two outfits would be supplemented on air by a 'band of the week', like Bert Ambrose's or Billy Cotton's.

For £250 a week, Payne committed to give three broadcasts for the Home Service and Forces Programme, plus a further three for the Overseas Service. Like a doctor, he agreed to be on call six days a week. As well as performing straight dance-band music, Payne's eighteen-piece outfit had a show called *Moods Modernistic*, which could include light classical pieces like Massenet's 'Elegy', as well as ballad hits of the day, like Billie Holiday's 'I Don't Want to Cry Anymore' (Bruce Trent, Payne's male vocalist, handled this one). *Melody Maker* described Payne's arrangements as 'overdone' and his brass section as 'weak . . . Jack's band never really swings a phrase, even by accident.'

Still, there was a reassuring familiarity to this heavy rotation of Payne and Geraldo, and besides, Geraldo had a certain slickness. One Columbia Records advert described him as 'polished and stream-lined . . . fastidious'. He didn't attempt to cover up his north London accent and enjoyed tinkering with his life story. The one-time Gerald Bright had studied piano at the Royal Academy of Music and led hotel bands in Blackpool during the 1920s, before apparently heading to Brazil in 1929 to study coffee plantations. While there – and there's no evidence he ever was – he became intrigued by the tango, and returned home to front the Gaucho Tango Orchestra, changing his name to Geraldo while he was at it and landing a residency at the Savoy in 1930. *Melody Maker* described his appearance as 'polished to the last demi-semiquaver'. He was open to swing, though, sneaking things like 'Stormy Weather' and 'Ain't Misbehavin'' into *Tunes We Shall Never Forget*, a BBC oldies show.

Geraldo spoke to the troops as well, who were turned off by Payne's pomposity as much as his straight-backed arrangements. 'I think the greatest kick I get out of my job these days is when we are broadcasting to you fellows,' he told them. His style was intimate and informal. On top of this, he was a genuine swing enthusiast, and among his innovations was a swing septet, made up of existing band members, which played relatively daring material, like guitarist Ivor Mairants's 'Sea Food Squabble' (1942).

Geraldo later reminisced on life during wartime with the jazz journalist and broadcaster Benny Green: 'We used to start broadcasting and then the warning would go, air raid warning. And then we'd go onto short wave and still continue broadcasting. We couldn't come out because there was an air raid going on outside, so we used to have mattresses on the floor at the bottom of the Paris cinema and try and sleep down there. When the all-clear went in the morning we'd get up, go back to our respective homes, have a shave and a bath, and come and start broadcasting again.'

Radio could reach nearly everybody, but live performances were also important. Geraldo played at factories around the country, where the reaction was 'second to none, they absolutely lavished in it'.

The difference between British and American wartime music was encapsulated not by Payne or Geraldo, or even *Radio Rhythm Club*, but by the BBC's *Dancing Club*, hosted by 'strict-tempo' ballroom phenomenon Victor Silvester. Aged fourteen, he had lied about his age to fight in World War I and unwillingly became part of a firing squad that shot fourteen deserters. A complete change of direction was necessary for his mental well-being, and it came after the war, when he attended a tea dance at Harrods. Realising his feet were his fortune, he then won the first-ever World Dancing Championships in 1922, and his book, *Modern Ballroom Dancing*, was a million-seller. By the late 1920s Silvester had his own dancing school in Bond Street, approved by the Imperial Society of Teachers of Dance. It was all about rules – slow, slow, quick, quick, slow – and to anyone outside of the ballroom scene, it was a form of dancing that seemed thoroughly joyless.

Silvester didn't like much of the recorded music he heard and was peeved by unnecessary solos, silly vocal refrains and (most of all) drummers doing silly paradiddles. So in 1935 he picked up a baton and started to record 'strict tempo' records for Parlophone, metronomic but catchy things like Sammy Cahn and Jule Styne's 'And Then You Kissed Me' and Joseph Meyer's 'You're Dancing on My Heart', which became his signature tune. In March 1941 the BBC Variety Department's Mike Meehan called him up and said, 'There are thousands of service men and girls at camps and gun sites miles from anywhere. It occurred to me that if you gave dance lessons on the air it would help them to pass the time.'

Silvester was there to help pass the time. His music was sensible. There were no vocals to interfere with the seamless glide of brushed drums, with just a piano and either a violin or clarinet as the cherry on top. No shocks or surprises at all – that was the point. Silvester was a tall, athletic man, a smoothie who started each *Dancing Club* broadcast with ten minutes of instruction; this appealed to both the BBC's conservative side and the British weakness for being gently told exactly how to behave. The *Radio Times* would print diagrams to accompany each broadcast so that people could practise in their parlours, feet rotating like helicopter blades. Silvester's band became the most popular in the land, and his regimented dancing became known (in Britain, at least) as the 'international style'.

You would think he considered the music to be entirely secondary, if it wasn't for a second band he started in 1943. Inspired by the influx of American GIs, he held the baton for a series of terrific recordings, under the name Victor Silvester's Jive Band. The sound was far from the suave, slick hum the public might have expected. With arrangements by pianist Billy Munn and players like ace trombonist George Chisholm and Silvester loyalist 'Poggy' Pogson on sax and clarinet, 78s like 'Crazy Rhythm' and 'There's No Honey on the Moon' sounded like jazz loyalists had finally been let loose at Abbey Road. Post-war, though, Silvester reverted to the minimal, tidy sound that had made his name, which earned him his own request show on the BBC World Service. By the time he died in 1978 he had sold some seventy-five million records.

* * *

If Vera Lynn was the forces sweetheart, Gracie Fields was everyone's big sister. 'Our Gracie' was at the height of her fame at the outset of World War II. In 1939, having just been given a CBE for services to entertainment, as well as the Freedom of the Borough of Rochdale, she became seriously ill with cervical cancer. The public sent her over 250,000 goodwill messages. Knowing she had a job of morale-boosting on her hands, she cut 'Old Soldiers Never Die' and the upbeat 'I'm Sending a Letter to Santa Claus', the biggest Christmas hit of 1939. Best of the lot was 'The Thingummybob (That's Going to Win the War)', which made mind-numbing manufacturing jobs seem a little less pointless. Then disaster struck. She fell in love with the Italian-born film director Monty Banks and married him in March 1940. Banks had been christened Mario Bianchi, across enemy lines, in Italy. As he remained an Italian citizen, he would have been interned in the UK, so the couple were forced to leave Britain for North America, and the public's affections for Our Gracie became understandably muted. Once the conflict was over, though, Gracie was forgiven and welcomed home, and she scored her biggest-ever hit with the stately 'Now Is the Hour' in 1948.

With Our Gracie abroad, Petula Clark became like another family member, Britain's daughter or kid sister. She toured the country with another child star called Julie Andrews, the two performing at the

Entertainments National Service Association (ENSA) shows put on for troops at all the training camps, airfields and bases around London and beyond. Julie was a little buttoned-up, very proper, performing with her parents as 'Ted and Barbara Andrews and their little girl Julie'. Petula, on the other hand, sang swing numbers, cracked jokes and did 'When That Man Is Dead and Gone'. 'The first show I did for the BBC was at the Criterion theatre on Piccadilly,' she recalled, 'which the BBC used because it was underground. It was full of sandbags; it was really "London in the war". Our mum was Welsh, so when things really got a bit too hectic we used to go off to Wales, which I loved.' She would travel from one camp to another in troop trains, never really knowing where she was, sleeping in the luggage rack. 'And, of course, there were no lights. It was kind of strange.' Still, she was a little envious of her fellow child star: 'She sang with this amazing voice. I'd think, "How does she do that?"' As it turned out, neither of them would need to worry about their future.

* * *

The majority of Britain's wartime hits were still American in origin, but this feels like a good place to salute Northern Ireland-born Jimmy Kennedy. He had been a career civil servant in the early 1930s, and a lyricist on the side, but he wrote such unlikely hits as 'The Teddy Bears' Picnic' (a Henry Hall hit in 1941). He had written the first indisputable classic of the war, 'We're Going to Hang Out the Washing on the Siegfried Line', in 1939, when the war still seemed like an abstract concept. Kennedy had turned a chain of fortifications along Germany's western border into something relatable to your back yard.

Kennedy would go on to write travelogue standards like Gene Autry's Mexican tear-jerker 'South of the Border'; 'Isle of Capri' (after he heard Gracie Fields gushing about her holiday home) and 'April in Portugal' (both of which Frank Sinatra went on to record); and 'My Prayer' and 'Harbour Lights' (which would give the Platters' adult-oriented doo-wop hits in the mid-1950s). His best-known song might be 'Red Sails in the Sunset', cut by everyone from Bing Crosby to Fats Domino and written about his home town of Portstewart, in County Londonderry. Even though he never sought publicity, it seems bizarre that one of the most successful songwriters Northern Ireland has produced – only Van Morrison can really come close – remains so obscure. On the promenade in Portstewart, the local hero and his 'Red Sails in the Sunset' are commemorated by an abstract copper sculpture of a fish and a sail, once reddish, now green.

Arguably the most popular song with the British troops was of German origin. 'Lilli Marlene' (originally called 'Song of a Young Sentry') had been recorded in 1939 by Lale Andersen and picked up by the Axis-run Radio Belgrade, which played it at the same time every night. It had a bewitching effect. Soldiers on both sides tuned in to hear it, and soon different countries had their own recording. Anne Shelton, one of Jack Payne's singers, recorded it with an English lyric by Tommie Connor, who had also written Gracie Fields's more jovial 'The Biggest Aspidistra in the World' and Vera Lynn's 'Be Like the Kettle and Sing'. Shelton, still a teenager when the war ended, also recorded Jerome Kern and Oscar Hammerstein III's Academy Award-winning 'The Last Time I Saw Paris', but Tony Martin scored the bigger UK hit with this; the lyric's familiarity with Parisian life somehow sounded more convincing coming from an American rather than an unworldly girl from Dulwich.* Also written from a safe distance was Eric Maschwitz's 'A Nightingale Sang in Berkeley Square', composed in 1939, while he was staying in Le Lavandou, in south-east France. It was placed in the London revue *New Faces* and sung by Vera Lynn, and would go on to become a standard.

On the home front, the war's ultimate soundtrack would be Vera Lynn's 'The White Cliffs of Dover', which had been written by New Yorkers Walter Kent and Nat Burton in 1941 to uplift the spirits of the British as the threat of a Nazi invasion seemed at its most imminent. Its American origins explain why bluebirds are included in the lyric,

---

* Shelton's career would survive well into the 1950s. She had a number-one hit with the Joe Meek-engineered 'Lay Down Your Arms' as late as 1956, the year of Suez, the Hungarian uprising and Gene Vincent's 'Be-Bop-a-Lula'.

even though they've never been spotted in Dover during wartime or peacetime, but it was a beautiful gesture from one side of the Atlantic to the other. Vera sang it on the very first broadcast of *Sincerely Yours* in November 1941. A month later came Pearl Harbour.

29

WHY DON'T YOU DO RIGHT: AMERICA AT WAR

For some time after Britain had declared war on Germany, the US lived in a phony peace. Everyone was aware of what was going on in Europe, but in 1940 the country carried on much as it had before. America danced on as European nations began to fall one by one to the Germans. Over the next half-decade the make-up of popular music would undergo accelerated change, taking on board previously hidden influences thanks to two factors: a foreseeable war and totally unforeseen music-industry turmoil.

In 1940 you could go to twenty different places in New York, any night of the week, and catch a big band. Ballrooms, supper rooms, hotels – they were everywhere, and they were very much what the young generation of 1940 wanted. The dance hits of the year were Glenn Miller's 'In the Mood' and 'Tuxedo Junction'; the romantic hit 'Darn That Dream' by Benny Goodman with Mildred Bailey; the big ballad was Tommy Dorsey's 'I'll Never Smile Again', featuring a vocal refrain from rising star Frank Sinatra. It was boom time in the New World.

If you were a teenage swing fan in 1940, you probably favoured the out-of-town venues, like New Jersey's Meadowbrook ballroom, and the amusement parks. You might also have been able to sneak into the uptown hotels, because the cover charge was usually no more than seventy-five cents, meaning kids could afford to catch the biggest bands in person. If your particular favourite was playing at a theatre, you could go in the morning, pay your seventy-five cents and stay all day; you would see the same feature film three or four times, but you would also get to see your favourite band three, four or even five times. Band loyalty remained fierce.

Bands that weren't in residency were on buses and trains, criss-crossing the country, nabbing musicians from each other with the lure of more money and greater prestige. Fletcher Henderson had been the man behind the curtain who wrote Benny Goodman's arrangements, and Sy Oliver performed the same role for Tommy Dorsey. In 1939 he was with black bandleader Jimmie Lunceford, when he got an offer from Dorsey that he couldn't refuse: an extra $5,000 per annum. 1939 was a good year for Oliver: he also wrote 'It Ain't What You Do (It's the Way That You Do It)', cut in the States by Ella Fitzgerald and in Britain by Nat Gonella. 'Bandleaders would pay much more than they could really afford to get a particular star,' reckoned Oliver. It was 'a matter of professional pride'. Dorsey also poached Frank Sinatra from Harry James's band; when Sinatra went solo, Dorsey then grabbed James's replacement, Dick Haymes. You could be a well-known singer, or cornet player, or arranger, but working with Tommy Dorsey would make you a household name. 'Tommy was a star-maker,' said Haymes. 'Consider the people he had in his band, my lord . . . The travelling arrangers were Axel Stordahl, Sy Oliver and Paul Weston. A showcase like you wouldn't believe.' Dorsey had not only Sinatra, but also Jo Stafford, who was known for her absolutely perfect pitch.

Big bands and swing had bossed the scene for six years straight, but the war would change this set-up for ever. This was partly down to conscription and partly gradually diminishing demand, but the real revolution – with singers like Sinatra and Stafford moving centre stage, the bandleader's role being diminished and the professional songwriter's role challenged – was due to what we would now call 'industrial action'.

* * *

The American Society of Composers, Authors and Publishers (ASCAP) had been set up by operetta writer Victor Herbert in 1914 to collect money from public performances. Early beneficiaries were Herbert himself, Jerome Kern and Irving Berlin, who probably heard their own songs played back to them by a band, without recompense, every time they sat down in a restaurant. ASCAP was a very exclusive club, and if you weren't a member, you got nothing. In 1940 an existing agreement was coming to an end, so ASCAP decided to ask broadcasters for more money. Heck, didn't Rodgers and Hart deserve it? The broadcasters decided they didn't and refused to accept the new rates; from 1 January 1941 they simply wouldn't play any ASCAP music over the air. All that was left for them were foreign songs, folk songs, hillbilly songs and the blues. Bands and singers were faced with the prospect of going off the air. Bands couldn't promote their new records; songwriters couldn't push their new songs.

ASCAP sat tight, believing that the public would complain. Nobody did. Nobody. What's more, ASCAP effectively handed the broadcasters a means to make money from the performing-rights business: between January and October 1941 virtually no ASCAP music would be heard on the air, as the broadcasters had set up their own licensing and collection agency – Broadcast Music Incorporated (BMI). And BMI wasn't snobbish about whether you could write your own sheet music: anyone with a guitar who could whistle a tune could have their song registered with the agency.

So what on earth were the radio stations playing? Clarinettist and bandleader Les Brown had to abandon his regular set and dig out some antiquities: 'We played [Stephen Foster's] "Jeannie with the Light Brown Hair" every show. We had to get a new book overnight if we wanted to play on the air. So we did, because we wanted the exposure.' Turning to out-of-copyright classical material, Brown also came up with a hit called 'Bizet Has His Day'. He remembered seeing a memo being passed around radio stations: 'People will never miss what they don't hear.'

In the long run, BMI helped to democratise the American music business. No matter how hot the new hillbilly writer from Tennessee, or how exciting the new blues talent from Alabama, they couldn't get into ASCAP in 1940 – the old school weren't interested. They considered Broadway shows and film scores to be a league above, and assumed the public agreed. Pretty soon, drummer Gene Krupa's band had to ditch Gershwin and write new arrangements for Stephen Foster's 'Old Black Joe' and 'My Old Kentucky Home', both close to a century old. Foreign songs worked for BMI too: Glenn Miller took a Russian folk melody, 'Song of the Volga Boatmen' (otherwise known as 'Yo Heave Ho'), to the top of the nascent *Billboard* chart; Guy Lombardo played the Viennese theme from the Ingrid Bergman movie *Intermezzo*; Xavier Cugat, who had been leader of the resident orchestra at the Waldorf-Astoria before the war, capitalised on the tango craze and hit with 'Perfidia' in 1940; while Jimmy Dorsey had umpteen new stamps on his passport, bringing 'Yours (Quiéreme Mucho)', 'Maria Elena' and 'Amapola' over from Spain.

By the end of October 1941 ASCAP relented and agreed to a lower licence fee. 'Jeannie with the Light Brown Hair' had been played so many times in the previous ten months that *Time* magazine noted that 'she was widely reported to have turned grey'. If the ASCAP boycott had unexpectedly broadened the American public's palate, then another was about to test its patience a little further.

* * *

In the spring of 1928 a new machine called the Orchestrope had been unveiled. It was a record player that could take twenty-eight records, and it came with a remote-control wall box with which you could select the record you wanted to hear. Made by the Capehart Automatic Phonograph Corporation, more than six hundred had been manufactured by October, in time for the Chicago Radio Fair, where the Orchestrope caused a sensation, equalling the gasps drawn by another new machine being exhibited at the fair: the television.

Within a year Orchestropes could be found in bars, sweet shops and drug stores across the country. The Capehart Corporation played music to its workers on one of the machines, which was also connected to speakers outside the factory. The company's newsletter said that 'every afternoon and evening', large numbers of cars parked in front of what Capehart called its Singing Tower 'to listen to the splendid programmes offered'. It's hard to think of a more classically American scene.

The jukebox – as it became known – would save the record player, record production and record companies. In 1934 the AMI, Seeburg and Mills companies were making 15,000 'automatic phonographs' between them, and they must have been pretty happy with those figures. Then, in 1936, Homer E. Capehart took his know-how to the Wurlitzer company, and they alone shipped 63,000 machines that year. Every bar, every café, every possible jukebox location had a machine. During the Depression, the black jukebox market was one of the main reasons record companies survived. They would be wheeled into houses, where 'rent parties' paid the bills for black Americans who weren't allowed into segregated clubs in the South; then, a week later, they would be taken to another rent party. They were in amusement arcades and drug stores and anywhere that served alcohol. Homer Capehart got rich and became governor of Indiana. Everybody loved a jukebox. Everyone was pretty happy with the situation.

Well, you'd think so, wouldn't you?

James Caesar Petrillo was the president of the American Federation of Musicians (AFM), a highly disciplined and well-organised union. By the start of 1942 60 per cent of Petrillo's members were out of work, and he vocally blamed the jukebox. No matter that the Pearl Harbour attack had dragged America into the war a few months earlier, decimating bookings for his musicians at home; Petrillo reckoned the jukebox was 'scab number one'.*

Petrillo's intentions were largely honourable, but as misguided as those of anyone from ragtime-baiting George Robey to microphone-hating Al Jolson to the high-horse ASCAP – other folks who had historically tried

---

* You might think that the AFM would have been better off going after radio stations, which were starting to play more records as it was so much cheaper than using live musicians. You'd be right, but the US government had legislated to stop the union doing this, and so the AFM focused on the record labels.

to jab a stick into the spokes of music-industry progress. There had been hundreds of dance halls and thousands of restaurants employing tens of thousands of musicians not so long ago, Petrillo reasoned. If they now couldn't get work, why couldn't they at least get a cut of the record companies' action? He had been arguing his case for years. Jukeboxes, and the unrestricted playing of records over the air without further payment, were reducing the amount of work for musicians. And so the grim logic for the union was that musicians should stop making records altogether. Eventually, Petrillo instructed artists across America not to take on any recording work after 31 July 1942.

There was a rush by record companies to get into the studio before the strike began. Peggy Lee recalled cutting a last-minute best-seller with Benny Goodman: 'I used to play Lil Green's "Why Don't You Do Right" constantly, and Benny's room was next to mine. It drove him up the wall. So he said, "Would you like to sing that song and get it out of your mind?" We were told there was about to be a record strike. Benny recorded everything he had in his book. "Why Don't You Do Right" was at the bottom of the barrel, and it was an instant hit.'

Once the new recordings had all been released, the record companies needed to find old stuff that they could pass off as new, so they dug around in their vaults. When *Casablanca* came out, Rudy Vallee's 1931 version of 'As Time Goes By' became a hit, as Dooley Wilson – who sang it on screen – was unable to record it for lack of players. Another way around the strike was to make a cappella recordings.

Indeed, the real winners of the strike weren't the musicians but the vocalists. The Mills Brothers – Donald, Harry, Herbert and bassman John Jr – were a black, jazz-fired barbershop quartet from Piqua, Ohio, where they had started out singing in cinemas between Rin Tin Tin features. Their 1930 recording of 'Tiger Rag', a three-minute slice of pure joy made up of just their muted yet zippy harmonies, backed by a single acoustic guitar, was a huge seller; very soon they became regulars on Rudy Vallee's *Fleischmann's Yeast Hour*, as well as having their own nationally networked show on CBS. Further beautiful records followed with Hoagy Carmichael's 'Rockin' Chair' (1932) and 'Lazy Bones' (1934), and Walter Donaldson and Gus Kahn's 'Sleepy Head' in 1935. These were international hits, and the Mills Brothers became the first black Americans to play a Royal Command Performance. They were playing in London again* when war broke out. Unable to sail back to the US, they went on to Australia and didn't get back to the States until 1941. By then the more lugubrious Ink Spots ('Whispering Grass', 1940; 'Do I Worry', 1941) had stolen their thunder as the new black vocal group of choice. Nevertheless, Decca welcomed them back with open arms: as a self-sufficient a cappella act, the strike had suddenly made the Mills Brothers one of the label's priority acts. They were rushed into the studio and recorded their biggest-ever hit, 'Paper Doll', which went to number one on the *Billboard* chart in November 1943 and stayed there for twelve weeks.† By the end of the war it had sold six million copies. The Mills Brothers sent a gold disc to James Petrillo.

The big bandleaders were not exactly in sympathy with Petrillo. They wanted to keep their names in the papers – they had investments to protect. Petrillo could claim he was just doing what he was employed to do – acting in good faith for the jobbing sideman‡ – but in doing so he was sacrificing the future of the big bands, and the progress of instrumental music would be hugely affected by the strike. In the end the dispute was settled without fuss, but only once both sides were exhausted. Decca gave in first in September 1943, with RCA Victor and Columbia finally caving more than a year later, on Armistice Day 1944 (either they had a sense of the theatrical or it was a good day to

---

* John Jr had died in 1936, aged just twenty-five, after falling ill during their first visit to Britain, and was replaced by John Sr. Dad had form, having led his own barbershop quartet – in his own barbershop! – in the 1910s.

† 'Paper Doll''s composer, Johnny S. Black, didn't live to reap the dividends. He had died after trying to break up a fight in his own Club Dardanella in St Louis, Missouri, five years earlier.

‡ Petrillo's union was choosy about which musicians it wanted to look out for. The AFM had 673 local branches across the US, of which thirty-two were 'coloured'. Of the 641 'white' local branches, eight had a subdivision for black musicians. Many, especially in the South, simply didn't allow black artists to join. Given the high percentage of jukeboxes in black-run venues, and the predominantly black musicians played on those machines, you have to wonder just who Petrillo thought was benefiting from the strike.

bury bad news). The record companies were now forced to pay a small royalty – roughly 1 per cent of the retail price of each record sold – into the AFM's fund. The balm of money did its job. Why did the strike end so suddenly? Simply because popular music was constantly evolving, and fobbing the public off with reissues and a cappella songs couldn't work for ever.

* * *

By the start of 1942 World War II had enveloped the American consciousness. The Andrews Sisters put themselves forward as something to fight for, and captured the thoughts and concerns of GIs abroad: 'Every little Dutch girl says, "*Ja, ja*," every little Russian girl says, "*Da, da*," why won't you say, "*Sí, sí*"?' A trio from Minnesota, Patty (the youngest, and the lead singer), LaVerne and Maxene modelled themselves strongly on the beloved Boswell Sisters, but sold far more records. After signing to Decca in 1937, they had quickly struck gold with 'Bei Mir Bist Du Schoen' (1938), a Yiddish song that has mapped the way for every close-harmony vocal group since; 'Beer Barrel Polka' (1939), 'Ferryboat Serenade' (1940) and '(I'll Be with You) In Apple Blossom Time' (1941) followed in short order. The breakneck-speed 'Boogie Woogie Bugle Boy', released a few months before Pearl Harbour, ensured that when war broke out, they became darlings of the troops, culminating in an eight-week USO tour in 1945.

The main difference between the Boswells and the Andrews Sisters was down to subtraction rather than addition. The Andrews' 'Bounce Me, Brother, with a Solid Four' was a terrific dancer with a telltale, mono-minded title. Did they have a slightly sweeter sound? Maybe, but more significantly they cut out the Boswells' wild tempo changes and trombone impressions and delivered streamlined dancefloor fillers that would still be getting played in clubs decades later. Their radio and film performances were so numerous that, at their peak, they were earning $20,000 a week. As long as there was a war on they were untouchable, there was no stopping them. Their golden era ended on VJ Day; 1949's 'I Can Dream, Can't I' would be their sole post-war number one.

The Andrews Sisters' major addition to the Boswells' harmonies was boogie-woogie. Originally a piano-based sound, with the left hand playing a walking bassline, it had been cemented as a style by Clarence 'Pinetop' Smith's 'Pinetop's Boogie Woogie' back in 1928, which itself had been mostly filched from Meade 'Lux' Lewis's 'Honky Tonk Train Blues' from a year earlier (Smith and Lewis lived in the same Chicago boarding house, so it's probably not a coincidence). The style was rhythmically irresistible, and by the turn of the 1940s every swing band had a couple of boogie-woogie numbers, with the bass and treble parts from the piano transposed to brass and reeds. The Andrews Sisters scored their biggest hit with 'Boogie Woogie Bugle Boy'; Will Bradley's band ('Boardwalk Boogie', 'Down the Road Apiece', 'Cryin' the Boogie Blues'), with star player Freddie Slack on piano, built a whole career around it. But not everyone was a fan. Fats Waller apparently had it written into his contract that he could not be forced to play boogie-woogie. He considered it cheap and unmusical, all repetition and lacking in harmonics (though that didn't stop him taking on Roosevelt Graves's boogie-woogie milestone 'Crazy About My Baby'). Aaron Copland, usually a champion of jazz, moaned that it didn't have 'any shred of melodic invention'.*

When swing died, boogie-woogie went back underground, a minority interest for 'race' record-buyers and, for the first time, the 'hillbilly' market. It switched from piano and big-band arrangements to electric guitar, working its way into R&B, with Big Bill Broonzy, and country, with Arthur Smith and his million-selling 1945 single 'Guitar Boogie'. Country boogie became an early-1950s craze: there was the Delmore Brothers' 'Hillbilly Boogie' – 'in the low-down way' – and Tennessee Ernie's early hits, such as 'Catfish Boogie' and 'Shotgun Boogie'.†

---

* Copland wasn't wrong. Boogie-woogie pointed to a future where rhythm and repetition were more significant than the tune. Ahead of it lay rock 'n' roll, disco, Krautrock, Status Quo. When American concertgoers shouted, 'Boogie!' at bands in the 1970s, they may as well have been shouting, 'Boogie-woogie!'
† There's some geographical intrigue here. Boogie-woogie's roots seem to lie in east Texas, where George Thomas wrote the confusingly titled 'New Orleans Hop Scop Blues', which sounds like primitive boogie-woogie, as early as 1910. In Houston, Dallas and Galveston, workers on the railroads and in the oil fields

The popularity of boogie-woogie was in line with a greater presence of black faces in the entertainment world during America's war years, even as forces abroad were being segregated in pure Jim Crow fashion. Lena Horne became the first black singer to be booked by the Savoy Plaza Café Lounge in Manhattan; the Ink Spots, working with black bandleader Lucky Millinder, played at the Palomar club in Norfolk, Virginia; and black punters were allowed into suburban as well as downtown theatres in Columbus, Ohio, for the very first time – *Billboard*, being an industry magazine, saw this as potentially '60,000 new customers'.

Industry economics, rather than any shift towards civil rights, dictated this change. A 1944 incident involving Cab Calloway showed how little had really changed. Calloway had been Duke Ellington's replacement bandleader at the Cotton Club back at the turn of the 1930s, had starred opposite Al Jolson in *The Singing Kid* (1936) and had written his own guide to jive speak, *Cab Calloway's Cat-ologue: A Hepster's Dictionary*, in 1938. By the early 1940s he was something of a superstar, a flamboyant figure nicknamed 'His Hi-De-Ho Highness of Jive' after the refrain from his million-selling record 'Minnie the Moocher'. 'People used to say I had forty suits and forty pairs of shoes,' he laughed. 'They were wrong. I had fifty suits and fifty pairs of shoes, with fifty pairs of pearl grey gloves to match.' Calloway was the snappiest dresser in Harlem, resplendent in long jackets that reached his knees, worn over voluminous trousers, and always with a long watch chain – an outfit that was tagged the 'zoot suit'. He was a fashion icon. Finding himself at a loose end in Kansas City one night in 1944, he bought a ticket to see Lionel Hampton, but when he got to the door, he was told, 'No Negroes admitted.' What happened next led to an NAACP investigation. A security guard claimed he was pushed to the floor, to which he reacted by pulling a gun and beating Calloway around the head. While recovering in hospital, the zoot-suited

---

called this style of playing 'fast western' or 'fast blues', marking out its difference to the 'slow blues' piano styles of New Orleans and St Louis. When George and his brother Hersal migrated from Texas to Chicago, they took boogie-woogie with them. Boogie-woogie heroes Albert Ammons and Meade 'Lux' Lewis both claimed the Thomas brothers' 1922 composition 'The Fives' as a major influence.

superstar was charged by the Kansas City police with intoxication and resisting arrest.*

Still, wartime economics meant that more black Americans had defence-work money to spend, and so more black clubs and cocktail bars began to open, playing more black music on stage and on the juke-box. Philadelphia's Town Hall switched from booking predominantly white bands to predominantly black as its clientele changed; the beneficiaries were acts like Fats Waller, Nat King Cole and His Trio and the bands of Jimmie Lunceford, Lucky Millinder, Jay McShann and Earl Hines. By 1945 small, black-owned independent record labels like Exclusive (Joe Liggins's 'The Honeydripper', covered with even greater success a year later by Cab Calloway on Columbia) and Gilt Edge (with Cecil Gant's beautiful blues-based piano ballad 'I Wonder') were finding themselves with million-sellers and struggling to keep up with demand. Before too long, smarter operators began to sense a potential gold mine, and the next generation of record labels aimed at black audiences, in both the jazz and the nascent R&B scenes, would be white-run.

* * *

* Taking Cab Calloway's lead, the zoot suit would come to be favoured by Mexican Americans in Los Angeles. After Pearl Harbour, white servicemen began to regard these dandies in oversized clothes as unpatriotic for wasting valuable American fabric. On 3 June 1943 a group of sailors in downtown Los Angeles were rumoured to have been attacked by a number of 'pachucos' – Mexican Americans clad in zoot suits. The next day two hundred uniformed sailors headed for the Mexican American community to take their revenge on any zoot-suiters they spotted. The violence lasted for several days. On 10 June, after playing at Philadelphia's Met Ballroom, two members of Gene Krupa's band were rushed to hospital after sailors took exception to the way they were dressed. Thousands of servicemen were by now prowling the streets of Los Angeles, attacking not only any unfortunate zoot-suiter, but also random members of ethnic minorities. The next day Los Angeles City Council banned the wearing of zoot suits, although copycat 'zoot suit riots' continued in Chicago, San Diego, Oakland and New York City. Six hundred Mexican Americans were arrested. Los Angeles mayor Fletcher Bowron was keen to state that the riots had been caused purely by 'juvenile delinquents'. The LA Times was all sympathy: 'Those gamin dandies, the zoot suiters, having learned a great moral lesson from servicemen, mostly sailors, who took over their instruction three days ago, are staying home nights.'

In early 1942 the US government rationed record production. The simple reason was that 78s were made of shellac, and the biggest supplier of shellac in the world was Burma, now occupied by the Japanese; any remaining stocks were to be requisitioned by the military. Record companies had to think on their feet and announced that they would pay for any unwanted records, even if they were chipped or cracked, so they could recycle the shellac. Heaven knows how many rarities were lost this way.

The armed forces, though, could still obtain strange hybrid records called V Discs. The 'V' was presumably for 'victory', though it could have been for 'vinylite'* or possibly 'Vincent'. Bob Vincent was a five-foot-four army captain who, after lobbying the Pentagon, convinced Army Special Services that music would boost morale and that they should press records expressly for the troops abroad. During World War I record companies had discovered that soldiers didn't particularly want to be sent blatantly patriotic songs; *Talking Machine World* had written in 1918 that 'Rag is the rage . . . a rag, or at least a song with some syncopation, that is what the boys always ask for.' So the V Disc was all about popular music, the very best available. It would be used to remind the troops of their friends back home and the towns, soda shops and ballrooms they were fighting for. All fees and profits were waived; government money paid for the recordings, which got around the AFM strike.

V Discs played at 78 rpm but were twelve-inch records rather than the usual ten, and were made of, for the most part, unbreakable vinyl. From 1943 until the immediate post-war period they would be shipped to conflict zones in boxes of twenty-five, along with hand-cranked record players. Bob Vincent was the director of production, and he delegated the selection of the music to half a dozen people, including George T. Simon, editor of *Metronome* magazine. 'A lot of the recordings were taken from the air, from broadcasts, or the record companies

---

* This was a new material, used initially because shellac was a scarce resource. It was also more durable, and if vinylite hadn't also become scarce during the war, it may have found its way into commercial production sooner than 1949.

gave us permission to reissue things that the guys had, like Artie Shaw's "Begin the Beguine",' remembered Simon. 'The really great thing about V Discs was the fresh material they couldn't possibly hear any place else [because of the AFM strike].' V Discs also gave musicians a rare opportunity to go into the studio during the strike. Many of them worked for nothing: not just out of patriotism, but because of the opportunity – they hadn't had a chance to cut a record, get their message across, be creative, in months or even years. Simon relished the opportunity, and made Vincent sound like a pretty fun boss: 'This little captain who was in charge of V Discs said, "Just record them wherever you want, whenever you want, as long as you can get them for free." Well, I talked to Goodman, I talked to Woody [Herman], I talked to Harry James . . . Louis Armstrong did a fantastic session. It was a ball for me.'

* * *

Back in Tin Pan Alley, Irving Berlin ran World War II just like he'd run World War I.

Aside from individual hit songs like 'When That Man Is Dead and Gone' (cut by Al Bowlly and Anne Shelton in Britain) and 'A Little Old Church in England' (written after he'd heard about the Blitz), Berlin wrote songs whenever he received requests and seemed incapable of turning them down; the hymnal 'Angels of Mercy', recorded by Glenn Miller, among others, was written for the Red Cross. On top of this, he took on an all-soldier Broadway show called *This Is the Army* (1943). He contacted General George Marshall and proposed the show as a way to channel his patriotism, as well as a means of raising money for Army Emergency Relief. Secretly, he also loved the idea of another revue in which he would be the sole producer and songwriter, with a cast of three hundred, including – unlike in World War I, when blackface had been used in *Yip Yip Yaphank* – black soldiers. He hoped that if any good were to come from the war, it would be to strike a blow for integration: the company of *This Is the Army* would be the US's only integrated service unit during World War II. Berlin also saw a different attitude while working alongside these soldiers, compared to those of World

War I: 'They are more serious and grim. They know what they are up against . . . all the stock standard forms of patriotism are out of this war. Nowadays, the fellows go off quietly and we watch them go quietly.'

Berlin had the main course; Georgia-raised Johnny Mercer mopped up the leftovers. Mercer also wrote a bunch of patriotic songs – 'GI Jive' (a hit for Louis Jordan and for Mercer himself) struck a chord – but most didn't hit. He had a theory about this: 'I wrote one called "Old Glory", a funny one called "He Loved Me Till the All-Clear Came". There was "I'm Doing It for Defence", "On a Swing Shift" . . . didn't mean a thing. I don't think people believed in wars any more, I don't think people believed in propaganda.' He had a point: in America, the biggest song to come out of the conflict was 'Don't Sit Under the Apple Tree', a huge hit for both Glenn Miller and the Andrews Sisters. Mercer didn't really need to worry, though, and we'll be hearing more from him in the post-war age.

The sound of imminent victory came with a silvery big-band burst called 'Skyliner' by Charlie Barnet and His Orchestra, with the marvellous Barney Kessel on guitar and a thrilling Neal Hefti arrangement. The optimism, the confidence, the absolute joy of this record are undeniable. Maybe the most potent American war song, though, was 'I'll Walk Alone', with music by Jule Styne and lyrics by Sammy Cahn, which was sung by Dinah Shore in the 1944 film *Follow the Boys*. Cahn was a true professional. 'We tried to stay one step ahead of the generals,' he recalled. 'One day I looked at the maps, and I said to Jule, "You know, I think this war might be turning." So we wrote "Victory Polka". A while later I looked at the maps again. I said to Jule, "You know, I think this war might be coming to an end."' The pair duly obliged returning soldiers with the warm hug of 'It's Been a Long, Long Time', a sensuous lullaby – just what America needed in 1945.

30

HOT LICKS WITH VANILLA: GLENN MILLER

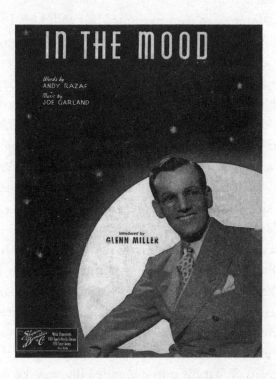

Glenn Miller occupies a unique position in the history of pop. He made music that was, and remains, so popular that it is almost never explored by critics (the jazz critic's default position is that it isn't jazz, so why bother?). The public never had any issue with it, though, and the roll call of Miller's wartime hits – 'In the Mood', 'Moonlight Serenade', 'Little Brown Jug', 'Chattanooga Choo Choo', 'A String of Pearls', 'Tuxedo Junction', 'American Patrol' – is as familiar as the Beatles' singles.

Miller remains a romantic figure. This has nothing to do with his slightly starched appearance, like Harold Lloyd without the jokes, his head bent slightly forward as if he were peering into a microscope. It has a lot to do with the evocative sound of 'Moonlight Serenade', and plenty with his disappearance in thick fog over the English Channel, aged forty, just before Christmas 1944. The combination of a forward-thinking sound with a withdrawn persona and opaque image foreshadows some of the greatest modern pop heroes, the likes of David Bowie and Scott Walker.

'In the half dozen or so conversations I had with him, I found Miller perfectly civil but staggeringly uninformed, and seemingly indifferent to practically everything,' wrote George Frazier in his 'Sweet and Low Down' column for the *Boston Herald*. Indifferent to everything, that was, 'except his music'. He played golf, apparently, and toyed with the stock market, occasionally. The 1954 movie *The Glenn Miller Story*, starring James Stewart, is an object lesson in making a little go a long way. 'I have this sound in my head,' says Stewart, many times, attempting to create mystique around a man who was undoubtedly devoted to his wife and adopted kids, but otherwise barely there.

None of this mattered to the millions who heard him on their radios playing at New York's Hotel Pennsylvania as winter set in; or on the BBC Light Programme, sounding impossibly American and futuristic; or on jukeboxes (Miller's career was made by jukeboxes) in drug stores and bars across America; or on portable gramophones, if you had the means, whistling along to 'In the Mood' as you opened a bottle of brown ale, while gazing across the tall grass blowing in the breeze on the South Downs. What his music sounded like was the world pulling together. Details were irrelevant; Glenn Miller's music sounded like a possible, and then a probable, future.

He loved jazz and had played fine trombone for Red Nichols's band, but he had a commercial heart and mathematical mind. He was obsessed in a scientific way with music, with how it could and should sound. Even the sound of his own name could be improved. Born in Clarinda, Iowa, he was originally Alton Glenn Miller, but he 'couldn't stand the name Alton. I can still hear my mother calling me from across the field. "Alton!" It was never 'Awlton.' "Alton!" she would call. "ALTON! Come on home!" I just hated the sound of that name. That's why I always used "Glenn" instead.'

Miller put himself through the University of Colorado by playing in a college band for two years. He took no music lessons; instead, he would stay up at night reading and re-reading Arthur Lange's *Arranging for the Modern Dance Orchestra*, a 1926 book that was the big-band equivalent of Bert Weedon's *Play in a Day*. A decade later, though, Miller was studying theory and arrangement with Professor Joseph Schillinger; one homework assignment turned out to be 'Moonlight Serenade'. In no way was he instinctive – possibly one reason why most jazz histories pass up on him completely – but new sounds obsessed him, the most exciting, the most commercial, the most modern.

The saxophone had been in plenty of military and minstrel bands but was an alien instrument in New Orleans jazz. The general line of thinking, according to trumpeter Bunk Johnson, was that 'it just runs up and down stairs with no place to go'. It would find a home in dance bands in the 1920s, who would play in spacious hotel rooms and needed its volume. With Fletcher Henderson laying out the blueprint, and Coleman Hawkins his chief architect, the big band used the saxophone to build its sound, tall and vast. By the time of the swing era, it bossed most reed sections.

The chief victim of the saxophone's rise was the clarinet. There were notable exceptions: the technique, virtuosity and New Orleans-influenced ornamentation of Benny Goodman's sound made him possibly the greatest clarinet player ever; and while Artie Shaw was self-taught, more of a melodist, his playing betrayed his suave smoothness (check out his sinuous solo on 'Frenesi'). Maybe more significant than either Goodman's or Shaw's clarinet-playing, though, was Miller's use of the saxophone. Sitting on top of his saxophone section, the clarinet was whipped cream on hot chocolate, luxurious, and while out of step with most of the bands around them, this sound defined the early 1940s. The band sounded like a humming engine, like a generator, very urban and machine-age.

This was a sound Miller had discovered while working for Ray Noble, the British bandleader who had crossed the Atlantic after his success with Al Bowlly. Noble had asked Miller to form a group for him to lead at the Rainbow Room, New York. Initially, Miller used Noble's trumpeter, Peewee Erwin, who played lead trumpet forcefully, an octave above the lead tenor saxophone. Erwin left just after Miller put Noble's small group together, and his replacement was weak. Miller decided to substitute the trumpet with a high clarinet lead. Noble was apparently unimpressed and used the sound only occasionally, but Miller took it and ran with it when he formed his own band in 1937.

The reeds were played with vibrato and had to be super-tight, creating a heat-haze effect.* Melody, above all else, was king. Miller incorporated melodic riffs – motorised and propulsive on 'In the Mood', gently throbbing on 'A String of Pearls' – played again and again with a rhythmic monotony, which allowed little room for soloing but gave the sound a hypnotic aspect. He disguised the repetition with a smooth sheen; melodic hooks would rise and fall, then conclude with a flourish. Miller understood pop.

For two years, the shimmering Miller sound was barely viable, with the band once earning itself a feeble $200 for an eight-hour performance at the Playland Casino in Rye, New York. Some players turned out to be drinkers or forgot to wear a handkerchief in their breast pocket – sackable offences to Miller's mathematically precise mind. At one point in 1938 he broke up the whole band and started from scratch. He hired two teenage singers, Ray Eberle and Marion Hutton, both born and raised in the Jazz Age, but it made little difference. Someone must have noticed Miller's band, though, as in 1939 they were booked to play a stint at Frank Dailey's Meadowbrook Ballroom in New Jersey. This meant ten broadcasts a week for NBC, and national exposure. That summer they were resident at the prestigious Glen Island Casino, meaning more broadcasts, more exposure; the pumping 'Little Brown Jug' was released as the Glen Island residency began, which sealed the deal.† By 1940 the Glenn Miller Orchestra was playing a hundred hours a week and recording a hundred songs a year. Not all were good, but its strike rate was incredibly high.

---

* Prototypes of the Miller reed sound can be heard in snatches of Fletcher Henderson's 1934 recordings 'Wrappin' It Up', 'Liza' and 'Hot and Anxious', which provided the blueprint for 'In the Mood''s riff.
† Originally a drinking song from the 1860s, in the 1950s it would be given a puerile lyric by the usually wonderful New Orleans writer Dave Bartholomew. As 'My Ding-a-Ling', it would give Chuck Berry a transatlantic number one in 1972.

Miller always looked professorial, his eyebrows raised as if to say, 'I'm in charge.' A mortar board and gown would have suited him well. But while his biopic makes him seem dull, mono-minded beyond belief, the musicians who worked with him early on remember he had a sharp sense of humour. In 1936 he wrote a song for Tommy Dorsey's band called 'Annie's Cousin Fannie', which was sung by Kay Weber (one of the earliest big-band female singers) and was risqué enough to get Dorsey and Weber's prom show in Stanford called off by the dean. Gil Rodin was the saxophonist in Ben Pollack's band, which Miller effectively ran: 'I remember Glenn had an attack of appendicitis. We tried to cure it with lots of orange juice and gin, but it didn't work, and finally one night I rushed him to the hospital for an operation. While Glenn was recuperating back in the apartment, we would have some free-for-alls among the musicians, who'd come in to try to make Glenn laugh so his scar would hurt.'

Miller was a shrewd judge, and some of his bit-part players were startlingly good choices. In 1939 sixteen-year-old Kay Starr briefly replaced the unwell Marion Hutton; her recordings with Miller that year included the cutesy 'Baby Me' and 'Love with a Capital You', but her rambunctious, older-sister voice would give her a string of major hits in the 1950s ('Comes A-Long A-Love', 'Side by Side', 'Rock and Roll Waltz'). Billy May was a trumpeter and an arranger for Miller's civilian band when he was just twenty-three, before becoming a much-coveted arranger and orchestra leader after that band broke up, and post-war going on to work with Frank Sinatra (including the career highlight *Come Fly with Me*), Bing Crosby, Rosemary Clooney and Anita O'Day. Trombonist Paul Tanner went on to produce experimental work with the theremin and played on the Beach Boys' 'Good Vibrations'.

The war made Miller bigger still. Not because of desperate things like 'The Booglie Wooglie Piggy', with Miller's Modernaires vocal group harmonising on the oinks, or the many sides he cut with brilliantine-voiced Ray Eberle, but because at the age of thirty-eight – after a decade of arranging and learning his craft – he asked to 'be placed in charge of a modernised Army band', entertaining the Allied forces with something more modern than Sousa marches. 'All members of the Miller band were handpicked,' said Bernie Privin, previously a trumpeter with Artie Shaw. 'One did not apply for the job, so to speak. Which was very flattering, I must say. From the start it was a marvellous orchestra, and very well received. It was a marvellous experience, really.'

Miller with his peaked army hat is the first image of him that comes to mind, which is a shame, as it squashes his very real links to the future. Those riffs without solos, which bored jazzers, thrilled dancers and prepared them for the purely rhythmic music of the late twentieth century that began with R&B, continued through rock 'n' roll and would find its purest form in house music. More specifically, Miller's 1939 hit 'The Little Man Who Wasn't There' ('Yesterday upon the stair I met a man who wasn't there') has been cited by Bowie scholar Chris O'Leary as the root of 'The Man Who Sold the World', and maybe *The Man Who Fell to Earth*. Miller must have felt like he was the man who owned the musical world of 1943.

As Captain Glenn Miller, he put together the Army Air Force Band and made some of his absolute best recordings: keeping the old brass reasonably happy, while frowning a little at this young people's music, he did a swing arrangement of W. C. Handy's 'St Louis Blues March'; 'My Buddy' had a similar glacial feel to Claude Thornhill's band, with an intimate, coddling sound, blanket-muffled and insulated against the cold outside; and at the other extreme was the thrilling, breakneck 'Mission to Moscow', which had been arranged for Miller by his pianist Mel Powell, who went on to become a Pulitzer Prize-winning avant-garde classical composer.*

On the back of umpteen number ones, in 1941 Hollywood called. The silver screen revealed his quiet, thorough confidence and studied

---

* Born Melvin D. Epstein, Powell is a fascinating character. Talking to *The New Yorker*'s jazz critic Whitney Balliett in the 1980s, he said, 'I had done what I felt I had to do in jazz. I had decided it did not hold the deepest interest for me musically. And I had decided that it was a young man's music, even a black music. Also, the endless repetition of material in the Goodman band – playing the same tunes day after day and night after night – got to me. That repetition tended to kill spontaneity, which is the heart of jazz and which can give a lifetime's nourishment.' Uniquely, he won *DownBeat*'s Jazz Pianist of the Year award in 1945 and a Pulitzer for 'Duplicates: A Concerto for Two Pianos and Orchestra' in 1990.

insolence to everybody, characteristics more associated with high clergy than jazz players. In one of his Hollywood vehicles, *Sun Valley Serenade*, Miller's permanent quarter-smile was undercut by his stentorian, monotone delivery, which gave the impression he had hearing problems. Films aside, the armed forces also gave him his own radio show, beautifully called *I Sustain the Wings*, which broadcast from Manhattan. Now an international name, he had permission to take the Army Air Force Band to Britain in the summer of 1944, where they gave an astonishing eight hundred performances.

The musicians in the flesh . . . Major Glenn Miller's Army Air Force Band. People couldn't believe it. To British fans, they were like messengers from another planet. American popular musicians had not played in the UK since the early 1930s, thanks to rows between the US's and UK's musicians' unions. The US Navy Band, led by Sam Donohue, was apparently the musicians' favourite. But there were more of Miller's men, heard by more people, and what's more, Miller stayed in Britain longer. They were loved. British bandleader Joe Loss reckoned that 'the only other time in my life I'd received such a thrill was in the early thirties, when I heard the Duke Ellington orchestra at the London Palladium. This magnificent orchestra . . . he [Miller] had a terrifically large string section, must have been fifty or sixty of them. So you've got every type of music, the lush sound of the strings, and you had the immaculate playing of the Miller music.' The effect was immediate and lasting. People were deeply impressed.

Miller had arrived in June, and by mid-December he was gone. He disappeared just after Paris had been liberated. Bernie Privin: 'We were all poised for take-off in Bedford. Our pilots wouldn't rev the engines; they weren't going anywhere. There was a hundred-foot ceiling – fog and rain and so forth. Major Miller elected to go in his one-engine plane, a pleasure plane. I remember waving goodbye as if it were yesterday. We left the next day and the sun was shining. It was beautiful.'

A lot of jazz history reads like romantic fiction. It comes down heavily on the dance-band era, while dabbing lavender around the sainted Louis and Bix. The combination of Miller's own romantic legend, combined with the critical jazz view, can obscure his importance as both the biggest star of his day and a progenitor of modern pop. His sound was futurist and prescient. Glenn Miller doesn't need jazz history on his side; he left his music frozen in time, like Buddy Holly, Eddie Cochran, Ian Curtis and Kurt Cobain. It is as permanent as stone.

31

SOMEONE TO WATCH OVER ME: VOCAL REFRAINS

Indoors, FRANKIE and NAN enjoy a quiet game of chess. Behind them : shelves of records.

As the big bands broke up at the end of the war, and jazz started to go down a dexterous path that would place virtuosity over audience interaction, the singers began to call the shots. Prior to this, they had been at the mercy of the bandleader, who had sole power over how commercially and artistically successful a singer could be, irrespective of their natural talent. Now it became tough work for a big-band hold-out like Stan Kenton to hang on to his canaries. Each time one of them had a big enough profile, they would inevitably go solo: Anita O'Day, June Christy and Chris Connor would all be among the biggest names of the 1950s.

The telltale sign was on record labels, where 'with vocal refrain' was replaced by 'with orchestral accompaniment'. Today it may seem like the privileging of singers in pop and rock is both normal and natural, that they are the obvious people to claim the main credit, but in 1945 it was new and strange.

Tommy Dorsey's orchestra was among the biggest of several big bands that broke up in the winter of 1946/7.* Their erstwhile 'vocalists' became new stars as 'singers'. Singers had been seen as less than secondary as recently as 1927, when Paul Whiteman's disc gave no clue as to the voice on 'Muddy Water'; it turned out to be Bing Crosby's first solo record.

Frank Sinatra was at the top of the pyramid, with newcomers Perry Como (formerly with the Ted Weems band) and the Irish Argentinian Dick Haymes – who had an exceedingly warm, all-enveloping voice – not far behind. Haymes remembered the point at which his world changed: 'Benny Goodman made a quip to me on the Astor roof, and I thought he was trying to be funny . . . as funny as Benny Goodman could get. He said, "What are you guys trying to do? Take over the damn business? You damn singers." And I said, "Oh, come on, Benny, you've had it good for a long time . . ." But he was right. He felt it happening. It was the end of the chapter.'

The new chapter had begun with the boys away and the girls at home, a new romantic era that was echoed in songs like Harry Warren's 'You'll Never Know', which was a warm, chocolatey 1943 hit for Haymes. As the war ended, he scored with Warren's 'The More I See You', which imagined clear blue skies ahead 'as years go by'. From the movie *Sing Your Way Home* came the delicious 'I'll Buy That Dream', which Haymes sang as a duet with Helen Forrest, looking as far ahead as possible: 'Imagine me with my head on your shoulder . . . a honeymoon in Cairo, then off to Rio for a drink . . . imagine you, ninety-two, making passes.' In reality, Hedda Hopper and Louella Parsons did their best to undermine the medically unfit Haymes as unpatriotic; that he wasn't American in the first place didn't deter the vultures. He cut two mid-1950s albums, *Rain and Shine* and *Moondreams*, with arranger Ian Bernard, which are highly recommended to any admirer of Frank Sinatra and Nelson

---

* Among the other orchestras to break up that winter were those of Benny Goodman, Harry James, Jimmy Dorsey, Les Brown and Glen Gray's Casa Loma Orchestra.

Riddle's work. But they didn't sell strongly. Haymes would be six times married, including to Rita Hayworth and Fran '*Harum Scarum*' Jeffries. By the early 1960s he was entirely out of fashion and had declared himself bankrupt. He's well worth rediscovering.

Of the female band vocalists, Haymes's duet partner Helen Forrest had been maybe the biggest star, singing with Artie Shaw, Benny Goodman and Harry James, but she struggled to maintain a profile post-war. By the mid-1950s she was looking backwards, guesting on the 1955 *Harry James in Hi-Fi* album, still in her thirties but with both feet already on the nostalgia carousel. She looked so 1940s that somehow it is hard to imagine her having hits, or even existing, beyond that decade.

By contrast, Doris Day – five years younger than Forrest, with blonde, atomic-age hair and laser-sharp blue eyes – was built for the 1950s. She had sung with Les Brown in the early '40s, and their sensuous 'Sentimental Journey' – with a two-note hook like a racing heartbeat – was one of the great homecoming hits of 1945. From here on in she was a singer and an actress, her movies affecting the hits she made ('Secret Love', 'Que Sera Sera'), her hits promoting her movies, and her persona inextricable from both.

'A normal family, just like yours,' ran the trailer for *Young at Heart* (1954), which found Day in Connecticut, one of three smiling, pastel-wearing blonde sisters. The movie started out like a more fun-loving *Virgin Suicides*. Day's character Laurie glowed like a Ready Brek kid, ripe and ready for Frank Sinatra's emaciated, chain-smoking bar-room pianist to throw her life into total confusion. The lighting is quite something: throughout, it enhances the three girls' round, healthy faces – Day, in particular, seems to be backlit with a blonde halo. The problem for Day was that the Laurie character stuck, something her husband/manager Marty Melcher encouraged, and eventually it became her default film role – a blonde, radiant, old world caricature of domestic goodness. As Sinatra snapped at her in *Young at Heart*, 'You come in here looking like a convention of angels . . . look at you!'*

---

* Laurie's pet dog in *Young at Heart* is called Number Nine. Maybe John and Yoko were fans.

It was a waste of her talent. Anyone who doubts Day's vocal jazz chops hasn't seen *Love Me or Leave Me*, the 1955 movie in which she bravely plays Ruth Etting. The catch in her voice, used as a giggle on *Calamity Jane* songs like 'The Deadwood Stage', proved incredibly effective on heartbroken ballads like 'Mean to Me' and the Depression-era morality play 'Ten Cents a Dance'. Here, she sounded beaten down, a beautiful loser, and it's a shame her later career – bossed by the manipulative Melcher, in an uncomfortable echo of the Ruth Etting story – was made up of so many soap bubbles and shiny-faced things like *Please Don't Eat the Daisies*. Her son Terry would produce her on a couple of great mid-1960s singles that showed her versatility ('Move Over Darling' was a UK Top 10 hit at the peak of the beat boom), but her husband scrapped a modern pop album, fearing anything that might harm her sainted housewife image. Maybe it's no surprise that, in her dotage, she wouldn't answer to the name of Doris any more, preferring to be called Clara.*

Though it was set twenty-odd years earlier, *Love Me or Leave Me* was an interesting mirror of the morals of early-1950s America. Etting's jealous gangster husband Martin Snyder had tried to murder her married arranger, Harry Alderman. In reality, Snyder went to prison, and Etting married the now-divorced Alderman, but at the climax of the movie she plays a 'thank-you' show for her supposed benefactor, Snyder, who somehow evades prison. In 1955 Hollywood, remaining loyal to a violent gangster was seen as morally preferable to marrying a divorced pianist.

* * *

In Britain, as the known dangers of war were replaced by the unknown dangers of peace, the West End desperately tried to wind back the clock.

By now in his early fifties, Ivor Novello had a huge hit in 1945 with *Perchance to Dream*, a musical that included 'We'll Gather Lilacs'. It's

---

* On the set of *Tea for Two* in 1950, actor Billy De Wolfe told her she looked more like a Clara Bixby than a Doris Day. It stuck, and close friends called her that for the rest of her life.

very hard to believe that this song had been written more recently than 'In the Mood'; it could easily have been an Edwardian smash. Novello was part of a swing back to an imagined pre-war idyll, by which I mean pre-World War I. *Perchance to Dream* ran for over three years, its writer and supporters – like Noël Coward and Vivian Ellis (whose 1947 show *Bless the Bride* was set in England on the eve of the Franco–Prussian war, its main protagonist called Lucy Veracity Willow) – glorying in the notion that such art would repel American colonialism.* The signifiers of safety and security that had been around in the 1890s were still in place: 'Primrose Hill' was a British number one on 1945's sheet-music chart, and its opening line ran, 'In an old world town, the moon looked down beside an old watermill,' painting a watercolour image of life way before the Nazis or the atomic bomb. The old world. The old ways. This method of wrestling with the demons of war trauma wasn't unique to Britain, of course: 'Among My Souvenirs', a hit in the same year for Frank Sinatra, similarly found him rummaging in his 'treasure chest'.

Natural selection can do strange things, and though swing had seemed so loudly modern, it had swung its last. Meanwhile, operetta – a signifier of mildew and bad eggs in most Judy Garland movies of the late 1930s and early '40s – outlived it, the music of the undead, a corpse with the powers of Frankenstein's monster. When Nelson Eddy and Jeanette MacDonald broke up, America simply found Kathryn Grayson, Jane Powell and Howard Keel to replace them. These were big, booming voices, with no possibility of gender confusion, or any chance of new artistic visions either. They weren't the place to go looking for fun.

As an antidote, Britain produced the lighter-voiced, owlish Donald Peers, who had scored a 1944 hit with 'In a Shady Nook (By a Babbling Brook)' and, after the war, had his own BBC Light Programme show, *Cavalier of Song*, which made him a star at the age of forty-two, with a weekly pay packet of £600. Another Welsh singer, Dorothy Squires,

---

* The big hit from *Bless the Bride* was 'This Is My Lovely Day', which was played heavily by the BBC around the time of Princess Elizabeth's wedding to Prince Philip in 1947. This helped it to become a *Housewives' Choice* favourite for years to come, as sung by the rubbery *Opportunity Knocks* winner David Whitfield or the operatic Goon Harry Secombe.

was way more intense, with long, arched eyebrows and a look that suggested she might have a steak knife behind her back. This was especially worrying when she sang 'I'm Walking Behind You', written for her in 1953 by her then husband, bandleader Billy Reid. In 1946 she was the highest-paid singer in Britain, scoring huge hits with the romantic fantasies 'The Gypsy' (1945) and 'A Tree in the Meadow' (1948), both also written by Reid. Squires was quite the romantic, later marrying aspiring actor Roger Moore, then breaking every window in his house when he left her in the 1960s.*

Away from pre-war fantasies, Geraldo's 1945 hit 'Kentucky' – 'where the sky is blue, and the grass is too' – acknowledged bluegrass, and the possible music of the near-future. There was also a strain of songs acknowledging that a new world had to be built, or at least rebuilt. Patrick Abercrombie and J. H. Forshaw, the chief architects for London County Council, looked to build new estates with green space to replace the terraces; Lewis Silkin sought to build entire new towns where before there had been fields – and possibly old watermills, rotting and derelict. Sentimentality was the enemy. The development of the town of Stevenage was approved in a 1946 government Act, without any consultation with the people who already lived in the area.

The people who were going to live in Stevenage had their own rebuilding to do. Bing Crosby sang 'The Land of Beginning Again' in 1945's *The Belles of St Mary's*: 'Though we've made mistakes, that's true, let's forget the past and start life anew.' The divorce rate spiked at the end of the war: there had been fewer than 10,000 in Britain in 1939, but more than 60,000 in 1945. It was easy to see why people were desperate to imagine how their lives had been before the conflict, why they tried really hard to wish the past back to life.

* To start a comeback in 1969, when she was fifty-five, Squires rented out the Royal Albert Hall and, impressively, managed to pack it. A ferocious, uncompromising version of 'My Way' was taken from the show and became a hit single in 1970. Her fondness for suing people led to the High Court declaring her a vexatious litigant in 1987. Most of her money would be lost in court cases, and she ended up living back in the mining area of Rhondda where she had started out. There's a hit movie in the Dorothy Squires story.

Things weren't so different in America. Bing Crosby and Dinah Shore both recorded the freshly laundered, milk-and-cookies 'Dear Hearts and Gentle People', Sammy Fain and Bob Hilliard's ode to folks who 'live in my home town' and 'will never, ever let you down'. There are mentions of 'picket fence and rambling rose', signifiers of safety, contentment and stagnation. What makes these people so dear and gentle? 'They read the good book from Fri till Monday, that's how the weekend goes.' You might think the antebellum idyll of Margaret Mitchell's 1936 novel *Gone with the Wind* had been safely dismantled by 'Strange Fruit', written in 1937, but here we were a decade on. The governor of Mississippi in 1945 was proud Ku Klux Klan member Theodore Bilbo, same as it had been in 1939, when he gave a speech on the floor of the Senate explaining how America's black population could be resettled in British and French African colonies. The land of 'Dear Hearts and Gentle People' was a dream home that never, ever really existed.

Between the modernists and the refuseniks was the large chunk of the population who whistled as they were clambering over the rubble. They had an anthem in a 1945 Sammy Kaye hit called 'Chickery Chick': 'Every time you're sick and tired of just the same old thing, saying just the same old words all day . . . open up your mouth and start to say, "Chickery chick, cha-la cha-la, chuckle-a-roony in a bananika".' Well, it wasn't going to get any new towns built, but you could see his point.

* * *

So, with Bing Crosby, Frank Sinatra, Dinah Shore and Doris Day bossing the silver screen and the hit parade, the world was safe for singers for the next few years. This implied it was also safe for songwriters. The bands may have gone, but performers still shopped for their songs on Tin Pan Alley and Broadway. How did the big songwriters of the 1920s and '30s fare in this shifting landscape? George Gershwin was by now long gone, Larry Hart had toasted his last toast in November 1943, and Cole Porter hadn't scored any significant hits during the war, in spite of long runs on Broadway for the now-forgotten *Panama Hattie* (1940) and *Let's Face It!* (1941).

Johnny Mercer, from Savannah, Georgia, had a holistic view of America, which was significant in 1945, something that could bring people from San Francisco and Savannah and Scarsdale together and remind them all about what they had been fighting for. What's more, he could sing, taking his own recording of 'On the Atchison, Topeka and the Santa Fe' to number one on the *Billboard* chart in 1945. He could sound as ribald and urban as the best of them on 'Blues in the Night', but wasn't above a little low humour – 1947's 'Huggin' and a-Chalkin'' was a cartoonish piece about making out with a fat girl. He sounded comfortable and familiar, and had a face to match, a gap-toothed fella wise beyond his years. The whole package – face, voice, music – was uniquely Johnny Mercer. In 1945 America hugged him close.

His melodies could be exercises in minimalism – think of the one-note chorus on 'Something's Gotta Give' – but that just helped you to focus on a more crafted lyric. If the melody was sweeter and swingier, as on Harold Arlen's 'Hit the Road to Dreamland', Mercer's lyrics took less of the load, but still had perfectly deployed bombs: 'It was divine, but the rooster has finally crowed . . . dig you in the Land of Nod.'

If there was a passing of the baton, it came with a brace of songs that Mercer wrote with Jerome Kern – by then in his late fifties – for the 1942 Fred Astaire film *You Were Never Lovelier*: 'I'm Old Fashioned' and the Oscar-nominated 'Dearly Beloved'. 'We hit it off right away,' remembered Mercer. 'I was in such awe of him, I think he must have sensed that. He was very kind to me, treated me more like a son than a collaborator.'

What Mercer had, what marked him out as a great songwriter, was a feel for the whole of America. This is a rare talent in music, something Mercer shares with giants like Louis Armstrong and Bob Dylan. He may not have sounded like your next-door neighbour, but you felt he could have been. He wasn't pure New York, or Broadway, and he didn't feel shoehorned into a Hollywood backdrop like wise-cracking, Eltham-born Bob Hope. He wrote for people 'from Natchez to Mobile, from Memphis to St Joe' on 'Blues in the Night', over Harold Arlen's none-more-Harlem melody. In 1944 the same team wrote 'Accentuate the Positive' – now there was a slogan America could live by. Maybe it was because he came from Savannah, which was another rare thing, a southern city that didn't define itself in black and white, a city so beautiful – with its hanging Spanish moss – that its buildings had been spared in the Civil War. Growing up, he had been obsessed with the family Victrola and had memorised his parents' Gilbert and Sullivan records, picking up W. S. Gilbert's English wit and sharp rhymes. Almost uniquely among his generation of songwriters, little Johnny played outside with black kids, so as a teenager it was no big deal for him to hang out in areas of town where he heard and absorbed blues and jazz. To grow up in Savannah was to understand American history and the country's ever-present fault lines: 'Have faith, or pandemonium's liable to walk upon the scene.'

Mercer had moved to New York after the family business in Savannah went belly up in 1929. He was a big drinker and made fast friends of people he had previously idolised from afar. Hanging out with the Whiteman band he got close to Bing Crosby, to trombonist–singer Jack Teagarden and to arranger Matty Malneck, with whom Mercer would write 'Goody Goody', a hit for Benny Goodman in 1936. Mercer was a natural, easy-going chap, and he couldn't believe his luck; he never thought of himself as a songwriter until he was several hits deep. His amiability explains how he could shift from one co-author to another without anyone seeming to stake a claim on him or get jealous. Everyone liked him. And so his song list – even leaving out the titles I've already mentioned – is like the Great American Songbook as bottled essence: 'Lazy Bones', 'Skylark' and 'In the Cool, Cool, Cool of the Evening' with Hoagy Carmichael; 'Hooray for Hollywood' and 'Too Marvellous for Words' with Richard Whiting; 'Jeepers Creepers' and 'You Must Have Been a Beautiful Baby' with Harry Warren; 'I Thought about You' with Jimmy Van Heusen; 'One for My Baby', 'That Old Black Magic' and 'Come Rain or Come Shine' with Harold Arlen. He didn't need A-listers, though: his exquisite lyrics on 'Fools Rush In' and 'Day in, Day Out' were written for melodies by Rube Bloom, previously best known as a sidekick pianist for jazz violinist Joe Venuti.

Mercer's casualness was legendary. By the time he presented Hoagy Carmichael with the finished lyric for 'Skylark', Hoagy had completely forgotten he'd written the song in the first place. But then their styles were close enough that maybe Mercer felt more pressure to deliver and impress.

Hollywood teamed him up with Harold Arlen in the 1940s: *Star Spangled Rhythm* (1942) gave us 'That Old Black Magic'; and *The Sky's the Limit* (1943) was the first home for the full fathom-deep 'One for My Baby (And One for the Road)', succinctly nailed by American chronicler John O'Hara as 'metropolitan melancholic beauty', and a song Sinatra revived with a grand nihilism in *Young at Heart*. Unlike many of his colleagues, Mercer kept on writing for the movies through the 1950s, and as late as 1961 Hollywood paired him up with Henry Mancini. Their 'Moon River' and 'The Days of Wine and Roses' would be outliers of Hollywood's golden age, but they also felt entirely contemporary to the 1960s. Both were quite beautiful, and 'Moon River' has the greatest lyric Mercer ever wrote.

In Britain, the black South African émigré Danny Williams took 'Moon River' to number one in December 1961, preceded by a Burt Bacharach/Bob Hilliard hit, Frankie Vaughan's 'Tower of Strength', and followed by Cliff Richard and the Shadows' 'The Young Ones'. The words were pulled from Mercer's childhood days, hanging around the black areas of Savannah, in a Spanish moss dream state. It has so much hope for whatever is 'waiting round the bend' that it functions as a song for any immigrant, any dreamer. It worked in the post-war age of uncertainty, and today, as a basic philosophy, 'there's such a lot of world to see' remains remarkably simple and wise.

* * *

It wasn't just the big bands that provided a source of new solo singers. Nightclubs, which primarily provided a space for small-group jazz, were bijoux enough for singers with rawer emotional styles than Helen Forrest or Bob Eberly to work without a big band. In Hollywood, the best known included Billy Berg's, the Bandbox and the beautifully named Club Hangover. The setting was intimate; you listened harder. Frankie Laine was the first, just about the biggest and almost certainly the loudest singer to emerge from this scene. He was an interval singer at Billy Berg's, there to fill in between the main acts while punters went to the bar. Seemingly out of nowhere, 'That's My Desire' became a number-one hit for him in 1947. Backed by Mannie Klein's eight-piece All Stars, Laine's fluid, intense style had zero to do with Sinatra, let alone Crosby. The man had size-twelve feet but wanted to be the male Billie Holiday: 'She was my doll. She was my inspiration from about 1937 or '38, when I went to New York.'

Laine's father had been Al Capone's barber. As a kid in 1920s Chicago, he had seen his grandfather – a mediator in the Mob's turf wars – shot dead in front of him. He got through the Depression by winning dance marathons, dehumanising events that sent America back to the days of the Romans. One of Laine's tricks was to not wear socks, thus minimising the risk of foot infections. He was always dehydrated; you could be disqualified if you wet your pants. In 1932 Laine danced with his partner Ruth Smith at Young's Million Dollar Pier in Atlantic City for 3,501 hours – or 145 days – which saw them enter the *Guinness Book of Records*. Twelve thousand sat and watched this cruel show. He finally quit in 1935, after dancing for hours on a bad ankle at the Arcadia Ballroom, Chicago, which left him hospitalised for eight weeks.

A Depression-era double threat, Laine also got to sing at these events, mostly Italian ballads, the current Crosby hit or his own jazz favourites, like Louis Armstrong's 'Sleepy Time Down South'. The fourteen-year-old Anita O'Day was a fan, peppering him with questions: '"Why did you pick that tune? Why did you phrase like that? How come . . .?" She would follow me around like a little puppy after every song I sang.'

For a full decade Laine had bad breaks, on the east coast, then the west. And so by 1947, aged thirty-four, he was plugging gaps at Billy Berg's, where he belted out torch songs with a blues base that drew on Billy Eckstine and Kansas City shouter Joe Turner. Eckstine might have had the deeper voice, Turner might have sounded brasher, but crucially Frankie Laine was white, and when 'That's My Desire' broke out, it began a decade of huge international hits for him. In his wake came new names – notably Johnnie Ray – and a new audience. They wanted something to chew on; they thought of singers as 'belters' and 'exciters', and had less time for the smooth croon. Down this road lay another music that would be entirely informed by R&B and country, but at the turn of the 1950s the belters and exciters would have their moment.

32

WE HAD TO BREAK UP THE BAND:
POST-WAR JAZZ

There's a dance pavilion in the rain, all shuttered down.
  'Early Autumn', Johnny Mercer

If you're in jazz and more than ten people like you, you're labelled commercial.
  Herbie Mann

All the way through this story, pop has been fighting class issues, race issues, classical snobbery. With the end of the war came a new battle-front, with jazz itself divided and factionalised.

Singers going solo was just one reason for the rapid demise of the big bands. They were also killed by a combination of union boss James Petrillo, the advent of television and the 'wartime entertainment tax', which lingered, unwanted, in the States until the 1950s, as mean and barely necessary as continued food rationing in the UK. On top of this, a lot of people, especially those returning from the fighting, didn't want to be reminded of the war years. Other factors included the rise of the drive-in movie theatre and the opportunities it gave to make out, eliminating the preliminaries of dancing to a band before you got to first base. Musicians – at least the ones who cared about music rather than those who saw it as a trade like any other – found themselves with hard decisions to make.

Duke Ellington's band soldiered on but was clearly a little lost. How else to explain his half-arsed recording of 'Singin' in the Rain', which was released by Columbia in 1947 and filled *DownBeat* with correspondence from indignant Ellington supporters who felt betrayed. Worse yet was the 1948 novelty 'Cowboy Rhumba' ('*Sí, sí, señorita*, yippy ki-i *olé!*'), which really did smack of commercial desperation. Everyone playing on it sounds apologetic; the muted trumpet sounds like it's crying to itself in the corner, saying, 'Don't look at me – I didn't write this stuff.' Astonishingly, Ellington himself had written 'Cowboy Rhumba'. He'd recover soon enough and ride on through the trauma, emerging with his best-ever work in the 1950s.

During wartime there had been plenty of big-band money in circulation. Many of the bands had added musicians, including string sections, the payroll growing three- or four-fold. After the war, things were different; dollars were harder to come by, so the bands cut down in size. In the interests of their clients, promoters insisted that ballrooms had to also book lesser bands in order to secure the big names. The result was that, little by little, the ballrooms closed down. They couldn't make any money from putting on big bands, and they couldn't operate at a loss for ever. Woody Herman saw the post-war scene as 'a strange re-evaluation . . . I could receive a lot more money to work with a sextet than I could to work with a big band.' His sextet included vibes player Milt Jackson, soon to be a leading light on the cool jazz scene. Herman, though, was happier exploring what was fast becoming the sound of yesteryear, putting the money he made with his small group aside to form a new big band.*

'Sweet' bandleader Guy Lombardo reckoned the final straw came with the 1949 Federal Communications Commission: 'They ruled that the stations in the outlying cities did not have to carry the network from seven until midnight, which allowed the stations to break away, and that started the disc jockeys. When prime time was over, they had a disc jockey to sell tyres and batteries and furniture. TV came along at the same moment. People just locked themselves away at home and wouldn't even turn on the lights! So the big ballrooms across the country – and there were hundreds of them – just died that slow death.'

It couldn't be denied that Lombardo's band had variety: their 1949 hits included 'Tennessee Waltz' (soon to be a massive hit for Patti Page) and 'Enjoy Yourself' (recorded thirty years later by the Specials). 'Still it has our Lombardo sound,' he reckoned. 'You may create a lot of attention with a new style, but you've lost them when that style goes out.' Lombardo's organisation was one of maybe a dozen big bands that survived into the 1950s.

* * *

Bebop, like Dada, was a silly name given to something of some seriousness. Its practitioners were obscure in the early 1940s, when they began to foment the overturn of swing, but stars by the '50s, the first underground musical heroes who were quite happy to stay underground. Charlie Parker, Bud Powell and Dizzy Gillespie related to a new, mid-century American style in the same way as Ernest Hemingway or Jackson Pollock. They were artists, not entertainers, and this was a large part of bebop's appeal. After the war, America was seen internationally as

* Herman kept building and rebuilding, creating new 'Herds'. By the mid-1970s his Thundering Herd were recording new jazz numbers, like Chick Corea's 'Spain', and sounding genuinely fresh.

the present and future of the free world, entirely modern and forward-looking, and the future part of this deal was bebop. For the people whistling 'Sentimental Journey' on their way to work, it made as much sense as a Pollock did alongside a painting of a horse – it was close to incomprehensible. Its relation to popular music was like that of a cross-word puzzle to its one-word answer; for those who liked to recognise melodies, it was hard work.

The foundation stone for bebop had been the Earl Hines band, which by 1942 featured a bunch of musicians bristling to break out, a revolutionary cell of top players brought in by arranger Budd Johnson and singer Billy Eckstine. Hines lacked the disciplinary streak of a Dorsey or a Goodman to keep them in strict formation. Among the players who liked to toy with flatted fifths were Charlie Parker and Dizzy Gillespie. 'We had a beautiful, beautiful band with Earl Hines. He's a master and you learn a lot from him,' said Gillespie, but that didn't stop him and other Hines players from mutinying come peace-time. Small groups and virtuosos now set the scene for jazz, away from Hollywood's influence and secure in the pages of *DownBeat*. The big names included Parker, Gillespie and Thelonious Monk; the second string included a trumpet player – still a teenager in 1945 – called Miles Davis.

* * *

The musicians' strike of 1942–4 had increased the opportunities for jazz players to amuse themselves in late-night after-hours sessions, at venues like Minton's in Harlem. The Hines band's theme tune, 'Rosetta', would be reworked in these sessions and eventually recorded as 'Yardbird Suite' by Charlie Parker in 1946. This was modernism in the style of Le Corbusier, with very little ornamentation. At this point, it was also danceable and not entirely self-contained. A resigned Hines admitted that he 'didn't like it . . . it was getting away from the melody. But we had to stay with what the young people were asking for at that particular time. I knew these boys were ambitious. Dizzy made some arrange-ments, so did Charlie, and I had about twelve bebop arrangements in my book. But I think what happened, the arrangers got out of hand. They got completely away from the melody, and the public didn't know what was happening. The music was fast! It was not danceable. That's what I think hurt bebop.'

The resentment of most jobbing big-band players, used to working under a boss, just as if they worked for the post office or on a building site, was understandable. They simply weren't welcome in this new world.* Bebop – or just 'bop' – was an attempt to exorcise popular music from jazz. Swing's huge popularity had come at the cost of its black innovators being sidelined. If watering down your art with commerce – like Ellington's 'Cowboy Rhumba' – wasn't guaranteed to translate into sales, then why not gravitate towards the undiluted? A mix of creative ambition, angry cultural frustration and basic racial dignity forged a new direction, heard in the strange, restless chords of Dizzy Gillespie's take on Jerome Kern's 'All the Things You Are' (1945), Monk's ''Round Midnight' (1947) and Parker's 'Scrapple from the Apple' (1947). Saying 'no' finally became an option for black musicians.

Bebop was necessarily exclusive. Dizzy Gillespie: 'There were always some cats showing up there who couldn't blow at all but would take six or seven choruses to prove it . . . On afternoons before a session [Thelonious] Monk and I began to work out some complex variations on chords and the like, and we used them at night to scare away the no-talent guys . . . After a while we got more and more interested in what we were doing as music and, as we began to explore more and more, our music evolved.'

Until this point, opportunities might have been afforded to black jazz players by white entrepreneurs and gatekeepers, but the tastes of these patrons could change very quickly. After a patron's change of heart, or

---

* Session work was always a possibility. Bernie Privin, a much-travelled trumpeter who had played with Artie Shaw and Tommy Dorsey before the war, became part of Glenn Miller's Army Air Force Band and then, still only twenty-seven, went back to Dorsey in 1946, saw the big-band scene collapse: 'Some went into insurance. Some studied new trades. Myself, I was very fortunate and I latched onto a studio job which held on for twenty-two years.'

lack of attention, black musicians could survive or be left stranded, while others would slip away unnoticed. So bebop was exclusive, but it wasn't simply self-segregation.

Mass popularity was not a concern for the new breed. They refused to be hemmed in by the usual structure of a melody or regular chord construction, instead working around angularity and dissonance. Very few swing-era musicians could make this transition, and quite likely many didn't want to. The practitioners of the new music pissed them off. 'They want to carve everyone because they're so full of malice,' said Louis Armstrong. 'All they want to do is show you up and any old way will do as long as it's different from the way you played it before. So you get all them weird chords which don't mean nothing.' Benny Goodman called bebop a 'catastrophe'.

* * *

The bebop musicians knew how good they were. They were inventing new languages, new habits and devices, and were very keen to move in circles that would acknowledge how much they had achieved. Jazz was now battling for a space in which it could be complex and contradictory, somewhere it could resist having Benny Goodman-shaped cartoons projected onto it. Bebop's moment would be surprisingly brief, though, and by 1950 its most talented contributors had set up their own new directions: Dizzy Gillespie began leading large Latin-style orchestras, moving gradually towards puffed-cheek, elder-statesman status; Charlie Parker would spiral towards addiction and an early death, aged thirty-four, in 1955; it was the relatively unheralded Miles Davis who would step forward as the most feared and fearless jazz sorcerer, always keeping his 'fuck-you' attitude intact.

Surprisingly, the splintering of bebop led mostly towards more discipline. At one calm end of the spectrum was Davis's nonet, including pianist/arranger Gil Evans and saxophonist Gerry Mulligan. Davis took the heat out of bebop's 'cutting contests' and musical arm-wrestling with a few Pete Rugolo-produced sessions for Capitol Records in 1949 and 1950, creating music – 'Moon Dreams', 'Jeru', 'Boplicity' – that would unexpectedly overlap with the world of exotica and film soundtracks in the dawning album era.*

Meanwhile, the wilder, screaming wing of bebop crossed over into the honking-sax end of early R&B, creating direct, three-minute-max songs, no time to waste, instant gratification. Illinois Jacquet had played with Lionel Hampton's band – most famously, he played the sax solo on the show-stopping 'Flying Home' (1942), which he would recut more than once with his own All Stars – before making rave-ups like 'Blow Illinois Blow' (1947). Big Jay McNeely was a big Jacquet fan; he ramped up his sound and scored an R&B number one with 'Deacon Rides Again' in 1949. At moments of the greatest raucous excitement, McNeely sounded like a goose trying to stop a runaway train, and through this cacophony he found a unique midpoint between jazz and R&B on records like 'Willie the Cool Cat' (1949) and 'Jay's Frantic' (1950). They were absolutely rollicking. Just where jazz ended and R&B began on these records was a moot point; it was pure party music, which meant that McNeely and his band also got paid to play it by the punters who wanted to hear it.

* * *

The future of jazz, post-swing, would be in small-group set-ups in small-group settings. 52nd Street, since the late 1930s, had been 'Swing Street' for white New Yorkers. People who had never dared venture into Harlem heard jazz there in a warm, intimate environment. The jazz club became a staple of cinema noir, the kind of place run by Kirk Douglas in 1947's *I Walk Alone*, with Lizabeth Scott purring a torch song while leaning on a piano.

Pianist, composer and arranger Claude Thornhill's 1940s band had helped to shape what came next. Thornhill wanted as little vibrato as possible. His sound hovered, heavy but thrilling, like an ominous cloud; part of the strangeness came from using eight clarinets, a set-up

---

* These sessions would first be compiled on an album – at Rugolo's insistence – in 1954, as *Classics in Jazz*, then again three years later as *Birth of the Cool*.

no other band could boast. The young Gil Evans wrote some complex, pretty arrangements for Thornhill – orchestral bop mixed with ethereal ballads – and the band's theme, 'Snowfall', was perfectly titled, a blanket of stillness. The sound belied the harshness of the post-war touring life. 'The road was grueling,' said trombone player Bob Brookmeyer. 'Claude's band in the early fifties was a hard-drinking band. You had to drink, given the pace. There were times on the road when we didn't check into a hotel for six days. You just rode the bus from gig to gig to gig. Buses didn't have toilets then, and the food on the road was terrible. When we traveled, there were two groups on the bus – one would sleep while the other was up semi-loaded and talking. Then the guys who were sleeping would get up, and the others would go to sleep. It was pretty rough.'

It's easy to think of the post-war jazz split as inevitable, its direction mapped out along minimalist versus maximalist lines or art versus commerce. But for one brief moment there was no obvious future, and recordings like Mary Lou Williams's 'Zodiac Suite' (1945) and the former Benny Goodman pianist and Glenn Miller arranger Mel Powell's extraordinary piano piece 'Sonatina' (1951) belonged to no tradition – no past, no future – at all. These were possibilities for future jazz that were simply left behind.

This feels like a good place to talk about Mary Lou Williams. She had been a heroine and inspiration to the new young jazz scene, a sounding board for the bebop innovators and a regular pianist at Barney Josephson's Café Society in the mid-1940s; her apartment in Harlem became a salon for the new breed. Originally, back in 1929, Williams had been the replacement pianist in Andy Kirk's band, which also employed her husband, saxophonist John Williams. Her teenage talent was greater than that of a mere replacement, but Kirk bristled at the idea of a woman in his band. When the band auditioned for Brunswick's Jack Kapp, though, Mary Lou happened to be playing, and Kapp was thrilled. The band travelled to Chicago to record for Brunswick, but somehow Williams was left behind. Kapp wouldn't record Kirk's band without her, so she was bundled onto a train from Kansas City, on which she was raped by the conductor. She went straight from the train to the recording session – the clock was ticking, after all – and played a jaw-droppingly exuberant piece called 'Nite Life', at once blue and beautiful, full of gorgeous block chords and dense atmosphere. It beggars belief, but she refused to let the trauma affect her triumphant moment in the studio.

Williams played her extended, twelve-part *Zodiac Suite* at New York City's Town Hall on New Year's Eve 1945, and it should have placed her at the forefront of jazz's new directions. But a terrible gambling habit held her back, and a 1951 trip to England turned into a two-year stay in Europe, where she became a member of America's expat post-war jazz movement. She would venture back, an outsider who didn't like to be seen simply as a female musician. Taking a wider view of jazz, even as it was developing, she recorded *A Keyboard History* in 1955; by 1964 *The New Yorker* was writing that 'Miss Williams' present work is an instructive history of jazz piano – a kind of one-woman retrospective of an entire movement.' To have achieved that, alone, was quite remarkable.

* * *

Some used the foundations of swing, as originally laid down by Fletcher Henderson, added the adventurousness of Billy Strayhorn and took it forward by adding bebop's sharp angles. The smoothness and the approachable nature of Benny Goodman or Glenn Miller largely disappeared, but the new sound had a metallic tang. Trumpeter Neal Hefti had played with Charlie Barnet and Charlie Spivak, then joined Woody Herman's band in 1944, just in time to be a part of what became known as the First Herd. He contributed his own 'Wild Root' and 'The Good Earth', which had the sharp simplicity of Barnet's 'Skyliner'; like Billy May's arrangements, they sounded like the jet age. Soon he had his own band, as well as turning out fifty original pieces for Count Basie and playing his part in Sinatra's 1960s, before creating the imperishable simplicity of the *Batman* theme in 1966.

Not all jazz adventurers wanted to travel down the small-group road. It wasn't just the modernisation that they railed against. Take Stan

Kenton. He wouldn't have anything to do with bop and sought a new direction by enlarging the jazz band, making it not only louder, but also symphonic – or 'neophonic', as he called it, the biggest of the big. Kenton unquestionably thought of this as a progressive move, but the sheer size of his band could get in the way of its swing. At least it gave more players employment, and on strange, atmospheric meanders like 1946's 'Intermission Riff' the cost seemed worth it.

Kenton's band had formed in 1940, when he was just shy of thirty. They got a break when they played at Roseland in 1942, signing with Capitol a year later, and members of the band during the war years included future cool jazz heroes like Anita O'Day and alto-sax player Art Pepper. Things got stranger post-war when arranger Pete Rugolo joined in 1945. A student of Debussy, Stravinsky and Ravel, he was the chief architect of Kenton's 'Artistry in Rhythm' (1946), a startling, super-brassy piece that sounded like a choreographed crime scene, with a moody piano breakdown at its heart. The restless Kenton soon altered his line-ups, creating the Progressive Jazz Orchestra from 1947 to 1948 and the gargantuan, thirty-nine-piece Innovations in Modern Music Orchestra in 1950. 'We tried to elevate jazz,' said Rugolo. 'The leaders we worked for allowed us to experiment. There was a healthy competition among us. I would hear something that Neal [Hefti] wrote and it would inspire me to try better.' Years ahead of Phil Spector, Kenton created a wall of sound – massive, complex, brass as heavy artillery. But Rugolo loved the challenge and felt like he 'had walked through the pearly gates' when he went to work for Kenton.

An alternative to this bombast was through softness. Working with Claude Thornhill, then Miles Davis, Canadian Gil Evans had developed a stripped-back, impressionistic sound that he described as 'a stillness that hung like a cloud . . . once this stationary effect, this sound was created, it was ready to have other things added to it'. Evans also wrote arrangements of Charlie Parker's 'Donna Lee' and 'Anthropology'. His sound was meticulous and refined. There were French horns and flutes – it was beautiful, modern and sophisticated. He continued to work with Miles Davis (1957's playful *Miles Ahead*), but maybe the greatest bene-ficiaries of Evans's delicate, beguiling tone colours in the 1950s were jazz vocalists like Helen Merrill and the less well-remembered Marcie Lutes and Lucy Reed.

One record epitomised a new softness in jazz. A quartet led by Battersea-born pianist George Shearing cut the exquisite 'Lullaby of Birdland' in 1949, selling just shy of a million copies and making you wonder what the fuss regarding feuding jazz factions was about. All manner of things in the late 1940s would be tagged 'New Look', after Christian Dior's post-war Paris fashions, but 'Lullaby of Birdland' genuinely matched the New Look's streamlined elegance. It sounded like rain on a warm evening: Denzil Best's brushed drums skipped like steady footfall on a wet pavement, while Margie Hyams's vibes and Shearing's piano – inseparable – played the brisk but oddly dampened melody in locked-hands unison, dancing between the raindrops. In the outside world, the Cold War was at its hottest. West Berlin had been blockaded in 1948, while Korea would explode in 1950. 'Lullaby of Birdland''s muted charms sounded full of promise, just around the corner, waiting in the shelter of a basement bar.

World War II was over, but there was still confusion and alarm around the world. Shearing's clarity of thought must have been reassuring: 'I think that everything, jazz or classical, literature, conversation, must have form, must have architecture, must have direction. And many people will criticise me because I confine my jazz to these requirements. I don't like undisciplined anything. I like abandon, yes, but lack of discipline? No.' Shearing wasn't alone. By 1954 things would become confused and combative enough for RCA to issue a compilation called *Jazz for People Who Hate Jazz*.*

Without the mid-1940s fracturing of jazz, it's quite possible that west coast, cool, free and Afro-Cuban jazz might never have happened. The styles of Oscar Peterson, Bill Evans, Gerry Mulligan, Stan Getz and Erroll Garner – even the beautifully named, easy-on-the-ear Modern Jazz Quartet – may have been quite different. In time, Ornette Coleman would receive a grant from the Guggenheim Foundation and official

---

* It was a fine, if uncontroversial, collection, including Ellington, Basie, Goodman and the relatively modern Sauter-Finegan Orchestra.

recognition in Britain as a concert artist, meaning he was treated as a classical performer – he was an artist. He was recognised as being beyond popular music, and maybe this was the final victory of bop. The mainstream moved on.

33

CALL ME IRRESPONSIBLE: FRANK SINATRA

> Having lived a life of violent emotional contradictions, I have
> an over-acute capacity for sadness as well as elation . . . What
> has been said about me personally is unimportant. When I sing
> I believe, I'm honest.
> Frank Sinatra

Frank Sinatra is the fulcrum of this book. He understood and assimilated much of what had happened in the past, he dictated what would happen in the immediate future, and the various phases of his career – pin-up boy vocalist, album-oriented adult singer, late-period duets – are still a blueprint for artists in the twenty-first century.

Technically – his pitch, his fluid phrasing – he could out-sing pretty much everyone, though it was when flaws crept into his singing in the mid-1950s that things got really interesting. Contradictory, true, but he was all about contradictions. The tenderness in his voice was all the more effective because of the flip side, the toughness that could mutate into drunken divorcee bitterness on something like 'That's Life'. Love and hate, kindness and intolerance in equal measure.

He was a storyteller, a genuine artist whom Wilfrid Sheed nailed as a 'romantic realist'. Lines flowed into each other; the story was told, quite naturally. Sinatra would sing a line almost without taking a breath. This was something he learned from the way Tommy Dorsey played the trombone, and he could go eight, ten, even sixteen bars without pausing.*

He claimed to practise breath control by swimming under water. It was also a sleight of hand. Some thought Dorsey was using 'circular breathing' – storing breath in his cheeks, breathing out through the mouth while breathing in through the nose – which would be hard enough for a trombone player but physically impossible for a singer. In fact, Dorsey would take tiny, almost imperceptible breaths – what he called 'pinholes' – and Sinatra did likewise.

Like all the best modernists, he borrowed selectively from past inspirations to create something new. His clarity of diction came from Burton-on-Trent-born cabaret singer Mabel Mercer, an acquired taste but the toast of Paris in the 1930s. Sinatra's 1955 masterpiece *In the Wee Small Hours* was a sixteen-track song cycle released in two volumes, as if it was intended to be a twentieth-century Tin Pan Alley take on Robert Schumann's *Dichterliebe*. His languor came directly from the greatest vocal stylist in this tale, Billie Holiday. He may have kept many secrets, but this wasn't one: 'Billie Holiday, whom I first heard in 52nd Street clubs in the early thirties, was, and remains, the single greatest influence on me.' His version of 'You Go to My Head' (1945) clearly borrows the phrasing of Holiday's 1938 version. It's no great shock to discover that Frankie and Billie had had a short, mad romance in the early 1940s. You'd be disappointed if they hadn't. The personal relationship between

---

* Listen to his 'April in Paris', from 1957's *Come Fly with Me*, and try singing along.

singer and listener – again, with Billie as the sole forebear – was something else that made Sinatra seem quite new.

Who did Britain have to compare? Who was our singing working-class actor, an underdog with relatability and wide emotional range? Norman Wisdom. This isn't even a joke. Both he and Sinatra were born in 1915, and both were huge box-office draws in the 1950s. Though Sinatra was always seen to be in control and would never be caught in a flat cap, being dragged around the garden by a runaway lawnmower, cuddly Norman really was the closest we had to him.* The only other comparisons were with crooners like Dickie Valentine, who were essentially aping Americanisms, or Frankie Vaughan, who was great but was basically a holdover from the variety theatres, the stereotypical 'all-round entertainer'. We also had Max Bygraves, of course. Frank Sinatra was one of the main reasons why so many people in 1940s and '50s Britain wished they were Americans.

* * *

What did Sinatra represent? The America that was created between the 1890s and 1920, when Woodrow Wilson folded America's welcoming arms. Some, like Richard Rodgers, were born rich; others, like Sinatra, climbed up from the lowest rung. But still he represented the whole nation. Beyond making a living and paying the bills, what did these newcomers have in common? What were they aiming for? Civilisation. Understanding. A shared human value.

His mother, an unashamed communist who performed backstreet abortions, took it on herself to run the neighbourhood. At one point, she considered running for mayor of New York, but was talked out of it by her husband. He had been a boxer, using the Irish pseudonym Marty O'Brien, before running a saloon with Mrs Sinatra during Prohibition. This way, they got tight with the Mafia.

* 'Don't Laugh at Me', Wisdom's biggest hit, was first heard in *Trouble in Store* in 1953, the year Sinatra was shockingly dropped by Columbia Records. In a parallel world, Wisdom would be offered the part of Angelo Maggio in *From Here to Eternity*, and Sinatra would be remembered only as a 1940s teen idol.

Born in December 1915, Frank Sinatra had been a forceps birth, which left him with a permanent scar behind his left ear and a punctured eardrum that would later excuse him from fighting in World War II and indirectly lead him to become the greatest star in the country come 1945. According to his daughter Nancy, he would learn compassion from Harry James and discipline from Tommy Dorsey. This didn't stop him from holding lifelong grudges (including one against his godfather, who had done no more than tell him off for being too cocky at work – by putting his feet up on the desk – when he was sixteen).

Harry James had hired the twenty-four-year-old Sinatra in 1939, and wanted to anglicise and glamorise his name. 'You're gonna be Frankie Satin!' he announced. Sinatra politely refused. His name was important to him, and this in turn would be important to his marked difference. Almost all of his contemporaries, from Dino Crocetti to Doris Kappelhoff, hid their foreign origins behind Americanised names, but not Sinatra. 'There was such spirit and enthusiasm in that band,' he told a friend a full twenty years later. 'I hated leaving it.' But within a year he was poached by Tommy Dorsey, and by 1941 was named best male vocalist in both *Billboard* and *DownBeat*, replacing the previously unstoppable Bing Crosby. He was inspired to go solo, much to Dorsey's chagrin, in 1942. Skinny and soulful, he became the idol of 'bobbysoxers' – teenage girls in white socks – who sighed when Sinatra's voice swooped down and screamed when he caressed the microphone stand. A run at New York's Paramount Theatre was a major sensation. The press labelled him the 'Sultan of Swoon', and a three-year-old recording of 'All or Nothing at All', from the Harry James years, sold a million in 1943. 'He's the most fascinating man in the world,' laughed Dorsey, 'but don't stick your hand in the cage.'

The seemingly malnourished Sinatra was mocked in cartoons. *Swooner Crooner* had him as a rooster. Tex Avery's *Little 'Tinker* featured a rabbit-wooing skunk in a shrink-to-fit 'Frankie suit', kissing and stroking the microphone as he sings 'All or Nothing at All', so thin he appears invisible behind the mike stand, falls through knot-holes in the floorboards, and eventually sings from inside an iron lung (everyone was quite aware that he could make the ladies scream while being too poorly to fight). At one point, an elderly rabbit dances herself literally into her grave, and a headstone appears, inscribed, 'Oh Frankie!'

During the war, GIs thought of him as 'Frankie Boy', the nation's kid brother, a whistling paper boy with a talent for crooning and soothing. Was he a danger to the gals back home? Surely not. He had a wonderful wife in Nancy (who turned out to be one of the most understanding and forgiving women in history); he was selling a dream, some apple pie for everyone to come home to. And, eventually, homecoming soldiers would buy into Sinatra's dream world. But not immediately.

In 1945, six years after his first recording with Harry James, and just before he turned thirty, Sinatra's debut album, *The Voice*, appeared. His was the voice in every girl's head as she thought of her boyfriend fighting abroad, and the voice of every GI who couldn't wait to get home. In a complex world of death and atrocities, he represented love and the simple pleasures. The downside of this for Sinatra was that once the war ended, he didn't have such an obvious purpose; the men were home, so no wireless substitute was necessary. Worse, the soldiers who had seen terrible things looked at him, staying at home since Pearl Harbour with his sore ear, and this gave them a reason to actively dislike him. He was the wolf who'd had the good fortune to escort Lana Turner behind his wife's back while they had been fighting the Japanese. Whose girlfriend would be safe from his philandering now? The nation turned against him. The gossip rags sensed blood. Lee Mortimer of the *New York Daily Mirror* described Sinatra's fans as 'imbecilic, moronic, screemie-meemie autograph kids'. The paper also ran stories about Sinatra hanging out with the Mafia – it later transpired that Mortimer was being fed information by the FBI, who had a file on Frank, suspecting him of being a communist. When Mortimer died, Sinatra took time out to visit his grave and piss on it. Why? 'Oh, he was a fink!' said Sinatra.*

---

* He could be as crass as he could be tender. One of his most enduring songs, 'Nancy with the Laughing Face', written by Phil Silvers and Jimmy Van Heusen and dedicated to his daughter, Nancy Jr, had an audible rustle of spring. As recorded for Columbia in 1945, it's one of Axel Stordahl's finest arrangements, couching Sinatra's 'mission bells ringing' in pizzicato strings, floating off the ground as we 'hear her say hello'. Older Frank re-recorded the song in 1963, with

His greatest sin, though, was to sell out on the dream he had promised everyone during the war. A dalliance with Lana Turner was maybe forgivable, but he chased Ava Gardner, wouldn't give her up, and rubbed his wife's nose in the dirt. No matter that every other man in America would probably have left his wife for Gardner, Sinatra was now reminding all the homecoming soldiers whose marriages had quickly soured of peacetime's grim normality.

* * *

For fans who kept the faith, he seemed like the embodiment of what it was to be a man. The flip side of 'Nancy with the Laughing Face''s fatherly joy was the hair-shirt 'I'm a Fool to Want You'. You could picture Frank – people had stopped calling him Frankie by 1949 – alone at the bar or eating dinner in a restaurant at a table set for one. He'd still look immaculate, would spend a good half an hour each day washing, shaving, dressing up clean and tight, but he'd be lost in his memories: Nancy, the good wife; Ava, the marriage-wrecking temptress. Melodies would haunt his reverie. He'd wince as he dropped some tomato sauce on his clean white shirt, and young girls would look over at him and well up. The poor man.

Still, he played the kid brother, dressed up in his sailor suit, in *On the Town*, Leonard Bernstein's hit musical, which became an equally successful movie in 1949. As the boyish Chip, Sinatra falls for a tough, sexy cab driver. This screen naïf was hard to square with his by now pugnacious public image, not to mention the possibility that he was a potential 'fellow traveller'. It would be Sinatra's last big movie for some time.

Biographer Arnold Shaw dates Sinatra's decline back to 1947 and 'an almost imperceptible change in public tastes'. Suddenly, reviews of his films, records and live performances were lukewarm. In 1949 *DownBeat*

---

a Johnny Mandel arrangement and rather unseemly swipes at Elizabeth Taylor and Audrey Hepburn, as if he felt the need to see a now-adult Nancy win a gold medal for having the best laughing face. By 1981 it had become 'Nancy (With the Reagan Face)', which I'm sure his daughter found even less charming.

wrote that "'Lost In The Stars" seems pitched too low for Sinatra, nor is
he able to make the rather complex lyric hang together. On the simple
"The Old Master Painter" he fares better, a hit song, though Sinatra's
is not the best record.' The pitching issues on 'Lost in the Stars" tricky
Kurt Weill melody fell around a clunking, semi-religious lyric: 'So long
as the Lord God's watching overhead, keeping track how it all goes
on . . . little stars . . . big stars.' Sinatra tripping up over clumsy words
didn't make anyone feel better.* The bobbysox fans were growing up,
and his poor health and marital problems weren't helping. In the 1949
DownBeat poll he was ranked only fifth, after years of being voted best
male singer.

In May 1950 his voice gave out spectacularly at the Copacabana, and
it took a while to recover. If Frank and Ava weren't getting drunk and
driving out into the desert, they were getting drunk and having blazing
rows – which caused too many sleepless nights. Some Columbia sides
were cut that made his problems painfully clear. Arranger George Siravo
said, 'If he'd ask for hot tea and lemon, you knew that he was messed up
with his voice. Axel [Stordahl] and I used to talk about it at the time.'
Siravo had a neat way of saying Sinatra was out of tune: 'There were
some times where he'd be singing in the cracks, the ones in between the
black keys and the white keys.'

Musically, the low point for Sinatra is usually seen as the day Mitch
Miller became head of A&R at Columbia in 1950. Instead of fully realised heartbreakers like 'All or Nothing at All', he was now forced to
record the Leadbelly song 'Goodnight, Irene'. When a DJ told him that
he should record more songs in the folk idiom, he muttered, 'Don't hold
your breath.' Still, it was a number-eight hit, at a time when he could
barely make the Top 20. He tried his hand at modern R&B with 'Bim
Bam Baby', a thrilling proto-rocker, though Sinatra wasn't really the best
choice for lines like 'Run your flim flam fingers through my greasy hair.'
Ultimately, there was 'Mama Will Bark', a duet with the briefly famous
blonde bombshell Dagmar, complete with animal noises.

---

* Clumsy or not, Sinatra was clearly fond of the song, reviving it for the showcase
The Concert Sinatra in 1963, his last album with Nelson Riddle.

Sinatra wasn't about to be dropped by Columbia, even if his halo was slipping. Miller claimed to have advanced him $150,000 in 1950, with the company president telling him, 'Mitch, I want to be sure you earn that money back for us. Give him the best songs.' Miller found two songs: one was the Weavers' nautical novelty 'The Roving Kind'; the other a ballad called 'My Heart Cries for You'. Sinatra was on his way from Hollywood to see Gardner in Africa for a few weeks, so Miller asked him to stop off in New York. 'I know your keys, I have two songs ready for you. We'll make them and you'll take the plane out that night.' He had the arrangements made, the backing singers primed, the orchestra hired, and he met Sinatra off the Los Angeles plane at seven in the morning. 'He came to the office, he listened to these two songs, we looked at each other . . . I don't know what mood Frank was in, God knows in those days. He said, "I won't do any of that crap." The musicians were hired, so in the back of my head I thought, "I'll show him."' Miller went into the studio at 5 p.m., with the previously untried Guy Mitchell replacing Sinatra, and emerged three hours later with a double A-side that proved so popular that both sides separately made the US Top 5, making Mitchell an overnight star.

In 1952 Sinatra played a show at the Cocoanut Grove that was so thinly attended that songwriter Sammy Cahn felt embarrassed to be there. That summer he was dropped by his booking agency and, finally, by an exasperated Columbia. He had no record label, no agent, no film studio contract, and he was massively in debt to the taxman. Frank Sinatra was thirty-six years old and washed up.

From Here to Eternity would be a turning point. It was a film he begged to be in, even offering to work for no fee. Ava pulled some strings, and it earned him an Oscar in 1953. But in a way his intense performance in *Young at Heart* (1954) is more significant, a reflection of where Sinatra had just been and where he might end up. In it he plays emaciated, chain-smoking bar-room pianist and would-be song-writer Barney Sloan ('The word is "hip", bub. Only Cubans say "hep"!'); cynical resignation was not something you would have associated with Sinatra – or with popular music at all – before this movie. His face is all angles and hard lines; not just his cheekbones but his eyebrows, even his unkempt hair. The setting is pure picket fence, all the better for Sinatra to hover over the movie like a drizzle; his misanthropy would make him a prototype Moe Szyslak if he wasn't so charismatic. He stands on the doorstep of post-war, pre-rock America and wisecracks that 'homes like these are the backbone of the nation'. The complete anti-hero, brilliantly alone, he gets the girl but still attempts suicide by driving his car at speed in a snowstorm, raising his eyes to the skies as he puts his foot down and turns off the windscreen wipers.

The character of Barney Sloan also allowed Sinatra to play songs like 'Someone to Watch Over Me', 'Just One of Those Things' and 'One for My Baby' with just piano accompaniment. To show just how much of an Eeyore Sloan is, he sings the latter in a packed, rowdy bar on New Year's Eve.*

The emotional complexity was there in Sinatra's performance of 'Young at Heart' and its audible sadness. Prematurely aged by his disastrous liaison with Gardner, was he too young, or already too old, to sing it? Two years later, he would carry off 'You Make Me Feel So Young' with heel-clicking ease.

By the time *Young at Heart* was in the can, Sinatra had signed a tentative new contract with Capitol Records (it was only for a year, initially), and his self-belief was partially restored. Still, nothing was a given. His first Capitol single was 'I'm Walking Behind You', Dorothy Squires's ballad about a jilted lover lurking in the shadow of his ex on her wedding day. It was a middling hit but was quickly covered by Eddie Fisher, who took it to number one in Britain and America. That was the new order – Fisher was a far bigger star in 1953. For his next single, 'I've Got the World on a String', Sinatra was teamed up with arranger Nelson Riddle for the first time, and between them they would go on to create the most emotionally expansive records of the mid-century. Like Jolson before him, and Presley and the Bee Gees after, Frank Sinatra now set about crafting a comeback that would make the first stage of

---

* Oddly, Sloan spends the film trying to finish writing his masterpiece, which turns out to be the middling 'You My Love', a Top 20 hit in 1955 but hardly a rival to the rest of the soundtrack.

his career look like a half-cocked warm-up. It makes absolute sense that when he sang Sammy Cahn and Jimmy Van Heusen's 'The Second Time Around', some ten years later, it was with a sensuous optimism, a softness and a gentle reverence.

34

SATURDAY NIGHT FISH FRY:
RHYTHM AND BLUES

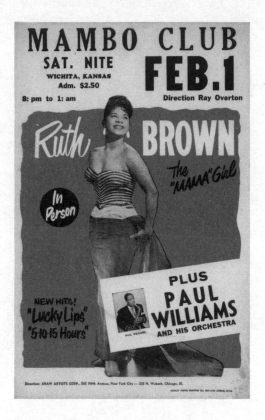

THE NEGRO MAKES ADVANCES. Edging into
Radio, Films, Bigger Than Ever in Music; And Despite
Many Obstacles.
Billboard, January 1943

On 24 October 1942 *Billboard* magazine inaugurated a sales chart
called the Harlem Hit Parade, the first acknowledged black music chart,
which came six years after the magazine's first all-encompassing Hit
Parade; by 1949 *Billboard* employee Jerry Wexler had given the chart

the more dignified and accurate name of Rhythm and Blues.* The original name also showed that *Billboard* wasn't casting its net very far, compiling the list from a tiny sample of six shops and a bunch of jukeboxes in one New York borough; the huge influx of black migrants to Chicago, Detroit and Los Angeles, and the tastes of the population in rural states like Mississippi and Alabama, would be ignored for some time yet. Moving into this gap in the market were new, independent record labels, many owned by Jewish entrepreneurs, all with names that had a strong whiff of class: Exclusive, Regent, Regal, Herald, Beacon, De Luxe, Keynote and – named after the Harlem theatre that billed itself as 'the world's most beautiful ballroom' – Savoy Records. Amplification, internal migration and a new (if reluctantly given) prominence for black music in the national press would add together to create a burgeoning alternative pop world.

The first Harlem Hit Parade number one was a thrilling call-and-response shouter called 'Take It and Git' by Andy Kirk and His Twelve Clouds of Joy. Already in his mid-forties, the elegant Kirk was a black bandleader and saxophonist who had introduced pianist Mary Lou Williams to the world and had scored successes in the 1930s, including the original hit recording of Sammy Cahn's 'Until the Real Thing Comes Along'.† Also charting on the early Harlem Hit Parades were records like Tommy Dorsey and Frank Sinatra's 'There Are Such Things', and even Bing Crosby's 'White Christmas'. Paul Whiteman's orchestra also featured on the new chart, though this was due to their loose, slouched

---

* The buzzword when the chart was first launched seemed to be 'sepia', with Louis Jordan advertised in *Billboard* as the 'Number one band in Decca Sepia Series', while a WNEW poll compiled by DJ Martin Block had Count Basie as 1942's 'Sepia King of Swing'. It was a weasel industry term, used to avoid the word 'black', just as the name 'Harlem Hit Parade' only dropped a hint as to what it represented.

† Kirk's band was never one of the biggest, which meant the loss of star players could be more noticeable and damaging. Sax player Dick Wilson died in 1941, and Mary Lou Williams left for a solo career in 1942. Kirk was sharp enough to put electric guitar up front, with the excellent René Hall joining in 1946, but his band finally broke up two years later and he left music for a career in hotel management.

recording of Johnny Mercer's 'Trav'lin' Light', featuring a significant credit on the label for a 'vocal by Lady Day'.* For the most part, though, the Harlem Hit Parade featured names that would rarely, if ever, cross over onto *Billboard*'s pop chart, like the Southern Sons. They were one of the great gospel groups of the era, formed by former Golden Gate Quartet member William Langford in 1940, and their version of Frank Loesser's 'Praise the Lord and Pass the Ammunition' was the most exciting, full of cheek. It reached number seven on the Harlem Hit Parade in December 1942, though Kay Kyser had the bigger pop hit.†

The introduction of a new instrument – the electric guitar – would not only hasten the demise of the big bands, but also point to myriad futures. In the short term, a hot new small-group style emerged called 'jump' – or 'jump blues' – based around a combo of sax, trumpet, piano, guitar, bass and drums. It wasn't far away from boogie-woogie or Count Basie's grooves, but the intensity of electric instruments and smaller club settings made the pulse race faster. It was a Saturday-night sound.

The absolute stars of the early Harlem Hit Parade,‡ and jump blues exemplars, were Louis Jordan's Tympany Five. When Jordan was born in Arkansas in 1908, his father was a saxophone player in a vaudeville act called the Rabbit's Foot Company. Young Louis borrowed the instrument and taught himself, getting a gig in 1936 with drummer and bandleader Chick Webb. A year later, Webb let his young alto-sax player take a vocal on the yearning 'Gee But You're Swell', which gave Jordan the courage to try and leave the band in 1938, with the intention of taking their singer Ella Fitzgerald with him. When Chick Webb died of TB soon after, Fitzgerald was nominated leader of the newly renamed Ella and Her Famous Orchestra and stayed on. 'No matter,' thought

---

* The V Disc pressing for the armed forces gave the more sober credit 'vocal by Billie Holiday'.

† True to the song's lyric, the Southern Sons disbanded come the draft. Langford then formed the Langfordaires, who introduced the lugubrious Brook Benton to the world.

‡ *Billboard* would switch the title of the listing several times in its early years. It would be called the Race Records chart from February 1945 until June 1949, when it was renamed Rhythm & Blues Records. In 1958 it became Hot R&B Sides, which the magazine stuck with until the 1970s.

the sharp-dressed Louis, and he put together his Tympany Five, which played Harlem venues like Elk's Rendezvous Lounge and slowly began to develop a loose, hard-driving sound, with no need for Webb. 'With my little band,' boasted Jordan, 'I did everything they did with a big band. I made the blues jump.'

Jordan bawled out the words over buccaneering call-and-response choruses that were more rhythm than blues. His band's songs were also the ultimate in good-time music, and during the war years they were the biggest mass-appeal jukebox hits in America: 'What's the Use of Getting Sober (When You're Gonna Get Drunk Again)' (1942); 'Ration Blues' and 'Five Guys Named Moe' (1943); 'GI Jive' and 'Is You Is or Is You Ain't (Ma Baby)' (1944); 'Mop Mop' and 'Caldonia' (1945). And then, in peacetime, he just kept right on, peaking in November 1946, when he had the top four records on *Billboard*'s chart: 'Choo Choo Ch'Boogie', 'Ain't That Just Like a Woman', 'Stone Cold Dead in the Market' and 'That Chick's Too Young to Fry'. He even made a guest appearance in a Tom and Jerry cartoon called *Smitten Kitten*. His combination of the raw rural South, earthy humour, hipster slang and swing's hard urban bounce was effectively the starting point for postwar R&B. James Brown, Ray Charles and Chuck Berry (whose riff on 'Johnny B. Goode' was pilfered from 'Ain't That Just Like a Woman') would all cite Jordan's jump blues as a primal influence.

Unlike most black-run big bands, Jordan had a sound that most white acts would have found almost impossible to mimic, and this held him in very good stead. The only notable Jordan cover was Woody Herman's terrific take on 'Caldonia', with unison brass replacing the Tympany Five's scream of 'What makes your big head so hard?' Incredibly, with segregation on the radio pretty absolute, Jordan was able to score a *Billboard* number-one single with 'GI Jive' in 1944, after the band were seen playing it in *Follow the Boys*, an all-star musical that featured everyone from George Raft to the Andrews Sisters. Bending his sound a little to appeal to – as he said in a 1974 interview – 'white crackers' didn't bother him, and decades later his musical compromises are barely discernible on something as gleeful and street-smart as 'Jack, You're Dead'.

Jordan would go on to spend more weeks at number one on *Billboard*'s black music chart than anyone else; stack those weeks on top of each other and he was at the top of the tree for more than two years. Not even James Brown comes close. As late as 1950, way after his swing contemporaries' combos had disbanded, he spent seven weeks at the top with 'Blue Light Boogie'. The distorted electric guitar he introduced to the world on the same year's prescient 'Saturday Night Fish Fry' ('It was rockin', it was rockin', you never seen such scufflin' and shufflin' till the break of dawn') would soon become widely adopted. He reacted contrarily by putting together his first big band in 1951. No one was interested. By the time he realised his mistake and put a new Tympany Five together in 1952, his star had dimmed.

* * *

With the demise of the big bands, and bebop's abstention from the pop world, there was a proliferation of black musicians hungry to find work and latch on to the next scene. The result was a fascinating period of flux and jazz/blues/jump/bop genre cross-pollination. Let me give you an example. This unlikely yarn starts with pioneering bebop saxophonist Charlie 'Yardbird' Parker. He had recorded the driving 'Now's the Time' with his Reboppers (including Dizzy Gillespie, Miles Davis and Max Roach) in late 1945. Ohio-born arranger Andy Gibson, who had worked with Duke Ellington, Count Basie and Charlie Barnet, as well as leading his own band during the war, was drifting towards jump blues by 1946 and heard Parker's riff on 'Now's the Time' as something to be retooled for the dancefloor. Rather than just arrange it, he also retitled it 'D'Natural Blues' and claimed the writing credit.

Gibson recorded it with an eight-piece band led by baritone-sax player Paul Williams and took it to Herman Lubinsky at Savoy Records in Newark, New Jersey. Lubinsky was incensed: he owned the publishing on Parker's 'Now's the Time' and spotted the similarity in a heartbeat. Gibson was sent packing. Williams would play the still-unreleased song live with his band, and it always went down well. When they played in Devon, Pennsylvania, he noticed the crowd began to do a peculiar dance to it. After the show, Williams discovered that the dance was called the hucklebuck, and he retitled 'D'Natural Blues' accordingly. A smooth-talking industry character called Juggy Gales, who had bought the publishing on 'The Hucklebuck', calmed Herman Lubinsky down and convinced him to release Williams's recording on Savoy. If it flopped, Gales said, he would buy Lubinsky 'a deluxe dinner'. So Savoy released Paul Williams's 'The Hucklebuck' in early 1949, and by March it was number one on the Harlem Hit Parade, where it stayed for a solid fourteen weeks. Lubinsky ended up buying Gales dinner.

On the west coast, a vocal version of 'The Hucklebuck' by Roy Milton's band ('Wriggle like a snake, waddle like a duck, that's what you do when you do the hucklebuck'), on Art Rupe's fledgling Specialty label, was a number-five hit, also in 1949. It sold well enough that Specialty then quickly recorded a faster, harder, wilder hit version with guitarist Jimmy Liggins and His Drops of Joy, calling it 'Shuffle Shuck', by which time it really didn't sound a whole lot like 'Now's the Time'. As far as I'm aware, no one ever asked Charlie Parker what he thought of the song.*

* * *

Los Angeles's Central Avenue in the late 1940s was the centre of jump blues, celebrated enough to earn the nickname of 'Little Harlem West'. The Avenue had been thriving since the beginning of the twentieth century; a developing district full of offices, shops and factories led to the opening of places where workers could unwind, spending the money in their pockets at the Lincoln Theatre or the Dunbar Hotel. In the early 1940s the massive influx of migrants, especially Texans and Oklahomans, led to a boom in small clubs, bars and new record labels on Central Avenue. Ivie Anderson quit Duke Ellington's band

* The vocal version would be covered by Frank Sinatra and Tommy Dorsey in 1949, and was a hit during the early-1960s twist era for Chubby Checker, before finally becoming a UK hit in 1981 for a group called Coast to Coast. Their milky version so incensed Mark E. Smith of post-punk group the Fall that, later that year, he wrote a parody version called 'Hassle Schmuck'. We are now a long way from Charlie Parker.

and opened her Chicken Shack restaurant, while Kansas City's Big Joe Turner, the 'Boss of the Blues', and boogie-woogie pianist Pete Johnson opened the Blue Moon Club.

Houston-born Amos Milburn was a pianist who played Central Avenue venues and got a deal with the local Aladdin label. 1949's 'Chicken Shack Boogie' entirely prefigured mid-1950s rock 'n' roll, with its rollicking piano, ninety-mile-an-hour backbeat and honking rhythmic sax. Milburn had started out as a jazz player but switched to jump blues in 1949, and he followed up 'Chicken Shack' with a string of booze-related party anthems: 'Bad, Bad Whiskey' (1950), 'Thinking and Drinking' (1952), 'One Scotch, One Bourbon, One Beer' (1953). Not yet thirty, Milburn seemed to stop recording at the height of his popularity in 1953, the same year he released 'Good, Good Whiskey', in which the explanation may lie. But then he wasn't alone.

How was jump blues covered by the industry press? Wynonie Harris's 'Young and Wild' was written up as 'good for the back rooms at the Harlem spots' by *Billboard*, which suggested they wanted it to be as far away from them as possible. Harris – of Omaha, Nebraska, before he moved to South Central LA – was loud-talking and fast-living, liable to walk into a bar, jump up on a table and shout, 'The blues is here!' before ending the evening with a fist fight. Between 1945 and 1950 he scored fourteen R&B hits, including three number ones: 'Who Threw the Whiskey in the Well' (with Lucky Millinder's Orchestra), 'Good Rockin' Tonight' (a leading contender in any first-rock-'n'-roll-record stakes) and 'All She Wants to Do Is Rock'. The rhythm was heavy, square on the beat, and irresistible, and the lyrics were often shamelessly filthy: 'Lolly Pop Mama' (1948); 'I Like My Baby's Pudding' (1950). In the October 1954 issue of *Tan* magazine, Harris boldly claimed he had 'started the present vogue of rocking blues tunes . . . As a statement of fact, clean of any attempt to brag about it, I'm the highest paid blues singer in the business. It's all because I deal in sex . . . I like to sing to women with meat on their bones and that long green stuff in their pocketbooks.' He was handsome, charismatic, outrageously confident, and like many jump-blues acts, his record sales seemed to stall overnight: after 'Lovin' Machine' made number five on the R&B chart in early 1952, there was nothing.

Why the precipitous decline? Thanks to the 1949 Federal Communications Commission, the early 1950s saw a growing number of smaller radio stations, with disc jockeys playing R&B records in the evenings. The changing listener demographic – now both black and white – required acts that would provide more teen-oriented material (in other words, more dancing, less jelly roll). The R&B charts would soon fill with records played by younger, airplay-savvy artists, like New Orleans's Fats Domino ('The Fat Man', 1950; 'Goin' Home', 1952; 'Going to the River', 1953) and Lloyd Price ('Lawdy Miss Clawdy', 1952). At the same time, the jukebox market, vital to the success of jump blues, went into decline. Amos Milburn's 'Good, Good Whiskey' and the blatantly sexual nature of Wynonie Harris's 'Keep on Churnin' (Till the Butter Comes)' might have worked well in bars, but they were never going to get played on commercial radio in between adverts for hot dogs and spark plugs. Milburn, Harris, Jimmy Liggins, Roy Milton and even Louis Jordan all suffered a freeze-out.

One artist who bucked this trend was Ivory Joe Hunter. He had been born in Kirbyville, Texas, in 1911 and was nicknamed 'Rambling Fingers', though you'd think a birth name of Ivory Joe negated the need for a nickname. With his round face and rimless glasses, he looked like a hip science teacher, and he suavely blended the sonorous jazz vocals of Billy Eckstine with a deep, slow blues feel, to huge commercial success. He first moved to Los Angeles in 1942, becoming a regular at the Sunset and Ciro's. By 1949 he had started working with a group of Duke Ellington sidemen (he had modelled his look on the dapper Duke), signing to MGM, and a year later he scored a major crossover hit with the slow blues of 'I Almost Lost My Mind', the sleepiest description of creeping insanity ever recorded. It was covered by Nat Cole, and later by Pat Boone, who took it to number one in 1956. Boone gave Hunter pop credence: after 'Since I Met You, Baby' became another hit for Hunter in 1957, Ed Sullivan would present him with a gold disc live on TV. It was hard to imagine Wynonie Harris in such company.

* * *

We last came across Jay Mayo Williams back in the 1930s, when he was the invisible man at Decca. He had stayed at the company until 1945, setting up his own Harlem Records a year later. Success was swift but brief: in January 1947 he recorded a smash with Stick McGhee's 'Drinkin' Wine Spo-Dee-O-Dee', and just like in the olden days, Williams grabbed himself an unearned slice of the writing credit.

This was a smart move, as the upstart Harlem label didn't have the funds to keep up with the public's demand for copies. McGhee was quietly poached by a new independent, Atlantic Records, who got him to re-record 'Drinkin' Wine' and then provided shops with the new version. Atlantic – previously a minor jazz label – would go on to become the most significant post-war independent label in the country.

Atlantic bossed east coast post-war R&B. It had been started as a jazz label in 1947 by Ahmet Ertegun, the son of a Turkish diplomat. In 1932, when he was nine years old, Ertegun had been taken to see Cab Calloway and Duke Ellington at the London Palladium. 'I had never really seen black people,' he later recalled. 'I had never heard anything as glorious as those beautiful musicians wearing white tails, playing these incredibly gleaming horns.' Two years later, Ertegun's father was posted to Washington as Turkey's first ambassador to the US.

With the profits from Stick McGhee's hit, Ertegun and the Atlantic family built an empire. His sidekicks were Herb Abramson, Miriam Bienstock, Tom Dowd and, later, Jerry Wexler, the man who had coined the phrase 'rhythm and blues', who joined from *Billboard* in 1953. All of them worked in both A&R and record production, and if they got a writing credit, they probably deserved it. They were fans and they wanted to be fully involved. 'We had bookkeepers,' said Ertegun, keen to distance himself from industry racketeers. 'We were people who went to universities.'*

---

* Ertegun would end up as one of the founding fathers of the rock-era record industry, but his dad Mehmet had an even bigger place in the formation of the modern world. In 1920 he was sent by the sultan of the crumbling Ottoman Empire to persuade Kemal Atatürk to give up his secular armed conflict. Instead, Mehmet decided to become Atatürk's legal adviser; as such, he would attend the signing of the Treaty of Lausanne in 1923, which set the borders and gave diplomatic recognition to the Turkish republic.

Ertegun signed Virginia-born Ruth Brown while she was in a hospital bed with two broken legs, on the understanding that she would learn to sight-read as she recuperated and sing songs he suggested rather than material he considered better suited to jazz singers like Sarah Vaughan. In October 1950 Brown had a number-one R&B hit with 'Teardrops from My Eyes'; three years later, she recorded another with the intense 'Mama, He Treats Your Daughter Mean'. People began calling Atlantic 'the house that Ruth built'.

In 1952 Ertegun signed Ray Charles, a singer and pianist in the vein of Nat King Cole and Charles Brown. Ertegun had plans for Charles too, and wrote the boogie-woogie-based 'Mess Around' for him. Charles had never played boogie-woogie piano before. The scenes in the studio were unprecedented – Ertegun said it was 'as if this great artist had somehow plugged in and become a channel for a whole culture that just came pouring through him'. Charles now became a conduit for all R&B, both new and old, with the fiery and rude 'I Got a Woman' (1954), the unzipped joy of 'Hallelujah I Love Her So' (1956) and, best of all, the brimstone and gelignite of 'What'd I Say', a *Billboard* Top 10 hit in 1959 that saw him cross over into the mainstream.

Charles left Atlantic for a big-money deal with ABC Paramount in 1960, and Ertegun put it about that he was now neutered. People continue to repeat this as fact. I'm guessing they've never heard Charles's exhausted, busted and beautiful reading of Hoagy Carmichael's 'Georgia on My Mind' (1960) or the hard-living, none-more-sassy 'Hit the Road Jack' (1961). In 1962 he recorded the *Modern Sounds in Country and Western* album, the king of R&B embracing a racially coded genre of music at the height of the civil rights struggle. It was brave, and it sold millions internationally. Brother Ray. Somehow, he's still underrated.

* * *

Based in Chicago, Lester Melrose was an A&R man of the old school. He was a talent-spotter; he supervised recording sessions; he was a music publisher and an artist manager. Yet Melrose was a freelancer and had invented his own sweet beat and kept it in his briefcase.

He scoured the bars and clubs of Chicago for talent, and if he couldn't be in two places at once, he would ask friendly musicians like singer Big Bill Broonzy to do the job for him. When Prohibition ended in 1933, rejuvenating nightlife and creating a high demand for jukebox records, Melrose wrote to the biggest labels in New York, saying he could independently produce black jazz and blues for them. RCA Victor (through its budget subsidiary Bluebird) and Columbia (on its similar Okeh label) took him up on the offer, and Melrose later claimed he had recorded 'at least ninety per cent of the rhythm and blues talent' on those labels between 1934 and 1951. It is almost certainly not an idle boast. He kept busy and made money, telling Alan Lomax: 'I wouldn't record anybody unless he signed all his rights over to me.'

So far, so typical. Where Melrose differed from his contemporaries was in the way he handled recordings: he used the same pool of backing musicians, and the sound was uniform and distinctive. The top floor of the Leland Tower hotel in Aurora, Illinois, was a nightclub used by a local radio station for live broadcasts of big bands; during off-hours it became a recording studio, a lab for Melrose and his commercially minded blues experiments. He smoothed over the rougher edges of country blues and the raucous shouts and added the hum of swing and the dancefloor-friendly rhythm of boogie-woogie to create something urbane and quite distinctive, a jazz-wise city blues. Though studio trickery was still years away, that distinctive sound made Lester Melrose the very first record producer. He would record major sellers for Big Bill Broonzy, Arthur 'Big Boy' Crudup, Lonnie Johnson, Memphis Minnie, Roosevelt Sykes and Sonny Boy Williamson. He only retired when a new, amplified, dirtier blues sound became more popular in the early 1950s, a sound popularised by a Mississippi singer called Muddy Waters. Nobody would call this sound 'urbane'.

In the summer of 1941 John Lomax had driven down from New York to the dirt roads of the Mississippi Delta. He'd heard about a blues singer called Robert Johnson, whose haunted sound had been captured on only a handful of dog-rare Brunswick 78s. Lomax wondered what else Johnson might have in his locker and wanted to record him. When he arrived, he was met by confused faces. Yes, Lomax was told, Johnson had been there, but that was years ago. He was dead; he'd been playing guitar at a house party, had his drink spiked after chatting up the wrong woman and died of poisoning three weeks later. Lomax was distraught. He'd missed his chance to capture part of the fast-vanishing rural blues world. 'But while you're here,' someone piped up, 'there's another guy down the street who plays bottleneck guitar and sings high just like Robert Johnson.' This other singer turned out to be Muddy Waters. Born McKinley Morganfield in 1913, Waters would be a one-man living link between the dusty, prehistoric Delta blues, recorded and coveted by big-city archivists and collectors like John and Alan Lomax, and the full flowering of the 1960s rock era.

In his shack on the Stovall Plantation in 1941, Waters sang 'Country Blues No. 1' into Lomax's tape recorder and was then asked some slightly intrusive questions by his curious visitor. How had he been feeling when he wrote it? What inspired it? Was it about a woman? Or something too personal or strange to discuss? Waters had a round, kind face and told Lomax straight: 'I just felt blue, and the song fell into my mind.' No pacts with the devil for Muddy. When Lomax sent him a 78 of the recording, Waters could not believe his ears: he sounded like a real singer; this sounded like a real record. He packed his case, left the plantation and took the train to Chicago in early 1943. By day he worked in a container factory, by night he played house parties, where people wanted to hear old-time music from the old South, just as the Irish, Italians and Russians of New York had done fifty years earlier, seeking out comforting memories of the old country. Moving from the plantation to the tenement, he swapped his broken Coke-bottle slide for a piece of steel tubing pinched from a factory.*

A transformation was under way.

Between 1940 and 1950 the black population of Mississippi dropped by 25 per cent, and – along with booming Detroit and Cleveland

---

* The first known recording of the bottleneck-guitar style had been in 1923 by Sylvester Weaver, on a brace of instrumentals: 'Guitar Blues' and 'Guitar Rag'. Western swing pioneer Bob Wills adapted 'Guitar Rag' in 1935 for his own 'Steel Guitar Rag', at a time when the distinction between country and blues was more fluid.

– Chicago was the obvious destination. It was the city at the end of the line, and for some the end of the rainbow. It was the final destination on the Illinois Central Railroad for romantically named trains like the Louisiane (which started out in Greenville, Mississippi), the Southern Express (from Birmingham, Alabama) and the Creole (which took a full twenty-four hours from New Orleans). Chicago was as far as you could go in a boxcar, if you were escaping the South. It had been a haven for black people looking for a new beginning since the industrial boom of the early twentieth century; the *Chicago Defender*, widely available across the South, painted the city as the height of sophistication, a place of freedom. In reality, it was rough, polluted, cold and frequently violent, especially if you were black.*

Decades of migration meant that black southern music – country blues, even songs passed down from the years before recorded sound – made its way to Illinois, where the cross-generational interplay and outside influence of jazz and ragtime helped it morph into Chicago blues. In 1948 a Chicago club-owner called Leonard Chess decided he'd had enough of letting his star turns make money for the record men who came by with their notebooks. He talked to Evelyn Aron, who ran a local record label called Aristocrat, and she signed his discovery, balladeer Andrew Tibbs. In exchange Chess got himself a job at Aristocrat.

Early Muddy Waters records must have sounded like ghosts of a long-dead past, even as they were being released. 'The first guitarist I was ever aware of was Muddy Waters,' Jimi Hendrix would say later. 'I heard one of his records when I was a little boy and it scared me to death.' Waters's first for Aristocrat, 'I Can't Be Satisfied', sold 100,000 copies, basically from the trunk of Leonard Chess's car. Fast becoming a local celebrity, Muddy swapped dive bars for nightclubs. As the crowds grew bigger and noisier, he bought himself an amplified electric guitar so that he

---

* In 1919 a black teenager called Eugene Williams had inadvertently strayed into an unofficial white swimming area. White sunbathers began throwing rocks at Williams and his friends. Williams was hit by one and drowned. Having escaped the South, Chicago's booming black population weren't about to take this quietly. Six days of rioting left thirty-nine people dead, and two thousand lost their homes.

could be heard above the din. Now the sound rang out over the voices of the audience. Waters liked the feeling, embraced the distortion and the feedback that transformed the sound of his guitar, and played the new electricity in his instrument as much as he played the strings.* He transformed country blues into Chicago blues.

By 1950 Aristocrat Records had become Chess Records, and Waters had been joined by rhythm guitarist Jimmy Rogers and a harmonica player called Little Walter Jacobs, who fed his instrument through an amplifier so it sounded like a demented train whistle. As a kid, Little Walter had run away from home, moving from Louisiana to New Orleans to Arkansas. Sometimes he had been so hard up that he slept on pool tables, but he always kept his harmonica – which no one thought of as much more than a kid's instrument – and mimicked the sounds he heard on the radio. He siphoned Louis Jordan and jazz solos through the harmonica, a wild mix all of his own making. Together, Little Walter, Jimmy Rogers and Muddy Waters made an intense, restless sound.

Little Walter quit the group in 1952 and immediately had a hit on his own with 'Juke'. His sound was rural but plugged-in, and unquestionably aggressive. 'My Babe' (1955), written by Chess's odd-job man Willie Dixon, was his biggest hit and would be widely covered; his best records were possibly the dense, muggy 'Temperature' (1957) and the shivery, distorted 'Blue and Lonesome' (1959). Unlike the sage Muddy Waters, Little Walter – with his heavily scarred forehead – always looked and sounded like he was never more than a few feet from trouble. In 1968, while playing dice in the street, he would rashly grab the winnings and get hit on the head with a pipe. He went to bed that night and never woke up.

Producer Leonard Chess had initially been loath to let Waters bring his live band into the studio – possibly because he didn't want to deviate from the simple, successful rural set-up; possibly because he was notoriously tight-fisted and didn't want to pay extra musicians – but

* The first recorded amplified guitar is thought to be Eddie Durham's, playing on Jimmie Lunceford's 'Hittin' the Bottle' in 1935. Charlie Christian, playing clean single notes with the Benny Goodman Sextet in 1939, had been the first prominent guitarist to use it as a solo instrument rather than a percussive time-keeper.

once he did the amplification increased, the drums became more upfront, the volume grew. Singles like 'Hoochie Coochie Man' (1954), 'Mannish Boy' (1955) and 'Got My Mojo Working' (1957) channelled an ancient sound, one that goes back beyond Bessie Smith or even Blind Lemon Jefferson to the earliest chapters of this book, acoustic, non-urban, faded, sepia. They also presaged the future, the British beat groups who would cover Waters' songs a decade later, juice them up, shake them, give them the instant glow of a Polaroid photo and somehow, through this time-travelling transformation, put London right back at the heart of the pop world. All the decades in between were as nothing – no jazz, no crooners, no swing, no jump blues. It was quite a feat.

* * *

John Lomax hadn't been the first industry man to head to Mississippi looking for Robert Johnson. Three years earlier, the omnipresent John Hammond had arrived, hoping to ask Johnson if he might appear at the Carnegie Hall in a major show called *From Spirituals to Swing*. Like Lomax, Hammond discovered he was too late, and so Big Bill Broonzy got the gig. A blues player and former Pullman porter who had started out playing fiddle in the 1920s, Broonzy had made generic blues records for Mayo Williams at Paramount in the early '30s, and gradually worked towards small-group blues as the decade progressed. Guitar- and piano-driven sides like 'Going Back to Arkansas' (1938) and 'Fightin' Little Rooster' (1939) sounded like Count Basie on a budget. Sticking around with Hammond in New York, Broonzy played alongside Louis Armstrong and the Benny Goodman Sextet in *Swingin' the Dream*, a jazz adaptation of *A Midsummer Night's Dream*. He turned out to be equally adaptable: he had moved to Chicago in 1939, getting himself an electric guitar in 1942 for up-tempo sides like 'Why Did You Do That to Me'; then leaping from jump blues to a rawer, slower Chicago sound after the war, recording with pianist Memphis Slim ('Where the Blues Began', 'Saturday Evening Blues'); and joining a touring folk revue in 1949 called *I Come for to Sing*.

In the Chicago clubs of the early 1950s, Broonzy, dressed in a sharp suit, hat tipped at a gently rakish angle, played hard, loud, electric party music. When he played for white European audiences who were expecting a folk-blues singer, he sang his old rural blues songs from the 1920s and wore patched-up dungarees with a tear in the knee. He understood how pop worked, and he knew on which side his bread was buttered.

He was a wise man. In Chicago, Broonzy gave advice to newcomer Muddy Waters and introduced Sonny Boy Williamson to Alan Lomax and Leonard Chess. His longest shadow, though, came with a song he wrote in 1946 called 'Black, Brown and White': 'Me and a man was workin' side by side. This is what it meant: he was making a dollar an hour, they was paying me fifty cent. I helped build this country, I fought for it too. Now I guess you can see what a black man have to do.' It would be recorded by Brownie McGhee in 1947 and Pete Seeger in 1948, just as he was becoming a prominent voice on the left. But Broonzy's own version stayed unreleased in his lifetime. He complained to Lomax that no company would release it: 'They would say to me, "You see, Bill, when you write a song and want to record it with any company, it must keep the people guessing what the song means . . . And that song comes right to the point and the public don't like that."' When the civil rights leader Reverend Joseph Lowery quoted 'Black, Brown and White' during President Obama's inauguration in 2008, there was no need to hide behind weasel words any more.

35

CALIFORNIA SUITE: THE LONG-PLAYER

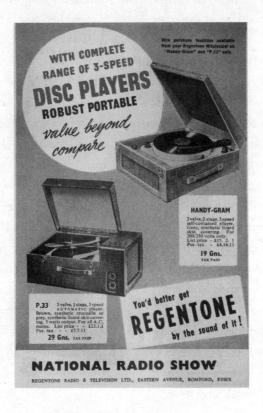

You couldn't just sling twelve songs together. You had to have
a concept and a reason for doing it. It made the production
of records a lot more professional and a lot more thought out.
Ron Goodwin, EMI producer and bandleader

Introduced by Columbia Records in 1948, the long-player – or LP –
was a new, nuanced and, for many, more rewarding way of listening to
recorded music. It was sedentary; it was adult. It was a new world. In
Absolute Beginners, Colin MacInnes saw people gazing into 'disc shops,
with those lovely sleeves set in the windows, the most original thing to

come out in our lifetime'. What would the album do to popular music? Could it create a new kind of artist out of someone who couldn't benefit from simple one-at-a-time singles?

It's easily forgotten that 'album' originally referred to the book that housed the discs, the same as a stamp or photograph album. It didn't make much sense once an album of six discs was replaced by a single long-player inside a cardboard protective cover, but the term stuck.* The Broadway cast of *Oklahoma!* recorded the score for a Decca album of six shellac 78s in 1943, a complete experience from beginning to end, from overture to finale, of song and narrative structure. With it, the cast album was invented. Broadway shows would usually have seen their ballads recorded by the stars of the day, but *Oklahoma!* was the first time everything was captured on shellac and people could listen to all of the show's songs sequentially. The cast album meant that quirkier songs which were entirely incorporated into the story – like 'The Rain in Spain' from *My Fair Lady* (1956) – could become as familiar as the more popular ballads. Never likely to be hit singles, they became 'album tracks'.

Since the 1890s the hardware and software for home listening had barely changed. Records had a maximum of three minutes playing time on each side, spun at seventy-eight revolutions per minute and were made of abrasive shellac; they had a lot of background noise, wide grooves and used a big, fat, steel needle, with a gramophone arm so heavy that the needles wore out after a few plays. The new 33 rpm album, made

---

* Including 78 rpm albums, here are some firsts: the very first album was Odeon's 1909 release of Tchaikovsky's *Nutcracker Suite* on four double-sided discs; the first musical revue album was UK Columbia's recording of the Hippodrome show *Business as Usual* in 1915; Victor put out the first jazz album, *The Bix Beiderbecke Memorial Album*, in 1936; while Decca's 1939 release *Chicago Jazz* was the first of newly recorded jazz. The father of stereophonic recording, Alan Blumlein, made his first test film and recording, *Trains at Hayes Station*, in 1933, while Audio Fidelity in the US issued the world's first stereo LP, *Stereodisc Demonstration LP* (AFLP 1872), in November 1957, with the Dukes of Dixieland on side one and railroad sounds on side two (it was sent free to anyone requesting a copy). The first commercially released stereo LP, *Marching Along with the Dukes of Dixieland Volume 3* (AFSD 5851), came out in 1958.

of smooth vinyl, required a much smaller-tipped microgroove needle
– or stylus – made of diamond or sapphire, with a diameter of one
thousandth of an inch. They could read a lot more information in the
record's grooves, and so the record had far greater clarity.

There had been attempts to create a long-playing album in 1932,
at RCA, but they didn't quite have the technology. According to John
Hammond, Columbia were set to begin vinyl production in the early
1940s, but the war stopped development in its tracks. Columbia 'still
recorded at 78 rpm, but all our safeties [disc masters] were on sixteen-
inch, thirty-three-and-a-third rpm discs', he said. 'So, we had a complete catalogue we could convert without having to change speeds or
anything. This was why Columbia, when it came out with the long-
playing record in 1948, had literally hundreds of albums ready to go,
classical and popular.'

The past provided a ready-made catalogue; record companies were
quick to see the potential of the long-player to corral stacks of old, out-
of-print, fragile 78s into one cleaner, clearer-sounding, more compact
package. Brunswick issued the first of eight volumes of Bing Crosby's
Collectors' Classics in 1950. In Britain, Decca put together the earliest
contemporary-hits compilation – a forerunner of *Now That's What I
Call Music!* – with their first *Decca Showcase* in 1954. The themes, content and sequencing of compilations became a minor art form, and
record companies used their back catalogues to create a demand for
'oldies' that was still being sated by box sets and super-deluxe editions
in the twenty-first century. The long-playing album would also become
a means of remaking the history of American popular music. In 1961,
John Hammond compiled Robert Johnson's *King of the Delta Blues
Singers* from a bunch of largely forgotten 78s from 1936 and 1937;
this began a process of critical rehabilitation and near-beatification for
Johnson.

* * *

The biggest early benefactors of the album boom were orchestras.
After six years of war, many were happy to sit down and drift into a

reverie for forty minutes. Arranger Paul Weston: 'Mood music – that's what people wanted. I remember that the first twelve-inch LPs were almost all instrumental. Percy Faith and Kosty and I were the three big artists at Columbia, and they did a monumental selling job on the three of us together as a unit. They had a big sales programme. They did a terrific job.'

'Kosty' was Andre Kostelanetz, born in St Petersburg in 1901, who was from an older generation and had established his reputation in light classical. He would release about four or five LPs a year – popular classics, some Cole Porter, and pieces he'd written himself, like 1941's *Grand Canyon Suite*, which sounded something like the *Calamity Jane* score, minus the gags about cowboys needing a bath. In 1961 he re-recorded it with an added narration from Johnny Cash. It was high-class exotica. Goddard Lieberson, the head of Columbia Records, understood Kosty's potential to provide a soundtrack for living: 'He created that whole world of super-arranged popular music. It was used as background music for love-making, for cooking to . . . I hesitate to think what else.'

Though it had a gently furrowed feeling of worth, commercial impulses drove this light music just as surely as they did three-minute Tin Pan Alley numbers. Richard Addinsell's *Warsaw Concerto*, from the 1941 film *Dangerous Moonlight*, about the Polish resistance to the 1939 Nazi invasion, was written purely because the producers couldn't license any of Rachmaninoff's work, and so Addinsell was commissioned to write a ten-minute soundalike piece. No matter that it was essentially a film soundtrack; latter-day recordings of the *Warsaw Concerto* have treated it just as seriously as if it were Rachmaninoff.

In Britain, the person to really benefit from the orchestral album boom was Annunzio Mantovani. He called his music 'pop light'; he didn't think he was selling to youngsters, but believed they would 'grow into it'. Born in 1905, Mantovani was, remarkably, from the same generation as Louis Armstrong. His mind-blowing, late-blooming success in the 1950s was largely thanks to his arranger, the light-music leviathan Ronald Binge. It was Binge who came up with the startling string chart for the 1951 single 'Charmaine', originally a 1927 hit for Guy

Lombardo.* The strings had a slightly unsettling, cascading sound, and Mantovani confessed his initial response to Binge's arrangement had been: 'There are a hell of a lot of chords in this piece, I don't know what Ronnie's up to. He said he was trying out something new. And when we played it, it really sounded beautiful, and the whole of the orchestra were delighted with it . . . we brought the record out and they sent it to America.'

Astonishingly, 'Charmaine' became a US Top 10 hit in 1951. No fool, Mantovani effectively trademarked 'cascading strings' and ran with it, recording whole albums of songs by Victor Herbert, Rudolf Friml and Sigmund Romberg, as well as Strauss, in the same style.† In the early 1950s he prospered with both the short- and the long-playing formats, scoring a UK number-one single with 'Moulin Rouge' in 1953, and almost repeating the theme with his none-perkier 'Swedish Rhapsody'.‡ Unlike British bandleaders such as Geraldo (the London-born Gerald Bright) and Chaquito (the Scottish Italian Johnny Gregory), Mantovani had a genuinely exotic background, having been born in Italy, with a father who had worked under Toscanini at La Scala in Milan. Figuring this wasn't enough to make him stand out as a bandleader in the 1930s, he had generated press by telling reporters he had a two-hundred-year-old violin that was 'cursed with evil power', and that he had once been forced to play his 'violin of death' at knifepoint by a crazed fan, until the neighbours came in and rescued him. It is hard to picture anyone who looked less likely to be cursed by an evil power; his albums are most definitely best enjoyed with a cardigan on and a mug of Ovaltine. And how they sold. Even today, it's hard to find a box of records in a charity

---

* Binge also wrote the swooning 'Elizabethan Serenade' to celebrate the Queen's ascension to the throne, and 'Sailing By', the music used by the BBC for its late-night shipping forecast, thought of by many as a secular, republican national anthem.

† It's hard to keep an exact tally, thanks to differing British and American releases, but starting with 1950's coyly titled debut *Musical Moments*, Mantovani recorded around fifty albums before the decade's end. He benefited hugely from the arrival of stereophonic sound, which had become standardised by 1958.

‡ Though it has always been an instrumental, people of a certain age will sing, 'Take me to Jamaica, where the rum comes from' to the melody.

shop that doesn't contain something by Mantovani. In this dusty way, he's strangely immortal.

* * *

Let's take a moment to think about concept albums, and the concept of albums, what makes them different from just a collection of songs or a faithful transcription of a show or classical piece. The Beatles rightly cop some credit with 1967's *Sgt Pepper's Lonely Hearts Club Band*, as it was such an overwhelmingly well-co-ordinated piece of work, right down to the Beatle-doll cut-outs, the gently psychedelic inner sleeve and the lock groove of mysterious squawks. Dig back further, and you have Frank Sinatra's astonishing run of themed Capitol albums, usually topped and tailed by something commissioned from Sammy Cahn and Jimmy Van Heusen.

Go back a little further yet, and there's *Manhattan Tower*. Gordon Jenkins would go on to have an incredible career as an orchestral arranger – working with Sinatra, Ella Fitzgerald, Louis Armstrong, Judy Garland and, in the 1970s, scoring *A Little Touch of Schmilsson in the Night* for Harry Nilsson – but back in 1946 he created history with a suite of four songs, linked by narration, about an apartment block called Manhattan Tower. It featured sound effects, which in itself was a novelty – a 'Beautiful Noise' symphony of car horns. The narration was ebullient ('The buildings were constant flames, and on the street below were the people who built that fire, stronger than the rain, seven million keepers of the flame'), and the overall effect quite Disney. It made New York sound like a make-believe world. If, listening to it now, the narrator sounds a lot like *Sesame Street*'s Guy Smiley, that only adds to its Gotham-like cartoonish appeal. This is Americana on a grand scale.

Manhattan Tower was originally issued by US Decca in 1946 as a double-78 set, with each track ('Magical City', 'The Party', 'New York's My Home', 'Love in a Tower') taking up one side. It was built around the technological limitations of 1946: a sixteen-minute suite was the capacity of two 78s, but with the launch of the 33 rpm long-player in

1948, Jenkins's work transferred neatly onto one seamless side of an album (side two was taken up by a new piece called 'California'). None of the songs had much of an afterlife, but 'New York's My Home' was later recorded with some style by Ray Charles, who gave it a swing that Jenkins, king of the Hollywood string sweep, wasn't really capable of.

There's one other contender. *Manhattan Tower* wasn't originally written and recorded for the vinyl age, so the tag of 'first concept album' could instead be affixed to Mel Tormé's 1949 *California Suite*, which took Jenkins's premise, switched the setting to the west coast and ditched the spoken parts. Unorthodox and ambitious, *California Suite* was created especially for the brand-new long-playing format.

Depending on your viewpoint, in 1949 Tormé was either a young hep cat set to conquer the world by the time he was twenty-three or a smart-arse who thought he was the new Sinatra. Laconic jazz-singing aside, he was a decent modern pianist, had been an arranger (for Ben Pollack's band), a songwriter ('The Christmas Song' – aka 'Chestnuts Roasting on an Open Fire' – is arguably the finest seasonal song of all) and a good-enough drummer that Tommy Dorsey and Stan Kenton both wanted him in their bands. He also idolised Stravinsky, Ravel, Percy Grainger and Frederick Delius. Generally, the kids loved him, but his apparent cockiness riled the old guard, and though his career didn't exactly turn out to be a struggle against the odds, this counted against him early on. He couldn't ever belt out a song; his cool voice was reliant on the microphone, which also pissed off the older generation. One reviewer alarmingly described it as 'intimate enough to convince you that your arteries have developed tonsils'.

Tormé was originally from Chicago but had moved to southern California in the 1930s, during its glorious years of growth and boom, before it became a fume-choked conurbation, and he loved it. His first big career break came when he was given a residency at New York's Copacabana in 1948. Unfortunately for the newly christened 'Velvet Fog', his opening-night crowd was made up of Broadway lags who fancied a bit of Al Jolson- and Eddie Cantor-style vaudeville. The Fog was cat-called all night, and Tormé flew back to California to lick his wounds and write tunes like 'West Coast Is the Best Coast'.

How does *California Suite* sound? Just as giddy and in love with a sense of place as Jenkins's suite, but more primary-coloured than *Manhattan Tower*; it also has the added bonus of guest singer Peggy Lee. Tormé was going through an obsession with Johnny Mercer and clearly had musical theatre in mind – you don't need a vivid imagination to picture the *Pink Panther* cartoon backdrops, the girls in Breton tops, the wide grins and the spinning choreography. The sleevenotes claimed that Tormé wanted a 'sweeping view, a panoramusical impression of the Golden State. The music had to be as modern as the daring new architecture of this fabulous land.' It was pretty innovative, no question, and there would be plenty of soft-rock and sunshine-pop acts pulling moves from the *California Suite* bag twenty years later. It's a cross between *The Pajama Game* and Spanky and Our Gang.

Jenkins rewrote large chunks of his suite, making it three times its original length in the process, and re-recording it as *The Complete Manhattan Tower* for Capitol in 1956. If you find a copy, this is the version you're most likely to see, as the mid-1950s was the first heyday of hi-fi, and a new wave of record collectors had been born since he first recorded it. Likewise, *California Suite* was expanded by Tormé to the length of a twelve-inch album and re-recorded in 1957 for the Bethlehem label, with a moody cover shot of Mel emerging from a mass of ivy in chinos, polo shirt and cardigan. Clearly, the lad knew what he was up to.

The hip, slick 'n' cool Tormé didn't want for confidence, but still came off like a confidant, a friend who'd made good, rather than a show-off. Strangely, he was treated as little more than a crooning pin-up by Capitol, who foolishly never followed up *California Suite*. He was a stylist, his voice warm and enveloping, almost liquid. The Bethlehem label was smart enough to see him as a jazz singer and signed him in 1955, when he was just shy of his thirtieth birthday, then set upon recording a string of beautifully recorded, performed and packaged albums. Bethlehem may have been inspired by the success of Sinatra's *In the Wee Small Hours* for Tormé's first outing, *It's a Blue World*; with a crew of fifteen players, and arrangers including André Previn and Marty Paich, it created more of a twilight feel, dusk at the end of a warm summer's day. There was no real darkness in his takes on 'Polka Dots and Moonbeams' and 'Stay as Sweet as You Are', but instead a deep, warm indigo. Tormé was a teetotaller, and you can kind of tell.

For *Blue World*'s sequel, he and Paich created a real masterpiece. They stripped the band back to a ten-piece – or a Dek-Tette. The peak of the Paich–Tormé sound might be the *Shubert Alley* album, which includes the greens and blues of 'Lonely Town' and an angular take on Cole Porter's 'Too Darn Hot' that pretty much defines vocal cool in spite of its breakneck pace. You can't really go wrong with any of the 1950s Tormé albums.

* * *

It hadn't been at all obvious that Duke Ellington would emerge as an albums artist. As far back as 1935, jazz critic and A&R man John Hammond had called out Ellington's extended works as pretentious. *Reminiscing in Tempo*, written that year as a tribute to his recently deceased mother, was thirteen minutes long and spread over four sides of shellac, and Hammond had called it 'a disaster, without the slightest semblance of guts'. With the war still raw, simple home-spun songs like 'Dear Hearts and Gentle People' dominated the hit parade, and the reaction to 1946's epic, openly political *Black, Brown and Beige* was, 'How dare he be so ambitious?' In trying to encompass so much in one piece, Ellington was publicly punished. The immediate post-war years were gruelling for him, from the lukewarm reception for his first Broadway show, *Beggar's Holiday*,* to the dwindling crowds paying to see his band. But he needed to keep the band together for composition, so that he could hear what his new work sounded like. He'd point to the band and say, 'That's my instrument' – his piano alone wasn't enough.

By 1949 *DownBeat* was putting the boot in with the cover-story head-line 'Reputation shredded, Duke should disband'. Fellow bandleader Charlie Barnet felt the need to leap to Ellington's defence a couple of

---

* Based on John Gay's *Beggar's Opera*, directed by Nicholas Ray, with choreography from Valerie Bettis, and with an interracial romance, it opened on Boxing Day 1946 and ran for 111 performances.

issues later: 'You're right that Ellington sounds dispirited and tired a lot of the time these days. But who the hell doesn't? Do you have any idea what it's like, night after night, playing to sparse crowds, and unenthusiastic ones at that? And don't forget for one minute, if Duke goes down, the whole horse show goes right down on a toboggan with him.' In the next issue, Duke himself wrote a letter to *DownBeat*, ever the cucumber: 'I've had worse reviews by better people . . . We're always looking to the future. The past and now are over, it's the future that counts.'

Columbia had initially been reluctant to afford prestigious album slots to their jazz musicians, preferring to reserve them for classical music or big-selling (and therefore white) pop acts like Doris Day and Dinah Shore. Still, Duke was in the perfect place when Columbia eventually relented. The future, as he probably knew, was in albums, and his longer compositions had been pushing the limits of 78 rpm's capability for years. He and Billy Strayhorn thought in terms of concepts, groups of songs; they were sharp enough to know that each new album would feel like an event if it had a unifying mood. *Masterpieces by Ellington* (1951) – made up of just four tracks over forty-seven minutes – and *Ellington Uptown* (1952) were landmark albums for both Columbia Records and the Duke. The former placed him, according to the self-consciously serious sleevenote, in the company of Gershwin, Stravinsky and Debussy; the latter was contemporary and thrilling.

'Skin Deep', featuring an exhausting drum solo, was catchy enough to be released as a seven-inch 45 rpm single in Britain in 1953, where – in spite of being almost seven minutes long – it gave the Duke his only Top 10 hit. *Ellington Uptown* also revisited Strayhorn's 'Take the "A" Train', with a saucy, husky vocal by Betty Roche, multiple tempo changes and a dreamily knackered saxophone solo. Taking his most famous swing-era recording and making it sound as mid-century modern as a George Nelson clock, Ellington put himself centre stage as an innovator once again. 'A Tone Parallel to Harlem (The Harlem Suite)' closed the album with an atmospheric fourteen-minute travelogue of the neighbourhood Ellington had grown up in. You could hear it as an affirmative, black take on *Manhattan Tower*, or you could think of it as Ellington's own 'Rhapsody in Blue'.

Duke was newly inspired. In July 1956 the Ellington band played the Newport Jazz Festival, and went down so well that Duke ended up on the cover of *Time* magazine. Two weeks later, Ellington, Strayhorn and the orchestra travelled to Canada to play at the Stratford Shakespearean Festival. Strayhorn and Ellington stayed a full two weeks, catching as many plays as they could and resolving to write some entirely new music for the next time they played there.

The critical attacks on the complex *Black, Brown and Beige* had only fired the Duke to make more conceptual pieces – though, admittedly, they rarely had the former's humanitarian reach. There had been *The Perfume Suite* in 1945 (which RCA Victor sat on for years), and after Newport the band cut a pocket history of jazz in 1956 called *A Drum Is a Woman*, which was a lot of fun ('My name is Madam Zajj, African temptress!'); it managed to mix up bebop's flattened fifths with calypso and more recognisably Ellingtonian jungle music.

Having had a year to work on it, Ellington and Strayhorn's Shakespeare tribute *Such Sweet Thunder* was eventually written in three weeks flat.* It is miraculous. Of all the Ellington 'suites' that emerged between *The Perfume Suite* in 1945 and *New Orleans Suite* in 1970, this is the one that most encapsulates everything there is to love about Ellingtonia: the cinematic motifs ('The Telecasters'); the transmogrifying instrumentation ('Half the Fun' is a black cat, chasing the mice of 'Up and Down, Up and Down'); and his beautiful, somehow under-valued piano-playing ('Sonnet in Search of a Moor'). Sometimes it was laugh-out-loud funny ('Hank Cinq'), sometimes a deep indigo atmospheric ('Sonnet for Caesar'). Everywhere, *Such Sweet Thunder* was melodic and up-with-people all-embracing. And you didn't need to see the orchestra live or on a TV special or even read Shakespeare to get its full impact. Clearly, thirty-odd years after his first recordings, the Duke still had ideas to burn.

---

* They didn't have time to write the finale before they performed it at the Shakespearean Festival, and so played Johnny Hodges's 'Cop Out' as the closing piece. Duke was disappointed that no one seemed to get this neat musical gag.

* * *

Ella Fitzgerald's manager Norman Granz was also wise to possibilities of the long-player. He had become a hero to jazz fans for his Jazz at the Philharmonic shows, a series of concert tours that had started in 1943, attracting exuberant kids out to listen to jazz musicians while the war was on and hooking them for life (previously, residencies were standard; Granz's blueprint for the one-night-only nationwide tour is still used by acts in jazz, rock and other genres today).

Granz was also responsible for the first curated compilation album, 1949's *The Jazz Scene*, a set of six 78s that featured Duke Ellington, Neal Hefti, Coleman Hawkins, Charlie Parker, Buddy Rich and Bud Powell. Jazzers could be sniffy about Granz popularising jazz, but he's a hero in this story. He produced Charlie Parker with string arrangements, almost made him a pop artist. He set up Verve Records and released Shelley Berman's comedy routines on the same label as Stan Getz's bossa nova breakthrough. Most significantly, he spotted the potential in anthologies of popular song, entrusting his client Ella Fitzgerald with 'songbooks' by Porter, Gershwin, Berlin, and Rodgers and Hart, both their major and their minor songs. It wasn't as if no one had thought to do this before. Bing Crosby had recorded anthologies of Stephen Foster, Victor Herbert and Cole Porter in the 1940s; even Ella herself had made *Ella Sings Gershwin* in 1950. The difference was the overall mood and the sense of occasion. By 1956 it felt like the door was closing on an era that, as yet, had no name; Ella's *Songbook* series defined the writers and the era. The writers who made it past her velvet rope were Porter, Rodgers and Hart, Ellington, Berlin, the Gershwins, Arlen, Kern and Mercer. Beginning with *Ella Fitzgerald Sings the Cole Porter Songbook* in 1956, and encompassing eight albums over the next eight years, the result was a library all of its own. Many listeners who had only been au fait with musicals via Broadway or Hollywood, those who were devoted to the art of the songwriter, found this crossover into the world of vocal jazz to be a revelation. It was the sound of two worlds colliding.

Granz, in his woollen cardigan and askew trilby, would shrug modestly about his achievement. 'I can't claim credit in the sense that I thought about it and deliberately did it that way. I liked the songs I did, I liked the idea of Ella doing those songs. It helped the composers, curiously enough . . . I think it really spawned a lot of records that followed, with tunes that people had completely forgotten.'

Though she had a sleepy, serene voice, Ella always sang as if she was having the utmost fun, something she had in common with Louis Armstrong (which explains why the 1956 *Ella and Louis* album, accompanied by the Oscar Peterson Quartet, is such an absolute treat). This – along with her perfect tone and easy glide between registers – made her the ideal choice for the songbooks. Porter's liberty-taking with language had what writer Fred Lounsberry called a 'rascality'. 'It's De-Lovely' was a scat song based out of real words. Porter felt easy covering current affairs ('You're the top, you're Mahatma Gandhi') and morality ('Love for Sale'), and Ella felt easy with songs that had such blatant cheek. Her albums were all about her voice and the songs; the arrangements came a distant third.

These albums were definitive, a folio series, and if you had one, you'd probably want to complete the set. Unlike Frank Sinatra's readings, these versions included the verses that would almost always be dropped in the modern pop era. The opening lines of 'I Get a Kick Out of You' on Ella's *Cole Porter Songbook* are: 'My story is much too sad to be told, but practically everything leaves me totally cold.' They are quite complete; what they lack is any real emotional punch. They are easy to admire and thoroughly enjoyable – her swing, inventive phrasing and enunciation were all spot-on – but on the more intense material, Ella never sounded as if she was living the lyric. It's not a fault, and I can't blame her for wanting to play her cards close to her chest and to just enjoy playing with her remarkable voice. But compared to Sinatra, or even someone as technically limited as Peggy Lee, Ella never feels like she's singing her life with her words. In this respect, she's closer to the past, to forebears like Sophie Tucker and Bing Crosby, than she is to her female jazz contemporaries of the 1950s. Still, when you hear the real joy in something like 'Love for Sale', then that joy is really enough. You want to hear a technically perfect 'Someone to Watch Over Me'? Listen to Ella. You want to hear the ultimate 'lost lamb' rendition? Go to Blossom Dearie. Barstool blear? Try Frank Sinatra. Who wants definitive anyway? Where's the fun in that?

The groundwork laid by Norman Granz, Gordon Jenkins, Duke Ellington and Mel Tormé led to Sinatra's run of Capitol albums, which are a world of their own. When we left him, Sinatra was a former bobbysox pin-up staggering through 1953 without a voice or a record deal; a year later, he was rescued by Capitol Records, by his synergy with arranger Nelson Riddle, and by the rise of the long-playing album. Starting with the yin and yang of *Songs for Young Lovers* and *Swing Easy* in 1954 – both eight-track, ten-inch albums, both arranged by Nelson Riddle – a run of fifteen albums took Sinatra through to 1960, when he quit Capitol to form his own Reprise label.

How and why did the Sinatra comeback happen? Why did it work so well? The modest Riddle reckoned that 'it was Frank's time for a renaissance; and the fact that I was at Capitol Records when Frank signed with Capitol Records; and the fact that somehow we hit it off together. I don't know whether it's the fact that we were both graduates of the Tommy Dorsey school of music – I sort of sensed what he would buy. The material we did was right for it, and the big explosion was *Songs for Swingin' Lovers* [1956]. That was the one the English people picked up on, and apparently enjoyed quite a bit.'

He's not wrong.

You want the bulk of this book inside three minutes? Try Sinatra's 'You Make Me Feel So Young'. If you want to know quite how revolutionary the performance and arrangement are on 'I've Got You Under My Skin', compare Sinatra's revisit in 1956 to the best-known British recording, Marjorie Stedeford's from 1937. Stedeford had a slight huskiness, and her version has a certain sensuality; she sounds like she's melting in someone's arms, despite her initial resistance. It's a fine record; it's just that Sinatra's is a painting exploding with colour and texture next to Stedeford's gentle pencil sketch.

The album that announced Sinatra as a force for the future and not just a former poster boy was 1955's *In the Wee Small Hours*. It may not have been the first concept album, but it was the first that could be called a masterpiece. This was a deep blue album, with an intensity and intimacy that was made all-enveloping by its length – sixteen songs, initially spread over two ten-inch albums. Harold Arlen's 'Ill Wind', Duke Ellington's 'Mood Indigo', Schwartz and Dietz's 'I See Your Face Before Me' – every one of the songs had been written in the 1930s and '40s, and maybe Sinatra needed that amount of distance to give these versions their art-song colouring. The damage wreaked by his personal life was on display here. Hushed and humbled, with *In the Wee Small Hours* Sinatra showed how the album could be used as a form of communal healing.

What I hear in Sinatra's best up-tempo Capitol performances, chiefly, is mischief. The title track of *Come Fly with Me* is an instant mood-enhancer; just the line 'Weather-wise, it's such a lovely day' is enough. The album cover is high modernism and 1950s Sinatra-world distilled in a single image. His ad libs may verge on the daffy – I'm not even sure what he's getting at with 'in old Brazil, in old Brazil, man, it's old, in Brazil' – but they don't irritate, as they would later in the Reprise era. Billy May's arrangements are none-brasher on 'Brazil', jet-set playful on the title track and 'It's Nice to Go Travellin'' (both peaks for Cahn and Van Heusen), while his strings are a cushion of warm air on the ballads. The brave placing of 'Autumn in New York' immediately after 'Moonlight in Vermont' on side one, then playing 'April in Paris' and 'London by Night' consecutively on side two, is inspired, creating mini-suites within a suite. And with 'make a pizza' as the unlikely and hilarious closing line, it's also Sinatra's funniest album.

* * *

The organisation of the swing band meant that innovation had largely been beyond the musicians' remit. Post-swing, a new kind of musician emerged: the arranger. This was a character we first came across back in Paul Whiteman's days, and Duke Ellington and Billy Strayhorn had been playing this game for years already, but after the war, the arranger's role grew in importance and originality. They became known as composer–arrangers.

Many musicians were readers rather than improvisers, and just needed stock arrangements. At the top end, though, were Gil Evans,

Neal Hefti, Quincy Jones, Pete Rugolo, Gerry Mulligan, Oliver Nelson, Nelson Riddle – a new breed. Their career paths had often begun with them as sidemen in a name band, for which they might have contributed a few songs, before writing for other outfits, writing arrangements for singers, and then writing soundtracks for TV and the movies. Pete Rugolo worked with Peggy Lee; Quincy Jones straddled the old and new pop worlds with Lesley Gore and, ultimately, Michael Jackson, as well as marrying the singer-songwriter and *Mod Squad* actress Peggy Lipton. He was tainted by commerciality in the eyes of the jazz world, but really, who cares?

Nelson Riddle had been a trombonist with Dorsey for a few months: 'We had some arrangements written by Sy Oliver, who had gravitated to the Tommy Dorsey band from the old Jimmie Lunceford orchestra. And though Jimmie Lunceford had no strings, Sy Oliver somewhere along the way had learned to write for strings.* And he would lay down this cushion of sustained strings over the pulsating rhythmic sound of the brass and the saxes for Tommy. I took that sound from my memory some ten years later and created, with the addition of a muted trumpet and a bass trombone, the same sound for Frank Sinatra.' He made it sound so simple, as if there could be no other setting for Sinatra, no other way to cushion Nat Cole's conversational vocal.

Nelson Riddle made his arrangements for Sinatra's albums seem effortless. Clearly, they weren't. Bing Crosby's 1956 statement album was *Bing Sings Whilst Bregman Swings*. On a dozen inter-war standards, he gave faultless, relaxed vocals (this was also the year of his super-laidback performance in *High Society*) over young Buddy Bregman's pin-sharp brass blasts and cooling woodwinds. They wanted to be in on the *Songs for Swingin' Lovers* action, no doubt, but there was little sympathy in the

---

* The Lunceford band wasn't as distinctive, but in the 1930s their technical ability and harmonic colouring was rivalled only by Basie and Ellington. A lot of their impact was down to their complex but delicate arrangements – usually by Sy Oliver, but occasionally by clarinet player Willie Smith or pianist Edwin Wilcox – which were always kept in place by the solid but unobtrusive Lunceford rhythm of guitar, hi-hat and string bass. Forceful but subtle, their clarity of sound gave them a sense of space without equal and set them apart – check out 1934's 'Rose Room' and 1937's 'He Ain't Got Rhythm'.

arrangements, and the album's best moments, with Bing and Buddy in sync, felt like they could have been accidental. By contrast, I can't think of a single moment on *Songs for Swingin' Lovers* that doesn't sound like total empathy.

You might have thought Bing was built only for singles, but then there was the absolute delight of 1958's *Fancy Meeting You Here*, a travelogue of duets with Rosemary Clooney. Billy May's swinging arrangements allowed the singers room, with occasional harp or banjo backing, then egged them on through a ninety-mile-an-hour chorus on 'Slow Boat to China' that sounded like so many comical spinning plates. Rosie had met Bing at Paramount in 1954, working on *White Christmas*, and loved him immediately. 'We had the same kind of sense of humour. Our ranges are totally compatible. I always found Bing was so sensitive to what I was going to do, and vice versa – it was fun. He's always fifteen minutes early, for every appointment – something that looks so easy is very well worked out and thought out.' Sinatra rarely sounded loose or spontaneous. The joy of Crosby's work is that you would never guess he'd be waiting outside the studio door a quarter of an hour before kick-off. He never sounded like he was having more fun than he did with Rosie.

* * *

So, with Nelson Riddle at the forefront, the work of the arranger was sneaking out of anonymity. The LP would bring them into prominence at the very end of the 1940s. Paul Weston was the arranger for Dinah Shore, then Jo Stafford: 'I think it occurred to some of us [arrangers] that conducting wasn't that tough, and why shouldn't we be up there conducting the session? It started when Frank left Tommy's band, and Axel Stordahl left Tommy's band to become Frank's arranger. A lot of it was nodding your head for the band to start and shaking it for the band to stop.'

The king of the 45 disagreed. Mitch Miller reckoned that most arrangers were 'lousy conductors, let's face it. If an arranger conductor comes in, you have 45 men in the studio and you want to make three or four sides in a session in those three hours and you only end up making one or two, that session is costing you twice as much. If you have an arranger and a conductor who knows his business, you can really get it done much faster.'

In 1956 Miller was the conductor working with arranger Ray Conniff, when one day Conniff stumbled upon the sound of wordless vocals doubling up with the brass section.* Miller was so thrilled with it that he let Conniff arrange and conduct; he knew what Conniff had discovered and happily relented control. The resulting 'S Wonderful album would be the first of twenty-eight straight Top 40 albums for Ray Conniff, His Orchestra and Chorus in the States between 1956 and 1968. Commerce always trumped art for Mitch. Besides, he wasn't really an albums kind of guy.†

---

* The Ray Conniff sound was maybe the easiest on the ear ever conceived by any arranger. One song at a time it isn't so bad, but as a body of work it defines 'white bread'. The sound would be gently damned by a doomed president: when Richard Nixon's phone calls were being recorded in 1972, he was caught describing the Conniff outfit as 'kinda square'.

† Were there any British equivalents to Miller or Riddle? The most versatile and interesting conductor/arranger in the 1950s was probably George Martin, a former tea boy at the War Department and the archetypal well-groomed English gentleman. He recorded dry, middlebrow wits Flanders and Swann ('Mud Glorious Mud', 'I'm a Gnu') and made more absurdist comedy records with the Goons, including whole albums with Peter Sellers, Spike Milligan and Michael Bentine. He engineered Sidney Torch's 'Barwick Green' (1951) – which became the theme tune to the BBC radio series The Archers – and arranged Ron Goodwin's film theme 'Murder She Said' (1961). Martin was also the producer on a series of miniature comedy masterpieces in the early 1960s with Bernard Cribbins ('Hole in the Ground', 'Right Said Fred', 'Gossip Calypso'), Joan Sims ('Spring Song') and Terry Scott ('My Brother'); the arranger on full-blooded hit ballads like Edna Savage's 'Arrivederci Darling' and Matt Monro's 'Portrait of My Love'; and he even helmed the earliest piece of Radiophonic Workshop electronica (Ray Cathode's 'Time Beat' b/w 'Waltz in Orbit'). Noël Coward once said that if he was on a desert island with a box of records, 'the only one I would never get sick of is "Hole in the Ground"'. Martin's ingenuity on these recordings is almost totally overlooked because of the music he worked on in the mid-to-late 1960s.

36

IT'S MITCH MILLER'S WORLD AND
WE JUST LIVE IN IT: THE 45

The album, housed in a paper inner bag within a chunkier, protective, full-colour outer sleeve, was for serious music. Record companies, musicians and the public were in broad agreement on this. Which meant the single – faster, smaller, cheaper, no fancy artwork – was for here-today-gone-tomorrow pop. When RCA launched the seven-inch, forty-five revolutions per minute single in 1949, they colour-coded the vinyl: black (popular), red (classical), midnight blue (popular classical), sky blue (international), green (country and western), cerise (blues and rhythm) and yellow (children). The effect was to make *all* singles – compared to the solid, sober, well-wrapped long-player – look like children's records, small bright discs of coloured plastic.* The hit parades of the

* It was only a combination of cost and the Korean War that led to all RCA 45s becoming black vinyl.

late 1940s and early '50s would become a Woolworth's pick 'n' mix of fizz bombs and sherbet lemons, with Mitch Miller the Willie Wonka of the recording studio.

Miller joined Mercury Records in 1949. He was a gnomic man with a pointy beard and a permanent half-smile, and had played oboe for George Gershwin, Andre Kostelanetz and Charlie Parker, before getting work as a classical A&R man. But what got him really excited was novelty – steam whistles, harpsichords, calliopes. He was also quite at home in the recording studio, eager to experiment with tape manipulation, and with the arrival of the 45 rpm single he saw a bright, candycoloured future for Mercury.

In his masterful 1966 essay 'Frank Sinatra Has a Cold', Gay Talese wrote: 'Many Italian-American boys of [Sinatra's] generation were shooting for the same star – they were strong with song, weak with words, not a big novelist among them; no O'Hara, no Bellow, no Cheever, no Shaw; yet they could communicate *bel canto*. No need for a diploma; they could, with a song, someday see their name in lights.'

Vic Damone was just such a boy. He was signed to Mercury in 1949, where Miller and engineer Bob Fine had just created an echo chamber to, as Miller put it, 'put a halo around the voice'. Damone was the first beneficiary. Fine 'rigged up a microphone and a loudspeaker in a toilet, sent the signal in there, and that did exactly what I wanted it to. That made the singer more of a performer in the home, where it is meant to be heard. The point was to make the performer sound more alive on the record.' Damone's 'You're Breaking My Heart' became a Miller-produced number one in 1949.

As he was signed to Mercury, the torch singer Frankie Laine also came under Miller's wing. Suddenly, he was given material that had zip to do with his 1947 heart-wringing breakthrough song 'That's My Desire'. He scored a second *Billboard* number one, spitting out fire on 'That Lucky Old Sun', in 1949, but for the follow-up Miller dressed him as a cowboy and gave him 'Mule Train', complete with whip-cracks, which proved an even bigger hit. At Miller's behest, Laine kept at the cowboy thing – 'Cry of the Wild Goose', 'High Noon' and 'Cool Water'. Then Miller gave him a dog collar so he could sing 'I Believe', 'Answer Me' (both 1953) and 'In the Beginning' (1955). Remarkably, Laine – built like a brick outhouse – could take Miller's medicine-show hokum and still turn these into some of the biggest and best records of the period. Or he could spin a yarn like a barfly in a western – 'The Kid's Last Fight' and 'Strange Lady in Town'. Best of all was the gothic murk, the siren wails and melodrama of 1950's 'Swamp Girl' and 'Satan Wears a Satin Gown', which anticipated Lee Hazlewood, the Cramps and Nick Cave. They were truly intense.

Like Laine, Johnnie Ray had also emerged from clubs that primarily featured black singers. He and Laine were labelled 'belters' by the press, almost physical in their emotive performances. He was also a pin-up. There was no emotion left to wring from the 1951 single 'Cry' once Johnnie had finished with it. He wore a hearing aid on stage and frequently wept; very quickly he built a huge and devoted female fanbase, and his best records – including a cover of the Drifters' 'Such a Night' – were a clear waymark for younger, country-based singers – Elvis Presley, Carl Perkins, Jerry Lee Lewis – who wanted to borrow from rhythm and blues.

Mitch Miller arrived at Columbia in 1950, having been head-hunted from Mercury and having already made stars of Vic Damone and Frankie Laine. He thought he was at least as important as the singers he was recording, but had a scientifically verifiable flair for making hit records on his own terms. Working with Rosemary Clooney, he found 'Come on-a My House', a saucy song written by Pulitzer-winning playwright William Saroyan that drew on his Armenian heritage.* Miller added a demented, over-amped harpsichord to the mix and knew at once that 'Come on-a My House' was a hit. The problem was that Clooney hated it. They had a long phone conversation the night before the studio date. Clooney explained that she was a jazz singer, that novelty songs weren't really her bag, while Miller listened carefully, murmuring concern. He told her that he understood. He also explained that if she didn't sing

---

* Hats off to Saroyan. He wrote the song with his cousin Ross Bagdasarian (who went on to write a brace of maddening US number ones in 'The Chipmunk Song' and David Seville's 'Witch Doctor'), and having copped a million-seller with his very first song, never wrote another.

'Come on-a My House' the very next morning at 9 a.m., Rosemary Clooney would be dropped by Columbia. She sang it, and it became her first major hit, staying at number one for eight weeks over the summer of 1951. So Miller was crude, rude and fond of gimmicks – *anything* that might sell. But he understood before anyone else that it wasn't about the singer or the song; it was about the sound.*

When Guy Mitchell recorded 'My Heart Cries for You' in 1950, at a Columbia recording session that Sinatra walked out on, he wasn't only unknown, he wasn't even Guy Mitchell. Twenty-three-year-old Croatian Al Cernik was one of the many chancers who had been hanging around on the pavement outside the Brill Building – the Broadway warren of publishing offices that became Tin Pan Alley's post-war hub – hoping for a break. That had earned him work from the music publishers behind the building's golden doors as a demonstration recording artist, but he had never cut a record of his own; he was brought in by Mitch Miller simply because Sinatra had walked out and the musicians were already assembled. On the way out of the session, Miller said to him, 'I don't think your name is a very good name for a hit singer. Let's think . . . you're a nice guy, and my name is Mitchell . . . let's call you Guy Mitchell.' Cernik had no say in this game, but the swaying, ultra-simple 'My Heart Cries for You' was an instant hit in December 1950, staying at number two for seven weeks, behind Patti Page's 'Tennessee Waltz'. 'The Roving Kind' on the flip side was almost as big, reaching number four. He took a while to adjust to overnight fame and said he didn't feel like 'Guy Mitchell' – 'You wouldn't want to wake up being somebody else, would you?' – but this was Mitch Miller's world, and Al Cernik was just playing a bit part.

Miller's favoured songwriter was Bob Merrill, who wrote all of his melodies on a child's xylophone. Merrill had struck a deal with his

---

* As for Rosemary Clooney, she never sounded more swinging and seductive than she did on 1956's *Blue Rose*, with Duke Ellington's orchestra and Billy Strayhorn's arrangements, a sophisticated record that was maybe overlooked because of the perception of her as a pop act known only for singles. Although she had been making hit records since 1951, *Blue Rose* was her first purpose-made studio album.

publisher that required four songs a week. He couldn't rely on inspiration to strike: 'I practised something called free association. I'd sit in a room and I'd see a plant and I'd see a glass, and I'd say "glass plant". Just trying to get the wheels to roll. The most successful application was when I had a toy dog someone had gifted me. I started saying "dog radio", "dog lamp", "dog window", "doggie window", "how much is that doggie in the window". I think Patti Page's "How Much Is That Doggie in the Window" was an exceptional recording.'

Merrill wrote reams of hits for Guy Mitchell that played on 'The Roving Kind'. Mitchell's character was often on a ship, or had just got off one, or he was a gamblin' man or a reformed character. They scored major hits with '(There's a Pawnshop on the Corner in) Pittsburgh, Pennsylvania', 'Pretty Little Black-Eyed Susie' and – daffiest of all – 'She Wears Red Feathers', a British number one in 1953, which imagined hula-skirted ladies serving tea on the hour to London's bankers. Mitchell was always jaunty (oddly, he never returned to the ballad style of his first major hit, 'My Heart Cries for You'), and if you didn't want anything that was even remotely demanding, his songs were thoroughly uplifting: 'Look at That Girl' (a UK number one in 1953), 'Cuff of My Shirt', 'Chick a Boom', 'Sippin' Soda'. OK, so they weren't *In the Wee Small Hours*, but then sometimes you might want to go on a picnic instead of a pub crawl.

Miller thought 'the essence of popular songwriting [is] to say a lot in very few words', and he believed Hank Williams had captured that rare essence. 'Here was this country singer, he had very little education but he wrote from the guts. I played his record ['Cold, Cold Heart'] with this scratching violin to Tony Bennett, and Tony says, "Are you kidding? You want me to do cowboy songs?" I said, "Wait a minute, I've got Percy Faith to do an arrangement," and of course that was the breakthrough.'

It seems odd that Tony Bennett started out as one of Miller's Italian boys – he outgrew the role so thoroughly. Cy Coleman later said that you knew a record was a hit once Bennett had recorded it. More than Crosby or even Sinatra, Bennett had his early-career voice and he had his 'Tony Bennett' voice. After starting out as another Italianite, Lanza-esque shouter, he eased off, relaxed and found he could still sing loud and true, but sounded comfortable. Not that there's too much wrong with the Bennett who was A&Red by Miller. His 'Stranger in Paradise' was the biggest hit version in a crowded field, a UK number one, though Bing Crosby's awe-struck, almost whispered take, with its autumnal woodwind backing, is the most beautiful: 'Somewhere in space I hang suspended until I know there's a chance that you'll care.'

Born in Queens in 1926, Bennett was all tan, all grin, all confidence. Given the high-end material he cut later on, he was surprisingly fond of his scuffling days with Mitch Miller: 'I liked his system of rotating the artists. He gave them all a shot. There were [Canadian vocal group] the Four Lads, and Rosemary Clooney and myself . . . we were trained to promote one another. Johnnie Ray would be out talking about Tony Bennett, and Tony Bennett would talk about Rosie Clooney. It was teamwork. When there was no dissention and nice involvement, things seemed to work.'

His most adventurous album was 1959's *Hometown, My Town*, a terrific six-part hymn to New York arranged by Woody Herman protégé Ralph Burns that started with 'Skyscraper Blues' and closed with 'The Party's Over'. On the cover Bennett, gabardine collar protecting him from the wind off the Hudson, screwed up his eyes and turned away from New York. Like almost every other singer of his generation he was feeling the heat by the late 1950s. One day he bumped into Count Basie, confiding to the philosophic bandleader that he was scared. What should he do? Basie paused, looked up and smiled. 'Why change an apple?' From then on, Bennett relaxed and sold a ton of penthouse-ready albums, all sleek as a Persian cat. When he sang 'I Left My Heart in San Francisco' (1962), you pictured a modern, minimally furnished apartment with a pristine, cream carpet and a view of the Golden Gate Bridge. You did not picture the ramshackle timber-frame structures that you'd associate with San Francisco if anyone else was your guide. He had golden, tanned tonsils, sang about 'The Good Life', and sold a ton of albums without sounding as if he was ever trying.

Bennett was the consummate singer; confidence, clarity, pitch – he had them all down pat. There's an unwritten rule of show business that says no matter how sad the song is, smile when you sing. It still holds today. You can hear Bennett smiling through 'I Left My Heart in San Francisco' and other heartbreakers. It should be said too that you can hear Bing Crosby smiling on 'Count Your Blessings' (but you can also sense those acute/grave eyebrows); likewise, Billie Holiday smiling on 'That Ole Devil Called Love' (but you can almost touch the pissed-off feeling of self-doubt); and you can hear Judy Garland smiling through 'The Trolley Song' (but you can read the panic in her eyes). You get that Bennett would take sadistic pleasure in his 1963 hit 'I Wanna Be Around' ('to pick up the pieces when somebody breaks your heart'), and he does a manful job, it works perfectly, but you don't believe his heart has ever been bruised, let alone broken. His biggest fan was Scott Walker, who in the late 1960s would borrow heavily from Bennett's delivery, but who had no trouble dialling everything down and downer.

* * *

DownBeat's best male vocalist of 1949 had formerly been a singer with Earl Hines and a revolutionary bandleader: Billy Eckstine. He would gracefully take to the stage in an all-white suit, and the women would gasp. His voice was powerful; the Eckstine baritone on 'Cottage for Sale' (1945) and an update of Russ Columbo's 'Prisoner of Love' (1946) turned out to be the forerunner of a modern pop trait: the big man down on his knees, the burly carpenter fighting back the tears. His 'My Foolish Heart' was a huge hit in 1950: a surprisingly straightforward, string-led ballad, it reached number six on the *Billboard* chart. It wasn't hard to fall for its seductive charm: 'There's a line between love and fascination that's hard to see on an evening such as this.' His insanely deep and resonant voice became a huge, underestimated influence: within a couple of years there was the ex-boxer Roy Hamilton with his heart-stopping 'Ebb Tide' and 'You'll Never Walk Alone'; further down the line were Chuck Jackson and P. J. Proby, who made hay in the mid-1960s reviving Eckstine's 'I Apologise'.

In 1950 there was also Bill Farrell's intense 'It Isn't Fair', which exaggerated the slight strangulation in Eckstine's voice and ran with it. It's such a strong performance that it's hard to believe that Farrell couldn't follow it up, not even with the solid, crushed-heart ballads 'Love Locked Out', 'Am I Blue' and 'Cry'.* His career path was an archetype for singers who arrived in the immediate pre-rock era; by 1956 he had signed to Imperial and tried to rejuvenate himself as 'Billy Farrell', cutting a slightly uncomfortable cover version of Little Richard's 'Slippin' and Slidin''.

Toledo-born Teresa Brewer was the biggest new name of 1950, and she was proof that women could also rise through the clubs. Impossibly apple-cheeked, her voice was simultaneously a roar and a squeak, a freak of nature, like an atomic-age mouse. Her lines curled up at the end just like her nose, and you could tell at first glance that her mum had wanted her to be the next Shirley Temple. Aged two, she had sung for candy and cupcakes on Toledo's *Uncle August Kiddie Show*; by five, she had graduated to tap-dancing; and in her teens she earned a residency at New York's Sawdust Trail nightclub, where she was spotted in 1949 and signed up by London Records, a newly formed US division of UK Decca. Aged eighteen and pregnant, she recorded the insanely catchy, old-timey 'Music! Music! Music!', a love song to the jukebox. It was relentlessly cheerful, and Brewer's 'cutesie-poo' image, as she called it, was set in stone. It was a number one in Britain and America, and London would feed her similarly bug-eyed novelties: 'Choo'n Gum', 'Cincinnati Dancing Pig', 'Molasses, Molasses (It's Icky Sticky Goo)'. These were not songs she would have sung at the Sawdust Trail.

After leaving London for Coral in 1952, things got a little better. They billed her as 'The little girl with the big voice', and producer Bob Thiele gradually edged her towards songs her voice deserved: the slow swinger 'Till I Waltz Again with You' (the title was slightly misleading) was a second US number one for her in 1952; the country weeper 'A Tear Fell' was her biggest UK hit, a number two in 1956; while her extraordinary 1955 take on Johnny Ace's 'Pledging My Love', over a drum track that seems to anticipate skittery 1990s beats, is country soul

---

* Even 'It Isn't Fair' stalled at number twenty on the *Billboard* chart, while Sammy Faye's 'swing and sway' version, with a smarmy Don Cornell vocal, reached number three. One version sounded clammily like the recent but dead past; the other indicated something much more enticing.

more than a decade ahead of the game. By all accounts as nice a person as she appeared to be, Brewer would end up singing lead on Chas & Dave's first album (when they were still called Oily Rags) in 1973, would be one of the first guests on *The Muppet Show* in 1977, and finally got the stage she deserved when Bob Thiele arranged for her to record an album of Bessie Smith songs, led by Count Basie. So she ended up a jazz singer, though she had to really go round the houses. And she married Thiele, who had transformed her reputation. It was a proper happy ending.

* * *

The early-1950s singles charts may have been the junk shop of twentieth-century American pop. Full of trinkets (Leroy Anderson's 'The Typewriter'), costume jewellery (Eddie Fisher's rose-scented ballads) and Mitch Miller's plastic baubles, it was light and easy, undemanding but fun. For Britain, creatively, the early '50s was a time of creative famine. Practically every British record was a cover of an American song, with Denmark Street, the BBC and Radio Luxembourg content to remain in a state of post-war inertia. In 1953, with a new queen on the throne, there was a brief flurry of activity, and a bunch of songs – Billy Cotton's fawning 'In a Golden Coach', Winifred Atwell's playful 'Coronation Rag', Ronald Binge's lush 'Elizabethan Serenade' – were written in celebration; there was even a new sandwich filling for the ages in coronation chicken. But the only significant change was in formats, with UK Decca introducing LPs in 1950, and EMI producing its first 45s in 1952. What these brought to Britain's meagre pop party was quite unexpected: record sales rose – it was a gold rush. Stranger yet, all three speeds benefited, as many records were still available only on 78.

This boom led to another American import: record-plugging, which became big business in the UK. There were broadcasting restrictions as the music publishers were, for now, still kingmakers. They had a release date for sheet music, and so all versions of a record had to come out on the same day. This meant that British covers and American originals were given a level playing field. Still, the modern pop world was sticking a cheeky foot in the door. Alan A. Freeman was a producer for the independent Polygon label, home to child star Petula Clark and the kind-faced balladeer Jimmy Young: 'The publishers used to put a release date on it . . . you could not go on the air before a date. Everybody was going for programmes like *Housewives' Choice*, which was very strong and was a morning show. That was the big plug to get, the first record of the day.'

On Saturday nights DJ Jack Jackson had a BBC Light Programme show called *Record Roundup*; if Jackson picked up on a record and played it three weeks in a row, 'you could bet your bottom dollar it would be in the charts', reckoned Alan A. Freeman. In June 1951 Freeman recorded Jimmy Young's version of 'Too Young' – which was already a major American hit for Nat King Cole – with Ron Goodwin's orchestration, and had it ready and waiting four weeks before the release date. Then, on the first day airplay was allowed, Freeman drove down to Southsea, where Jackson was appearing in a summer show: 'I played him the record, and he slapped me on the back and said, "My boy, you've got a big, big hit here." He said, "Can you give me an exclusive on it?" Three or four programmes that day wanted to play the Jimmy Young in preference to the Nat King Cole, and I had to turn them down – it was heartbreaking! Of course, Jack came in with a fanfare of trumpets and said, "The greatest British record of the year." And the thing took off.'

Jack Jackson was a harbinger. He was the first UK radio presenter to treat a 'record programme' as entertainment. He would get behind acts and records, give them his personal treatment, play the same record six weeks running; previously, radio presenters who had a weekly show would create a totally different programme each week. Jackson also had a nose for unlikely hits: Rose Murphy's Helen Kane-redux recording 'Busy Line'; *Opportunity Knocks* winner David Whitfield's 'Bridge of Sighs'; Yma Sumac's wordless, glass-shattering 'Taita Inty'. He nourished the career of Alma Cogan, helping her to get a slot on *Take It from Here*, a comedy show interspersed with music.

British popular music revolved around the London Palladium. With union restrictions lifted in 1950, the stars were brought over from America – Duke Ellington, Lena Horne, Guy Mitchell, Frank Sinatra – and they appeared alongside old-school variety acts like Tommy Trinder and Bruce Forsyth. If you appeared on a Sunday night at the London Palladium, you would sell records. Mitchell, Frankie Laine and Johnnie Ray played there and outsold all the home-grown acts.

Not all of the traffic was one-way. Columbia producer Norrie Paramor discovered a hit when his au pair told him about a record she'd heard in Austria. She sent home for the music, and Norrie liked it enough to place it on the B-side of trumpet player Eddie Calvert's 'Mystery Street'. An independent-record-label man called Dave Miller was over from the US and heard this track, 'O Mein Papa'. 'He immediately went into ecstasies,' remembered Paramor, 'and called his office in Philadelphia for a rush release.' It sold a million. There was also former forces sweetheart Vera Lynn and her single 'Auf Wiedersehen', which, coinciding with the escalation of the Korean War, became the first British recording to top the American charts. But these were very much the exceptions. It would be another decade before British pop finally regained its influence on America.

For pop in the UK, the most significant new arrival of 1952 was the *New Musical Express*. The fading weekly *Accordion Times and Musical Express* had been bought by Maurice Kinn, a former concert promoter. A sharp-eyed pop enthusiast called Andy Gray became managing editor of the *NME*: he knew that, as a paper for dance-band musicians, it was doomed to die. *Melody Maker* could survive as the weekly job centre for jazz musicians, but the scene couldn't handle two papers, so Gray decided the best thing to do was to turn the *NME* into something Britain didn't have: a record paper. The first thing he did was to run the charts from American *Billboard*, including the best-selling (sheet) music. As he was struggling to get sales figures from the record companies, Gray devised his own chart system by asking retailers how many records they were selling. Anybody could get into the *NME* hit parade: the very first had Al Martino's Italian tear-jerker 'Here in My Heart' at number one and stretched from Mario Lanza to Johnnie Ray to Max Bygraves.

The charts appealed to a British sensibility; they were league tables of what amounted to a new sport. Record shops were still something of a rarity, and anything from a toy shop to a hardware store to a chemist would stock items on the new 'hit parade'. Shop owners could now look at the chart and make sure they had a Jo Stafford as well as an Al Martino, ten packs of AA batteries and five cans of Brasso. The singles chart's founding father Andy Gray understood their significance: 'They were taken up by the national papers, they were taken up by the BBC, and so for the first time the music business had a barometer, a spokesman for the outer world.'

* * *

The singles-buying public formed a different social grouping to theatregoers; shows were not just about a three-minute hit song. As we'll soon see, musical theatre was still a huge force; it continued to evolve oddly in the 1950s, with a different fresh ingredient in each hit show: Berlin's *Annie Get Your Gun* (gun-toting female protagonist); *Paint Your Wagon* (proto-beatniks, the original drop-outs); Rodgers and Hammerstein's *The King and I* (spoiler – the hero dies on stage); and Alan J. Lerner's *My Fair Lady*, which had no element of dance in it – I mean, how could you dance to *Pygmalion*? Singles buyers were much more likely to buy something they could at least nod along to, something party-ready.

What was happening in Britain and America was a divergence between 'pop' as a three-minute burst of emotion and 'pop' as a more immersive album or show-length experience. Take one record, Les Paul and Mary Ford's 'How High the Moon'. The song was the sole survivor of a vanished musical from 1940 and was a lilting country ballad. But Paul made it sound very different. He had built a makeshift recording studio in the couple's garage, where spools of tape squeezed their automobile out onto the driveway. By the time he had finished with 'How High the Moon' it sounded like it was being beamed into your front room by a Sputnik. After multitracking sounds and manipulating the speed of his recorded guitar, the song sounded *entirely* electronic; even Ford's close-miked, double-tracked voice sounded weirdly present, almost as if she was inside your ear. It had no semblance of a natural, live performance. It wasn't a one-off, either: the couple followed it with similarly mind-warping takes on 'Mockingbird Hill', 'Smoke Rings' and 'Vaya con Dios', and by 1954 Paul and Ford were hosting their own syndicated TV show. Country producer Chet Atkins later complained that Paul 'talked Ampex into building an eight-track machine, back in the fifties. He made about five times as much work for me and every other producer in the country.' Maybe so, maybe no. But he had also conceived the sound of the next decade and beyond.

37

BREAKS A NEW HEART EVERY DAY:
PEGGY LEE

Somebody asked me recently if I always dress up, and I do, even
for rehearsals. But when I plant roses, or paint, I wear karate
clothes.
    Peggy Lee

On Christmas Eve 1941 the Benny Goodman Sextet went into the
studio to record Rodgers and Hart's 'Where or When'. The lyric was
romantic, charged by its own confusion: 'It seems that we have met
before, and laughed before, and loved before. But who knows where or
when?' Given that America had entered World War II a fortnight earlier,

the recording – so hushed and uncertain, its celeste suggesting a child's music box, a quiet storm of pasts – was doubly poignant. The vocalist on 'Where or When' was twenty-one-year-old Peggy Lee.

Two years later, she appeared with Goodman in the movie *Stage Door Canteen*, walking onto the crowded bandstand for a couple of choruses of 'Why Don't You Do Right'.* Short of space, Lee's arms hung by her side, and the only movement she allowed herself was a rhythmic twitch in her hip throughout the song. She was smiling, as was the custom for band vocalists in the early 1940s, but under piled-up platinum hair, her eyes were looking around the room, telling a different story, one that went with the hard-line lyric. She had the languid phrasing of Billie Holiday and she looked like mischief. *DownBeat* and *Metronome* had described her as 'cold' when she had first appeared in 1941; now they considered her Goodman's finest canary. Though doing very little, she was clearly in charge. While Goodman's other girl singer of the time, Martha Tilton, had a not dissimilar voice, it was far less authoritative; her face was a monochrome photo, snapped and trapped in the early 1940s. Martha Tilton was the girl waiting patiently at home. Peggy Lee wasn't going to wait for anyone.

Originally, she was Norma Delores Egstrom, a North Dakota farm girl with Norwegian and Swedish blood. The full weight of Lee's furs and jewels and compound-eye sunglasses could never entirely hide her roots. Even after moving to Greenwich Village in the 1940s, she didn't feel at home unless she had a twenty-five-pound sack of potatoes in the kitchen. She would still make her own bread, leaving the dough to prove in a warm closet while she skipped town to see a boyfriend two hours away in Washington DC. Norma Delores Egstrom was a small-town girl, but she represented the height of metropolitan elegance.

'Why Don't You Do Right' had peaked at number four on the *Billboard* chart in January 1943, and no matter how much Benny Goodman thought canaries were little more than a necessary evil, to be kept in their

---

* I always imagine Lee singing 'Why Don't You Do Right' to actor Dan Duryea, the go-to Hollywood creep for roles like the slimy blackmailer in Fritz Lang's *Woman in the Window* and the lazy-ass pimp in the bleak noir *Scarlet Street*. He always came to a sticky end.

cage whenever possible, it was Lee who made the record a hit. While she was filming *Stage Door Canteen*, though, she discovered she was pregnant. Dave Barbour had been the guitarist in Goodman's band; fraternising with the girl singers was strictly forbidden, but Peg 'had to chase him for a year! He's the type who wouldn't admit he was attracted to me . . . but at night after the shows he was always there to drive me home.' When Goodman found out about the pregnancy, he was furious. Pianist Mel Powell and arranger Eddie Sauter had just left him – now this? Barbour was sacked, and married Lee in a shotgun wedding. He carried on working; she stayed at home playing mother. 'I'm retired,' she told Dave Dexter of Capitol Records, America's hottest new label. 'I don't sing any more.'

But what she did while she was changing nappies and washing dishes was write her own songs, with Barbour coming up with guitar accompaniment. Domesticity couldn't hold her. By 1945 Peggy was a solo star: 'Waitin' for the Train to Come In' ('I'm waiting for my life to begin, waiting for the train to come in') and the coy 'I Don't Know Enough About You' were both self-penned and both reached the US Top 10, and by 1946 she had been voted top female singer by *DownBeat*. Biographer James Gavin said she had an 'enticing sense of the forbidden', which was part of Peg's appeal, but so was the darkness that drew her towards material like Willard Robison's 'Don't Smoke in Bed' ('Goodbye, old sleepy head, I'm packing you in like I said') and the daffiness that led her to sing like Speedy Gonzales on 'Mañana' (a number-one hit for nine weeks) at the very same session in 1948.*

* * *

Peggy Lee's voice was about minimalism. Her range wasn't huge, but she knew exactly how to use it. Unlike the crooners of the 1920s and '30s, she was sparing with vibrato and most effective when she seemed to

---

* Robison had been a bandleader in the 1920s, and at one point employed Bix Beiderbecke. But by 1948 he was drinking heavily and getting by on the royalties from his biggest hit, 'A Cottage for Sale'. When he discovered Lee was going to record a song of his, he went to her home town of Jamestown, North Dakota. 'I just sat on a curb and thought about you,' he told her, 'and then I went home.'

have run out of breath, dipping at the end of a line and stopping dead.
You could hear her wink, cock her head. She was funny, sensual, and
one of the definitive jazz vocalists. She worked around a melody, picked
out off-beats, audibly teased and put her hand on her hip, all the while
keeping the rhythm ticking so you barely noticed. The door was always
left slightly ajar so that you could enter her world and get lost in her
mink jazz; or you could just as easily walk on by and never know what
you'd missed. Lee was never going to try too hard to lure you in; she'd
rather just lie there and wait. 'We are Siamese if you please,' she'd say.
'We are Siamese if you don't please.'

Throughout the 1950s and '60s she remained pop's Mona Lisa,
unknowable, enigmatic and most desirable. Playing at Hollywood's
Ciro's nightclub in 1951, she experimented with the lighting, employing sudden blackouts to crank up the mystique. On record she could
disinter Little Willie John's hot and heavy 'Fever' one minute, getting
to the nub of its sensuous strength, then melt like a butter statue on
'Mr Wonderful' the next. She could swing hard too: 1959's 'Jump for
Joy' was packed with some of Nelson Riddle's brassiest arrangements,
and Peg sassed her way through the Boswell Sisters' 'When My Sugar
Walks Down the Street', Billie Holiday's 'What a Little Moonlight Can
Do' and Fred Astaire's 'Cheek to Cheek'. On darker ballads – her narcotic takes on Ray Davies's 'I Go to Sleep' (1965) and Michel Legrand's
'I Was Born in Love with You' (1971), or the unsettling 'I Can Sing
a Rainbow' (from 1955's *Pete Kelly's Blues*) – she employed a numb
patience, a scary sense of resignation. Whether upbeat or low, it was
a hypnotic sound, a cocoon of all-enveloping breathiness; at all times
she sounded as if she was reclining into a huge consignment of furs. 'I
have a lot more voice than I ever use,' she would say. 'I ration it, and
it's lasting very nicely.'

* * *

Miss Peggy Lee never sounded girlish, though there was a sense of artificial sweetness on some of her earliest recordings with Goodman. This
had gone by the time of *Black Coffee* (1954) and *Dream Street* (1955),

two intimate song cycles that revealed Lee as an ideal singer for the album age. The title track of *Black Coffee* features the definitive 1950s jazz vocal; Lee's opening note is preceded by an intentionally audible breath, a subtlety that simply wouldn't have been possible on a pre-war recording, let alone something from the acoustic era. How far things had moved along! And what was more 1950s, more stylish, than a pot of fresh black coffee, preferably French or Italian strength?

Though *Black Coffee* would become a touchstone LP over the years, cited as a favourite by Joni Mitchell, among others, *Dream Street* was even better. A lot of its mood could be put down to arranger Sy Oliver's light touch, using harp and glockenspiel to add sweet perfume to Lee's delicate vocals and cushioning many of the verses with nothing but solo piano. The opening to 'Street of Dreams' created an empty nocturnal cityscape; there was a heavy frost on the woodwind-and-plucked-guitar intro to 'Too Late Now', with the brushed drums a carpet of snow that Lee delicately tiptoed over; and her 'What's New' was quietly devastating, her sad smile failing her – head bowed – on the climactic 'I haven't changed, I still love you so.'

More uncompromising yet – and eventually shelved by a nervous Decca – was the avant-garde folk of *Sea Shells*, recorded by Lee in 1956 and only released two years later, when she left the label. Throughout, Lee was accompanied by just harpist Stella Castellucci and harpsichord player Gene DiNovi. The lyrics referenced 'ruined old forts', 'green habitation' and 'butterflies powdered with gold'. 'The White Birch and the Sycamore' opened with 'One day, when I was feeling very low', before incorporating a conversation between a field mouse and a wren. Four of the tracks were entirely instrumental; two more were translated Chinese poems. In places it sounded like muzak from forty years hence; at the very least, it left a marker for 'new age'. It's hard to think how odd it must have sounded to the A&R men (and they would have all been men) at Decca. It's as singular as Mel Tormé's *California Suite*, the Beach Boys' *Smile* or Herbie Flowers' *Plant Life*, and I'll lay good money on Stevie Nicks owning a copy.

Having *Sea Shells* rejected by Decca wasn't Lee's only disappointment in 1956. A year earlier, Walt Disney's *Lady and the Tramp* had afforded her a chance to write for a movie for the first time, and she sang 'He's a Tramp' ('What a *dog!*') like the Mae West of old. It's quite shocking that none of her contributions – 'He's a Tramp', 'Siamese Cat Song', 'Bella Notte' – was even nominated for an Oscar (the 1956 winner was Sammy Fain and Paul Francis Webster's gooey theme for *Love Is a Many-Splendored Thing*). In sympathy, *DownBeat* wrote that 'few contemporary figures possess her many applied talents and fewer still can match her consistent record'.

Still, the real treasure was in the down-tempo albums. No Peggy Lee album was more seductive than 1957's *The Man I Love*, which celebrated her return to Capitol after Decca had rejected *Sea Shells*. It was produced and conducted by Frank Sinatra, at a time when both singers were at the top of their game. Here, however, Sinatra played host, getting the studio ready for Peg, dimming the lights just so, a gin and tonic ready for her as soon as she walked through the door. Her voice was so intimate, so hushed and breathy, that it felt like she was somehow inside you, right there, inside your thoughts. Nelson Riddle's unobtrusive arrangements provided a warm cocoon – it was just you and Peg. She sang, 'Someday we'll build a home on a hilltop high, you and I,' the opening line of Jerome Kern and Oscar Hammerstein's 'The Folks Who Live on the Hill', and the message was one of impossible hope. Maybe it's just me, but I hear the song from the perspective of a woman stuck in the city, with no obvious way out, nowhere to go other than her internal Dream Street. Maybe she's in a new, post-war tower block, isolated in the sky, scared to meet the new neighbours, killing time. It has an unreal quality, and it gets me every time.

Twin totems of 1950s vocal jazz, Sinatra and Lee were peers, equals, and clearly admired the heck out of each other, but their approaches were opposite extremes. Sinatra laid his life out for you; that was what he did, and that's why he was so relatable. Lee, on the other hand, was a deep and impenetrable mystery. She sang of life, but not her life; it was quite abstract. She was a farm girl from North Dakota, but one who wore space-cadet shades and beaded headdresses. Songwriter Mike Stoller called her 'a nice bunch of gals'. When the rock wave threatened to engulf the post-war stars, Peg adapted with the twanging guitar and (slightly staid) doo-wop backing on 1957's 'Every Night'. It wasn't a hit, but her sizzling, stripped-back take on 'Fever' went Top 10 in Britain and America the following year. Peg's purr aside, there was nothing to it apart from finger clicks, stand-up bass and strategically placed bongos that got animated in all the right places. She even added a couple of new verses – one about Pocahontas and one about Romeo and Juliet – which gave it an added wink. As a bridge between vocal jazz and modern R&B, it couldn't be bettered, and Elvis Presley would copy Peg's version almost note for note on his 1960 album *Elvis Is Back*.

Atmosphere and mystery, smoke and mirrors – Lee didn't want to open up about herself. She wanted the listener to absorb her experience and use it to delve into their own half-buried memories and complex emotions. 1961's *If You Go* was arranged by jazz's golden boy, Quincy Jones, a couple of years before his pop crossover with Lesley Gore's 'It's My Party', the hit single that would ultimately lead to him producing *Off the Wall* and *Thriller*. *If You Go*, though, with its almost apologetic, half-finished title, was as sensitive and controlled as 'It's My Party' was brassy and blubby. In fact, it featured no brass at all, with just woodwind and string arrangements cosseting a downcast Peg as she sang 'As Time Goes By', 'Chaplin's Smile', Cahn and Van Heusen's 'Here Comes That Rainy Day' and Frank Loesser's 'I Wish I Didn't Love You So'. She could break a new heart every day. Clearly, she had been places and seen more than any of us ever would, probably more than we would care to. There was never any emoting for the sake of it, though; Lee's power was in her restraint, which, even on a feline novelty like Chip Taylor's 'Sneakin' Up on You', was absorbing. Her intensity was always intimate; the climactic note, bathed in echo, towards the end of 'Don't Smoke in Bed' was as close as she would ever get to belting.

Lee also diverged from Sinatra in her taste and take on modern pop in the 1960s and '70s. Sinatra audibly hated having to record Petula Clark's 'Downtown' in 1966, and sang it like someone's creepy uncle. Peg would turn to Ray Charles ('Hallelujah, I Love Him So') and Leiber and Stoller (the delicious 'I'm a Woman') in the early 1960s; then to Tim Hardin, the Lovin' Spoonful and the Kinks in the mid-'60s; Goffin and King ('Natural Woman') and Sly Stone ('Everyday People)' at the decade's end; and back to Leiber and Stoller for her ultimate party piece, 'Is That All There Is', in 1969.

* * *

Jerry Leiber and Mike Stoller had been slightly put out that Miss Peggy Lee never got back to thank them for 'I'm a Woman', a rollicking, blues-based, first-wave feminist anthem that came out in 1963, just as Merseybeat was breaking. Both thirteen years Lee's junior, the pair had repositioned her career with the song's quickfire, hard-line lyric: 'I got a twenty-dollar gold piece says there ain't nothing I can't do. I can make a dress out of a feed bag and I can make a man out of you.' She never bought Leiber and Stoller a bottle of Scotch, never took them out to a ball game, never even asked them for another song – 'I'm a Woman' had been Grammy-nominated, for Chrissakes! A few years later, immersed in the chaos of late-1960s America and looking for something deeper than the teenage pop that surrounded him, Leiber read a Thomas Mann piece called 'Disillusionment'. He peered into the existential emptiness within and began to write – not a song, but a narration. Your house burns down. So what? You fall in love. So what? You die. Whatever! Stoller decided the perfect musical setting for this über-cynical spiel would be the 1930s cabaret feel of Brecht and Weil. First off, they offered it to Marlene Dietrich. 'That is who I am,' said the great singer, when Leiber sang it to her, 'not what I do.' Next, Barbra Streisand received a demo, but never responded. It was too bad that Peggy Lee wouldn't be interested, they sighed – she'd be perfect. But they thought, 'What the hell,' and handed her a tape after a show at the Copacabana. A week went by. Then she called them up and said, 'If you give this song to anyone but me, I will kill you. This is my song. This is the story of my life.'

'Is That All There Is' was arranged by another Jewish smart alec and master of the observational, Randy Newman, a kid who had been born the year 'Why Don't You Do Right' made Peg a star. Between them Leiber, Stoller and Newman created something that was warm, funny and entirely death-haunted. It was released in 1969, a few months before Lee turned fifty, and a few months after Sinatra recorded his

winter-of-my-years, 'and now the end is near' epic 'My Way'. That was
chewy and bombastic. Lee's summation of life was very different – an
eye-roll, a shrug – and the message of her song was not endless libertar-
ian defiance, but 'Let's break out the booze . . . let's keep dancing.'

In 1974, as Sinatra relived the good old days with shows at Caesar's
Palace, Lee would be given a tailor-made Paul McCartney song called
'Let's Love' – written just after Wings' *Band on the Run* album had been
released – that ached in all the right places. With its minor-chord piano
backing and weightless, seductive, dream-state lyric ('Lover, let's be in
love and discover that night is the flight of the butterfly'), 'Let's Love',
as much as 'Is That All There Is', was Lee's perfect late-career coda. The
world's greatest and most famous songwriters visiting her misty house
on the hill, paying their respects, bearing her gifts – it was exactly what
she deserved.*

* McCartney was paying tribute to one of his favourite singers. He had sung
'Till There Was You' on *With the Beatles* in 1963, a song from *The Music Man*
that Lee had made her own in 1961. In the same year as 'Let's Love', puppet-
maker Bonnie Erickson came up with a slightly less flattering tribute: she created
a puppet called Miss Piggy Lee, in part as an homage to a famously strong and
independent woman. 'But as Piggy's fame began to grow, nobody wanted to
upset Peggy Lee, especially because we admired her work,' recalled Erickson. 'So,
the Muppet's name was shortened to Miss Piggy.'

38

ALMOST LIKE PRAYING:
POST-WAR BROADWAY

In 1922 a play called *Abie's Irish Rose* opened on Broadway and became a major hit. It celebrated New York's melting pot by telling the story of a nice Jewish boy and a sweet Catholic colleen, and it was pure corn, sentimental mush in the nascent, agnostic Jazz Age. The papers ridiculed it. Each week in *Life* magazine, critic Robert Benchley had to write a one-line capsule review, and he had much joy at the play's expense: 'Just about as low as good clean fun can get'; 'Shows that the Jews and the Irish crack equally old jokes'; 'Will the Marines never come?'; 'People laugh at this every night, which explains why democracy can never be a success.' Benchley set a readers' competition for a review of *Abie's Irish*

Rose, and Harpo Marx won it with 'No worse than a bad cold.' Still, it showed no sign of closing.

The best pot-shot taken at the dreaded play wasn't from Benchley or Harpo, but Lorenz Hart. The original lyric for 'Manhattan' ran: 'Our future babies we'll take to *Abie's Irish Rose*, let's hope they'll live to see it close.' It did, eventually, in 1927, but Larry Hart wouldn't live to see a longer-running play. Oscar Hammerstein would never have written a line as catty, as specifically targeted or as funny. Like Berlin, he didn't make fun of the masses. His lyrics were broad sweeps, with the broadest message, for the broadest audience, and though his thoughts on *Abie's Irish Rose* were never recorded, he would have been more likely to write songs for a play about society's great patchwork than to take it down with a sassy one-liner.

Post-war, the emergence of new formats – in particular, the long-playing album – would eat into Broadway's space, at both its 'pop' and its 'serious' margins. Its self-segregation would be as much imposed from outside as pursued from within. The likes of Hart would disappear from the scene, replaced by writers with loftier aims – both lyrically and for Broadway itself – like Hammerstein and Stephen Sondheim. They felt the weight of Broadway's history when they wrote; their task was to create new musicals while elevating the genre's past. For Sondheim, 1981's *Merrily We Roll Along*, based on a 1934 book, was maybe the show he had always aspired to. It awkwardly toyed with time itself, and became a famous flop.* For Hammerstein, there was nothing but success, all the way from 1941's *Oklahoma!*, when he was forty-six years old, to 1959's *The Sound of Music*, which opened just before his death in 1960. Commercially, this was a totally unmatched late-career flowering.

---

* *Merrily We Roll Along* ran on Broadway for just sixteen performances. Sondheim was bitter. 'The delight and the joy that people took in the failure of *Merrily We Roll Along*, it was the hostility that had built up towards Hal [Prince, the producer] and me because we committed the unpardonable crime of being mavericks who were successful. And everybody hated us. It would have been fine if we'd just been hacks and made a lot of money, that's OK. Or to be really original and starve, that's OK. But it's not OK to be both, and they didn't forgive us. I thought, I've got to get out of this.' Sondheim and Prince wouldn't work together again until *Bounce* in 2003.

The Theatre Guild had been set up in 1918 'to present classic and contemporary dramatic works on Broadway'. It had always been sniffy about musicals, condescending in its view of the musical comedy's audience as 'tired businessmen'. By the early 1940s, though, it was on the verge of bankruptcy. One of its directors was Theresa Helburn, who had the notion of turning a 1931 Theatre Guild production called *Green Grow the Lilacs* into a musical. It was a folksy piece about the Oklahoma Territory at the turn of the century. Rodgers and Hart were approached by Helburn, but Larry turned it down flat for being too corny. Rodgers approached Oscar Hammerstein, who hadn't pulled up many trees since *Showboat* way back in 1927, but had recently won an Oscar for 'The Last Time I Saw Paris' (sung by Ann Sothern in the 1941 film *Lady, Be Good*). Hammerstein would go on to be credited with the musical's 'book and lyrics', the first major American lyric writer to take on both roles. When Hart bailed out, he unintentionally opened the door for a new and very different version of musical comedy. *Green Grow the Lilacs* was retitled *Oklahoma!*, and it was huge.

Rodgers and Hammerstein changed Broadway. They took it forward by making it less a geographical location where the hits were born, and more a stand-alone genre with new rules and regulations. With their exotic but defiantly non-metropolitan locations, they also took it back to a time when the book drove the songs, back to the time of light opera and operetta. Hammerstein was a liberal with a message for the masses. 'I knew what his words meant,' said Rodgers, 'and I thought I could match them. The first song we wrote went, "There's a bright golden haze on the meadow".' Certainly, 'Oh, What a Beautiful Mornin'' didn't have the urban smarts of Rodgers and Hart, but as Sondheim would later respond, 'It's not about being smart, it's about being alive.' *Oklahoma!* was celebrating a living America that had existed before Pearl Harbour, and was about to exist again after welcoming its homecoming heroes. It may have been broadly corny, but it was broadly true. Betty Comden, writing for 1944's *On the Town*, was quite aware that *Oklahoma!* had rewritten the rules of Broadway: 'What comes first, the music or the lyrics? What comes first is the *book*. The character, the situation. You have a situation where a character is in a town and he's lonely. So you write "Lonely Town".'

Hammerstein's son William once described his father's philosophy: 'The world needed somebody to tell [it] about these simple fundamental things like love, faith and justice and honour. That was pretty much the basis of his work.' Before *Oklahoma!*, Hammerstein, writing with Jerome Kern, had endured ten years of relative failure. When Kern had a heart attack in 1939 and was advised by his doctors to write less demanding incidental music, Hammerstein's own heart must have sunk. The enormous success of *Oklahoma!* in 1943 brought out his black humour. He took an ad out in the trade papers, listing all the flops he had written between *Show Boat* and *Oklahoma!*, with the strapline 'I did it before, and I can do it again'. That wasn't likely; all he had to do was repeat the triple threat of *Oklahoma!*'s production by revealing the characters' dreams and their fears through song, dance and acting. Integration became the new watchword.

Integration meant that all the elements – book, lyrics, music, dancing – should have equal input on the overall effect of the work. The show's choreographer, Agnes de Mille, had wanted it to be a ballet. It had to be integrated, with all the principals dancing, and it had to reflect American folklore. 'I kept nudging Oscar, "Integrate! Integrate! Bridge it!"' The dialogue, she said, 'needed to be rhythmic'. De Mille came from classical dance, something Richard Rodgers had ventured into a whole seven years earlier with the 'Slaughter on Tenth Avenue' sequence in *On Your Toes*, but this time it caught fire. Everybody had been convinced *Oklahoma!* would be an utter flop. Instead, it ushered in a golden age of choreography for Broadway. Jerome Robbins (*West Side Story*), Bob Fosse (*The Pajama Game*) and Michael Kidd (*Guys and Dolls*) all owed their chance to *Oklahoma!*'s runaway Broadway success – 2,212 performances in almost six years.

Oklahoma! did to the Broadway musical what *Jaws* would do to American cinema three decades later. It was so expansive and all-consuming, such an exciting spectacle, that nuance was steamrollered. New Broadway musicals could now work only if they were sufficiently post-*Oklahoma!*, harking back to the familiarity of the past while appearing to be groundbreaking and modern. The very biggest hits of the next twenty years would have Rodgers and Hammerstein's names on them: *The King and I*, *The Sound of Music*, *Carousel*, *South Pacific*.

Every Rodgers and Hammerstein musical seemed to begin in the highest of spirits ('Oh, What a Beautiful Mornin'', 'June Is Bustin' Out All Over', 'I Whistle a Happy Tune'), wholesomely buoyant, before diverting into romance ('Shall We Dance', 'Some Enchanted Evening', 'If I Loved You') and then meandering through a gradually darkening storyline, before climaxing in pain, death and – if you were lucky – some kind of redemption ('You'll Never Walk Alone', 'Climb Ev'ry Mountain'). In 1949 Hammerstein's lyric for 'You've Got to Be Carefully Taught' felt confrontational and shocking. Next to 'Strange Fruit', though, it sounded hectoring. Wolcott Gibbs in *The New Yorker* called it 'a poem in praise of tolerance that somehow I found a little embarrassing'. Still, when *South Pacific* reached Wilmington, Delaware, and Rodgers and Hammerstein discovered that the theatre was racially divided, they threatened to cancel the performances unless the audiences were integrated – and they got their way.

The film adaptations of Rodgers and Hammerstein's musicals are a tough twenty-first-century watch. A real problem is the gap between Hammerstein's simplistic progressive messages, always hammered home, and the more nuanced aspects in the script, which are often left unresolved. In *Carousel* (1956), Billy Bigelow is an ox of a man, and Julie his pretty blonde wife. He can't find work and he hits her. She lets him off. The men wear tight-fitting polo necks; the girls are in dresses that look as if they are made from sacks but are still figure-hugging. The colours are luminous, but the storyline drags and the pacing is awful; until the last thirty minutes it is less involving than Elvis Presley's fairground romp *Roustabout* (a bonus is that Elvis doesn't punch his love interest). The film came out in 1956, when, up against *High Society*, *And God Created Woman* and *Baby Doll*, it was an embarrassment.

As a film, *Carousel* made no sense at all, unless you were already familiar with the Broadway version (in which Billy Bigelow ascends to heaven after his death, rather than jauntily telling the story while sitting on St Peter's lap) or the original Hungarian story, Ferenc Molnár's *Liliom*, a cautionary tale about the violent, thieving anti-hero who eventually realises that, dead or alive, his actions have caused, and can still cause, nothing but harm. Common sense may tell you that the ending will be sad, but though Rodgers and Hammerstein's 'You'll Never Walk Alone' makes for a heart-stopping moment after Bigelow's death, he ends up finding redemption when spending a single day back on earth. Even then, he still manages to strike his fun-loving daughter, after which she claims that 'it didn't hurt, it didn't hurt at all. It was just as if he kissed my hand.' Shirley Jones is pretty but given an entirely one-dimensional, flatly besotted character ('Anywhere he leads you, you will walk,' she simpers); she would reprise the role of a single mother, with considerably more strength, in *The Partridge Family* fourteen years later. Writer Andy Zax remembered being taken to a 1972 production of *Carousel* when he was seven years old: 'It made me miserable. I think it was the first time I ever encountered adult level bleakness in a cultural artefact. When it finished I couldn't believe that that was actually the end – I remember asking my mother if there was more. It left me upset for days.'

1949's *South Pacific* ('Bali Hai', 'Happy Talk', 'Some Enchanted Evening') was compromised in a different way: Nellie is a nurse from Arkansas who falls in love with Emile, a French plantation owner raising two children alone since his Polynesian wife died. Hammerstein's message is that Nellie's love for Emile can just about overcome her prejudice against his mixed-race children. You wait in vain for the issue of plantations and an occupying force to be raised. But confronting racism and empire on Broadway could only go so far in 1949.

Rodgers and Hammerstein threw a cloak of seriousness over musical theatre that at least could be gleefully subverted by snappier writers. *Guys and Dolls* was an instant success in 1950. Combining Damon Runyon's stories and former newspaper man Frank Loesser's songs, it put the emphasis back on comedy. It was as sharp as a zoot suit and earned Loesser two Tony Awards. Bob Fosse would call *Guys and Dolls* 'the greatest American musical of all time'.

Jo Sullivan, Loesser's widow, later recalled his writing technique: 'His style was getting up at four in the morning, working till eight-thirty in the morning. Then he would have a Martini and he would have breakfast and take a nap. He said nobody could bother him at four in the morning. He had an electric piano with earphones, so he wouldn't wake up the neighbourhood.' Daughter Susan remembered other times when the muse wasn't with him: 'He would swear. He would jump up and down like an obscene Rumpelstiltskin.'

In the opening sequence of Richard Adler and Jerry Ross's *The Pajama Game* (1954), you hear, 'When will old man Hassler break down and come up with our seven-and-a-half-cent raise?' sung with exactly the same precision, verbosity and gumption as 'Oh, What a Beautiful Mornin''. Adler and Ross were protégés of Frank Loesser, and their songs shared his relaxed, six-in-the-morning spontaneity. Future Broadway legends choreographer Bob Fosse and producer Hal Prince worked on the show, both of whom would get progressively more heavyweight over the next twenty years. Maybe Ross was the one with the light touch, but we'll never know: after one more show co-composed with Adler, 1955's equally joyous *Damn Yankees*, he died of a lung infection, aged twenty-nine.

The Pajama Game – with union shenanigans, factory-floor gossip, 'Hey There' and a bull-headed (but depressingly handsome) boss – was perfect movie material for Doris Day, one to follow 1953's *Calamity Jane*, in which the hard-hitting messages about class and race that Hammerstein was so keen to promote were comically trumped by the hysterical attempts to feminise 'Calam' against her will. James O'Hanlon's screenplay and Sammy Fain and Paul Francis Webster's songs created multiple scenes of cross-dressing and gender confusion ('Of course I'm a woman. You thought I was a *man*? Ah-hahahaha!'), without coming close to finger-wagging. The actress Frances Fryer, singing 'Hive Full of Honey', turns out to be the actor Francis Fryer in a wig and make-up. 'We don't want it!' yells a redneck when he realises what's going on. Then he pauses. 'No!' he yells even louder. 'We *don't want it*!'

By the 1960s Calamity Jane herself had become a gay liberation pin-up, and 'Secret Love' an anthem for people who were still on the wrong side of legality. Underpinning this playful subversion, Fain and Webster's score was all killer: it mixed the intensely catchy and upbeat ('The Deadwood Stage', 'I Can Do Without You'), vaudeville songs that sounded decidedly saucy ('It's Harry I'm Planning to Marry', 'Keep It Under Your Hat') and drop-dead-gorgeous ballads ('Secret Love', 'The Black Hills of Dakota').

No one felt short-changed. Even a piece of blatant exposition like 'Just Blew in from the Windy City' had a life of its own. Roll over, Oscar Hammerstein, tell George O'Dowd the news – this was rich in subversion *and* funny with it. OK, so it ends with a double wedding sequence, but it was 1953, and anyway that's over and done with in thirty seconds. No one would have guessed at the time that decades later, *Calamity Jane* would be studied for its gender politics, while the morbid earnestness of *South Pacific* would be good for nothing much beyond karaoke turns of 'I'm Gonna Wash That Man Right Out of My Hair'.

One of Rodgers and Hammerstein's other traits – setting musicals in old-timey America – led not only to *Calamity Jane*, but also convinced a couple of familiar yet unlikely faces to join the parade. Irving Berlin had once said, 'I hate that term "integrated score". If you have a great song, you can always integrate it into any show.' In 1945 Dorothy and Herbert Fields called him in at short notice, following Jerome Kern's unexpected death, to write a musical about Wild West sharp-shooter Annie Oakley. They then sat back in wonder as the master came up with 'Doin' What Comes Naturally', 'Anything You Can Do I Can Do Better' and 'There's No Business Like Show Business'. In theory, any of them could have fitted just as easily into an Astaire and Rogers high-society Manhattan setting as *Annie Get Your Gun*, but happily no one seemed to notice. The show was total entertainment, with none of *Carousel*'s existential drag. Richard Rodgers called it the greatest show score ever written.

Similarly disinclined, Cole Porter had always shown zero interest in writing songs to fit a book. So in 1948 he was an extremely left-field choice for Bella Spewack's musical adaptation of *The Taming of the Shrew*. 'I swore it could not be done,' Porter said, feeling both cut off from the new heaviness of Rodgers and Hammerstein and intimidated by the source material. Spewack told him to think of it as Yiddish theatre, with a younger sister unable to marry until her older sister gets hitched. He came back with 'Always True to You in My Fashion' and 'Too Darn Hot', two of his best songs in years, and *Kiss Me, Kate* was in business.

The 1950s would see both a new golden age and an over-ripening of the form. The integration of the musical took another step forward with the rise of Stephen Sondheim. Just as progressive rock bands would shun hit singles in favour of the immersion offered by a forty-minute album, so Sondheim was interested in the entirety of the show. Cole Porter or Irving Berlin would have measured the success of a musical by how many weeks it ran and the number of hit songs taken from it; Sondheim's shows ran for years without one hit single emerging. His first break had come as the lyricist for Leonard Bernstein's *West Side Story*, but he preferred to work alone and considered himself a musical theatre writer, not a writer of popular songs. Every word he wrote for *West Side Story* was on the beat, with little room for jazz. It was extraordinarily formal, and in time would set musical theatre apart from popular music.

Bernstein's music for *West Side Story* (1957) was modern classical, with the emphasis on modern: the Jets were New York Italian, with a bebop vocabulary and staccato sounds; the Sharks were Latin American, their songs rhythmic and lush. With three murders on stage, this was not the New York of *On the Town*, and the music ('Somewhere', 'Maria', 'Something's Coming') had the drama and sky-scraping emotion to match. Bernstein must have thought he was mentoring Sondheim, but the lyricist didn't see it that way. 'Lenny never lectured me. He was very fond of changing my lyrics. I was twenty-five years old, he treated me like a kid! Always, that condescension was there.' Instead, Sondheim considered Oscar Hammerstein to be his 'surrogate father and mentor'.

In *Gypsy* (1959), they were still shouting from the stage like the megaphone hadn't been invented. The Warner Brothers movie was released three years later. 'Vaudeville is dead in the water,' says actor Karl Malden, more than once. The film took almost two and a half hours to make a star out of Gypsy Rose Lee and focused almost entirely on her hideous mother, giving plenty of time for us to absorb the notion that while vaudeville was dead in the water, there will always be the horror show of a pushy parent screaming in the background. The result was a musical that had the vulgarity and volume of music hall but the portentous feel of Rodgers and Hammerstein. There have been more cast recordings of *Gypsy* than any other show, yet it sets my teeth on edge.

Gypsy was the birth of Sondheim's super-enunciated, one-syllable-per-note style, which came to dominate Broadway musicals – 'In-to-the-woods-I-have-to-go.' It sounded important. It was letting us know, one syllable at a time, that in spite of Elvis and Bill Haley and whatever England was brewing up, musical theatre was not dead in the water. Whether it had anything to do with forward-looking popular culture was another question. Sondheim was probably unaware that the first Book of Common Prayer, issued by the Church of England in 1549, had stated, 'for every syllable a note, so that it may be sung distinctly and devoutly', but his approach was just as zealous. Jerry Herman was a more playful presence who blended Irving Berlin's brio and every-day touch ('We're baking pecan pies again, tonight the chicken fries again') with Busby Berkeley wham-bam choruses. *Mame* and *Hello, Dolly!* sounded ancient in the early 1960s, outrageous throwbacks to a time before Astaire, let alone Sondheim, yet the title song of the latter hogged the hit parade in early 1964, at the height of Beatlemania, because Herman was a populist.

By the mid-1960s things were different. Sondheim understood that some changes had to be made, and his solution was to wall Broadway theatres off from the rest of popular culture, to make them – he hoped – a higher art form, in the image of his mentor Hammerstein. It wasn't just that Sondheim and his followers wanted to self-isolate – after all, the likes of Harold Arlen were still writing shows like *House of Flowers* and getting little traction – but the big bands and late-night radio broadcasts that had helped to make hits out of a stage show's songs no longer existed. This was an era of rapid pop-culture progression, when even Duke Ellington was bawled out for using a big-band backdrop for his 1965 album *Concert for the Virgin Islands*. Just ten years previously, Broadway had still been a steady source of pop hits – *The Pajama Game* alone had produced two number-one hits in 1954 with 'Hey There' and 'Hernando's Hideaway' – but now it felt reactionary, conservative. The form had ossified.

It wasn't only Sondheim. Another child of Hammerstein was Sheldon Harnick, who was initially a comic-song writer. His parents had spoken in Yiddish at home to keep secrets from the kids, and in the mid-1960s Harnick turned his childhood puzzlement into *Fiddler on the Roof*. Among the ballads, *West Side Story* had 'America', contemporary and danceable, which would even speed up and mutate into a psychedelic hit single by the Nice in 1968. But *Fiddler on the Roof* was desperately

444 Let's Do It

serious, with only Topol's 'If I Were a Rich Man' emerging as a hit, monstrously out of step with what was filling discotheques in 1967.

There was still some fun to be found on Broadway. A relatively new songwriting kid on the block was Cy Coleman, though he had been around long enough to have entertained the troops in the war. In 1966 he wrote *Sweet Charity* with the by-now-veteran lyricist Dorothy Fields. It was based on Fellini's *Nights of Cabiria*, though this being an American stage show, the central character of a prostitute was replaced by a dancer. Coleman kept the faith. He thought of curtain calls and rouge as he wrote; he wouldn't write songs without having a show in one corner of his mind. He trusted that living in the here and now would make his music sound contemporary, even though he harked back to hits he had heard on the radio in the late 1930s and early '40s.

He frequently worked with lyricist Carolyn Leigh,* and they turned out their best work when they chopped the rhythms and contorted the melodies with a jazz singer in mind. The snaking, sinuously structured 'Witchcraft' was a hit for Frank Sinatra in 1959, at the height of rock 'n' roll's Top 40 omnipresence, when he had no right to be scoring hit singles. Three years later, Coleman and Leigh wrote the super-modern, super-optimistic 'The Best Is Yet to Come' ('Out of the tree of life I just picked me a plum'), based on one of Cy's most demanding piano warm-up exercises; he refused to believe it was even a real song (somehow pooh-poohing Tony Bennett's 1962 version) until he heard Frank Sinatra and Count Basie's recording of it in 1964. The Cy Coleman songs that would be best remembered were the one-dimensional roars: 'Hey, Look Me Over' could have been written for Sophie Tucker, but was instead purpose-built for Lucille Ball to belt out in the 1960 musical *Wildcat*; 'If My Friends Could See Me Now' and 'Big Spender', from *Sweet Charity*, became karaoke standards.†

* Born in the Bronx in 1926, Leigh was in many ways Dorothy Fields's successor, with a similar Algonquin sharpness and a deep romantic streak ('Young at Heart', 1954). Broadway didn't particularly inspire her, but her own tough upbringing did; one of her best lyrics is the hard but accepting 'The Rules of the Road', recorded by Nat King Cole with Billy May in 1963.
† Beyond Cy Coleman and Alan Jay Lerner, and into the 1970s, there would

By the late 1960s Broadway shows were being released on the Columbia Masterworks and RCA Red Seal labels, as if Glenn Gould were trying his hand at *Oliver!* It was a way of keeping the Great White Way immune to the passage of time. There were attempts to realign Broadway with popular culture through 'rock operas' that mostly had little to do with either rock or opera. *Hair* (1968) managed to acknowledge the existence of hippies and feature on-stage nudity, yet was still a massive hit thanks to its groovy, hit-laden score: the title song ('Grow it! Show it!') was a US number-two hit for family band the Cowsills; the ditsy 'Good Morning Starshine' would go on to be performed by Petula Clark, the Strawberry Alarm Clock and Bob from *Sesame Street*; Nina Simone tore through 'Ain't Got No – I Got Life' and had a British Top 3 hit in 1969; and biggest of all was 'The Age of Aquarius', a US number-one single for the Fifth Dimension in 1969. *Hair* engaged with modern pop, with drugs and Vietnam and sex, and was a genuine smash hit – the cast recording sold three million copies. It was raucous, not at all prissy, and also featured a kind of integration – racial – that Broadway sorely needed.

The wild success of *Hair* led to a brief flurry of left-field Broadway musicals. *Earl of Ruston* (1971) was about an average guy called Earl from a small town called Ruston, and that was pretty much it. The country-based score detailed how he was ill, checked himself out of the hospital, then died at home. 'He just wanted to go home,' wails a chorus. 'He just wanted to go . . . [big pause] . . . home.' It felt like a Dadaist experiment in minimising a storyline to the point where it doesn't exist. In its own way *Earl of Ruston* was remarkable and, unsurprisingly, it closed within a week. A brace of musicals capitalising on rock's brief dalliance with Christianity in 1970 ('Let It Be', 'Spirit in the Sky', 'My Sweet Lord') were noticeably bigger: America produced *Godspell*, which had a solitary memorable song in 'Day by Day', while Britain came

---

be Kander and Ebb, who wrote *Cabaret* and *Chicago*, big theatrical hits full of memorable songs (that 'Razzle Dazzle' dates from 1975 blows my mind). They weren't entirely disengaged from modern conversation: the edge of fascism in *Cabaret* was grimly topical, while Sally Bowles's image fed into the nascent glam rock scene, even if the music didn't.

up with *Jesus Christ Superstar* (both 1970). The latter was riddled with hits: the title song was an instant playground singalong, with words changed appropriately to include jokes about bras; 'I Don't Know How to Love Him' had the feel of a French hymn and was covered with serenity by Petula Clark; while the organ-led 'What's the Buzz' and grubby-riffed 'Heaven on Their Minds' suggested underground club scenes from Hammer movies (this was a good thing). *Jesus Christ Superstar* encouraged critics to consider its writers – Tim Rice and Andrew Lloyd Webber – as Britain's kings of rock opera. They had already scored a surprise religio-musical hit with the school-friendly *Joseph and the Amazing Technicolor Dreamcoat*, as well as writing and producing psychedelic pop flops for Ross Hannaman and Tales of Justine. Unlike *Hair*, there was no nudity in *Jesus Christ Superstar*; ultimately, it was still closer to *Pirates of Penzance* amateur dramatics than actual rock music. Still, it suggested an intriguing future for the British musical. (We'll encounter Rice and Lloyd Webber again later.)

Broadway survived, then, on its own peculiar terms. The notion of going to see a show, making a night of it, has never gone away. Revivals of *Oklahoma!* and *Hair* have shown how not only the form has endured, but also its biggest hits. Stephen Sondheim would receive the Presidential Medal of Freedom from Barack Obama at the White House in 2015; he would have shrugged at my indifference to his work and to Hammerstein's solemnity. Myself, I'm happy sniggering along to *42nd Street* on TV or singing 'Whip-crack-away' with my five-year-old sitting on my back. Oscar Hammerstein had a philosophy – and the trophies to back it up – but Irving Berlin had a better one: 'Trouble's just a bubble and the clouds will soon roll by. So let's have another cup of coffee, and let's have another piece of pie.'

39

SQUEEZE ME: VOCAL JAZZ

When you clap your hands or tap your feet on the second and
fourth beat of the bar, that is jazz.
   Alan Jay Lerner

A jazz singer simply makes whatever he or she sings swing.
Ethel Merman was not a jazz singer. Doris Day is.
   Whitney Balliett

When we talk about jazz vocalists, we are usually talking about women.
The 1950s was the first time women really came to the fore in jazz – and
pretty much the first time they come to the fore in this whole story, so
it's worth dwelling on the best names.

   What had it meant to be a canary, the girl singer in an all-male big
band? How did it feel to be Peggy Lee or Dinah Washington, loaded
with talent and energy, and only getting to sing two or three songs a

night? The band was the star in the 1930s and early '40s; you had to sit by the side of the stage until you were called.

Many bandleaders – not to mention swing fans – thought of their vocalists as an insignificant concession to the listeners who wanted a lyric to sing along to. They did not consider them integral to the ensemble at all. The Musicians' Union strike – and the resulting a cappella discs – had pushed singers to the fore, but there was also the development of small groups, like Benny Goodman's sextet. When Peggy Lee sang 'Where or When' with Goodman in 1941, she had been more than just a part of this cosier ensemble; she was the absolute heart of it. This wasn't about ten silver saxes and dancefloor-ready arrangements; this was music designed for careful listening. What Lee, Anita O'Day and June Christy had in common was a private, intimate style, a new thing in pop after years of being canaries and having to project, unsupported, while standing in front of a blaring horn section. Cut loose from their big-band perch in the 1940s, they became some of the finest jazz singers of the '50s. Finally, they had agency. With this new freedom, it seemed like dozens, scores, maybe hundreds of fine new singers emerged, happily coinciding with the birth of the album and the new hi-fi generation of record fans.

For a while, it felt like there was an endless supply of jazz vocal albums – almost always by women – which featured moody shots, a handsome font and a glossy, full-colour, thick card sleeve. None of them looked like an unmade bed; these records looked wantable. The best of them had a jazz musician's phrasing, melded with woodwinds or strings, or just the small combo sound of brushed drums, piano and strolling stand-up bass. On up-tempo records, the sound was a clear continuation of swing, with the added benefit of recording-tape technology. Swing may no longer have been pop's dominant force, but as with disco three decades later, it had become part of the musical language, pervasive and assimilated, the palette rather than the paint. The best post-war vocal jazz albums still sound entirely modern.

Vocal jazz also benefited from jazz's bifurcation into traditional and modern, and the hardening attitudes on both sides – 'the beret-and-dark-glasses boys and the mouldy figs', as Philip Larkin called them. Many jazz fans had lost touch with the music – and, almost certainly, with their record collections – during the war. Trying to reacquaint himself in the early 1950s, the Bix-loving Larkin found that trad had developed a 'slightly unreal archaism', while modern caused him 'disbelief, alarm . . . Something fundamentally awful had taken place to ensure that there should be no more tunes.' On hearing Charlie Parker, Battersea pianist George Shearing wrote, 'America has gone mad!' Working with a singer at centre stage, an arranger or musician could stay in touch with all of the chunks splintering from the jazz glacier; you remained in touch with everyday human life, you were relatable. Unsurprisingly, the move towards vocal jazz in the early 1950s also went down very well with the general public.

* * *

Ella Fitzgerald was regarded as being in a class of her own. Her only rival among the deep-jazz cognoscenti – essentially white audiences – was Sarah Vaughan, who had originally been with the proto-modern Earl Hines band, then Billy Eckstine's, and went solo in 1944, when she was just twenty years old; by March 1953 *Tan* magazine was calling her 'the nation's number one female vocalist!' Her pitch-perfect voice sounded almost electronic in its accuracy, a human theremin with its swoops and bends; when it reached the lower notes, it sounded closer to a clarinet. It was truly uncanny, highly impressive, and somehow seemed closer to modern classical music than pop. Technically, she was beyond compare. On a real, emotional level, she had plenty of rivals.

At the gutsier, bluesy end were Della Reese, Carmen McRae and, toughest of the lot, Bessie Smith's heir apparent Dinah Washington; at the softer, lounge-bar end there was a sliding scale from Dakota Staton and Ethel Ennis to Anita O'Day and June Christy, gliding smoothly down to Jeri Southern, the Mogadon queen Chris Connor and, ultimately, the whispering saucepot Julie London, who purred more than she sang.

Dinah Washington was simply known as 'the Queen' – queen of the jukeboxes, queen of the crossover hit. 'She had a voice that was like the pipes of life,' said Quincy Jones. 'She could take any melody in her hand, hold it like an egg, crack it open, fry it, let it sizzle, reconstruct it, put the egg back in the box and back in the refrigerator, and you would've still understood every single syllable of every single word she sang.' The amount of sass in her voice was quite overpowering. No question, she owned Noël Coward's 'Mad About the Boy' – no one else will ever be able to go near it. She was nineteen years old when she first sang with vibes player Lionel Hampton's band in 1943, having been given solo spots in church since she was fifteen. Hampton described her as 'raggedy' when they started out – Dinah had been borrowing her mother's nylons to get work in nightclubs – and his band would rib her about her weight, leaving Dinah with ongoing issues. Still, her very first publicity shot found her in high heels and a dress with a slit up the side, her hair in a pageboy cut with a gardenia pinned to it. Not only did she look far from raggedy, she was also clearly taking her cues from Billie Holiday.

Jet magazine featured her as a cover star in 1953, with the tag line 'Famous blues singer is all time favourite recording star'.* Labelled as a blues singer, she was effectively hemmed in, ignored by *DownBeat* and other magazines, until she tore the 1955 Newport Jazz Festival apart. The record that truly established her with a white audience was 1959's 'What a Difference a Day Makes', with its celestial string arrangement, wonderfully high on love, which won Washington a Grammy. She began to earn more money; she began to spend more, on the occasional mink but mostly on her family. According to her attorney, future mayor of New York David Dinkins, the IRS was basically camped out in his office. There was a brace of hit duets with Brook Benton ('A Rockin' Good Way', 'Baby, You've Got What It Takes') and a UK success with 'September in the Rain'. And then suddenly she was gone, killed by an accidental overdose of sedatives just before Christmas 1963. Her bassist Paul West described her as 'a very lonesome person, afraid to be alone, a little girl caught in a storm, can't find shelter. That's when I realized

---

* Washington racked up twenty-seven Top 10 hits on the R&B chart between 1948 and 1955, with 'Am I Asking Too Much' (1948) and 'Baby Get Lost' (1949) both reaching number one.

how vulnerable she was, as opposed to this image she presents onstage, an image offering her protection.'

Carmen McRae was another huge admirer of Billie Holiday, and had even got her heroine to record one of her own songs – 'Dream of Life' – in 1939, when McRae was still a teenager. After working as a pianist, with occasional stints in the Benny Carter and Count Basie bands, she finally signed to Decca as a solo singer in 1956 and cut a swathe of lounge jazz albums. 1957's *After Glow* was the pick, McRae always hanging just behind the beat, with knowing, sensuous curlicues on songs like Richard Whiting and Leo Robin's 'I Can't Escape from You', and with only a piano, brushed drums and bass to support her. She even recorded a whole album of Noël Coward songs, 1958's orchestrated *Mad About the Girl*, and it turned out they were perfectly matched on the dry cynicism of something like 'World Weary' – 'I could kiss the railroad tracks.'

Almost uniquely, McRae carried on cutting contemporary material, making modern and emotionally powerful records right through the 1970s. Her 1976 rewrite of James Taylor's 'Music', from his largely soporific *Gorilla* album, is the sound of a bar to which Warren Beatty and Julie Christie might go for a secret liaison. She slayed Carole Bayer Sager's 'Come in from the Rain' on her 1980 album *I'm Coming Home Again* with an extraordinarily sensual performance, thunderclouds hovering above, McRae waiting in the doorway, head cocked and with a soulful smile. Someone once described her singing to me as 'extremely romantic': they were being overly English.

* * *

If McRae or Washington slipped, there were plenty of rivals-in-waiting, talented women whose arrangements and voices were imaginative and seductive, and yet who are now largely forgotten.

Take Toni Harper, who had begun as a child star. Back in 1945 her unnervingly mature voice had earned her a spot at the same Los Angeles theatre where Judy Garland had been discovered. She appeared on an early Ed Sullivan TV show in 1949, then in 1955, aged eighteen, hit the jazz big time when she recorded *Toni Harper Sings* with the Oscar Peterson Trio for Verve. It's a wonderfully warm record, and Harper went on to record two more fine albums with Marty Paich, toured Japan with saxophonist Cannonball Adderley in 1963, before retiring completely in 1969, aged just thirty-two. Chicago singer Lurlean Hunter was singing in clubs before the war, accompanying big bands, and she cut four albums between 1956 and 1960 with such ace arrangers as Al Nevins, Quincy Jones (who described her voice as 'like clothing') and Al Cohn. Cohn also worked with the lovely Irene Kral, a regular vocalist on *The Steve Allen Show* in 1959. This led to a brace of fine albums for United Artists; two years later, Kral moved to Tarzana, California, to raise a family, and she was off the scene until the mid-1970s. 'Now when I'm old enough to appreciate them,' she sighed, 'almost all the really good bands are gone.'*

Plenty of talented singers had just one or two cracks at fame. Sally Blair made it into *Variety*'s 'New Acts' column in June 1956, when she debuted at the Apollo, just as 'Don't Be Cruel' was topping the *Billboard* Hot Hundred. Under the headline 'Negro songstress has the essentials for a big time break-in', *Variety* wrote about her 'sizzling gyrations . . . derriere shaking . . . her neat chassis that gets broad outlining in a skin-tight, off-the-shoulder gown', but concluded: 'It's OK for the Apollo and kindred locations but could be detrimental in classier surroundings.' She was OK for black folks, in other words, but not for what *Variety* considered its 'classier' readers. Sure enough, she made the cover of *Sepia* magazine in February 1960, but never got beyond a black audience.

You have to wonder what the nimble-voiced Ethel Ennis had to do to keep her name in the papers. A lifelong Democrat, she sang an a cappella 'God Bless America' for Richard Nixon's inauguration that stopped the clocks, recorded the cod-Bond theme for the 1967 movie *Mad Monster Party* and sang with Louis Armstrong, Benny Goodman, Duke Ellington and Miles Davis. She had emerged from Baltimore, Billie Holiday's home town, aged twenty-two, with her minimal 1955 debut, *Lullabies*

---

* Nevertheless, she cut a trio of small-group albums, including 1977's neatly titled *Kral Space*, before her untimely death in 1978.

for Losers. Ennis later heard that Lady Day was asking, 'Who's this new bitch from Baltimore?' One night, her hairdresser called to say that she had Billie Holiday on the line. Ennis snorted, but then heard a familiar voice: 'I like your voice. You're a musician's musician – you don't fake. Stay with it, and you'll be famous.' Ennis never became famous; unusually, fame really held no interest for her, which explains the slightly quizzical, laughing look she holds on almost every record cover. For many years she didn't even want to perform outside of Baltimore. Her legacy was a happy family and a small catalogue of near-perfect albums (top tip: 1964's *Eyes for You*), so who's to say she was wrong?

Who sold the most records? Quite possibly Julie London, who was content to smoulder on a series of album covers that, unquestionably, helped her sales to go through the roof and in turn established the newly formed Liberty Records. *Billboard* listed her as the most popular female vocalist in 1955, 1956 and 1957. A statuesque blonde who occasionally even dressed up as a scantily clad Greek statue, London had been a humble elevator operator when she was discovered by Hollywood (I'd guess by someone bald and half her height). She went on to specialise in playing mean girls but was still pretty alluring. Her most significant film appearance was as a sultry ghost in *The Girl Can't Help It*, in which she sang 'Cry Me a River', a track from her first album, written by an ex-boyfriend. It became a huge hit single; the rest of the score was unfiltered rock 'n' roll, but who could resist spectral Julie? Her twenty-odd albums over the next fifteen years were largely interchangeable; all perfect 11 p.m. soundtracks, the one with the best title was *Nice Girls Don't Stay for Breakfast*. Just in case you didn't think there was anything tongue-in-cheek about her work or her opinion of herself, she recorded a seductive, quarter-speed cover of the Ohio Express's bubblegum hit 'Yummy Yummy Yummy' in 1968. When the nightclub circuit closed to her in the 1970s, she got a role as a nurse in TV's *Emergency!* and spent the rest of her time with her kids in her Encino home, inviting over friends like Frank Sinatra and Donny Osmond. It must have been fun being Julie London.

She didn't sell anywhere near as heavily as Julie London, but one of the very best singers was Helen Merrill, who said she preferred to be 'a voice within the music rather than being accompanied'. Her voice was 80 per cent vapour, an all-enveloping sound, like a sea mist. She used her voice as an instrument, and while there was a lot of Sarah Vaughan in her delivery, her idols were saxophonists – Ben Webster, Lester Young, Johnny Hodges. She said her mother, from the Croatian island of Krk, was her biggest influence: 'She felt music from a very spiritual place. A private place that was all her own. This kind of music can have no teacher.' Quincy Jones played on her 1954 debut and convinced Claude Thornhill's arranger Gil Evans to come out of semi-retirement for Merrill's exquisite *Dream of You* in 1956. Her recording career was as hard to pin down as air, and she was peripatetic, flitting from a bad romance in New York and heading to Italy (where she recorded with Ennio Morricone), and then Japan, where she is still regarded very highly indeed; their nickname for her is the 'Sigh of New York'.

Quincy Jones also worked with Shirley Horn, a fine pianist who likewise could do extraordinarily seductive things with her breathy tones, beginning with her 1960 debut *Embers and Ashes*. Unlike Merrill, Horn's voice, and her piano, were the whole story; everything else was garnish. She could swing hard, but her reputation was made by tracks like Howard Dietz and Arthur Schwartz's 'Confession', an almost embarrassingly sexual piece of music: 'I always go to bed at ten, oh isn't that a bore?' she sings, half an inch from your face, all satin and perfume, and you'd roll your eyes if she hadn't got you completely absorbed, almost holding your breath. When the Beatles took over and everybody was living in their world, Ella Fitzgerald cut 'These Boots Are Made for Walking', and Peggy Lee worked on Kinks and Lovin' Spoonful songs. Horn, though, would do nothing of the sort: 'I will not stoop to conquer,' she said, stubbornly sticking to what were by now jazz standards.*

Blossom Dearie was something else. Unlike Shirley Horn or Helen Merrill, there was no earth, wind or fire in her voice. Instead, she sounded girlish and naive, and her quizzical eyebrows and askew glasses

---

* It was a moot point, given that she recorded only one album between 1965 and 1978. That was *Where Are You Going*, which included pre-rock titles like 'A Taste of Honey' but also the entirely modern – in the year of Roberta Flack's breakthrough – 'LA Breakdown' and 'Consequences of a Drug Addict Role'.

as she sat at the piano went beyond the far-out pixie image her name suggested; she looked like she had been drawn by Charles Schulz. No matter, her recordings were high urban romanticism, and her repertoire dug into lesser-known Broadway shows and pulled out gold. Broadway hadn't been killed off by high seriousness after all, it transpired. As late as 1975 she co-wrote 'I'm Shadowing You' with Johnny Mercer, and it was delicious, backed by nothing more than electric piano and skipping brushed drums. Off the cabaret stage, Dearie lived in an apartment filled with sheet music. She was warm and modest, quite happy in the knowledge that she was a true original and very good indeed.

If push comes to shove, in a crowded field, Nebraska-born pianist–singer Jeri Southern gets my vote. Like Helen Merrill, she felt detached from the smoke rings and gentle hubbub of bars and clubs; her music helped her to escape into her own private world. Though she had a smoky, melancholy and quite individual voice, Southern's name is largely forgotten. Partly this is because she gave up performing and recording in 1962, while still in her thirties, after years of paralysing stage fright. Just the thought of going on stage or seeing her name in lights made her enormously anxious. She hated performing in front of anyone; even her daughter Kathryn had to sneak into the room to hear her practising Beethoven sonatas and Debussy's *Images*, or improvising and composing her own melodies, which no one else would ever hear.

Two of her own songs did appear on *The Southern Style*, her second album, released in 1955. It was an unadorned affair, but the tangible warmth of the recording stems from the notion that Southern was playing for her own pleasure, becoming totally lost in songs such as the atmospheric 'I'll Wear the Green Willow'. She sang in something close to her speaking voice, with no obvious mannerisms, which – given her extreme shyness – could create an almost unsettling intimacy. Like Nat King Cole, she believed in finding the right interpretation of a song and sticking with it. No scat-singing for Jeri Southern.

She could do playful too – on standards such as 'Let's Fall in Love' and 'It's De-Lovely' – but she was at her best when yearning, anxious or in despair. Take Johnny Mercer's 'Too Marvellous for Words': Frank Sinatra's version sounded ring-a-ding happy, as if he had just emerged from his new belle's house at 7 a.m.; Doris Day had sung it with her beaming face turned to heaven; Jeri Southern sounded in complete awe. Her piano chords should have been there to underpin her voice, but instead they seemed on edge. When she sang, 'It's all too wonderful,' she was implicitly suggesting panic, quite aware that it really was too wonderful to last.

Dave Barbour, Peggy Lee's arranger and former husband, provided the cello, splash cymbals and bongos on another of *The Southern Style*'s highlights, the eerie 'One Day I Wrote His Name Upon the Sand', and his arrangement ended up sounding closer to late-1960s chamber folk than anything from the early '50s. Of her self-composed recordings, 'My Letters' was extraordinary, with a wayward, restless chord structure underneath a spooked lyric about 'dead paper, mute and white'.

Singing aside, Nat King Cole also rated Southern as one of the great pianists. She would end up more popular in Britain than in the US – American stars almost never travelled to the UK in the 1950s, so her stage fright didn't count against her – and even scored a Top 30 hit in the UK with 'Fire Down Below' in 1957. It's a nice record, with a peppy Latin backing, but not a patch on the eeriness of 'I'll Wear the Green Willow' or 'My Letters'. At a time when a singer's worth was often measured by the cost of their gowns or the size of their orchestra, records such as 'Fire Down Below' were closer to the norm. We should be grateful that *The Southern Style* even exists, recorded in much the same way as she would have played in clubs, backed by only a small rhythm section and her own piano.

When the photo calls and the blare of orchestration started to bore her, Southern quit. After she died in 1991, jazz promoter and former Chess Records executive Dick LaPalm said: 'More people should have known about her. She should have stayed, remained in show business and gotten the recognition she deserved.' I know what he means, but I'm pleased for her that she let the weight of expectation go and liberated herself. Southern spent the rest of her life giving piano lessons by day and smoking and drinking beers with her friends by night.

* * *

Stan Kenton's operation uncovered three of the biggest names in vocal jazz: Anita O'Day, who quit his band in 1945; June Christy, who stayed until 1953; and Chris Connor. All three are like characters in a film noir: the wisecracking hard nut, the shy girl next door and the ice-cool blonde.

O'Day was sassy and confident. She drank, she drugged, she ended up in jail and could not care less. 'I sort of became one of the guys because that was the only way to play it,' she recalled in the 1980s. 'I mean, I guess you could play it "girl". But I haven't played "girl" yet. Let's see, I'm sixty-eight. I've been wearing slacks since 1932.' She had been with Gene Krupa's band and recorded the thrilling back-and-forth vocal on 'Let Me Off Uptown' with trumpeter Roy Eldridge, which had sold a million in 1941: 'If it's pleasure you're about and you feel like stepping out, oh, you've got to shout it – let me off uptown! If it's rhythm that you feel, then it's nothing to conceal, oh you've got to spiel it – let me off uptown!' Her life didn't change overnight, 'because at that time there was no union for girl singers. I made $7.50. [Krupa] built a house in Yonkers!' She was always smiling a very knowing smile when she sang and looked like a hipster Barbara Stanwyck. Along with Mel Tormé, she pretty much invented the cool jazz vocal, holding a botched tonsillectomy as a child responsible for her inability to hold long notes; it was patently untrue, but she was always good for a yarn. In 1952 she cut a song of her own called 'Rock 'n' roll Blues', which, aside from a dab of scat towards the end, and Roy Eldridge on trumpet sounding like the entire *Aristocats* band, was mostly definitely a forerunner of the teen wave three or four years hence. Her phrasing was outrageous, super-percussive, and the cool breath from her voice always hit you before the note.

No snob, she liked to record 'songs that ordinary people as well as jazz buffs liked'. When she appeared in the 1958 Newport Jazz Festival movie *Jazz on a Summer's Day*, she stole the show singing 'Sweet Georgia Brown', wearing a big picture hat with real ostrich feathers and white gloves that came up to her elbows. Was she high? asked a prurient interviewer. 'I would say, yes,' laughed O'Day. People would come to gawp at the jailbird on stage, and she thought it was fine – more bums on seats.

The freewheeling Anita O'Day. She lived to be eighty-seven and was a walking advert for fun and positivity.

O'Day's stay with the highly regimented Kenton band had been just long enough to cut another monster hit, 'And Her Tears Flowed Like Wine', in 1944, but she got sick of singing it every night. 'We were in the middle of a job in St Louis,' Kenton recalled, 'and all of a sudden Anita comes up to me and says, "I've had it!" And I said, "You've had what?" She says, "I'm leaving!" I said, "You're leaving right now?" She says, "Right now!" So I said, "So long," and she walked off the bandstand.' She hung around to give her timid-looking replacement the once-over. O'Day already regarded June Christy as a soundalike; she looked at her similar hairdo and laughed, 'And bangs too?'

Christy had a naivety that O'Day never possessed. In 1945 – twenty years old, out of work and 'living on tuna fish sandwiches in Chicago' – she heard a rumour that O'Day had quit and presented Kenton with a tape. He liked it; his only issue was her real name – Shirley Luster – which he thought 'sounded something like a hair-shampoo'. So she became clean-haired, sad-eyed, anxious June Christy; if she had been English, she could have played Pinky's girlfriend in *Brighton Rock*. She always sounded slightly nervous, never fully surrendering to a song in case her tuning wobbled (which it often did, and this was a large part of her charm). For this reason, jazz-heads are less likely to side with Christy in an argument than with her predecessor or successor. She never learned to read music and had no training at all, which gave her husky voice a highly personal style. Her 1954 solo debut *Something Cool*, with a title that telegraphed its intent, sold in huge numbers. She had a permanent look of fighting back tears, and you would listen to an album, willing her on. This didn't mean she couldn't turn winter into spring with albums like *Gone for the Day* (its gorgeous leafy cover representing the freshness of 'It's a Most Unusual Day' and 'Give Me the Simple Life') or *The Cool School* (essentially vocal jazz for kids, but a grown-up treat too). You'll feel a tug when Christy sings 'mashed potatoes' on 'Give Me the Simple Life' and imagine her jumper snagging on the mike stand.

Chris Connor, with her white blonde hair and peachy skin, seemed to physically glow and didn't lack for confidence. She was the Kim Novak of the crowd, the huskiest of the Kenton three, but with a positive force that came across like the bright sliver of light through curtains in the morning. Two years younger than Christy, she replaced her as Kenton's main vocalist in 1954, but went solo after just one year. On her own, Connor was an instant success: one week in 1955, her first two albums – *Lullabys of Birdland* and *Lullabys for Lovers* – were numbers one and two on the *Billboard* jazz chart. She went on to record almost twenty albums for the Atlantic label between 1956 and 1962; they are exquisite, inexpensive and always worth picking up. In between her sets at the Birdland club on Broadway she would nip across the road to Colony Records and look for material to work on. She was devoted, and it came across on her 1956 album *He Loves Me, He Loves Me Not*, a cool, crisp career peak.

Anita O'Day's performance may have been the highlight of *Jazz on a Summer's Day*, but the future arrived with the closing set from Chuck Berry and his electric guitar – the first amplified instrument that anyone had used all day. He sang 'Sweet Little Sixteen', and it sounded crude, rubbed raw, juvenile and messy in comparison to everything around it. But its physical drive, its boisterous *joie de vivre* were undeniable. He sounded more like a descendant of the Original Dixieland Jazz Band, with their motley percussion boxes and rhythmic anarchy.

Some days, it isn't so hard to see why rock 'n' roll pissed off so many people. Vocal jazz, an urbane, sophisticated music, a luscious new American art form, would be swept aside by self-sufficient guitar bands. Unless these singers had already hit the big time – the TV and radio and sponsorship tie-in big time – unless they were bigger at any rate than Anita O'Day, whose career tanked in the mid-1960s, then their careers would be badly wounded by rock 'n' roll. They would then be killed off by the speed, volume and rapid innovation of the Beatles age. The enormous intimacy of their music – best appreciated with a warm brandy (preferably in a Finnish glass) in a hushed room, while reclining on a Hans Wegner sofa – would simply be trampled underfoot.

40

EXPERIMENTS WITH MICE:
BRITISH BIG BANDS

In America, the big-band era had never been allowed to peak, swell and become overripe. Strikes and the end of World War II prematurely accounted for it. In Britain, though, it entered its peak phase after the war, still blasting away on the deck in the mid-1950s, while the ship's crew plotted revolution below.

A remarkable number of the 1930s heroes were operating on the main stage in the late '40s. Joe Loss, Lew Stone, Bert Ambrose, Billy Cotton and Harry Roy were all still working, still getting BBC airplay, and were generally popular. Far from shrinking, by the 1950s the British band scene had added new star attractions. In 1952 the BBC formed its own show band under the direction of Cyril Stapleton, a Nottingham-born violin player who had first played with Henry Hall. After the war, he played with the London Symphony Orchestra, before building his own band in 1947, and he was soon regarded as a dependable fixture on the scene; indeed, Frank Sinatra chose Stapleton's set-up to back him when he was in town. Stapleton players who became names in their own right included pianist Bill 'Scruffy' McGuffie, singer Matt Monro and guitarist Bert Weedon, whose *Play in a Day* book would contribute to bringing down the curtain on the British big-band era. Stapleton's recorded output was more varied and intriguing than his BBC band work might suggest: his version of 'Blue Star', the theme from the TV show *Medic*, was a thing of wispy beauty, McGuffie's cascading piano parts lifted into the ether by Julie Dawn's ghostly vocal; 'The Italian Theme' was 1950s British exotica *in excelsis*, an insistent, impossible-to-ignore harpsichord melody that suggested black coffee and polka-dot skirts, sounding 'foreign' but no more genuinely Italian than Peter Sellers's accent in *The Wrong Arm of the Law*.

Johnny Dankworth started the Dankworth Seven in 1951 and expanded to a full orchestra two years later. His sound was cooler, in both the west coast sense and in terms of knowing nods. Their first press release described them as 'couth, kempt and shevelled'. The Dankworth band was jazz-inclined, as opposed to being strictly for the dancefloor, but straddled both worlds; in another era they would have been called 'underground' or 'alternative'. Dankworth remembered the band as 'tre-mendously popular in a minority sort of way. 10 per cent of the three thousand people who turned up really listened very carefully; most of them wanted to dance or be sociable or find a girl. Nevertheless, they got to be brainwashed by our sort of music, and we became quite pop-ular as a result of that.'

Their popularity led to a thirty-nine-week radio series: ninety min-utes every Wednesday on the BBC Light Programme. Showing their smarts, each week the band would play 'Three Blind Mice' in a different jazz style – Gerry Mulligan, Sauter-Finegan, Stan Kenton, Glenn Miller ('He was a romantic little mouse,' squeaked Dankworth), Billy May, Benny Goodman . . . This shtick led to an unlikely Top 10 hit record in 1956, under the title 'Experiments with Mice'. When he wasn't showing off, Dankworth wrote some terrific British swing in the 1950s. 'Cole Storage', for example, neatly fused small-group bass, brushed drums, ticklish piano and paint-stripping brass.

Dankworth's wasn't the only outfit to manage the occasional hit record. The biggest British band, undoubtedly, was that of Ted Heath, the veteran trombonist for Geraldo, who had formed his own band in 1944, when he was already in his forties. He became a regular on the early *NME* hit parades with 'Vanessa' (1953), 'Hot Toddy' and the roaring 'Dragnet' (both 1954). Like the American bands, Heath decided to feature vocalists. His wife Moira said that he 'regarded them as a necessary evil. He didn't really want vocals, but from the point of putting on a show, for entertainment, you had to have vocalists. He was very lucky because he got Lita, who was first-class.' Liverpool-born, half-Spanish Lita Roza had got the job because Ted liked the photos she'd sent him; her smoky voice suited her ahead-of-the-curve boyish haircut. Heath's male singer, Dickie Valentine, was apparently terrified of Ted, but with some coaxing his boss made him a star; after going solo he became a major pin-up, scoring UK number ones with 'Finger of Suspicion' and 'Christmas Alphabet' in 1954.

Sharing a name with a Tory prime minister might not have helped his legacy, but Ted Heath was a cut above any of his rivals and way more adaptable than most of his American heroes, turning out a Nelson Riddle-esque finger-snapper with 'Swinging Shepherd Blues' (a Top 3 hit in 1956) and a decent version of the Champs' 'Tequila' in 1958, after rock had taken over. The best of his later 45s was 1959's 'Frog March', the sound of a giant metal Slinky falling down a flight of stairs while the band plays a TV theme for a hard-boiled East End detective.

Heath's outfit was also the only one that meant anything in the States, and they toured as a package with Nat King Cole, June Christy and the Four Freshmen (the unions worked it out as a swap for Stan Kenton's contemporaneous tour of Britain). They even did a show at Carnegie Hall, which had a touch of the improbable about it. The band could scarcely believe it was happening. Trombonist Don Lusher: 'Benny Goodman and Tommy Dorsey were there. I remember meeting Gerry Mulligan on the staircase. Everyone became quite emotional. For Ted it was a real major success – I remember seeing him with tears running down his cheeks.'

The Ted Heath Orchestra was no one's idea of confrontational, but when the tour reached the southern States, it turned ugly. They were booked to play in Birmingham, Alabama, with Nat King Cole. Ronnie Chamberlain, who played sax for Heath, recalled Cole's trio were 'absolutely scared stiff, saying, "We don't want to go there, man." We did our show first, and when Nat came on they insisted that the curtain was drawn in front of us so they couldn't see the white band accompanying this "nigger" singer, as they called him. That's how they talked down there – "Are you with this nigger group?" We couldn't believe it.' At one point a man ran down the aisle, jumped onto the stage 'and was on top of Nat and got him on the floor. The concert stopped immediately and we all went off. I felt really sick and went outside and puked, it frightened me so much.'

Previously the star drummer of the Ted Heath band, Jack Parnell struck out on his own in 1951. Back in 1933, when he was ten, Parnell had been taken to see Duke Ellington's band at the Palladium. He had been overwhelmed, and thereafter bought every Ellington record he could afford as it came out, with the drum-led 'Skin Deep' a favourite. Parnell recordings like 'The Hawk Talks' (from the great 1958 album *Trip to Mars*) were American-inspired but clearly British-made, and the band's twin-drummer line-up – with Parnell and Phil Seamen – anticipated Adam and the Ants. 'It was a very smooth band,' said Parnell, 'very good, very accurate, and we had great players.' He wasn't kidding: Seamen, Don Lusher (who followed Parnell out of the Ted Heath band), pianist Max Harris and sax players Ronnie Scott and Pete King were the cream of the British crop. 'We decided to go out on the road and we did very well, all the time,' said the pragmatic Parnell. 'I never made the money Ted Heath made but I made a very good living and kept sixteen men together.' They could blend modernism with their big brass blasts – take 'Cottontail' or 'Catherine Wheel' (both 1958). Parnell ended up working on ITV shows and recording library music for KPM, a one-man link between Duke Ellington, Russell Harty and *The Muppet Show*.

Ray Ellington (no relation) was another bridge between the old world and the new. Born to an African American father and a Russian Orthodox–Jewish mother in working-class Kennington, he had got his first break as a drummer in Harry Roy's band in 1937. He was also the featured vocalist on 'Swing for Sale', which swung more freely than any other British record in 1938. After the war, Ellington's own band added a comedy element and ended up in residence on the Goons' radio show. But Ellington was cool, a Louis Jordan fan who could sniff the incoming rhythm-and-blues revolution – his was the first British band to include an electric guitar – and by 1955 his outfit was stripped back to guitar, piano, bass and drums – essentially a rock 'n' roll line-up. A few years later, Ellington's guitarist, the Trinidad-born Lauderic Caton, became an informal tutor to a teenager from Newcastle called Brian Rankin, who had just moved to London and changed his name to Hank Marvin. Tectonic plates were shifting.

In his autobiography *Free Association*, the actor Steven Berkoff remembered Ellington's band as being the kings of the Tottenham Royal, where Teddy Boys and Teddy Girls – pre-rock 'n' roll – would jive to things like 'The Creep', 'Too Many Chicks' and 'Dracula's Three Daughters' – all titles that cast some distance between Ellington and the staid likes of Billy Cotton. The Royal, wrote Berkoff, 'had a particular aroma of velvet and hairspray, Brylcreem and Silvikrin lacquer, cigs, floor polish. When you entered the Royal, the band, usually Ray Ellington, would be up the far end . . . Dancing was the thing and as the clock ticked away until the terrible hour of 11 p.m. when the band would stop, you became more and more desperate to find someone you could crush for half an hour of fierce kissing and squeezing and creating sparks as your gaberdine rubbed against her taffeta.'

Bands in the mid-1950s, then, were in reasonable health; British audiences had plenty of music to listen and dance to. The advent of TV would squash the live scene considerably, as it had in America a decade earlier, but it gave the bigger names – Heath, Parnell, Stapleton – a new family-friendly platform. What's more, when you heard their albums in the comfort of your own home, the improvements in recording technology gave their sound a crispness that the American bands of the 1930s had never benefited from.

Still, even the most vigorous bands would have admitted that they based their sound heavily on American source material, and one thing the British public hadn't seen or heard for twenty years was a real-life American outfit. They'd been here in wartime, but a tour that was open to the paying public hadn't happened since the mid-1930s. You could be forgiven for thinking that there were no bands left to hear. There was one newcomer, though, whom the British public was especially keen to see. Stan Kenton had achieved remarkable success with a policy that seemed to contradict itself: making musical revolution respectable. Pete Rugolo's complex arrangements on Kenton sides like 'Intermission Riff' could sound like a chaotic blare of brass, like Tweetie Pie trying to cross Broadway in the rush hour, but they were a big influence in Britain.

One Kenton devotee was John Barry, who was doing national service in the mid-1950s, having worked as a projectionist at his dad's cinema in York, where he'd absorbed the sounds of Dimitri Tiomkin and Elmer Bernstein alike. He killed time in the army by sending off for a Stan Kenton-sponsored course on 'Composition and Orchestration for the Jazz Orchestra' by Bill Russo, who by 1955 was Kenton's main arranger. He got to practise with musicians in the camp, making his mistakes in private, and when he got out after a year, he sent his arrangements to Johnny Dankworth, Ted Heath and Jack Parnell. None used them, but Parnell advised Barry to set up his own band, don't be afraid to take the popular route, advised the sage Parnell, as there would always be time to experiment later on. And so the John Barry Seven was born. As a singer, Barry sucked, but soon he was writing brass-blare soundtracks with British rock elements for rough-cut movies like *Beat Girl* and *Never Let Go* (both 1960). Two years on, 'The James Bond Theme' was released, and the British big band had found itself both an international hit and a way forward. The John Barry Orchestra – with organist Alan Haven and guitarist Vic Flick – was about to take the British big-band sound to worldwide success. Without Stan Kenton's transatlantic correspondence course, it might never have happened.

41
REVIVAL: TRAD JAZZ AND FOLK

Britain's jazz following split itself neatly down the middle at the turn of the 1950s: one half became fascinated by new, complex jazz made by Charlie Parker and other revolutionaries, and eagerly went in pursuit; the other was much more interested in where it had come from and headed back to its roots, starting a New Orleans revival that became known as 'trad', which soundtracked 1950s Britain much more than anything modern. Scared of bop's alien futurism and turned off by light-weight hit-parade regulars like Guy Mitchell, British youth experienced its first bout of pop revivalism. Possibly coincidentally, America did much the same, but instead found solace in its own folk culture. With the Cold War entering a deep freeze, people in both countries wanted an alternative future to what their governments – and the hit parades – were offering. These alternative futures drew heavily on the past.

In 1950s Britain, where visiting American jazz acts had always been a rarity, first-wave jazz still had a raw thrill. But in '50s America, where

'Dixieland' was seen as hokey, the term itself problematic, and Louis Armstrong was now largely viewed as Bing Crosby's fishing companion, it no longer had a revolutionary texture for college kids. The same impulses that made trad so popular in Britain – rooting for the underdog, a sense of community, a sense of being alive that professionally written songs by professional singers didn't provide, the DIY thrill of amateurism, and teenage one-upmanship – led American students towards folk and country blues, gospel and labour songs. This was also music that was easy to both play and sing, and that spoke about real lives. It was simple to adapt, to rework with a topical theme, and so later down the road came Bob Dylan, who used the folk revival as a springboard for one of the greatest American stories. The kids getting into this stuff should have been natural jazz hounds, like their British cousins, but modern jazz ignored or bored them, and early-1950s pop gave them no social or aesthetic anchor. So instead they became self-taught on the Spanish guitar, learned from each other and found a new language that eventually fed into '60s pop – the Byrds, Jefferson Airplane – and then into the '70s Laurel Canyon acts.

The point at which America had to pay attention was when Leadbelly's 'Goodnight, Irene' provided the Weavers, a leftist New York folk quartet led by Pete Seeger, with a *Billboard* number-one single in 1950. Leadbelly himself, who had died a year earlier, had recorded the song first, while he was in prison. His story is most peculiar.

Huddie (pronounced like 'Judy') Ledbetter had been in Angola State Penitentiary, Louisiana, in 1933 – the year Bessie Smith made her final recordings – when musicologist and archivist John Lomax came knocking with his (barely) portable Edison cylinder machine. Lomax said he was hoping to find the true voice of southern black America, in songs that were 'the least contaminated by Negro jazz' and 'most unlike those of the white race'. He was well-intentioned, to a point. He worked for the Smithsonian rather than Columbia or Brunswick, and put in the miles to record obscure musicians who would otherwise likely be lost to history, visiting work farms and fishermen's shacks. Still, when he realised that Huddie – or Leadbelly, as his fellow inmates called him – had the voice and the songs to reach the crowds in New York, he decided to cut himself a third of all the singer's income, with another third going to his son, Alan. It would become a grim experiment in dominance and control. The Lomaxes would insist Leadbelly wore prison garb when performing, forbade him from singing anything that could be construed as white or urban, and explained his songs to the audience on stage, one at a time. For years, they forced him to sing 'rough', even though, as a musician, Leadbelly was developing and improving naturally. It was demeaning in the extreme. None of them got rich, either.

By 1939 Leadbelly was back in prison. This time, Alan Lomax, now twenty-four, left graduate school to help pay for the legal costs, and soon had Leadbelly on his new CBS radio show, *Back Where I Come From*. Co-hosted by film director Nicholas Ray and broadcast nationwide, *Back Where I Come From* was base camp for the folk scene, and other guests included Josh White, Woody Guthrie, Pete Seeger and the jazz/blues duo Sonny Terry and Brownie McGhee. At nightclubs, Leadbelly would explain the songs, something he had picked up from John Lomax on their lecture tours. This hadn't gone down well in Harlem in the 1930s, but in late-'40s Greenwich Village, it was a different story.

A spell was broken when John Lomax died of a heart attack at a party in honour of his eightieth birthday – while singing a blues piece called 'Big Leg Rose' – in January 1948. A few months later, Leadbelly was approached by a jazz historian and music critic called Fred Ramsey. Ramsey didn't see Leadbelly as some kind of zoological exhibit. The Lomaxes had recorded his songs on disc for the Library of Congress; Ramsey invited Leadbelly over for dinner and showed him the Magnecord tape recorder he had just acquired, one of the first in America, and asked if he'd like to sing a few songs. Sure, said Huddie.

One reason the session worked so well was that Ramsey could play back Leadbelly's songs on the tape recorder as he recorded them. Leadbelly could hear how good he sounded, and it encouraged him to let loose, to sing things like Gene Autry's 'Springtime in the Rockies' just because he liked it. He recorded thirty-four songs straight, a cappella, anything he felt like; the irony was that this unfiltered version of Huddie Ledbetter – no prison garb, no studious Lomax insights – was exactly what the public wanted. Ramsey's tape included 'Stewball' (later recorded by the Beatles and the Hollies), 'I Want to Go Home' (better known as 'Sloop John B'), a stomp 'n' holler called 'Black Betty' (a transatlantic hit for Ram Jam in 1977), 'Rock Island Line' (which effectively kick-started the modern pop era in Britain after Lonnie Donegan recorded it in 1954) and 'Goodnight, Irene', which became the biggest-selling record of 1950 for the Weavers. Leadbelly wouldn't live to see any of this: he died in Belle Vue hospital of Lou Gehrig's disease in December 1949.

'Goodnight, Irene' wasn't exactly Tin Pan Alley. It could be regarded as a watershed moment for the folk movement, the point at which a nascent political, roots-of-America movement was born; it was seen by others as a novelty. 'Goodnight, Irene' spawned a raucous answer song by the deliciously named Ziggy Talent called 'Please Say Goodnight to the Guy, Irene' ('and let me get some sleep!'). Frank Sinatra was strong-armed into recording a cover (which reached number five on the *Billboard* chart, his biggest hit of the era), but he loathed its repetition, monotony and simplicity, the three things that made it a hit as a group singalong. It would be adopted by Bristol Rovers fans and is still sung at their home games today,* giving it a special place in football folklore, up there with Chicory Tip's 'Son of My Father' and the White Stripes' 'Seven Nation Army'.

The Weavers' new highly public profile meant that, in the paranoid atomic age, Joseph McCarthy was on them like a ton of bricks. Everyone kept their politics a little closer to their chest, and the movement sank back underground as quickly as it had risen. Burl Ives survived the whole ordeal. He had spent the 1930s travelling with his banjo after dropping out of college, but was savvy enough to finish his education at Juilliard. By 1940 he had his own radio show, *The Wayfaring Stranger*, on which

---

* It was first sung by Rovers' fans in November 1950. Plymouth Argyle had arrived for a match at Rovers' Eastville Stadium with their own accordion player, whose job was to play popular songs to Plymouth's travelling fans before kick-off. One of the hits he played that day was 'Goodnight, Irene', best known in Britain via Jo Stafford's 1950 recording. Argyle scored first, and their fans started to sing 'Goodnight, Irene', but in the second half Rovers scored three goals in eight minutes, prompting the home fans to quickly adapt it to 'Goodnight, Argyle'.

he popularised traditional songs, including 'The Blue Tail Fly' and 'Big Rock Candy Mountain', and in 1942 a starring role in Irving Berlin's *This Is the Army* cemented his fame. Post-war – having been blacklisted, like the Weavers, for un-American activities – he co-operated with the House Un-American Activities Committee in 1952 and named names to save his neck. This taints his music, which is a real shame, because he had one of the great American voices, somehow simultaneously deep and high. Whether he's singing 'Home on the Range' or the beautiful Christmas song 'The Friendly Beasts', or even the Disney novelty 'The Ugly Bug Ball',* you can't avoid his big-rock-candy-mountain voice. He commands your full attention, like Elvis or Johnny Cash. But he was a grass. It's too bad really.†

Away from the mainstream, Woody Guthrie had been the most profound influence on folk's future, playing a guitar that had the direct message 'This machine kills fascists' painted onto it and singing about union rights, farm workers' causes and other places the hit parade just didn't visit. Guthrie represented, after too long a post-war stasis, just what the restless, Kerouac-reading generation of the 1950s wanted, rather than Tin Pan Alley entertainers from their parents' era who gently embraced jazz, or the polite Broadway politics of Oscar Hammerstein. Guthrie was non-pop, but in 1944 he recorded 'This Land Is Your Land', and it remains the closest thing to an alternative American national anthem. His music, his whole persona had real grit and in the 1950s resonated with young Americans who questioned why 'duck and cover' was being taught in schools. There had to be a better way, and Guthrie carried the torch. By the late '50s the run-down New York district of Greenwich Village had become full of Guthrie imitators and acolytes. Among them was the cuddly, ursine Dave Van Ronk, whose voice and songs were tough but tender; the Clancy Brothers, whom Bob

---

* The song has easily outlived the Disney movie it was taken from, 1963's *Summer Magic*, which only Disney nerds could name. 'Ugly Bug Ball' was one of the first Sherman brothers songs to appear in a Disney film.
† In the 1970s he was the face of America's equivalent of the 'Keep Britain Tidy' campaign; no small irony that it was called 'This Land Is Your Land – Keep It Clean'.

Dylan called 'musketeer-type characters', and who sang rebel songs in improbably strong Irish accents; and Dylan himself, a questing kid from a Minnesota mining town who absorbed the scene like a sponge.*

The fear of the atomic bomb – which would lead to Dylan's 'A Hard Rain's Gonna Fall' and Malvina Reynolds's 'What Have They Done to the Rain', both written in 1962 – had been soundtracked in Britain by the home-grown revival in Dixieland, or 'traditional', jazz. For Pete Seeger, Dave Van Ronk and Liam Clancy read Humphrey Lyttelton, Chris Barber and George Webb. Cornet player Muggsy Spanier – a veteran of Ted Lewis's and Ben Pollack's bands – had inspired a Stateside Dixieland revival in 1939, when his Ragtime Band recorded several standards for Bluebird, later compiled as *The Great Sixteen*; the revival grew in popularity when Spanier formed the Big Four quartet with the forty-three-year-old Sidney Bechet in 1940. Guitarist Eddie Condon had likewise kept the flame of New Orleans jazz burning: his shows at the New York Town Hall had, remarkably, been broadcast by the BBC,† and British trumpet player Ken Colyer joined the merchant navy just so he could make it over to Condon's, the nightclub on Greenwich Village's West 3rd Street that was home to a sophisticated variant of Dixieland in the 1940s.

The roots of UK trad can be traced more prosaically to a pub in Kent: the Red Barn, Barnehurst, which was home to George Webb's Dixielanders. They were a bunch of like-minded enthusiasts who had been thrown together during wartime at the Vickers munitions factory, in nearby Crayford, where they had assembled machine guns together. Word got out, the band built up a following, and soon they were joined by trumpeter Humphrey Lyttelton. Pianist Webb – who wore his father's

---

* Incapable of joining them, Guthrie himself was in a psychiatric hospital by 1956, suffering from undiagnosed Huntington's disease. As if this wasn't bad enough, a few years earlier his arm had been badly hurt in a gasoline explosion, leaving him incapable of playing the guitar. His health gradually deteriorated, and he died in 1967.

† The shows ran from May 1944 to April 1945 and were broadcast in the US as *Eddie Condon's Jazz Concerts*. Condon was joined regularly by singer Lee Wiley and surrounded himself with some of the brightest stars in jazz: Louis Armstrong, Jack Teagarden and Willie 'The Lion' Smith.

overcoat, which looked like a tent on him – was by most accounts a very shy man, and in 1947 his band effectively became Lyttelton's. The puritanical Webb stayed on as a pianist; Lyttelton said he admired his 'Cockney directness, which scorned compromise'.

Traditional jazz wasn't by any means unknown in late-1940s Britain: the Squadronaires had been playing the odd Dixieland song during the war, and trumpeter Freddy Randall's band had been doing very well in the late '40s, playing vintage Armstrong tunes. But Humph's band felt more like they were on a mission, that they represented something real and exciting that was missing in contemporary music.* The Lyttelton band now became part of the mainstream very quickly, while signifying their gentle outsider status; as residents on *Melody Maker*'s New Dance Band tour in 1949, they were told off for not dressing properly, as a dance band should. Webb's famous blue overcoat seemed to be an inspiration to their fans, who donned Cossack hats and sheepskin waistcoats. Lyttelton himself was slightly baffled by their crowd's oddball behaviour: 'People who had been dancing to Ted Heath, and American bands during the war, had this modification of jitterbug dancing which was called jiving. When we started, we had a lot of people coming from art schools, and it was really like a primitive way of teaching people how to swim – we started to play and they flung themselves on the floor and literally flailed about.'

Art schools would provide a place for a post-war British youth revolution to foment. Universities were still an impossible dream for working- and lower-middle-class Britain, and the new plate-glass institutions – Lancaster, Warwick, Sussex, York, Kent, Essex and East Anglia – wouldn't open until the mid-1960s. For now, art school was where you went to shock your parents and hang out with contemporaries who had the same ideas as you about everything, including art and politics, but especially jazz and popular music. What drew them to old-time jazz was an inversion of the cultural hierarchy: its roots were in poor, black America, and the BBC wouldn't touch it.

* It's worth remembering that Britain had never really experienced Dixieland – or even 1920s – jazz without it being translated by Jack Hylton or Bert Ambrose.

The saxophone, seen as a modernist weapon, was anathema to student purists. So when alto-sax player Bruce Turner joined the Lyttelton band in 1953, a section of their fans unfurled a banner at a Birmingham Town Hall show that read: 'Go Home Dirty Bopper'. It was a sign of hardening borders: a new scene based around 'traditional jazz' was forming, which subdivided jazz further still. The musical distinction between 'Dixieland' and 'trad' was that while Freddy Randall and Humphrey Lyttelton had favoured 1920s Chicago jazz, the trad hard-liners claimed that the authentic New Orleans sound was only to be found with musicians who, unlike Louis Armstrong and Jelly Roll Morton, had never left New Orleans to head north. This puritanism– with barely capable players bashing out the tunes in Soho coffee bars and cellars – was gently mocked by some; cultural theorist Jeff Nuttall recalled that 'Uncle John Renshaw, a bandleader of the time, used to say with some irony, "I'm in the sincerity racket, meself."'

Record labels were happy to release trad to its burgeoning middle-class fanbase, and Lyttelton's 'Out of the Galleon' was one of the first four 45s to be released by EMI in January 1953. Like other jazz releases, though, it was relegated to EMI's Parlophone label – largely seen as a home for novelty and comedy records, before the Beatles made it their own – rather than the more mainstream HMV or Columbia. It was an underground scene – literally, in this instance. Trad jazz blossomed away from the ballrooms that welcomed Ted Heath, and often found a home in subterranean clubs.

In London, the proliferation of coffee bars in mid-1950s Soho provided a home for young British musicians with plenty of zeal but little technique. This would be the proving ground for skiffle, a very British DIY boom spearheaded by Chris Barber's old banjo player Lonnie Donegan, which is essentially where modern British pop begins, and its story can be found in my companion book, *Yeah Yeah Yeah*. One such coffee bar is worth dwelling on here, though. This was the Freight Train, opened by Chas McDevitt with the profits from his 1957 transatlantic Top 10 skiffle hit of the same name. 'Freight Train' had been sung by a Scottish art student and folk singer called Nancy Whiskey, who was signed to hardcore folk label Topic. The song was a bridge between the British and American traditionalists. It had been written, astonishingly, by an eleven-year-old called Elizabeth Cotten in 1904. Cotten was working at a department store in the late 1940s, when she helped a lost girl find her mother, and on the spot was offered a job as a maid for the family. The little girl was Peggy Seeger. Cotten sang songs around the Seeger household, playing guitar in a distinctive two-finger, left-handed style, and astonished her folklore-loving employers. It's a safe bet that she inspired siblings Pete and Peggy, future totems of the American folk revival.*

The real fire-starter for trad's popularity was trombonist Chris Barber, who had been born in the model community of Welwyn Garden City in 1930. He had formed his Jazz Band with clarinettist Monty Sunshine in 1953, and they wrote their own pieces ('Blue Sunshine'), as well as digging up relative obscurities like Papa Celestin's 'Tuxedo Rag' or Jimmy Blythe's State Street Ramblers' 'Brownskin Mama'. As well as being fine players, they weren't as hemmed in by regulations on what they could or couldn't do, recording an EP of Duke Ellington compositions and becoming the favoured band of the CND-following beatnik set. They even took a Sidney Bechet song, 'Petite Fleur', into the British and American Top 10s in 1959, which was quite an achievement. Somehow, their sound still suggested the Home Counties or suburban London, and Barber was probably quite happy about that.†

One of the main reasons why the trad jazz favoured by Barber blossomed in the 1950s was its direct opposition to the route modern jazz

---

* Growing up in Chapel Hill, North Carolina, Cotten had taught herself to play guitar when she was eight by turning her brother's banjo upside down, playing the treble notes with her thumb and the bass notes with her fingers. She called the style 'Cotten-picking'.
† Barber would horrify some of his fans by bringing in blues guitarist John Slaughter in 1964. He also brought blues musicians over from the States, thus introducing attendees like the Kinks' Ray Davies to R&B. Barber was no purist: he recorded the Paul McCartney obscurity 'Cat Call' in 1967, signed to the progressive Marmalade label for the driving 'Battersea Rain Dance' in 1969, and made an unlikely but terrific trad jazz/blues rock fusion album with guitarist Rory Gallagher in 1972. He was a modest but key figure in the development of British pop.

had taken. Its ragged nature and playfulness meant that anyone at school or college with the basic ability to play a clarinet, trumpet or piano could make a fair stab at jazzing up a tune. It was a world that was open to amateurs, and the continuing popularity of trad into the mid-'60s had a lot to do with participation. For someone to take a chance on a modern jazz arrangement, it would have helped to be as au fait with the rapidly developing codes of the avant scene, or maybe even Stravinsky, as Louis Armstrong. It was played by players for players. Trad was for underdogs and outsiders, students in duffel coats, Berkshire beatniks. It wasn't necessarily for public consumption.

British revivalism of aged American music wasn't always as inventive or desirable. Take George Mitchell's Black and White Minstrels, whose enduring popularity seems mystifying today. In 1952 John Abbott, in his history of the publishers Francis, Day and Hunter, had written that blackface entertainment 'was almost the only alternative to the doubtful humour of the music hall of the period. Minstrelsy was a form of family entertainment where husband and wife could take their children without fear of being asked embarrassing questions afterwards.' There was no danger of catching a glimpse of stocking in minstrelsy, after all. Just four years after the *Windrush* policy had been implemented, it was still possible to think and write like this because people who were so casually turned into caricatures (by blackface and the golliwog on the labels of jars of Robinson's marmalade) had only recently begun to arrive in the UK in large numbers. There had been black communities in the country for centuries – mainly in the port cities – but only in the 1950s did numbers grow significantly. The BBC commissioned *The Black and White Minstrel Show* in 1958, and it ran and ran – with peak viewing figures of over twenty million and two number-one spin-off albums – until 1978. The show continued to tour theatres after that, finally running aground after a 1989 tour of Butlin's holiday camps in Minehead, Bognor and Barry Island. It ended not because of its insensitivity primarily, but because it was seen as dated.

The mid-1950s also saw a new vogue for ragtime. Del Wood's 'Down Yonder' was a surprise American hit in 1951, while in Britain there was Trinidad-born Winifred Atwell, a classical pianist who sold millions of records, on which she played what she called her 'other piano'. Winnie was a helpful corrective to the Black and White Minstrels. She was a regular on the '50s hit parades, with things like 'Britannia Rag', 'Coronation Rag', 'Flirtation Rag' (all 1953) and 'Poor People of Paris', a number one in 1956 that also featured a musical saw. Winnie went on to set up the first hairdressers for black Britons (the Winifred Atwell Salon, 82A Railton Road, Brixton, opened in 1956*) and was a welcoming face for the *Windrush* generation.† Meanwhile, a German pianist called Fritz Schulz-Reichel reinvented himself as 'Crazy Otto' and joined the neo-ragtime craze – a medley of German songs became 'Crazy Otto Medley', a number-two US hit in 1955 – and was then exalted by Hoagy Carmichael, of all people, with the nutty but joyous 'Crazy Otto Rag': 'Mister piano player, you should be the mayor!'

* * *

By the late 1950s Greenwich Village was known across America, and folk music had become a commercial concern. The Kingston Trio were a nightclub act based at San Francisco's Purple Onion, and in 1958 they spent five weeks at number one with 'Tom Dooley', a nineteenth-century song about a murder in North Carolina. The Trio went on to record five number-one albums, and they spent their money wisely, buying an eight-storey office block in San Francisco and starting their own men's clothing line of slacks, belts and raincoats. Seattle's Brothers Four described their style as 'Hootenanny Folk' and in 1960 scored a number-two hit with 'Green Fields' – almost an answer song to Irving

---

* The building – by then a welding shop – was so badly damaged in the 1981 Brixton riots that it had to be demolished.
† Winnie was first in line for a number of hugely popular pianists. When her profile faded in the late 1950s, she was usurped by the debonair, non-jazz Russ Conway, who scored number-one hits with 'Side Saddle' and 'Roulette'; by the mid-'60s the jovial, mumsy Mrs Mills had replaced Conway, selling millions of albums with her boogie-woogie-flavoured pub-piano medleys; and in the '70s a long-haired lad called Bobby Crush took the crown, looking more like Arsenal's zippy new winger than someone usually glued to a bar stool. It seemed as though British TV couldn't take more than one ever-smiling pianist at a time.

Berlin's 'Blue Skies'. While the latter had a melancholy tune with an
optimistic lyric, there is nothing optimistic at all about 'Green Fields'.
It talks about a land 'parched by the sun' and 'valleys where rivers used
to run'; though it's essentially a love song, it feels post-apocalyptic and
has a gently disturbing power. At this point folk was the only genre
that could handle the concept of atomic apocalypse – a continuation of
its role during the dustbowl and other social calamities – even though
the threat of the bomb was a reality, right there on the news every day.
Rock began to shoulder the burden, with added twists from the literary
Dylan: 'Where black is the colour, where none is the number.' Brothers
Four never recorded anything as unsettling as 'Green Fields' again; they
would go on to record a bizarre, almost whispered cover of the Beatles'
'Revolution', which notably omitted the line about 'carrying pictures of
Chairman Mao'.

The most commercially successful single to emerge from the folk
revival was the Tokens' 'The Lion Sleeps Tonight' at the end of 1961,
a reworking of a South African song called 'Wimoweh' and an early
example of pop beyond purely Anglo-American boundaries. A four-
piece ranging in age from fourteen to twenty-one, the Tokens – Hank
Medress, Jay Siegel, Mitch Margo and Phil Margo – were New York–
Jewish songwriters in the Irving Berlin tradition, and 'The Lion Sleeps
Tonight' was to African folk what 'Alexander's Ragtime Band' had been
to 'Maple Leaf Rag'. Not long before 'The Lion Sleeps Tonight' became
'the great new folk sound that's sweeping the country!', the Tokens had
been in the US Top 20 with the heart-pumping doo-wop hit 'Tonight
I Fell in Love'; five years later, they would cut a delightful, Beach Boys-
harmonised update of Matt Monro's 'Portrait of My Love'. The week
'The Lion Sleeps Tonight' entered the Top 40, on its way to number
one, Bob Dylan spent two days recording his debut album at Columbia's
Studio A, and the folk revival was about to be transformed, once again
a political force.*

---

* In Britain, a folk revival would grow out of the trad and skiffle scenes in the
early 1960s. Mostly, it would be an underground, beatnik phenomenon. Its
commercial wing sprang largely from one man, Hampstead-born Dionysius
O'Brien, who was a fan of Latin American music, ragtime and barbershop

The unfiltered paradise of the UK's underground jazz scene – which had been documented in Karel Reisz and Tony Richardson's wonderful 1956 film *Momma Don't Allow*, shot with Chris Barber's band at an energetic jazz night held in the Fisherman's Arms, Wood Green – would also, naturally, become commercial property. Fortunately, this did at least give one of the scene's leaders his due: Humphrey Lyttelton's 'Bad Penny Blues' was made into a 1956 Top 20 hit single by DJ Jack Jackson and the pop-minded engineer Joe Meek, who emphasised the bottom end of the piano to give it real propulsion.* At the tail end of the decade the alliterative trio of Barber, Ball and Bilk stamped their names on the hit parade. Chris Barber had been playing to two hundred people, three nights a week in 1952; four years later, the Barber band sold out Newcastle City Hall for five consecutive nights.

There was nothing worryingly authentic about Kenny Ball and His Jazzmen, and they wouldn't have claimed any fake ancestral connection to Kid Ory. More at home on ITV's *Sunday Night at the London Palladium* than at Wood Green's Fisherman's Arms, they scored number-one hits with both their trad take on 'March of the Siamese Children' (1962), from *The King and I*, and 'Midnight in Moscow' (1961), a genuinely misty bit of contemporaneous Cold War soundtracking. Clarinet player Acker Bilk's Paramount Jazz Band initially got the public's attention with their bowler hats and waistcoats – 'but', argued Bilk, 'we were good. People only come once to see a guy in a bowler hat and a waistcoat.' Born in rural Somerset in 1929, Bilk had worked in a sawmill and

---

harmonies. Changing his name to Tom Springfield, he formed a harmony trio called the Springfields with Dusty, his sister, and their friend Tim Feild. They scored major hits with 'Silver Threads and Golden Needles', 'Island of Dreams' and 'Say I Won't Be There', before splitting in 1963, when Dusty went solo. Tom then discovered an Australian group called the Seekers, wrote and produced 'I'll Never Find Another You' and 'A World of Our Own' for them, and saw them become the biggest new act in Britain in 1965. Judith Durham's voice was schoolma'am-like, and there was a definite Salvation Army whiff about their sound, but they were rarely off the chart ('The Carnival Is Over', 'Morningtown Ride', 'Georgy Girl') before splitting in 1968.
* Later, it was clearly an influence on the Beatles' 'Lady Madonna', though that was meant to be channelling Fats Domino.

a smithy, and done a stint with the army in Egypt, before forming his band in 1958. He had a rumbling, tipsy piano and fellow West Country boy Joe Meek's engineering skills to thank for his first Top 10 hit, the evocative 'Summer Set', in 1959. He wouldn't be off the singles chart for the next three years. Unlike many of his British trad contemporaries, he was also openly political, recording the rousing 'Marching Union' ('When it comes to wages and holidays with pay, we're marching along with the union!') in 1960 for the National Union of Boot and Shoe Operatives.

Bilk's biggest hit was the orchestrated 'Stranger on the Shore', a trans-atlantic 1962 success that had started out as 'Jenny', a tune written for his daughter. It was almost a lullaby, and operated as balm for a world living through the Cuban missile crisis; in this respect, it could have been regarded as a modern folk piece, no less authentic than Louis Armstrong's 'Savoy Blues' or 'Potato Head Blues' had been in the late 1920s. Like 'Green Fields' and 'Tom Dooley', Bilk's 'Stranger on the Shore' used the feel of historical folk song to capture the aura of impending apocalypse; its odd, ominous chords towards the end sug-gested – even predicted – an uncertain future.* It wasn't wrong. Within a few months, the Beatles released 'Love Me Do', and the trad boom died overnight.

---

* Years later, 'Stranger on the Shore' would be heard on the Apollo 10 lunar module; later still, it made a sampled appearance on the KLF's ambient landmark, *Chill Out*. It remains a hugely evocative, lonely piece of music.

42

IN A RESTLESS WORLD: NAT KING COLE

On a warm LA night in 1947, jazz pianist and singer Nat King Cole was relaxing backstage after a show at the Lincoln Theatre, when his manager, Mort Ruby, was accosted in the gentlest possible way by a long-haired man in a tunic leaning on a battered bicycle. 'I want to see Mr Cole,' he said. 'I have a song for him.' As he nudged this fruitcake away from the stage door, Ruby was handed a rolled-up score that looked more like ancient parchment than a music score. Ruby went back into the dressing room and handed the soiled piece of paper to Cole. I don't know who that guy was, Ruby laughed, but he looked a lot like Jesus.

The song was called 'Nature Boy', and it would transform Nat King Cole's fortunes. It could have done the same for its writer, eden ahbez (no capitals – he thought only the divine were worthy of capitals). Cole recorded the song in August 1947, though Capitol soon realised they couldn't release it, as they had no idea how to contact ahbez. After scouring the city, Capitol executives eventually found him living under-neath one of the 'L's in the Hollywood sign. Initially, 'Nature Boy' was released as the B-side to 'Lost April' in April 1948, but after WNEW in New York championed the flip, the station was overwhelmed by callers. Knowing a smash when they heard it, Frank Sinatra, Sarah Vaughan and Dick Haymes rushed out cover versions, with the second Petrillo recording ban just days away.

Both Cole and ahbez were outsiders. The media regarded ahbez as a freak, a punchline to a Bob Hope joke. He was a minor legend in Hollywood, noted for living out under the stars, with not much more than a bicycle, a sleeping bag and a juicer.* As a kooky figure whom everyone seemed to know, he was an east coast equivalent of New York's street-jazz genius Moondog, though ahbez's commercial reach went far deeper. 'Nature Boy' earned him a profile in a 1948 issue of *Life* magazine, and it would eventually be covered by everyone from John Coltrane to Celine Dion, a constant rebuke to ego and consumerism, a gentle, simple philosophy that, twenty years after Nat Cole recorded it, may as well have been the new bible for American youth. To the Don Drapers of wipe-clean, consumerist, late-1940s America, its spiritual message and timeless melody must have created nagging doubt.

* * *

Nat Cole had been born in Montgomery, Alabama, and his family had moved to Chicago when he was four. Originally, Nat was a virtuoso pianist who played with Johnny Miller, on bass, and Oscar Moore, on guitar, and the results were magical – total synergy. He was sympathetic to the moderns. Adding Jack Costanzo, the bongo player from Stan

---

* The success of 'Nature Boy', and the addition of a family, didn't change him much, and he seems a remarkably prescient figure from a 2021 viewpoint. Hassled by a cop who assumed from his wild appearance that he deserved to be hauled off to a mental institution, ahbez remarked calmly, 'I look crazy, but I'm not. And the funny thing is that other people don't look crazy, but they are.' The cop thought this over and said, 'You know, bud, you're right. If anybody gives you any trouble, let me know.'

Kenton's band, they became Nat King Cole and His Trio. Nat played notes emphatically, as if they were speaking, and each one had its own articulation. But when Nat sang, it was over the relaxed block-chord stylings of a George Shearing; it was a luxurious, apartment block, cocktail party of a sound.

Cole was also king of the process. Until the Afro became an acceptable look of liberation, black hair was there to be tamed; curls had to be transformed into waves using irons, fire and grease. The grease came in jars labelled Murray's, Duke and Bergamot, the last marked out by its image of a beautiful black woman. But Nat's process didn't look greasy; it looked clean, sleek and effortless, like he'd just got out of bed and there it was, a perfect match for his voice.

He had written 'Straighten Up and Fly Right' while he was working in a café in Omaha, Nebraska. Based around an expression his dad used, it crossed the bridge from jazz to pop and sounded like Yves Klein producing Louis Jordan – simple, nothing unnecessary, but hip and lots of fun – and it went to number one on *Billboard*'s R&B chart in 1944. Soon after it came out, Nat and the Trio had the chance to appear in an MGM movie starring Lucille Ball. They played the song to a stony-faced Lucy; three minutes later, hands on hips, she declared, 'That's the filthiest song I ever heard in my life.' She could obviously hear something in the lyric about the monkey encouraging the buzzard to get his act together that Nat hadn't thought of – but she was the comedian, so he wasn't about to argue.

'Straighten Up''s follow-ups sold like billy-o and placed Nat's voice front and centre. Gradually, his style became sleeker, soft and comforting but slightly rough, like corduroy. His delivery, like his piano-playing, was relaxed, economical and emphatic. When he sang, you felt like you could trust him completely, and when he told a story, it sounded as if he was making it up off the top of his head. Very soon, his singing was seen as more significant than his piano-playing, and before too long many thought he was the finest singer in America. In 1946 he was talked into recording Mel Tormé's brand-new 'Christmas Song', backed by strings rather than his trio, and from this point on he became a universally loved balladeer: 'Mona Lisa' (1950), 'Unforgettable' (1951), 'Pretend'

(1953), 'Smile' (1954), 'A Blossom Fell' (1955), 'When I Fall in Love' (1957). He outsold everyone.

Nat was signed to the familial Capitol Records. Its artists, founders (Johnny Mercer, Buddy De Sylva, and record-store owner Glenn Wallichs) and even executives would hang out at the Radio Recorder studio on Santa Monica Boulevard, go for drinks after a recording session and play softball for the Capitol team. It had the best arrangers. It had the coolest reputation. It felt like a well-heeled co-operative to artists like Cole, Jo Stafford, Paul Weston, Stan Kenton, Margaret Whiting, Mel Tormé, Peggy Lee and Kay Starr. Capitol was the singer's label, the premier record company of the 1940s and '50s. It had started with the ideals of Johnny Mercer and grown with the sales of Nat King Cole, and that was why Frank Sinatra moved there in 1953. Three years later, Capitol unveiled its stunning new HQ: the cylindrical, thirteen-storey Capitol Tower, which was designed to look like a stack of records. The money had come largely from the sales of Cole's albums, and it quickly became known as The House That Nat Built.

As a solo act, Nat decided he needed a look, so he began sporting a narrow-brimmed tweed hat made by Thomas Begg – the same model that Rex Harrison wore. He would wear one for the rest of his life. There was a more substantial life change too: he left his wife Nadine after falling in love with the sharply intelligent Maria Ellington, who had sung with Duke Ellington for two years.* While on their honeymoon in Mexico, Nat and Maria received a telegram saying that 'Nature Boy' was a hit all over the world.

* * *

Cole attempted to live out 'Nature Boy''s philosophy of life and always tried new things – singing, acting, different arrangers, different cities. He bought a house of his own, in LA's white, old-money enclave Hancock Park. The neighbours were unfriendly – 'Bedlam,

* Maria used to laugh that Duke 'didn't mind [sharing a surname] as long as they didn't think I was his daughter'.

everywhere,' is how Maria described it – and a meeting was called about undesirables moving into the area. Cole attended and told them that if he came across any, he'd be the first to let them know. One neighbour asked him to sing at her daughter's birthday party; Cole did, then sent a bill that the woman clearly wasn't expecting.

In a position of rare privilege, with an audience that included both blacks and whites, Nat was criticised for not being an activist. But speaking out wasn't his style. He was always restrained, always maintained his cool, even after the incident in Birmingham, Alabama, that so shocked the supporting Ted Heath Orchestra, when five men rushed the stage, one hitting Cole with such force that he fell back onto the piano stool, breaking it in two. 'I think this is one out of a million,' Cole told the press. 'I don't think it was a personal affront to me, personally.' Backstage, though, he was heard to say, 'Man, I love show business, but I don't want to die for it.' He never went back to Alabama.

His nationally broadcast *Nat King Cole Show*, launched in 1956, was the strongest indication yet of 'America beginning to awaken itself', according to Harry Belafonte. Nat was used to censorship. One time, he sang Cole Porter's 'Anything Goes' and was forced to change the words: 'Good authors too who once knew better words now only use four-letter words writing prose – anything goes,' was too racy for America, even in the 1950s. Cole was forced to sing that the 'good authors' now used 'three-letter words', which was funny enough in its way, but you have to wonder which TV executive seriously thought he could do a better job than Cole Porter.

Anyway, Nat had been given his own TV show, becoming the first black man in America to have his own full-length variety show, and Rheingold beer was the sponsor. Southern TV stations pulled out; soon the sponsor pulled out too. 'The show was flawless,' Tony Bennett remembered, but as Cole said privately, 'Madison Avenue's afraid of the dark.' It wasn't just in the South where Cole had problems: Madison Avenue, he drily pointed out, was in the North.

When he was back in New York, far away from his miserable Hancock Park neighbours, Nat would go to a barber's in Harlem, in a building owned by Sugar Ray Robinson, and eat spare ribs in a diner. Even here, though, he got heat from civil rights activists, who discovered he wasn't a paid-up member of the NAACP – though he had played several NAACP fundraisers – and some black-owned bars removed Nat's records from their jukeboxes. He found this heartbreaking. In 1951 he had instituted a $62,000 suit against a hotel in Rock Island, Illinois, that had refused him a room because of his skin colour. He testified that the hotel treated him 'like a little fly that might be in the way'. Cole had won, though he didn't court publicity; that wasn't how he wanted to navigate America's maze of racism and stupid segregation etiquette. No fool, though, he joined the NAACP after the Alabama attack. Sometimes it paid to go with the crowd.

Along with critics who wanted him to take a vocal stand on racism – as if sticking it out in Hancock Park wasn't enough – there were jazz fans who constantly complained that he had abandoned his roots. It is hard to imagine how cloth-eared you'd have to be not to spot a masterful jazz singer on 'When Your Lover Has Gone', from 1959's *Just One of Those Things*, but it was a constant niggling complaint. Another way of looking at it is that Cole had already become an exemplary pianist, and his voice was a new avenue for him to explore. No question, he worked at it, in the same way he practised knotting his ties for hours until they looked just right. If you listen to a Trio recording like 'That Ain't Right' (1942) and compare its phrasing and pronunciation to solo Cole on 1950's 'Mona Lisa' ('Are you warm, are you rill, Mona Lisa?'), the derivative and generic elements are gone; his voice has become burnished and conversational, unlike any other. The older he got, the deeper and richer his voice became.

As sales of his singles started to dip in the mid-1950s, Cole, like many of his contemporaries, would concentrate on the long-player: in 1957 alone he released *Love Is the Thing* (arranged by Gordon Jenkins, including his best-loved UK hit, 'When I Fall in Love', and a definitive, sky-reaching 'Stardust'); *After Midnight*, the one to please the jazzers, which had Nat back on the piano stool playing fresh versions of the old Trio hits 'Sweet Lorraine' and 'Route 66'; and the swinging, Billy May-helmed *Just One of Those Things*. Those three albums alone would have been a substantial legacy. 1960's *Wild Is Love*, all originals by the largely unknown pair of lyricist Dottie Wayne (who went on to write Bobby Vee's 'The

Night Has a Thousand Eyes') and songwriter Ray Rasch, was a brave and dizzy song cycle. With each track linked by his narration, it chronicled Cole's sometimes gauche attempts to pick up girls ('There are hundreds of thousands of girls . . . it's confusing, but I like it so!'), until he settles down on the head-cocked, misty-eyed 'Wouldn't You Know (Her Name Is Mary)'. The album was followed by a live show called *I'm with You* – a musical that was almost entirely music – which developed the *Wild Is Love* storyline. It had a racially mixed cast, and Cole's main love interest was future Motown act Barbara McNair. *I'm with You* never made it to Broadway, was never even recorded, and it lost Cole a small fortune.*

* * *

In 1957 TV presenter Ed Morrow visited what he called the Coles' 'English Tudor-style' house in LA. Daughter Cookie had a handwritten sign on her door: 'Humans can *NOT* enter this room! Signed . . . Elvis'. 'I explained to Daddy that us teenagers like rock 'n' roll better than any other kind of music,' she told Morrow, quite deadpan. 'I finally got him into making "Send for Me", and it made a big hit.' 'Send for Me' was a beauty, mellow and soulful, his biggest American hit in three years, and he followed it a year later with the similarly cool 'Midnight Flyer'. Generally, though, Nat felt negatively towards the new beat, cutting the rather silly 'When Rock 'n' Roll Came to Trinidad' in 1956 (no, it doesn't anticipate reggaeton), and a couple of years later recording the Sherman brothers' 'Mr Cole Won't Rock 'n' Roll', which thankfully stayed in the vaults. He agonised over whether to cut material that was similar to 'Send for Me', but sadly blues-based tracks, like the fine doo-wop shuffler 'Thank You, Pretty Baby', remained the exception.†

---

* A TV special based on *Wild Is Love* was screened in Canada in 1961 but was not shown in the US until 1964, thanks to a brief moment of physical contact between Cole and white actor Larry Kert. Even that was enough to be taken as offensive by commercial sponsors.
† As Cole didn't want to venture in this direction, Brook Benton picked up the slack and put a huge list of armchair R&B hits together, all of which you could imagine Nat singing.

He was much happier putting his suites of songs together. Arranged by Gordon Jenkins, who had been behind the ornate, autumnal turns of Sinatra's 'Where Are You' and 'No One Cares', *Where Did Everyone Go?* (1963) was Cole's last great album. Sat in a bar on the title track, Cole was – as so often – somewhere in the background, listening to another drinker's tale of woe: 'I was the host. Everyone loved me. I was the most . . . Jokes by the yard, I was a card.' Cole's voice pauses thoughtfully, responding to the azure richness of Jenkins's orchestration. 'Nothing lasts for ever,' he sings, almost to himself, 'and the deepest well runs dry.'

The closing track, 'That's All There Is, There Isn't Any More', is one of his very best: 'I put a sign that says "For Sale" on all my dreams.' There is something about Cole's voice as he sings, 'Call me, baby . . . call me,' that transcends his usual husky smoothness – it is unsettlingly deep. As the very last moment of an album that became in effect a memorial to Cole – perfectly arranged, a melancholic celebration, 'a drink for monsieur, a drink for us all' – it has an oddly permanent feel of the present, like the singer is reaching out from wherever he may now be, almost making it through the speaker, trying desperately, vainly, to make contact with the living world.

Billy Eckstine once said of Nat: 'He's one of the two guys who took a style and made a voice out of it – the other is Louis [Armstrong].' To this list of stylists you could probably add Frank Sinatra. He and Cole had great respect for each other and a kinship: they smoked, enjoyed cold drinks and spent half their lives doing shows for charity. At the end, Sinatra was a regular visitor to the ailing Nat, who had been diagnosed with lung cancer in late 1964, after he had started to worry about unexplained back pain and weight loss.

Cole died on 15 February 1965, aged forty-seven, and the world was deeply shocked. He was the first major figure that people knew who had been killed by a heavy smoking habit. Given everything he'd gone through – stage invasions by racist thugs, TV shows cancelled by timid sponsors, lawsuits from neighbours to scare him out of his home, hateful slurs burned into his lawn – it seemed particularly cruel. He was always such a dignified figure, even when he was adding a gentle cockney twang to 'With a Little Bit of Luck' or jazzing 'Old MacDonald Had a Farm' on 1948's *King Cole for Kids*. 'There was something magical about him as a person,' said Buddy Greco. 'I never read anything derogatory about Nat King Cole.' As a black entertainer, he wasn't just accepted, he was really loved.

After Nat's death, his wife Maria secured the rights to 'Nature Boy', contacted eden ahbez and made sure they were returned to him. Still living in LA, ahbez would see it become a city full of soft-spoken peace-niks, then watch that dream fall away in the 1970s and '80s. He died in 1995, aged eighty-six. Cole's voice and ahbez's message have survived for future generations, and quite possibly will never leave us nor become any less human or profound: 'The greatest thing you'll ever learn is just to love and be loved in return.'

My music has always been like fiction, no authenticity. I didn't
want to make African music – I only wanted to suggest how
African music might sound.
    Martin Denny

In 1947, just two decades after the authorities had seen electronically
enhanced crooning as a grave threat that could emasculate men and
impregnate women, twenty-five-year-old bandleader Les Baxter released
Music Out of the Moon, an album that attempted to imagine sounds
from another planet altogether. Titles included 'Celestial Nocturne' and
'Mist o' the Moon'. Baxter was accompanied by Dr Samuel J. Hoffman
on a futuristic and eerie instrument called a theremin, which had no
keys or strings; its music was literally plucked from the air. Dr Hoffman's
involvement implied that you would have to be a man of science, preferably of the Professor Frink variety, to truly master the theremin. This

was highly artificial, rootless music, partly the result of Americans having been briefly acquainted with the farthest-flung corners of the globe in the early 1940s. After World War I, Sophie Tucker's question had been 'How Ya Gonna Keep 'Em Down on the Farm (After They've Seen Paree)'; the answer to the same question after World War II would be by creating worlds that could be explored via the gramophone in your living room, fictionalised versions of places – Hawaii, rainforests, outer space – and things that were foreign, historical or hiding just beyond the clouds.

Post-war, there was a desire to make the world more united. It seemed natural at the time that the dream would emanate from New York, capital of the free world. The United Nations briefly offered real hope of making sense of the world, reducing it to gentle signifiers – flags, desks, microphones – in a purpose-built modernist home. If U Thant and Dag Hammarskjöld had got together to make an album in the 1950s, it probably would have sounded a lot like the Buddy Collette Septet's *Polynesia*.

Potential apocalypse underpinned America's turn to human rights-based folk in the 1950s and young Britain's flirtation with the certainties of aged jazz. Exotica yearned for cartoonish adventure. The strangeness and decidedly un-American scent of the music had been in the air since the ASCAP strike of 1941 let Latin music, Swedish whimsy and Russian folk moans infiltrate the radio. Early sightings of exotica* came with Vaughn Monroe's 1950 single 'Bamboo', a dense, thick, oppressive sound with the most minimal instrumentation. 'Nature Boy''s success had convinced Nat King Cole to be adventurous in his choice of singles, leading to his 1951 single 'Jet', a mass of minor chords and gently Middle Eastern percussion, and 'Hajji Baba (Persian Lament)' in 1954, which wore its heart on its sleeve.

'Jet' was the vocal version of an instrumental from Les Baxter's 1948 album *Perfume Set to Music*. Cole's version, produced by Baxter, wasn't

---

* The term 'exotica' probably wasn't used until 1957, when it was coined by Liberty Records founder Si Waronker, who produced Martin Denny's album of the same name.

daring enough to feature the theremin, but it did have the female siren sound that Baxter would make his own and anticipated the *Star Trek* theme of the 1960s. Baxter was also a fiend for percussion, and he would generally be happier evoking tropical climes rather than the cold dark of space. In 1951 came his landmark *Ritual of the Savage* LP, which included his calling card, 'Quiet Village' – a humid thing, barely a melody at all, that worked entirely on atmosphere and would become a number-two hit in America when it was covered in suitably small, unhurried fashion by Martin Denny.

Capitol's house arrangers were often allowed to record albums of their own arrangements and compositions. Some were pet projects (Frank de Vol's *A Symphonic Portrait of Jimmy McHugh*, 1955), some were surprisingly flat-footed (Nelson Riddle's *Sea of Dreams*, 1958), while others were inspired (Gordon Jenkins's *Night Dreams*, 1957). Mostly, it was quite obvious that the arrangers didn't feel the need to put as much energy into these albums as they would for premier acts like Cole, Sinatra, Lee or Stafford. Les Baxter was the exception; he used them as an excuse for all manner of genre-trashing, sonic experiments, daydreams and travelogues. As he had had a number-one single with his version of 'Unchained Melody' in 1955, he was allowed to release more than any other arranger.

Bongos pounding under the half-speed sensuality of a cooing siren, harpsichords and finger cymbals defying the rules of time and space . . . Mostly what I hear in Baxter's best albums, like *Ritual of the Savage* (1951), *Tamboo!* (1955) and *Caribbean Moonlight* (1956), is shadow – trees in the moonlight, a serene slick of lake, invisible creatures making noises in the darkness. Tales of mystery and imagination. It's no surprise that Baxter was later asked to score *The Pit and the Pendulum*.

The best-selling exotica act was Martin Denny, whose albums – *Forbidden Island* (1958), *Hypnotique*, *Afro-Desia* (both 1959) – were, said a wag at *Time* magazine, 'labelled like bargain-counter perfumes'. New York-born Denny had picked up a fascination for Latin rhythms when he toured South America with the Don Dean Orchestra in the 1930s. He collected unusual instruments and introduced them into his jazz group, which had regular gigs in the hotels of Waikiki. Denny's main addition to the Baxter sound was the 'wild animal' noises – birdsong, chattering monkeys – that litter his albums, and which had begun by chance when his group were playing in an open-air bar that had a pond full of noisy bullfrogs close by. 'Some of the boys in the band got carried away and started doing bird calls. The next day someone came up to me and said, "Mr Denny, would you get that arrangement with the birds and the frogs?" I thought, "What is he talking about?" Then I suddenly realised he had a point.'* The noises can get a little wearing over the length of an album, and can sound unpleasantly reminiscent of 1980s student high jinks, but in the '50s Denny's albums made Hawaii incredibly fashionable.

Whether it was meant to evoke Hawaii or Burma, the Denny smallgroup sound rarely changed. 'My music is all make-believe . . . it's what people think the islands might be like,' he would say. And people heard exotica, erotica, liberation. He was no ethnographer, just a chubby New Yorker with an ear for the unusual, but Denny was partly responsible for the success of the tiki bars that exploded across America, after the Trader Vic's franchise began spreading outwards from California in 1949.

Not all exotica came in twelve-inch square packages. Caterina Valente's 'The Breeze and I' was a wild and evocative noise on the British and American singles charts in 1955. Quite the polyglot, Valente had been born in 1931 to Italian parents, grew up in Paris and recorded 'The Breeze and I' with the Werner Müller orchestra. Her first husband was a German juggler; her second Croydon-born jazz pianist Roy Budd, who would create new sonic worlds of his own with the soundtracks to *Get Carter*, *The Black Windmill* and *The Internecine Project* in the 1970s.

A form of domestic exotica came from Leroy Anderson, a classical pianist and composer who never had the nerve to share his symphonies with the world. Instead, he came up with bite-size work-time novelties like 'The Syncopated Clock' and 'The Typewriter', which used – yes! – a typewriter as a percussion instrument. There was also 'Blue Tango', a huge hit single in 1952; it was an instrumental, but listeners in Britain

---

* It is also quite likely that Denny was inspired by the bird noises and monkey calls on *Ritual of the Savage*, the 1951 album by his mentor, Les Baxter.

added their own words to the chorus: 'I've got my woolly woofs on.' The reason why seems lost to time. And for the homebody, Anderson had 'The Waltzing Cat' and the DIY-soundtracking 'Sandpaper Ballet'. Best of all was 'Sleigh Ride', an evergreen Christmas hit which – like nearly all of Anderson's efforts – was quite utopian in its perkiness.

For the most part, though, exotica was defined by something entirely out of the ordinary. Zither player Anton Karas didn't know it in 1951, but he was about to change the art of the film soundtrack with his 'Harry Lime Theme' from *The Third Man*, a piece of music that evoked the Viennese underworld and the beginnings of the Cold War with an instrument that was completely alien to Anglo-American pop.

Les Baxter also produced and largely wrote *Voice of the Xtabay*, the hugely successful first album by Yma Sumac, a Peruvian singer with a five-octave range who could growl or emit a siren wail in a hitherto unknown language. Sumac was such an unlikely figure, her music so unprecedented, that the legend persisted that the whole thing was a gag and she was really a New Jersey housewife called Amy Camus.

The twenty-four-year-old Sumac and her husband, Moisés Vivanco, were hoping to make it as Andean folk musicians when they arrived in New York in 1946. Quite soon, they realised they would do better if they played up to American preconceptions about the exotic. Sumac's face and voice were attention-grabbing, and seemed all the more so with the addition of Baxter's Polynesian rhythms and tribal chanting. She was billed as an Incan priestess, wore colourful gowns and casketfuls of Peruvian jewellery and began to sing in a vaguely operatic style. She was even given a part in *Secret of the Incas*, the 1954 movie that became the inspiration for the Indiana Jones films.* It was about as authentically Peruvian as Groundskeeper Willie is Scottish. It was a shame as, in the long term, all of this artifice obscured the genuinely extraordinary power of Sumac's voice, the true exoticism of her high notes, and made her seem more of a circus act. Still, the chances are that, without

---

* Depressingly, Sumac's scenes weren't filmed in Machu Picchu; they were shot on Hollywood soundstages. The music is credited to her husband Vivanco, but it seems pretty unlikely that Sumac had no input into her performances.

Baxter's involvement, Sumac and her husband would never have got to Hollywood, would never have sold a million records, and instead would have been stuck playing to a dozen people in Greenwich Village, before flying back to Lima, broke and depressed, in the mid-1950s.

* * *

After the exotica boom died down in the early 1960s, Les Baxter moved into movie scores: anything from Frankie Avalon and Annette Funicello's camp classic *Beach Blanket Bingo* to H. P. Lovecraft's *The Dunwich Horror*. There was one exotica classic left in him: 1970's surprisingly moody and quite beautifully produced *Bugaloo in Brazil* employed most of the typical Baxter traits that had taken him to quiet villages all around the world. By then, people were familiar enough with the actual sounds of Brazil, but Baxter's take was a blend of real Brazilian percussion with the dark, the atmospheric and the dissonant. He knew that authenticity was as much of a move as wearing a gaudy paste necklace and claiming regal Incan heritage. There was much fun to be had in artifice. This was pop music, after all.

44

SHARKS IN JETS CLOTHING: ROCK 'N' ROLL

A very good friend in America, at the RCA Victor company, was a man called Steve Sholes. And he wrote me one day and sent me six sides. And he said to me, 'You won't understand any of this, you won't like it, but issue a couple of sides because this man is going to be tremendous.' So I listened, I put my head in the speaker, and I couldn't make out a word except 'heartbreak hotel'. I realised two things. One, it was the first time anything had been successful, in terms of records or sheet music, via writing, via articles, not by hearing. Second thing, I realised a new era was upon us, in which I could take no part.

Wally Ridley, HMV Records

In 1955 *Variety* magazine worried about 'the cheap cynicism of the song-smiths' in an ominous piece titled 'A Warning to the Music Business'. 'What are we talking about? We're talking about "rock and roll", about "hug" and "squeeze" and kindred euphemisms which are attempting a total breakdown of all reticences about sex . . . dirty postcards have been translated into songs.' The Juvenile Delinquency and Crime Commission in Houston, Texas, set up a 'wash out the air' committee, which effectively banned R&B songs like Ray Charles's 'I Got a Woman' and Wynonie Harris's 'Good Rockin' Tonight'. All nine Houston radio stations complied. Cultural events in America almost always have a racial dimension, but it's not known what Houston's authorities made of Elvis Presley's covers of both songs.

White covers of black R&B songs had often been a way of nullifying black progress in American culture: in 1955 Georgia Gibbs had a pop hit with LaVern Baker's 'Tweedlee Dee'; Pat Boone castrated Little Richard's 'Long Tall Sally' in 1956, rendering it nonsensical; Teresa Brewer would later say she felt guilty for her recordings of Fats Domino's 'Bo Weevil' and Johnny Ace's 'Pledging My Love', though the approach was always exuberant enough to at least make her versions a worthwhile listen. Elvis Presley's blending of R&B, country boogie, gospel, folk ballads and Hawaiian songs popularised by Bing Crosby, while incorporating the stylings of Dean Martin and Mario Lanza, blurred racial and cultural issues in a single unifying noise – which, in the conservative, post-Korean War Eisenhower years, made him appear highly non-conformist.

* * *

What had changed? Why were British and American youths no longer satisfied by the croon of Crosby, the sweep of a Gordon Jenkins arrangement or the blast of ten silver saxes? Murray the K, a rock 'n' roll DJ on New York's WINS in the late 1950s, reckoned it was partly to do with the McCarthy era, an era of doubt and hateful line-toeing. After this, young people did not try to emulate the older generation. What's more, the age of the record-buyer had lowered each decade; in the 1930s there would hardly have been anyone under twenty buying records – they didn't have any money. Much as they had after World War I, teenagers were building their own world, and now some of them had the financial clout to make it stick.

The new sounds were 'amateurish', according to Ted Heath. 'It sounds like amateurs . . . Mickey Mouse music.' He was right on all counts. Mickey Mouse was partially responsible too: the arrival of 45s in late-1940s America had created a separate market for smaller children, and those children were now teenagers, locked into a new path of dependency as consumers. In a July 1954 edition of *Cashbox* magazine, Atlantic Records' Jerry Wexler and Ahmet Ertegun wrote a prescient article on an emergent form of R&B, popular with teenagers, that they labelled 'cat music'; that same month, Atlantic had its first Top 5 hit on the *Billboard* pop chart with the Chords' 'Sh Boom'. Rock 'n' roll was emerging, though it was not yet a recognised term.

The young Paul Gambaccini remembered a Saturday morning in Westport, Connecticut, 1957. His father had left the breakfast table and left the radio on. He controlled the dials; it was his favourite radio station, and on a Saturday morning, after nine o'clock, it ran the American hits. The show had suddenly taken on a new complexion with rock 'n' roll. Elvis Presley's 'Teddy Bear' came on, and Gambaccini's father vaulted down the stairs, jumped across the room and flipped the dial in one fluid motion. 'He stood on the threshold of the kitchen – I can see him now – and said, "How can you listen to such damn music?" And that was the first time I heard my father swear. I thought, "There must be something to this."' Gambaccini started listening to the radio three hours a day, in time to hear all of the great rock 'n' roll DJs in the New York area.

Gambaccini's father wasn't alone. There was a lot of griping, and some real anger. Johnny Mercer compared rock's rise to 'a ten cents store taking over a great, luxurious department store'. British jazzer George Chisholm said, 'It's like putting a funny hat on and saying you're going to sing "Stardust", in a funny hat and a red nose. You just don't do that.' The charges against rock 'n' roll included monotony, though the repeated three-note riff of Glenn Miller's 'In the Mood' would prove adaptable enough to become a transatlantic 1959 hit for the honking sax and dustbin drums of Ernie Fields.* Irving Berlin was more conciliatory; he even heaped praise on Kay Starr's clunky 'Rock and Roll Waltz', saying he wished he'd thought of the idea. Given her ease with R&B on singles like her 1950 hit 'Oh Babe', Starr was wasted on 'Rock and Roll Waltz', which attempted to bridge generations ('One, two and then rock! One, two and then roll!') and briefly – commercially, at least – seemed to have done the trick. A massive hit, number one in both Britain and America in 1956, it has been buried by history. Berlin was a lot less well disposed to Elvis Presley's 1957 recording of 'White Christmas', though, and tried vainly and foolishly to get it banned from the radio.

The rise of rock 'n' roll coincided with Berlin's near-terminal depression. His last film musicals had been in 1954, and *White Christmas* had turned out to be the biggest-grossing film of that year. Still, the rise of rock 'n' roll gave his fragile confidence a shock from which it took him eight years to recover. He had always been an observer of American life; overnight he felt out of touch and redundant. He laid low until 1962, when he returned with *Mr President*, gamely keeping on top of American trends with 'Washington Twist', but the show bombed with the worst reviews of his career, and Berlin went into a decades-long retirement.†

Ella Fitzgerald was less proscriptive and would write and sing 'Ringo Beat' in the mid-1960s: 'It's the younger generation's kind of rhythm. So don't be a creep, come on and get with 'em!' In 1956, the year of Elvis's breakthrough, she released her first *Songbook*, with thirty-two Cole Porter songs split over two albums. It was also the year of Sinatra's *Songs for Swingin' Lovers*, which sold so well it confusingly entered the singles chart; and Mel Tormé's album with Marty Paich, which included

---

* What's more, 'Sentimental Journey''s two-note hook line pre-dated Buzzcocks' 'Boredom' and, in turn, Orange Juice's 'Rip It Up', while also providing the title track of Ringo Starr's first solo album. And there's always 'One Note Samba'.
† Later, Berlin would say how much he liked the Beatles' 'Michelle' and Bobby Russell's 'Little Green Apples', though he frowned: 'A professional songwriter would never have rhymed "little green apples" with "it don't snow in Minneapolis"; he would have said, "We don't pray in churches and chapels."'

a revival of 'I Like to Recognize the Tune' aimed at bop players (presumably), but it could just as easily have been sung to the Hillbilly Cat who mumbled his lyrics and seemed to sleep in an echo chamber – Elvis Presley was a total mystery to the establishment. Bing Crosby, alone of his contemporaries, had time for Elvis. 'Don't underestimate this boy. The boy's here to stay,' he told the *Hollywood Reporter* in 1956. 'He's got talent and he can sing.'

With all the teenage noise of 1956 – the panting, the howls, the heat of 'Be-Bop-a-Lula', 'Long Tall Sally' and 'Heartbreak Hotel' – the high album sales of the established stars are easily overlooked. As the older generation – older overnight – built a definitive reference shelf in their libraries for Ella's recordings of the Gershwins (fifty-three songs over five albums), the new generation got their kicks from bite-size, portable 45 rpm discs. Pity the poor Ella fan going to a party with his library shelf under his arm. In Britain, 1956 also saw an import ban on jukeboxes lifted, just in time for 45s like 'Hound Dog' and 'Be-Bop-a-Lula' to come blasting out of Wurlitzers and Rock-Olas in Soho milk bars and suburban caffs. The different vinyl formats enhanced the age gap.

The 45 rpm boom meant records were no longer confined to record shops but could now also be found in American supermarkets and drug stores. In Britain, W. H. Smith the newsagent, Boots the chemist and Woolworths the pick 'n' mix sundries chain became three of the biggest distributors, while by the 1960s corner shops, camera repair shops and even greengrocers could have a carousel of records.*

The broad brush of history suggests the mid-1950s were a total wipeout for pre-rock popular music. But a broad brush can sweep plenty under the carpet – many names survived and thrived after the advent of rock. The coming of rock 'n' roll certainly didn't mean the previously

---

* Danny Baker remembers Starr's, in London's Surrey Docks, in the late 1960s: 'They only had one small browser with a pretty random selection of LPs and a rack of singles behind the counter. The other seven-eighths of their floor space was given over to balls of wool, knitting needles and knitting-pattern booklets. If the instructions for a certain type of cardigan came out the same day as the new Jethro Tull album, the queuing clientele ratio would be 92 per cent fastidious blue-rinsed grandmothers to 8 per cent stoned hairy hippies.'

popular suddenly wasn't. Top 10s of the late 1950s, in Britain and America, were split roughly 60/40 between pre-rock and the new wave. The first British chart of July 1958, with rock 'n' roll at its commercial peak, featured the likes of Frank Sinatra's 'The Lady Is a Tramp' and Perry Como's 'I May Never Pass This Way Again', while *Record Mirror*'s Top 10 looked like this:

1 Everly Brothers – 'All I Have to Do Is Dream'/'Claudette'
2 Vic Damone – 'On the Street Where You Live'
3 Max Bygraves – 'Tulips from Amsterdam'/'You Need Hands'
4 The Four Preps – 'Big Man'
5 Connie Francis – 'Who's Sorry Now'
6 The Mudlarks – 'Book of Love'
7 Michael Medwin, Bernard Bresslaw, Alfie Bass and Leslie Fyson – 'The Army Game'
8 Don Lang – 'Witch Doctor'
9 Michael Holliday – 'Stairway of Love'
10 Elias and His Zig Zag Jive Flutes – 'Tom Hark'

Kentucky's Everly Brothers were a grade-A rock act, albeit their record had a ballad on one side that Gene Austin could have sung thirty years earlier. What about the rest? Max Bygraves's double A-side comprised a brace of music-hall songs; the Four Preps were a barbershop update; Connie Francis's revival of Isham Jones's 1923 hit 'Who's Sorry Now', in spite of its thudding snare and insistent piano, had been a more raucous affair when Johnnie Ray released it in 1953; 'The Army Game' was a TV theme; the former merchant seaman Michael Holliday, his sincere and balm-like voice making him Liverpool's answer to Bing Crosby, had recently topped the charts with a cover of Marty Robbins's country hit 'The Story of My Life' and would take the tinkling, featherweight 'Starry Eyed' to number one in 1960; Elias and His Zig Zag Jive Flutes provided a rare early appearance for African music, seemingly unadulterated, and 'Tom Hark' would go on to become a football terrace chant decades later.

Then there's a pair of barely rock numbers: 'Book of Love' – a squeaky, RADA-trained cover of the Monotones' DIY doo-wop hit – and 'Witch Doctor'. If you were being generous, you could call 'Witch Doctor' 'novelty rock 'n' roll'. It was written by Ross Bagdasarian, who had co-written Rosemary Clooney's 'Come on-a My House', and performed by Don Lang, a jazzer whose Frantic Five were an early British attempt to capture the heat of Bill Haley's Comets. Essentially, it was for children.

This leaves Alan Jay Lerner and Frederick Loewe's 'On the Street Where You Live', from *My Fair Lady*, soon to become a number one for Vic Damone, which proved there was still very much a market for well-crafted ballads. Lerner later recalled: 'At the time *My Fair Lady* opened, rock 'n' roll was the musical currency of the moment. We finished making the album, and I thought if it sells 50,000 copies, I'll be delighted. I thought it'd be a triumph in that market. So I was very surprised when it suddenly swept the world as it did.' Who was buying 'On the Street Where You Live'? Some teenagers, undoubtedly. But one look at the charts reveals that they didn't become a teenage domain overnight.

If the charts weren't quite overrun by rock, the theatres were entirely untouched by it. It's hard to believe, but *Salad Days* and Presley's pomp shared the same era. Julian Slade and Dorothy Reynolds's musical came out of Bristol's Old Vic, where it initially had a three-week run. It was born old-fashioned, a total contrast to the big American shows and to rock 'n' roll. Slade considered it would have been 'very foolish to ape them. We had to find an indigenous style.' The *Guardian* called it 'the gayest piece of entertainment since *The Mikado*', and it couldn't have been more in denial of everything that 1950s Britain was going through.

At the cinema, *The Good Companions* also gave fingers-in-the-ears a go. Based on a book by J. B. Priestley, it starred Janette Scott and told the story of a struggling touring troupe called the Dinky Doos. It was a film about the good-heartedness of variety acts in the face of abusive northern audiences. At one point an operatic lady is cat-called, and she splutters, 'I've never been so insulted in all my life. Not since that time in Grimsby, when they were drunk and threw fish.'

* * *

In 1937 Ernie Ford, gifted with a beautifully rounded and clear bass-baritone voice, began his career as a radio announcer in Bristol,

Tennessee. After the war, he got work in San Bernardino and Pasadena, but when he began playing up his southern accent, acted the hillbilly and called himself 'Tennessee Ernie', things took off. He went on tour with west Texan bluegrass act the Mayfield Brothers, became the breakfast show DJ on radio station KXLA and sang on their country show *Dinner Bell Round-Up*, which led to him signing with Capitol in 1949. Tennessee Ernie would release a couple of dozen terrific singles that blended country and boogie-woogie, his resonant voice backed by Speedy West's out-there slide guitar and a solid 4/4 beat. Essentially, things like 'Blackberry Boogie', 'Shotgun Boogie' (a *Billboard* country number one) and 'Catfish Boogie' (with its clear double entendre) were rock 'n' roll before the fact. Still, to become a bigger star Ford had to appear on *I Love Lucy* in 1954 as the hick Cousin Ernie, which would lead to huge crossover hits with 'The Ballad of Davy Crockett' and the finger-clicking bleakness of 'Sixteen Tons' in late 1955.

'Sixteen Tons' was a transatlantic number-one hit in the year of Suez and the Hungarian uprising, a wintry piece that was as reflective on poverty and pessimism as 'Ten Cents a Dance'. But Ernie had to jump over hayricks and crack corn to appease New York, to make himself relatable. It's hard to believe he was happy to appear on TV for laughs as Ernie Ford and His Four Hot Chicken Pickers, doing rooster impressions or clucking at Lucille Ball, 'You got quite a hitch in your git-along!' Off stage, he drank heavily, though never let it show.

Compare this to a Capitol Records signing from 1956, Gene Vincent, who went into the studio with his mates, recorded the unadorned, sexually charged 'Be-Bop-a-Lula' and saw it reach the American Top 10 and British Top 20 within weeks. Vincent looked and dressed like a no-goodnik. His hoodlum mates sang in teenage jive speak, and the instrumentation was sparse and harsh. But they didn't need to dress it up in any other way to become an instant success. No false self-deprecation, no kowtowing, no *I Love Lucy* embarrassments.

The truth that Tin Pan Alley and Broadway were deaf to was that the roots of this new music went back years, beyond Tennessee Ernie's country boogie of the late 1940s, back past the groove-thump and repetition of Louis Jordan, all the way to the pre-swing days of Kansas City and New Orleans. If there was one man who linked the old and new, it was saxophonist Earl Bostic, one of the most important names in this entire book.

Why doesn't anyone talk about Earl Bostic? He's a bridge between jazz, R&B, rock 'n' roll and easy listening, and really good at all of them, in a very idiosyncratic way. It's not as if he's Robert Johnson, either: Bostic was big; he sold many records, and all of them are now worth nothing. He gets no respect at all from jazz guys because he plays too simple, and none from R&B guys because he plays too sweet. Bostic was a mentor to John Coltrane, who was in his band for a few formative years. But his music combines a sense of simplicity, beauty and playfulness that keeps Coltrane acolytes and other jazz fans far, far away. He has been written out of history partly because, like Paul Whiteman or Louis Jordan, he doesn't fit easy racial narratives. Nevertheless, pretty much everything he did – especially in the 1950s – was great.

Born in Tulsa in 1913, Bostic was thirty-two years old by the time he got to lead his own band, a six-piece with piano, bass and drums in the rhythm section, and trumpet and tenor saxophone alongside Bostic's alto. At a session in late 1947 he recorded the old Bing Crosby hit 'Temptation' and made merry with his 'growl' technique, humming or singing into the sax as he played. The interference gave a raw, buzzing roughness; this, combined with Bostic renouncing virtuoso moves for gut-level impact, meant a new sound was born. 'Temptation' made the Harlem Hit Parade Top 10 in 1948, and he was soon signed to Syd Nathan's King label in Cincinnati. Bostic's commercial peak came in 1951, when his version of Duke Ellington's 'Flamingo' hit number one on the R&B chart. There are vibes, but they don't sound clean like they do on George Shearing's 'Lullaby of Birdland'. They sit on top of a loose groove of splashy drums and walking bass; soaking the whole thing like a shaken can of beer is Bostic's echo-laden sax, exaggerated and electrified by King's studio engineers. 'Flamingo' is loaded with excitement, the promise of something illicit, maybe dangerous, maybe violent, but most definitely modernistic. It was a futuristic R&B sound, an early roar of rock, predicting everything from Tommy Steele's 'Rock with the Caveman' to the intro to 'Da Doo Ron Ron' and the solo on 'Born to

Run'. Earl Bostic is maybe the secret pop-futurist of this book, a half-forgotten hero whose music is full of elements that art music – classical or jazz – can never touch or discover. Only deep R&B diehards seem to treat him with due reverence.

* * *

Disgruntlement with rock 'n' roll was understandable when it meant instant unemployment. Song-pluggers, the ones who turned up in your office and played something on the piano, were suddenly out of a job; rock 'n' roll hit-makers were given fresh material on a one-off acetate or 'dub plate' with a ready-made backing. Beyond this, struggling publishers took matters into their own hands and recorded their own songs, which they then licensed to the myriad new independent record labels. It didn't always pan out, but a morning's work could net you a Top 20 hit and thousands of dollars. This was the direction publishing companies in the Brill Building and in the offices of nearby 1650 Broadway took. They were spearheaded by Don Kirshner and his company Aldon Music, and an in-house studio would be built into 1650's basement by the late 1950s.

Barry Mann was an Aldon writer. He was a former architecture student who, with his wife, Cynthia Weil, wrote future standards like 'On Broadway', 'You've Lost That Lovin' Feelin'' and 'Up Where We Belong'. In a 1963 *New York Post* interview, he bemoaned the perceived generation gap. He saw more that connected rather than divided pop's old and new schools, and the attitude of some older writers he admired seriously irked him: 'The old-time songwriters like Sammy Cahn and Jimmy Van Heusen sit there collecting their ASCAP royalties, saying, "Wait till melodic music comes back." I don't want to knock Cahn and Van Heusen because they're great writers. These old-time songwriters put down rock 'n' roll – they say it isn't music. But let me see them try to write it. I could write music the way they wrote it, but could they write it the way I do? I'd be able to do both, but they don't understand it.'

Mann tried and failed to become a hit recording artist in the early 1960s. He tried and failed again with a brace of mid-1970s albums. His ultimate aim, he told the *New York Post* a year before the Beatles blew into town, was to write a Broadway musical: 'I guess that's the dream of every songwriter.' That never happened, but Mann and Weil would go on to win a brace of Grammys and an Oscar nomination in 1987 for 'Somewhere Out There', from *An American Tail*; in 2011 they received the Johnny Mercer Award, the Songwriters Hall of Fame's most prestigious honour.

After the teenage revolution of the mid-1950s, some pre-rock singers would head down a dark street marked 'easy listening', full of potholes for the unsuspecting, with the odd twist cash-in. Apart from the biggest names, jazz singers became a niche concern almost overnight. But what didn't disappear was the love song; as Sammy Cahn said, 'Whatever the market, whatever the vogue, the ballad remains inviolate. If a man has food in his stomach, a roof over his head, he'll want to hear a ballad.' While Cahn felt edged out by the likes of Barry Mann and Don Kirshner's Aldon Music, sensing the end of the road for his style of popular songwriting, it turned out that Kirshner's take on pop was almost exactly the same as Cahn's: 'I believe a great song is basically a great idea, a message. I don't think today's music is "junk" songs or rock and roll, per se. People buy feels, ideas, sounds. They want a great storyline, a fresh melody line.' Both, it turned out, were correct.

With rock 'n' roll, pop got back in touch with its sense of immediacy and barrier-breaking, which had been there since the turn of the century, only now it was much faster, with a constant hunger for newness that would survive until the 1990s. What pop lost was a lot of melodic and lyrical subtlety and its cross-generational pleasures. 'For the life of me I can't understand it,' cried Harold Arlen, 'because it's horrible. Outside of eight or ten writers, there's nothing you can really care about. If you know the wealth of the twenties, thirties, forties and the early fifties, it puts to shame what's being written today. Percussive instruments have taken the place of the melodic line.' But Harold Arlen wasn't wrong to sound mournful. Rhythm and raw noise had become more desirable to many than whistleability. Sheet-music sales went through the floor; careers foundered. Pop music, for now, was divided against itself.

45

THE SUMMIT: FRANK, DINO AND SAMMY

In January 1957 Humphrey Bogart died. The last film he saw, on tele-vision at home, was the Frank Sinatra musical *Anchors Aweigh*. Sinatra had been a regular guest at Bogie's evening get-togethers, which started with cocktails at six. Other A-list faces at these soirées included Judy Garland and Sid Luft, Katharine Hepburn and Spencer Tracy, David Niven, George Cukor, Cary Grant and songwriter Jimmy Van Heusen. Bogart's place in Holmby Hills was a shelter where Hollywood's A-listers could laugh, gossip and drink, at their own pace, and not have to worry about B-listers, C-listers and the fast-spinning world beyond. One after-noon, when they had gathered to see Noël Coward perform, all still suffering from the night before, Lauren Bacall described them as a 'rat pack'. When Bogie died, she turned to Sinatra for support, and – his divorce from Ava Gardner having just been filed – the two comforted each other, which developed into a fast romance. The Rat Pack parties moved over to Sinatra's house, with Bacall as co-host. The baton had been passed.

At this point, aged forty-two, Sinatra was probably the highest-paid entertainer in the world. Creatively, his life could hardly have been sweeter. He was on Capitol, the classiest record label in the world. He was labelmates with two of the very few singers who could deservedly be called his peers, Peggy Lee and Nat King Cole. His albums, produced and arranged exactly as he wanted, were instant classics, everyone agreed. But it wasn't enough. What rankled with Sinatra was that he was on only a 5 per cent royalty, and he thought he deserved more. I want my own label, he told Capitol. They refused. I want out of my contract, he told them, more angrily. They said OK, but you need to give us four more albums. Sinatra considered this a price worth paying, and the Capitol era – almost a decade of unimpeachable greatness – was over.*

* * *

Sinatra's Reprise label – so called because you'd want to play the records again and again – overshadows the Beatles' Apple and every other vanity project-cum-record company set up by a pop singer at the peak of their powers. In its first year it made a profit of $4 million. Its huge commercial success, combined with Sinatra's allure, allowed him to sign almost anyone who had ever influenced or inspired him – Bing Crosby, Count Basie, Duke Ellington, the Hi-Los, Jimmy Witherspoon, Les Baxter,

---

* All of his Capitol albums are good-to-excellent, but his Capitol singles are much more of a mixed bag. He recorded around eighty tracks specifically for singles, taking only a handful ('My Funny Valentine', the title track of 1960's *Nice 'n' Easy*) from albums. Sometimes – like 'Young at Heart' (1954), 'Love Is the Tender Trap' (1956) and 'Witchcraft' (1958) – they were a match for any of his album tracks; other times he tried to keep pace with doo-wop ('Two Hearts, Two Kisses', 'From the Bottom to the Top'), got in a children's choir and enough apple pie to out-cutesy Tommy Steele (1960's desperate 'High Hopes'), or sang rubbish on purpose just because he could – how else to explain 'with a little wiggle here and a little wiggle there, man, this chick had wiggles to spare' on his 1960 hip update of 'Old MacDonald'?

his daughter Nancy – as well as all his mates. They didn't even have to be alive: check out his 1961 *I Remember Tommy* tribute to the recently departed Tommy Dorsey. Sinatra committed himself to three albums a year, on top of the A&R work and company chairman business, on top of all his live shows. Pleasure and business inevitably mixed. It was an insane workload; he was never off duty.

At the start of the 1960s Sinatra ran not only Reprise, but four music publishing companies based at the Brill Building, a string of radio stations in the Pacific North-West and a hotel-cum-casino in Reno, Nevada. He also had a large stake in the Sands Hotel, Las Vegas, and a film production company called Essex Productions. He was a big-time operator; as far back as 1962 he was making predictions about the movie business that wouldn't be realised until the twenty-first century: 'The way I see it is that pay-TV has got to come. It could give the film industry a terrific shot in the arm. I can see us making one picture a year, doing it really properly, but it's got to be a good product as well as lavish, of course. Then you show it on colour TV to forty million people at, say, fifty cents a head. Do that three times – pow pow pow – and you're really in business.'

Sinatra was literally in business – a tycoon, a magnate. He was also an in-demand actor in undemanding films like *Ocean's Eleven*, as well as a few better ones, like *The Manchurian Candidate*. He enjoyed his extracurricular work, but he was also realistic and objective enough to know that his voice was beginning to falter. Reprise looked slick, its artwork bright and contemporary, but still there was a suggestion of closing windows, of breathing in the air of memories, of knowing how things should be done. With exceptions like the proto-soul singer Hillard Street and Keely Smith's occasional stab at the Goffin and King songbook, early Reprise didn't exactly embrace the 1960s.

This shouldn't be a surprise; Sinatra had been less than generous to the music of the modern age during the later Capitol years. In 1960, when Elvis Presley left the army, Sinatra invited him onto his *Frank Sinatra Timex Show* for a 'Welcome Home Elvis!' special. 'Where the heck are his sideburns?' mugged Joey Bishop. 'Well, *IIIIII'll* be a hound dawg!' screamed Sammy Davis. 'I may pass out,' gasped daughter

Nancy, before Frank turned to the camera, totally deadpan, mumbling, 'And that's the opening, friends.' The show's awkward highlight was a duetted medley of 'Love Me Tender' and 'Witchcraft', during which Elvis did his best not to laugh and Sinatra finally seemed to register that Elvis could actually sing. 'Man, that's pretty,' he whispered. It was almost certainly scripted, but you knew he meant it.

The two signings most important to Reprise, and its least surprising, were Sammy Davis Jr, a song-and-dance man who was almost exactly ten years younger than Sinatra, and the crooner's crooner, Dean Martin. It wasn't just the venue that changed for the Rat Pack when Bogart died, the clientele changed too. Sinatra hated the name; he wanted the gang's get-togethers to be called 'the Summit', like it was a conference of top-end entertainers.* Given his socialist upbringing and outlook, Sinatra was surprisingly clear about the hierarchy: he was chairman – he knew how to get things done; Dino (who wasn't bothered) and Sammy (who was just happy to be in Sinatra's company) were second- and third-in-command, though neither got to make any real decisions; comedian Joey Bishop was usually around to crack jokes; and gawky Peter Lawford with the empty eyes was the sniggering tea boy. Sharp-suited, semi-resident in Las Vegas, the main trio gave the impression that their drinking, gambling and partying knew no bounds. With Sinatra as the record-label boss, and Reprise's two other best-selling acts in tow, who was ever going to say no to them?

Sammy Davis was stick-thin and wiry with energy, doubled-up with finger-snapping hipness, a virtuosic performer who could do anything he turned his hand to – singing, tap-dancing, mimicry, comedy – and make it look easy. Born on 8 December 1925, he had been on the road since childhood, a reminder of the days of minstrel shows. He had worn blackface, danced on street corners and dealt with the Mob, prising doors open by ignoring his blackness. Originally, he had been in a

---

* It wasn't the first time around for this type of semi-official Sinatra coterie. Back in the 1940s there had been 'the Varsity'; its floating membership was partly made up of Columbia A&R man Mannie Sachs; Sinatra's regular confidant, sometime songwriter and sometime bodyguard Hank Sanicola; music publisher Ben Barton; and his favourite songwriter, Sammy Cahn.

vaudeville dance act called the Will Mastin Trio with his father, who had appeared on a bill with Sinatra in 1947. Davis Jr made an impression, and Sinatra encouraged him to develop his singing and go solo. He signed to Decca in 1952, and his elastic, frivolous style soon made hit singles out of 'Love Me or Leave Me', 'Something's Gotta Give' (both 1955) and 'In a Persian Market' (1956). Some of his Reprise records are among the label's best, like his jet-propelled version of Jimmy Webb's 'Up, Up and Away' – 'This is your captain, prepare for take-off!'

In 1960 Sinatra was best man at Sammy's wedding to the Swedish actress May Britt. This was no small thing: in 1957 interracial marriage had still been illegal in half the American states, and a 1958 Gallup poll had showed that just 4 per cent of Americans approved of it. 1960 also saw the showdown in Little Rock, Arkansas, over integration in schools. The country was uptight with racial tension, and Sammy's 1960 album was pointedly called *I Gotta Right to Swing*, as if black America had to remind white America of the fact.*

If you're looking to find evidence of Sammy's magic on record, there are plenty of places to start: any tracks he cut with Marty Paich's jazz ensemble, including the minimal snap of his 'Begin the Beguine'; *When the Feeling Hits You*, cut in Vegas with Sam Butera and the Witnesses, which could well be the coolest forgotten record of 1965; and best of all, 1957's *Mood to Be Wooed*, with Sammy upfront and exposed, singing ballads, the only accompaniment coming from jazz player Mundell Lowe on electric guitar. Ella Fitzgerald and Tony Bennett had recorded albums with just piano, but *Mood to Be Wooed* was brave and unique. The only jazz vocal album to compare, from a decade later, is the sublime *Sammy Davis, Jr. Sings, Laurindo Almeida Plays*, this time with Spanish guitar. In both cases, his natural instinct to lark about, to scat right out of his hat, is quashed by the record's intimacy. The results are hushed and exquisite.

He's undervalued, for sure. Part of the reason for this is what he got up to in the 1970s. For black America, his cosying up to President Richard

---

* Sinatra and Davis would drift apart in the 1970s. Frank strongly disapproved of Sammy's fondness for cocaine and his advocacy of pornography, which led Davis to cultivate a friendship with porn star Linda Lovelace.

Nixon was unforgivable. The Anthony Newley-penned children's song 'The Candy Man', Sammy's sole US chart-topper in 1972, was perky as you like, but the kind of late-career smash that – like Chuck Berry's 'My Ding-a-Ling' from the same year, or Sinatra's 'My Way' for that matter – can cast a pall over a career; with time it can completely erase all cultural memory of everything that went before. Still, it wasn't a one-off for Sammy. For enthusiasts of kitsch, it got no better than 'I Am Over 25 but You Can Trust Me' (can you even say that with a straight face, let alone sing it?); a vocal version of the theme from *Hawaii Five-O*; his pained attempt at soul with the 'Theme from *Shaft*'; and his two recordings (rock and big band – he was versatile to the end) of the 'Plop Plop, Fizz Fizz' jingle for Alka-Seltzer.

The other reason his stock has dropped is precisely because of this versatility – subsequent generations haven't quite known what to latch onto. Everybody understands who Frank Sinatra and Dean Martin were, but Sammy Davis is much harder to define. There was his unlikely membership of Anton LaVey's Church of Satan, for a start. The shtick and gimmicks and doolally politics (he had also been initiated into the hardcore Black Power group the Blackstone Rangers) cloud the picture. He is a fascinating figure, but if you were a catalogue marketing executive who wanted an easy life, you'd stick to grinding out Dino's greatest hits.*

Dean Martin seemed the most affable of the three king rats, as well as the most conventionally handsome, but he remained the most unknowable. Neither Sinatra nor Davis are easy listening; you're always aware of their perfectionism; almost physically, they demand your attention. Martin couldn't have been more different. He had scored nonchalant hit singles right through the 1950s (the ramped-up Italo-ballad 'Return to Me'; the heartbreaking 'Young and Foolish'; the castanet-led shaggy-dog story 'The Naughty Lady of Shady Lane'), more consistently than Sinatra, but his albums would be mostly thrown together in a moment. One of his biggest hits was 'Memories Are Made of This' in 1956, a

---

* It's also hard not to be reminded of the scene in *This Is Spinal Tap* where the band's limo driver is talking to them about Sammy Davis's autobiography *Yes I Can*. It should, he tells them, have been called *Yes I Can, If Frank Sinatra Says It's OK*.

number one in Britain and America; with its creamy backing harmonies and almost folksy acoustic guitar, it was a bridge between the old world and the young idea that was just emerging. 'One girl, one boy, some grief, some joy, memories are made of this.' It's tempting to say it's haiku-like, but it's way simpler and more succinct. It might even be facile, but the song is so well suited to Dean's ultra-relaxed deportment that it's irresistible. Was there any more to this story? Of course, but Dino couldn't be bothered to elaborate.

Sinatra was obsessed with longevity, competition, quality, legacy. He frequently returned to old songs and made alterations to the phrasing, chipping away, capturing the perfect Sinatra vision. Martin didn't give a fuck about legacy. He was cavalier, seemed almost jaded from the outset. On stage with hard-working Sammy and Frank, his routines were improvised, and duly forgotten by the next show. Starring as an irritable singer in the 1964 movie *Kiss Me, Stupid*, he is presented with an Italian song and rolls his eyes – as if he hadn't sung a thousand of them already! But in real life he kept on singing them. A large part of his appeal, naturally, came from his perceived ease, his laziness even. Dino – even his nickname required the minimum of effort. He may not have cared, but other people really did, because his voice could entrance women, charm golden eagles down from their eyries and calm raging bulls, seemingly without any effort whatsoever. Elvis Presley once excitedly told Martin's daughter Deana that 'your dad is the king of cool'.

Even more than Bing Crosby, Dino enjoyed spending most of his time playing golf and wasn't remotely embarrassed by letting everyone know, unlike the sociable Bing, that this may have been because of the distance between people on a golf course, the minimal interaction and the game's quiet and solitary nature. Oddly, while most of Crosby's achievements and almost all of his hits are forgotten, and Sammy Davis is hardly mentioned except in his yes-man role for Sinatra, Dino's presence is still strong. Pizza parlours have 'That's Amore' on a loop; 'Sway', 'Mambo Italiano' and 'Volare' pop up in adverts for cars, furniture, pasta. As shorthand for mid-century Italian cool, Dino is your go-to man.

A brace of albums show just how good he really was. 1958's *Sleep Warm* was conducted and produced by Sinatra. You can sense his insecurities and work ethic being channelled into it, the power of his presence bringing out controlled, beautiful performances from Dean. It genuinely works best late at night, and insomniacs could do a lot worse than give *Sleep Warm* a listen before turning in. Then there's *Dream with Dean*, from 1964, one of the finest vocal jazz albums there is, with Dino's deep, seductive voice backed by guitarist Barney Kessel on an excellent romantic selection that includes Johnny Mercer's 'Fools Rush In' and Dick Haymes and Helen Forrest's 'I'll Buy That Dream'. The pace never changes; the odd piano trill or tinkle of a celeste can make you jump, like a thunderstorm. The effect is soothing, the vocals deeply resonant, and Jimmy Bowen's careful production has Dino right there with you, warming you a cognac. It's only thirty minutes long, but it helps you to imagine what Martin might have achieved had he become a jazz singer.

In 1964 he had an unexpected hit with a twenty year-old song called 'Everybody Loves Somebody', which knocked the Beatles' 'A Hard Day's Night' from the top of the *Billboard* chart that October. This led to two things happening: first, an unexpected, and largely dreary, set of Dino-goes-country albums; second, and more predictably, Frank Sinatra felt a twinge of envy.

Sinatra's early-1960s catalogue was messy. Often he would be trying to recall the snap of *Songs for Swingin' Lovers* (1961's *Come Swing with Me!*) or the emotional depth of *Only the Lonely* and *Where Are You?* (1962's weighed-down, miserable, Gordon Jenkins-arranged *All Alone*). Singles? 'The Coffee Song' and 'Granada' revisited 1940s travelogues, while 1962's 'Everybody's Twistin'' was a fascinating sub-Chubby Checker knees-up.

Sinatra's 1961 album *Point of No Return* had been his last for Capitol. It was, in every sense, a contractual obligation. Reprise had been up and running for a few months, and Sinatra already had three new Reprise albums under his belt. Capitol made the best of the situation: Axel Stordahl would once again be the arranger, Dave Cavanaugh would pro-duce it, and the songs would all share the theme of farewell. Everyone wished it well – except, naturally enough, Sinatra. He didn't want to be in the Capitol studio at all; he had his own label to run. Stordahl's wife, who knew her husband was ill, had to beg him to work just once more with his old partner. Sinatra acquiesced. He did every track in a single take. On one song there was a technical hitch, and Cavanaugh asked him if he could sing it again. 'Didn't you hear me?' snapped Sinatra, tearing his lead sheet in two. 'Next number.'

Miraculously, *Point of No Return* is a great album. Cavanaugh's song selection is inspired, mixing classics – 'September Song', 'As Time Goes By', 'These Foolish Things' – with less well remembered but equally affecting ballads like Eubie Blake's 'Memories of You' and Noël Coward's 'I'll See You Again'. Stordahl's arrangements are something else, the best he ever wrote for Sinatra, vividly colourful, almost modern classical, but never grave or overwhelming. Sinatra was too proud a singer to toss off a vocal on a song as revered as 'These Foolish Things' and performed well, but the secret of *Point of No Return*'s success was that everyone bar Sinatra was doing what they wanted and didn't need the singer's consent. He wasn't their boss.

Sinatra's pique when Dino's 'Everybody Loves Somebody' reached number one spurred him on to try harder, to try and sound relevant. Why had the Capitol records worked so well? Because, unlike the work of almost any performer before, you could hear his life in his music. Martin's Top 40 success indirectly led Sinatra to record 'It Was a Very Good Year' in late 1965. It blended deep melancholy and resignation with knotted braggadocio, and felt autobiographical. The emotional colour was as tangible as it had been on 'I'm a Fool to Want You'.

His fiftieth birthday had just gone, marked by TV specials, as well as one of the most lavish career retrospectives ever conceived – the triple-disc *A Man and His Music*. Sadly, this overshadowed his best mid-1960s albums. *Autumn of My Years* was a collection that hovered moodily around the sad core of 'It Was a Very Good Year'. Better yet was *Moonlight Sinatra*, which had a rotten pun for a title, a lunar theme that might have caused a raised eyebrow when you picked up the sleeve (phew – at least he didn't do 'Blue Moon'), and wasn't even an original idea – Mel Tormé had done something very similar with *Swingin' on the Moon* back in 1960. But it contained some of Sinatra's and Nelson Riddle's finest work – the bossa reimagining of 'The Moon Was Yellow', the aching violin- and woodwind-led 'Moon Song' – plus most of the selections were refreshingly obscure. 'I Wished on the Moon' had been written by Ralph Rainger and Dorothy Parker in 1935, and recorded by Bing Crosby, Al Bowlly, Billie Holiday and June Christy, but never with such richness and twilit darkness, never with such a deep velvet and mahogany sound.

It didn't sound young, though, and by now Sinatra was dating twenty-year-old Mia Farrow, so he really didn't want to seem like a piece of mahogany. As if Dino's surprise chart-topper hadn't been enough, in early 1966 Sinatra's daughter Nancy finally scored a number-one hit after five solid years of flops. 'These Boots Are Made for Walking' was a monster, indirectly referencing Emma Peel and Cathy Gale, with a fierce feminism that would still sound fresh decades later. What to do? A German song called 'Strangers in the Night' came Frank's way in 1966; all the care he'd taken over *Moonlight Sinatra*, released just weeks earlier, was dashed against the wall. Sinatra galumphed his way through a Euro Disney song that was undoubtedly catchy and cheaply evocative. It was always going to be a hit, no matter how he treated it, and the 'dooby-dooby-dos' on the fade-out had a strong whiff of sarcasm. It worked. In May 1966 'Strangers in the Night' dislodged the Rolling Stones' 'Paint It Black' from the top of the British singles chart; two months later, it replaced the Beatles' 'Paperback Writer' at number one in America. Still, he struggled to follow it. 'That's Life' roared and spat, with a lurching Sinatra struggling to stay in tune, and somehow it caught the mood of a section of the American public that was confused and angry about the way the world was turning, how long its hair was growing. There were versions of Petula Clark's 'Downtown' and Simon and Garfunkel's 'Mrs Robinson', and an ill-advised scrap with 'Winchester Cathedral' – all tossed out with less care than 'Mama Will Bark'. He called modern pop 'Beatleland', as if it was a foreign country to him. That much was clear to anyone listening.

The clue to a modern Sinatra sound lay outside of Anglo-American pop and in *Moonlight Sinatra*'s dalliance with bossa nova. The graceful economy of Antônio Carlos Jobim's music was a perfect fit on a brace of albums, *Francis Albert Sinatra & Antônio Carlos Jobim* (1967) and

Sinatra & Company (recorded in 1969, released in 1971). With liquid
arrangements from Claus Ogerman (who was simultaneously knocking
out bubblegum pop productions like 'Bend Me, Shape Me' and 'Hi Ho
Silver Lining'), Sinatra couldn't have sounded more different than he
had when growling his way through 'That's Life'; on songs like 'Quiet
Nights of Quiet Stars' he was entirely persuasive, so soft he was almost
whispering in places.

There are two records that end the Frank Sinatra story. One of them
is 'My Way',* with its histrionics and overtones, which can be seen as
either Italian American machismo or slightly fascist; he took the blows,
and told us about them as loudly as possible. Horribly immodest, it
peaked at number five on the UK singles chart in 1969 but ended up
staying in the Top 50 for a never-been-beaten 122 weeks. The other
record is *Watertown*, released in 1970. A song cycle about an everyday
Joe living in the suburbs who is separated from his wife, it was written by Bob Gaudio of the Four Seasons and jingle writer Jake Holmes.
Each song was effectively a letter to the missing Mrs Smith: there was
the title song, setting the scene in a town where 'everyone knows the
perfect crime – killing time'. 'Michael and Peter' starts off talking about
their kids but soon veers into domestic mundanities ('The roses that we
planted last fall climb the wall. I think the house could use some paint
– you know your mother's such a saint, she takes the boys whenever she
can'). Climactically, there's 'The Train', in which the narrator excitedly
anticipates his wife's return; it isn't really a spoiler to say that the train
comes and goes, and his wife doesn't alight.

You know she isn't coming back. You can hear it in his voice. She may
even be dead. *Watertown* is an incredibly bleak but beautiful album,
heightened by a vulnerability in Sinatra's voice. He wasn't the boyish
crooner, the jet-setting playboy or even the barking cynic any more. He
was a man coming to terms with middle age and a voice – his voice, the
Voice – that was reaching the end of the line. *Watertown* would become
a bookend. It was a masterpiece; the humility and self-doubt that had

* Actually, there was an even more bravado coda to this called 'I Will Drink the
Wine', his farewell single in 1971.

always been there to counter the bluster, the affairs and the bullying was more present on *Watertown* than on any other record in Sinatra's catalogue, but it also sold the fewest copies. That was enough of a sign. Frank Sinatra retired in 1971, having just made arguably the greatest album of his career.

46

TV IS THE THING: THE RISE OF TELEVISION

If the youth were taking over radio in the 1950s, then the older generations would switch to a medium that wasn't portable and wasn't cheap, something teenagers could only dream of controlling: television.

When we think about our memories of pop music, the first medium we think of is the record. The next one, ahead of radio even, is probably television – *Top of the Pops*, *Soul Train*, *Ready Steady Go!*, MTV, Christmas specials with Johnny Cash, Andy Williams or Girls Aloud. Once things were recorded on film and could be re-broadcast, a narrative could be shaped. Unlike radio stations or record companies, with television there was no chance of any independent alternatives, there was no possible parallel path. It was super-mainstream.

Before the advent of TV there had been enough of a mass media to create pop stars – venerated bandleaders, singers to have crushes on, people whose photos you could tape to the wall – but they became famous through ephemeral sources like cigarette cards, radio broadcasts and shellac 78s. With the advent of TV you now had an archive that would build, enforce and keep re-enforcing a canon. Major moments in pop-culture history – Elvis's pelvic thrusts, David Bowie putting his arm around Mick Ronson – would be repeated for ever. If television had come along twenty or thirty years earlier, names like Ina Ray Hutton and Harry Warren would not have been forgotten. Television would change the telling of pop history.

* * *

Prior to the TV revolution, it was sometimes hard to tell the difference between pre- and post-war Britain. In the late 1940s big bands would play concerts up and down the country on a Sunday, in town halls and ballrooms, to which literally the whole family would come. There would usually be a comedian, a ventriloquist and a couple of singers on the bill too. It would be a Sunday variety show, the last gasp of music hall, in a way. It wasn't until the beginning of commercial 'telly' – with the launch of ITV in 1955 – that people began to stay at home on a Sunday. Virtually no one in the UK had a TV set for the Queen's coronation in 1953; 90 per cent of American households would have one by 1960, a figure Britain didn't reach until 1968.

British TV's biggest showcase for music was ITV's *Sunday Night at the London Palladium*. It first aired in 1955, with cockney comedian Tommy Trinder as host. Its guest stars that night were Gracie Fields, whose career went back even further than Trinder's, and Guy Mitchell, one of the few American stars who made frequent trips to Britain when Musicians' Union regulations allowed. It was very much a boxed replacement for the Sunday family concerts. Concessions to youth were few, but in November 1955 a whole episode was dedicated to the *Daily Mirror* Disc Festival: singing comedian Max Bygraves presided over the best Britain had to offer, with a cast including Ted Heath and his band, Heath's former singer turned pin-up Dickie Valentine, Eddie 'The Man with the Golden Trumpet' Calvert and blonde balladeer Joan Regan, who would go on to marry the Palladium's box-office manager three years later. It was the first-ever 'poll winners' concert' put together by the British press, something that would be a staple of the rock era, but here it was, at the Palladium, which suggests that British pop had yet to split definitively into teenage and grown-up.

America had a weekly popularity poll of its own. *Your Hit Parade* had been on the radio since 1935,* switching to TV in 1951, with the hits of the day sung by the stars of the show. In the radio era the programme had largely featured anonymous singers, before striking gold with Frank Sinatra in 1943, then Doris Day in 1947. The TV series had a competent quartet of singers: Dorothy Collins (formerly with Raymond Scott's band), the actor Russell Arms, Snooky Lanson (Sinatra's replacement on the radio show) and Gisèle MacKenzie, a protégée of comedian Jack Benny. It worked when Arms had to tackle Frankie Laine's 'I Believe' or MacKenzie sang 'Secret Love' sweetly, but with rock 'n' roll taking up so much of the hit parade from 1956 onwards, the performance becoming more important than the song alone, the show looked slightly surreal. Snooky Lanson was called on to sing 'Hound Dog' week after week in 1956 – no one was happy. The show limped on for another two years. No one seemed to twig that there might be an audience for a show featuring Elvis Presley's hits and another that wanted to hear George Gershwin songs.

* * *

At the end of World War II television had been a toy for just a few thousand wealthy Americans. There were just three networks: NBC and CBS, both launched in 1941, both springing out of existing radio networks; and ABC, which launched in 1945 and was effectively a part of NBC that had to be sold off. By 1948 television was booming, and Milton Berle was the reason most Americans bought a TV set. He was so popular that he earned the nickname 'Mr Television'. On paper, he was just a vaudeville comedian who had a variety show, but after he

* The number-one record on the very first show was Bing Crosby's 'Soon'.

received 400,000 letters of protest when Elvis Presley appeared on his programme singing 'Heartbreak Hotel' in 1956, Berle was placed at the centre of an American moral panic.

An even less likely arbiter of morality was the *Ed Sullivan Show*, also launched in 1948, and presented by a man so hunched and uncomfortable that he appeared to have no neck or shoulders. When he declared Elvis to be a 'real fine boy' and that the show's producers had 'never had a nicer experience' working with a guest, he inadvertently set the ball rolling for *Blue Hawaii* and a decade of family-friendly entertainment from the King of Rock 'n' Roll. When he allowed the Beatles to appear in 1964, he heralded the British Invasion of the American hit parade. Could anyone have been a less likely revolutionary?

Kraft Television Theatre had launched in 1947, and for soldiers wondering what they'd been fighting for, it must have compared very poorly with Busby Berkeley. The show was sponsored by a company that manufactured 'TV dinners': pre-packaged convenience foods, like Kraft macaroni cheese, designed to be eaten while you watched. So this was the atomic age.

The demise of the big-band concert circuit led some singers to concentrate on TV. Newer faces saw it as an opportunity to bypass the gruelling bus journeys altogether. One of the first was bright-eyed squeaker Teresa Brewer. When 'Music, Music, Music' gave her a number-one hit in 1950, the timing was bad: she was pregnant with her first child. Given such a golden opportunity, though, Brewer was determined to combine a singing career with motherhood, which led her to concentrate on television rather than club shows and concert tours; as a result, she became a TV star. In the early 1950s she always seemed to be on one network show or the other – on *The Colgate Comedy Hour* with Abbott and Costello, out-smiling hosts like Perry Como and Jackie Gleason – and by 1953 she had her own twice-weekly programme, *Summertime USA*, with lugubrious co-host Mel Tormé. Each week Mel and Tess were seen in a different studio-simulated resort – Atlantic City one week, Rio de Janeiro the next. By the standards of the day, it was pretty high-concept.

Liberace was the most TV-ready presence of all. He had started out in the 1940s as a classical pianist who could play 'Chopsticks' in the style of Rachmaninoff for a laugh, but his glitz, his flamboyance and the candelabra on his piano weren't really built for radio. He was a true showman, never afraid to flaunt his growing wealth from nightclub appearances, and by 1955 he had his own TV series, *The Liberace Show*. His hands ran up and down the keyboard at a rate of knots on songs like 'Stella by Starlight' (a beautifully odd song from the 1944 film *The Uninvited*), Vera Lynn's 'Auf Wiedersehen' or his own 'Ballet for the Clouds'. He smiled constantly. 'Thank you very much,' he would say, often, slowly and unctuously. He was also handsome, in a waxy way, knew his audience well and in 1956 did a Mother's Day Special: 'It's no secret how I feel about my mum. She's the most wonderful person in all the world.' So he was shrewd, hard-headed and horribly sentimental, but he wasn't boring, and he became a constant TV presence through the 1950s. He would be namechecked in both the Chordettes' 'Mr Sandman' (1954) and Nina Simone's version of 'My Baby Just Cares for Me' (1959), which gives you some idea of just how famous he was.

* * *

Older generations found a comforting TV host in the rather less charismatic Lawrence Welk. Milton Berle and Ed Sullivan seemed positively edgy compared to Welk. He had led a sweet dance band in the 1930s and '40s, playing polka music on an accordion he had bought as a teenager. In one way, Welk's story was a classic American tale. He had grown up on a North Dakota farm, speaking only German until he was twenty-one, yet ended up as one of the biggest stars on TV.

The Lawrence Welk Show had been picked up by ABC from a local LA channel in 1955, and it would make Welk the king of old people. The opening scene featured a bubble machine, to give the impression of champagne. He would dance with his 'champagne lady' (there were many over the show's three-decade run) to operetta or Dixieland music or even a Polka-ised version of Saint-Saëns' 'The Swan'. The show was out of touch enough that when they performed a contemporary song in 1962 – the Orlons' girl-group dancer 'Wah Watusi' – the band dressed as beatniks. By the mid-1960s the show would be in colour, embracing this jump as lustily as T. Rex and Slade would on early colour episodes of *Top of the Pops* a few years later. The polka beat would play as men in sweaters of all the colours of the rainbow sang Sigmund Romberg's 'Stout Hearted Men'. Welk always looked awkward, only truly happy with his accordion strapped across his chest. He had one catchphrase – 'A-wunnerful' – and that was enough for ABC to air the show from 1955 to 1971. His show wasn't for you or for anyone you knew; it was for other people's grandparents and was a major outlet for non-rock pop.*

It seemed like even the most uncharismatic old white dude could carry an American TV show. Surely, in this brave new world, TV could shame Hollywood and show some respect to a potential audience of fifteen million black Americans? It had started out looking promising. Ethel Waters had been given her own show as early as 1939. 'When it was good it was quite good. When it was bad it was capital B,' said *Variety*. With a couple of minor exceptions (*The Bob Howard Show*, hosted by the little-known pianist, which ran for one season; *The Laytons*, which featured Amanda Randolph playing a black maid) that would be it until *The Hazel Scott Show* in 1950. Scott was a phenomenon, a charismatic, confident woman and a terrific jazz pianist who had been one of the major attractions at Barney Josephson's Café Society. She had powerful friends, too, being married to Congressman Adam Clayton Powell. *Variety* loved the show: 'Most engaging is the Scott personality, which is dignified yet relaxed and versatile.' What could go wrong? The McCarthy witch-hunts, for a start. Appearing before the House Un-American Activities Committee, Scott would speak up for art and music and love. She would not be cowed by 'the vicious slanders of little and petty men'. She was glamorous and outspoken, and within three months her TV show would be cancelled. Scott moved to France, where un-American activities were positively encouraged.

Instead of Hazel Scott's virtuoso piano-playing, America got Perry Como, formerly the singer with Ted Weems's sweet band, who sang

---

* Welk was also a more than competent businessman. He may have had no time for the music they released, but he wound up owning the Sugarhill and Vanguard labels, among others.

gently while shuffling packets of cigarettes on NBC's *Chesterfield Supper Club*. He was an informal, entirely calming presence in comfortable knitwear who could handle soft ballads ('Idle Gossip', 1954) and semi-rock jivers ('Juke Box Baby', 1955) with equal ease. Como was also the first singer to release an album of television-related songs, 1952's *TV Favourites*, which gave some idea of the medium's most popular reper-toire: 'Over the Rainbow', 'Summertime' and 'You'll Never Walk Alone'. Safe as houses. His female counterpart was Dinah Shore: she sang things like 'Goodnight Captain Curly Head' ('of the high-chair brigade') with such sincerity and goodwill that, like Perry, it was impossible to dislike her. Titles like 'Sleigh Ride in July' and 'At the Candlelight Café' saw her in full blue-skies regalia; that her name sounded a lot like 'dinosaur' didn't matter. She sang 'It's So Nice to Have a Man Around the House' in 1950: 'Just a guy in carpet slippers who will share your breakfast kippers and will help you zip your zippers . . . it's so nice!' Dinah and Perry: civility in a hostile world. *The Dinah Shore Show* ran from 1951 to 1963; by the 1970s Shore was hosting an afternoon talk show called *Dinah's Place*, on which she shared recipes and cooked with her guests. There was no cosier programme.

Andy Williams would be defined by his 1970 hit 'It's So Easy' and by the woollen ski-wear he donned every Christmas on TV, annually ushering in the season with 'It's the Most Wonderful Time of the Year'. Though his voice had Crosby's loose swing, he had first broken through as a milky rock 'n' roller, with hits like 'I Like Your Kind of Love' and 'Butterfly', a transatlantic number one in 1957, when he was already thirty years old. Williams thought so little of his early recordings – for Cadence, whose only other major act was the Everly Brothers – that he bought the master tapes so they could never be reissued.

These early recordings didn't make the most of Williams's caramel voice, and he wasn't wrong to be a little embarrassed about them. After signing to Columbia in 1962, his records got much better, as he merged Brill Building pop (Doc Pomus and Mort Shuman's 'Can't Get Used to Losing You') with film music ('Moon River', 'The Days of Wine and Roses') and lush but supportive arrangements from Robert Mersey. *The Andy Williams Show* would run from 1962 to 1971 and would make stars of regular guests the Osmond brothers. By 1965 he was in Hollywood, starring alongside Maurice Chevalier, Sandra Dee and Robert Goulet in *I'd Rather Be Rich*, a film that would be totally forgotten now were it not for the moving 'Almost There'. Williams started the song low and rumbling, climbed the melody in slippered feet until he reached its summit, taking in a view that showed him 'how wonderful, wonderful the world could be'. It looks pretty glib on paper, but it was all about Williams's delivery.

More than any of his contemporaries, Williams knew how to use television to his advantage. He sang 'Moon River' at the 1962 Academy Awards show, which was watched by more than forty million people; he then made sure it wasn't released as a single, in spite of the huge demand, and smiled to himself as hundreds of thousands of his *Moon River and Other Great Movie Themes* LP flew out of the shops, all retailing at three times the price of a 45. The industry gave him a round of applause.

47

I COULD GO ON SINGING:
THE NEXT GENERATION

Bongo Herbert was a fictional rock 'n' roller, with the kind of late-period Martin Amis name that suggested his creator, Wolf Mankowitz, thought rock 'n' roll was a rather gormless business. Played by a saturnine, unsmiling Cliff Richard, Bongo was the central character in *Expresso Bongo*, a 1959 film that luridly captured London's feverish coffee-bar scene at the end of the 1950s. Neither Cliff nor Soho's coffee-bar scene nor indeed any of the frenetic teenage activity in London that would eventually morph into the billion-dollar British rock boom meant a thing in America in 1960. Which makes the character of Dixie Collins (played by Yolande Donlan) all the more interesting. Dixie is a torch singer, all furs and purrs, highly American, who arrives in London in the customary limousine but is privately scared by the rock explosion. She hooks up with Bongo, and indirectly with rock 'n' roll, as a way of keeping her career afloat

– because Dixie knows that cool-headed pop is losing oxygen to hot and heavy teenage music.

If rock 'n' roll didn't impact directly on the sound and style of pop at the turn of the 1960s, its supercharged noise was always rumbling in the background. You had to adapt your image in a pop world that cohabited with rock. Bing's pipe and slippers didn't cut it in 1962; Sinatra's loosened tie and Vegas lifestyle did. The music industry – radio, the singles chart – may have been turned on its head by rock 'n' roll, but market research showed that teenage girls thought it was perfectly OK to buy Perry Como records along with Elvis's; they were different sounds for different moods. The rise of 'tweens like Paul Anka and Bobby Rydell, teenage rockers with half an eye on Vegas who straddled the old and new worlds, gave hope to the old school that rock was in abeyance, and by the early 1960s – in America at least – it certainly felt like more of a fringe concern. 1960's American number ones included the heavenly strings of Percy Faith and His Orchestra's 'Theme from a Summer Place', Marty Robbins's cowboy duel 'El Paso', Ray Charles's take on Hoagy Carmichael's 'Georgia on My Mind' and Brenda Lee's Italian ballad 'I Wanted to Be Wanted', while Elvis Presley stuck a Latin beat under 'O Sole Mio' and called it 'It's Now or Never', before pumping new life into Vaughn De Leath's 1927 hit 'Are You Lonesome Tonight'. For a few short years there was a truce, and it worked like this: Bobby Rydell sang Harold Arlen and Johnny Mercer's 'That Old Black Magic'; Arlen and Mercer pretended Bobby Rydell wasn't there. But in 1963 the Beatles arrived, and you couldn't ignore them. You had to pick sides. No one under twenty-one picked Perry Como's side, while Anka and Rydell were treated as collaborators.

* * *

There would still be room at the top table for newcomers. Notably, none of them would come over like Mario Lanza. The operatics were toned down; the mood was easy. Let the rockers sit in the sun – there was still fun (and Martinis) to be found in the shade.

'Easy listening' was a term that had first been introduced (though never really defined) by the radio industry after World War II. It wasn't 'hot' (as in rock or ragtime, or as jazz could be), and by definition it was also not 'difficult' (so it wasn't 'cool' in the sense of intellectual, musicianly music like bebop or Miles Davis, but it could include cool vocal jazz). It began life as a marketing category, but after the convulsion of rock it started to become used as a term for pop that suggested possible futures, a positive way forward for the many who saw rock as a catastrophe.

The kids hadn't taken over the wireless completely. The Federal Communication Committee's licensing of stereo radio stations on FM airwaves in 1960 would be a launchpad for a new format of soft instrumentals called 'beautiful music'. Philadelphia's WDVR would be set up for more mature listeners in 1963, while other local stations concentrated on teenagers; within four months it had become the number one-rated FM station in Philadelphia. This was a key moment, proving the viability of pop stations on FM.

With many over the age of twenty covering their ears at the predominance of rock on AM stations, 'beautiful music' stations were quickly set up on FM radio across America. Essentially, this was the birth of easy listening as a genre rather than just a background hum, and these stations would be the older siblings to Radio 2, the great-grandparents to Magic FM. Instrumental versions of popular tunes were the default. Duke Ellington's version of 'Never on Sunday' was about as edgy as it got, but more often you'd hear Lawrence Welk's 1961 number one 'Calcutta', with its decidedly non-Indian lead harpsichord.*

By 1961 'easy listening' was a common enough term for *Billboard* to use it as the name of their first 'adult-oriented' chart, though this was the first official industry recognition given to something most people would only have been dimly aware of. Likewise, this was a wax stamp on the notion that youth and non-youth had created two parallel pop

---

* The 'beautiful music' format had largely been replaced with 'adult contemporary' by the mid-to-late 1970s; in the '90s, as FM stations switched en masse to modern country, it expired. However, the basic format – relatively few advert breaks, nothing musically outré, only familiar tunes – survives with smooth jazz stations in America and the hugely popular, lower-middlebrow Classic FM in Britain.

worlds. *Billboard* had effectively designated a market space for acts who were neither future-centric nor pining for Jolson and the good old days, a market for music that was (by choice) gentle and sentimental and soothing. Delicate, even. And that was OK. New singers plugged right in.

Judy Garland's short-lived CBS TV show would introduce us to a new star in 1964. With her hair straightened into a Mary Quant bob and wearing nautical chic, Barbra Streisand seemed to be demanding attention. The part of Miss Marmelstein in the Broadway show *I Can Get It for You Wholesale* had made her name. Its director, Arthur Laurents, wrote of Babs: 'When she sang, she was simple; when she sang, she was vulnerable; when she sang, she was moving, funny, mesmerizing, anything she wanted to be.' Just nineteen, she wrote her own bio for the theatre programme, adding a little exoticism: 'Born in Madagascar and reared in Rangoon, educated at Erasmus Hall High School in Brooklyn. She is not a member of the Actors' Studio.' If her bio had said she was born in Flatbush, nobody would have taken any notice. Streisand set herself up in opposition very early on. 'Everything was so pompous and serious . . . everybody said they were a member of the Actors' Studio.'

Already, she seemed ridiculously comfortable with her talent, something that is perfectly audible and frequently off-putting. On the small screen, Garland could see her as the future, smiling and egging her on as she sang 'Happy Days Are Here Again', just as Sophie Tucker had doted on the young Judy in *Broadway Melody of 1938* nearly thirty years earlier. But Streisand didn't need the applause or the sense of continuity. She didn't crave praise; she may have been mannered in the extreme but she was entirely self-sufficient, her own planet, and it was one that plenty of people were happy to orbit.

In 1962 her very first single had been a half-speed, miserabilist take on 'Happy Days Are Here Again' – an ancestor to every *authentique* John Lewis ad – signalling how much emotion she could wring from apparently basic material. Vocally, she used the same odd trick that Judy Garland herself had used to great effect at key moments in *Easter Parade* ('Better Luck Next Time') and *A Star Is Born* ('The Man That Got Away'): each line became louder and bendier as it went on. Garland had always sounded as if she was dredging something up from a deep well of dreadful memories – when she was separated from her sisters aged five, for instance, or being drugged by MGM aged fourteen – and was inches away from a breakdown. Streisand, by comparison, was projecting technique; each of these lines sounded more and more pleased with itself as it grew louder and louder. Tackling difficult material like Laura Nyro's 'Stoney End' (1970), she would be all technique, devoid of nuance, but she would thrive when given tag-team material ('No More Tears' with Donna Summer in 1979, 'Guilty' with Barry Gibb in 1980) or ballads written specifically with her rubbery Bronx honk in mind (Gibb's 'Woman in Love', Paul Williams's 'Evergreen', 'Papa, Can You Hear Me' from *Yentl*). One of her very best recordings was the New York beat ballad 'Our Corner of the Night' (1966), a nocturnal Gotham love song expertly arranged by Charles Callelo that Streisand apparently hated and has never allowed to be reissued.

Johnny Mathis could have been an Olympic athlete. In 1956, when he was twenty years old, he had to choose between the high jump and music. His sweet, high voice and pristine vibrato won out over his long, lean legs. There was a slight country lilt to his debut hit 'Chances Are' in 1957, but mostly his music sounded like it had been ushered in from Eden on a perfumed breeze. 'Look at me, I'm as helpless as a kitten up a tree' is not a line you would ever expect from Tom Jones. Mathis's voice was androgynous and his racial identity a blur. It turned out he had Choctaw heritage on his mother's side, and he suspected his grandfather – whom he never met – was white. In a *Washington Post* interview, he later said: 'I had to find out who I was. So I decided that I was everything.' Hits like 'A Certain Smile' (1958), 'Misty' (1959) and an extraordinary Dimitri Tiomkin song called 'Wild Is the Wind' (which David Bowie would later extend and effectively own) were as clearly enunciated and moving as Nat King Cole's best moments.

He became a hero to some unlikely fans. Hard hippie Arthur Lee, singer with the band Love, would model his voice on Mathis's for their *Da Capo* and *Forever Changes* albums in the late 1960s; Philly soul arranger Thom Bell called him a 'leader' and rebuilt Mathis's career with gently autobiographical songs like 'I'm Coming Home' in the mid-1970s; Chic's Nile Rodgers and Bernard Edwards produced his *I Love My Lady* album in 1981, which – for no good reason – stayed in the vaults until 2017. You can precis his career to make Mathis sound like a giant for our times, a gender-fluid, pan-racial being with the voice of an angel and a face both handsome and kind who surely arrived decades too early. The problem with this reading of his life is all the material you have to leave out: not just his vaguely right-wing politics or the lack of commitment to anything beyond his voice, but the albums. Dozens of them. For every album track like 'Life Is a Song Worth Singing' (his 1974, Bell-produced masterpiece) there is a pile of sedate, sterile songs like 'When I Need You' or 'Those Were the Days' or 'When a Child Is Born' (his only UK number one, in 1976) that were vapour-soft, a waft of air, barely there and ultimately boring. He had an amazing voice, one of the very best, but much of the time he didn't know what to do with it.

At his best, though, Mathis was the make-out king, a romantic lead who had taken on and beaten all newcomers in the late 1950s. And there was a surprising number of them, singers who carried on as if rock 'n' roll were happening in some foreign country. There was Robert Goulet, whose name made him sound like a lugubrious gourmet. Buddy Greco was a post-Mel Tormé finger-snapper who turned 'The Lady Is a Tramp' into a smug soufflé; more impressively, in 1971 he sang 'Cardboard California', a riposte to Tormé's *California Suite* some twenty years on.* Jack Jones was born the night his dad, the stentorian actor Allan Jones, recorded the Neapolitan-sounding 'Donkey Serenade', a huge hit in 1938 and allegedly the third-best-selling single in RCA Victor's history. Both blessed with matinee-idol looks, father and son were singing together at the Thunderbird Hotel and Casino in Las Vegas by the late 1950s.

Even when he was given contemporary material – like Burt Bacharach and Hal David's hip but uproariously sexist 'Wives and Lovers' (1964) – Jack Jones sounded twenty years older than he was. Twenty years out of time, that is, rather than a sage forty-something. He was signed to Kapp in 1961 and recorded a ballad called 'Lollipops and Roses', which

* My favourite Buddy Greco fact is that Jimmy Webb once stayed in his house and wrote 'MacArthur Park' on his piano.

won him a best male vocal Grammy straight out of the blocks. He was extraordinarily well groomed, almost unreal, as if he'd emerged from a spray-can, and his voice sat somewhere between Mel Tormé and Andy Williams, without ever suggesting much affinity with either jazz or rock 'n' roll. He was born for Vegas. It is quite impossible to get excited by anything he ever recorded; he simply existed to fill a gap that was exactly Jack Jones-shaped. My favourite thing about him is that he recorded a swing album in 1997 called 'New Jack Swing'.

Matt Monro had all the emotion that Jones lacked. Though he was often called Britain's Sinatra in the 1960s (as Dickie Valentine, rather generously, had been in the '50s), there was never anything other than kindness and warmth in his singing. He was closer in tone to Perry Como, but sounded considerably more engaged. I love photos of Monro, with a slight paunch, a hint of double chin, a couple of beads of sweat on his brow, a few hairs on the crown of his head sticking up. He still looked the bus conductor he had been before turning pro, like he'd just given the school bully a clip round the ear and chucked him off the 68 to Chalk Farm. No matter what the exotic setting on his album covers, you could cut the shot of Monro out and place it on a Watney's pub backdrop and it would fit just as well. A pint of bitter at his side, a fag in his hand. Never a cigar. Part of his classiness was that he never looked down on his own; Monro was a working man's hero. In this respect, certainly, he was Sinatra's equal. His 1962 hit 'Softly as I Leave You' was one of the greatest songs and productions of the decade, a heartbreaking tale of separation that might even be about death. It would be trashed by a sleepwalking Sinatra a couple of years later.

Jazz vocalists struggled as these new easy-listening performers took the middle ground, and jazz would continue its post-bop move from popular music into the realm of art. As for the classical audience, the vast majority were still pretending that jazz – let alone popular music – simply didn't exist. A couple of olive branches were held out by the Swingle Singers – a group of Parisian session singers – and the Jacques Loussier Trio, who turned Bach into a smoky-cellar-bar concern.

Loussier had signed to Decca in 1959 as a classical pianist. While they were trying to think of something that could launch his recording career, he 'started to play some Bach with my improvisations and they said, "What is that? Why don't we make a record of that?" I was still doing it out of fun. I never thought the public would like it. I was wrong.' The jazz input was sparing, never too assertive, and Loussier sold some six million albums. The *New York Times*' classical critic called his smooth sound 'tiresome and offensive'. In Britain, his 'Air on a G String' would become synonymous with lighting up a Hamlet cigar and drifting off into a reverie.

The Swingle Singers were assembled in 1962 by Mobile, Alabama's Ward Swingle, who came up with the idea of applying wordless scat vocals to Bach, as well as to Vivaldi and Rodgers and Hart. The softest brushed drums underpinned cleverly layered da-buh-da harmonies, and the sound was all very Christmas shopping. It was either captivating or the most infuriatingly featherweight music in the world – a buzzing fly of scat-singing, circling the temperature-controlled departure lounge of easy listening.

One post-war jazz musician who crossed over into the mainstream was pianist Dave Brubeck. His quartet had a sound that was fresh but not too out there, novel but somehow familiar. It was about clarity and simplicity. It was very cool. In 1953 they recorded a song called 'At a Perfume Counter', and it sounded exactly like Saks Fifth Avenue on a Tuesday afternoon in May.

Compared to Duke Ellington or Glenn Miller, nothing very exciting happened in Brubeck's world, but it was both inventive and relaxed. Brubeck and drummer Joe Morello loved to try out wild time signatures – 1961's 'Unsquare Dance' was in 7/4 time and was still a UK Top 20 hit single. It was pop, but a little scientific, hardly pop as anyone would recognise it. A Brubeck album track like 'Blue Rondo à la Turk' – with piano and sax harmonising over a 9/8 rhythm derived from Turkish street musicians – anticipated Steve Reich and Philip Glass. Things like 'Unsquare Dance' would later be given a nod of recognition by progressive-rock acts (Keith Emerson was a Brubeck devotee) in the 1970s and math-rock performers (Polvo, Mars Volta) in the 2000s. So Brubeck occupies a rare place where pop, jazz and modern classical intersect.

There was nothing to indicate what fired him. Unsurprisingly, he chose to put twentieth-century modern art on the covers of his albums rather than his blank, bespectacled face. To look at, Brubeck could have been anything – a dentist, a maths teacher, a jazz virtuoso, a Stasi agent. His anonymity was a plus, and people projected onto this blank canvas. He also had a sense of humour: 'Kathy's Waltz' was mostly in 4/4 time.

The Brubeck Quartet's most famous recording, 1958's 'Take Five', was initially built around a Morello drum solo in 5/4 time; sax player Paul Desmond added the melody, and Eugene White's walking bass glued it together. It was incredibly popular, while also a work of groundbreaking experimental jazz. To his discomfort, Brubeck was on the cover of *Time* magazine in 1954; he was convinced it was only because he was white, and he was probably right. (The article claimed he was 'described by fans as a wigging cat with a far-out wail and by more conventional critics as probably the most exciting new jazz artist at work today'.) In the long run, the *Time* cover might have worked against his legacy: Brubeck is mostly ignored in jazz circles today. Given his one-time stature, it now feels like his work is well regarded only by those in the know – and buskers, who can't get enough of 'Take Five'.*

* * *

If you wanted the new easy-listening sound in a nutshell, there was Billy May's 'beautiful music' version of the Brazilian song 'So Nice (Samba de Verão)', which was basically an ice-rink organ playing over a pitter-pat of Latin brushed drums, with nothing else audible. It was an astonishing piece of minimalism from the man who had arranged *Come Fly with Me*'s globe-spanning roar five years earlier.

In spite of the quality of these emerging singers and the continued improvements in recording technology, there was a lack of newness, a feeling of continuity, of status quo. The new sound would emerge when

* Brubeck attempted to cross over into the post-Beatles, modern pop era by working on a handful of experimental jazz/pop singles with a singer called Ranny Sinclair. Long, breathy New York whispers, they would finally be collected on an album called *Another Autumn* in 2017, which I can't recommend highly enough.

bossa nova travelled up-continent thanks to floppy-haired, scholarly-looking guitarist Antônio Carlos Jobim. For most Britons and North Americans, the sleepy, sensual shuffle of bossa nova seemed to have come from nowhere. As far as they were concerned, it had been discovered by sax-playing expeditionist Stan Getz, who had scored a surprise hit single in 1962 with a recording of Jobim's 'Desafinado', but its roots were in plain sight. Jobim's heroes were Dorival Caymmi (who had written the songs for Carmen Miranda that helped her become a Hollywood star) and Ary Barroso, composer of 'Baìa' (adapted for Disney's *The Three Caballeros* in 1945) and 'Brazil', an instrumental US hit for Xavier Cugat during the ASCAP dispute in 1942.*

The subtleties of samba music might have been steamrollered by Tin Pan Alley, but Jobim – a one-time architecture student – said Caymmi and Barroso 'left a *rastro*, a track of beauty for us to follow'. Brazilian music was traditionally hot and percussive, peppered with joyous shouts; bossa nova was cool, restrained, considered and lyrical. With fellow writer João Gilberto, Jobim created a cleaner sound – water on pebbles, a breeze through green leaves – and this Brazilian 'new wave' (the literal translation of 'bossa nova') made an international impact with 'The Girl from Ipanema' in 1964. Sung by Gilberto's wife Astrud, who strangely wasn't credited on the record, it would provide a soothing balm in the overheated year of Beatlemania. Astrud became a major star off the back of it, singing everything from 'Fly Me to the Moon' to Randy Newman's 'I Think It's Gonna Rain Today' in her flat, breathy, *desafinado* voice that somehow sat perfectly over Gil Evans's and Eumir Deodato's arrangements.†

* 'Brazil' would later be recorded, with the addition of Bob Russell's English lyrics, by everyone from Frank Sinatra to Kate Bush to 1970s disco outfit the Ritchie Family.
† Jobim's best-known songs – 'The Girl from Ipanema', 'Meditation', 'How Insensitive' – featured English lyrics by Norman Gimbel, a model writer who had sidestepped rock 'n' roll after first having written pre-rock hits like Teresa Brewer's 'Ricochet', Andy Williams's 'Canadian Sunset' and Dean Martin's 'Sway'. Along with his Jobim lyrics, he put words to Marcos Valle's 'Summer Samba' (aka 'So Nice'), Michel Legrand's 'I Will Wait for You' and 'Watch What Happens', wrote kids' bubblegum for the TV soundtracks to *The Bugaloos* and *H. R. Pufnstuf,* and

'When bossa nova first appeared in Brazil it had so many adversaries,' Jobim told jazz writer Bob Blumenthal, 'so many *puristas* full of animosity. Yet the US loved us. With hindsight, I can see that the more the US said yes, the more Brazil said no.' His sound may have been light, minimal and unvarnished, so soft it could be bruised by marshmallows, but it featured unsettling chords and harmonies, and flatted fifths borrowed from American bebop – one reason it garnered so much opposition from the *bossa velho* in Brazil. 'How Insensitive' borrowed as much from Chopin as Gerry Mulligan, but that didn't stop the old guard from saying that bossa nova had 'crooked melodies'.*

Streisand, Mathis, radio and TV helped a non-rock popular-music tradition to continue; Jobim added a new dimension. But when Cole Porter died in 1964, aged seventy-three, it felt like a certain type of song really had died with him. Hart and Hammerstein were already gone, leaving just Rodgers, and writer's block had effectively put Berlin into retirement. Porter, born in the lap of luxury, had moved in a milieu that was way above that of most of these contemporaries, living and working where the air was rarefied. 'It came natural to him to write about it,' said Johnny Mercer. 'He wrote about society people, he wrote about the Riviera, he wrote about chic places. He just was a very elegant, chic man.' The number-one album on the day Porter died was the soundtrack to *A Hard Day's Night*, the number-one single was Roy Orbison's 'Oh Pretty Woman', and top of the easy-listening chart was Gale Garnett's folksy 'We'll Sing in the Sunshine'. For now, at least, it felt like pop no longer needed a sophisticated vocabulary like Cole Porter's.

---

ultimately came up with 'Killing Me Softly with His Song', which he wrote for singer Lori Lieberman after she showed him a poem she had written about going to a Don McLean concert.

* In Brazil, upsetting the old guard had worse consequences than Irving Berlin getting the hump with your treatment of 'White Christmas'. The government put Jobim in jail in 1970, along with fellow groundbreaking musicians like Gilberto Gil and Caetano Veloso. The politicians were convinced that their songs were written in some underground code, and they wanted them silenced. When Sergio Mendes sent the imprisoned musicians a telegram written in slang to announce his son had been born, the authorities took it as evidence that they were sending secret messages to each other.

48

THE STRENGTH OF STRINGS: FILM SOUNDTRACKS

By the late 1950s many singers had walled themselves behind the TV screen to keep the teenage hordes at bay. They thrived and, for now, had the albums market sewn up. But if you were a player in a big band or a jazz arranger, the '50s offered slim pickings. In Britain, the success of Ted Heath's band might have heralded an Indian summer for swing, though even here the trad revival saw it off before the decade was out. In America, Stan Kenton aside, jazz was strictly for small groups, and arrangers were working exclusively for singers like Frank Sinatra, Ella Fitzgerald and the dozens of jazz-influenced vocalists who came in their wake. There was another lucrative, progressive way out of the post-war jazz malaise that didn't involve supporting a club singer or diving blind into rock, and that was cinema.

Back in the early days of Hollywood, when there was no dialogue, the score had been of huge significance in keeping the action ebbing and flowing. The soundtrack in a movie theatre had usually been provided by a solo piano, with different music for every film. When the talkies began, the paying audience were, understandably, more interested in hearing the cast's dialogue; music was prominent only in the opening and closing credits and love scenes. While it was necessary, unobtrusiveness was rewarded, its background quality making it more effective when you had dialogue writers like Anita Loos to compete with. To be unobtrusive, it also helped if it was familiar, and so soundtracks tended to be semi-classical, heavily derivative of Tchaikovsky, Debussy and Ravel. Unless you were filming a musical, there was no need or demand for originality.*

Three things ushered in a change: firstly, the emergence of the independent film producer, willing to try a new sound; secondly, the new composer–arranger, who emerged from the ashes of the swing era; and thirdly, the breakthrough of television. TV shows were not films, and their scores required something closer to everyday life, something more contemporary than *Seven Brides for Seven Brothers*. There was also a lot of them; work was not thin on the ground.

While Hollywood was fighting the post-war American appetite for home entertainment, soundtrack writing was coming into its own. Fred Zinnemann's *High Noon* (1952) had a generic Dimitri Tiomkin soundtrack but achieved a hypnotic state by effectively repeating a single song, sung by Tex Ritter in the film and a hit single for Frankie Laine.† Influential soundtracks included *The Third Man*, which utilised Anton Karas's 'Harry Lime Theme' throughout. No mush of strings was needed for the sinister but charming Lime, just a zither to create one of

---

* Here are a few soundtrack milestones. The first soundtrack album to be commercially released was Disney's *Snow White and the Seven Dwarfs* in 1938; issued as a set of 78s, it was essentially a musical. As for an album of purely orchestral score, the first was for Alexander Korda's version of *The Jungle Book* (1942), with music composed by Miklós Rózsa. And the first jazz-based film score? In Hollywood, at least, it was Alex North's music for the 1951 movie *A Streetcar Named Desire*.

† Sheb Wooley, who had a bit part in the film, would go on to score a number-one single with the novelty hit 'Purple People Eater' as rock 'n' roll entered its decadent phase in 1958.

the best-selling movie themes of all time, a UK sheet-music number one in 1951, a year before the first British singles chart was launched. Most influential of all was 1955's drug-pocked, low-life drama *The Man with the Golden Arm*. With director Otto Preminger, Frank Sinatra in a new, mature acting role, Saul Bass's Blue Note-comes-alive opening credits, composer–arranger Elmer Bernstein's theme and Shorty Rogers's score, here was a world that didn't need to look to dance halls or jazz clubs for its future, something adult but forward-looking and thoroughly reward-ing – a viable, parallel existence to rock 'n' roll America. The drums slunk, the brass alternately snapped and growled. It sounded like a knife fight between Woody Herman and Gene Krupa, shirts torn and blood-ied. Covered by Billy May, the theme became a transatlantic Top 10 sin-gle, and would be revisited with similar floor-shaking thunder by British bass player Jet Harris in 1962. Put simply, *The Man with the Golden Arm* invented both the modern movie theme and its score.*

In the film's wake came a swarm of imitations and homages. Among the best were *Peter Gunn*, a TV detective series that should by rights be entirely forgotten but which has lived on thanks to an exceptionally murky, growling Henry Mancini score. Duane Eddy had a hit single with the theme, emphasising the menace on his bottomless bass guitar, while Mancini's album of the soundtrack did even better, with its neat appropriation of west coast cool jazz written large in the titles: 'Session at Pete's Pad', 'Sorta Blue', 'Not from Dixie', 'Dreamsville'.† Beyond this were Laurie Johnson's bold, sensual music for *The Avengers* (1964), Lalo Schifrin's itchy Latin score for *Mission: Impossible* (1968) and Neal Hefti's nyah-nyah *Batman* theme (1966), camp as a row of tents but

---

* Elmer Bernstein had an even bigger impact on the UK singles chart with the explosive 'Staccato's Theme', from the short-lived TV crime drama *Johnny Staccato*, in 1960. It seems appropriate that the glowering Staccato, both jazz pianist and private detective, was played by John Cassavetes, who, as an independent director, would become a singular voice in Hollywood.
† Mancini was smart enough to employ some of the best west coast musicians to create this most modern sound: Pete Candoli (trumpet), Ted Nash (reeds), Dick Nash (trombone), Larry Bunker (vibes), Jack Sperling (drums) and pianist John Williams, who would, though no one could have guessed, go on to be the villain of this particular sub-story.

with a cat-like bassline whose paw prints led right back to *The Man with the Golden Arm*.

All of these films and shows were crime-related. The ultimate conjunction might be *I Want to Live*, which featured Gerry Mulligan's music and a condemned woman who talked to her cellmate about being a Mulligan fan – a very literal association between the cool and crime, since Mulligan had done time for narcotics offences.

Jazz certainly wasn't the only way in for the generation of soundtrack writers who would underscore the shape-shifting cultural world in the 1950s and '60s. Michel Legrand's break came in 1954, when Columbia commissioned a suite of chanson and accordion music with English lyrics called *I Love Paris*. Designed to sate the appetites of the growing number of American tourists heading to the French capital, the album sold an astonishing eight million copies and spawned dozens of imitators. Legrand had left the Paris conservatoire in 1949 as a jazz pianist and walked into work with local stars Juliette Greco and Zizi Jeanmaire. The wild success of *I Love Paris* at the age of twenty-two derailed him, and Legrand followed it with *Bonjour Paris*, *Paris à la Hi Fi*, *Rendezvous à Paris* and – yes – *The New I Love Paris*, before descending into the less-than-kosher travelogues *Holiday in Rome*, *Legrand in Rio*, *Castles in Spain* and *Vienna Holiday* (*Time*'s review called the latter 'a major atrocity that should cause Vienna to break diplomatic relations with Paris').

Fortunately, Legrand's success led to a parallel career in soundtrack-scoring. First came 1955's chanson-lite *Les Amants du Tage*; more memorable was the lonesome harmonica-led score for Marcel Carné's suburban rebel flick *Terrain Vague* (1960). The French New Wave came along at exactly the right time for Legrand, with his deliciously cheeky songs for Agnès Varda's *Cleo from 5 to 7* and a slapstick score for Jean-Luc Godard's *Une femme est une femme*, but it was Jacques Demy who let him run riot, with 1964's *Les Parapluies de Cherbourg* (*The Umbrellas of Cherbourg*) – all songs, no dialogue, everything rainbow-coloured. It also featured a gold-plated standard in 'I Will Wait for You', which would be recorded by Frank Sinatra, Scott Walker, Tony Bennett, Matt Monro, Bobby Darin, Astrud Gilberto, Andy Williams, Gil Evans . . . everyone. The song was exquisite, and deathlessly romantic. Legrand drew deep from a well of melancholic melody – Oscars for *Summer of '42* and *Yentl* were the least he deserved – and he gleefully showed how you could progress as a jazz player, without sacrificing tunes or a sense of identity.

Bernard Herrmann's work was not deathlessly romantic. He had been to Juilliard and founded the New Chamber Orchestra of New York by the time he was twenty, before working his way up at CBS. He scored Alfred Hitchcock's *North by Northwest* (1959) and *Psycho* (1960), while his sawing, monotone string theme for François Truffaut's *Fahrenheit 451* (1966) influenced the Beatles' 'Eleanor Rigby' and, in turn, the whole baroque-pop genre. He also wrote an opera (*Wuthering Heights*), a cantata (*Moby Dick*) and a beautiful, almost pastoral *berceuse* dedicated to those killed in World War II ('For the Fallen'). He could afford to fall out with Hitchcock, who wanted a pop soundtrack for *Torn Curtain*, knowing that the likes of Martin Scorsese and Brian De Palma would be on the phone sooner or later. Herrmann knew what he was doing. 'I have the final say or I don't do the music,' he said.

Like Herrmann, *Peter Gunn* composer Henry Mancini had also studied at Juilliard. After the war, he had been the pianist and arranger for Tex Beneke's re-formed Glenn Miller Orchestra, while studying under Czech composer Ernst Krenek.* Working at Universal Pictures, Mancini somehow became the go-to man for goofy horror films (*The Creature Walks Among Us*, *Creature from the Black Lagoon*, *It Came from Outer Space*), but soothed his soul by arranging the music for *The Glenn Miller Story* and *The Benny Goodman Story*. He had a huge sentimental streak, writing a late-period side for that old smoothie Guy Lombardo ('I Won't Let You Out of My Heart', 1957), which was followed by an Oscar nomination for *The Days of Wine and Roses*. Almost alone among his Hollywood contemporaries, he was smart enough to sign a record deal, with RCA, who made him a major albums artist. He looked progressively more tanned, more Californian, more smiley.

---

* Krenek's own work veered between neo-romantic, atonal and jazz, a diversity which rubbed off on Mancini: compare *Experiment in Terror* (1959) to *A Shot in the Dark*'s 'Pink Panther Theme' (1964) to *Two for the Road* (1967).

Sometimes he recorded his own songs, soft melodic things with deceptive bends like 'How Soon', with its delicate harpsichord melody swamped by what could be the Mormon Tabernacle Choir (it would be Mancini's only UK Top 10 hit, in 1964). He was just as happy knocking out easy-on-the-ear things, whether by Scott Joplin, Antônio Carlos Jobim or the Beatles. A chuckling, quite possibly stoned John Lennon introduced him on the BBC's *The Music of Lennon and McCartney* in 1965: 'Here's Henry Mancini, known to his friends as Hank . . . Take it away, Henry!' Hank should care. Eventually, he had a deserved US number-one single in 1969 with the Rachmaninoff-inspired 'Love Theme from *Romeo and Juliet*' (better known to Radio 1 listeners in Britain as the music from Simon Bates's *Our Tune*). By the 1970s Mancini had earned eight gold discs and twenty Academy Awards, and had a catalogue deep enough for a TV-advertised compilation on Arcade called *40 Greatest*. At their worst, soundtracks can resemble popular music but sound like a facsimile, closer to telephone hold music, a musical chloroform, and Mancini at his soupiest edged towards this non-music.

In the 1960s he had scratched his jazz itch on 1965's *A Shot in the Dark*, which sat alongside contemporary scores by Herbie Hancock (*Blow Up*), Neal Hefti (*Barefoot in the Park*), Quincy Jones (*The Pawnbroker*, *In the Heat of the Night*, *In Cold Blood*) and Lalo Schifrin (*Bullitt*). All of these were jazz-based, but soundtracks are too tightly restricted for innovation, so they weren't exactly jazz. They were more like a conjunction of American and old European; not 'Third Stream', but a third way.

The *Gesamtkunstwerk* would be 1967's *The Graduate*, where Dave Grusin's score and Simon and Garfunkel's songs were a counterpoint to Mike Nichols's uncomfortable love story. It was quite possible to believe that Dustin Hoffman's character was responsible for the songs, although he never sang a note (the polar opposite of this had been *The Umbrellas of Cherbourg*, which had been closer to operetta than rock). Elsewhere, Grusin soundtracked the mock-Tudor mundanity of the parents' pool party and the humiliation of Elaine Robinson (played by Katharine Ross) in a strip club. The soundtrack sold like billy-o, and the artwork was totemic. Two years later came its only rival in straddling the old worlds and the very new – *Midnight Cowboy*. The soundtrack mixed psychedelic rock ('Old Man Willow'), nursery-school Latin jazz ('Florida Fantasy'), country folk ('Everybody's Talkin'') and John Barry's weary, lucid dream of a title song – New York through the eyes of Old York.

Barry had become the ultimate soundtrack writer. In the mid-1960s his Cadogan Square flat was the epicentre of all that Swinging London represented. His young wife Jane Birkin stirred his cocktails as he sat in his Eames chair wondering whether his next project would be a fifth Bond score (Was that idea played out? No, he decided, and wrote *You Only Live Twice*) or a musical version of *Brighton Rock* (which he finally completed in 2004). He never moved. By the 2000s the modern furnishings had been replaced with his parents' antiques, but history weighed heavily in the air: this was the place where he had conceived the themes for *On Her Majesty's Secret Service*, *Midnight Cowboy* and *The Persuaders*.

While it would be a little outlandish to say that Barry lived a James Bond lifestyle, it wasn't hard to imagine him in the world of *The Persuaders*, driving an open-topped sports car to the south of France, immaculately turned out, eloping with the au pair. He was, more than many familiar faces, a film star. The movies were bound to be central to his life. His father had run a string of eight cinemas in the north of England, including the Rialto in York. Old York was where John Barry Prendergast grew up. His dad first took him into the theatre 'when I was four or five, and I saw this big black-and-white mouse on the screen. And I thought, "I like it here."' At home he acted out dramas with Dinky toys, as Sibelius played in the background. By the time he was a teenager he was in charge of publicity for the cinemas. The Rialto remained his favourite. It had burned down in the 1920s, and his father had redesigned it with a stage. Nat King Cole and His Trio, Stan Kenton, Lionel Hampton and Count Basie all played there, and all of them had dinner at the Prendergasts' home. These memories would be used to great effect when the newly rechristened John Barry started to write his own music in the late 1950s.

He was always hungry to learn, to find new sounds. On the cusp of the 1960s he had travelled to America to discover why the studios there sounded so much richer than those at Abbey Road or Decca. He hung around during sessions by Phil Spector and Lee Hazlewood (when neither were household names in America, let alone Britain), and was shocked to discover that they used not one but seven mikes on a drum kit! A diligent worker, and confident with it, Barry took his Parlophone label-mate and would-be rocker Adam Faith under his wing in late 1959 and put his studies to use on a song called 'What Do You Want'. As he recalled in 2001: 'He'd done one or two things before, dismal failures. We had four violins and one mike, very close, and we goosed it up on the board so it sounded almost electronic – tok tak tok. I got a phone call from [record producer] Norman Newell at EMI the day after we recorded "What Do You Want", and he said, "This is the worst record I ever heard." So I kept away from EMI. I thought, "Fuck them." Finally, Norman Newell called again: "Well, what do you know, we're number one!" I said, "Yeah, I'd noticed that." He said, "Isn't it amazing, this business, you never know what's going to happen, do you?" I said, "No, you don't, do you?" We followed that with another ten Top 5 hits.'

It was scoring *Dr No* in 1962 that took Barry into the big league, making him an internationally known name, and the 'James Bond Theme' is still underrated. It's like air, like it's always been there, but let's try and listen to it fresh. It looks back with its Stan Kenton full brass blast, forward to the growling bass guitar of the Shadows and the Stranglers; after a minute or so there's a sassy interlude that recasts Sophie Tucker in *Sweet Charity*; intercutting these sections are sudden rhythmic jumps and a loud/quiet aesthetic that still sounded new when the Pixies and Nirvana adapted it three decades later. Barry was always a little wary of becoming too closely associated with the Bond soundtracks – 'million-dollar Mickey Mouse music', he called them. Likewise, he didn't want to score *Born Free* when he first saw it: 'I felt it was just a big, sentimental family romp,' he told biographer Eddi Fiegel. He decided 'the only way I can have some fun with it [is] if I can do it as a pastiche on a Disney-type movie.' On one particularly memorable day in 1966 his wife Jane Birkin gave birth to their daughter, Kate, and they drove back to Cadogan Square in the early hours to discover he had won two Oscars for *Born Free*.

Young, handsome and naughty, Barry made the most of the time he spent on set with Shirley Anne Field (*Beat Girl*) and Carol White (*Never Let Go*); Shirley Bassey was an on–off girlfriend; Charlotte Rampling and Britt Ekland were dinner dates. Adding to his hip credentials, Michael Caine had been his flatmate when he wrote the theme for *Goldfinger* in 1965, helpfully pointing out, after Barry had spent an all-night session coming up with the main hook, how much it sounded like 'Moon River'.

Barry's distinctive sound was not just in the strange beauty of his chord sequences, but also his taste for unusual instrumentation: there were plucked harps, there was African percussion and there were Moog synthesizers, ahead of pretty much everyone. He would use the Moog to heighten suspense and mystery, creating basslines and fearsome drones on the themes for *On Her Majesty's Secret Service* (1969) and TV shows *The Persuaders* (1971) and *Orson Welles' Great Mysteries* (1973); in 1969 the majority of musicians could only get the weird new instrument to sound like an electronic swanee whistle. Most significant in Barry's musical instrument cupboard was the cimbalom. Once *The Ipcress File* reached the cinema in 1965, this Hungarian hammered dulcimer, played by Barry's friend John Leach, became the definitive sound of the Cold War. 'John Leach was always a great daydreamer,' said Barry. 'I'd crawl into his place, step over sheet music and zithers and cimbaloms. He'd pick up all these weird things nobody knew how to play. Just amazing stuff. So if I wanted a freaky sound he was the only one, the only game in town.'

Photos of Barry in the late 1960s and '70s are usually heavily shadowed, monochrome, dark. As one decade melted into the next, he would provide a host of similarly haunting, very simple scores: the pipe organ and cimbalom waltz of (legendarily awful Richard Burton and Elizabeth Taylor movie) *Boom* (1968); a TV adaptation of Tennessee Williams's *The Glass Menagerie*; the melancholy music-box theme for *A Doll's House* (both 1973). Almost John Barry music in miniature, these small-scale triumphs sounded like a coda and would presage an eighteen-month-long complete break from music. The plan was to set up home in Spain, but in 1976 he recorded a jazz homage in Los Angeles called *Americans*. While in LA he was offered the scores to *Eleanor and Franklin*, *Robin and Marian* and the remake of *King Kong*. The six-week job turned into a thirty-five-year stay, and this is the era thought of by American John Barry fans as his prime period. Among the highlights would be the soundtrack to 1981's *Body Heat*; it was erotic, slow and steamy, with an easy-sleazy sax pegged back by a subtly threatening fog of strings, brushed drums and woozy danger. The American years were less musically adventurous but defined what would become thought of as 'Barryesque': the sound of sweeping romantic strings, which would go on to win him more Oscars for *Out of Africa* (1985) and *Dances with Wolves* (1990).

His last album, 2001's *Eternal Echoes*, saw Barry using his life, and cinema, as the storyboard. You could hear the child playing with his gramophone and Dinky toys, the teenager in the projection room of the York Rialto falling in love with Leslie Caron. 'Saturday night and the theatre would be full, everyone smoking,' he recalled, years later. 'Then the film would end, everyone would go, we'd walk from the offices at the back through the theatre and . . . it was all ghosts. Imagine it! Twenty minutes ago there were two hundred people looking at *An American in Paris* or *Sunset Boulevard*, and they'd all gone. I could see things in the air. There's something that people leave behind when they exit a room. That's what stays with you through life.'

49
WHAT KIND OF FOOL AM I: LIONEL BART AND ANTHONY NEWLEY

England would have been happy if the clock had stopped for ever on VE Day; even now, it clings to the memory like a comfort blanket. We only had piles of rubble and ration books, but we were happy. This became a permanent English mindset; attempt to get above your station, and someone would always be there to take great pleasure in pulling you back down into the rubble. Sid James was there to deflate Tony Hancock; Dave Davies would keep brother Ray in check; ultimately there's Baldrick and Blackadder. However much we try, we can't escape the fact that we're still essentially damp people in damp houses who like eating fry-ups.

Lionel Bart and Anthony Newley were both born at the turn of the 1930s, both grew up poor in Jewish east London, both sought an escape from the stultifying Britain that was unable or unwilling to leave the 1940s. They didn't shrink at the sound of rock 'n' roll; they were smarter, recognised its long-term implications. Both started out by walking down rock's still-unmapped streets, and both ended up on Broadway.

Bart and Newley were counter-examples of the English archetype. They were ambitious and should have lived longer, at least long enough to be feted as songwriting legends, with a dedicated evening on BBC4. Both had enormous success in the 1960s, were household names in Britain and America, but their legacies are under-appreciated, grounded – if not ground down – by their English roots. They have ended up stranded somewhere in the Atlantic, equidistant from the Hollywood hills and Hackney Wick. Had they stayed in London, like Ray Davies, there might be guided tours now and South Bank retrospectives. But in their lifetimes they did what mattered: they found a way out of the English straitjacket, out of working-class post-war austerity London, onto the stage, the silver screen and eventually the Academy Awards.

Just as Bart and Newley were making their names, Tony Hancock was breaking with the BBC's variety radio format and state-sponsored mediocrity, fulminating from within the confines of 23 Railway Cuttings, East Cheam, once a week on *Hancock's Half Hour*. His depressed shuffle from one potential escape route to another – a poetry society, art classes – would be foiled by the outside world of petrol rations and train strikes. Notes from a rainy island, resigned and angry, aiming for the profound in a self-reflective drear. Hancock's 'Sunday Afternoon at Home' ('What's on at the other place?' 'It's closed down') reached number two on the album chart in 1960 as one whole side of *This Is Hancock*, a solipsistic piece about absolutely nothing happening. It has often been said that everything in Britain was black and white before the Beatles, but as musical counterparts to Hancock, Bart and Newley did their best to cut through with a mixture of surrealism, slapstick and manic depression. All three were self-destructive.

The British rock 'n' roll scene gave both Bart and Newley a bunk-up. If you were expecting the sheer sexual magnetism of Elvis Presley or the easy-rolling New Orleans piano thud of Fats Domino, then you'd have been disappointed by the works of home-grown Terry Dene and Wee Willie Harris; if you were looking for updated music hall, sardonic and self-aware, or barely disguised gay fantasy pop, then you'd have been much happier. Bart's break came writing songs for Bermondsey's Tommy Steele, a working-class merchant seaman who had a guitar and a good ear for things he'd heard in New Orleans, New York and the West Indies. Never let anyone tell you otherwise – Steele was Britain's first rock 'n' roll star, and most of his early sides ('Rock with the Caveman', 'Doomsday Rock', 'Elevator Rock') were written by Lionel Bart with his actor sidekick Mike Pratt.

The son of an East End tailor, Bart was born Lionel Begleiter in 1930, the youngest of eleven. He had no formal musical training. Aged sixteen he got a scholarship to St Martin's School of Art, then started hanging around the left-wing Unity Theatre, working as a set painter. One of their productions needed some songs, so Bart – having renamed himself after the London hospital – had a go. Unable to write music, he would tap out the melody on a piano with one finger and someone else would orchestrate it. His first full show, *Lock Up Your Daughters* (with music by future *Avengers* score writer Laurie Johnson), opened at the Mermaid Theatre in 1959. In 1960 came *Fings Ain't Wot They Used to Be*, which was bigger. Then there was *Oliver!*, which took Bart off the scale.

1960 also saw him writing his last collection of songs for a Tommy Steele vehicle. *Tommy the Toreador* gave us the immortal 'Where's the Birdie' (sung in the film by the gorblimey-trousered trio of Steele, Sid James and Bernard Cribbins) and 'Little White Bull'. Steele was aware on set that Bart was finessing songs for *Oliver!*. He heard 'Consider Yourself'. Could I have that? he asked. No, said Bart. He had outgrown Tommy. Bart's songwriting heroes were Lorenz Hart, W. S. Gilbert and Noël Coward, and he was soon hanging out with the latter, the only one of the three who was still around. Coward loved Bart and introduced him to the likes of Marlene Dietrich, who thought – with his blunt fringe and shaggy sideburns – that he looked like 'an Egyptian beatnik'.

Oliver! ran in London from 1960 to 1965. It went to Broadway and was turned into a film in 1968. It even had a hit ballad in 'As Long as He Needs Me', a tear-jerker of the old school that was a hit single for a young singer who had emerged at the beginning of the rock 'n' roll era, Shirley Bassey. *Oliver!* was big enough to become a problem. 'The phone never stops ringing,' Bart told the *Sunday Dispatch*. 'I am inundated with offers. But listen, mate, I've got to know what to take on, what to turn down. It's a headache. I have just rejected a Hollywood offer to write all the songs for Elvis Presley's next picture. I can't repeat myself, see? That's fatal.'

All he kept from *Oliver!* for his follow-up was the exclamation mark. *Blitz!* was a sentimental, autobiographical musical set on Petticoat Lane, a cockney *West Side Story*, with rivalry between the Blitzsteins, who sell pickles and gefilte fish, and the Lockes, who have a fruit-and-veg stall. They end up united under falling bombs, singing 'As Long as This Is England', a patriotic windsock of a song, but also an ode to multiculturalism that deserved a longer shelf life. It did OK, but there was no transfer to Broadway or film. Still, Bart was now a millionaire and could indulge himself. 'Success and other drugs had persuaded him that he could do anything,' said his former theatre cohort Joan Littlewood. 1965's *Twang!!* had two exclamation marks and a massive budget that Bart was blowing night after night playing poker. The idea of a *Carry on Robin Hood*-style musical didn't sound at all bad in theory, but as the cast – including Barbara Windsor and Ronnie Corbett – were constantly being asked to improvise, and the songwriter had just discovered LSD, it ended up as less than commercial. Windsor remembered its disastrous opening night in November 1965: 'We all went out for the big finish and performed to the backs of hundreds of people flocking to the exits. By the time we got to the last number, the theatre was empty.'

* * *

There was little to suggest that Anthony Newley, from Clapton Park, in the deepest East End of London, would become a pop star. He was an actor, for a start, and didn't really think of himself as a singer. The 1959 movie *Idle on Parade* (or sometimes *Idol on Parade*) was an extremely British take on the Elvis Presley legend: a pop star is called up to do national service; there are chases around bedrooms and a couple of swooning grannies. Newley played Jeep Jackson, who at one point gets to sing a rock-a-ballad called 'I've Waited So Long'; released as a single, it was taken at face value. By late 1959 it nestled in a Top 10 that also included Marty Wilde's 'Donna' and Ricky Nelson's 'Never Be Anyone Else but You', where it wasn't remotely disgraced. Newley, suddenly, was a pop star: for three years he was barely off the charts with sly, comedic updates of folk songs ('Strawberry Fair', 'Pop Goes the Weasel'); American rock 'n' roll covers (Frankie Avalon's simpering 'Why' and Lloyd Price's strutting 'Personality'); beyond-melodramatic ballads ('And the Heavens Cried', 'If She Should Come to You'); self-penned hip jazz ('Bee Bom', covered by Sammy Davis Jr); and in 1960 a cockney-vowelled, finger-clicking number one 'Do You Mind', which had been written by his spiritual twin Lionel Bart. That same year he got his own TV show. *The Strange World of Gurney Slade* saw suburbia as life-denying, routine for the sake of routine, but full of frustrated individuals with rich internal lives, celebrated in Newley's surreal, deadpan skits.

Things caught fire when he teamed up with Leslie Bricusse, a Cambridge graduate who had written Matt Monro's sauntering 'My Kind of Girl'. *Stop the World – I Want to Get Off*, their 1962 musical, gave us two instant standards in 'Once in a Lifetime' and 'What Kind of Fool Am I', along with the cod-gospel 'Gonna Build a Mountain'. Three years later, Bricusse and Newley's *The Roar of the Greasepaint – The Smell of the Crowd* opened on Broadway, and again three of its numbers almost immediately became jazz standards: 'Who Can I Turn To', 'A Wonderful Day Like Today' and 'Feeling Good' (quickly turned into a blues classic by Nina Simone), with a minor hit in the smoking-jacket groove of 'The Joker'. This was quality writing barely seen since the American Songbook had been closed shut more than a decade earlier. 'Who Can I Turn To' would be covered by dozens of pop singers and jazz instrumentalists, and remains vital today. Along with Newley's own RCA album of the songs, there were two jazz interpretations of the entire show by Ahmad Jamal and Herbie Mann. Both were recorded before the show had even opened on Broadway, such was Newley's standing. At least that's what Newley and Bricusse would have you think. Against all expectations, the show had bombed in Britain, not even making it to the West End.

The Roar of the Greasepaint's success in America was down to luck and an ingenious marketing campaign. American producer David

Merrick had seen the show early on in Liverpool, and decided he could afford to put it on in the States. He started out with a pre-Broadway tour, with Newley himself in the lead role, which seemed like a coup, and convinced RCA to record and release the cast album before the show reached New York. The persuasive Merrick also convinced other labels to record versions; learned from Newley's demo, Tony Bennett's stand-out recording of 'Who Can I Turn To' was released in November 1964, months before *The Roar of the Greasepaint* reached Broadway. If anyone ever uncovered Merrick's subterfuge, they kept quiet about it. Newley was a constant guest on American TV shows after the show made Broadway.

Newley's Stateside popularity was also down to the magic dust that seemed to cling to anyone associated with James Bond. He recorded a demo of the theme from *Goldfinger* in April 1964, just before the soundtrack version was cut, and part of you wishes Cubby Broccoli had heard it and said, 'We've got it, boys. Nooley nailed it!' He laughs as he sings, 'but don't go in', and subtly elevates the comedy in lines like 'such a cold finger'; there's a cheekiness that's lost in Shirley Bassey's crumbling-skyscraper version. You're also more aware that calling the villain 'Mr Goldfinger' indicates he was based on a real person – very loosely, the architect Ernö Goldfinger, presumably because Ian Fleming had rather conservative views about modern architecture, as well as feminism. The demo would have made a very different yet coolly effective Bond theme.

'On stage or off,' wrote *Life* magazine, 'he [Newley] vibrates in an electric state of perpetual performance.' In London, he recorded 'Moogies Bloogies', an electronic single with Delia Derbyshire of the BBC Radiophonic Workshop that was deemed too experimental by a timid Decca Records and left on the shelf. In Hollywood, Newley's versatility and ambition was accepted: he won a Grammy for 'What Kind of Fool Am I' and appeared in 1967's appalling but nevertheless Oscar-winning *Doctor Dolittle*. Given free rein, his confidence presumably in high cockalorum, in 1969 Newley made the film *Can Heironymus Merkin Ever Forget Mercy Humppe and Find True Happiness?* When I say 'made', I mean he scripted it, directed it, wrote the songs, starred in it and roped in his real-life wife Joan Collins and their kids to play Merkin's wife and kids. Occasionally, Newley (as Merkin) broke the fourth wall to talk to Newley (the director, a voice off screen) and complain about how the critics were going to hate the film. He was channelling Fellini, and it was fascinating. I'd love to say it was his masterpiece – which was screamingly his intention – but I can't. He was on more watchable form in a 1972 Burt Bacharach TV special, performing with Sammy Davis Jr, with whom he batted Newley/Bricusse songs back and forth. 'Look at that face of yaaaaars!' sang Newley in that voice which had taken his East End vowels and contorted them into an entirely invented accent. There was also a Beatles tribute, in which he wrapped those same vowels around George Harrison's 'Within You Without You'. Watching it, your head feels light, your breathing alters – these are worlds colliding, and neither performer nor viewer is on solid ground.

Lionel Bart's late-1960s blow-out would be an extraordinary album that was psychedelic, abstract and autobiographical. *Isn't This Where We Came In* came out on the progressive Deram label – like Procol Harum's 'Whiter Shade of Pale' – in 1968, and was as dense, confusing and unwieldy as its mirrored, multicoloured sleeve and prosaic type-writer font. Bart's voice sounds closer to Nat Gonella than any of his contemporary Deram label-mates, a semi-spoken, breathless cockney. John Cameron's arrangements are vast. If it had been made into a film, it could have been either the best or the worst ever made. But at least the record got released. Though the film version of *Oliver!* was a huge hit in 1968, Hollywood had started to tire of Bart by the turn of the 1970s. Not long before, they had been pampering him horribly: he had demanded a car (though he couldn't drive) and a giant teddy bear, which was to be permanently installed in the passenger seat. He got both.

Like Bart, Newley didn't translate into the post-Beatles world, much as he wanted to. 1972 gave him an American number one with Sammy Davis's recording of 'The Candy Man', taken from Newley's ace soundtrack to *Willie Wonka and the Chocolate Factory*. He was still on American TV, but being a regular guest on *Celebrity Squares* didn't suggest a cutting edge; nonetheless, he played Vegas when he could, hammered the Borscht Belt and in 1971 put out *For You*, an album of erotic poetry for which he posed topless on the cover. By the 1990s he was back where he started, working as a cockney archetype – his last role would be in *EastEnders*. It is touching to know that Bart spent years working on a musical version of *Richard III*, presumably to be called *Hump!* But by the 1990s he would be even worse off, living in poverty, having long ago sold the rights to *Oliver!* for a pittance.

Too Much Woman, Newley's last album, from 1992, included the odd decent romantic ballad, alongside 'Centrefold' (yes, an inappropriate song about a *Playboy* model) and 'White Boy', a pensioner's complaint about the state of popular music – 'Will someone tell me what the hell is rap?' he asks, exasperated, almost tearful. His time was up. He sounded like he knew his legacy was already shot. You could snigger, but mostly it made you feel sorry for him.

50

WHIPPED CREAM AND OTHER DELIGHTS: ADVENTURES IN BEATLELAND

Since the rise of Elvis in the mid-fifties, the popular music
scene has been divided in half . . . onto this scene the Tijuana
Brass came like a healing, swinging salve.
  Tijuana Brass concert programme, 1966

Elvis had riled the biggest names in popular music. If they didn't regard
it as some fitful vision, more baffling than exciting, then they found
rock 'n' roll actively offensive. For a while, pop's evolution had continued as if rock hadn't arrived, but Elvis in particular and rock in general
were taking up plenty of its space. The arrival of the Beatles in 1964

used up even more of the available air. When this next wave of rock emerged from England, the (by now) old guard weren't only prepared for it, they sat down, poured a stiff brandy and set about embracing it.

You knew some kind of rapprochement was coming when Shirley Horn, the grand dame of jazz purists, recorded Paul McCartney's 'And I Love Her' in 1965. For the first time in half a century, the English influence was swaying the American sound. 'Pop' and 'mod' were British terms that, overnight, became accepted as American cultural terminology. The Beatles were at the epicentre, but in the same sphere of influence were Mary Quant and Twiggy, David Hockney and Richard Hamilton, Emma Peel and James Bond. If *Sammy Davis Sings the Hits of the Dave Clark Five* was found in the vaults, you wouldn't be that surprised.

The Beatles and the Rolling Stones were one arm of young Swinging London, but as far as most people in Paris and New York were concerned, two women – Julie Andrews and Petula Clark – were equally key players. Both appeared as ready-made international stars in 1964; both were around thirty years old and had enough experience to make the most of their breakthrough. Petula Clark had been born Sally Clark but was given her nickname by her father, who joked that it combined the names of two ex-girlfriends, Pet and Ulla. After her wartime childhood stardom, she had scored irregular hits on the UK charts ('Sailor', notably, was a number one in 1961), but became an even bigger star in France after she married Vogue Records' publicist Claude Wolff. 'Downtown', an extraordinary evocation of big-city glamour, was an international hit for her at the tail end of 1964. Significantly, it reached number one in America, where she had been previously unknown, giving the parents of Beatles-crazy kids an English face they could relate to; the 'gentle bossa nova' club scene Clark sang about promised champagne rather than rum and coke. Also, 'Downtown' had a sensuality. A woman wants to take your hand and show you all *this*? Who could refuse? 'I Know a Place', she would wink on the follow-up.

Julie Andrews's speaking voice was similarly cut crystal – a hard 'a' would never pass her lips. Having never made a film before, she found herself in the odd position of waiting for three to open almost simultaneously: any one of *Mary Poppins*, *The Americanisation of Emily* or *The Sound of Music* would have made her a huge star. She was head-girl material and always spoke as if she was gently correcting you.* Both Andrews and Clark had perceptible sophistication, the ring of the international airport.

By 1966, as the Beatles and Bob Dylan egged everyone in rock on to fresh heights, a new Californian sound emerged that was part American exotica, part Brazilian revolution, and it was ushered in by LA smoothies Herb Alpert and Jerry Moss on their A&M label. Their adventure had begun with an inconsequential instrumental called 'The Lonely Bull', which sounded like an offcut from Lionel Bart's *Tommy the Toreador* but – credited to Herb Alpert and the Tijuana Brass – became a Top 40 hit in 1962. This got the label off the ground, and far from it being a one-off novelty hit, they discovered there was an endless appetite for the sweet simplicity of the Tijuana Brass sound. They would record sixteen albums over the next ten years, all of which were million-sellers.†
Alpert, with looks to melt, became a star, and the A&M label tried different ventures based on the same west coast, balloon-weight Tijuana Brass aesthetic: the Baja Marimba Band were led by Julius Wechter, who had once been in Martin Denny's combo; Chris Montez, a 1962 rock 'n' roll one-hit wonder with 'Let's Dance', was reborn with a soft, feminine sound on his Hispano-Cali cover of Dick Haymes's 1945 hit 'The More I See You'; Claudine Longet was so wispy-voiced she made Astrud Gilberto sound like Bessie Smith, though her reputation was somewhat altered after she shot dead her ski champion boyfriend.

A fan in Pennsylvania sent Alpert a card that read: 'Merry Christmas to the man who has given happy music back to the world.' Alpert was a cool presence on the scene. 'All music is getting together,' he said,

---

* Interviewed by Dick Cavett, she was asked if she was tired of her 'pure image', which probably had little to do with the real-life Julie Andrews. 'Damn right!' she replied, in a slightly embarrassed, most proper voice. It was very endearing.
† In Britain, the Torero Brass were a London studio cash-in concoction who recorded six albums of their own and, unlikely as it may sound, made arguably the most exhilarating version of the Beatles' 'Please Please Me'. They also cut a single as Bert Farrell's Marijuana Brass, which deserves a hat-tip.

'symphony, folk, jazz, far eastern, country and western, everything . . . music from all over the world.' On a TV special called *The Brass Are Comin'*, he played a scene with Petula Clark as a parody of Fellini and Warhol, and still pulled in an incredible 57 per cent of American viewers. In 1967 he was awarded the golden ticket of a James Bond theme, recording the Burt Bacharach-penned 'Casino Royale'. That summer the *Saturday Evening Post*'s Alfred G. Aronowitz wrote that America's pop music scene had become 'as incomprehensible to the people who dreamed it all up as it is to the people who are sleeping through it . . . It is as if some magician had started pulling tricks out of a hat and found, to his amazement, that the hat contained more surprises than his magic could account for.'

* * *

John Gabree in *DownBeat* tried to explain to his readers why the Beatles had affected the musical climate in a way none of the first wave of rock 'n' rollers had: 'They were safe, being white, and having none of the aggressive sexuality that had been so upsetting in the likes of Elvis – all they wanted to do, remember, was hold your hand.' Others in the jazz world were less sniffy and recognised a new direction that was worthy of investigation. Vibes player Gary Burton, guitarist Gábor Szabó and saxophonist Charles Lloyd all began to blend instrumental sophistication with the rhythms of soul and rock; Miles Davis would embrace jazz rock fully with *In a Silent Way* (1969) and *Bitches Brew* (1970). Arranger Gary McFarland moved from Brazilian jazz to something approaching soft rock with his excellent albums *Today* (1970) and *Butterscotch Rum* (1971); his cover of the Beatles' 'Because' is profoundly affecting, even more so with the knowledge that it was one of the last things McFarland did before his mysterious death from poisoning.

The two leading jazz magazines in America, *DownBeat* and *Jazz*, both opened up to pop in 1967. The former vowed, with its usual qualified generosity, 'to include the musically valid aspects of the rock scene' in June. *Jazz* went considerably further that August, changing its name to *Jazz & Pop*. The editorial read: 'Jazz, pop and folk are children of the streets: without official recognition, scuffling for survival at times, they still go on speaking to the largest audience in the world. Let's face it. Jazz needs popular music. Economically as well as aesthetically, they have always interpenetrated each other, the pop song becoming the jazz vehicle, the jazz artist becoming popular musician.'

What about the hundreds of thousands of office-bound folkniks who had been OK with the Brothers Four and the Kingston Trio, and maybe liked Bob Dylan's poetry but were alarmed by either his political stance or his nasal whine? They were among the devotees of Rod McKuen, a former actor who sensed his moment and dug in, selling not just millions of records, but becoming a best-selling poet in the process. He may be almost forgotten now, but until Fleetwood Mac's *Rumours*, McKuen's album *The Sea* was the Warner Brothers group's best-selling LP of all time. That catalogue included every album by Frank Sinatra, Dean Martin and Sammy Davis on Reprise, not to mention those by Neil Young and Joni Mitchell. McKuen was huge, and now his music is forgotten. He is worth a short diversion here.

Rod McKuen had started out on a radio show in Oakland when he was sixteen or seventeen, reading dramatic recitations over music – this was in the early 1950s. He then talked himself into a contract at Universal Studios, featuring in the rock 'n' roll exploitation picture *Rock, Pretty Baby* as one Ox Bentley, starring alongside Sal Mineo and Shelley Fabares and singing over a non-rock Henry Mancini score. 'Exploitation' is the key word here. You could have taken 1960's narrated *Beatsville* album ('Just for kicks, we all went to the self-realisation café and had mushroom burgers') at face value, but two years later McKuen had a novelty hit with 'The Oliver Twist'.* It was a dire record but a minor success, and it led to McKuen touring bowling alleys in the Midwest for a couple of months, wrecking his vocal chords in the process. This was fortunate, because when he switched to poetry a year after that, he had developed a rough whisper that suited his flowery

---

* A generous reading here is that the twist craze led to more cash-in records than any fad before or since: Count Basie's 'Basie Twist', Keely Smith's 'Peppermint Twist', Louis Prima's 'Tag That Twistin' Dolly', Duane Eddy's alarmingly titled 'Twisting Off a Cliff'. As Frank Sinatra said, 'Everybody's Twistin''.

poesies, with their frequent suggestions of sex. He had discovered the Rod McKuen Voice.

Robert Shelton, who had given Dylan a helping hand in the papers, reviewed McKuen at folk club the Bitter End for the *New York Times* in 1965 and said he was the next big thing – a 'chansonnier' with a 'foggy voice'. That's when McKuen's self-published poetry took off, and by the end of the decade he was the best-selling poet in all human history.

Finally, he had his niche. Released under the name the San Sebastian Strings, *The Sea* was an album of his poetry set to music by arranger Anita Kerr and narrated by *Bye Bye Birdie* actor Jesse Pearson. It was the ultimate make-out record, proto-ambient and shockingly strange for a multi-million-selling LP. Kerr's arrangements, on a relatively small budget, were really skilled. 'Whoops, here come the violins,' deadpanned Pearson on 'Body Surfing with the Jet Set', a sardonic surf song that pre-dates the Beach Boys' sardonic takes on their own youth culture. The poetry was one thing, but the package was made whole by a minimalist sleeve that anticipated the new-age album covers of the 1980s. With this artwork, McKuen's pillow talk and the elemental sounds of wind, rain and waves that join the tracks, *The Sea* was an American phenomenon. No fools, McKuen and Kerr followed it up with two more San Sebastian Strings albums, *The Earth* and *The Sky*, both of which featured McKuen's own cracked but appealing voice. Just in case Jesse Pearson fans felt aggrieved, they also released *The Soft Sea* and *Home to the Sea*, with Pearson's voice instead of McKuen's, to cover all bases. Clearly, Rod had poems to spare.

One track on *The Earth* was called 'The Mud Kids', and it nailed McKuen's appeal for people too old to be kids but not old enough to instinctively kick against the rapid social progression of the 1960s: 'We blame it all on Freud, the Madison Avenue cult of youth, urban non-renewal, Dylan's songs that taught them how to think, England, anything but what it is . . . They're turning from homes that weren't quite right. They're getting up from TV dinners to eat the snow. They're playing with each other instead of dolls.'

The Poetry Society of America's president labelled McKuen's work 'a social plague'; *McCall's* magazine said that 'there is no other figure on the cultural scene in this country who is so utterly revered by fans and held in such mocking contempt by non-fans'. *Life* profiled McKuen in February 1968, saying his poems 'skip prettily like a flat stone across a sea of poetic clichés', but that didn't mean people wouldn't see depth in them: the magazine saw McKuen's philosophy as, 'Be sentimental. Be natural . . . Don't fear to bare your emotions. Don't stay cool, stay warm.' On the rock side of the fence, within a few weeks Paul McCartney showed a similar philosophy on the Beatles' single 'Hey Jude': 'It's the fool who plays it cool while making the world a little colder.' The boundaries between hip and straight were becoming fluid enough in 1967. McKuen wanted to write a poem about his cat Sloopy? That was absolutely fine.

Beyond this, he set up his own mail-order label, Stanyan Records, licensing from Britain (Tony Hancock, Vera Lynn), as well as releasing even more of his own music – sometimes ten LPs a year. He wrote an album for Frank Sinatra in 1969, another (unreleased) for Diana Ross. In the 1970s he produced a Rock Hudson album in London and taunted anti-gay campaigner Anita Bryant with a comedy song about boycotting Florida oranges, for which she was the figurehead. There was a *musique concrète* record under the pseudonym Heins Hoffman-Richter (*Music to Freak Your Friends and Break Your Lease*) and a version of the Moody Blues' 'Legend of a Mind', with a gigantic arrangement that he got cold feet on, pressing up two hundred copies on Stanyan and including a covering letter that said, 'We're not sure on this one.' Towards the end of his life McKuen would walk to Tower Records and buy classical CDs every night, which he never opened or played. When the store closed in the 2000s, he wrote a poem called 'Is There Life After Tower Records?' Rod McKuen was a one-off.

People like McKuen weren't any part of the Dylan/Beatles/Grateful Dead rock axis, but they were as radical as many in the counter-culture. Aside from the irony of the music industry being intensely capitalist and swallowing small bands and smaller rock labels at a rapid rate at the end of the 1960s – an issue rock wouldn't confront until the DIY boom of the punk era – the official counter-culture presences left less room for such popular and outspoken figures.

Eartha Kitt had been one of the most intriguing stars of the early 1950s, who had survived a poverty- and abuse-wracked upbringing to become a pulse-quickening presence on stage. Orson Welles, who had cast a twenty-two-year-old Kitt as Helen of Troy in *Time Runs* back in 1950, called her 'the most exciting woman on Earth'. She made Julie London seem shy and retiring on records like 'Mink Schmink' (1954), 'I Want to Be Evil' (1958) and 'Bad but Beautiful' (1962). Her voice was entirely feline, her records both funny and sexy, and it made perfect sense when she played Catwoman in *Batman*. Off stage, the CIA kept tabs on Eartha, as she had the audacity to try and help black kids in impoverished inner-city areas like Watts. At a White House dinner in 1968, she reduced Lady Bird Johnson, the president's wife, to tears when she was asked what she thought of the Vietnam War. 'You send the best of this country off to be shot and maimed. No wonder the kids rebel and take pot,' replied Eartha. 'There are so many things burning the people of this country, particularly mothers. They feel they are going to raise sons – and I know what it's like, and you have children of your own, Mrs Johnson – we raise children and send them to war.' She was rewarded with a CIA dossier that labelled her a 'sadistic nymphomaniac'. Effectively blacklisted, she spent most of the 1970s in Europe, recording her best song, the extraordinary, anti-racist 'Paint Me Black Angels', while exiled on Denmark Street in 1970.*

The Juilliard-trained Nina Simone had started out professionally as a nightclub pianist in Atlantic City, where the owners encouraged her to throw the occasional vocal into her blend of Bach and cocktail jazz. In 1959, when she was twenty-five, her first album came out on Bethlehem Records, at a time when vocal jazz was struggling to stay afloat in a sea of teenage noise, but remarkably Simone's *Little Girl Blue* not only sold heavily but produced a US Top 20 hit single with her recording of the Gershwins' 'I Loves You, Porgy'. That's how strikingly different and unavoidable Simone was. Her voice was deep and smoky, almost androgynous. The album also contained a slow-burn classic in her cool jazz take on Walter Donaldson and Gus Kahn's 'My Baby Just Cares for

* Kitt had sung it in the original Spanish in 1955, as 'Angelitos Negros'.

Me', which would eventually become acknowledged as a standard in the 1980s through – of all things – a perfume advert. Why did it take so long for her to receive a public seal of approval? One reason was that Simone's style would always be difficult to categorise. Her first album may have been solid piano and vocal jazz, but what were its fans to make of 1961's 'Rags and Old Iron', a blues with a junkyard backing of nothing beyond electric guitar, drums and the odd finger-click? Or the monotonous flute-and-chant-led 'See-Line Woman'? Or her groovy take on the Bee Gees' 'To Love Somebody' (a UK Top 10 hit in 1969) or her disassembling of Leonard Cohen's 'Suzanne'?

Another reason for her relatively low profile in the 1960s was that a lot of people wanted Simone to be quiet and go away. She said the civil rights movement gave her 'a state of grace . . . I was needed. I could sing to help my people, and that became the mainstay of my life.' 1964's 'Mississippi Goddam' was a reaction to the murderous situation in the South – 'We're too damn lazy, our thinking's crazy . . . we're all gonna die, and die like flies' – but the lyric was placed over a razzmatazz melody that could have been written by George M. Cohan in 1905. This vaudeville disguise made it easier to get the lyric's revolutionary politics across: 'Doing things gradually will bring more tragedy.' By the late 1960s she would be asking black audiences if they were 'ready to kill' for the cause. She certainly wasn't trying to get an invite to the White House or a knockabout role on *Batman*.

A subtext of civil rights could be read into her 1964 single 'Don't Let Me Be Misunderstood'* and even covers of Anthony Newley's 'Feeling Good', George Harrison's 'Here Comes the Sun' and Sandy Denny's 'Who Knows Where the Time Goes'. That's how transformative she could be, almost supernaturally so. She took Screaming Jay Hawkins's 'I Put a Spell on You' and switched it from a Halloween R&B novelty into something intense and thoroughly, witchily believable. Simone had

---

* The melody and chorus hook were written by soul arranger/producer Horace Ott, with the rest of the lyric coming from the team of Bennie Benjamin and Sol Marcus, who had written the wartime standards 'I Don't Want to Set the World on Fire' (the Ink Spots, 1941) and 'When the Lights Go on Again' (Vaughn Monroe, 1943), both of which were associated with Vera Lynn in Britain.

unique powers. In 1967 she recorded an album called *High Priestess of Soul*; she also claimed to be a reincarnated Egyptian queen. No one was going to argue. It's remarkable in retrospect just how commercially successful Nina Simone was in the 1960s.

Harry Belafonte, meanwhile, had bankrolled the civil rights movement on the back of his huge exotica hits 'Mary's Boy Child' and 'The Banana Boat Song' (both 1957). He had to deal with such horrors as sponsors pulling out of a 1968 TV show after he dared to let English rose Petula Clark touch his arm. The same year, Herb Alpert had been booked to play Brigham Young University, but publicly announced he was cancelling the show when officials baulked at his choice of support act, A&M's interracial Checkmates Ltd. Alpert, Belafonte and Barbra Streisand would play a fundraiser for the Southern Christian Leadership at the Hollywood Bowl in the wake of Martin Luther King's assassination. Streisand later played a show to raise money for the legal defence fund of Daniel Ellsberg, the whistle-blower who effectively brought down Nixon. These people weren't squares.

* * *

In 1967 the Beatles' *Sgt Pepper's Lonely Hearts Club Band* did the impossible: it appealed equally to jazz, serious- and popular-music critics. Frederic V. Grunfeld of *Horizon* magazine described the final chord of 'A Day in the Life' as the most definitive final chord in the history of music, 'worth the price of admission alone; nobody else, not even Rachmaninoff, carried off a *Schlußakkord* with such panache'.

Sgt Pepper's revelatory magic – combining tapes played backwards, found sound from a circus tent, 'She's Leaving Home''s baroque strings and the tea-dance woodwinds of 'When I'm Sixty-Four' – suggested to everyone involved in the myriad forms of popular music that overlap, interplay, historical reflectiveness and stepping outside your comfort zone could be just as commercially successful as playing safe. And a lot of fun. Also, maybe if you did this, you might become the next big thing, the next Beatles! (It didn't happen for anyone, but as we'll see, it took several years for people to twig this.) *Sgt Pepper's* effect on pop's old guard was immediate and sometimes extraordinary: Bing Crosby made the space-race protest single 'What Do We Do With the World'; Dickie Valentine attempted an escape from the cabaret circuit with a splendid beat ballad called 'The Way of a Fool'; Johnnie Ray turned to British songwriter Tony Macaulay, who had scored a brace of number ones for the Foundations and Long John Baldry in 1967, for the bubbly 'The Ways of a Woman in Love'; Anthony Newley and Lionel Bart both made concept albums that were wild and autobiographical; and Frank Sinatra, who had been making concept albums of his own since 1954, went the whole hog with both the Rod McKuen-penned song cycle *A Man Alone* (1969) and the exceptional late-career high *Watertown* (1970).

Largely thanks to the Beatles, Britain's standing in popular music was suddenly back where it had been in 1900. Anything from England was automatically seen as superior in the States. For reasons we will soon encounter, this state of affairs did not last for long, and by 1969 British pop (though not rock) had essentially returned to being a niche interest. Just for a moment, though, it felt like the future of pop was wide open to all-comers, with London leading the way. If you wanted London's moment of kaleidoscopic optimism summed up in a shade over two minutes, there was Des O'Connor's 1969 single 'Dick-a-Dum-Dum', written by the Disney actor Jim Dale and performed in a style that could have somehow slotted into any decade in the twentieth century. It was quite a sleight of hand.

51

THE LAST WALTZ: TOM JONES AND THE NEW BALLADEERS

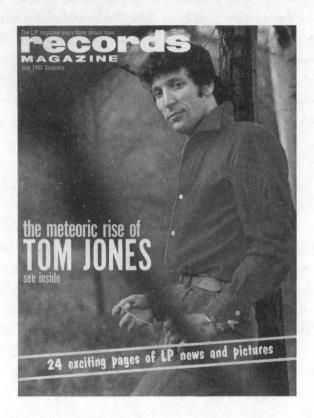

While the Beatles would single-handedly affect the climate of the 1960s, Philip Larkin had noted early on that their move into experimentation around 1966 had 'lost the typists in the Cavern'. Who did the typists turn to if 'Paperback Writer' didn't give them the same glow as 'This Boy'? *Fabulous* magazine photographer Fiona Adams, who had taken the famous image of the Beatles leaping in the air on a Euston Road bombsite, was typical of the fans who would have switched allegiances after *Sgt Pepper*. Her misgivings about modern pop's new direction, seen from the epicentre of the *Fabulous* offices, were that 'things were getting peculiar, druggy, a bit hairy'. Alternatives were plentiful, and none of them had guitar–bass–drums line-ups.

The album that replaced *Sgt Pepper* at number one on the UK album chart was *Val Doonican Rocks, but Gently*. If you listened to all the number-one LPs in sequence, the first thing you'd hear after the final chord of 'A Day in the Life' would be a mournful string swell leading into a heartbreaking reading of Harry Belafonte's early-1950s hit 'Scarlet Ribbons' (a hard song to get wrong, but still). Here, the forty-year-old Doonican could have been the father on 'She's Leaving Home', checking in on his daughter, intruding (but gently) on her space, some years before she thought she'd had enough. But was it a logical successor to *Sgt Pepper*? Doonican was a fine singer,* but from a rock perspective, he was no one's idea of the future of anything. No, the forward motion of rock had fractured, its atomisation had begun, and an unexpected result of this was that both youth-oriented and classic pop – running largely on separate rails since 1956 – slowly began to come to terms with each other.

Petula Clark's biggest-selling single in Britain wasn't 'Downtown' but 1967's 'This Is My Song', a track she derided as 'old-fashioned' and which sounded like a travel agent's precis of 'the Continent', with dashes of Frenchification and the odd balalaika. Like the flowery shows of George Edwardes, the strict tempo of Victor Sylvester or the giddying string lines of Mantovani, 'This Is My Song' didn't need a great amount of complexity to succeed; it only had to suggest sophistication, with a broad sweep of romance and international appeal. In Britain, the counter-reaction to the Beatles' questing music would be a return to something more delicate and maybe unexpected in its own way – music that saw looking backwards as a value. This explains why Engelbert Humperdinck ended up as the break-out act of 1967, the year of *Sgt Pepper*. The three biggest-selling singles in the UK in 1967 were all by a singer known a couple of years earlier as Gerry Dorsey. I love the notion

---

* There's a strong case for reading his 1966 hit 'What Would I Be' as a 1960s forebear to Joy Division's 'Love Will Tear Us Apart', with its quiet despair on a catchy chorus disguising lines like 'Unspoken thoughts we both regret, forgive the past but can't forget.'

that he had recorded and performed under his real name for years,* playing the saxophone in working men's clubs and doing impressions of Jerry Lewis, before one day waking up and deciding to rename himself after a bearded German composer who made an opera out of *Hansel and Gretel* and had the most oompah name known to man.

His ex-flatmate Gordon Mills had been in a minor British harmony act called the Viscounts, but by 1965 was managing Tom Jones and doing very well. Taking his old pal under his wing in 1966, Mills initially let the newly renamed Engelbert record his own left-field song, a slightly R&B-flavoured, psychedelia-adjacent single called 'Stay'. It flopped badly, so next he sent him off to compete in the Knokke song contest in Belgium, where Engelbert managed to score a local hit with a throwback ballad called 'Dommage, Dommage'. Nobody could have foreseen what came next. Engelbert recorded 'Release Me', a country song from the late 1940s that had been recorded by everyone from Patti Page to Kitty Wells, the Everly Brothers to Dean Martin. It struck a chord in 1967, when divorce rates in Britain were soaring and the idea of staying together simply because you were married was, for the first time, starting to be widely acknowledged as cruelty. The former Gerry Dorsey, the handsome Anglo-Indian from Leicester who had pawned his saxophone for a mid-Victorian frock coat, unexpectedly found himself at number one. He did the unthinkable and kept 'Strawberry Fields Forever' b/w 'Penny Lane', the single by which all modern pop singles would be judged, at number two in the British chart, breaking the Beatles' otherwise consecutive run of seventeen chart-toppers.

Humperdinck's voice was powerful but clean, rich but lacking the greasy humour of Tom Jones or the warmth and common touch of Matt Monro. With hits like 'A Man Without Love' (also cut in the original Italian, 'Quando m'innamoro', by A&M act the Sandpipers) and the twinkling Francophile film theme 'Les Bicyclettes de Belsize' (1969), he was the definition of 'middle-of-the-road', or MOR, a newly coined non-rock industry term that superseded 'beautiful music' and

---

* Actually, his first name was Arnold, so even Gerry Dorsey was a partial reinvention.

was rather less circumspect about the music's intentions. There was no kerb or camber to Engelbert; in 1967 he only needed to stand there and well up to charm the knickers off Great Britain, a country confused by the turn those lovable moptops had taken. 'Turning and turning the world goes on, we can change it, my friend,' he sang on 'Les Bicyclettes de Belsize', as if he wanted to stop the world.

In the context of Elvis and the Beatles, Engelbert's sudden rise made no sense. But in the context of Caruso or Crosby, he was more easily understood, as a signifier of stability and a certain gentle strength in uncertain times. Engelbert told the short-lived monthly *Music Maker* in November 1967, 'I think glamour is coming back into the business, and the public was ready for what I had to offer.' *Music Maker* wrote that he parried questions 'with the skill of an Alekhine countering an opening gambit'. Did he like jazz? 'So long as it is not too modern.' Did he want to act? 'Of course. All singers want to be actors. My pantomime, *Robinson Crusoe*, has given me my first acting chance, and I shall gain a lot from it, particularly working with such a seasoned performer as Arthur Askey.' Gordon Mills's management? 'They know how to handle me and I leave it to them. I'm completely satisfied the way things have worked out.' He had a tendency to sound like he was filling in a Sainsbury's customer survey.

Tom Jones was Engelbert's only major rival in 1967, and his albums – with supermarket-ready titles like *Thirteen Smash Hits*, *From the Heart* and *This Is Tom Jones* – were equally far away from the Beatles' mind expansion. He had come out of the South Wales clubs, and early on was a soul-singing beefcake who based his style on New York baritone Chuck Jackson. His stentorian voice was something else, and from the late 1960s through to the mid-'70s he was an old-school sex symbol, the Valentino of the Valleys. His biggest hit was 1966's 'Green, Green Grass of Home', a country ballad about a man awaiting execution, and from the opening line Jones's stone-quarrying voice commanded you to listen: 'The old home town looks the same, as I step down from the train.' Its death-haunted lyric, and Jones's Welsh heritage, gave the single added poignancy when it was released close to the time of the Aberfan disaster, in which a primary school was engulfed by a coal-mining spoil tip. Unexpectedly, it became that year's Christmas number one. During the spoken part, though, Jones was so hammy that it sounded like he was laughing at the song's big reveal – 'Ye-e-es, I was only *dreaming*.'

Though he was a genuine music fan (recording songs by undervalued singers such as Charlie Rich, Mickey Newbury and Bobby Bare), Jones was also a showman of the Jolson school and often seemed to use his voice as nothing more than an adjunct to his gyratory stage show. When he sang straight and deep (Les Reed and Barry Mason's 'I'm Coming Home', a UK number-two hit in 1967), it was as effective and impressive as Elvis had been on Neapolitan hits like 'It's Now or Never'; when he yucked it up (the outrageous 'I'll Never Fall in Love Again', also 1967), Jones the Voice was camp enough to raise Susan Sontag's eyebrows. More often, though, he sounded like a poolside pest. His biggest hit of 1968 was the lecherous 'Help Yourself' – 'Love is like candy on a shelf, you want to taste and help yourself' – which suited his meaty persona but was quite repulsive.

He never let go, again like Jolson, revelling in his role as the 'come-back kid'. 'The fire is still in me,' he said in 2008. 'Not to be an oldie, but a goodie. I want to be a contender.' Keen as a puppy to appear relevant, he used the lingo of a boxer* and seemed to misunderstand his own career completely. No one has ever taken him seriously, and that's why people like him. He's an entertainer, Vegas-standard, a sweatier Frankie Vaughan. Over the decades he's been happy to do a limited Record Store Day seven-inch with Jack White, cover the Archies' 'Sugar, Sugar', record John Lee Hooker songs with Booker T, open a tour for Morrissey and sing über-schlager like 'Love Me Tonight' and 'Daughter of Darkness'. In becoming all things to all people I'm sure he's had a lot of fun, but he's no Scott Walker.

What did people hear in funereally paced Jones ballads like 'I'll Never Fall in Love Again' or 'I'm Coming Home'? Or Engelbert's 'The Last Waltz', a mother-of-pearl-inlaid musical box of a song that spent five weeks at number one in late summer 1967? For a start, 'The Last Waltz' defied time and place; it could have been Vienna in the 1880s

---

* Jones did once sing the national anthem before a Ricky Hatton fight.

or the Mecca Ballroom, Enfield, in the 1960s. The revenant fondness for Old Vienna's merry widows and the folk-memory footpaths of the Old Country (Ireland, Italy or the American frontier) had been there since the first flush of ragtime. It remained strong; the old songs and the old shows didn't necessarily register as conservative (which is certainly how the rock press regarded these strange old/new hit-makers), but as a readdressing of grown-up complexities, vanished social support networks and pragmatic wisdoms. The teenagers that had bought 'She Loves You' in 1963 would have been young adults by 1967, possibly even parents. This being late-1960s Britain, the women would mostly have been housewives. It's easy to see how the LSD visions of Pink Floyd's contemporaneous *Piper at the Gates of Dawn* would have confused them or just left them cold. At home behind privet hedges or isolated on freshly built new-town housing estates, with all mod cons on HP to help them through the day's housework, thousands of child burdened, lonely housewives rested their heads on Engelbert's mock-velvet shoulder. If their ambitions had been dashed by Electrolux, Hotpoint, school runs and cooking the tea, then the voice of a tall, dark gentleman in a ruffed collar could make broken dreams easier to take.

Tom and Engelbert aside, Britain was also in thrall to former Butlin's redcoat Des O'Connor, who had a UK number one with 'I Pretend' in 1968, and Coventry's big-voiced Vince Hill, who almost scored a number one in 1967 with Rodgers and Hammerstein's 'Edelweiss', only kept from the top by Engelbert's 'Release Me'. As surely as the Beatles' 'A Day in the Life' was inspired by acid, the prescription drug Valium instructed 'If I Only Had Time', a 1968 number-three hit for the tanned New Zealander John Rowles: 'Time, like the wind, goes hurrying by and the hours just fly.' These singers were all of a type, lugubrious, dressed either as Jane Austen heroes or Cointreau-drinking, sad-but-worldly holiday romancers.

* * *

Engelbert and his fellow balladeers foreshadowed a downward turn for Britain's standing in the world. 1968 was a year that felt like it had been

left in the sun – overripe, slightly off. Julie Andrews's new vehicle was
Star!, based on the life of Gertrude Lawrence, which featured 125 costume changes for its leading lady, more than Joan Crawford, Tallulah
Bankhead or anybody else had ever got through, but that didn't stop
it tanking. Overnight, London became a cold city: the pirate radio stations had been shut down, the Beatles were fragmenting, its film studios were serving up Technicolor pantomimes (*The Breaking of Bumbo*)
or movies uncovering the grimy cogs that had made the city swing
(*Joanna*, *The Untouchables*), all unedifying spectacles that revealed, as
ever, Britain's seething class war. Andrews decided to lie low for a few
years, re-emerging in slightly saucier roles, and even going topless in
Victor/Victoria.

Petula Clark's run of hits began to slow in 1968. She would make five
wonderful albums, the best of her career, in quick succession at the end
of one turbulent decade and start of the next.* None sold in quantity,
and Pet moved to Switzerland to spend time with her kids and play
shows in casinos and all-seater concert halls. Sadly, her recording career
was sidelined.

This sudden abandonment of London as pop's epicentre was tough
on three new British talents who emerged seconds too late: Jake
Thackray, Barry Booth and Pete Atkin. Booth released just one album
– 1968's *Diversions!* – of melancholic, suburban character sketches, all
dashed commuter dreams and soured milk on the doorstep; the lyrics
were written by Michael Palin and Terry Jones, whose TV show, *Monty
Python's Flying Circus*, was just a year away. Like Palin and Jones, Pete
Atkin was at Cambridge and his melodies were accompanied by lyrics
from another Cantab alumnus, Clive James; the baroque *Beware of the
Beautiful Stranger* (1970) had tales of borrowed biros, of lives wasted
in flats above newsagent's, and fiery visions of escape. Of the three,

---

* The Michel Colombier-arranged, gently psychedelic *Just Pet* (1969); the brumal
Conversations on the Wind, her last with long-time writer/arranger – and author of
'Downtown' – Tony Hatch, which remained unreleased until the 1990s; *Memphis*
with Chips Moman, fresh off recording 'Suspicious Minds' with Elvis Presley
(1970); *Petula '71* with soundtrack composer Johnny Harris; and the soulful
Warm and Tender, produced by Atlantic Records' Arif Mardin, also in 1971.

Thackray was the most singular, a Leeds schoolteacher who syphoned Georges Brassens' *chansons* through tales of West Yorkshire grotesques and sex comedies wrapped in chip paper. He would become an influence, decades later, on fellow Yorkshireman Jarvis Cocker, and he was the only one of the three to sell in numbers, thanks to his regular appearances on British TV, where his face, somehow both chiselled and hangdog, would be a worried and worrying presence right through the 1970s.

The same couldn't be said of Shirley Bassey, one of Britain's few black stars of the 1960s, a true internationalist who always seemed to be on board a jet plane – often in the cockpit, pinching the captain's cheek – in the opening sequence of her many TV shows. Back in 1962, while in her mid-twenties, she had placed herself in the Vegas mould with a BBC special called *Shirley Sings and Riddle Swings*. But later she would find her sweet spot ripping chunks out of John Barry's themes to James Bond movies (*Goldfinger* in 1964, *Diamonds Are Forever* in 1971) and turning on her flamethrower voice. When she sang *Sweet Charity*'s 'Big Spender' in 1967 ('Wouldn't you like to have *fun, fun, fun*?'), it was like the hardest girl in school had taken a shine to you and was repeatedly slamming you against her locker door.

Bassey had been raised in Cardiff's tough dock area, Tiger Bay. Her voice, presence and lavish outfits were reminiscent of Sophie Tucker and Mildred Bailey, shouters from decades earlier. And like post-war Welsh heroine Dorothy Squires, she was attractive, in a rather terrifying way. No one was ever going to argue with her. Who was the only person to get two Bond themes? Our Shirl.* *Fabulous* photographer Fiona Adams once attempted to do a shoot with her in Glasgow. After waiting outside her hotel room for several hours, she was startled to hear Bassey's voice call her as the lift doors opened: 'Be quick! This is all you're getting.' Adams took a single shot of a fully made-up and fur-lined Bassey, before

---

* She actually recorded three, with 'Mr Kiss Kiss Bang Bang' being the original title theme for *Thunderball*; all concerned believed you couldn't write a song called 'Thunderball' that made any sense. Cubby Broccoli disagreed and asked Don Black to try harder. The new song's chorus ran: 'He looks at this world and wants it all, so he strikes like thunderball.' Who could sing it with such volume and ferocity that you wouldn't notice it was pure hokum? Tom Jones, of course.

the lift doors began to close again and she was whisked off to somewhere far more glamorous.

* * *

The *New York Times Review of Books* had declared that *Sgt Pepper* marked 'a new and golden Renaissance of song'. Jack Kroll of *Newsweek* compared the Beatles to other artistic writers: '. . . loss of innocence is, increasingly, their theme and the theme of more "serious" new art from the stories of Donald Barthelme to the plays of Harold Pinter'. The *Washington Post* declared that 'music may never be the same again'. No record would ever unify the serious and pop culture universes again in quite the same way, but the collision was very brief.

After their manager Brian Epstein's death in the summer of 1967, the Beatles had splintered almost immediately, and their spell over pop was broken. In November Britain's postmaster general, Anthony Wedgwood Benn, was behind government legislation that outlawed pirate radio stations and effectively split the BBC's Light Programme in two, giving one channel – Radio 1 – a monopoly on modern pop and rock, and another – Radio 2 – specialist programmes like *The Organist Entertains*, *Big Band Special* and *Dance Band Days*. Unashamedly nostalgic, *The Grand Hotel* featured Reginald Leopold and the Palm Court Orchestra, and there was a weekly hour-long show of 'old time and sequence dancing' called *Those Were the Days*. *Sgt Pepper* had been a counter-cultural attempt to grasp and reanimate the past that had led to it, but ultimately it had failed. Its full-spectrum impact was killed off by, on one side, the BBC's sundering of pop's past, present and future; at the same time, instead of embracing everything, rock's boomer generation decided it would indulge in a Great Forgetting.

In the British front room, meanwhile, the deep brown family radiogram was being replaced by the man-of-the-house's Bang & Olufsen hifi, with hip-high Wharfedale speakers. The kids had Dansettes in their bedrooms. On the wife's Roberts radio in the kitchen, Radio 2's Jimmy Young was being asked, 'What's the recipe today, Jim?' by a squeaky Goon-like voice. The Valium world of Engelbert Humperdinck began to be usurped by other, younger sounds, American-based, with some roots in the rock era, but also a soft, smiling, pre-Beatles appeal. This was a new kind of 'beautiful music'; the Carpenters, John Denver and Olivia Newton-John would provide a low hum throughout the international suburbs of the 1970s.*

* Before we move on from the late 1960s I'd like to give a nod to one of the early kings of Radio 2, a songwriter called Jack Fishman, who had quite a back story. He would unearth hits from continental Europe, add an English lyric to them, and let Denmark Street do its worst. Fishman was the lyricist on both Tom Jones's 'Help Yourself' and John Rowles's 'If I Only Had Time', as well as Petula Clark's 'My Friend the Sea' and Amen Corner's 1969 number one '(If Paradise Is) Half as Nice'. Primarily, though, he was a political journalist, and so embarrassed about his songwriting that he initially used the pseudonym Larry Kahn (as Kahn he wrote 'Ev'rywhere', a 1955 hit for David Whitfield, which won him an Ivor Novello Award). Film music was another sideline: Fishman worked on everything from classic war film *The Best Years of Our Lives* (1946) to *Get Carter* with jazz pianist Roy Budd in 1971. In between the hits and film scores, he found time to write several books, including *The Life of Joseph Stalin* (1962) and *My Darling Clementine* (1963), a biography of Winston Churchill's wife. He also acquired the literary rights to *The Man from UNCLE* after being blown away by the TV pilot, editing and co-publishing all the related paperbacks and annuals. Most remarkably, Fishman was credited with the exposure of the spy Kim Philby in 1963. British libel laws had prevented his hunches about Philby from being published in Britain, so with the aid of friends on the *New York Daily News*, he broke the story in America. The issue was then raised in Parliament, and Philby defected to Moscow. There were rumours that Fishman was working for the CIA or MI5, but he always denied them. Whether he was or not, once you know this, it's hard to hear 'Help Yourself' in quite the same way.

52

SOME KIND OF RAPPROCHEMENT:
THE 1970s

Here is pop's greatest conundrum: how does the present tackle the ever-increasing mass of the recorded past? Pop has always included large numbers of people who are invested in what is, or will soon be, a vanishing genre, and they are often disinclined to scramble around in order to keep up. We have met plenty in this story – George Robey, Al Jolson, Shirley Horn, Stan Kenton. Some of the greatest practitioners and most talented musicians in this book – Armstrong and Crosby, Holiday and Garland, Ellington and Sinatra – have made peace with the past by using it as a shared landscape to express evolving maturity. That's one way of measuring the scale of their own achievements, and also of ensuring that things aren't lost. The hurtling present can be thrilling, it's always there, but even the Beatles had their 'you'll be older too' moments.

In 1972 songwriter and critic Alec Wilder published *American Popular Song: The Great Innovators 1900–1950*. What Wilder's book did – for the very first time – was to partition 'popular song' from both 'serious music' and 'rock'. It snorted at Mitch Miller's kiddie-pop 1950s recordings, which Wilder thought had destroyed a tradition, but also glowered at Gershwin for his classical pretensions. The Beatles didn't even warrant a snide aside. The funny thing was that Wilder wrote like the grumpiest classical die-hard: he didn't crack a smile throughout the hundreds of examples he cited of great pop songs, and the acres of musical notation shuttered out potential converts who couldn't read music.* Still, it's a fascinating book. This was the first time anyone had chalked out the boundaries of what is now commonly referred to as the Great American Songbook, or sometimes just *the* Songbook.†

Soon after Wilder's landmark, Kenneth Tynan wrote in his diaries that the serious music tradition had 'died of sterility and malnutrition; and that the greatest composers of the twentieth century are Berlin, Rodgers, Porter, Kern, Gershwin, et al.'. This was still a contentious view in the 1970s, but like Wilder, his target was classical music rather than latter-day pop. Tynan didn't think it was worth mentioning anything that had happened in the decades since the Songbook was apparently closed shut at the turn of the '50s. No one raving to Jethro Tull at the Isle of Wight festival, no one watching Bob Dylan and George Harrison at the Concert for Bangladesh, no one in the audience for Harry Nilsson's BBC *In Concert* show in the '70s would have been surprised by Tynan's stance: 'They don't like us, and we don't like them.' Professional songwriters were seen as passé at best, reactionary at worst, by the Woodstock generation.

* * *

The bold, unifying promise of the mid-to-late 1960s hadn't really been broken up by the old guard, scared of their younger usurpers, but by American youth, who decided that they had worked hard at

---

* Confirming his own ill temper, Irving Berlin refused to have a bar of his music reprinted. When Wilder's collaborator James Maher told Berlin that Harold Arlen and Richard Rodgers had given permission, Berlin responded: 'You guys are lying to me. I goddamn well don't believe for one minute that they let you use their music. That's bullshit!'
† Wilder was well qualified for the job. It's a neat irony that Frank Sinatra conducted *The Music of Alec Wilder* for an early Capitol album in 1955, emphasising Wilder's own classical leanings. It's doubly ironic that the oboe and English horn player on these sessions was Sinatra's soon-to-be nemesis Mitch Miller.

building a cultural generation gap and were quite happy with their barricades. While Joni Mitchell's 'Both Sides Now' would be recorded by Andy Williams, Frank Sinatra, Nana Mouskouri, Cilla Black and Neil Diamond by the end of the '60s, there was no desire on the part of Laurel Canyon's voyagers to travel forward with their parents and grandparents. After the Beatles had found a song for everyone to sing and an instrument for everyone to play in their 1967 Lonely Hearts Club Band, Bob Dylan and the Band took things back to basics a year later, adding a denim-clad rootsiness to rock and dismissing both the dayglo frivolity of psychedelia and the tux-wearing old school. In rock discourse terms, *Sgt Pepper* had been the genre's north star for only a fairly short time; the '70s would be spent shaking this off as a vision and a delusion.

In reality, the sundering of the pop worlds had itself been delusional. Carole King may have seemed firmly in the 'rock' camp, an international earth mother with 1971's *Tapestry*, but her catalogue of songs from the early '60s belied her influences; 'It Might as Well Rain Until September' could have been sung by Judy Garland in *Meet Me in St Louis*. The Brill Building writers of the early '60s had been as close spiritually to the Songbook writers as they were to Buddy Holly or the Beatles. King's lyricist and husband in the '60s had been Gerry Goffin, who idolised Lorenz Hart – something you can identify on urban mini-dramas like the Drifters' 'Up on the Roof'.

Paul McCartney was coolly aloof from these pop wars. It seemed he had been on a mission to break down the border between rock 'n' roll and pop from the word go: his sweet arrangement of Peggy Lee's 'Till There Was You' had been included as far back as 1963 on the second Beatles album, alongside songs by Chuck Berry and Smokey Robinson. In 1968 McCartney wrote a tune called 'Thingummybob', conceived for a traditional brass band, and recorded it with Yorkshire's prize-winning Black Dyke Mills Band. 'When I'm 64', from *Sgt Pepper* and never released as a Beatles single, would be covered by Kenny Ball, Claudine Longet and Bernard Cribbins, while McCartney's 1965 song 'Yesterday' would become the most-covered song of all time, Matt Monro's version scoring the biggest UK hit. John Lennon disparagingly referred to these efforts as Paul's 'granny music'. But who doesn't love their granny? In 1973 McCartney would close the circle by writing the woozy, dimly lit 'Let's Love' for his beloved Peggy Lee.

Pop's intermingling, and rock's failure to keep out Old Pop interference, had an odd case study in the Who and their 1969 double album *Tommy*. On release, it was seen as a grand rock statement – a 'rock opera', if not the very first, then the first to be widely acknowledged – and it became a commercial monster that stayed on the charts in Britain and America for more than two years. Their manager Kit Lambert, son of composer Constant Lambert, was pleased that 'classical influences are being absorbed by pop . . . the impetus has passed to the younger generation'. Pete Townshend might have wanted *Tommy* to be treated with artful reverence – like the works of Joplin or Gershwin before him – but he similarly found that the pop world took his idea and ran with it. Within a couple of years came *Flectric Tommy*, a 1971 American synthesizer rendition; a year later came a version recorded by the London Symphony Orchestra, with star turns from Rod Stewart, Sandy Denny and Ringo Starr; Les Grands Ballets Canadiens performed it as a rock ballet; the music was scored for brass bands as *Marching Tommy*; and, ultimately, there was Ken Russell's grotesque 1975 film version. In 1977 Townshend glumly acknowledged that *Tommy* had 'become rock's *Pirates of Penzance*'.

* * *

Once the world of popular music had rowed out into rock's waters – even if it was only to touch base with 'Yesterday' rather than 'I Am the Walrus' – it realised it couldn't easily find its way home. Someone had changed the locks. It wasn't as simple as calling Nelson Riddle and getting the old gang back together. By the 1970s what had been 'popular music' was uniformly tagged 'middle-of-the-road', a phrase that could now encompass Sondheim's 'Send in the Clowns', as well as the Rat Pack, Rod McKuen's poems or medley-crazed German bandleader James Last. In early-'70s Britain, Vegas-era Elvis, Tom Jones and Shirley Bassey became the blueprint for a new wave of big-voiced popular entertainers, like Sheffield's Tony Christie and Liverpool's Marti Caine, who, Vegas-aspirations or not, felt as geographically grounded as George Formby and Gracie Fields had been. Their natural home was the working men's or social club, rather than the halls, and light-entertainment TV shows like *Seaside Special*.

The TV variety show continued to be a cross-generational safe house for the middle-of-the-road. In 1971 America had *The Sonny and Cher Comedy Hour*, hosted by an unlikely TV couple who had initially found fame in 1965, when 'I Got You Babe' was a transatlantic number one at the height of the weeks-long protest-music boom. Sonny Bono was short and thin and looked like he was made of balsa wood, a weedy, needling presence with greasy hair. Cher was originally Cherilyn Sarkisian, part Armenian and part Cherokee, tall and slim, with long dark hair, black pools for eyes and a permanent knowing half-smile. Her voice was rich and powerful; his was high, nasal and carried as far as a few inches in front of his face. Somehow Sonny worked as a counterbalance to Cher – presumably because he inspired many male viewers to dream the impossible dream. Guests included Dinah Shore, the Supremes and Burt Reynolds, while Steve Martin made his name as part of the regular cast. The show ended only in 1974, when the odd couple's divorce came through.

In Britain, *It's Cliff Richard* effectively saw the ex-rocker start the 1970s as part of a singing comedy duo with Hank Marvin, welcoming names like Petula Clark, John Rowles and Aretha Franklin onto the show, while introducing the world to Olivia Newton-John. It was very much like cleaned-up music hall; Oswald Stoll would have approved. The show was also used to promote the Eurovision Song Contest, a compressed and strange world of its own that looked back to the days of variety and vaudeville, as well as forward to the all-conquering TV talent shows of the twenty-first century. Eurovision was initially a very continental affair and had almost no impact on Anglo-American pop when it began in the mid-'50s.* The music on the show

---

* A notable exception was Domenico Modugno's 'Nel blu, dipinto di blu', which only came third in 1958, but became a huge hit, and a Grammy-winner, once it was successfully covered by Dean Martin and retitled 'Volare'.

remained unaffected by modern developments until 1965, when Serge Gainsbourg wrote the winning song, a self-parodic teen galloper called 'Poupée de cire, poupée de son' that was clearly influenced by contemporary American Brill Building pop, notably the Crystals' 'Then He Kissed Me'. Eurovision would become a genre in its own right, a melange of continental tropes (balalaikas, oompah rhythms, internationally recognisable nonsense lyrics) that inspired ridicule from the British rock press but would provide at least one major British hit single a year from the late 1960s to the mid-'80s. It was pop music as sport, and even if the sport itself was often at the level of a garden fete kickabout, some major stars emerged, notably Abba, who – like Gainsbourg – used a Phil Spector blueprint for their 1974 winner, 'Waterloo'. By the mid-'80s the group's Björn Ulvaeus and Benny Andersson had worked their way through Eurovision, disco and epic downer pop and into musical theatre, writing *Chess* with British veteran Tim Rice in 1985. They were doing him a favour.

* * *

What of the long-lived, the names that had survived through several decades? Bing Crosby was quite happy to stay in semi-retirement, a living period piece. On March 1977's *Bing! A 50th Anniversary Gala* TV special, he joshed with his wife Kathryn: 'I originally had this suit put together for the inaugural.' 'Carter?' 'No, Roosevelt . . . Teddy!' Guests included Bob Hope, Rosemary Clooney, Paul Anka and the fast-emerging Bette Midler. With the crowd giving him a standing ovation, Bing turned and exited the stage the wrong way, falling into the orchestra pit and ending up in hospital. His final album, *Seasons*, also in 1977, would conclude with Michel Legrand's 'Yesterday When I Was Young', which, rather neatly, was the most recently written song on it.

Long-lived didn't have to mean long in the tooth. Someone else deserving of a first-name-only celebration was Eubie Blake, the ragtime pianist born in 1887, who would receive greater recognition in the 1970s than ever before. He attended the Grammys (and said he was disappointed to lose out to someone who was already dead), and in

1979, aged ninety-two, would appear on *The Tonight Show* with Johnny Carson, sitting next to the Flying Nun Sally Field and celebrating a new Broadway show called *Eubie*. Doris Day, the jazz singer turned cowgirl turned eternal virgin, would similarly live to a grand age and see her reputation do somersaults; by the time she died in 2019 she was widely seen as a heroine, as well as a victim. 1975 had found her on the *Doris Day Today* TV special, aged fifty-three, in a sparkling blue jumpsuit, singing effervescent duets with John Denver – Cole Porter's 'Anything Goes' and Stevie Wonder's ubiquitous 'You Are the Sunshine of My Life'. Still, she couldn't be persuaded back into the studio, and her last album would remain 1965's *Sentimental Journey*, which was a rotten shame.

How about the original king of Tin Pan Alley? By the 1970s Irving Berlin, like Doris Day, was out of the loop, out of confidence and in need of encouragement. But no one could get through to him. He would spend hours on the phone to Harold Arlen, the two of them bemoaning the standard of contemporary songwriting. All his life, Berlin had been citing the man on the street as the only critic that counted. Now, whenever he opened his Upper East Side window, he could hear something blasting out of an open-topped car, another New York-born and -raised act. Neil Diamond! Carole King! A band called Steely Dan, fer Chrissakes! But still he wouldn't write a competitive note. 'The music began to leave him,' said writer Wilfrid Sheed, 'and not the other way round.'* When Berlin died in 1989, aged 101, the UK's number-one single was 'Ride on Time' by Black Box; an academic could argue that he had, just about, made it through to the other side of the rock era. At least that might have given him pause to smile.

* * *

Jazz had almost disappeared as a popular-music form by the mid-1970s. The death of Duke Ellington in 1974 felt like a full stop. To the end, he

---

* Steven Spielberg got in touch with Berlin in the 1980s to ask for permission to build an entire movie around his song 'Always'. Berlin refused to let him use it, saying he had 'other plans' for the song. He didn't share these plans with anyone.

had been pushing forward, experimenting, working on new material, and 1971's evocative *New Orleans Suite* contained some of his most extraordinarily moving work; the rain-soaked 'Bourbon Street Jingling Jollies' was part celebration, part requiem for a music that had been transformed entirely over the decades. At the cinema, *The Sting* (1973) uncovered a huge appetite for Joshua Rifkin's takes on Scott Joplin's rags, all recorded in the proscriptive classical style. This didn't stop 'The Entertainer' from being souped up with brass, clarinet and drum rolls on the film's soundtrack. Marvin Hamlisch was the man responsible, and his adaptation saw him rewarded with an international hit single in 1974. At the same time, there was a new vogue for the R&B that had fed into rock 'n' roll, with reissued albums on new labels like Sonet and Charly appearing in British record shops by the mid-1970s, introducing names like Amos Milburn and Wynonie Harris to impressionable kids. Clubs in the south of England found another aspect of the past to project onto an unfulfilling present: as Abba dominated the radio in 1976, a raft of Glenn Miller reissues piled into the bottom end of the UK charts, propelled there by spins at venues in forgotten corners of the country, like the Goldmine in Canvey Island. 'In the Mood' turned out to still be dancefloor-friendly, more than three decades after it was first released, New Pop *avant la lettre*.

What had become of the music once dismissively known as hillbilly? Demographics had altered it considerably. By 1970 only 7 per cent of people in the southern states worked on the land. 'You see, there's no country left,' singer-songwriter Tom T. Hall told writer Gene Guerrero in 1971. 'It used to be people had outdoor johns, but it's all gone. Country music is the music of the average working man or the intellectual who cares to look at the problems of the working man – they become fans. There's no country left. Try to drive out in the country sometime! You're going to see colour television, steam baths . . . there's no country left, so country music simply became the music of the people.'

Kris Kristofferson was part of a new breed of country writers who were severed from the Nashville establishment and known as the 'outlaws'. In 1973 sixty-year-old Perry Como recorded Kristofferson's 'For the Good Times', a desperately sad song about a couple spending their

last night together ('Make believe you love me one more time'). It was
an olive branch: Como, the crooner from the Ted Weems band and
innumerable Christmas TV specials, gave Kristofferson a huge hit and
quietly, effectively rolled several genres and generations into one. Like
the country people Hall spoke about, Como was a hard-working family
man, a star who married just the once – he would have been a fixture on
country folks' colour TVs at Christmas. Making life look easy was his
shtick, and it worked. People believed him.

It may have been dismissed as an easy-listening hit at the time, but
Como's 'For the Good Times' blurred decades of disparate American
popular musics – the songs of the Italian immigrant, of the train-riding
country boy, of the broken-hearted Tin Pan Alley melodist – from the
earliest years of the century and made them new, made them a single entity. It was impossible to imagine Como – or even Sinatra, for
that matter – singing a song so wearily suggestive of casual sex at any
time before the 1970s. 'For the Good Times' may not have been the
best record of 1973, but it was one of the most important. Alec Wilder
might not have understood why, nor the *NME*, but several million
record-buyers did. It was all showbiz, it was all pop.

EPILOGUE

One night in November 1972 I was watching a TV programme with my parents. It was called *Fifty Years of Music* and featured such stalwarts as dance-band leader Henry Hall and forces sweetheart Vera Lynn, alongside contemporary names like Lulu and Cliff Richard. Bearded, smiley men and long-haired blonde women in a troupe called the Young Generation were dancing to the music, every song instantly familiar, decade by decade. When the music reached the 1960s, the host suddenly looked very glum and told the audience that the music had pretty much died by then – which must have been news to Cliff and Lulu – but there was still the odd good song, he said. Grudgingly, the house band then played 'Ob-La-Di, Ob-La-Da'.

This show stuck in my memory for years. I couldn't understand what the host could possibly have meant – the charts of November 1972, never mind the whole of the 1960s, were stacked with great records. It was possibly a case of ignoring the truth in order to create a convenient arc in the programme's narrative. But I think the nameless, long-forgotten host had an agenda that would have been widely shared: he was assuming that everyone watching would believe proper music had ended circa 1957, with the rock 'n' roll era, and that everything since (except 'Ob-La-Di, Ob-La-Da') had been somehow improper.

History has shown the host to have been quite wrong. Clearly, he was very wrong about the music of the 1960s being worthless, but also the rupture of 'rock' seems ever less significant as time goes by. Another guest on the show was Gilbert O'Sullivan, who earlier in 1972 had a substantial hit with 'Alone Again Naturally'. It's hard to think of many songs that better incorporated the tricks and wit of the Songbook age, while adding contemporary production. Lorenz Hart, for one, would have been proud to win a Grammy for such a drily written, beautifully structured song about, of all things, contemplating suicide.

The more years that have passed, the more the hard border between the modern pop era – the period that began with rock 'n' roll in 1956 – and the pre-rock era has become porous. I wouldn't often cite Jive Bunny as a cultural bellwether, but the cartoon rabbit's 'Swing the Mood' medley – the UK's biggest-selling single in 1989 – casually mixed the hook of Glenn Miller's 'In the Mood' (1941) with Elvis Presley, Little Richard, Bill Haley and Everly Brothers hits from between 1956 and 1958. Old Teds must have been fuming, but given the record's success, it seemed like most people didn't notice the anomaly, or just didn't care.

As the twenty-first century has progressed, the previous one has understandably become a progressively more distant land, where dates blur and old rivalries and standpoints are forgotten. A surprising beneficiary of this cultural forgetting has been musical theatre. The huge success of *Jesus Christ Superstar* in 1970 had drawn back the curtain to reveal the gargoyles Tim Rice and Andrew Lloyd Webber, who, over the next twenty years, would become the biggest show writers since Rodgers and Hammerstein. They were the privet-hedged, middlebrow result of Hammerstein's good intentions – wasn't it all better when we went to church on Sundays? Borrowing Sondheim's preciousness and Hammerstein's hauteur, they went on to write some of the worst popular music of the late twentieth century for musicals like *Cats*, *Phantom of the Opera* and *Starlight Express*.* Gradually, the West End musical became completely bossed by people from Surrey with a fearful mistrust of beards and the Open University.

By 2000 it seemed like the jukebox musical would be the weak finale

---

* I'd be a boor, though, if I didn't give Lloyd Webber some props for 1978's winking prog-pop collection *Variations*, a whole album based around a theme by Paganini, which apparently he was forced to write because he lost a football bet. The main theme would become the opening music to TV arts programme *The South Bank Show* for many years. The musicians on *Variations* were members of progressive rock band Colosseum, plus Lloyd Webber's cellist brother Julian, rather than the light opera likes of Sarah Brightman and Michael Ball. Maybe that helped to give the album an unpretentious and genuinely charming feel. Also, losing a bet on Leyton Orient probably made the task of composing it seem less onerous than having to work up a Broadway musical that would employ dozens of people.

in the story of musical theatre, as Queen and Ben Elton's plain stupid *We Will Rock You* ran and ran. But the Freddie Mercury statue outside the Dominion Theatre on Tottenham Court Road would be toppled soon after the Iraq War. Arriving in short order, *Mamma Mia* and *Jersey Boys* were still jukebox musicals, but they were sharper and slightly knowing. Then the detoxification of the musical began in earnest, with off-Broadway, Edinburgh Festival fodder like *Jerry Springer the Opera*, *The Book of Mormon*, *Avenue Q* and *Enron*. At the time of writing, musical theatre is thriving. The racially and politically sassy *Hamilton* and the mental-health storyline behind *Dear Evan Hansen* have given the genre an artistically and commercially successful, teen-led revival. Why is this? Partly because of the AI blankness of much pop in the digital age, its disconnect from live singing and orchestration. Kids who dug Taylor Swift as a big sister with bright ideas have rediscovered the roar of the greasepaint and smell of the crowd.

* * *

What of the Great American Songbook? Did the combined hippie energies of Laurel Canyon, blindly associating Tin Pan Alley with the military-industrial complex, kill it off? It would be abandoned en masse by many of its traditional flag-wavers in the 1970s and '80s, something singer Buddy Greco put down to 'collective insanity', but it merely went underground. Harry Nilsson was someone who wasn't happy with Laurel Canyon's stance at all, and he attempted to merge the rock and non-rock worlds in 1973, when he released *A Little Touch of Schmilsson in the Night*. It was a seamless suite of Alec Wilder-approved songs, topped and tailed by 'As Time Goes By'; the track listing stretched all the way back to Al Jolson's 'You Made Me Love You (I Didn't Want to Do It)' from 1913. Nilsson even called in Gordon Jenkins for the orchestration, which had strong shades of both Jenkins's 1940s concept album *Manhattan Tower* and his 1957 arrangements for Nat King Cole's *Love Is the Thing*. 1973 also saw Bryan Ferry manage a delicious, high-camp take on 'These Foolish Things', but Nilsson was quite serious in his love for this music. He had already been dismissed as a 'dilettante' by the *NME* and saw the album panned, but while it sold reasonably well, it didn't sell as many as his raucous, barely listenable *Pussy Cats* collaboration with John Lennon in 1974.

A Little Touch was a bold album, though, far ahead of its time. Four decades later, Rod Stewart would be singing 'It Had to Be You', Van Morrison would have a crack at 'A Foggy Day', and Bob Dylan – who has maybe done more to unbottle the ghosts and the magic of old-time music than anyone else in the rock era – would be brave enough to tackle Sinatra's dolorous 'I'm a Fool to Want You'. If Gary Barlow, Taylor Swift or Nick Cave sang 'You Made Me Love You' or 'They Didn't Believe Me' on stage tomorrow, no one would bat an eyelid. Nilsson's groundbreaking rapprochement is largely forgotten now, but he should retrospectively be awarded a medal for valour.

Another line in the sand that seems to get fuzzier with time is punk rock, which posited 1977 as a year zero. Though it was infra dig for the punk generation to suggest too much familiarity with blues-based rock, it turned out to be quite acceptable to peer behind the curtain into pre-rock time. In the UK, Elvis Costello had a good grasp of the older tradition thanks to his club singer dad; in 1981 Joe Jackson recorded a whole album of Louis Jordan songs called *Jumpin' Jive*; Jools Holland of Squeeze kept demonstrating his love of boogie-woogie, whether people wanted to hear it or not. In New York, Kid Creole and the Coconuts and the Ze Records collective looked to Cab Calloway, zoot suits and a Cotton Club aesthetic, which was perfectly audible on their 1982 hit 'Stool Pigeon'. The same year brought ABC's classicist *Lexicon of Love*, with strings straight from the 1950s heyday of Capitol Records; a year later, a new wave of jazz-influenced post-punk singers like Sade, Carmel and Tracey Thorn heralded what *NME*'s Ian Penman called 'the return of the torch song'.

A handful of 1970s acts would pick up on a single aspect of the past and run with it. The Pointer Sisters harked back to the days of Adelaide Hall, more in look than sound, but were very sharp indeed as they sang 'Yes We Can Can' (1973), taking ownership of art deco stylings as if they were repossessing the Cotton Club and putting it under black ownership. Disco would hark back to the big-band sounds of the

1930s and '40s: Chic's image recalled the Roseland, and they quoted Basie's 'Stompin' at the Savoy' in their million-seller 'Le Freak'; their 'Dance, Dance, Dance' and Donna Summer's 'I Remember Yesterday' (both 1977) managed to blend the '30s and '70s musically as well as visually. Maybe dancing had become an escape from the three-day week, stagflation and the oil crisis, economic echoes of the '30s. 'Glamour' and 'escape' were two words that had described the swing age; equally, they suited the disco experience.

Both black and gay culture would play a large part in weaving pop's past into the present day. Bette Midler initially made her name performing at New York's Continental Bath House in 1970, singing the Andrews Sisters' 'Boogie Woogie Bugle Boy' for the towel-clad gay clientele. Her following became big enough to make her 1972 debut album, *The Divine Miss M*, a platinum-seller. Her musical director at the Bath House was a grinning, tanned fellow from Williamsburg called Barry Manilow.

If one person put chunks of this book into a blender and served it up for the 1970s and '80s, it was Manilow. His 1975 single 'It's a Miracle' sounded like Busby Berkeley had got his hands on *Annie Get Your Gun* and choreographed it under a giant mirror ball. Originally Barry Pincus, Manilow had started out off-Broadway in the mid-'60s, was singing jingles by the turn of the '70s ('All across the nation, it's the Pepsi Generation!') and had his finger on the pop pulse by the middle of the decade. Ballads like 'I Made It Through the Rain' sounded like climactic Rodgers and Hammerstein moments mulched with 'Let It Be' or 'Bridge Over Troubled Water' – the boy Pincus knew his pop history. Ultimately, there was 'Copacabana', his cautionary tale of showgirl Lola, which sounded like an entire musical inside three minutes.

A *Vanity Fair* writer once claimed to be shocked that Manilow didn't write one of his best-known hits, 'I Write the Songs'. When he sang it, the journalist asked, did he feel as if he was living a lie? 'No,' said Manilow, 'because the song isn't about me or anybody else. It's about the spirit of music. The first line says, "I've been alive forever," so it can't be about me.' There's a wit, a sense of fun and a knowingness to Manilow, learned from Cole Porter, Frankie Valli and Randy Newman in equal measure. When he wrote 'Copacabana', he wasn't trying to be Leonard

Cohen and getting it wrong.

Acts like Midler and Manilow showed how the recorded pop era was a form of time travel. In the 1980s British TV viewers would be serenaded on a weekly basis by Irving Berlin's 'What'll I Do', repurposed as the theme to *Birds of a Feather*, a sitcom about two women whose husbands were in prison. The late '90s saw Al Bowlly appearing in ghostly form at the top of the UK charts, his 'My Woman' primitively sampled for 'Your Woman' by a Leicestershire bedroom-pop act called White Town. Even the stentorian voice of light opera resurfaced, with the fabled Three Tenors – Pavarotti, Carreras, Domingo – crossing over into the pop charts of the 1990s, before the Viennese whirls of Katherine Jenkins, Il Divo and Russell Watson became as familiar to British TV audiences as Simon Cowell or Ant and Dec.

Frank Sinatra did stage a full-blown comeback, of course (sorry if I left you holding your breath). The early 1970s would find the former modernist marooned in the post-Beatles era, his musical direction as flappy as his political allegiances. Out of step with the modern pop of his (and his daughter Nancy's) time, the inevitable comeback album – 1973's weak *Ol' Blue Eyes Is Back* – began a sad, extended adjunct to a tumultuous career. Yet he would score one of his signature tunes in his career's third – or was it fourth? – act with his 'Theme from *New York, New York*'; so closely did it mimic the brassy Billy May years that almost no one guessed it was a brand-new song in 1977. For the most part, though, it's a shame he didn't really quit for good in 1971. He knew his voice was strained, with little nuance, permanently set in its fairground barker 'That's Life' mode. The last twenty-five years of his recording career spoiled what had been a perfect arc. The *Trilogy* set from 1980 – a triple album split into 'Past', 'Present' and 'Future' – earns my respect for its Mars-reaching levels of pretentiousness (not an insult), but I'm afraid it works better if you imagine it in your head. Towards the end, Frank was duetting with Bono. Myself, I'm happy to stick with *Watertown* as his final album and pretend the rest never happened.

Something I only touched on in the main body of the book is the time slippage between when the songs on Frank Sinatra's Capitol albums were written and when he recorded them. *In the Wee Small Hours* was made up of torch songs written in the 1930s and '40s, while his *Songs for Swingin' Lovers*, cut in 1956, were on average twenty years old. Just as Charles Dickens had set most of his novels in the recent past, so Sinatra created a form of time travel to make hip, adult pop music for the early rock era. And decades later, how many people listening to his versions of 'Night and Day' (1932), 'Isle of Capri' (1934) or 'Pennies from Heaven' (1936) know or care when they were written?

I wrote this book to make sense of the different times, eras and genres that gave us Frank Sinatra and Sophie Tucker, *Sweet Charity* and *Showboat*, Billy May and Count Basie, 'Moon River' and 'What'll I Do', to sort out the chronology for myself and for anyone else who was interested. Though pop has to constantly reinvent itself, the miracle is that the original time frame of the music in this book hasn't stopped much of it from time-travelling to become a part of the current century. That's quite magical, and it reminds me that the most important thing to do, of course, is to listen to the music and enjoy it for what it is while we can.

In my head as I wrote the last few chapters was a beautiful Rosemary Clooney song called 'Time Flies', written by Jimmy Webb, which puts the strange and unlikely longevity of pop music, and its place in our lives, into context: 'Life begins and spirits rise, and they become memories that vaporise, and the vapour becomes all the dreams we devise. And while we are dreaming, time flies.'

ACKNOWLEDGEMENTS

With special thanks to Lee Brackstone for commissioning the book in the first place; my agent David Godwin and everyone at DGA; my extremely patient editor Alexa von Hirschberg, Mo Hafeez, Dan Papps, copy-editor Ian Bahrami and the rest of the team at Faber who have made the process of finishing a very large book seem remarkably straightforward; and wise owl Mark Sinker, who was always capable of making sense of my conflicting thoughts, happy to read and re-read my drafts.

A special thank you to Catherine Eccles, Jean Petrovic, Cara Rodway and Dr Polly Russell at the Eccles Centre. Access to their American collections, held at the British Library, was invaluable. Many thanks also to Olivia Laing and Alison MacLeod for pointing me in the direction of the Eccles Centre. In particular, I'm grateful to Phil Davies for his warmth and enthusiasm, and for putting me in touch with the wonderful writer and music historian Brian Ward.

Over the last ten years I've had a huge amount of help and encouragement from friends, and strangers who have become friends. I would like to especially thank the late Fred Dellar, an absolute gentleman, whom I'd known since my cub writer days at the *NME* in the late 1980s. He sent occasional emails recommending things from the era that I might not know, like the unique small group sound of Artie Shaw's Gramercy Five or hidden gems like Patti Page's 'No Moon at All', as well as suggesting I include moments like the 'zoot suit riots'. I wish we'd had more time to talk.

I'm very grateful to Matthew Lees, Pete Paphides and Daniel Scott for going through half-finished manuscripts, giving me confidence and keeping me sane; Jonny Trunk for coming up with the title; the sagacious Jon Savage for his further reading suggestions; and, for help on specific pieces of the jigsaw, a big hat-tip to industry legends Mark Ellen (Duke Ellington), Jerry Jaffe (Al Jolson), Lenny Kaye (crooners), Russ

Titelman (Harry Warren), Geoffrey Weiss (Earl Bostic) and Andy Zax (Rodgers and Hammerstein). Many thanks to Russell Drury for the kind gift of his father's swing 78s, which were the perfect accompaniment when I was writing the middle-period chapters. Thanks also to Roger Spiers for sourcing so many albums, which were fifty times more enjoyable to listen to than streaming.

For support and inspiration, direct and indirect, I am indebted to Danny Baker, Rob Baker, Pete Baran, Jeff Barrett, Gus Bousfield, James Brown, Ken Bruce, Liz Buckley, Derek Burbage, Sheila Burgel, Ian Catt, Alex Conway, Ossie Dales, Matt Dixon, Alan Dobrin, Travis Elborough, Paul Gambaccini, Tariq Goddard, Martin Green, Michael Hann, Brian Henson, Tim Hopkins, Johan Kugelberg, Andres Lokko, Anneliese Midgley, Caitlin Moran, Alex O'Connell, Gail O'Hara, Siân Pattenden, Tris Penna, Lisa Jane Persky, Rob Prior, Michael Robson, Jude Rogers, Andy Rossiter, Andrew Sandoval, Neil Scaplehorn, Ian 'Vic' Smith, James Turner, Kate Turner, Kieron Tyler, Adam Velasco, Audun Vinger, Anne-Marie White, Harvey Williams and Jason Wood.

Thanks again to the Saint Etienne extended family – Sarah Cracknell, Pete Wiggs and Debsey Wykes – and to James Ball, Joe Bennett, Robin Bennett, Gerard Johnson, Martin Kelly, Paul Kelly, Mike Monaghan and Andrew 'Pep' Peppiatt, who keep three wheels on our wagon.

To my mum and dad and my sister Jules, lots and lots of love to you.

And finally, to my gorgeous girlfriend Tessa Norton and our handsome lad Leonard, you are the best family in the world and I couldn't have written this without you (I mean, I could have done, but it would have been a lot more like homework). I love you both so much.

SOURCES

Many thanks to Karen Bevan for sourcing tapes of BBC Radio 2's 1974 series *Ragtime to Rock 'n' Roll*, written by Benny Green and narrated by Kenneth More, which had multiple wonderful interviews with song-writers and performers – Irving Caesar being particularly quotable – that have found their way into this text.

My subscription to *The New Yorker* was invaluable and allowed me to access Gary Giddins's fine pieces on Bing Crosby, Glenn Miller and Fats Waller.

I'm indebted to Marc Myers's excellent Jazzwax blog and the Jazz Profiles site, to Tyler Mahan Coe's *Cocaine and Rhinestones* podcast, and to current writers who weren't directly connected to my subject matter but whose new work kept up my enthusiasm: Tom Breihan (Stereogum), Marcello Carlin (Then Play Long), Tom Ewing (Freaky Trigger) and Simon Goddard.

Thanks also to Barney Hoskyns and rocksbackpages.com, which saved me hours of searching for the right issue of *Melody Maker* for a quote from Chris Barber or Duke Ellington.

The American chart positions I have used come from *Billboard* maga-zine and Joel Whitburn's invaluable Record Research books. UK chart positions are those recognised by the Official Charts Company and, prior to that, the Guinness books of *British Hit Singles* and *Albums*.

Images are from the author's collection, with the exception of:

p. 62: 'When you're a long, long, way from home.' British Library, London, UK. British Library Board. All Rights Reserved/Bridgeman Images. p. 86: Louis Armstrong and family. PVDE/Bridgeman Images. p. 111: Al Jolson. Granger/Bridgeman Images. p. 139: Columbia Race Records advert, *c.*1935. Pictorial Press Ltd/Alamy Stock Photo. p. 240: the Boswell Sisters, *c.*1934. Everett Collection Inc./Alamy Stock Photo. p. 264: Fats Waller and Ada Brown, 1943. Masheter Movie Archive/

Alamy Stock Photo. p. 288: George Gershwin at the piano with Fred Astaire, Ginger Rogers, Hermes Pan, Mark Sandrich, Ira Gershwin and Nathaniel Shilkret, 1937. © Giancarlo Costa/Bridgeman Images. p. 337: Glenn Miller, 'In the Mood' sheet music, c.1930s. Everett Collection/Bridgeman Images. p. 368: José Iturbi and Frank Sinatra on the set of *Anchors Aweigh*, 1945. Everett Collection/Bridgeman Images. p. 412: In-ear monitoring in a record store, Copenhagen, Denmark. colaimages/Alamy Stock Photo. p. 506: Frank Sinatra, Dean Martin, Sammy Davis Jr, 1960. Bridgeman Images. p. 547: Anthony Newley, 1959. Photo by John Pratt/Getty Images. p. 555: Eartha Kitt. Courtesy of SWNS and the Bradford *Telegraph & Argus*.

Scanning courtesy of PDQ Fotos in Shipley. Thanks to Odele Ayres, Emma Clayton and Duncan Seaman for helping me to source the Eartha Kitt image from the Bradford *Telegraph & Argus* archive.

SONGWRITER CREDITS

CH. 3: 'Alexander's Ragtime Band' by Irving Berlin. 'Life Begins at Forty', 'I Don't Want to Get Thin' lyrics by Jack Yellen.

CH. 6: 'Take Me Back to Dear Old Blighty' by Bennett Scott, Fred Godfrey, Arthur J. Mills. 'Stay Down Here Where You Belong' by Irving Berlin. 'I Didn't Raise My Boy to Be a Soldier' lyrics by Alfred Bryan. 'Naughty! Naughty! Naughty!' lyrics by Joe Goodwin and William Tracey. 'Let's All Be Americans Now' by Irving Berlin

CH. 9: 'Nesting Time in Flatbush' lyrics by P. G. Wodehouse. 'Everything Stops for Tea' by Al Hoffman, Al Goodhart and Maurice Sigler. 'Old Man River' by Jerome Kern/Oscar Hammerstein II © Universal Music Publishing Group, Songtrust Ave

CH. 16: 'The Whiffenpoof Song' by Meade Minnigerode and George S. Pomeroy

CH. 18: 'Remember My Forgotten Man' by H. Warren/A. Dubin © WB Music Corp., Four Jays Music Publishing Company, M. Witmark & Sons

CH. 19: 'Mississippi Mud' by Harry Barris/James Cavanaugh © Reservoir Media Management Inc.

CH. 20: 'Yes, Yes' by Con Conrad and Cliff Friend

CH. 22: 'Why Did She Fall for the Leader of the Band' by Jimmy Kennedy/ Michael Carr. 'Dinner at Eight' by Jimmy McHugh/Dorothy Fields. 'Life Is Just a Bowl of Cherries' by Ray Henderson/Lew Brown

CH. 23: 'Slap That Bass' written by George and Ira Gershwin. 'Housequake' by Prince Nelson © NPG Publishing. 'You're the Top' written by Cole Porter © WB Music Corp. 'They Can't Take That Away from Me' by George and Ira Gershwin

CH. 26: 'All of You' by Cole Porter © Sony/ATV Music Publishing LLC, Warner/ Chappell Music, Inc. 'Too Marvellous for Words' by Richard Whiting/Johnny

Mercer. 'Love Is Here to Stay' by Ira Gershwin/George Gershwin © Ira Gershwin Music, George Gershwin Music, Nokawi Music, Frankie G. Songs, Chappell & Co., Inc.

CH. 27: 'Play That Barbershop Chord' by Lewis Muir/William Tracey. 'I Remember You' written by Victor Schertzinger/Johnny Mercer. 'The Man That Got Away' by Harold Arlen/Ira Gershwin. 'Strange Fruit' written by Abel Meeropol

CH. 28: 'Let the People Sing' by Noel Gay/Frank Eyton/Ian Grant. 'God Bless You, Mr Chamberlain', song by Harry Roy. 'We'll Meet Again', song by Ross Parker and Hughie Charles

CH. 29: 'Say Si, Si', songwriter Ernesto Lecuona © Carlin America Inc.

CH. 30: 'The Man Who Wasn't There' written by William Hughes Mearns

CH. 31: 'I'll Buy That Dream' lyrics by Herb Magidson and Allie Wrubel. 'Primrose Hill' written by Chester, Morris and Lynton. 'The Land of Beginning Again' by Grant Clarke and George W. Meyer. 'Dear Hearts and Gentle People' lyrics by Bob Hilliard. 'Chickery Chick' written by Sidney Lippman/Sylvia Dee. 'Hit the Road to Dreamland' by Harold Arlen/Johnny Mercer. 'Blues in the Night' by Harold Arlen/Johnny Mercer. 'Accentuate the Positive' by Harold Arlen/Johnny Mercer. 'Moon River' by Johnny Mercer/Henry Mancini

CH. 32: 'Early Autumn' by Johnny Mercer. 'Cowboy Rhumba' by Don George, Ellington & Reif

CH. 33: 'Nancy with the Laughing Face' written by Phil Silvers and Jimmy Van Heusen. 'Lost in the Stars' lyrics by Maxwell Anderson. 'Bim Bam Baby' by Sammy Mysels

CH. 34: 'Caldonia' by Louis Jordan/Fleecie Moore. 'Saturday Night Fish Fry' by Louis Jordan/Ellis Walsh. 'The Hucklebuck' by Roy Alfred. 'Black, Brown and White' by William Lee Conley Broonzy © Warner Chappell Music, Inc.

CH. 35: 'Manhattan Tower' by Gordon Jenkins. 'You're the Top' by Cole Porter © WB Music Corp. 'I Get a Kick Out of You' by Cole Porter. 'Come Fly with Me' by Sammy Cahn and Van Heusen. 'Brazil' lyrics by Bob Russell

CH. 36: 'Stranger in Paradise' by Robert Wright/George Forrest © Warner Chappell Music, Inc. 'I Wanna Be Around' by Sadie Vimmerstedt and Johnny Mercer. 'My Foolish Heart' by Victor Young and Ned Washington

CH. 37: 'Waitin' for the Train to Come In' by Sunny Skylar/Marty Block © Universal Music Publishing Group. 'Don't Smoke in Bed' by Willard Robison/Peggy Lee/Dave Barbour. 'What's New?' by Johnny Burke/Bob Haggart. 'The White Birch and the Sycamore' by Willard Robison, Hubert Wheeler. 'The Folks Who Live on the Hill' by Jerome Kern and Oscar Hammerstein © Universal Music Publishing Group. 'I'm a Woman' by Jerry Leiber/Mike Stoller © Sony/ATV Music Publishing LLC, Warner/Chappell Music, Inc. 'My Way' by Claude François and Jacques Revaux; English lyrics by Paul Anka. 'Let's Love' by Paul McCartney

CH. 38: 'Witchcraft' by Cy Coleman, with lyrics by Carolyn Leigh. 'The Best Is Yet to Come' by Cy Coleman, with lyrics by Carolyn Leigh. 'Earl of Ruston' by C. C. Courtney and Ragan Courtney. 'Let's Have Another Cup of Coffee' by Irving Berlin

CH. 39: 'World Weary' by Noel Coward © Warner Chapell Music, Inc. 'Let Me Off Uptown' by Earl Bostic/Redd Evans © Universal Music Publishing Group

CH. 41: 'Crazy Otto Rag' by Edward R. White/Mack Wolfson/Emile Trent/ Fred Lawrence. 'Green Fields' by Terry Gilkyson/Frank Miller/Richard Dehr © Sony/ATV Music Publishing LLC, BMG Rights Management. 'A Hard Rain's A-Gonna Fall' by Bob Dylan © Sony/ATV Music Publishing LLC. 'Revolution' by John Lennon/Paul McCartney

CH. 42: 'Anything Goes' by Cole Porter. 'Mona Lisa' by Ray Evans/Jay Livingston. 'Hundreds and Thousands of Girls' by Dotty Wayne/Ray Rasch. 'Where Did Everyone Go?' by Mack David/Jimmy Van Heusen. 'That's All There Is, There Isn't Any More' by Marty Robbins © BMG Rights Management, Warner Chappell Music, Inc. 'Nature Boy' by eden ahbez

CH. 44: 'Rock and Roll Waltz' by Roy Alfred/Shorty Allen © Jonroy Music Company, Sony/ATV Music Publishing LLC. 'Ringo Beat' by Ella Jane Fitzgerald

CH. 45: 'Old MacDonald' by Marilyn Bergman/Lew Spence/Alan Bergman. 'Up, Up and Away' by Jimmy Webb. 'Memories Are Made of This' by Terry Gilkyson/Richard Dehr/Frank Miller © Campbell Connelly & Co. Ltd. 'Watertown' by Jake Holmes/Bob Gaudio/Robert Gaudio. 'Michael & Peter' © WB Music Corp., Universal Music Corp., Pw Arrangements, Devalbo Inc.

CH. 46: 'It's So Nice to Have a Man Around the House' by Harold Spina/John Moon Elliott © Music Sales Corporation, Edwin H. Morris & Co. Inc. 'Almost There' by Gloria Shayne/Jerry Keller © September Music Corp., Lynn Hatch Music. 'Chances Are' by Al Stillman/Robert Allen © Reservoir Media Management Inc., Sony/ATV Music Publishing LLC

CH. 49: 'Sunday Afternoon at Home' by Tony Hancock. 'Goldfinger' (theme song) by Anthony Newley/John Barry/Leslie Bricusse © Sony/ATV Music Publishing LLC. 'White Boy' by Anthony Newley

CH. 50: *Beatsville* lyrics by Rod McKuen. 'Body Surfing with the Jet Set' lyrics by Rod McKuen. 'The Mud Kids' by Rod McKuen. 'Hey Jude' by Lennon–McCartney. 'Mississippi Goddam' by Nina Simone.

CH. 51: 'What Would I Be' by Jackie Trent © M and M Music, Darren Music Ltd. 'Les Bicyclettes de Belsize' by Barry Mason/Les Reed. 'Green, Green Grass of Home' by Curly Putman © Tree International, Tree Publishing Co. Inc. 'Help Yourself' by Carlos Labati Donida/Giulio Rapetti/Jack Fishman © Universal Music Publishing Group. 'If I Only Had Time' by Christopher Coyne/Kris Dollimore/Michael Gibson/George Mazur/Peter Coyne © Valley Music Ltd., Sony/ATV Songs LLC, Godfathers Music. 'Big Spender' by Cy Coleman/Dorothy Fields © BMG Rights Management, Words and Music A Div Of Big Deal Music LLC. 'Thunderball' by John Barry © Sony/ATV Music Publishing LLC

CH. 52: 'For the Good Times' by Kristoffer Kristofferson © Universal Music Publishing Group

EPILOGUE: 'Time Flies' by Jimmy Webb

BIBLIOGRAPHY

Michael A. Amundson, *Talking Machine West: A History and Catalogue of Tin Pan Alley's Western Recordings 1902–18*, University of Oklahoma Press 2017

Gage Averill, *Four Parts, No Waiting: A Social History of American Barbershop Harmony*, Oxford University Press 2003

Christina L. Baade, *Victory Through Harmony: The BBC and Popular Music in World War Two*, Oxford University Press 2012

Rob Baker, *Beautiful Idiots and Brilliant Lunatics*, Amberley 2015

Louis Barfe, *Where Have All the Good Times Gone: The Rise and Fall of the Record Industry*, Atlantic 2004

Tony Bennett, *Life Is a Gift*, HarperCollins 2012

Billy Bragg, *Roots, Radicals and Rockers: How Skiffle Changed the World*, Faber & Faber 2017

Matt Brennan, *Kick It: A Social History of the Drum Kit*, Oxford University Press 2020

Donald Clarke, *The Rise and Fall of Popular Music*, Penguin 1995

Peter Cliffe, *Fascinating Rhythm: Dance Tunes from Between the Wars and the Stars Who Made Them Magical*, Egon 1990

Harvey G. Cohen, *Duke Ellington's America*, University of Chicago Press 2017

Rich Cohen, *Machers and Rockers*, W. W. Norton 2004

Nicholas Dawidoff, *In the Country of Country*, Faber & Faber 2005

Robin Douglas-Home, *Sinatra*, Grossett & Dunlap 1961

Susan and Lloyd Ecker, *I Am Sophie Tucker*, Prospecta Press 2014

Travis Elborough and Nick Rennison, *A London Year*, Frances Lincoln 2013

Ken Emerson, *Doo-Dah! Stephen Foster and the Rise of American Popular Culture*, Simon & Schuster 1997

Daniel Farson, *Marie Lloyd and Music Hall*, Tom Stacey Ltd 1972

Will Friedwald, *The Great Jazz and Pop Vocal Albums*, Pantheon 2017

Philip Furia, *Irving Berlin: A Life in Song*, Schirmer 1998

Peter Gammond, *Scott Joplin and the Ragtime Era*, Abacus 1975

Rolan Gelatt, *The Fabulous Phonograph*, Cassell 1956

Gary Giddins, *Bing Crosby: A Pocketful of Dreams*, Little, Brown 2000

Isaac Goldberg, *Tin Pan Alley*, John Day 1930

Leslie Gourse, *Unforgettable: The Life and Mystique of Nat King Cole*,
    New English Library 1991

Tim Gracyk with Frank Hoffmann, *Popular American Recording
    Pioneers 1895–1925*, Haworth Press 2000

Benny Green, *Let's Face the Music: The Golden Age of Popular Song*,
    Michael Joseph 1990

Kitty Grime, *Jazz at Ronnie Scott's*, Robert Hale 1979

Charles Hamm, *Yesterdays: Popular Song in America*, W. W. Norton
    1979

Roy Hemming and David Hajdu, *Discovering Great Singers of Classic
    Pop*, Newmarket 1991

Eric Hobsbawm, *The Jazz Scene*, Faber & Faber 1959

Eric Hobsbawm, 'On the Reception of Jazz in Europe', in Jazz und
    Sozialgeschichte, Chronos 1994

Adrian Horn, *Juke Box Britain: Americanisation and Youth Culture
    1945–60*, Manchester University Press 2009

Alan Hyman, *The Gaiety Years*, Cassell 1975

Chris Ingham, *The Rough Guide to Frank Sinatra*, Penguin 2005

Mark Katz, *Capturing Sound: How Technology Has Changed Music*,
    University of California Press 1974

Lenny Kaye, *You Call It Madness: The Sensuous Song of the Croon*,
    Villard 2004

Charles Keil, Angeliki V. Keil and Dick Blau, *Polka Happiness*, Temple
    University Press 1992

J. J. Kennedy, *The Man Who Wrote the Teddy Bears' Picnic*, Author
    House 2011

William Howland Kenney, *Recorded Music in American Life: The
    Phonograph and Popular Memory 1890–1945*, Oxford University
    Press 2003

John Lahr, 'Come Rain or Come Shine: The Bittersweet Life of
   Harold Arlen', *The New Yorker*, September 2005

Frankie Laine and Joseph F. Laredo, *That Lucky Old Son*, Pathfinder
   1993

Philip Larkin, *All What Jazz: A Record Diary 1961–68*, Faber & Faber
   1970

Philip Larkin, *Reference Back: Uncollected Jazz Writings 1940–1984*,
   University of Hull Press 1999

Peggy Lee, *Miss Peggy Lee*, Bloomsbury 1990

Geoff Leonard and Pete Walker, *Hit and Miss: The Story of the John
   Barry Seven*, Redcliffe Press 2018

Bruce Lindsay, *Shellac and Swing: A Social History of the Gramophone
   in Britain*, Fonthill 2020

Anita Loos, *Kiss Hollywood Goodbye*, Viking 1974

William McBrien, *Cole Porter*, Vintage 2000

Allison McCracken, *Real Men Don't Sing: Crooning in American
   Culture*, Duke University Press 2015

Sara Maitland, *Vesta Tilley*, Virago 1986

Karl Hagstrom Miller, *Segregating Sound*, Duke University Press 2010

Judah Mirvish, 'Albert Sandler: A Life and Discography', Atavist.com
   (accessed 20 June 2017)

Jerrold Northrop Moore, *A Matter of Records: Fred Gaisberg and the
   Golden Era of the Gramophone*, Taplinger 1976

John Mullen, *Propaganda and Dissent in British Popular Song During
   the Great War*, Université de Bourgogne 2011

Stuart Nicholson, *Billie Holiday*, Weidenfeld & Nicolson 1995

Paul Oliver, *Conversation with the Blues*, Cassell 1965

Paul Oliver, *Songsters and Saints: Vocal Traditions on Race Records*,
   Cambridge University Press 1994

Richard Osborne, *Vinyl: A History of the Analogue Record*, Ashgate
   2012

Richard A. Peterson, *Creating Country Music: Fabricating Authenticity*,
   University of Chicago Press 1997

Claudia Roth Pierpont, 'Jazzbo: Why We Still Listen to Gershwin', *The
   New Yorker*, January 2005

Henry Pleasants, *Serious Music and All That Jazz*, Simon & Schuster 1969

Henry Pleasants, *The Great American Popular Singers*, Simon & Schuster 1974

J. P. Robinson, *Fanatics and Collectors*, Few Press 2020

Clarkson Rose, *Red Plush and Greasepaint: A Memory of the Music Halls*, Museum Press 1964

Steve Roud, *Folk Song in England*, Faber & Faber 2017

Robert Rushmore, *The Life of George Gershwin*, Crowell-Collier Press 1966

Jon Savage, *Teenage: The Creation of Youth: 1875–1945*, Faber & Faber 2008

Meryle Secrest, *Somewhere for Me: A Biography of Richard Rodgers*, Alfred A. Knopf 2001

Arnold Shaw, *The Jazz Age: Popular Music in the 1920s*, Oxford University Press 1987

Wilfrid Sheed, *The House That George Built*, Random House 2008

Alyn Shipton, *A New History of Jazz*, Continuum 2001

David and Caroline Stafford, *Fings Ain't Wot They Used t'Be: The Lionel Bart Story*, Omnibus 2011

Mark Steyn, *Broadway Babies Say Goodnight: Musicals Then and Now*, Faber & Faber 1997

Richard M. Sudhalter, *Stardust Melody: The Life and Music of Hoagy Carmichael*, Oxford University Press 2002

David Suisman, *Selling Sounds: The Commercial Revolution in American Music*, Harvard University Press 2009

David Suisman and Susan Strasser, *Sound in the Age of Mechanical Reproduction*, University of Pennsylvania Press 2010

Nicholas E. Tawa, *The Way to Tin Pan Alley: American Popular Song 1866–1910*, Schirmer Reference 1990

Terry Teachout, *Duke: A Life of Duke Ellington*, Avery 2013

Melanie Tebbutt, *Making Youth: A History of Youth in Modern Britain*, Palgrave 2016

Robert C. Toll, *Blacking Up: The Minstrel Show in Nineteenth-Century America*, Oxford University Press 1974

Sheila Tracy, *Talking Swing: The British Big Bands*, Mainstream 1997

Ted Vincent, *Keep Cool: The Black Activists Who Built the Jazz Age*, Pluto Press 1995

Brian Ward and Patrick Huber, *A&R Pioneers: Architects of American Roots Music on Record*, Vanderbilt University Press 2018

Joel Whitburn, *Pop Memories 1890–1954*, Record Research Inc. 1986

Ian Whitcomb, *After the Ball*, Penguin 1972

Ian Whitcomb, *Irving Berlin and Ragtime America*, Ebury 1987

Jonny Whiteside, *Cry: The Johnnie Ray Story*, Barricade 1994

Alec Wilder, *American Popular Song: The Great Innovators 1900–1950*, Oxford University Press 1972

P. G. Wodehouse and Guy Bolton, *Bring on the Girls*, Herbert Jenkins 1954

INDEX

A&M (record label), 557, 564
Aaronson, Irving, 279n
Abba, 581, 583
Abbott, John, 475
Abbott, Robert S., 142n
ABC (network): TV launch, 520; *The Lawrence Welk Show*, 522–3; *Philco Radio Time*, 226
ABC (band): *Lexicon of Love*, 588
Abercrombie, Patrick, 350
Aberfan disaster, 569–70
Abie's Irish Rose (play), 434–5
Abramson, Herb, 386
Academy of Motion Picture Arts and Sciences, 262–3
Ace, Johnny, 419, 496
Accordion Times and Musical Express, 422
Acuff, Roy, 171
Adams, Fiona, 566, 573
Adderley, Cannonball, 452
Addinsell, Richard: *Warsaw Concerto*, 397
Adler, Richard, 440; see also *Pajama Game, The*
'After the Ball', xix, 28n, 96, 151
ahbez, eden, 480–1, 488
'Ain't Misbehavin'', 91–2, 265, 269, 317
Ain't Misbehavin' (revue), 106, 269
albums/LPs: cast, 395; concept, 399, 564–5; origins, 394–5, 396; 33rpm vs 78rpm, 395–6
Aldon Music, 504, 505
'Alexander's Ragtime Band', 24, 39, 42, 44–6, 477
Alexander's Ragtime Band (film), 48
Alford, Kenneth, *see* Ricketts, Freddie
Allen, Chesney, 55n
Allen, Steve, 278, 452
Allen, Woody, 90, 176
Alpert, Herb: and civil rights, 564; 'Casino Royale', 558; 'The Lonely Bull', 557
Altman, Robert, 107
Ambrose, Bert, 248, 251, 314, 316, 460, 472; 'Cryin' for the Carolines', 251
American Civil War, 9, 169, 170
American Federation of Musicians (AFM), 166, 327
American Quartet, 34, 39, 68, 82; 'Casey Jones', 35; 'Oh You Beautiful Doll', 39; 'Play That Barbershop Chord', 35
American Society of Composers, Authors and Publishers (ASCAP), 26, 166, 325; dispute (1941), 325, 326, 490, 535

American Tail, An (film), 505
American Telephone & Telegraph Company (AT&T), 152
Americana (revue), 207
Americanisation of Emily, The (film), 557
AMI (company), 327
Ammons, Albert, 332n
Ampex: *see under* recording technology
Anchors Aweigh (film), 506
Anderson, Ivie, 92n, 175, 383–4
Anderson, Leroy, 420, 492–3
Anderson, Sherwood, 272
Andersson, Benny, 581
Andrews, Julie, 319–20, 556–7, 571
Andrews, Maxene, 225, 245
Andrews Sisters, the, 225, 244, 245, 336, 381; vs the Boswell Sisters, 330–1; 'Bei Mir Bist Du Schoen', 330; 'Boogie Woogie Bugle Boy', 330, 589; 'Bounce Me, Brother, with a Solid Four', 330; 'Don't Sit Under the Apple Tree', 336
Andy Williams Show, The, 524–5
Angelou, Maya, 307
Animal Crackers (film), 294
Anka, Paul, 527, 581
Annie Get Your Gun (musical), 423, 441
Ansermet, Ernest, 78
Applause (musical film), 204
Apple Sauce (revue), 311
'April in Paris', 212, 369n, 408
Archies, the: 'Sugar, Sugar', 570
Aristocrat (record label), 390, 391; *see also* Chess Records
'Arkansas Traveler, The' (comedy sketch), 32–3
Arlen, Harold, 180–1, 238, 289, 291, 302, 443, 577n; and Mercer, 352, 353, 354, 527; on rock 'n' roll, 505, 582; 'Blues in the Night', 182, 352; 'Ill Wind', 179n, 408; 'One for My Baby', 180–1; 'Over the Rainbow', 180, 299, 524; 'Stormy Weather', 180, 256
Arluck, Samuel, 180, 181
Arms, Russell, 520
Armstrong, Lil Hardin, 89, 90, 92, 168
Armstrong, Louis, xii, 85, 136, 146, 254, 306, 335, 352, 355, 392, 576; assassination attempt, 93, 94; on bebop, 361; on Beiderbecke, 137; and civil rights, 93; cornet-playing, 87, 88, 89; criticism, 94–5; and Crosby, 222, 467; early life, 36, 86–7; and

Ethel Ennis, 452; and Fitzgerald, 406; and
    Hot Five/Seven, 90–1, 95; and Hines, 267;
    and King Oliver's Creole Jazz Band, 88–90;
    Miles Davis on, 95; moves to Victor, 214;
    musical style, 87–8; in New York, 90, 91;
    radio broadcasts, 155, 191n, 266, 471n; vocal
    style, 91n, 92n, 406, 487; 'Ain't Misbehavin'',
    91, 92; 'Heebie Jeebies', 90–1, 144; 'Lazy
    River', 91; 'Potato Head Blues', 90, 479;
    'Shine', 277; 'Sleepy Time Down South', 355;
    'Stardust', 92; 'Weather Bird Rag', 89; 'What
    a Wonderful World', 93–4
'Army Game, The' (TV theme), 500
Arnold, Eddy: 'Cattle Call', 172
Aron, Evelyn, 390
Aronowitz, Alfred G., 558
arrangers: and bebop, 360; record own
    arrangements, 491; rise of, 408–9; vs
    conductors, 410–11
'As Time Goes By', 290, 431, 514, 587
ASCAP, see American Society of Composers,
    Authors and Publishers
Askey, Arthur, 569
Astaire, Adele, 85
Astaire, Fred, vii, 85, 259, 269, 272, 428; and
    Dorothy Fields, 231; and Ginger Rogers, 259,
    296n; in Blue Skies, 260; in The Gay Divorcee,
    263, 269; in Holiday Inn, 224; in Lady, Be
    Good, 85; in Second Chorus, 284; in Shall We
    Dance, 259, 296; in Swing Time, 231; in Top
    Hat, 259; in You Were Never Lovelier, 352
Astley, Edwin, 314
Atkin, Pete, 572
Atkins, Chet, 424
Atlantic City, 81, 355, 562
Atlantic Monthly, 124
Atlantic Records, 386–7, 459, 497, 572n
Atwell, Winifred, 475–6
Austin, Gene, 185, 188, 266, 500; 'My Blue
    Heaven', 188
Autry, Gene (Oklahoma Cowboy), xii, 171–2,
    320, 468; film career, 172; 'At Mail Call
    Today', 172; 'Home on the Range', 171–2
Avalon, Frankie, 494, 551
Avengers, The (TV series), 539
Avery, Tex, 371
Ayer, Nat, 39–40; 'If You Were the Only Girl in
    the World', 39; 'Oh You Beautiful Doll', 39
Ayler, Albert, 95

Babes in Arms, 236
Babes in Toyland, 96
Bacall, Lauren, 506–7
Bacharach, Burt, 176, 289, 354, 531, 553, 558
Bacon, Max, 249, 250
Bagdasarian, Ross, 414n, 501
Bailey, Mildred, 146, 243–4, 323, 573
Baines, Sidney: 'Destiny Waltz', 60
Baja Marimba Band, the, 557
Baker, Belle, 48

Baker, Danny, 499n
Baker, Helen, 282
Baker, Josephine, 78, 105
Balanchine, George, 238
Balcon brothers (producers), 236
Baldry, Long John, 565
Ball, Kenny: and His Jazzmen, 478; 'Midnight
    in Moscow', 478; 'When I'm 64', 578
Ball, Lucille, 225, 444, 482, 502; 'Hey, Look Me
    Over', 444
Ball, Michael, 586n
Balliett, Whitney, 342, 447
ballrooms, 272, 323, 473, 519; post-war decline,
    357, 358
Band Wagon, The (revue), 210
Bankhead, Tallulah, 126, 202, 261
Barber, Chris, 471, 473; Jazz Band, 474, 478
'barbershop' music, 34–5, 36
Barbour, Dave, 427, 456
Bard, Wilkie: 'I Want to Sing in Opera', 55–6
Bare, Bobby, 570
Barnet, Charlie, 271, 382, 402; defends
    Ellington, 403; 'Skyliner', 336, 364
Barris, Harry, 220
Barroso, Ary, 535
Barrow, Tony, ix
Barry, John, 465, 573; Academy Awards, 546;
    dalliances, 545; distinctive sound, 545; early
    life, 543; film soundtracks, 543, 544, 545–6;
    Eternal Echoes, 546; 'James Bond Theme', 544
Bart, Lionel, 547–8, 551, 565; musicals,
    549–50, 554; and Noël Coward, 126, 549;
    and Tommy Steele, 549; Isn't This Where We
    Came In, 553
Bartholomew, Dave, 340n
Barton, Ben, 509
Basie, William James 'Count', xi, xiii, 214, 271,
    293, 304, 305, 379n, 420, 444, 451, 507,
    543, 559n; in Kansas, 215; musical style,
    280; and Neal Hefti, 364; recording sessions,
    215–16, 280; at Roseland Ballroom (NY),
    280; and Tony Bennett, 417
Bason, Fred, 196
Bass, Saul, 539
Bassey, Shirley, 545, 573–4, 579; Bond themes,
    552, 573; 'Goldfinger', 552; 'As Long as He
    Needs Me', 549
Batman (1966 film), 364, 539, 562
Bauduc, Ray, 284
Baxter, Les: movie scores, 494; and Yma Sumac,
    493–4; Bugaloo in Brazil, 494; Caribbean
    Moonlight, 491; 'Jet', 490–1; Music Out of the
    Moon, 489–90; Perfume Set to Music, 490;
    'Quiet Village', 491; Ritual of the Savage, 491,
    493n; Tamboo!, 491; 'Unchained Melody',
    491
Bayer, Carole, 451
Bayes, Nora, 38n
BBC: Dance Orchestra, 160, 192, 250; against
    crooners, 193, 310n; against song-plugging,

249; censorship, 193, 255; Dance Band Scheme (WWII), 316–17; Dankworth band at, 461; and dance music, 248–9, 316–18; early programming, 157–160; formation, 156; hotel broadcasts, 158, 159n, 250; Light Programme, 338, 349, 574; Radio 1, 542, 574; Radio 2, 290; 574; Radio 3, 286; Radiophonic Workshop, 411n, 552; shipping forecast theme, 398n; Stapleton's band at, 460–1; in World War II, 310–14, 315, 316–17, 318, 320; *The Black and White Minstrel Show*, 118n, 475; *Cavalier of Song*, 349; *Children's Hour*, 315; *Dancing Club*, 317–18; *Desert Island Discs*, 158; *Fifty Years of Music*, 585; *The Grand Hotel*, 574; *Hancock's Half Hour*, 548; *In Concert*, 577; *In Town Tonight*, 158; *It's Cliff Richard*, 580; *The Music of Lennon and McCartney*, 542; *Music While You Work*, 252n, 312; *Opportunity Knocks*, 421; *Our Tune*, 542; *Pot Black*, 21; *Private Smith Entertains*, 310; *Radio Guide*, 193; *Radio Rhythm Club*, 312–14; *Radio Times*, 160n, 261, 318; *Record Roundup*, 421; *Shirley Sings and Riddle Swings*, 573; *Sincerely Yours*, 311; *Sing Something Simple*, 290; *Take It from Here*, 421; *This Is Hancock*, 548; *Top of the Pops*, 522; *Tunes We Shall Never Forget*, 317
Beach Blanket Bingo (film), 494
Beach Boys, the, xviii, 560; 'God Only Knows', 251; 'Good Vibrations', 341; *Smile*, 429
Beatles, the: counter-reaction to, 566–8; influence, 556, 557, 558, 565; 'Because' (cover), 558; 'A Day in the Life', 564, 571; 'Eleanor Rigby', 541; 'A Hard Day's Night', 513; 'Hey Jude' 561; 'Lady Madonna', 478n; 'Paperback Writer', 515, 566; 'Please Please Me', 557n; 'Revolution' (cover), 477; *Sgt Pepper's Lonely Hearts Club Band*, 399, 564–5, 574, 578; 'She Loves You', 571; 'Strawberry Fields Forever' b/w 'Penny Lane', 568
'Beautiful Dreamer', xvii–xviii, 159
'beautiful music', 528, 574; *see also* 'easy listening'
bebop, 358–9; and Earl Hines, 359–60; exclusivity, 360–1; splintering of, 361–2
Bechet, Sidney, 11, 78, 82, 471; 'Petite Fleur', 78, 474
Bee Gees, 376; 'To Love Somebody', 563
Beecham, Thomas, 157
Beerbohm, Max, 5, 58
Beery, Wallace, 300
'Begin the Beguine', 231, 261, 278, 291
Beiderbecke, Bix, 89, 136–7, 145, 201, 209, 427n
Belafonte, Harry, 295, 484, 567; and civil right movement, 564; 'The Banana Boat Song', 564; 'Mary's Boy Child', 564
Bell, Thom, 530
Belles of St Mary's, The (film), 350
Benchley, Robert, 434

Beneke, Tex, 541
Benjamin, Bennie, 563
Benn, Anthony Wedgwood, 574
Bennett, Arnold, 18–19
Bennett, Tony, 222, 416–17, 444, 484, 510, 540, 552; vocal style, 416–17; *Hometown, My Town*, 417; 'I Left My Heart in San Francisco', 417, 418; 'Stranger in Paradise', 417
Benny, Jack, 520
Benny Goodman Story, The, 286, 541
Benson, Ivy, 314–16
Bent Eagle, 209
Benton, Brook, 380, 450, 486n
Berg, Alban, 71
Bergman, Ingrid, 326
Berigan, Bunny, 242, 283; 'I Can't Get Started', 283
Berkeley, Busby, 90, 208, 230, 236, 263, 443, 521, 589
Berkoff, Steven, 464
Berle, Milton, 190n, 520–1, 522
Berlin, Irving, xii, 42, 68–9, 162, 166, 237n, 259, 289, 325, 405, 446; Broadway musicals, 46, 335; death, 582; depression, 50, 498; early life, 44; film scores, 49–50, 259–60; on integrated scores, 441; Kern on, 51; 'King of Ragtime', 39, 46; marriage, first, 46, 50; marriage, second, 47; on modern music, 498, 582; musical style, 45; patriotic/war songs, 49, 65, 69, 335; retirement, 498, 536; and Ruth Etting, 207, 208; self-doubt, 47–8, 49, 50; social/seasonal songs, 51; on soldier attitudes, 335–6; and 'White Christmas', 48, 49, 51, 224–5, 498; 'All Alone', 46, 83, 130; 'All By Myself', 130; 'Always', 47, 582n; *An American in Paris*, 231; 'Angels of Mercy', 335; 'Anybody Can Write', 50; 'At Peace with the World', 47; 'Blue Skies', 48, 476–7; 'Count Your Blessings (Instead of Sheep)', 50; 'Easter Parade', 51; 'Everybody's Doin' It', 46, 55; 'God Bless America', 51; 'Heat Wave', 274; 'He's a Rag Picker', 45; 'How Deep Is the Ocean', 262; 'I'll See You in C-U-B-A', 50; 'I've Got My Love to Keep Me Warm', 243; 'Manhattan Rhapsody', 231; 'Mine Was a Marriage of Convenience', 106; 'My Little Feller', 50–1; *Music Box Revue*, 244; 'Oh How That German Could Love', 62; 'Remember', 47; 'Revival Day', 116; 'Shaking the Blues Away', 207; 'Stay Down Here Where You Belong', 65; 'That Mesmerising Mendelssohn Tune', 24; 'Shaking the Blues Away', 207; 'There's No Business Like Show Business', 50; *Watch Your Step*, 46; 'What'll I Do', 46, 130, 590; 'When I Lost You', 46, 227–8; *see also* 'Alexander's Ragtime Band'; 'White Christmas'
Berman, Shelley, 405
Bernard, Ian, 346
Bernard, Mike, 23

Bernard, Sam, 62
Bernhardt, Sarah, 197
Bernie, Ben, 133n, 279
Bernstein, Artie, 242
Bernstein, Elmer, 465, 539
Bernstein, Leonard, 373, 442
Berry, Chu, 256
Berry, Chuck, 578; at Newport Jazz Festival,
    459; 'Johnny B. Goode', 381; 'My Ding-a-
    Ling', 340n, 511
Best, Denzil, 366
Bethlehem (record label), 401
Betsy (musical), 48
Bettis, Valerie, 402n
Betty (musical), 67
Betty Boop, 132
Beware of the Beautiful Stranger (film), 572
Bianchi, Mario, 319
Bibbs, Joseph, 143
Biberman, Herbert, 306–7
Bidgood, Harry, 252
Bienstock, Miriam, 386
Big Broadcast, The: 1932, 114, 206, 221, 223,
    242; 1936, 282; 1937, 281; 1938, 237
Big Store, The (film), 294
Bilbo, Theodore, 351
Bilk, Acker, 478–9; Paramount Jazz Band, 478;
    'Marching Union', 479; 'Stranger on the
    Shore', 479; 'Summer Set', 479
Billboard (magazine), xvii, 166, 332, 386, 422;
    best male vocalist (1941), 371; easy listening
    chart, 528–9; Harlem Hit Parade, 378–80;
    Hot C&W Sides, 173; Jukebox Folk Records
    chart, 172; most popular female vocalist
    (1955–7), 453; R&B chart, 379, 385, 482
Bing Boys Are Here, The, 40
Binge, Ronald, 397–8, 420
Bioscope (magazine), 203
Birkin, Jane, 543, 544
Birds of a Feather (TV series), 46n, 590
Birmingham Town Hall, 473
Birth of the Blues (film), 281
Bishop, Joey, 508, 509
Bitter Sweet (musical), 65
Black, Cilla, 578
Black, Don, 573n
Black Box: 'Ride on Time', 582
Black Dyke Mills Band, the, 578
Black Swan (record label), 143
Black Windmill, The (film), 492
Blair, Sally, 452
Blake, Eubie, 17–18, 20–1, 26, 269, 581;
    'Bugle Call Rag', 17; 'Charleston Rag', 21;
    'Memories of You', 106, 514; Shuffle Along
    (musical), 105
Bland, James, 31, 59–60
Bless the Bride (musical), 349
Blind Blake, 144
Blind Lemon Jefferson: see Jefferson, Blind
    Lemon

Blind Willie Dunn: see Lang, Eddie
Blind Willie Dunn's Gin Bottle Four: 'Jet Black
    Blues', 145
Blitz! (musical), 550
Block, Martin, 150, 266, 379
Blondell, Joan: 'Remember My Forgotten Man',
    208, 237
Bloom, Rube, 353
Blue Hawaii (film), 521
'Blue Moon', 233
Blue Rockets, the, 314
Blue Skies (film), 220, 227, 260
Bluegrass Boys, 134
blues 75, 139–46, 378; Chicago, 141, 142, 145,
    390–3; 'fast' vs 'slow', 332n; 'jump', 380,
    385; and technology, 147; see also rhythm
    and blues
Blumenthal, Bob, 536
Blumlein, Alan, 395
Blythe, Jimmy: 'Brownskin Mama', 474
Bob Howard Show, The (TV), 523
Boer War, 11, 64
Bogart, Humphrey, 506
Bolden, Buddy, 79, 88, 90
Boles, John, 199, 222
Bolton, Guy, 101, 102n, 123
Bombo (musical), 115
Bono, Sonny, 580
boogie-woogie, 331–2, 502, 588
Book of Mormon, The, 587
Boom (film), 545
Boone, Pat: 'I Almost Lost My Mind', 385;
    'Long Tall Sally', 496
Boop, Betty, 132, 281
Booth, Barry: Diversions!, 572
Boots! Boots! (film), 235
Born Free (film), 544
bossa nova, 515–16, 535–6
Bostic, Earl, 503–4; bridging music, 503, 504;
    'Flamingo', 503; 'Temptation', 503
Boston, 155, 295, 305
Boston American, 295
Boston Herald, 338
Boswell, Connee, 146, 233n, 241, 242, 245
Boswell Sisters, the, 114, 240–1; early life, 241;
    on film, 223, 242; influence, 245, 330; studio
    recordings, 241–3; 'Sentimental Gentleman
    from Georgia', 245; 'There'll Be Some
    Changes Made', 240–1; 'We've Got to Put
    That Sun Back in the Sky', 212; 'When My
    Sugar Walks Down the Street', 428
Botsford, George, 21
Bowen, Jimmy, 513
Bowie, David, xiii, 127, 338, 519, 530
Bowlly, Al, 192–3, 246, 250, 282, 335, 339,
    515, 590; 'Dinner at Eight', 248
Bowron, Fletcher, 333
Bradley, Will, 331
Brass Are Comin', The (TV show), 558
brass bands, 3–4, 54n

Brassens, Georges, 573
Breakfast Club, The (film), 4
Breaking of Bumbo, The (film), 572
Breen, Bobby, 300
Bregman, Buddy, 409
Breil, Joseph Carl, 196
Brennan, Walt, 232
Brent, Earl, 289
Brewer, Teresa, 419–20, 521, 535n; covers, 419, 496; TV shows, 521; 'A Tear Fell', 419; 'Music! Music! Music!', 419, 521; 'Pledging My Love', 419–20; 'Till I Waltz Again with You', 419
Brice, Fanny, 38
Bricusse, Leslie, 551, 553
Bridge on the River Kwai (film), 4
Bright, Gerald (Geraldo), 252, 316–17, 398
Brightman, Sarah, 586n
Bristol Rovers, 469
Britt, May, 510
Broadcast Music Incorporated (BMI), 325–6
Broadway, 11, 58, 69–70, 207; in Jazz Age, 137; Kentucky Club, 176; post-war, 434–5, 446; Princess Theatre, 102; 'rock operas', 445; Theatre Comique, 97–8; Theatre Guild, 436; at turn of twentieth century, 96–9; Viennese revival, 137; vs Hollywood, 232; *see also individual musicals*
Broadway Melody (1929), 200
Broadway Melody of 1938, 41, 529
Broccoli, Cubby, 552, 573
Brockman, Polk C., 166
Brookmeyer, Bob, 363
Brooks, Michael, 242
Brooks, Russell, 265
Broonzy, Big Bill, 142, 331, 388, 392; in Chicago, 392–3; 'Black, Brown and White', 393; 'Brother, Can You Spare a Dime', 207, 212, 291
Brother, Can You Spare a Dime? (film), 283
Brothers Four, the, 476–7; 'Green Fields', 476–7
Brown, Charles, 385, 387
Brown, James, 191, 381, 382
Brown, Lawrence, 253
Brown, Les, 271, 325, 346n, 347
Brown, Lew, 201
Brown, 'Nacio Herb', 198–9
Brown, Roy, 385
Brown, Ruth, 387; 'Mama, He Treats Your Daughter Mean', 387; 'Teardrops from My Eyes', 387
Brown, Tom, 80n
Browne, Sam, 208n, 249
Brox Sisters, the, 200, 222
Brubeck, Dave, 533–4; 'At a Perfume Counter', 533; 'Blue Rondo à la Turk', 533; 'Take Five', 534; 'Unsquare Dance', 533
Brunswick (record label): music catalogues, 143–4, 227, 396; Teddy Wilson at, 304–5
Bryant, Anita, 561

Buchanan, Jack, 107–8; 'And Mother Came Too', 107, 108; 'Everything Stops for Tea', 108n
Budd, Roy, 492
Buffalo Bill Cody, 169
Bugaloos, The (TV show), 535n
Bunch of Blackberries, A, 141
Bunker, Larry, 539n
burlesque, 97
Burns, Ralph, 417
Burr, Henry, 28, 32, 36, 65
Burton, Gary, 558
Burton, Nat, 321; *see also* 'The White Cliffs of Dover'
Bush, Kate, 535n
Business as Usual (show), 63
Butera, Sam, 510
Buzzcocks: 'Boredom', 498n
Bygraves, Max, 370, 422, 519; 'Tulips from Amsterdam'/'You Need Hands', 500
Byrds, the, 467

Cabaret (musical), 445n
Cabaret Voltaire, 209
Cadence (record label), 524
Caesar, Irving, 57, 84, 109, 111; on Romberg, 109
Cagney, James, 208
Cahn, Sammy, 265, 318, 375, 377, 399, 504, 509; on ballads, 505; war songs, 336; 'Until the Real Thing Comes Along', 379
Caine, Marti, 580
Caine, Michael, 545
Calamity Jane, 348, 397, 440–1
Calder, Alexander, 107
Callelo, Charles, 530
Calloway, Cab, 128, 180, 332–3, 386, 588; Cotton Club band, 128; *Cab Calloway's Catologue: A Hepster's Dictionary*, 332
Calvert, Eddie, 519; 'Mystery Street'/'O Mein Papa', 422
Cameron, John, 553
Can Heironymus Merkin Ever Forget Mercy Humppe and Find True Happiness? (film), 552–3
Candoli, Pete, 539n
Cantor, Eddie, 38, 97, 189, 207; hits, 163; on Jolson, 119–20; radio show host, 163; writer, 163; *Palmy Days*, 230; *Whoopee!*, 199, 207, 208n, 230
Capehart, Homer E., 327
Capitol Records, 361, 365, 376, 427, 480, 483, 491, 502, 507, 588; Sinatra at, 302, 407–8, 483, 507, 513–14, 577n
Capone, Al, 41, 128–9, 265, 355
Carlisle, Elsie: 'My Kid's a Crooner', 189n
Carmel, 588
Carmichael, Hoagy, 42, 145, 209–10, 244, 289; 'Crazy Otto Rag', 476; 'Georgia on My Mind', 387, 527; 'Lazy Bones', 210, 328, 353; 'Skylark', 353; 'Stardust', 91, 92, 485

Carné, Marcel, 540
Caron, Leslie, 297, 546
Carousel (musical/film), 438–9
Carpenters, the, 575
Carraway, Nick, 122
Carson, Fiddlin' John, 165–6, 167, 169; 'The Little Old Log Cabin in the Lane', 165, 166, 167
Carson, Johnny, 582
Carter, Benny, 216, 256, 261, 451
Carter Family, the, 167
Carus, Emma, 39
Caruso, Enrico, 2, 30–1, 32, 56, 113, 116; 'Liberty Forever', 17; 'Over There', 68, 247; 'Vesti la giubba', 32
Caryll, Ivan, 7
Casa Loma Orchestra, 133, 244, 346n
Casablanca, 290
Casement, Roger, 68
Cash, Johnny, 223, 397, 470, 518; 'I Walk the Line', 223
Cash, Morny: 'I Live in Trafalgar Square', 4
Cashbox (magazine), 497
Cassavetes, John, 539n
Cassidy, David, 189
Castellucci, Stella, 429
Castle, Vernon and Irene, 21
Caton, Lauderic, 464
Cavanaugh, Dave, 513
Cave, Nick, 94, 414, 588
Cavett, Dick, 557n
Caymmi, Dorival, 535
CBS (Columbia Broadcasting System): Cotton Club broadcasts, 155–6; Judy Garland's TV show, 529; radio network launch, 154; radio shows, 114, 180, 186n, 242, 468; TV network launch, 520; *Back Where I Come From*, 468
Celestin, Papa: 'Tuxedo Rag', 474
Cernik, Al: *see* Mitchell, Guy
Chamberlain, Ronnie, 462
Champion, Harry, 55; 'Any Old Iron', 55; 'Boiled Beef and Carrots', 55; 'A Little Bit of Cucumber', 55
Chandler, Anna, 24; 'The Dance of All Nations Ragtime Ball', 24
Chandler, Dee Dee, 79n
Chaplin, Charlie, 115
Chaquito, 398
Charisse, Cyd, 259
Charles, Ray, 381, 431, 496; at Atlantic, 387; move to ABC Paramount, 387; 'Georgia on My Mind', 387, 527; 'I Got a Woman', 496; *Modern Sounds in Country and Western*, 387; 'New York's My Home', 400
'Charleston, The', 131–2, 152n
Charters, Ann, 18n
Chas & Dave, 420
Checker, Chubby, 383n
Checkmates Ltd, 564

Cheever, John, 210
Cher, 580
Chess, Leonard, 390, 393
Chess (musical), 581
Chess Records, 391, 456
Chesterton, G. K., 3
Chevalier, Albert: 'My Old Dutch', 4
Chevalier, Maurice, 118, 204, 232, 525
Chicago: Arcadia Ballroom, 355; blues, 141, 390–3; Civic Opera Company, 151; Convention of Local Phonograph Companies, 9; Grand Terrace, 253, 267, 268; Hawthorne Inn, 265; jazz, 73, 76, 81n, 89, 142–3, 395n; jazz, vs New Orleans, 473; ragtime school, 15; underworld, 128–9; *see also* KDKA; KYW; WLS-AM
Chicago (musical), 445n
Chicago Defender, 142, 282, 390
Chicago Whip (newspaper), 143
Chilton, Charles, 313
Chisholm, George, 314, 319, 497
Chocolate Soldier, The (operetta), 57, 58
Chordettes, the: 'Mr Sandman', 522
Chords, the: 'Sh Boom', 497
Christensen, Axel, 15
Christian, Charlie, 286, 391
Christian Science Monitor, 175
Christie, Julie, 451
Christie, Tony, 580
Christy, June, 345, 448, 449, 457, 458–9, 462, 515; *The Cool School*, 458; *Gone for the Day*, 458; *Something Cool*, 458
Chu Chin Chow (film), 67
cinemas, 52–3, 54, 195
Civil Rights Act (US, 1964), 93
civil rights movement (US), 393, 485, 563, 564
Claes, Johnny, 314
Clancy, Liam, 471
Clancy Brothers, the, 470–1
Clark, Petula, 49, 319–20, 421, 431, 515, 556, 558, 564, 580; final albums, 572; 'Downtown', 556; 'I Don't Know How to Love Him', 445; 'This Is My Song', 567
classical music 2–3; 'light music', 157
Clayderman, Richard, 267
Cleo from 5 to 7 (film), 540
Cliff Adams Singers, 290
Clifford, Nat: 'John Bull's Little Khaki Coon', 64
Clooney, Rosemary, 50, 225, 228, 284, 341, 417, 581; and Crosby, 410; and Mitch Miller, 414–15; *Blue Rose*, 415n; 'Come on-a My House', 414–15, 501; 'Time Flies', 591
Clorindy: The Origin of the Cakewalk (musical), 11, 269
CND, 474
Coast to Coast, 383n
Coates, Eric, 124, 157–8; signature tunes, 158; 'Devon to Me', 157; *London Suite*, 158
Coborn, Charles: 'The Man That Broke the Bank at Monte Carlo', xx

Cochran, Charles 'CB': Revues, 213, 255
Cochran, Eddie, 344
Cocker, Jarvis, 573
Cogan, Alma, 421
Cohan, George M., 29–30, 563; 'Life's a Very Funny Proposition', 30; 'Yankee Doodle Dandy', 29
Cohen, Harvey G., 176
Cohen, Leonard, 216n, 563, 589
Cohn, Al, 452
Colbert, Claudette, 276
Cole, Cozy, 280
Cole, Gracie, 315
Cole, Nat King, 302, 333, 385, 409; activist criticism, 484, 485; balladeer hits, 482–3; death, 487; and His Trio, 481–2, 485, 543; on Jeri Southern, 455; in LA, 483–4, 486; and Maria Ellington, 483–4, 488; and rock 'n' roll, 486; and Sinatra, 487; vocal/piano style, 482, 485; *After Midnight*, 485; 'A Blossom Fell', 483; 'Christmas Song', 482; 'Hajji Baba (Persian Lament)', 490; 'Jet', 490–1; *Just One of Those Things*, 485; *King Cole for Kids*, 488; *Love Is the Thing*, 485, 587; 'Midnight Flyer', 486; *Nat King Cole Show*, 484; 'Nature Boy', 480–1, 488, 490; 'Send for Me', 486; 'Straighten Up and Fly Right', 482; 'That's All There Is, There Isn't Any More', 487; 'When I Fall in Love', 483, 485; *Where Did Everyone Go?*, 487; *Wild Is Love*, 485–6
Coleman, Blanche, 315
Coleman, Cy, 416, 444
Coleman, Ornette, 315, 366–7
Coleridge, Samuel, 82
College Humour (film), 192
Collette, Buddy (Septet): *Polynesia*, 490
Collins, Arthur, 32, 36, 75; 'The Leader of the German Band', 62; 'The Preacher and the Bear', 32
Collins, Dorothy, 520
Collins, Joan, 553
Colombier, Michel, 572n
'Colonel Bogey', 4
Coltrane, John, 87, 95, 201, 481, 503
Columbia Broadcasting System: *see* CBS
Columbia Records: introduces LP, 394–5, 396; in Jazz age, 124–5, 145, 146; Masterworks label, 445; and musicians strike 330–1; recording technology (78s), xvi, 161; sets up CBS, 154; Sinatra dropped by, 370n, 375; UK arm of, 161, 216; US Marine Band recordings, 16; *see also* Okeh Records
Columbo, Russ, 191, 193, 224, 418; Crosby rivalry, 191–2; 'Prisoner of Love', 191
Colyer, Ken, 471
Comden, Betty, 436
Come Fly with Me (film), 228, 341, 369n, 408, 534
Come Out of the Pantry (film), 107n
Commodore (record label), 306

Communications, Federal, 358, 385
Como, Perry, 191, 222, 346, 521, 523–4, 527, 583; and Dinah Shore, 524; TV specials, 524, 584; 'For the Good Times', 583–4; 'I May Never Pass This Way Again', 500; *TV Favourites*, 524
Concert for Bangladesh, 577
Condon, Eddie, 145, 471
Connecticut Yankee, A (musical), 110
Connelly, Reg, 305
Connie's Hot Chocolates (revue), 91–2
Conniff, Ray, 411; *'S Wonderful*, 411
Connor, Chris, 345, 449, 457, 458–9; *Lullabys of Birdland*, 459; *Lullabys for Lovers*, 459
Connor, Tommie, 321
Conqueror (record label), 171
'Continental, The', 262–3
Conway, Russ, 476n
Cook, Will Marion, 11, 30, 78, 269
Cooke, Sam, 109; 'A Change Is Gonna Come', 109
Cooley, Spade, 285
Coolidge, Calvin, 151
'coon' music, 9–10, 20, 117
Cooney, Celia, 127–8
Cooper, Gladys, 58
Copland, Aaron, 84, 331
Corbett, Ronnie, 550
Corea, Chick, 358
Cornell, Don, 419n
Cortlandt, Peter, 232n
Costello, Elvis, 588
Cotten, Elizabeth, 474
Cotton, Billy, 316, 420, 460, 464
Cotton Club, The (film), 179n
Cotton Club Parade (revue), 179n
Count of Luxembourg, The (musical), 58–9
country music: borrows from R&B, 414; 'country'/'western' traditions, 169–71, 285; exclusions/resistance to, 166; hillbilly origins, 166–7; hillbilly renamed, 173; in films, 172; in 1970s, 583–4; 'outlaws', 583; paradox, 173; and radio, 168–9, 173; and WWII, 172–3; yodelling in, 167, 168, 172
Cowan, Odessa: *see* Hutton, Ina Ray
Coward, Noël, 65, 108, 125–7, 202, 256, 292, 411n, 506, 549; 'I'll See You Again', 514; *see also Bitter Sweet*; *Bless the Bride*; *Private Lives*; *The Vortex*
cowboys, 169, 170–1
Cowsills, the, 445
Cox, Ida, 141, 142
Coyne, Joe, 57
Cramps, the, 414
Crawford, Joan, 200
Crazy Otto: 'Crazy Otto Medley', 476
Creole Jazz Band (King Oliver's), 88–90
Cribbins, Bernard, 411n, 549, 578; 'Hole in the Ground', 411n
Crocetti, Dino: *see* Martin, Dean

Crombie, Tony, 309
crooning, 185–92, 221–2; criticism, 193; technologised intimacy, 189, 219, 221
Crosby, Bing, xi, xiii, xviii, 136, 201, 207, 243, 245, 279, 346, 351, 353, 467, 503; anthologies, 405; and Armstrong, 222; and Astaire, 224, 260; covers, 238, 320, 351, 515; death, 228; drinking, 222; ear for music, 219; on Elvis, 499; in films, 192, 222, 223–4, 260, 281; goes solo, 221–2; golfer, xi, 226–7, 228, 512; and Hope, 224; legacy, 227; marriage, 187; Oscar (*Going My Way*), 224; popularity, 220, 221, 224; popularity, decline in, 227, 496; radio presenter, 221, 225, 226; and recording technology, 219, 221, 225, 226; and the Rhythm Boys, 219–21; and Rosemary Clooney, 410; and Russ Columbo, 191–2; throat operation, 223; vocal style, 219, 222–3, 409; and 'White Christmas', 49, 50, 224–5; *Bing! A 50th Anniversary Gala*, 581; *Bing Sings Whilst Bregman Swings*, 409–10; *Call Me Lucky* (autobiography), 219; *Collectors' Classics*, 396; 'Count Your Blessings', 418; 'Dear Hearts and Gentle People', 351; *Fancy Meeting You Here*, 410; 'Galway Bay', 227; 'The Land of Beginning Again', 350; *Seasons*, 581; *Songs I Wish I Had Sung (The First Time Around)*, 228; 'Soon', 520n; 'Stranger in Paradise', 417; 'Too Marvellous for Words', 296; 'True Love', 228, 292; 'What Do We Do with the World', 228, 565; see also *Big Broadcast, The*; *High Society*; *King of Jazz, The*
Crosby, Bob, 219, 278–9, 283, 314; Bob-Cats, 279; 'Big Noise from Winnetka', 283; 'My Inspiration', 279
Crosby, Harry, 220
Crudup, Arthur 'Big Boy', 388
Crush, Bobby, 476
Cugat, Xavier, 151, 275; 'Brazil', 535; 'Perfidia', 326
Cukor, George, 506

Dagmar, 374
Dailey, Frank, 151, 272, 340
Daily Chronicle, 58–9
Daily Mirror, 130n; Disc Festival, 519
Daily Telegraph, 130
Dairymaids, The (musical), 100
Dale, Jim, 565
Dall, Evelyn, 249
Dames (film), 237
Damn Yankees (musical), 440
Damone, Vic, 413, 414; 'On the Street Where You Live', 500, 501; 'You're Breaking My Heart', 413
dances/dancing: cakewalk, 19; Charleston, 131–2; dance halls, 249, 283; foxtrot, 248; hucklebuck, 383; jitterbug/jive, 313, 472; marathons, 355; 'sweet'/'hot', 211; 'strict

tempo', 257; turkey trot, 22; twist, 559n; two-step, 23; waltz, 23
Dangerous Nan McGrew (film), 133
Daniels, Bebe, 199
Daniels, Charles Neil, 21; 'Hiawatha', 21–2
Dankworth, Johnny, 465; Seven, 461; 'Cole Storage', 461; 'Experiments with Mice', 461
'Danny Boy', 63, 157n
Darin, Bobby, 540
David, Hal, 176, 531
Davies, Dave, 547
Davies, Ray, 108, 428, 474, 548
Davis, Ben, 250n
Davis, Kay, 92n
Davis, Miles, 126, 359, 382, 452, 528; on Armstrong, 95; Capitol Records sessions, 361–2; and Gil Evans, 296n, 361–2; 365; *Bitches Brew*, 558; *In a Silent Way*, 558; *Miles Ahead*, 365
Davis Jr, Sammy, 508, 509–10, 512, 551; marriage, 510; political beliefs, 510–11; and Sinatra, 510; singles, 510, 511, 553; *I Gotta Right to Swing*, 510; *Mood to Be Wooed*, 510; *Sammy Davis, Jr. Sings, Laurindo Almeida Plays*, 510; *When the Feeling Hits You*, 510
Dawn, Julie, 461
Day, Doris, 347, 351, 371, 403, 456, 520, 582; in *Calamity Jane*, 348, 440, in *Love Me or Leave Me*, 208, 348; in *The Pajama Game*, 440; TV special (1975), 582; in *Young at Heart*, 347; 'Secret Love', 347, 440, 520; 'Sentimental Journey', 347
Day, Edith, 137
Days of Wine and Roses, The (film), 541
De Courville, Albert, 59, 77
De Forest, Lee, 197
de Leath, Vaughn, 161–2, 164, 185, 186, 189, 527
de Mille, Agnes, 437
De Palma, Brian, 541
De Sylva, Buddy, 82, 125, 159, 191, 196, 201, 483
de Vol, Frank: *A Symphonic Portrait of Jimmy McHugh*, 491
De Wolfe, Billy, 348n
Dean, Don, 491
Dear Evan Hansen (musical), 587
Dearborn Independent, 122
Dearie, Blossom, 406, 454–5; 'I'm Shadowing You', 455
Decca, 255, 395, 419, 451, 510, 532; introduces LPs/45s (UK), 420; and musicians strike, 329–30; Sepia Series, 379n; shelves Newley, 552; shelves Peggy Lee, 429; *Decca Showcase*, 396
Dee, Sandra, 525
'Deep Forest', 253, 267
Delicious (film), 231
Delius, Frederick, 400
Dell, Dorothy, 224

Delmore Brothers, the, 168; 'Hillbilly Boogie', 331

Demi-Tasse (revue), 84

Demy, Jacques, 540

Dene, Terry, 548

Deniz, Joe, 313

Denmark Street, 62–3, 63n, 235, 420, 562

Dennis, Matt, 289

Denny, Martin, 490n, 491–2, 557; *Afro-Desia*, 491; *Forbidden Island*, 491; *Hypnotique*, 491

Denny, Sandy, 563, 579

Denver, John, 169, 574, 582

Deodato, Eumir, 535

Depression, the 118, 138, 146, 206–7, 208–9, 211, 214, 216, 291, 327

Deram (record label), 553

Derbyshire, Delia, 552

Desert Song, The (operetta), 137–8

Design for Living (musical), 256

Desmond, Paul, 534

Dexys Midnight Runners: 'Come On Eileen', 68

Dial, The (magazine), 155–6

Diamond, Neil, 578, 582

Diamonds Are Forever (film), 573

Dickens, Charles, 591

Dietrich, Marlene, 432, 549

Dietz, Howard, 98, 291, 454; 'Dancing in the Dark', 210–11

Dinkins, David, 450

Dion, Celine, 481

Dior, Christian, 366

disc jockeys, 150n, 285, 379n, 421, 496, 478

disco, 588–9

Disher, Willson, 4n

Dixieland, 72, 255, 467, 471; vs 'trad' jazz, 473; *see also* jazz, traditional; Original Dixieland Jazz Band

Dixon, Willie, 391

Dockstader, Lew, 112

Doctor Dolittle (film), 552

Dodd, Ken: 'Tears', 190n

Dodds, Johnny, 88, 90, 274

Dodds, Warren: 'Baby', 88, 90

Doll's House, A (film), 545

Domino, Fats, 177, 321, 385, 478n, 496, 548; R&B hits, 385, 496; 'Bo Weevil', 496

Don Juan (film), 197–8

Donaldson, Walter, 98, 199, 207n, 211; 'Love Me or Leave Me', 199, 207, 208n; 'My Baby Just Cares for Me', 562–3; 'Sleepy Head', 328–9

Donegan, Anthony James 'Lonnie', 145, 469, 473

Donlan, Yolande, 526

Donohue, Sam, 343

Doonican, Val, 567

Dorsey, Gerry: *see* Humperdinck, Engelbert

Dorsey, Jimmy, 80, 242, 271, 274n, 326, 346

Dorsey, Tommy, 136, 141n, 242, 271, 360n, 462; breath control, 369; and Dick Haymes, 324; on Ma Rainey, 141; orchestra breaks up, 346; and Sinatra, 324, 371, 379, 383n, 508; and Sy Oliver, 324, 409; 'Annie's Cousin Fannie', 341; 'I'll Never Smile Again', 323; 'I'm Getting Sentimental Over You', 283

Dowd, Tom, 386

Downbeat, 342n, 359; on best male vocalists, 371, 418; on black bandleaders, 281; on Beatles success, 558; on the Boswell Sisters, 245; on Ellington, 357, 402–3; on Holiday, 426; on Lee, 427, 430; and the Melodears, 282, 283; on Sinatra, 373–4; opens up to pop, 558

Dr No (film), 544

Dramatic Mirror, 99

Dreiser, Theodore, 29

Dresser, Paul, xix, 28n, 29; 'My Gal Sal', 28–9, 151; 'On the Banks of the Wabash', 8

Dreyfus, Max, xix

Drifters, the: 'Such a Night', 414; 'Up on the Roof', 578

Drifting and Dreaming, 227–8

drive-ins (movie theatres), 357

drum kits, 79n

Drummond, Bill: 'Doctorin' the Tardis', 45; *The Manual*, 45

'dub plates', 504

Dubin, Al, 118, 208, 237, 238, 263, 293

Duchin, Eddy, 281

dulcimer, 545

Dumont, Margaret, 294

Dunne, Irene, 135

Dunwich Horror, The (film), 494

Durbin, Deanna, 299

Durham, Eddie, 280, 391

Durham, Judith, 478n

Duryea, Dan, 426n

Dylan, Bob, xviii, 30, 174, 216n, 352, 467, 477, 557, 559, 577, 588; and the Band, 578

Earl and the Girl, The (musical), 99

Earl of Ruston (musical), 445

Early to Bed (musical), 269–70

Easton, Sheena, 238

easy listening, 505, 527–32, 534–6

Eberle, Ray, 340, 341

Eberly, Bob, 354

Eckstine, Billy, 191, 272, 286, 355, 359, 385, 418, 449, 487; vocal style, 418; 'My Foolish Heart', 418

Ed Sullivan Show, The, 385, 451, 521, 522

Eddy, Duane, 559n; 'Peter Gunn Theme', 539

Eddy, Nelson, 138, 223; and Jeanette MacDonald, 293, 294

Edinburgh Festival, 587

Edison, Thomas, xvi, 30, 74–5, 197

Edison cylinder machine, xvi, 8–9, 467

Edison Phonograph Monthly, 75

Edward VII, King, 37, 52, 53, 56, 125

Edwardes, George, 3, 6, 53, 57, 63, 567; *The Girl on the Film*, 59

Edwards, Bernard, 531
Edwards, Bettie, 313
Edwards, Cliff 'Ukulele Ike', 91, 200, 244, 305
Edwards, Eddie, 74
Edwards, Gus, 38–9; 'By the Light of the Silvery
   Moon', 38
Ekland, Britt, 545
Eldridge, Roy, 457
Elen, Gus, 5
Elgar, Edward, 157
Elias and His Zig Zag Jive Flutes: 'Tom Hark',
   500
Elite (record label), 283
'Elizabethan Serenade', 398n
Elizalde, Fred, 250
Ellington, Edward Kennedy (Duke), 25n, 92n,
   106, 262, 268n, 275, 295, 343, 405, 407,
   408, 483; as ambassador, 183–4; Artie Shaw
   on, 279; and Bubber Miley, 177; at Cotton
   Club, 155, 178–80, 181; criticism, 402–3;
   death, 582; early life 174–5; 'Ellingtonia',
   280; and Foresythe, 253, 254; and His
   Washingtonians, 155; on jazz/swing, 175; at
   London Palladium, 386, 421, 463; NAACP
   award, 183; at Newport Jazz Festival (1956),
   404; tours Europe, 182; Truman letter, 183;
   Black, Brown and Beige, 175, 183n, 402;
   'Caravan', 293; Chocolate Kiddies, 181–2;
   Concert for the Virgin Islands, 443; 'Cowboy
   Rhumba', 357; 'Creole Love Call', 177, 179;
   'Creole Rhapsody', 179; 'Diminuendo and
   Crescendo in Blue', 182; A Drum Is a Woman,
   404; Ellington Uptown, 403; 'Flamingo', 503;
   The Hit Parade, 281; 'It Don't Mean a Thing
   (If It Ain't Got That Swing)', 175; 'Manhattan
   Murals', 176; Masterpieces, 176; Masterpieces by
   Ellington, 403; 'Mood Indigo', 243; 'Never on
   Sunday', 528; 'The New East St Louis Toodle-
   Oo', 177, 182; New Orleans Suite, 583; The
   Perfume Suite, 404; Reminiscing in Tempo, 402;
   'Singin' in the Rain', 357; 'Skin Deep', 403,
   463; Such Sweet Thunder, 404; Symphony in
   Black, 281; 'Take the "A" Train', 176
Ellington, Maria, 483–4, 488
Ellington, Ray, 463, 464
Ellington, Ruth, 176
Ellis, Vivian, 349
Ellison, Ralph, 183–4
Ellsberg, Daniel, 564
Elrick, George, 250
Elsie, Lily, 57–8
Elton, Ben, 586–7
Emergency! (TV series), 453
Emerson, Keith, 533
EMI: Gramophone Company, 30–1; first 45s,
   420; Parlophone label, 473
Engle, Vic, 273
Ennis, Ethel, xiv, 449, 452–3
Enron (play), 587
'Entertainer, The', 18, 583

Entertainments National Service Association
   (UK), 320
Epstein, Brian, 188, 574
Epstein, Vladimir, 122
Erickson, Bonnie, 433n
Erlanger, A. L., 104
Ertegun, Ahmet, 386–7, 497
Essex Productions, 508
Etting, Ruth, 47, 199, 207–8, 348; and Martin
   Snyder, 208; Favourite Melodies, 201; 'Love
   Me or Leave Me', 199, 207, 208n; 'My
   Mother's Eyes', 201; 'Ten Cents a Dance',
   207, 208, 348; 'That's Him Now', 201
Etude (magazine), 149
Europe, James Reese, 17, 21
Eurovision Song Contest, 580
Evans, Bill, 366
Evans, Gil, 296, 361, 363, 365–6, 408, 454,
   535, 540
Evans, Herschel, 280
Eveready Hour, The (radio show), 153
Everly Brothers, the, 500, 568
Every Sunday (film), 299–300
Everybody Sing (film), 299
Everybody's Welcome (musical), 290
Exclusive (record label), 333
exotica, 489–94
Expresso Bongo (film), 526–7

Fabares, Shelley, 559
Fabulous (magazine), 566–7, 573
Fagen, Donald: Eminent Hipsters, 245
Fahrenheit 451 (film), 541
Fain, Sammy, 351, 430, 440
Faith, Adam: 'What Do You Want', 544
Faith, Percy, 397, 416; 'Theme from a Summer
   Place', 527
Faithfull, Marianne, 308
Fall, the: 'Hassle Schmuck', 383n
Fame, Georgie, 575n
Famous Jazz Band, 79
Farmer, Frances, 224
Farrell, Bert, 557; Marijuana Brass, 557n
Farrell, Billy, 418–19; 'It Isn't Fair', 418–19
Farrell, Charles, 201
Farrell, Marguerite, 68
Farrow, Mia, 515
Fay, Harry: 'Bravo Little Belgium', 64
Faye, Alice, 190n
Faye, Sammy, 419n
Fazola, Irving, 279
Federal Communications Commission (FCC):
   radio station licensing (1960), 528; ruling
   (1949), 358, 385
Feild, Tim, 478n
Ferera, Frank, 74–5, 82; 'Drowsy Waters', 74
Ferry, Bryan, 187; 'These Foolish Things', 587
Fiddler on the Roof (musical), 443–4
Fiegel, Eddi, 544
Field, Sally, 582

Field, Shirley Anne, 545
Fields, Dorothy: and Berlin, 441; and Cy
    Coleman, 444; and Jimmy McHugh, 80,
    188n, 231, 263; and Kern, 231–2
Fields, Ernie: 'Sentimental Journey', 498n
Fields, Gracie, 234, 246, 319, 321, 519, 580
Fields, Herbert, 441
Fields, W. C., 97
Fifth Dimension: 'The Age of Aquarius', 445
Finck, Henry T., 1–2, 10
Fine, Bob, 413
Fisher, Eddie, 376, 420
Fitzgerald, Ella, 146, 304, 399, 449, 510; and
    Her Famous Orchestra, 380; vocal style, 243,
    406; 'Ev'ry Time We Say Goodbye', 292; 'It
    Ain't What You Do (It's the Way That You Do
    It)', 324; 'Ringo Beat', 498; Song Book series,
    288, 405–6, 498; Songs for Swingers, 135;
    Sweet Fine and Dandy, 135; 'These Boots Are
    Made for Walking', 454
Fitzgerald, F. Scott, 46, 122, 138, 205, 272
Five Kings of Syncopation, the, 61
Flack, Roberta, 454n
Flamingos, the, 237
Flanagan, Bud, 55
Flanagan and Allen, 55n
Flanders and Swann, 411n
flappers, 130, 132, 189
Fleming, Ian, 210n, 552
Fleming, Rhonda, 224
Florodora (1900 musical), 6–7, 101
Florodora Girl, The (1930 musical), 7
Flowers, Herbie, 429
Folies Bergère, 104
folk: Andean, 493–4; UK revival, 473–4; US,
    466–7, 468, 469–71, 476–7, 490
Follow the Boys (film), 336, 381
Fontaine, Joan, 224
Forbes, Sandy, 255
Ford, Ernie ('Tennessee Ernie'), 501–2; on
    radio/TV, 502; 'The Ballad of Davy Crockett',
    502; 'Catfish Boogie', 331, 502; 'Sixteen
    Tons', 502
Ford, Ford Maddox, 3
Ford, Henry, 122
Ford, Mary, 226, 423–4
Forde, Florrie: 'Down at the Old Bull and Bush',
    28; 'It's a Long Way to Tipperary', 61, 63;
    'Take Me Back to Dear Old Blighty', 65
Foresythe, Reginald, xiv, 252–4; musical style,
    252, 253, 254; and World War II, 255
Forever and a Day (film), 236
Formby, George, 66, 234–5, 252, 580
Formby Sr, George, 235n
Forrest, Helen, 305, 346, 347, 354, 513
Forshaw, J. H., 350
Forsyth, Bruce, 422
42nd Street (film), 112, 118n, 230, 237, 446
Fosse, Bob, 437, 439, 440
Foster, Stephen, xvii–xviii, 9, 31n, 44, 46, 60,

326, 405; 'Jeannie with the Light Brown
    Hair', 159, 325; 'Old Folks at Home', 9, 84;
    'Swanee River', xvii, 45
Foundations, the, 565
Four Lads, the, 417
Four Preps, the, 500
Fox, Ed, 268
Fox, Roy, 222, 248
Fox Movietone Follies (film), 200
Francis, Connie: 'Who's Sorry Now', 500
Franklin, Aretha, 216n, 580
Frazier, George, 338
Freed, Arthur, 198, 199, 200
Freeman, Alan A., 421
Friml, Rudolf, 137, 293, 294, 398
Frohman, Charles, 99
From Here to Eternity (film), 370n, 375
From Spirituals to Swing (film), 392
Fryer, Francis/Frances, 440
Fuller, Earl, 79–80
Funicello, Annette, 494
Funny Face (film), 110, 123

Gabree, John, 558
Gainsbourg, Serge, 581
Gaisberg, Fred, 77n
Gales, Juggy, 383
Gallagher, Rory, 474n
Gambaccini, Paul, 497
Gant, Cecil: 'I Wonder', 333
Gardner, Ava, 373, 506
Garfunkel, Art, 237
Garland, Judy, viii, 41, 259, 260, 349, 399, 451,
    506; child star, 300; death, 303; gay icon,
    303n; James Mason on, 302; late albums,
    302–3; marriages, 301; at MGM, 300,
    301–2, 530; return to stage (1950s), 301;
    and Sophie Tucker, 61, 529; TV show (CBS),
    529; vocal style, 299, 300, 301, 529–30; vs
    Holiday, 298–9, 303; 'Play That Barbershop
    Chord', 301; 'Broadway Rhythm', 300; 'The
    Man That Got Away', 302; 'Meet Me in St
    Louis', 28, 308; 'Over the Rainbow', 180,
    299, 524; 'The Trolley Song', 300, 418
Garner, Erroll, 366
Garnett, Gale: 'We'll Sing in the Sunshine', 536
Gaucho Tango Orchestra, the, 252, 317
Gaudio, Bob, 516
Gavin, James, 427
Gay, John, 402n
Gay, Noel, 235, 293
Gay Divorcee, The (film), 263, 269
Gaye, Gloria, 315
Gaynor, Janet, 201
General Electric, 152
Gennett Records, 89
George V, King, 58
George, David Lloyd, 206
George, Prince (Duke of Kent), 202
'Georgia on My Mind', 387, 527

Geraldo, 316, 252, 310n, 316–17, 398; 'Kentucky', 350

Gershwin, George, xix, 42, 72, 83, 101, 259, 289, 405, 413; and Ann Pennington, 122–3; Broadway musicals, 84, 85, 110, 123, 210; early life, xvi, 42, 84; Hollywood films, 42, 135, 231, 236, 295–6; illness/death, 296–7; and Kay Swift, 134–5; *An American in Paris*, 231; 'Dawn of a New Day', 135; 'I Got Rhythm'/'Embraceable You', 295; 'I Loves You, Porgy', 562; 'I'll Build a Stairway to Paradise', 82; 'Manhattan Rhapsody', 231; *Melting Pot*, 122; *New York Concerto*, 85; 'Rhapsody in Blue', xii, 47, 83, 84, 122; 'Slap That Bass', 259; 'Swanee', 42, 84, 117

Gershwin, Ira, 82, 110, 135, 210, 236, 259, 302

Get Carter (film), 492

Getz, Stan, 366, 405; 'Desafinado', 535

'GI Jive', 336, 381

Gibb, Barry, 530

Gibbons, Carroll, 213, 248, 261, 290

Gibbons, Stella, 126

Gibbs, Arthur, 132, 152n

Gibbs, Georgia: 'Tweedlee Dee', 496

Gibbs, Wolcott, 438

Gibson, Andy, 382

Gideon, Melville, 24

Gil, Gilberto, 536n

Gilbert, Fred, xx

Gilbert, John, 200

Gilbert, W. S., 7, 353, 549

Gilbert and Sullivan, 3, 7, 157, 353

Gilberto, Astrud, 535, 540, 557; 'The Girl from Ipanema', 535

Gilberto, João, 535

Gillespie, Dizzy, 92n, 95, 358, 359, 360, 361, 382

Gilt Edge (record label), 333

Gimbel, Norman, 535n

Gimble, Charles: 'Old Black Joe', 18n

Girl Can't Help It, The (film), 453

Girl Crazy (musical), 123, 135

Girl from Utah, The (musical), 100

Glass, Louis, 8–9

Glass, Philip, 533

Glass Menagerie, The (film), 545

Gleason, Jackie, 521

Gleason, Ralph, 219

glee clubs, 36

Glenn Miller Story, The (film), 338, 541

Globe, The, 101–2

Gluck, Alma, 31n

Glyndebourne Festival, 257

Go into Your Dance (film), 119

Godard, Jean-Luc, 540

Godfrey, Fred, 66; 'Good Luck, Little French Soldier Man', 64

Godspell (musical), 445

Goffin, Gerry, 431, 578

Going My Way (film), 224, 227

Gold Diggers of Broadway (film), 199

Gold Diggers of 1933 (film), 208, 213, 237

Gold Diggers of 1935 (film), 263

Goldfinger, Ernö, 552

Goldfinger (film), 545, 552, 573

Goldwyn, Samuel, 230, 296, 297

Goldwyn Follies, The, 297

Gone with the Wind (novel), 351

Gonella, Nat, 249, 324, 553

Gonzelle White travelling show, 215

Good Boy (musical), 133

Good Companions, The (film), 501

'Good Morning Starshine', 445

Goodhart, Al, 108n

Goodman, Al, 117

Goodman, Benny, 80, 88, 244, 261, 268, 271, 272, 279, 281; band members, 277, 286, 347, 363; on bebop, 361; biopic, 278, 286, 541; as bridge for jazz, 286–7; at Carnegie Hall (NY, 1938), 277–8; clarinet player, 274, 286; and Foresythe, 254; and Hammond, 215, 216, 254; and Henderson, 273, 275, 324; and Holiday, 147, 304, 305; 'King of Swing', 274; in *Let's Dance*, 275, 276; musical style, 274–5, 277; at Palomar Ballroom (LA, 1935), 275–6; at Paramount Theatre, (NY, 1937), 276; and Peggy Lee, 276–7, 328, 425–7, 428, 448; recording sessions (NY), 254; Sextet, 277, 286, 391n, 392, 425–6; on singers, 346; and splintering of jazz/popular music, 285–6; Trio/Quartet, 285; 'Flying Home', 286; 'Goody Goody', 353; 'King Porter Stomp', 273, 275–6; 'Sing, Sing, Sing', 276, 277, 293; 'Your Mother's Son-in-Law', 304; 'Where or When', 425–6, 448

'Goodnight, Irene', 467, 469

Goodwin, Ron, 394, 411n, 421

Goons, the, 411n

Gordon, Mack, 238, 289

Gordy, Berry, 142

Gore, Lesley, 409, 431

gospel music, 116

Gott, Tommy, 82

Gould, Glenn, 162, 445

Goulet, Robert, 525, 531

Graduate, The (film), 542–3

Graham, Sheilah, 296n

Grainger, Percy, 124, 174, 400

Gramophone, The (magazine), 130

Gramophone Company, 30–1

gramophones: Dansette player, 574; decline during Depression, 212; Orchestrope player, 326–7; outsell sheet music, 123; Sonora, 132; as women's domain, 34, 131, 132; *see also* albums/LPs; singles/45s

Grand Ole Opry (Nashville), 173

Grant, Cary, 506

Granz, Norman, 405, 407

Grappelli, Stéphane, 314

Graves, Roosevelt: 'Crazy About My Baby', 331

Gray, Andy, 422, 423
Gray, Glen, 133, 346n
Grayson, Kathleen, 349
Great American Songbook, 288–91, 577, 587
Great Gatsby, The (film), 122
Greco, Buddy, 488, 531, 587
Greco, Juliette, 540
Greeley, Horace, 10n
Green, Abel, 180
Green, Benny, 290, 317
Green, Freddie, 280
Green, Johnny, 107
Green, Sadie: 'Cakewalk', 19
Green Grow the Lilacs (play), 436
Greenwich Village Follies, 80
Gregory, Johnny (Chaquito), 398
Griffith, D. W.: *Birth of a Nation*, 196
Grimethorpe Colliery Band, 315
Grofé, Ferde, 81, 136
Grunfeld, Frederic V., 564
Grusin, Dave, 542
Guardian, 501
Guarnieri, Johnny, 284
Guggenheim Foundation, 366
guitars: bottleneck style, 389; electric, 216n,
    331, 379n, 380, 382, 390, 459; Spanish, 467
Gunther, Mitzi, 57
Guthrie, Woody, 468, 470; 'This Land Is Your
    Land', 470
Guys and Dolls (musical), 439
Gypsy (musical), 442–3
Gypsy (film) 442

Haggard, Merle, 285
Haggart, Bobby, 284
Hahl, Adolph J., 69
Haig, General Douglas, 66
Hair (musical/film), 445, 446
Hale, Sonnie, 236
Haley, Bill, 443, 501, 586
Hall, Albert: *see* Hahl, Adolph J.
Hall, Henry, 148, 159–60, 249, 250, 254, 320,
    460, 585; 'It's Just the Time for Dancing',
    160; 'Radio Times', 160
Hall, Tom T., 583
Hallelujah, I'm a Bum (film), 118, 233
Hamilton, Roy, 418
Hamilton (musical), 587
Hamlisch, Marvin, 583
Hammerstein II, Oscar: Academy Award, 321;
    and Harbach, 137; and Kern, 108–9, 232,
    321, 430, 437; and Rodgers, *see* Rodgers
    and Hammerstein; and Romberg, 137–8;
    Sondheim as mentor, 442, 443; writing style,
    108, 435, 436, 438
Hammerstein, William, 437
Hammond, John, 244, 256, 280, 304, 392, 396,
    402; Basie recording sessions, 215–16; and
    Bessie Smith, 146–7; and Goodman, 215,
    216, 254

Hampton, Lionel, 253, 271, 277, 286, 332,
    450, 543; 'Flying Home', 362
Hancock, Herbie, 542
Hancock, Tony, 547, 548, 561
Handy, W. C.: 'Beale Street Blues', 80;
    'Memphis Blues', 139, 140; 'St Louis Blues',
    17, 140, 342
Hannaman, Ross, 446
Hanshaw, Annette, xiv, 133–4, 305
Happiness Boys, the, 152–3
Harbach, Otto, 137
Harburg, Yip, 98, 103, 291, 297, 299
Hardin, Lil, 88, 89, 90, 92, 168
Hardin, Tim, 431
Hardy, Emmett, 241
Hare, Ernie, 152–3
Harlan, Byron G, 75; 'Wait 'Til the Sun Shines,
    Nellie', 28
Harlem Records, 386
Harlow, Jean, 233, 248
harmonica, 170, 391
Harms, Thomas B., xix, 196
Harney, Ben, 14–15, 18, 33; 'You've Been a
    Good Ole Wagon but You've Done Broke
    Down', 33
Harnick, Sheldon, 443
Harper, Toni, 451–2; *Toni Harper Sings*, 452
Harrigan, Edward, 97–8
Harris, Augustus 'Druriolanus', 6
Harris, Charles K., xix; 'After the Ball', xix, 28n,
    96, 151; 'Mid the Green Fields of Virginia',
    167
Harris, Gus: 'Sergeant Solomon Isaacstein', 64
Harris, Jet, 539
Harris, Johnny, 572n
Harris, Marion: 'The Blues Have Got Me', 132;
    'I'm Gonna Do It If I Like It', 130
Harris, Max, 463
Harris, Phil, 32
Harris, Wee Willie, 548
Harris, Wynonie, xiv, 147, 385, 583; 'Good
    Rockin' Tonight', 496; 'Young and Wild', 384
Harrison, Charles: 'Ireland Must Be Heaven for
    My Mother Came from There', 68
Harrison, George, 553, 563, 577
Harrison, Rex, 192, 483
Hart, Lorenz, 48, 97, 98, 100, 104, 105, 202,
    233, 585; on *Abie's Irish Rose*, 435; on Astaire,
    259; death, 239, 351; influence, 549, 578,
    lyricist, 105, 203; Rodgers on, 101, 105; *see
    also* Rodgers and Hart
Hart, Max, 76, 182
Hart, Moss, 69–70
Hart, Tony, 97–8
Harvey, Morton: 'I Didn't Raise My Boy to Be a
    Soldier', 66
Hasse, John Edward, 183
Hatch, Tony, 572n
Havana (musical), 58–9
Hawaiian music, 74–5

Hawkins, Coleman, 81, 146, 256, 273, 305, 339, 405

Hawkins, Screaming Jay: 'I Put a Spell on You', 563

Hayden Quartet, 29, 32, 34, 35; 'In the Shade of the Old Apple Tree', 35; 'Sweet Adeline', 35

Hayes, Isaac, 305n

Haymes, Dick, 222, 324, 346–7, 481, 513, 557; 'I'll Buy That Dream', 346; 'The More I See You', 346, 557; 'You'll Never Know', 346

Hayworth, Rita, 29, 259, 347

Hazel Scott Show, The (TV), 523

Hazlewood, Lee, 414, 544

Healy, Dan, 133

Hearst, William Randolph, 127, 129

Heath, Ted, 266n, 461–2, 472, 519, 537; on rock 'n' roll, 497; singles, 462; US tour, 462–3, 484

Hefti, Neal, 336, 364, 405, 409, 542; and the Woody Herman band, 364; *Batman* theme, 364, 539

Helburn, Theresa, 436

Hello, Dolly! (musical), 443

Henderson, Fletcher, 81n, 90, 146, 181, 216, 281, 339, 340n, 364; band disbands, 273; at Black Swan, 143; and Ethel Waters, 273; and Goodman, 273, 275, 324; musical style, 155, 273; radio broadcasts, 155; 'Big John's Special', 277; 'Camp Meeting', 273; 'Harlem Madness', 273; 'The Meanest Blues', 83; 'Radio Rhythm', 214; 'What Did I Tell Ya', 125; 'Wild Party', 273

Henderson, Ray, 201

Hendrix, Jimi, 147, 185, 390

Hepburn, Audrey, 373

Hepburn, Katharine, 506

Herbert, Victor, 29, 83, 96, 102, 278, 325, 398, 405; *The Fortune Teller*, 29; 'The Gypsy Love Song', 2, 29

Herman, Jerry, 443

Herman, Woody, 271, 280, 282, 306, 357, 364, 381, 417; First Herd (band), 364

Herrmann, Bernard, 541

Hewitt, John Hill, xvii; 'The Minstrel's Return'd from the War', xvii

Hickman, Art, 80–1; and His Orchestra, 80; New York London Five, 81

Hicks, Seymour, 7–8

High Noon (film), 170, 538

High Society (film), 228, 292, 409

High, Wide and Handsome (film), 232

Hill, Vince: 'Edelweiss', 571

hillbilly music, 165–7, 583; becomes country, 173; naming, 166; *see also* country music

Hilliard, Bob, 289, 351, 354

Hillier, Hope, 57–8

Hi-Los, the, 507

Hines, Earl 'Fatha', 168n, 254, 304, 333, 418, 449; band members, 269, 359; and bebop, 359–60; at Grand Terrace (Chicago), 253,

267–8; musical style, 304; nickname, 267; radio broadcasts, 154–5, 267–8; tours the South, 268; 'Deep Forest', 253, 267; 'Rosetta', 359

Hinton, Milt, 128–9

Hirsch, Louis A.: 'Bacchanal Rag', 24

Hit the Deck (musical), 110

Hit Parade, The (film), 281

Hitchcock, Alfred, 64, 541

Hitler, Adolf, xi, 49, 225

HMV, 24, 77, 473, 495

Hobsbawm, Eric, 257

Hobson, J. A., 56

Hodges, Johnny, 277, 404n, 454

Hoey, William 'Old Hoss', xx

Hoffman, Al, 108n

Hoffman, Dr Samuel J., 489

Hoffman Hayride, The (TV show), 285

Hoffman-Richter, Heins, 561

Hogan, Ernest, 17, 20; 'All Coons Look Alike to Me', 20

Hohner, Matthias, 170

Holiday, Billie, x, 80, 146, 216n, 243, 244, 261, 316, 380, 428, 515, 576; and Artie Shaw, 305; in Britain, 307; at Café Society (NY), 306; death, 308; and drugs, 244, 307, 308; early life, 303; on Ethel Ennis, 453; film career, 306–7; and Goodman, 147, 304, 305; influence, 303–4, 355, 369, 450, 451; musician, 304; nickname, 305; and Spike Hughes, 256; studio recordings, 305, 308; and Teddy Wilson/Lester Young, 304–5; vocal style, 303–4; vs Judy Garland, 298–9, 303; 'Any Old Time', 305; *Lady in Satin*, 308; 'Strange Fruit', 306, 351; 'That Ole Devil Called Love', 418

Holiday Inn (film), 49, 224

Holland, Jools, 588

Holliday, Michael: 'Stairway of Love', 500; 'Starry Eyed', 500; 'The Story of My Life', 500

Holly, Buddy, 28, 344, 578

Hollywood, 110, 195, 236; Bandbox, 354; Bowl, fundraising concert, 564; during Depression, 229–30; famous residents (1930s), 205; Motion Picture Production Code (1930), 154; nightclubs, 354, 428; songwriters move from Broadway, 201–2, 236; vs Broadway, 232

Hollywood Party (film), 233

Hollywood Reporter, 499

Hollywood Revue of 1929, 200, 244

Holmes, Jake, 516

Homesick James, 141

Hood, Basil, 57

Hoover, J. Edgar, 41

Hoover, Herbert, 216

Hope, Bob, 225, 237, 285, 352, 481, 581

Hopper, Hedda, 346

Horizon (magazine), 564

Horn, Shirley, 454, 576; 'And I Love Her', 556;

'Confession', 454; *Embers and Ashes*, 454; *Where Are You Going*, 454n
Horne, Lena, 304, 332, 421
Horowitz, Vladimir, 267
Hot Chocolates (revue), 91–2, 265
House, Son, 144
House of Flowers (musical), 444
House Un-American Activities Committee (US), 470, 523
Housewives' Choice (radio show), 149
Houston, 331n; song censorship, 496
Howard, Paul, 253
Hudson, Rock, 561
Hughes, Spike, 255–6; and His Negro Orchestra, 256
Hullo Ragtime (revue), 22, 39, 59
Humperdinck, Engelbert, 567, 574; *Music Maker* interview, 569; voice, 568; 'Dommage, Dommage', 568; 'The Last Waltz', 570–1; 'Les Bicyclettes de Belsize', 568, 569; 'A Man Without Love', 568, 'Release Me', 568, 571; 'Stay', 568
Hunter, Alberta, 91n, 141, 142, 146
Hunter, Ivory Joe, 385; 'I Almost Lost My Mind', 305, 'Since I Met You, Baby', 385
Hunter, Lurlean, 452
Hupfeld, Herman, 290
Hutchinson, Leslie 'Hutch', 261–2; 'These Foolish Things', 261
Hutton, Betty, 151, 224, 259
Hutton, Ina Ray, xiii, 281–2, 519; Emmy award, 283; film shorts, 282; *Ina Ray Hutton Show*, 283; and the Melodears, 282–3
Hutton, Marion, 340, 341
Hyams, Margie, 282, 283, 366
Hylton, Jack, 80, 213, 249, 251, 290, 472

I Can Get It for You Wholesale (musical), 529
I Come for to Sing (revue), 392
I Could Go on Singing (film), 302
I Love Lucy (TV sitcom), 502
I Love Paris (film), 540
'I Only Have Eyes for You', 237
I Walk Alone (film), 362
I Want to Live (film), 540
'I Will Wait for You', 535n, 540–1
I'd Rather Be Rich (film), 525
Ifield, Frank, 168n, 301
Il Divo, 590
Illinois Central Railroad, 390
I'm with You (musical), 486
In Old Santa Fe (film), 172
In the Good Old Summertime (film), 301
'In the Mood', 323, 338, 340, 497–8, 583, 586
'In the Shade of the Old Apple Tree', 28, 29, 35
Ingham, Beryl, 235
Ink Spots, the, 329, 332, 563n
International Copyright Act (1891), xx
Ipcress File, The (film), 545
Ireland, John, 303

Irwin, May: 'The Bully', 10
Is Everybody Happy? (film), 80
'It Ain't What You Do (It's the Way That You Do It)', 324
'It's a Long Way to Tipperary', 61, 63, 68
'It's Been a Long, Long Time', 224, 336
ITV, 93, 463; see also *South Bank Show, The*; *Sunday Night at the London Palladium*
Ives, Burl, 469–70
Ives, Charles, xviii

Jackson, Chuck, 418, 569
Jackson, Jack, 248, 250; DJ, 421, 478; 'Make Those People Sway', 250–1
Jackson, Joe: *Jumpin' Jive*, 588
Jackson, Mahalia, 183n
Jackson, Michael, 300, 409
Jackson, Milt, 357
Jacobs, Little Walter: see Little Walter
Jacquet, Illinois, 362
Jaffa, Max, 159
Jamal, Ahmad, 551
James, Clive, 572
James, Harry, 272, 277, 324, 346n; and Sinatra, 324, 371; *Harry James in Hi-Fi*, 347
James, Paul: see Warburg, James Paul
James, Sid, 547, 549
James, Skip, 144
Jarvis, Al, 285
jazz: Age, start/end, 122, 209; bandleaders, decline of black, 281; bandleaders, female, 281–3; big band swing era (US), 271–9, 285–6; birth of, 71–8; blends with rock/soul, 558; Chicago, 73, 76, 81n, 89, 142–3, 395n, 473; clubs, London, 575n; clubs, New York, 362; 'cocktail', 304; cool, 357, 366, 528; criticism/censorship, 123–4; and early R&B, 362; Hawaiian, 74–5; hot, 124, 209–10, 528; Kansas, 214; looseness of term, 82n; New Orleans, 72, 73, 87, 88, 138, 241; New Orleans vs Chicago, 473; notation, 72; origin of name, 74; post-war, 356–67; post-war, big band decline, 286, 345–6, 357–8, 380, 521, 537; post-war, split, 285–6, 363, 366, 448–9, 466; and rock 'n' roll, 459, 505; 'soft', 365–6; 'sweet', 124, 211–12, 358, 503; 'symphonic', 82, 83; 'tenor band', 212; traditional (UK), 471–6, 478–9; traditional vs Dixieland, 473; traditional vs modern, 448–9, 472–3, 474–5; vocalists, 123, 447–8, 451–9, 532–3; west coast, 80, 284–5, 366, 539, 557; see also bebop; skiffle
Jazz/Jazz & Pop (magazine), 558–9
Jazz on a Summer's Day (film), 457, 459
Jazz Singer, The (film), 41, 113, 116, 118, 119, 195–6, 216, 217
Jeanmaire, Zizi, 540
'Jeannie with the Light Brown Hair', 325, 326
'Jeepers Creepers', 92, 266, 353
Jefferson, Blind Lemon, 143n, 144; 'Got the Blues', 144

Jefferson Airplane, 467
Jeffries, Fran, 347
Jeffries, Herb, 172
Jenkins, Gordon, 236, 302, 407, 485, 487,
    491, 496, 513, 587; *The Complete Manhattan
    Tower*, 401; *Manhattan Tower*, 399–400, 587;
    Night Dreams, 491
Jenkins, Katherine, 590
Jerry Springer the Opera, 587
Jersey Boys (musical), 587
Jessel, George, 198
Jesus Christ Superstar (musical), 446
Jet (magazine), 450
Jethro Tull, 499, 577
Jewell, Derek, 301
Jive Bunny: 'Swing the Mood', 586
Joanna (film), 572
Jobim, Antônio Carlos, 515, 535, 536, 542;
    'The Girl from Ipanema', 535
Johnson, Budd, 359
Johnson, Bunk, 339
Johnson, Eldridge, 30, 31
Johnson, James P., 25n, 146, 152n, 176, 265
Johnson, Lady Bird, 562
Johnson, Laurie, 539, 549
Johnson, Lonnie, 145, 388
Johnson, Pete, 384
Johnson, Robert, 147n, 388–9, 392, 503; *King
    of the Delta Blues Singers*, 396
Johnstone, Clarence 'Tandy', 125
Jolson, Al, xiii, 15, 42, 50, 76, 84, 295, 305n,
    332, 576; on Broadway, 113–14, 115; Cantor
    on, 119–20; catchphrase, 113; character,
    111–12, 114–15, 117, 119–20; death, 120;
    dislike of microphones, 119; early life, 112;
    hit-maker, 117; and *The Jazz Singer*, 116, 118,
    119, 196, 198, 219; and *The Jolson Story*, 119;
    and Keeler (wife), 112, 119; kneeling pose,
    113–14; on *La Belle Paree*, 113; legacy, 117;
    minstrelsy, 112, 117–18; and the ODJB, 76;
    sees Eddie Leonard sing, 112–13; vocal style,
    116; Warren on, 114; world tour (WWII),
    119; 'My Mammy', 117; 'Sonny Boy', 115,
    117, 196; 'Swanee', 42, 84, 117; 'You Made
    Me Love You', 117, 587, 588; see also *Bombo*;
    Hallelujah, I'm a Bum; *Go into Your Dance*;
    The Singing Fool; *The Singing Kid*
Jolson Sings Again (film), 119
Jolson Story, The (film), 119
Jones, Ada, 32, 38
Jones, Allan: 'Donkey Serenade', 531
Jones, Billy, 78, 152–3
Jones, Isham, 17, 125, 290, 500
Jones, Jack, 531–2; 'Lollipops and Roses',
    531–2; 'Wives and Lovers', 531
Jones, Joe, 280
Jones, Julian, 59
Jones, Quincy, 409, 431, 450, 452, 454, 542
Jones, Terry, 572
Jones, Tom, 530, 568, 569, 573, 579; 'Green,

Green Grass of Home', 569–70; 'Help
    Yourself', 570; 'I'll Never Fall in Love Again',
    570; 'I'm Coming Home', 570
Joplin, Scott, vii, 13, 18, 19, 21, 45, 76, 182,
    542; blocking/shut-outs, 26; death, 26; early
    life, 19; 'The Entertainer', 18, 583; 'Maple
    Leaf Rag', 18, 19; 20, 477; 'Pine Apple Rag',
    23; *The Ragtime Dance*, 19; *Treemonisha*, 25–6
Jordan, Louis, 216n, 259, 336, 379n, 385, 503;
    Joe Jackson covers, 588; and Tympany Five,
    380, 381, 382; vocal style/sound, 381; war-
    time hits, 381; 'Blue Light Boogie', 382; 'GI
    Jive', 336, 381; 'Saturday Night Fish Fry', 382
Joseph and the Amazing Technicolor Dreamcoat
    (musical), 446
Josephson, Barney, 306, 363, 523
Joy Division, 127, 567
jug music, 74
jukebox musicals, 586–7
jukeboxes: decline (1950s), 385; Orchestrope,
    326–7; origins, 8–9; post-Prohibition boom,
    388; UK import ban lifted, 499
Jungle Book, The (film), 538n

Kael, Pauline, 258
Kahlo, Frida, 245
Kahn, Gus, 98, 125, 199, 208n, 290, 328; 'Love
    Me or Leave Me', 199, 207, 208n; 'My Baby
    Just Cares for Me', 562–3; 'Sleepy Head',
    328–9
Kahn, Roger Wolfe, 211–12
Kahn-a-Sirs, 212
Kálmán, Emmerich, 57
Kander and Ebb, 445n
Kane, Helen, xi, 132–3, 421
Kansas City, 20, 88, 214–15; Blue Moon Club,
    384; Cab Calloway in, 332–3; jazz and
    Prohibition, 214, 216n; Reno Club, 215; *see
    also* W9XBY
Kapp, Jack, 143–4, 227, 242, 363
Kappelhoff, Doris: *see* Day, Doris
Karas, Anton: 'Harry Lime Theme', 493, 538–9
Kaufman, George S., 47
Kaye, Sammy: 'Chickery Chick', 351
KDKA (Chicago radio station), 149–50, 155
Keel, Howard, 349
Keeler, Ruby, 112, 119, 263
Kelly, Gene, 260, 297
Kelly, Grace, 228, 292
Kelly, Pete, 428
Kennedy, Jimmy, 320
Kent, Walter, 321; see also 'The White Cliffs of
    Dover'
Kenton, Stan, xiii, 271, 345, 364–5, 461, 462,
    537, 543; Anita O'Day quits band, 458;
    arrangers, 465; band vocalists, 365, 457,
    458–9; big bands, 365, 457; 'And Her Tears
    Flowed Like Wine', 458; 'Artistry in Rhythm',
    365; 'Intermission Riff', 365, 465
Kentucky Club Orchestra, 178

Keppard, Freddie, 88

Kern, Jerome, xi, xix, 42, 96, 181, 263, 289, 325, 352, 360, 430, 441; appearance, 98, 99; arranger, 100, 101; on Berlin, 51; biopic (*Till the Clouds Roll By*), 99; Broadway musicals, 96, 97, 98, 99–101, 102–3, 106, 108–9; early life, 98–9; 4/4 time, 102; and Gershwin, 42; and Hammerstein, 108–9, 232, 321, 430, 437; heart attack, 437; in Hollywood, 231–2, 352; influence, 98, 101, 110; marriage, 99; and Mercer, 352, 405; personality, 98; and Prohibition, 103; on singers, 101; and Wodehouse, 102, 103, 109–10; 'How'd You Like to Spoon with Me', 99; 'The Last Time I Saw Paris', 321; 'Old Man River', 109; 'They Didn't Believe Me', 67–8, 100–1, 288

Kerr, Anita, 560

Kersands, Billy, 60

Kert, Larry, 486n

Kessel, Barney, 336, 513

KFWB (radio station), 241

Kid Creole and the Coconuts, 588

Kidd, Michael, 437

Kincaid, Bradley, 168–9; 'The Little Shirt My Mother Made', 169; 'A Picture from Life's Other Side', 169

Kinetophon, 197

King, Carole, 431, 578; 'It Might as Well Rain Until September', 578; *Tapestry*, 578

King, Eddie, 187

King Jr, Martin Luther, 183, 564

King, Pete, 463

King (record label), 503

King and I, The (musical), 423, 438, 478

King of Cadonia, The (musical), 100

King of Jazz, The (film), 200–1, 218, 222, 244

'King Porter Stomp', 273, 275–6

Kingston Trio, the, 476, 559

Kinks, the, 431, 454

Kinn, Maurice, 422

Kirk, Andy, 363, 379; 'Take It and Git', 379

Kirshner, Don, 504, 505

Kiss Me, Kate (musical), 441

Kitchener, Lord, 63

Kitt, Eartha, 562; and CIA, 562; 'Paint Me Black Angels', 562

Klein, Mannie, 355

KLF: *Chill Out*, 479n

Korda, Alexander, 538n

Korean War, 412n, 422

Kostelanetz, Andre, 397, 413; *Grand Canyon Suite*, 397

Kral, Irene, 452

Krell, William Henry: 'Mississippi Rag', 18n

Krenek, Ernst, 541

Kristofferson, Kris: 'For the Good Times', 583–4

Kroll, Jack, 574

Krupa, Gene, 212, 254, 271, 276, 277, 326, 333n; 'Let Me Off Uptown', 457

KVOO (radio station), 284

KXLA (radio station), 502

Kyser, Kay, 380

KYW (Chicago radio station), 151

La Belle Paree (show), 113

La Gioconda (opera), 82

LA Times, 333n

Ladies Home Journal, 123–4, 154

Lady, Be Good (film), 436

Lady, Be Good (musical), 123

Laine, Cleo, 262

Laine, Frankie, 285, 354–5, 422, 520; and Mitch Miller, 413–14; 'High Noon', 538; 'Mule Train', 413; 'That Lucky Old Sun', 413; 'That's My Desire', 354–5

Lamb, Joseph, 21

Lambert, Kit, 579

Lamour, Dorothy, 224, 301

Lang, Don: Frantic Five, 501; 'Witch Doctor', 500–1

Lang, Eddie, 134, 145, 212, 221, 242

Lange, Arthur: *Arranging for the Modern Dance Orchestra*, 339

Langford, William, 380

Lansbury, Angela, 99

Lanson, Snooky, 520

Lanza, Mario, 31, 422, 496, 527

LaPalm, Dick, 456

Larkin, Philip, 121, 137, 315, 448, 566

LaRocca, Nick, 74

Las Vegas: Sands Hotel, 508; Thunderbird Hotel and Casino, 531

Lasky, Jesse, 104

Last, James, 579

Latin music, 490

Lauder, Harry, 31, 32, 55, 56–7, 63; 'I Love a Lassie', 56; 'Keep Right on to the End of the Road', 56; 'Roamin' in the Gloamin'', 56

Laurel Canyon, 467, 578, 587

Laurents, Arthur, 529

LaVey, Anton, 511

Lawford, Peter, 509

Lawrence, Gertrude, 202, 571

Layton, Turner, 125

Laytons, The (TV show), 523

'Lazy Bones', 210, 328, 353

Leach, John, 545

Leale, Eva, 99

Ledbetter, Huddie 'Leadbelly', 467–8; death, 469; Fred Ramsey session, 468–9; and John Lomax, 467–8; 'Goodnight, Irene', 467, 469

Lee, Arthur, 530

Lee, Brenda, 300, 527

Lee, Dixie, 187

Lee, Peggy, viii–ix, xii–xiii, 302, 401, 409, 447, 454, 456, 483, 507; at Ciro's nightclub, 428; covers, 428, 431–2, 454; and Goodman, 276–7, 328, 425–7, 428, 448; and Leiber/Stoller, 432; and McCartney, 433, 578, 579; marriage, 427; mystery, 430, 431; self-penned hits, 427; vocal style, 300, 427–8, 431; vs Sinatra, 430, 431, 432–3; *Black Coffee*, 428–9; *Dream Street*, 428, 429; 'Every Night', 431; 'Fever', 431; *If You Go*, 431; 'I'm a Woman', 432; 'Is That All There Is', 432–3; 'Let's Love', 433, 579; *The Man I Love*, 430; 'Mañana', 417; *Sea Shells*, 429; 'Till There Was You', 578; 'Why Don't You Do Right', 328, 426–7, 432

Leedy, Harry, 243, 245

Legrand, Michel, 428, 540, 581; Oscars, 541; *I Love Paris*, 540; 'I Will Wait for You', 535n, 540–1

Lehár, Franz, 53, 57, 58

Leiber, Jerry, 431, 432

Leigh, Carolyn, 289, 444

Leigh, Vivien, 234

Lennon, John, 542, 578, 588

Leonard, Eddie, 112

Leopold, Reginald, 574

Lerner, Alan Jay, 423, 444n, 501

Les Amants du Tage (film), 540

Les Parapluies de Cherbourg (*The Umbrellas of Cherbourg*), 540

Let 'Em Eat Cake (film), 210

Let's Face It! (musical), 351

Levey, Jules, 306–7

Lewis, Jerry Lee, xviii, 300, 414, 568

Lewis, Meade: 'Honky Tonk Train Blues', 331; 'Lux', 306, 332n

Lewis, Ted, 79–80, 471; and His Band, 80; 'In a Shanty in Old Shanty Town', 80

Leyton, John, 91n

Liberace, 521–2

Liberty Records, 453, 490n

Lieberman, Lori: 'Killing Me Softly with His Song', 536n

Lieberson, Goddard, 397

Life (magazine), 434, 481, 552

Liggins, Jimmy, 383

Liggins, Joe, 385; 'The Honeydripper', 333; 'Shuffle Shuck', 383

Lilley, J. J., 50

'Lilli Marlene', 321

Lincoln, Abraham, 104, 253

Lipton, Peggy, 409

Liszt, Franz, 18

Little, Little Jack, 188n

Little Cherub, The (musical), 100

Little Show, The (revue), 135

Little 'Tinker (cartoon), 371–2

Little Walter, 391

Littlewood, Joan, 550

Lloyd, Charles, 558

Lloyd, Harold, 199, 337

Lloyd, Marie, 5, 6, 12, 22, 54, 55, 99, 235n; 'The Boy I Love Is Up in the Gallery', 5; 'Piccadilly Trot', 22

Lloyd Webber, Andrew, 446, 586

Loads of Coal (revue), 265

Lodger, The (film), 64

Loesser, Frank, 380, 431, 439–40

Loewe, Frederick, 501

Lomax, Alan, 25, 388, 389, 393, 468

Lomax, John, 17, 171, 388, 389, 392; death, 468; and Leadbelly, 467–8; *Cowboy Songs and Other Frontier Ballads*, 171

Lombardo, Guy, 211, 212, 326, 541; on FCC ruling, 358; hits, 211, 358; Royal Canadians, 211; 'Charmaine', 397–8; 'Enjoy Yourself', 358; 'Tennessee Waltz', 358

London: Adelphi Theatre, 58, 203; Café Anglais, 248; Café de la Paix, 253; Café Malmaison, 262; Carlton Hotel, 250n; County Council, 350; Criterion theatre, 81, 320; Dorchester hotel, 248; Drury Lane, 137; Embassy Club, 77, 251; Empire Leicester Square, 53; Freight Train (coffee bar), 473; Gaiety Theatre, 3, 6, 57, 63; Garrick theatre, 54–5; Hammersmith Palais, 249; Hippodrome, 40, 53, 59, 77; Mayfair Hotel, 248; Palace Theatre, 232; Palladium, 77, 160, 301, 311, 343, 386, 421–2, 478, 519–20; Paramount Ballroom, 312; Pavilion, 213; Philharmonic Hall, 78; Queen's Hall, 159; Rector's, 77; Ronnie Scott's (club), 575n; Royal Albert Hall, 350n; Savoy Hotel, 213, 247, 248, 250, 317; Soho coffee bars, 473, 499, 526; Strand Theatre, 64; Unity Theatre, 549; West End vs Broadway/Tin Pan Alley, 62–3

London, Julie, xi, 449, 453, 562; 'Cry Me a River', 453

London Records, 419

London Symphony Orchestra, 250n, 579

'Londonderry Air', 157

Longet, Claudine, 557, 578

Look Up and Laugh (film), 234

Loos, Anita, 202n

Lopez, Vincent, 150–1; *Vincent Lopez's Jazz Concert*, 83

Loraine, Violet, 40, 64

Lorca, Federico Garcia, 250

Los Angeles: Broadway refugees, 201; Hancock Park, 483–4; Palomar Ballroom, 275–6; *see also* Hollywood; Laurel Canyon

Los Angeles Examiner, 233

Loss, Joe: 'Let the People Sing', 310

Louise, Helen, 74; 'Drowsy Waters', 74

Loussier, Jacques, 532–3; 'Air on a G String', 533

Love, Bessie, 200

Love (band), 530

Love Me or Leave Me (film), 348

Love Me Tonight (film), 118, 205, 232, 233

Love o' Mike (musical), 101

Love Parade, The (film), 204

Lovelace, Linda, 510n

Lovin' Spoonful, 454

Lowe, Mundell, 510

Lowery, Rev. Joseph, 393

LPs (long-players): *see* albums/LPs
LSD, 550, 571
Lubetkin, Berthold, 179
Lubinsky, Herman, 382, 383
Lubitsch, Ernst, 204
Lucas, John, 245
Luft, Sid, 506
'Lullaby of Birdland', 355, 366, 503
'Lullaby of Broadway', 237, 263
Lulu, 585
Lunceford, Jimmie, 271, 324, 333, 391, 409
Lusher, Don, 462, 463
Luster, Shirley: *see* Christy, June
Lutes, Marcie, 366
Lyman, Abe, 279
lynchings, 88n, 306
Lynn, Vera, 249, 310, 311–12, 321, 522, 561, 563, 585; 'Auf Wiedersehen', 422, 522; 'A Nightingale Sang in Berkeley Square', 321; *Sincerely Yours*, 311; 'The White Cliffs of Dover', 311, 321–2
Lyon, Ben, 202
Lyttelton, Humphrey, 92, 471, 473, 478; 'Bad Penny Blues', 478; 'Out of the Galleon', 473
Lytton, Mary, 313

McCarthy, Joseph, 469, 523
McCartney, Paul, 561; and Peggy Lee, 433; 'Cat Call', 474n; 'Thingummybob', 578
Macaulay, Tony, 565
McCormack, John, 31n, 68, 115, 116, 153n, 223
McDevitt, Chas, 473
MacDonald, Jeanette, 204, 293, 294, 349
Macdonough, Harry, 34, 36
McFarland, Gary, 558
MacFarlane, George: 'A Little Bit of Heaven (Sure They Call It Ireland)', 68
McGhee, Brownie, 468; 'Black, Brown and White', 393
McGhee, Stick: 'Drinkin' Wine Spo-Dee-O-Dee', 386
McHugh, Jimmy, 80, 180, 188n, 231, 263, 491
MacInnes, Colin: *Absolute Beginners*, 394–5
Mack, Cecil, 152n
Mackay, Ellin, 46–7
McKee, Margaret, 82
Mackenzie, Compton, 5, 130, 310
MacKenzie, Gisèle, 520
McKuen, Rod: early career, 559; poet, 559–61; and San Sebastian Strings, 559, 560; songwriter, 561, 565; *Beatsville*, 559; 'The Oliver Twist', 559
McNeely, Big Jay, 362
Macon, Uncle Dave, 11n
McPartland, Jimmy, 135–6
McRae, Carmen, 449, 451; 'Come in from the Rain', 451; 'Music', 451
McShann, Jay, 333
McWhorter, John, 269

Madden, Cecil, 310
Madden, Owen 'Owney', 178
Magic FM, 528
Magnet, The (music hall publication), 6
Maher, James, 577n
Maid of the Mountains, The (musical), 67
Maid of Salem (film), 276
Mairants, Ivor: 'Sea Food Squabble', 317
Malden, Karl, 442
Malneck, Matty, 353
Mame (musical), 433
Mamma Mia (musical), 587
'mammy' songs, 117
Mamoulian, Rouben, 200, 204, 205, 232
Man with the Golden Arm, The (film), 539
Manchurian Candidate, The (film), 508
Mancini, Henry, 354, 541, 559; film/TV scores, 539, 541, 542; 'How Soon', 542; 'Love Theme from *Romeo and Juliet*', 542; 'Moon River', 289, 354, 524, 525, 545; 'Pink Panther Theme', 541n
Manhattan (film), 90
Manhattan Melodrama (film), 233
Manila Symphony Orchestra, 250
Manilow, Barry, 589; 'I Made It Through the Rain', 589; 'I Write the Songs', 589; 'It's a Miracle', 589
Mankowitz, Wolf, 526
Mann, Barry: on rock 'n' roll, 504; songwriter/artist, 504–5; 'Somewhere Out There', 505
Mann, David, 289
Mann, Herbie, 356, 551
Mann, Thomas, 432
Mantovani, Annunzio, 397–8; 'Charmaine', 397–8; 'Moulin Rouge', 378
'Maple Leaf Rag', 18, 477
Marbury, Bessie, 102n
marching music, 2, 15–16
Marconi, 52, 149, 156
Mardin, Arif, 572n
Margo, Mitch, 477
Margo, Phil, 477
Marion, George, 269
Marsala, Joe, 128
Marsh, Roy, 313
Marshall, General George, 335
Martin, Dean, 220, 222, 238, 290, 302, 371, 496, 509, 511, 535n, 568; hit singles, 511–12, 513; vs Sinatra, 511; *Dream with Dean*, 513; 'Everybody Loves Somebody', 513, 514; 'Let's Put Out the Lights (And Go to Sleep)', 290; 'Memories Are Made of This', 511–12; *Sleep Warm*, 512–13; 'That's Amore', 237, 512; 'Volare', 580n
Martin, Freddy, 212
Martin, George, 411n
Martin, Steve, 580
Martin, Tony, 294, 299, 321
Martino, Al: 'Here in My Heart', 422
Marvell, Holt: *see* Maschwitz, Eric

Marvin, Hank, 464, 580
Marx Brothers, the, 97, 233n, 244, 294
Marx, Groucho, 65n, 117
Marx, Harpo, 435
Mary Poppins (film), 557
Maschwitz, Eric, 158, 261, 321; *see also* 'These Foolish Things'
Mason, Barry, 570
Mason, James, 302
Mastin, Will, 510
Matcham, Frank, 53
Mathis, Johnny, 530–1; *Love My Lady*, 531
Matthews, Jessie, 203, 235–6
May, Billy, 341, 364, 408, 461, 485, 590; arranger, 410; 'Man with the Golden Arm' theme, 539; 'So Nice (Samba de Verão)', 534
Mayer, Louis B., 160n, 293n, 294, 301
Mayfield Brothers, the, 502
Mayflower Burlesque Company, 112
Mayo, Sam, 5
Maytime (film), 293–4
Me and My Gal (musical), 293
Medic (TV theme), 461
Medress, Hank, 477
Meehan, Mike, 318
Meek, Joe, 321, 478, 479
Meeropol, Abel, 306
'Meet Me in St Louis', 28, 308
Meet Me in St Louis (film), 28, 578
Melba, Dame Nellie, 156
Melcher, Marty, 347
Melodears, the, 282–3
Melody for Two (film), 293
Melody Maker, 216, 227, 250, 253, 256; Cavendish Swing Concert review, 313; Geraldo review, 317; Ivy Benson review, 315; Jack Payne review, 316; launch, 130; New Dance Band tour, 472; on US bands in UK, 262
Melrose, Lester, 387–8; first record producer, 388
Memphis, 88, 93, 140, 146, 281; *see also* WMC
Memphis Minnie, 141
Mendelssohn, Felix, 24
Mercer, Johnny, 210, 243, 289, 296, 301, 356, 380, 401, 455, 483, 497, 505, 513, 536; and Arlen, 352, 353, 354, 527; early life, 352–3; and Kern, 352, 405; patriotic songs (WWII), 336; songlist, 353; 'Moon River', 289, 354, 524, 525, 545; 'On the Atchison, Topeka and the Santa Fe', 352; 'Something's Gotta Give', 352; 'Too Marvellous for Words', 204, 296, 353, 455–6
Mercer, Mabel, 369
Mercury, Freddie, 587
Mercury Records, 413
Merman, Ethel, 201, 447
Merrick, David, 551–2
Merrill, Bob, 415–16
Merrill, Helen, 366, 453–4; *Dream of You*, 454
Merrily We Roll Along (musical), 435

Merry Widow, The (musical), 53, 57–8
Mersey, Robert, 524
Meyer, Joseph, 318
Mezzrow, Mezz, 136
MGM, 226, 231, 233, 293–4, 385, 482; and Deanna Durbin, 299; and Judy Garland, 300, 301, 302, 530; *Broadway Melody* (1920), 199; *Hollywood Revue of 1929*, 200
Miami Daily News-Record, 162
Michael, George, 189
microphones, 119, 186; directional, 230; and intimacy, 161, 162, 168
middle-of-the-road music, 579, 580; *see also* easy listening
Midgley, Bobby, 313
Midler, Bette, 581, 589
Midnight Cowboy (film), 543
Milburn, Amos, 147, 384, 385, 583; 'Chicken Shack Boogie', 384
Miley, Bubber, 177
Miller, Dave, 422
Miller, Emmett, 167n
Miller, Glenn, 35, 151, 271, 273, 280, 335, 541; Army Air Force Band, 341–2, 343, 360n; character, 338, 340, 341; early life, 338–9; influence on modern pop, 345; musical style, 338, 339–40, 343, 344; reissues, 583; vocalists, 340, 341; 'Chattanooga Choo Choo', 237; 'Don't Sit Under the Apple Tree', 336; *I Sustain the Wings* (radio show), 343; 'In the Mood', 323, 338, 340, 497–8, 583, 586; 'Little Brown Jug', 337, 340; 'The Little Man Who Wasn't There', 342; 'Moonlight Serenade', 337, 339; 'Song of the Volga Boatmen', 326; 'A String of Pearls', 337, 340; *Sun Valley Serenade* (film), 237–8, 343; 'Tuxedo Junction', 323
Miller, Johnny, 481
Miller, Marilyn, 106–7, 201, 203
Miller, Mitch, viii, 4, 284, 374, 417, 420, 577n; on arrangers, 410–11; at Columbia, 374, 375, 414–15; criticism, 576; and Frankie Laine, 413–14; at Mercury, 413–14; and Ray Conniff, 411; and Rosemary Clooney, 414–15
Miller, Ruby, 6, 58, 63
Mills, Gordon, 568, 569
Mills, Irving, 182, 256, 282, 305
Mills Brothers, the, 190n, 223, 328–9
Milton, Roy, 385; 'The Hucklebuck', 383
Mineo, Sal, 559
Ministry of Labour, 262
Minnelli, Liza, 303
Minnelli, Vincente, 301
minstrelsy, 2, 9, 10n, 19, 20, 117–18; George Mitchell's Black and White Minstrels, 475; Georgia Minstrels, 59–60; Haverly Minstrels, 59–60; Lew Dockstader's Minstrels, 112; Nigger Minstrels, 59; Tyrolese Minstrels, 36
Miranda, Carmen, 535

Miranda, Jack, 250
Mission: Impossible (1968 film), 539
Mississippi: basin, 13; black population migrate from, 389–90
'Mississippi Mud', 220–1
Mitchell, Guy, 415, 421, 466, 519; hits, 416; 'My Heart Cries for You'/'The Roving Kind', 375, 415; 'My Truly, Truly Fair', 212; 'She Wears Red Feathers', 416
Mitchell, Joni, 429; 'Both Sides Now', 578
Mitchell, Margaret, 351
Mobile Register, 168
Modern Jazz Quartet, 366
Modugno, Domenico, 580
Moenkhaus, William 'Bunkhaus', 209
Moman, Chips, 572n
Momma Don't Allow (film), 478
Monckton, Lionel, 7
Monk, Thelonious, 274, 359
Monotones, the, 500
Monro, Matt, 411n, 460, 477, 532, 540, 568, 578; 'My Kind of Girl', 551; 'Softly as I Leave You', 532
Monroe, Marilyn, 50
Monroe, Vaughn, 563n; 'Bamboo', 490
Monte Carlo (film), 204
Montez, Chris: 'Let's Dance', 557
Monty Python, 234n
Monty Python's Flying Circus (film), 16, 572
Moody Blues, 561
Moog (synthesizer), 545
'Moon River', 289, 354, 524, 525, 545
Moondog, 481
Moore, George, 3
Moore, Oscar, 481
Moore, Roger, 350
Moore, Unity: 'I'm Mary from Tipperary', 63
Morello, Joe: 'Unsquare Dance', 533
Morgan, Helen, 204
Morley, Sheridan, 127n
Morricone, Ennio, 454
Morris, Lily: 'Don't Have Any More, Mrs Moore', 4
Morris, William, 40–1, 83
Morrison, Van, 321, 588; 'A Foggy Day', 588
Morrow, Ed, 486
Morse, Lee, 134
Mortimer, Lee, 372
Morton, Jelly Roll, 24–5, 89, 473; 'King Porter Stomp', 273, 275–6
Moss, Jerry, 557
Moten, Bennie, 214, 215
Motion, Andrew, 315n
Motion Picture Production Code (1930), 154
Mountbatten, Lady, 262
Mouskouri, Nana, 578
Mr President (musical), 498
MTV, 518
Mudlarks, the: 'Book of Love', 500
Mueller, Paul, 297

Müller, Werner, 492
Mulligan, Gerry, 361, 366, 409, 461, 462, 540
Mulligan Guard Ball, The (musical), 97–8
Mullin, Jack, 225–6
Munn, Billy, 319
Munson, Ona, 202
Muppets, the, 220, 433n; *The Muppet Show*, 94, 420, 463
Murphy, Rose: 'Busy Line', 421
Murray, Billy, 28, 32, 38, 39, 169; 'Casey Jones', 35
Murray, Kel, 275, 276
Music Box Revue, 244
music hall, xiii, 2, 3, 4–6, 9, 53, 56; acts move to film, 234–5; demise, 54–6, 519; London venues, 53; militarism (WWI), 63, 66; patriotism affects, 11, 52; and ragtime, 13, 15, 22, 60; strike (1907), 54–5; vulgar reputation, 54
Music Maker (magazine), 569
Music Man, The (musical), ix, 433n
musical theatre, 2, 3, 38; post-war integration, 437, 441
mutes, 88n
My Fair Lady (musical), 67, 69, 395, 423, 501
My Gal Sal (film), 29
'My Way', 350n, 433, 511
Myrow, Josef, 289

Nanton, Joe 'Tricky Sam', 177n, 182
Nash, Dick, 539n
Nash, Ted, 539n
Nathan, Syd, 503
National Association of Orchestra Directors (US), 124
National Association for the Advancement of Colored People (NAACP), 183, 332, 485
National Barn Dance Show, 169
National Prohibition Act (US, 1919), 154
Naughty Marietta (film), 293
NBC (National Broadcasting Corporation): censorship, 124; launch, 154, 520; *The Bugaloos*, 535n; *Chesterfield Supper Club*, 524; *The Colgate Comedy Hour*, 521; *The Dinah Shore Show*, 524; *Fleischmann Yeast Hour*, 164, 190, 328; *Kraft Music Hall*, 225; *Kraft Television Theatre*, 521; *Let's Dance*, 275, 276; *Maxwell Hour Coffee Time*, 153; *Maxwell House Show Boat*, 133; *The Tonight Show*, 581
Neame, Ronald, 302
Nelson, Oliver, 409
Never a Dull Moment (musical), 135
Nevins, Al, 452
New Chamber Orchestra (New York), 541
New Jersey, 21, 82, 161, 215, 269, 272, 290, 323, 382, 493; Frank Dailey's Meadowbrook Ballroom, 340
New Moon, The (operetta), 109
New Musical Express (*NME*), 462, 584, 587; hit parade, 422–3

New Orleans, 11, 35, 79n; bans integrated
    bands, 93; jazz, 72, 73, 87, 88, 138, 241; jazz
    vs Chicago jazz, 473; legalised prostitution,
    73; Storyville closure, 73
New Orleans (film), 306–7
New York: Biltmore Hotel, 81; Bossert Hotel,
    212; Brill Building, 415, 504, 508, 578; Café
    Society, 306, 363; Capitol Theatre, 224; as
    centre of music industry, 140; Club Alabam,
    155; Colonial Theatre, 152n; Cotton Club,
    155, 177–8, 221; 52nd Street, 217, 362,
    369; 400 Club, 75; Glen Island Casino, 272,
    340; Greenwich Village, 80, 102, 256, 426,
    468, 470–1, 476, 494; Heigh Ho Club, 188;
    Hotel Pennsylvania, 338; Lafayette Theatre,
    92; Manhattan nightclubs, 80, 332; Minton's
    Playhouse, 286; Paramount Theatre, 151, 241,
    276, 371; Playland Casino, 340; Radio City
    Music Hall, 135; Reisenweber's Restaurant,
    76, 251; Ritz-Carlton Hotel, 127; Roseland
    Ballroom, 155, 272, 280, 365; Savoy Plaza
    Café, 332; Sawdust Trail nightclub, 418;
    songwriters move to Hollywood, 201–2, 236;
    Tony Pastor's Theatre, 15, 23; Town Hall,
    364; *see also* Broadway; Tin Pan Alley; WABC;
    WHN; WOR
New York Daily Mirror, 372
New York Evening Graphic, 175
New York Herald Tribune, 175
New York Post, 504, 505
New York Times, 38, 85, 92, 96, 103, 239, 295,
    533, 560, 574
New Yorker, The, 47, 82, 131, 342n
Newbury, Mickey, 570
Newcastle: Balmbra's Music Hall, xviii; City
    Hall, 478
Newell, Norman, 544
Newley, Anthony, viii, 307, 511, 547–8, 563,
    565; actor, 550; film, 552–3; hit singles,
    550–1, 552; musicals with Bricusse, 551–2;
    TV shows, 551, 552, 553; *For You*, 553–4;
    Goldfinger theme, 552; 'I've Waited So Long',
    550–1; 'Moogies Bloogies', 552; *Too Much
    Woman*, 554; 'What Kind of Fool Am I', 551,
    552
Newman, Randy, 432, 535, 589
Newport Jazz Festival: 1956, 404; 1958, 457,
    459
Newsweek (magazine), 574
Newton-John, Olivia, 575, 580
Nice, the: 'America', 443
Nicholls, Basil, 311
Nichols, Mike, 542
Nichols, Red, 212, 338; and His Five Pennies,
    201
Nicks, Stevie, 429
'Night and Day', 248, 259, 291, 591
Nightingale, Annie, 262
Nilsson, Harry, 577; *A Little Touch of Schmilsson
    in the Night*, 399, 587–8; *Pussy Cats*, 588

Niven, David, 506
Nixon, Richard, 411, 452, 510–11, 564
NME: see *New Musical Express*
Noble, Ray, 192–3, 280, 305n; and Miller,
    339–40; on popular music, 208–9; 'Love Is
    the Sweetest Thing', 251; 'Midnight, the Stars
    and You', 247; 'The Very Thought of You',
    192
Nobody Home (musical), 102n
Noone, Jimmy, 274n
Normand, Mabel, 22
North, Alex, 538n
North by Northwest (film), 541
Northcliffe, Lord, 156
Norton, Frederic, 67
Norvo, Red, 243, 244
Norworth, Jack, 38n
Novello, Ivor, xi, 64–5, 107, 126; actor, 64;
    'And Her Mother Came Too', 107; 'Keep the
    Home Fires Burning', 64, 107; 'Some Day
    My Heart Will Awake', 64; 'We'll Gather
    Lilacs', 348–9
Nuttall, Jeff, 473
Nyro, Laura: 'Stoney End', 530

Obama, Barack, 393, 446
Oberon, Merle, 261
Observer, 203
Ocean's Eleven (film), 508
O'Connor, Des: 'Dick-a-Dum-Dum', 565; 'I
    Pretend', 571
O'Day, Anita, 341, 345, 355, 365, 448, 449;
    character, 457–8; at Newport Jazz Festival
    (1958), 457, 459; quits Kenton band, 458;
    'And Her Tears Flowed Like Wine', 458; 'Let
    Me Off Uptown', 457; 'Rock 'n' roll Blues',
    457
ODJB: *see* Original Dixieland Jazz Band
Of Thee I Sing (musical), 210
Ogerman, Claus, 516
O'Hanlon, James, 440
Oh Boy (musical), 103
Oh, Kay! (musical), 123, 134–5, 195
Oh I Say (musical), 100
Okeh Records, 90, 165, 168, 283, 388
Oklahoma! (musical), 269, 395, 435–6, 437, 446
Oklahoma Cowboy: *see* Autry, Gene
Olcott, Chauncey: 'Too Ra Loo Ra Loo Rai', 68
Oliver, Joe 'King', 145, 274n; Creole Jazz Band,
    88–90
Oliver, Paul, 153
Oliver, Sy, 324, 409
Oliver! (musical/film), 549–50
On Her Majesty's Secret Service (film), 543, 545
On the Town (musical), 373, 442
On the Town (magazine), 436
On with the Show (film), 199
On Your Toes (musical), 238–9, 437
'One for My Baby', 180, 353, 354, 376
opera, xvii, 25, 31, 37, 151, 152, 295

operetta, 2, 7, 57, 62, 64, 67, 97, 137, 349, 436
Orange Juice: 'Rip It Up', 498n
Orchestrope (record player), 326–7
Original American Ragtime Octet, 22, 24
Original Dixieland Jazz Band (ODJB), 74, 75–7, 459; in London, 77, 247, 249; 'Darktown Strutters Ball', 79; 'Livery Stable Blues', 74, 75; 'Tiger Rag', 76, 77, 223, 249, 328
Orson Welles' Great Mysteries (TV show), 545
Ory, Kid, 82, 90, 478
Osmond, Donny, 453
Osmond brothers, the, 525
Ossman, Vess, 22, 32, 33, 75
O'Sullivan, Gilbert: 'Alone Again Naturally', 585
Ott, Horace, 563n
'Over the Rainbow', 180, 299, 524
Owen, Wilfred, 67
Owens, Tex: 'Cattle Call', 172

Pace, Harry H., 143
Pacific Phonograph Company, 8
Page, Anita, 200
Page, Dorothy, 172
Page, Oran: 'Hot Lips', 214
Page, Patti, 568; 'How Much Is That Doggie in the Window', 416; 'No Moon at All', 593; 'Tennessee Waltz', 358, 415
Page, Walter, 214, 280
Paich, Marty, 401–2, 452, 498, 510
Paint Your Wagon (musical), 423
Pajama Game, The, 401, 437, 440, 443
Pal Joey (musical), 239
Paley, William S., 114, 242
Palin, Michael, 572
Palm Court Orchestra, the, 158–9, 247
Palmer, Olive, 153
Palmerston, Lord, xviii
Palmy Days (film), 230
Panama Hattie (musical), 351
pandemic (1918–19), 77n
pantomime, 2
Paramount Records, 142, 143, 144, 236, 392
Parker, Charlie 'Yardbird', 358, 359, 361, 365, 405, 413, 449, 466; and the Reboppers, 382; 'Now's the Time', 382, 383; 'Yardbird Suite', 359
Parker, Col. Tom, 188
Parker, Dorothy, 106, 130, 205, 515
Parks, Larry, 119
Parnell, Jack, 463, 465
Parry, Harry: Radio Rhythm Club Sextet, 313
Parsons, Louella, 233n, 346
Passing Show of 1919, The (revue), 80
Pastor, Tony, 9, 15, 23
Pathé: news, 157, 262; Records, 133
Patton, Charley, 142, 144
Paul, James (James Paul Warburg), 135
Paul, Les, 226, 227, 423–4; 'How High the Moon', 423
Payne, Jack, 192, 193, 316, 321

Payne, Norman, 250
Pearson, Jesse, 560
Pearson, Ted, 267
Peer, Ralph, 165, 166, 168
Peerless Quartet, 34, 35, 36, 75, 'I Didn't Raise My Boy to Be a Soldier', 66; 'Let Me Call You Sweetheart', 35; 'On Moonlight Bay', 35
Peers, Donald: 'In a Shady Nook (By a Babbling Brook)', 349
Pendergast, Tom, 214, 215
Penman, Ian, 588
Pennington, Ann, 122–3
Pennsylvania, Hotel Grill, 150
Pepper, Art, 365
Perchance to Dream (musical), 348–9
Perkins, Carl, 145, 414
Perry, Mark, 174–5
Persuaders, The (TV series), 543, 545
Peter Gunn (film), 539
Peterson, Oscar, 366, 452; Quartet, 406
'Petite Fleur', 78, 474
Petrie, George, 157n
Petrillo, James Caeser, 327–8, 329, 357
Philadelphia: Met Ballroom, 333n, Town Hall, 333, WDVR (radio station), 328
Phillips, Bob, 226n
phonographs: Edison wax cylinder, 8–9; Victrola, 30, 31; *see also* gramophones
Photoplay (magazine), 200
Pigskin Parade (film), 299
Pilcer, Murray: Jazz Band, 77n
Pink Floyd: *Piper at the Gates of Dawn*, 571
Pinkard, Maceo: 'Sweet Georgia Brown', 106, 133n, 457
Pit and the Pendulum, The (film), 491
Please Don't Eat the Daisies (film), 348
Pogson, 'Poggy', 319
Pointer Sisters, the: 'Yes We Can Can', 588
Pollack, Ben, 128, 135–6, 274, 278, 341, 400, 471
Polo, Danny, 248
Polygon (record label), 421
Pomus, Doc, 524
popular music: early UK, 2, 3–8; early US, 8–10, 11; early, UK vs US, 10–11; origin of 'pop', 2; 'pop' vs 'mod', 556; short vs long formats, 423; tagged 'middle-of-the-road', 579, 580; and TV, 518–20, 524; UK influences US (1960s), 521, 555–7, 564–5; US accent in 37; *see also individual genres*
Popular Radio (magazine), 152
Porgy and Bess (musical), 42, 295–6
Porter, Cole, xix, 42, 259, 261, 279n, 289, 293; anthologies, 405; Broadway musicals, 278, 351, 441; death, 536; Fitzgerald's *Songbook*, 405, 406, 498; lifestyle, 291–2, 536; lyricist, 406; Mercer on, 536; riding accident, 292; and *The Taming of the Shrew*, 441; 'All of You', 292; 'Anything Goes', 484, 582; 'Begin the Beguine', 231, 278, 291; 'Ev'ry Time We Say

Goodbye', 292; 'It's De-Lovely', 406, 455; 'Let's Do It', 236; 'Night and Day', 248, 259, 291, 591; 'Too Darn Hot', 402; 'True Love', 292; 'You're the Top', 260, 291, 406

Porter, Linda, 291, 292

Powell, Adam Clayton, 523

Powell, Bud, 358, 405

Powell, Dick, 263

Powell, Jane, 349

Powell, Mel, 271, 342, 363, 427

Powell, William, 233n

Pratt, Mike, 549

Preminger, Otto, 539

Presley, Elvis, ix, 180, 226, 233n, 414, 438, 496, 497, 555, 572n; Crosby on, 499; Ed Sullivan on, 521; on *Frank Sinatra Timex Show*, 508–9; on Martin, 512; walk-on music, 276; 'Are You Lonesome Tonight', 188, 527; 'Be-Bop-a-Lula', 499; *Elvis Is Back*, 431; 'Heartbreak Hotel', 499, 521; 'I Want You, I Need You, I Love You', 292; 'It's Now or Never', 31, 527, 570; 'Long Tall Sally', 499; 'That's Alright Mama', 145n; 'White Christmas', 498

Priestley, J. B., 234, 501; on ragtime, 60

Prima, Louis, 241, 276, 559n

'Primrose Hill', 349

Prince, Hal, 435n, 440

Prine, John, xviii

Private Lives (play), 125, 127

Privin, Bernie, 342, 343, 360n

Procol Harum: 'Whiter Shade of Pale', 553

Prohibition, 41, 103, 127, 138, 154, 177, 206, 291, 370; end of (1933), 178, 181, 216–17, 388

Proms, the, 159

psychedelia, 446, 553, 568, 578

Psycho (film), 541

punk rock, 561, 588

Pupin, Prof. Michael, 198

'Puttin' on the Ritz', 50, 260

Quealey, Chelsea, 250

Queen, 586–7

Rachmaninov, Sergei, 267

radio: advertising/sponsorship, 150, 152–3, 154, 162–3; censorship, 154, 255, 496; and country music, 168–9, 173; cultural influence, 148–9, 156, 518; in Depression, 212; early nightclub broadcasts, 150–1, 155–6; first black musicians, 154–5; first UK stations, 156–7; first US shows, 152–3; first US station, 149–50; FM stereo, 528; intimacy, 189; networks, 154; 'oldies' shows, 151; pirate, shut down, 571, 574; Radio Act (US, 1927), 154; station licensing (US, 1960), 528

Radio Age (magazine), 151n

Radio Broadcast (magazine), 149, 152, 153

Radio Corporation of America: *see* RCA

Radio Luxembourg, 213n, 420

RAF, 245, 255, 312, 314

Raft, George, 263, 381

Rag Time Instructor (Harney), 15

Raga, Henry, 77n

ragtime, 12–14, 60; criticism, 13, 18–19, 24; decline/resurgence, 24–5; early recordings, 23; musical style, 13–14; origins, 13; Priestley on, 60; ragging the classics, 24; revival (1950s), 475–6; 'rules', 13, 15; spreads to Europe, 22–3

Ragtime Reception (variety show), 15

Rainey, Ma ('Mother of the Blues'), 141–2

Rainger, Ralph, 515; *see also* 'Thanks for the Memory'

Ralton, Bert, 124, 125

Ram Jam: 'Black Betty', 469

Rampling, Charlotte, 545

Ramsey, Fred, 468

Randall, Freddy, 472, 473

Randolph, Amanda, 523

Rasch, Ray, 486

Ravel, Maurice, 231

Ray, Johnnie, 355, 414, 417, 422, 500, 565; 'Such a Night', 414

Ray, Nicholas, 402n, 468

Razaf, Andy, 106

RCA (Radio Corporation of America), 149, 152, 171, 366, 404, 445, 541, 551, 552; Bluebird (subsidiary), 388, 471; LP attempt (1932), 396; and musicians strike, 329; and NBC/Victor, 154; recording technology, 230, 412; Red Seal, 445; *Jazz for People Who Hate Jazz* (compilation), 366

Record Mirror, 500

recording industry: during Depression, 209; first record producers, 388; independent record labels, 379, 386; record/song-plugging, 8, 209, 249, 420–1, 504; *see also* arrangers *and individual record companies*

recording technology: 'acoustic' vs 'electric', 186; Ampex 200 (tape recorder), 226; and Crosby, 219, 220, 221, 225, 226; echo chamber, 413; Edison cylinder machine, xvi, 8–9, 467; German (WWII), xi, 225–6; Kinetophon, 197; LPs, 396; Magnecord (tape recorder), 468; Magnetophon (tape recorder), 225–6; microphones, directional, 230; multitracking, 423, 424; piano, bottom end, 478; radio, 161; 78s, xvi, 161; sound-on-disc (film), 154; stereophonic sound, 398n; Stroh violin, 33–4; V Discs, 334–5; Vitaphone (film), 154, 197, 201; *see also* gramophones

Red Barn (pub), Kent, 471

Redman, Don, 273

Reed, Donna, 278

Reed, Les, 570

Reed, Lucy, 366

Reese, Della, 449

Regal Zonophone (record label), 235

Regan, Joan, 519–20
Reich, Steve, 533
Reid, Billy, 350
Reid, Gordon K., 192
Reisz, Karel, 478
Reith, Lord John, 156–7, 158, 159, 193, 248
Remick, Jerome H., 21–2
Renshaw, 'Uncle' John, 473
Reprise (record label), 228, 407, 507–8, 509, 513
Reser, Harry, 134
revues, 97
Reynolds, Dorothy, 501
Reynolds, Malvina: 'What Have They Done to the Rain', 471
Reynolds, Wynford, 310
'Rhapsody in Blue', xii, 47, 83, 84, 122
rhythm and blues: *Billboard* chart, 378–9; censorship, 496; early, 362; modern, 374; origin of name, 386; post-war, 381; white covers of black, 496; *see also* blues
Rialto (cinema), York, 543
Rice, Tim, 446, 581, 586
Rich, Buddy, 405
Rich, Charlie, 570
Rich Mr Hoggenheimer, The (musical), 100
Richard, Cliff, xvi, 526, 580, 585; 'The Young Ones', 354
Richard, Little, 419, 496, 586; 'Long Tall Sally', 496
Richards, Johnny, 289
Richardson, Tony, 478
Richardson, Walter, 252n
Richman, Harry: 'Puttin' on the Ritz', 260
Ricketts, Freddie, 3–4; 'Colonel Bogey', 4
Riddle, Nelson, 302, 409, 410, 428, 430, 573; and Sinatra, 251, 374n, 376, 407, 409, 514–15; *Sea of Dreams*, 491
Ridley, George 'Geordie': 'Blaydon Races', xviii
Ridley, Wally, 495
Rifkin, Joshua, 26, 583
Rinker, Al, 221, 243
Rinker, Mildred: *see* Bailey, Mildred
Ritchie Family, the, 535n
RKO (film company), 199, 259
Road to Singapore, The (film), 224
Road to Utopia, The (film), 227
Roar of the Greasepaint, The – The Smell of the Crowd (musical), 551–2
Roaring Twenties, 25, 177, 209
Robbins, Jack, 181, 233
Robbins, Jerome, 437
Robbins, Marty, 500; 'El Paso', 527
Roberta (musical), 263
Roberts, 'Ragtime' Bob, 38, 169
Robeson, Paul, 105, 109n, 115, 141
Robey, George, 40, 55, 63, 77, 327
Robichaux, John, 79n
Robin, Leo, 29, 305, 451; *see also* 'Thanks for the Memory'

Robinson, Bill (Bojangles), 40n
Robinson, J. Russel, 77, 78
Robinson, Smokey, 578
Robison, Willard: 'Don't Smoke in Bed', 427
Roche, Betty, 176, 403
rock and roll: criticism, 496, 497, 504, 521; emergence, 499–503, 505, 526–7; first UK star, 549; fracture of, 567; and jazz, 459, 505; porosity with pre-rock era, 586; on TV, 521
rock opera, 445–6
Rockettes, the, 135
Rockwell, Norman, 36; *Barbershop Quartet*, 36
Rockwell, Tommy, 91
Rodgers, Dorothy, 232
Rodgers, Jimmie, 167–8, 169, 170, 171; 'Standin' on the Corner' ('Blue Yodel No. 9'), 168
Rodgers, Nile, 531
Rodgers, Richard, xix, 42, 97, 108, 370, 437, 441, 536; early life, 168; in Hollywood, 201–2; Kern influence, 98, 104, 110; in London, 202–3; on Wodehouse, 101; *Musical Stages* (memoir), 104–5
Rodgers and Hammerstein: *Carousel*, 430–9, *Oklahoma!*, 269, 395, 435–6, 437, 446; *The Sound of Music*, 435, 438, 557; *South Pacific*, 438, 439, 441
Rodgers and Hart, 100, 207, 229, 289; early years, 104; 1937 hits, 294; *Betsy* (musical), 48; 'Bewitched, Bothered and Bewildered', 239; *Ever Green* (musical), 202–3; *Hallelujah, I'm a Bum* (film), 233; *Hollywood Party* (film), 233; *The Hot Heiress* (film), 202, 203, 232; 'I Could Write a Book', 239; *Love Me Tonight* (film), 118, 205, 232, 233; *On Your Toes* (musical), 238–9, 437; *Pal Joey* (musical), 239
Rodin, Gil, 341
Rogers, Billie, 282
Rogers, Ginger, 259, 263, 269, 296n
Rogers, Jimmy, 391
Rogers, Shorty, 539
'Roll Out the Barrel', 310
Rolling Stones, the, 147n, 515, 556
Rollins, Sonny, 238
Romberg, Sigmund, 109, 137, 293, 398, 523; *The New Moon*, 109
Ronson, Mick, 519
Rooney, Mickey, 288, 302
Roosevelt, Franklin D., 216
Ropes, Bradford, 118, 119
Rose, David, 301
Rose Marie (musical), 137
Rose Marie (film), 231, 294
Rosing, Val, 160
Ross, Diana, 561
Ross, Jane, 157n
Ross, Jean, 261
Ross, Jerry, 440; see also *Pajama Game, The*
Ross, Katharine, 542
Ross, Shirley, 237; 'Prayer', 233

Roustabout (film), 438
Rowles, John, 571, 580
Roy, Harry, 248, 249, 460, 463; the Tiger
    Ragamuffins, 249; 'God Bless You, Mr
    Chamberlain', 311; 'My Girl's Pussy', 251
Royal Academy of Music, 157, 252, 317
Royal Canadians, the (Lombardo's), 211
Royal Command Performance (Palace Theatre),
    55
Royal Hawaiian Quartet, 74
Royal Ordnance Army Corps Dance Orchestra
    (The Blue Rockets), 314
Roza, Lita, 462
Rózsa, Miklós, 538n
Ruby, Mort, 480
Rugolo, Pete, xiv, 361, 365, 409, 465
Runnin' Wild (musical), 152n
Rushing, Jimmy, 215, 280
Russell, Bobby, 498n, 535n
Russell, Gilbert, 160n
Russell, Ken, 579
Russo, Bill, 465
Rust, Brian, 255
Rydell, Bobby, 527

Sachs, Mannie, 509
Sade, 588
Sager, Carole Bayer, 451
'Sailing By', 398n
St Louis: Club Dardanella, 329n; World's Fair,
    28
Salad Days (musical), 501
Sally (musical/film), 106, 203
Sally in Our Alley (film), 234
samba music, 535; *see also* bossa nova
Sampson, Edgar, 305
San Francisco: Panama–Pacific Exposition
    (1915), 74; Purple Onion (nightclub), 476; St
    Francis Hotel, 80
San Sebastian Strings, the: *The Earth*, 560; *The
    Sea*, 559, 560; *The Sky*, 560
Sandberg, Carl, 170
Sandler, Albert, 125, 158–9
Sanicola, Hank, 509
Sarkisian, Cherilyn: *see* Cher
Sarnoff, David, 149
Saroyan, William, 414
Saturday Evening Post, 36, 558
Saturday Review, 58
Sauter, Eddie, 427
Sauter-Finegan Orchestra, 366n, 461
Savannah, Georgia, 352–3
Saville, Victor, 235
Savoy Havana Band, the, 124–5, 248; 'What
    Did I Tell Ya', 125
Savoy Hotel Orpheans, the, 213
Savoy Records, 379, 382
Savoy Quartet, the, 79
saxophone, 80n, 124, 339; and traditional jazz,
    473

Scala, Primo, 252
scat singing, 91
Scharf, Walter, 114–15
Schifrin, Lalo, 539, 542
Schillinger, Prof. Joseph, 339
Schulz-Reichel, Fritz ('Crazy Otto'), 476
Schumann, Robert, 22, 369
Schwartz, Arthur, 98, 100–1, 291, 454; on
    Kern, 110; 'Dancing in the Dark', 210–11
Scorsese, Martin, 541
Scott, Hazel, xiii, 523; *The Hazel Scott Show*,
    523
Scott, James: 'Frog Legs Rag', 20
Scott, Janette, 501
Scott, Raymond, 252, 277, 520
Scott, Ronnie, 463, 575n
Screenland (magazine), 191
Seamen, Phil, 463
Seasame Street (TV show), 237, 445
Seaside Special (TV show), 580
Secret of the Incas (film), 493
'Secret Love', 347, 440, 520
Sedalia, 11, 19; Maple Leaf Bar, 19
Sedes, Gilbert, 266
Seeburg and Mills, 327
Seeger, Peggy, 474
Seeger, Pete, 467, 468, 474; 'Black, Brown and
    White', 393
Seekers, the, 478n
segregation, xii, 36, 183, 286
Seldes, Gilbert, 155, 292n
Selmi, Dante, 159n
Selvin, Ben, 237, 248
Sennett, Mack, 22, 221
Seven Lively Arts, 292
78s, x, xvi, 161, 395–6
Seville, David: 'Witch Doctor', 414n
'Shadow Waltz, The', 238
Shall We Dance (film), 259, 296
Sharp, Cecil, 17
Shaw, Artie, 151, 212, 271, 272, 278, 339; band
    members, 284, 342, 347, 360n; on Ellington,
    279; and the Gramercy Five, 284; and His
    Orchestra, 284; and Holiday, 305; 'Summit
    Ridge Drive', 284; *see also* 'Begin the Beguine'
Shaw, Lucy Bernard, 58
Shearer, Norma, 200
Shearing, George, 267, 283, 313, 449, 482;
    'Lullaby of Birdland', 355, 366, 503
Sheed, Wilfrid, 238, 369, 582
Shell Chateau Hour, 300
Shelton, Anne, 321, 335
Shelton, Robert, 560
Shields, Ella: 'Burlington Bertie from Bow', 4
Shields, Joey, 255
Shields, Larry, 74, 76
'Shine on Harvest Moon', 38
Shocking Miss Pilgrim, The (film), 135
Shop Girl, The (musical), 7
Shore, Dinah, 220, 285, 351, 403, 410, 580;

and Como, 524; TV shows, 524; 'Dear Hearts and Gentle People', 351; 'I'll Walk Alone', 336
Showboat (musical), 108–9, 141, 146
Shubert Organization, 104
Shuffle Along (revue), 21
Shuffle Along (musical), 105–6
Shuman, Mort, 524
Siegel, Jay, 477
Sigler, Maurice, 108n
Silkin, Lewis, 350
Silver-Masked Tenor, the, 153
Silvers, Phil, 372n
Silvertown Orchestra, the, 153
Silvester, Victor, 318–19, 567; Jive Band, 319
Simon, George T., 334
Simon and Garfunkel, 542
Simone, Nina, 208, 445, 522, 551; and civil rights, 563; 'Ain't Got No – I Got Life', 445; 'Don't Let Me Be Misunderstood', 563; *High Priestess of Soul*, 564; 'I Put a Spell on You', 563; *Little Girl Blue*, 562–3; 'Mississippi Goddam', 563; 'My Baby Just Cares for Me', 522, 562–3; 'To Love Somebody', 563
Simpson, Wallis, 251
Sinatra, Frank, x, xii, 46, 149, 251, 285, 320, 323, 351, 399, 421, 453, 460, 481, 535n, 537, 561; actor, 375–6, 508, 539; and Ava Gardner, 373, 506; birth, 371; boxer, 370; breath control, 369; business interests, 508; at Capitol Records, 302, 407–8, 483, 507, 513–14, 577n; and Cole, 487; comebacks, 376–7, 407, 590; covers, 469, 540, 578; and Crosby, 227, 228; dalliances, 372, 373, 374, 515; and Dorsey, 324, 371, 379, 383n, 508; dropped by Columbia, 370n, 375; and Elvis, 509–10; excused from WWII, 371, 372; fans, 371, 372, 373; hit singles (Capitol), 507n, 513; goes solo, 371; grooming, 373; and Harry James, 324, 371; and Holiday, 369–70; and Lauren Bacall, 506–7; and the Mafia, 370, 372; and Martin, 511, 512, 513, 514; and Mitch Miller (Columbia), 375, 415; mocked in cartoons, 371–2; nicknames/pseudonyms, 370, 371, 372; Oscar (*From Here to Eternity*), 375; at Paramount Theatre (NY), 371; and Peggy Lee, 430, 431; popularity, decline in, 372, 373–4, 375; and the Rat Pack, 506–7, 509; recorded standards, 289; representing America, 370; and Reprise label, 507–8, 509; and Riddle, 251, 374n, 376, 407, 409, 514–15; and Sammy Davis Jr, 510; vocal style, 368–9; voice fails, 374; in *Young at Heart*, 347, 354, 375–6; *All Alone*, 46n, 513; 'All or Nothing at All', 371; 'Among My Souvenirs', 349; *Autumn of My Years*, 514; 'The Best Is Yet to Come', 444; 'Bim Bam Baby', 374; *Come Fly with Me*, 341, 408; *Francis Albert Sinatra & Antônio Carlos Jobim*, 515; *Frank Sinatra*

Timex Show, 508; 'Goodnight, Irene', 374, 469; *In the Wee Small Hours*, 135, 369, 401, 407–8, 590; 'It Was a Very Good Year', 514; 'I've Got the World on a String', 376; 'I've Got You Under My Skin', 407; 'The Lady Is a Tramp', 500, 531; 'Lost in the Stars', 373; 'Mama Will Bark', 374; *A Man Alone*, 565; *A Man and His Music*, 514; *Moonlight Sinatra*, 514–15; 'My Way', 433, 511, 516; 'The Old Master Painter', 373; 'Please Say Goodnight to the Guy, Irene', 469; *Point of No Return*, 513–14; *Sinatra & Company*, 516; *Songs for Swingin' Lovers*, 297n, 407, 409, 410, 498, 590–1; *Songs for Young Lovers*, 407, 409, 410; 'Strangers in the Night', 515; *Swing Easy*, 407; 'That's Life', 369, 515; 'Too Marvellous for Words', 455–6; *The Voice*, 372; *Watertown*, 516–17, 565; 'Witchcraft', 444, 507n; 'You Make Me Feel So Young', 407
Sinatra, Nancy (daughter), 40, 371, 372n, 373, 508; 'These Boots Are Made for Walking', 508
Sinatra, Nancy (wife), 372
Sinbad (musical), 84
Sinclair, Ranny, 534n
Sing as We Go (film), 234
Sing Your Way Home (film), 346
'Singin' in the Rain', 199, 200, 244, 357
Singing Cowgirl, The (film), 172
Singing Fool, The (film), 115, 196
singles (45s), xvi(n), 412–13, 420, 499; first UK charts, 227, 422–3, 500
Sissle, Noble, 21, 105, 269
Six Brown Brothers, the, 80n
Sizzlin' Syncopators, the, 133
skiffle, 91n, 473
Skyrockets, the, 314, 316
Slack, Freddie, 331
Slade, Julian, 501
Slaughter, John, 474n
'Slaughter on Tenth Avenue', 238–9
Sly and the Family Stone, 147
Smiley, Guy, 399
Smith, Arthur: 'Guitar Boogie', 331
Smith, Bessie 'Mamie', 77, 90, 145–6, 155, 256, 420, 467, 557; Hammond recordings, 146–7; and Holiday, 147; and Ma Rainey, 141–2; 'Cake Walking Babies from Home', 146; 'Crazy Blues', 165; 'Do Your Duty', 147; 'I'm Wild About That Thing', 145; 'Poor Man's Blues', 212
Smith, Clara, 141
Smith, Clarence 'Pinetop': 'Pinetop's Boogie Woogie', 331
Smith, 'Whispering' Jack, 186–7; in Hollywood, 187–8; radio broadcasts, 187; vocal style, 187; 'Gimme a Little Kiss, Will You, Huh', 133n; 'Me and My Shadow', xi, 187
Smith, Keely, 508, 559n
Smith, Laura, 141n

Smith, Patti, 106
Smith, Ruth, 355
Smith, Trixie, 141n
Smith, Willie 'The Lion', 25n, 78, 176, 265, 409n, 471n
Smitten Kitten (cartoon), 381
Snow White and the Seven Dwarfs (film), 538n
Snyder, Joe, 23
Snyder, Martin, 208, 348
Society Orchestra, the, 21
Son of the Sheik, The (film), 138n
Sondheim, Stephen, 98, 289, 435; and Bernstein (*West Side Story*), 442; and *Gypsy*, 442–3; on Hammerstein, 442; and integration of the musical, 441–2; lyrical style, 442–3; Medal of Freedom, 446; 'Send in the Clowns', 579
song plugging, 8, 209, 249, 420–1, 504
'Sonny Boy', 115, 117, 196
Sonny and Cher Comedy Hour, The (TV show), 580
Sontag, Susan, 570
Soul Train (TV show), 518
Sound of Music, The (film), 435, 438, 557
Sousa, John Philip, xix, 15–16, 22; marches, 15–16; suites, 16–17
South Bank Show, The, 586n
South Pacific (film), 439
South Pacific (musical), 438
Southern, Jeri, 449, 455; vocal style, 455, 456; 'Fire Down Below', 456; 'My Letters', 456; *The Southern Style*, 455, 456; 'Too Marvellous for Words', 456
Southern Christian Leadership, 564
Southern Sons, the, 380
Southern Syncopated Orchestra, 78, 247
Spanier, Muggsy, 80, 274, 471
Spargo, Tony, 76
Spasm Band, the, 73
Specials, the: 'Enjoy Yourself', 358
Specialty (record label), 383
Spector, Phil, 255, 365, 544, 581
Spencer, Len, 32–3; 'Arkansas Traveler', 32; 'A Hot Time in the Old Town', 33; 'Ta Ra Ra Boom De Ay', 33
Spencer, Platt Rogers, 32–3
Sperling, Jack, 539n
Spewack, Bella, 441
Spielberg, Steven, 582n
Spivak, Charlie, 151, 364
Spivey, Victoria, 141, 209n
Spread It Abroad (revue), 260
Springfield, Dusty, 307
Springfield, Tom, 478
Squadronaires, the, 314, 315, 316, 472
Squeeze Me (revue), 106
Squires, Dorothy, 349–50; 'The Gypsy', 350; 'I'm Walking Behind You', 350; 'A Tree in the Meadow', 350
Staccato, Johnny, 539
Stafford, Jo, 324, 410, 423, 469, 483

Stage, The (trade paper), 2
Stage Door Canteen (film), 427
Stamper, Dave, 38
Stanwyck, Barbara, 112, 457
Stanyan Records, 561
Staples, Mavis, xviii
Stapleton, Cyril, 460–1; 'Blue Star', 461; 'The Italian Theme', 461
Star! (film), 572
Star Is Born, A (film), 301–2, 529
'Stardust', 91, 92, 485
Stark, John, 18, 19, 20, 24, 25–6
Starr, Kay, 305, 341, 483; 'Rock and Roll Waltz', 498
Starr, Ringo, 498n, 579
Staton, Dakota, 449
Stedeford, Marjorie: 'I've Got You Under My Skin', 407
Steele, Tommy, 507n, 549; 'Rock with the Caveman', 503, 549
Stein, Charlie, 73
'Stein Song, The', 189–90
Sterling, Louis, 161
Steve Allen Show, The, 452
Stewart, James, 338
Stewart, Rod, 579, 588
Sting, The (film), 18, 26
Stoeckel, Gustav, 36
Stoll, Oswald, 6, 54, 580
Stoller, Mike, 430, 431, 432
Stone, Lew, 249, 460
Stop the World – I Want to Get Off (musical), 551
Stordahl, Axel, 324, 372, 410, 513–14
Story, Sidney, 72–3
Strachey, Jack, 261; *see also* 'These Foolish Things'
Strange World of Gurney Slade, The (TV show), 551
Stratton, Eugene: 'Lily of Laguna', 5
Straus, Oscar, 57, 58; *The Chocolate Soldier*, 58
Strauss, Johann, 3, 159
Strayhorn, Billy, 176, 179, 364, 403, 408, 415; 'Take the "A" Train', 403
Streetcar Named Desire, A (film), 538n
Streisand, Barbra, xiii, 432, 529; duets, 530; fundraising concerts, 564; singing style, 529, 530; 'Happy Days Are Here Again', 529; 'Our Corner of the Night', 530; 'Stoney End', 530
Strike Up the Band (musical), 123, 236
Stroh, John, 33–4
Stuart, Leslie, 6
Student Prince, The (operetta), 138
Styne, Jule, 318, 336
Suesse, Dana, 135, 188
Sullivan, Ed: see *Ed Sullivan Show, The*
Sullivan, Jo, 439
Sumac, Yma, xi, 493; 'Taita Inty', 421; *Voice of the Xtabay*, 493
Summer, Donna, 530, 589
Summer Magic (film), 470n
Sun Valley Serenade (film), 237–8, 343

Sunday Night at the London Palladium (ITV), 422, 478, 519–20
Sunderland Empire, 63
Sunny (film), 203
Sunny Side Up (film), 201
Sunshine, Monty, 474
Supper, M. A., 143
Supremes, the, 580
'Swanee', 42, 84, 117
Sweet Charity (musical), 444, 573
'Sweet Georgia Brown', 106, 133n, 457
Swift, Kay, xiv, 134–5
swing, 254, 255; at the BBC, 312–13; big band era (US), 271–9, 285–6; black bands swept aside, 281; Cavendish Swing Concert, 313; post-war decline, 286, 345–6, 357–8, 380, 521, 537
Swing Magazine, 313
Swing Time (film), 231–2
Swingin' the Dream (musical), 392
Swingle, Ward, 533
Swingle Singers, the, 532, 533
Swooner Crooner (cartoon), 371
Sykes, Roosevelt, 388
Symphony in Black (film), 281
syncopation, 13–14
Szabó, Gábor, 558
Szyslak, Moe, 376

Taft, William H., 30
Talent, Ziggy: 'Please Say Goodnight to the Guy, Irene', 469
Tales of Justine, 446
Talese, Gay, 413
Talking Machine World, xvii, 30, 131, 132, 161, 166, 334
Tan (magazine), 384, 449
tape recorders: *see under* recording technology
Tatler (magazine), 203
Tauber, Richard, 2, 31
Taylor, Buck, 169
Taylor, Chip: 'Sneakin' Up on You', 431
Taylor, Elizabeth, 373, 545
Taylor, James: *Gorilla*, 451
Teagarden, Jack, 80, 147, 212, 353, 471
television: *see* TV
Temperance Seven: 'You're Driving Me Crazy', 211
Temple, Shirley, 300, 419
Tennessee Ernie: *see* Ford, Ernie
'Tennessee Waltz', 358, 415
Terrain Vague (film), 540
Teschemacher, Frank, 274n
Thackray, Jake, 572–3
Thaler, Irving, 236
'Thanks for the Memory', 204, 236–7
theremin, 489, 491
There's No Business Like Show Business (film), 49
'These Foolish Things', 260, 261, 514, 587
Thiele, Bob, 93, 419, 420

Third Man, The (film): 'Harry Lime Theme', 493, 538–9
This Is the Army (musical), 335, 470
Thomas, George, 331n
Thomas, John Charles, 223
Thomas brothers, the: 'The Fives', 332n
Thompson, Leslie, 255
Thomson, Virgil, 295
Thorn, Tracey, 588
Thornhill, Claude, xi, 286, 342, 362, 365, 454; band, 362–3; 'Snowfall', 363
Thoroughbreds Don't Cry (film), 299
Three Caballeros, The (film), 535
Thunderball (film), 573
Tibbett, Lawrence, 223
Tibbs, Andrew, 390
'Tiger Rag', 76, 223, 249, 328
Tiger Ragamuffins, the, 249
Tijuana Brass, 555, 557
Tiller Girls, the, 230n
Tilley, Vesta, 63, 197
Tilton, Martha, 426
Time (magazine), 183, 212, 534
Time Runs (film), 562
Times, The, 125
Tin Pan Alley, 13, 22, 27–8, 38, 67, 159, 195, 415, 502
Tiomkin, Dimitri, 465, 530, 538
Titheradge, Dion, 107
Tokens, the: 'The Lion Sleeps Tonight', 477; 'Portrait of My Love', 477; 'Tonight I Fell in Love', 477
'Tom Dooley', 476, 479
Tommy (film), 579
Tommy the Toreador (film), 549
Tonight Show, The (NBC), 581
'Too Marvellous for Words', 204, 296, 353, 455–6
Top Hat (film), 234, 259–60, 263
Topic (record label), 473
Torch, Sidney: 'Barwick Green', 411n
Torero Brass, 557n
Tormé, Mel, 400, 407, 457, 483: co-hosts *Summertime USA*, 521; *California Suite*, 400–1; 'I Like to Recognize the Tune', 498–9; *It's a Blue World*, 401–2; *Shubert Alley*, 402; *Tosca*, 82
Torn Curtain (film), 541
Townshend, Cliff, 314
Townshend, Pete, 314, 579
Tracy, Arthur, 114, 115
Tracy, Sheila, 315, 316
Tracy, Spencer, 506
Transatlantic Merry-Go-Round (film), 242
Trent, Bruce, 316
Trevathan, Charles, 'The Bully', 10
Trinder, Tommy, 421, 519
Trotter, John Scott, 227
Trouble in Store (film), 370n
'True Love', 228, 292

Truman, Harry, 183
Truman, Margaret, 183
Tucker, Sophie, xi, xiii, 10n, 38, 40–1, 60–1, 76,
    77, 201, 490, 573, 591; and Judy Garland,
    61, 529; nicknames, 40, 61; 'I Don't Want
    to Get Thin', 41; 'Life Begins at Forty', 41;
    'My Extraordinary Man', 41; 'My Yiddishe
    Momme', 41; 'Oh You Beautiful Doll', 60;
    'Second Hand Rose', 41; 'Some of These
    Days', 41
Tulsa, Oklahoma, 284
Tune Times, 254
Turner, Big Joe, 355, 384
Turner, Bruce, 473
Turner, Lana, 372, 373
Turpin, Tom: 'Harlem Rag', 18n
TV: and demise of big bands, 357, 358, 521;
    'dinners', 521; first public transmission,
    242; and pop music, 518–20, 524; shows vs
    films, 538; singers turn to, 521; US networks
    launched, 520; variety shows, 580
Twain, Mark, 8
Twang!! (musical), 550
Twisting the Dials (radio show), 153
Tynan, Kenneth, 577

ukulele, 75
Ulvaeus, Björn, 581
Umbrellas of Cherbourg, The (film), 540, 542
Une femme est une femme (film), 540
United States: Army, 49; Marine Band, 16; Navy
    Band, 343; Navy orchestra, 81
Universal Studios, 541, 559
Untouchables, The (film) 572

Valente, Caterina: 'The Breeze and I', 492
Valentine, Dickie, 370, 462, 519, 532; 'The Way
    of a Fool', 565
Valentino, Rudolf, 138n
Valle, Marcos, 535n
Vallee, Rudy, vii, 82, 164, 185, 187–8, 193,
    201, 207, 213, 224, 290, 328; radio star,
    190; sees Crosby perform, 219–20; sound
    system, 190; 'Goodnight Sweetheart', 199;
    'The Stein Song', 189–90; 'Tears', 190; 'The
    Whiffenpoof Song', 190
Valli, Frankie, 589; 'My Mother's Eyes', 201
Van Alstyne, Egbert: 'In the Shade of the Old
    Apple Tree', 28
Van Brunt, Walter, 33
Van Heusen, Jimmy, 289, 353, 372n, 377, 408,
    431, 504, 506
Van Ronk, Dave, 470, 471
Variety (magazine): Ellington review, 180; on
    hillbilly, 166–7; Jolson review, 112; Sally Blair
    review, 452; on Seymour Hicks, 8; 'A Warning
    to the Music Business', 496; TV show reviews,
    523
vaudeville, xvii, 2, 9–10, 20, 21, 33, 38, 39, 75,
    97, 114; see also music hall

Vaughan, Frankie, 370, 570; 'Tower of Strength',
    354
Vaughan, Sarah, 387, 449, 454, 481
Vee, Bobby: 'Night Has a Thousand Eyes', 485–6
Veloso, Caetano, 536n
Venuti, Joe, 212, 216, 242, 353
Very Good Eddie (musical), 102–3
Victor Recording/Talking Machine Company,
    30, 79, 168; merges with RCA, 154; Military
    Band, 17, 139; moves to production of radios,
    212; recording technology (78s), 161; Red
    Seal label, 30–2, 34; Victrola, 30
Victor/Victoria (film), 572
Victoria, Queen, 60
Victoria, Vesta, 53
Viennese Nights (film), 203
Vincent, Bob, 334
Vincent, Gene, 321, 502; 'Be-Bop-a-Lula', 502
Vincent Lopez's Jazz Concert, 83
Viscounts, the, 568
Vitaphone (film technology), 154, 197, 201
Vogue (record label), 556
von Bismarck, Otto, xviii
Von Tilzer, Harry (Harry Gumm), 28
Vortex, The (film), 125–6

WABC (radio station): This Is New York, 266
Wagoner, Porter, 173
Walker, Robert, 99
Walker, Scott, 338, 418, 540, 570
Wall Street crash, 146; see also Depression
Waller, Thomas 'Fats', 25n, 80, 106, 201, 212,
    243, 277, 304, 333; on boogie-woogie, 331;
    on Broadway, 269; early life, 264–5; and
    His Rhythm, 265; radio broadcasts, 266;
    'Ain't Misbehavin'', 91–2, 265, 269, 317;
    Ain't Misbehavin' (revue), 269; Early to Bed
    (musical), 269–70; London Suite, 266
Wallichs, Glenn, 483
Warburg, James Paul, 134–5
Ward, Dorothy: 'Take Me Back to Dear Old
    Blighty', 65
Waring, Fred, 262
Warner, Jack, 198
Warner Brothers, 154, 202; best-selling LPs,
    559; Show of Shows, Paramount on Parade, 200
Waronker, Si, 490n
Warren, Harry, xiv, 237, 238, 353, 519;
    on Jolson, 114; 'At Last', 237–8, 289n;
    'Chattanooga Choo Choo', 237; 'I Only Have
    Eyes for You', 237; 'Jeepers Creepers', 92, 266,
    353; 'Lullaby of Broadway', 263; 'The More I
    See You', 346, 557; 'Remember My Forgotten
    Man', 208; 'September in the Rain', 293;
    'Shuffle Off to Buffalo', 118n, 237; 'That's
    Amore', 237, 512; 'You'll Never Know', 346;
    see also 42nd Street
Washington, Dinah, 449–50; 'Mad About the
    Boy', 450; 'What a Difference a Day Makes',
    450

Washington Post, 530, 574
Waters, Ethel, 50, 123, 155, 523; TV show, 523; 'Ain't Goin' Marry', 273; 'Heat Wave', 274; 'I Got Rhythm', 123; 'Oh Daddy', 143
Waters, Muddy, 388, 393; band members, 391; birth, 389; Hendrix on, 390; as link between blues and beat/rock, 389, 392; moves to Chicago, 389; singles, 390, 392; use of electric guitar, 390–1; 'Country Blues No. 1', 389; 'I Can't Be Satisfied', 390
Watson, Russell, 590
'Way You Look Tonight, The', 231, 261
Wayne, Dottie, 485–6
WCAE (Pittsburgh radio station), 155
WDVR (Philadelphia radio station), 528
We Will Rock You (musical), 586–7
WEAF (radio station), 152, 153
Weatherly, Frederic, 63–4; 'Danny Boy', 63, 157n; 'Roses of Picardy', 63–4
Weaver, Sylvester, 389
Weavers, the: 'Goodnight, Irene', 467, 469; 'The Roving Kind', 375
Webb, Chick: 'Gee But You're Swell', 380
Webb, George, 471; Dixielanders, 471–2
Webb, Jimmy, 510, 531, 591
Weber, Kay, 341
Webster, Ben, 454
Webster, Paul Francis, 430, 440
Wechter, Julius, 557
Weedon, Bert, 339, 460
Weems, Ted, 346, 523, 584
Weil, Cynthia, 504, 505
Weill, Kurt, 374
Weir, Frank, 313
Weisman, Scott, 168
Weiss, George, 94
Welk, Lawrence, 522–3; 'Calcutta', 528
Welles, Orson, 545, 562
Wells, Kitty, 568
'We're Going to Hang Out the Washing on the Siegfried Line', 312, 320
'We're in the Money', 213
West, Mae, 10n, 97, 134, 204, 430
West, Paul, 450–1
West Side Story (musical), 442
Western Electric, 161, 229
Westinghouse, 149, 150
Weston, Paul, 324, 410, 483
Wexler, Jerry, 378–9, 386, 497
'What a Little Moonlight Can Do', 305, 428
'When I Grow Too Old to Dream', 234
Whirl of Society, The (musical), 113
Whiskey, Nancy: 'Freight Train', 473–4
Whitburn, Joel, 224
White, Carol, 545
White, Eugene, 534
White, George, 123
White, Gonzelle, 215
White, Jack, 570
White, Josh, 468

'White Christmas', 48, 49, 51, 224–5, 379, 498, 536n
White Christmas (film), 49–50, 225, 410, 498
'White Cliffs of Dover, The', 311, 321–2
White Rose, The (film), 64
Whiteman, Paul, 17, 89, 127, 201, 253; Aeolian Hall concert, 47, 83; band members, 136, 221, 243, 353; and Crosby, 218, 219, 220, 221; early career, 81; 'King of Jazz' (nickname), 82; and *King of Jazz*, 200, 222; radio broadcasts, 82; 'symphonic' style, 82; 'Dance of the Hours'/'Avalon', 81–2; 'I'll Build a Stairway to Paradise', 82; 'Mississippi Mud', 136; 'Muddy Water', 346; 'There Ain't No Man That's Worth the Salt of My Tears', 136; 'Trav'lin' Light', 379–80; 'Whispering', 82, 132, 187
Whitfield, David, 349n; 'Bridge of Sighs', 421
Whiting, Margaret, 296, 483
Whiting, Richard, 204, 296, 305, 353, 451; *see also* 'Too Marvellous for Words'
Whitman, Slim, 137
WHN (New York radio station), 155; *Barn Dance*, 170
'Who Can I Turn To', 551, 552
Whoopee! (film), 199, 207, 208n, 230
Widow Jones, The (musical), 10
Wilbur, Joe, 79
Wilcox, Edwin, 409n
Wildcat (musical), 444
Wilder, Alec, 45, 289, 584, 587; *American Popular Song: The Great Innovators 1900–1950* (book), 576–7
Wiley, Lee, 471n
Williams, Andy, 518, 532, 535n, 540, 578; hits, 524, 525; in *I'd Rather Be Rich*, 525; *The Andy Williams Show*, 524–5; 'It's So Easy', 524; 'Moon River', 524, 525; *Moon River and Other Great Movie Themes*, 525
Williams, Cootie, 177n, 277
Williams, Danny: 'Moon River', 354
Williams, Eugene, 390
Williams, Frances, 290
Williams, Hank, 168n, 416
Williams, Jay Mayo, 142–3, 386, 392
Williams, John, 192, 363, 539n
Williams, Mary Lou, 363–4, 379; *A Keyboard History*, 364; 'Nite Life', 364; *Zodiac Suite*, 364
Williams, Paul, 530; 'The Hucklebuck', 382–3
Williams, Robbie, 115
Williams, Spencer, 106
Williams, Tennessee, 545
Williams Sisters, the, 274
Williamson, Sonny Boy, 388, 393
Wills, Bob, 171, 389; and His Texas Playboys, 284–5; musical style, 285; 'New San Antonio Rose', 284, 285n
Wilson, Dick, 379n
Wilson, Dooley, 290, 328

Wilson, Teddy, 216n, 261, 267, 277, 304, 305
Wilson, Woodrow, 71, 176, 370
Winchell, Walter, 150
Windrush (policy), 475, 476
Windsor, Barbara, 550
Wings: *Band on the Run*, 433
Winnick, Maurice, 248
Wintor, Marius B., 250n
Wisconsin Chair Company, 142
Wisdom, Norman, 370
Witherspoon, Jimmy, 507
Wizard of Oz, The (film), 299
WJZ (NJ radio studio), 82
WLS-AM (Chicago radio station), 169; *Barn Dance*, 171
WMC (Memphis radio station), 146, 155
WNEW, *Make Believe Ballroom*, 266
W9XBY (Kansas radio station), 215
WOR (NY radio station), 155
Wodehouse, P. G., 7, 38, 96, 101–2, 123; and Kern, 102, 103, 109; *Bring on the Girls* (memoir), 101, 103
Wolff, Claude, 556
Wolverines, the, 136
Wonder, Stevie: 'You Are the Sunshine of My Life', 582
Wong, Anna May, 261
Wood, Del: 'Down Yonder', 475
Wood, Harry M., 305n; 'What a Little Moonlight Can Do', 305
Wood, Henry, 159
Wood, Natalie, 160n
Woodstock (festival), 147
Wooley, Sheb: 'Purple People Eater', 538n
World War I, x, xi, 23–4, 54, 62, 69–70, 71; post-war dance scene, 247–55; war songs, 24, 62, 63–9
World War II: BBC cuts music, 310; German recording technology, xi, 225–6; post-war jazz, 356–67; post-war jazz split, 285–6, 363, 366, 448–9, 466; post-war rise of vocalists,
345–6; post-war UK songs, 348–50, 354; post-war US songs, 346–8, 351–2, 353–6; rise in black US music, 332, 333; and TV, 520–1; UK dance music, 312–19; US country music, 172–3; US musicians (AFM) strike, 327–30, 335; war songs, 4, 49, 66, 310–12, 319–22, 335–6
World's Fair (1939), 135
Wray, Fay, 107n
Wren, P. C., 138n
WSB (Atlanta radio station), 155, 166, 167, 173
Wurlitzer, 327
Wu-Tang Clan: 'The Forest', 94

Yale (university), 36, 188, 190, 191n, 216
Yentl (film), 530
'Yesterday', 578, 579
Yip Yip Yaphank (musical), 335
yodelling, xii, xvii, 167, 169
'You Are Too Beautiful', 233
'You Made Me Love You', 117, 587, 588
'You Make Me Feel So Young', 289, 376, 407
You Were Never Lovelier (film), 352
'You'll Never Walk Alone', 418, 438, 439
'You're Driving Me Crazy', 211
Youmans, Vincent, xix, 110, 181
Young, Brigham, 564
Young, Jimmy, 421, 574; 'Too Young', 421
Young, Victor, 236
Young at Heart (film), 347
Your Hit Parade (radio/TV programme), 520

Zappa, Frank, 174
Ze Records, 588
Ziegfeld, Florenz, 7, 37, 48, 97, 207, 213
Ziegfeld Follies, 37–8, 40, 81, 106, 122, 207; *Ziegfeld Follies of 1918*, 106; *Ziegfeld Follies of 1934*, 211
Zinnemann, Fred, 538
zoot suits, 332–3, 588
Zunser, Florence, 175